WOMEN IN CONTEXT

WOMEN IN CONTEXT

Toward a Feminist
Reconstruction
of Psychotherapy

Edited by

MARSHA PRAVDER MIRKIN

Forword by MONICA McGOLDRICK

The Guilford Press
New York London

© 1994 The Guilford Press
A division of Guilford Publications, Inc.
72 Spring Street, New York, NY 10012

Printed in the United States of America

This book is printed on acid-free paper.

Last digit is print number: 9 8 7 6 5 4 3 2

Library of Congress Cataloging-in-Publication Data
Women in context : toward a feminist reconstruction of
     psychotherapy / edited by Marsha Pravder Mirkin
          p.   cm.
     Includes bibliographical references and index.
     ISBN 0-89862-095-3
     1. Feminist therapy. 2. Women—Mental health.
     3. Women—Medical care—Social aspects. 4. Women—
     Social conditions. I. Mirkin, Marsha Pravder, 1953–
     RC489.F45W664 1994   94-5534
     616.89'14'082—dc20   CIP

For Allison and Jessica,
with love and appreciation

Contributors

Roberta J. Apfel, M.D., M.P.H., is an associate professor of clinical psychiatry at Harvard Medical School, The Cambridge Hospital, and a consultant to the Faulkner Breast Centre, Boston, MA, on psychosocial issues. She has worked in public health settings, especially on women's health, and is also engaged in the private practice of psychiatry and psychoanalysis. She is coauthor of *To Do No Harm: DES and the Dilemmas of Modern Medicine* and *Madness and Loss of Motherhood: Sexuality, Reproduction, and Long-term Mental Illness,* as well as numerous articles about women's physical and mental health.

Anne C. Bernstein, Ph.D., is a professor of psychology at the Wright Institute in Berkeley, CA, where she is also a practicing family psychologist. She is the author of *Yours, Mine and Ours: How Families Change when Remarried Parents have a Child Together* and *The Flight of the Stork: How Children Think (and When) About Sex and Family Building.* She has served on the boards of directors of the American Family Therapy Academy and the Stepfamily Association of America, for which she chairs the Clinical Committee. With Diane Ehrensaft, Ph.D. she is founding the Center for the Changing Family in Oakland, CA.

Jill Betz Bloom, Ph.D., is on the faculty of the Massachusetts School of Professional Psychology; has a private practice in Brookline, MA; and has written numerous articles on psychological theory and treatment concerning women.

Ellen Cole, Ph.D., is the dean of the Master of Arts Program at Prescott College, Prescott, Arizona. She is a psychologist and sex therapist with a long-standing interest in women's mental health. The author and editor of numerous publications, she coedits the journal *Women and Therapy* and the Haworth Press book program "*Innovations in Feminist Studies,*" and is the recipient of a Distinguished Publication Award from the Association for Women in Psychology.

Priscilla Ellis, Ph.D., is a clinical and community psychologist with Newton Psychotherapy Associates, Newton, MA, and cofounder of the Social Research Institute of New England. In collaboration with her colleagues, she strives to understand and counteract the impact of toxic social and environmental forces on people's mental health.

Mindy Thompson Fullilove, M.D., is an associate professor of clinical psychiatry and public health at Columbia University, and a research psychiatrist at the New York State Psychiatric Institute. She also conducts research on women and trauma, and is codirector of a study on health in the household population of central Harlem. Previously, she was the director of Multicultural Inquiry and Research on AIDS (MIRA), a part of the University of California at San Francisco Center on AIDS Prevention Studies.

Helen Lettlow Gasch, M.P.H., is the director of Women's Health Services at the New York State Department of Health AIDS Institute, where she coordinates community-based HIV prevention programs and hospital-based counseling and testing programs. She is a doctoral candidate at Columbia University School of Public Health, where she received her master's degree. She is involved with AIDS prevention and community-based behavioral research with women of color; she is interested in assessing the community and social dynamics that create the context for women's sexual health behavior.

Sarah Greenberg, Ed.D., M.S.W., is an assistant professor at Salem State College, School of Social Work, Salem, MA, where she is participating in the development of a gerontology concentration. She provides consultation and training in the field of aging and is the author of several articles about older families. She is currently involved in a study of older women's friendships.

Beverly Greene, Ph.D., is a clinical psychologist in private practice in New York City, and associate clinical professor of psychology at St. John's University. She is coeditor with Gregory Herek of the series *Psychological Perspectives on Lesbian and Gay Issues;* coeditor with Lillian Comas-Díaz of *Women of Color: Integrating Ethnic and Gender Identities in Psychotherapy;* and an author of *Abnormal Psychology in a Changing World.* In addition to being a Fellow of the American Psychological Association, she is also a recipient of the 1991 Women of Color Psychologies Publication Award and the 1992 Award for Distinguished Professional Contributions to Ethnic Minority Issues.

Alice K. Johnson, Ph.D., is an assistant professor at the Mandel School of Applied Social Sciences, Case Western Reserve University, Cleveland, OH. Since 1986, her research has focused on homeless women and the development of shelter-based services. She is currently completing a study of formerly homeless women. Her recent articles published in the *Journal of Community Practice: Organizing, Planning, Development and Change* explore integrating case management and group work methods with homeless women, and propose a scholar–advocate role for professionals working with community organizations on behalf of homeless persons.

Barbara Hansen Kalinowski, R.N., M.S.N., O.C.N., is an oncology clinical nurse specialist at the Faulkner Breast Centre, Boston, MA. She has practiced oncology for 14 years in a variety of outpatient and inpatient settings, specializing in women with cancer. She was assistant professor at Rush University, Chicago, IL, and project director of a study of nutrition and breast cancer at the Harvard School of Public Health.

Elana Katz, M.S.W., is the coordinator of on-site training and a member of the teaching faculty at the Ackerman Institute for Family Therapy, New York. She recently served as the chairwoman of the Ad Hoc Committee for Reproductive Choice within the American Association for Marriage and Family Therapy. She has published several articles on systemic work in medical settings, and she is in private practice in New York City and Englewood, NJ.

Jodie Kliman, Ph.D., is on the faculty of the Massachusetts School of Professional Psychology, Boston, where she teaches family therapy and serves on a curriculum transformation project to integrate gender, class, race, ethnicity, and sexual orientation into the curriculum. She also teaches family therapy at the Center for Multicultural Training in Psychology at Boston City Hospital. She has recently joined the faculty of the Family Institute of Cambridge, Watertown, MA. She has written on social network therapy and has a psychotherapy practice in Brookline, MA.

Joan Laird, M.S.W., Ph.D., a family therapist, is a professor at the Smith College School for Social Work. She has written on myth, ritual, story, secrets, and silence, particularly in relation to women's experiences in family life. Most recently, she has been engaged in research and writing on lesbian couples and families. She organized the first Women's Institute for the American Family Therapy Academy.

Joyce R. Lappin, M.A., is the teen coordinator for Planned Parenthood, Greater Camden Area, Camden, NJ, where she supervises the Peer Teen Center and directs the Teen Information Life Theater. She has been a sexuality educator and trainer since 1978.

Molly Layton, Ph.D., is in private practice in Philadelphia. She is a contributing editor for the *Family Therapy Networker* and is on the editorial board of the *Journal of Feminist Family Therapy*. She has written on mothering, and presented the keynote address on the maternal presence in the therapy room for the American Family Therapy Academy's Women's Institute.

Judith A. B. Lee, D.S.W., is a professor of social work at the University of Connecticut School of Social Work, the chair of the Casework Sequence, and a member of the Women's Substantive Area. She has written numerous articles and chapters on practice with oppressed groups, and a book entitled *The Empowerment Approach to Social Work Practice.* Since 1982, she has provided consultation and direct practice with homeless women in New York City and Hartford, CT.

Karen Gail Lewis, A.C.S.W., Ed.D., is in private practice in Washington, DC. She has edited three books, including *Siblings in Therapy;* she has also written many articles on gender issues for married and single women and men, eating disorders, group therapy, and family therapy. She is currently working on a book on single women, and is on the editorial board of three professional journals.

Susan M. Love, M.D., is a surgeon specializing in breast diseases. She is director of the UCLA Breast Center, Los Angeles, CA, and is an associate professor of clinical surgery at UCLA. She was founder and former director of the Faulkner Breast

Centre, Boston, MA. She is cofounder of the National Breast Cancer Coalition, and the author (with Karen Lindsey) of *Dr. Susan Love's Breast Book*.

Marsha Pravder Mirkin, Ph.D., has a psychotherapy, consultation, and training practice in Newton, MA. She edited *The Social and Political Contexts of Family Therapy*, and coedited *The Handbook of Adolescents and Family Therapy*. She is a supervisor in the Couples and Family Program at Cambridge Hospital, serves on the editorial board of the *Journal of Feminist Family Therapy*, and is a clinical instructor at Harvard Medical School.

Aluma Kopito Motenko, Ph.D., M.S.W., is an assistant professor and chair of the Older Adult Concentration at the Salem State College School of Social Work, Salem, MA. She is the former director of the Area Agency on Aging, Brockton, MA. Her articles concern caregiving and normal dependency in old age.

Bianca Cody Murphy, Ed.D., is an associate professor of psychology at Wheaton College, Norton, MA, and is also a clinician with Newton Psychotherapy Associates, specializing in work with lesbian couples. She has published extensively on clinical issues with lesbian women and gay men, as well as on family responses to radioactive exposure and the psychological effects of environmental contamination. She is currently a member of the Committee for Women in Psychology of the American Psychological Association.

Margaret Nichols, Ph.D., is a licensed psychologist and diplomate in sex therapy. She is the founder and executive director of the Institute for Personal Growth, Inc., New Brunswick; New Jersey's largest psychotherapy agency specializing in work with the gay/lesbian/bisexual community.

Barbara Okun, Ph.D., is a professor and training director of the Counseling Psychology Program at Northeastern University; a supervisor in the Couples and Family Program at Cambridge Hospital; and a clinical instructor at Harvard Medical School. She is the author of numerous articles, chapters, and books, the latest being *Effective Helping* (4th ed.) and *Seeking Connections in Psychotherapy*.

Myrtle Parnell, M.S.W., is an adjunct faculty member at New York University and the Smith College School of Social Work. She is a 1992 Lydia Rappaport Lecturer at Smith, and a consultant to the Homeless Project at Bellevue Hospital. She does family therapy training at Kings County Inpatient Adolescent Psychiatry Unit and is presently working on a book about service delivery. She is on the board of directors of the American Family Therapy Academy.

Barbara Pressman, Ph.D., is an American Association of Marital and Family Therapy-accredited therapist, with a feminist marriage and family therapy private practice. She has spent the last thirteen years developing group treatment programs for abused women and battering men, and she counsels (both individually and in groups) abused women and survivors of child sexual abuse. She supervises marriage and family therapists; lectures and consults on violence against women and children; and is an adjunct faculty member of Wilfrid Laurier University in Waterloo, Ontario, Canada.

Irene Pierce Stiver, Ph.D., is the director emirita of and a senior consultant to the psychology department at McLean Hospital; a visiting scholar at the Stone Center at Wellesley College; and a lecturer on psychology at Harvard Medical School. She is author of numerous articles and coauthor of *Women's Growth in Connection: Writings from the Stone Center*.

Jo Vanderkloot, M.S.W., is an adjunct faculty member at New York University and the Smith College School of Social Work. She is a 1992 Lydia Rappaport lecturer at Smith, and a consultant to the Homeless Project at Bellevue Hospital. She provides family therapy training at Kings County Inpatient Adolescent Psychiatry Unit and is presently working on a book about service delivery.

Marianne Walters, M.S.W., is the founder and director of the Family Therapy Practice Center in Washington, DC. She is one of the founders of the Women's Project in Family Therapy and a coauthor of *The Invisible Web: Gender Patterns in Family Relationships*. Her numerous writings and lectures focus on feminism and family therapy. She is on the editorial boards of the *Journal of Feminist Family Therapy and Contemporary Family Therapy*.

Foreword

Women in Context: Toward a Feminist Reconstruction of Psychotherapy is a tour de force. This book reflects a complete transformation of traditional psychological ideology. It goes much further: It transforms even the developing literature on women and psychotherapy by considering culture, race, class, and gender as basic to any consideration of women, their problems, the life cycle, and psychotherapy. Having read this book, no one should ever be able to go back to the standard texts without a profound awareness of their glaring inadequacy. Every chapter in this book addresses women in all their multifaceted complexity. Each author has done her homework in re-viewing the subject at hand from the standpoint of diversity. What a boon to our field to read so many clear, well-informed authors who are able to steer our thinking in the new and important direction of overcoming our racism, sexism, classism, and heterosexism. The authors move comfortably among theory, the complexities of our sociopolitical world, and real women in their everyday lives. The theoretical discussion is tied brilliantly to case implications, and the chapters range over the life cycle and through a broad array of issues central to women's lives. The writing draws you in—no dry treatises that preach a new vision, but human and practical discussion, with all the lumps and difficulties of real life that do not fit well together.

Women in Context is an extraordinary resource for clinicians on women's issues, as well as a brilliant rethinking of many of the issues we have only been taught about until now from a white, male, privileged perspective. It is a rethinking of women through the life cycle, of women's health, of women in relation to therapy. Perhaps for the first time, mainstream dicussion of psychological issues includes all kinds of women: poor women, black and Puerto Rican women, lesbians, single women—women whose lives are embedded in structures organized by the norms of patriarchy, which are such a poor fit with their actual lives.

This book shows how we can develop and share a collective consciousness with other women about the patriarchal, hierarchical context of all our behavior. It shows ways to move beyond this context, which privileges certain groups over others. *Women in Context* offers specific, realistic, detailed suggestions about the treatment implications of these ideas. For one thing, it emphasizes ways of restorying families to allow women who are often at odds—mother and daughter, sister and sister—to be on the same side. Even stepmothers and biological mothers can be brought into inclusive coalitions (Bernstein, Chapter 9). For another thing, it suggests ways in which we can help to bond on-line service providers to the poor women they serve by making clear the hidden forces of the system that control them both.

As Walters (Chapter 1) demonstrates so powerfully, when women as gatekeepers for families seek services for their family welfare, they become dependent on and are often placed in opposition to social service workers, who are almost always women who are poorly paid, have limited resources, and have marginal social status. There is never enough of anything to meet the needs, and women are turned against one another in a system in which both the workers and the clients are relatively powerless, and the rules and benefits are controlled by men. As Walters puts it, "The system itself, which is devalued, employs people who are devalued, whose purpose is to provide services to people who are devalued—and the majority of people struggling to achieve their ends within this system are women" (p. 13). It positions the oppressed in opposition to one another and divides them functionally and emotionally. The system maintains the disadvantage of the disadvantaged.

The book articulates the sociopolitical context of women in families and the experiences in women's lives—menarche, abortion, menopause, living alone, and the politics of societal attitudes toward women's bodies and their lives. There are no pat answers here, just solid transformative thinking and illustrations from the real lives of women to back it up. Discussions like Greene's (Chapter 15) on the influences of racism on feminism should be required reading for all family therapists, so that we can never again attempt to deal with feminism without at the same time contending with racism. She places the issue squarely in its historical context. Parnell and Van der Kloot (Chapter 17) also take us far past the usual ignoring of poor women, who, if they are mentioned at all, tend to be sidelined with a passing reference that ignores the complex details of their actual dilemmas. Instead, they show a knowledge of the lives of poor women, commit themselves on the issues, and offer specific ideas of how to work.

I have myself only recently become aware of the constraints of class, culture, gender, and race on the structure of who I am. I have been coming to realize that most of us have never been safe, since home in our society has not been a safe place for women, children, or people of color, in light of the pervasiveness of abuse in the form of corporal punishment of children, child sexual abuse, mistreatment/devaluing of women, and the appalling institutionalized racism of our society. I had no awareness of these issues until a very few years ago. They were, to borrow a phrase from Betty Friedan, issues with "no name"—invisible issues that I only now realize defined the entire construction of relationships in my family, my schooling, and the communities in which I have lived. None of these issues was ever mentioned in my childhood, my adolescence, my college or graduate experience, or in my study of family therapy.

I have only recently come to appreciate the women in my family in ways that are very different from my understanding as a child. I grew up not seeing that my devaluing of my mother was a function of society's generalized attitudes. Now that I know this, I am realizing my ongoing responsibility to change the attitudes that lead to devaluing women. I think we are all pressed to try to "pass" for the dominant group—to accommodate, to fit into images, to keep invisible the parts of ourselves that do not conform to the dominant culture's values. I also did not realize that I benefited from the effects of slavery and racism, and do to this day. I am coming slowly and painfully to realize what it means that we who are white carry around, in Peggy MacIntosh's terms, a kind of "invisible knapsack of privilege" containing special provisions, maps, passports and visas, blank checks, and emergency gear. We cannot see it, but those who do not have one can.

I have been trying to think differently about these issues. I am beginning to see the racism in much of my work—when I spoke about couples or families and did not really mean black couples or families; when I spoke about women and did not really include nonwhite women.

I am also realizing how pervasively and how insidiously the rules of class influence our feeling of otherness, of not being "okay" in one situation or another, and how much we feel the need to lie about who we are—whether to hide WASP roots or money that would distance us socially in the mental health field, or whether to hide our poverty or working-class origins.

The multidimensional perspective presented by Mirkin and her colleagues reflects a profound paradigm shift. We must radically change our training to encourage us to have the courage to acknowledge and deal with this complexity.

Mirkin and her thoughtful and creative colleagues have taken a major leap forward in helping us to think in more inclusive ways—they are lighting the way for this crucial paradigm shift. Bravo and good luck to all who will read this book for the new paths it suggests for our work and our lives!

—MONICA McGOLDRICK

Acknowledgments

The inspiration for this book is a river fed by many tributaries, coming from many directions and crossing time. I was inspired by the stories of my grandmothers, Annie Olarnik Prafder and Sadie Goldman Erlich, who left behind the world they knew and came to this country—one setting up a business here and the other becoming actively involved in community affairs, both supporting their children's strivings to make this country their home while maintaining the strength of their religious culture. I am also appreciative of my parents, Sid Pravder and Ann Goldman Pravder, whose dedication to education and social justice supported my own development and made it possible for me to write this book.

I also want to acknowledge the women friends who have encouraged me throughout my life and who have shown me so many models of what it means to be a woman. In particular, I'd like to thank Chris Nevins Bright, Anne Hartman, Judy Libow, Rachel Mele, Joann Joseph Moore, Pam Raskin, Bronna Romanoff, Deborah Samet, Karen Stutman, and Marion Weinberg.

I would like to thank the women, men, and children who have come to my practice and taught me so much about strength and resilience. Likewise, I thank the contributors who generously shared their ideas and time—their wisdom and compassion are inspiring. A special thank you to Jodie Kliman for putting up with all the minicrises, and giving me such sound advice, as I edited this book. I also appreciate the guidance given to me by Nancy Boyd-Franklin as I searched for women to contribute to this text. A thank you also to Joyce and Jay Lappin for their sense of humor when I lost mine, to Donna DeMuth for her faith in my editing skills, and to Prill Ellis and Bianca Cody Murphy for their inexhaustible supply of names for this book!

A true blessing is to have an editor who is knowledgeable, supportive, and available, I couldn't ask for a better editor than Sharon Panulla, senior editor at The Guilford Press. I appreciate all her help. I want to thank Marie Sprayberry, my copy-editor at Guilford, for her careful and helpful copy-editing. I never realized how many errors my "perfect" final draft had until I looked at her red marks! And thanks to my production editor, Jodi Creditor, for getting the manuscript through the production process.

My deepest gratitude goes to my husband, Mitch Mirkin, and to my daughters, Allison and Jessica. Mitch—my heartfelt thanks for all the years of encouragement and nurturance. Your faith in me nourishes me and every project I undertake! And Allison and Jessica—I'm so proud of the two of you for being who you are, and so completely happy that you are my daughters.

Contents

PART III
WOMEN AND HEALTH

PART IV
PROBLEMS PRESENTED IN THERAPY:
THE IMPACT OF THE
SOCIOPOLITICAL CONTEXT

WOMEN IN CONTEXT

Half asleep bells
mark a butterfly's birth
over the rubble
I crawl into dawn
corn woman bird girl sister
calls from the edge of a desert
where it is still night
to tell me her story
survival.
—AUDRE LORDE (1986)

From Lorde, A. (1986). Naming the stories. In *Our dead behind us: Poems by Audre Lorde*. New York: W. W. Norton. Copyright 1986 by Audre Lorde. Reprinted by permission of W. W. Norton.

Introduction

I am sitting here at my word processor wondering how to write an introduction for this book. How do I explain the intellectual and emotional meaning to me of editing this volume? How do I introduce the idea that we as therapists need to reconstruct the meaning of psychotherapy so that it looks beyond the individual, beyond the family, to a society where privilege is based on gender, race, and class? My musings were interrupted by the newspaper lying open before me, which told me that Iranian women were sentenced to 74 lashes for not dressing in the prescribed manner, while on the flip side of the coin, unclad girls and women continue to be exploited in U.S. pornography. I realized what an important role statistics and newspaper articles had in motivating me to write this book. How could I remain silent when a woman is battered by her partner every 15 seconds?[1] When one of three girls is at risk for sexual abuse?[2] When Alice Walker informs us that girls continue to be victims of genital mutilation not only in other countries, but here in the United States?[3] When women's pay lags behind men's at every educational level, and black households with children earn 52 cents for every dollar earned by white households with children?[4] When girls report not wanting to go to school in order to avoid sexual harassment?[5] When we rarely hear about the reality of AIDS spreading at a fast rate among women? We then see these misogynist societal patterns replicated in the therapy room. For example, mothers continue to be blamed for sexual abuse perpetrated by fathers; more subtly, therapists may frame questions in ways that support the patriarchal status quo. It became obvious to me that while I may not be able to take on the entire society, I can begin by challenging our thinking and practice as psychotherapists, so that we can begin a journey that avoids mirroring—and may even have an impact on—the sexism, heterosexism, racism, and classism in our society.

During the same year as this book was conceived, I decided to take on the challenge of writing our family's Haggada, the book that celebrates the Jewish emancipation from slavery in Egypt and provides the means by which we ritualize each year the joy of and yearning for freedom. This task took on great importance and urgency for me. It became a way of further understanding myself as a woman and as a Jew. Every year, we as Jews are asked to recount the story of emancipation, to make the story our own, and to recount it in our own way. I envisioned the unspoken story of emancipation—the story of Miriam, singing and dancing across the sea to freedom. I resonated with the images of struggle and dance, of the rejection of silence and the bursts into song. Yet, for those whose lives do not match the dominant North American culture, how wide the sea remains that we need to cross!

At the same time, the Haggada is also a story about my roots, about the contexts from which I became who I am today. I saw myself first as a young Jewish child, nurtured in the loving environment of a religious school, and taking out of that experience the mandate so central to Judaism—that of challenging, questioning, and helping in the healing of the world *("tikkun olam")*. At the height of the civil rights movement, I was a child at camp, participating in our camp play—James Baldwin's *The Fire Next Time*—and spending Sunday mornings in structured debates about the social issues of the early 1960s. I came of age with the deaths of Martin Luther King Jr., and Bobby Kennedy; with the protests against the war in Vietnam, folk music resonating within me the hope and outrage of the era. My mother's community leadership, combined with my cousin's outspoken political activism, paved the way for my own political emergence in the antiwar movement.

This value of challenging and participating in social change brought me to feminism in the early 1970s. Since then, my Judaism has fed my feminism, and my feminism has fed my Judaism. The threads were woven together, so that I could no longer respond to the persistent question of whether I was first a "Jew" or first a "feminist." As Letty Cottin Pogrebin wrote in *Deborah, Golda, and Me* in 1991, I need to be vocal within the Jewish community about injustices against women, and I need to be vocal within the feminist community about injustices against Jews. In my Haggada, the two come together: Women's voices are heard along with men's voices, and attention is paid to women's stories as well as men's stories, while the themes of justice and responsibility, of unkept promises and still-to-be-realized dreams, resound.

In the 1980s, my husband, Mitch, and daughters, Allison and Jessica, entered my life, adding so much richness, beauty, and meaning. Having a true partner and soulmate in my life has made me even more aware of and sensitized to how differently most other women experience their relationships—how misogyny and patriarchy work together to oppress women. My Haggada reaffirms that although we may celebrate our freedom, we cannot rejoice and relax in freedom as long as any person remains enslaved. I am sobered by the experiences of many women that I know. Something I wrote in my last book is equally applicable to this book: "The birth of my daughters provided me with a sense of urgency that motivated me to edit a book on this theme. Watching them grow balances that urgency with hope that enables me to hold onto a feeling of optimism in spite of all the threatening issues addressed in this book."[6]

There are many contexts beyond my Jewishness and feminism which define my life. I am acutely aware of the privilege of having white skin in a country that devalues all other skin colors. As I hold that knowledge in one hand, in the other I hold my female Jewishness in a country governed by male Christians. This is the hand that holds my refusal to "pass": I want to have my bumpy nose and curly hair (which I spent so many adolescent years trying to straighten) and Jewish name in a country whose models, with the few exceptions that prove the rule, look nothing like me.

I am also writing this introduction on a computer in my suburban home. The new-found privilege of class is another thread that runs through my life. My mother and her parents left the pogroms of Poland to begin a new life in America. My father was born in this country to courageous Russian immigrants; he grew up in the tenements of the lower East Side of New York, sharing bathrooms with many other families. I grew up first in a lower-middle-income and then in a middle-income neighborhood, hearing the stories of oppression in the old land and promise in this land. I marvel at all that my grandparents had to sacrifice, endure, and initiate so that generations to come would be the recipients of that promise, while I also remain painfully aware that the promise is much more likely to be held out to people with white skin. As my grandfather worked the docks through the night, and my grandmother raised four children in a country so different from the one she knew, could their imaginations have wandered beyond the rules of class and gender, and held the possibility that their granddaughter would earn a doctorate?

So here are the many contexts that make up my life, the threads of my tapestry: the religious/ethnic thread of Judaism in an anti-semitic world; the thread of womanhood in a patriarchal world; the thread of being white in a racist country; the thread of being upper-middle-class in a country where many are starving; the thread of being heterosexual in a heterosexist society. This spinning together of privilege and discrimination reveals the message that I need to use my privilege to work for equality, and my lack of equality to fight for equal privilege. This book is my attempt to begin to respond to that message by bringing women together to examine psychotherapy practice in a broader sociopolitical context, and to begin to formulate psychotherapies that respond to women in that larger context. For many of us, it feels as if our field has taken a long time to begin to appreciate the issues facing women and the difficulties women have in psychotherapy. However, the recent growth of feminist approaches to psychotherapy has been striking, as one extraordinary text after another has explored, critiqued, and deconstructed psychotherapy from feminist perspectives.

Yet, as we know, with every step we take, many paths open and much more is available to be explored. Although I remain excited about the incredible work being done to understand women, and the importance of exploring our commonalities as women, I also want to avoid defining "woman" by the standards of the dominant culture: as white, middle-class, Christian, Western European, heterosexual. I want to look at what we have in common as women, but I also know that it is critical for us to understand our diversity, and not simply to assume sameness—or difference. This can lead us to reconstruct a therapy that is useful to all women and to particular women, to couples, and to families. In the long run, this reconstruction has a message about the society we want to build, and for the future we want to see.

The first section of this book, entitled "The Larger Story: Naming the Contexts," sets the stage for the rest of the volume. It is a look at the larger therapy system and the context of therapy; at the impact of living in a patriarchal society; and at the weaving together of gender, class, race, and sexual orientation. The section not only challenges some of our deeply ingrained assumptions, but challenges us to think in ways that allow us to reconstruct those assumptions and the clinical work that emerges from our conceptual models.

The second section of this book, "Women in Context through the Life Cycle," explores life cycle issues through a sociopolitical lens. This section begins with a study of adolescent females, which challenges the long-accepted idea that separation is the goal of this phase of the life cycle; argues that societal norms and stereotypes have a huge impact on how girls navigate adolescence; and puts forth the idea that this stage is moderated by gender-, class-, and race-based experiences. In the following chapters, the authors challenge the way we understand and work with women who are often marginalized and pathologized. Lesbians, bisexual women, single heterosexual women, aging women, and stepmothers are just some of the women who, by differing from the dominant culture's image of women as young, heterosexual, and married without divorce, are often marginalized and silenced. These chapters construct an understanding and a basis for working with women whose experiences do not match the expectations of the dominant culture.

The third section of this text, "Women and Health," views women's health concerns from multiple perspectives. These contexts include the financing (or lack thereof) of research on women's health; the male-dominated medical system; the influence of patriarchy on what appear to be medical decisions; the pathologizing of female life cycle changes; and the personal and familial impact of some feared illnesses. Again, some of our most deeply held assumptions are challenged: Are new reproductive technologies in the service of women or of patriarchy-supported myths about women? Is the fight against reproductive rights being waged for the sake of unborn children or for that of maintaining male supremacy over women?

Are immediate and radical decisions in response to breast cancer life-enabling or insensitive to women? Can we break the silence surrounding the spread of AIDS among women? How can we study so little about menopause when every women who is lucky enough to live into late middle age will experience menopause? This section not only challenges many of the myths surrounding women's health issues, and argues for the inclusion of sociocultural context in understanding the health needs of women; it also offers ways of both understanding the health issues confronting women today and developing a clinical practice that is responsive to and responsible about the health needs of women.

The final section of the book, "Problems Presented in Therapy: The Impact of the Sociopolitical Context," deals with issues typically presented in therapy by widening our lens so that we see these issues from a sociopolitical context. It is in this section that we see the impact on women of governmental policies and of deeply imbued belief systems. Violence, poverty, homelessness, and teen pregnancy are explored as issues that extend beyond both the individual and the family and can be better understood by including a societal perspective. The problems women encounter in the workplace and with money—both traditionally male realms—are re-examined with this wider lens. And finally, in the epilogue chapter, we "bring it all home" by presenting a way of actively engaging in an intimate and empowering psychotherapy with women who come to our office. Although there are many different models of feminist therapy, this chapter asks us to question the models we have learned from, and to develop a model more compatible with the way we view our patients and our world.

This reconstruction of psychotherapy with women is by no means completed. Some of the contexts have not yet been identified or integrated into our understanding; others need to be moved from background to foreground. I leave it to many of my sister therapists to continue this challenging, precious, and urgent work.

MARSHA PRAVDER MIRKIN

NOTES

1. Fund for a Feminist Majority, 1991.
2. From Judith Herman (1987). *Sexual violence.* Paper presented at Learning from Women: Theory and Practice, a Harvard Medical School Department of Continuing Education conference, Boston.
3. From Alice Walker (1992). *Possessing the secret of joy.* New York: Harcourt Brace Jovanovich.
4. From the 1992 Center for the Study of Social Policy's "Kids Count: State Profiles of Child Well-Being."
5. *Boston Globe,* June 2, 1993.
6. From Mirkin, M. (Ed.). (1990). *The social and political contexts of family therapy.* Needham, MA: Allyn & Bacon.

I

THE LARGER STORY: NAMING THE CONTEXTS

Service Delivery Systems and Women: The Construction of Conflict

MARIANNE WALTERS

Lucy came early for her appointment and immediately expressed her annoyance at the "smoke-free" rules of the Family Therapy Practice Center. Her small, tightly wound frame emanated belligerence. Through pursed lips she complained about having to make out forms, about not being seen right away, and about the decaffeinated coffee—protesting that she was in sore need of some caffeine. Weighing about 100 pounds, and not more than 5 feet tall, she looked young, angry, and vulnerable. It was hard to believe that she was the mother of five children ranging in age from 17 to 6.

Lucy and her five children had been referred to our Center for family therapy by child protective services following the disclosure by her oldest daughter, Rose, age 17, that her stepfather had been sexually abusing her for 6 years. Lucy, a waitress, had alerted the authorities and had her husband, Joe, removed from the home; Rose was put in temporary foster care. The four other children were all under age 13. The 11-year-old suffered from cerebral palsy, requiring considerable amounts of physical care; the 9-year-old had a learning disability and was in a special class in school.

With the removal of Joe and Rose from the home, Lucy had, in one fell swoop, lost her entire child care support system. She had borrowed enough money from a brother in Detroit for the down payment for an attorney. She had filed for divorce and for custody of the children. Joe had filed a countersuit for divorce and custody, claiming that Lucy was negligent with the children and sexually promiscuous. He had been remanded to an offenders' group, and was also being seen by a male court-appointed psychiatrist. Nonetheless, he continued to harass Lucy and force entry into the house.

When she called the police they would get him to leave, but there was nothing they could do about keeping him from doing it again. He owned the house the family lived in.

The foster care worker, a woman, received complaints from the foster mother with whom Rose had been placed that Lucy was inconsistent, demanding, and impulsive in making arrangements to visit her daughter. When the foster care worker saw Lucy and her daughter together, she felt there was a lot of unresolved conflict between them, and supported Rose in expressing anger at her mother for not protecting her from the sexual abuse of her stepfather.

The child protective services worker, also a woman, needed to determine whether Lucy could protect her daughter in the future, care for her other children, and provide for the family. This worker was concerned that Lucy's employment resulted in irregular times at home with her children, and that her child care arrangements were disorganized and haphazard. She thought that Lucy needed to be home more, and especially to spend more time with her two younger children. Lucy would also need to demonstrate that she could provide financially for her family. The worker was concerned that other placements might be needed for Lucy's children.

A "family preservation" team, under the supervision of a male family therapist, was brought in. The team, as a specially funded unit in the service delivery system, was able to function outside of the regular bureaucratic loop. Members of the team were critical of the workers who had been assigned to the case. The team leader felt that the workers were becoming triangulated in "turf" conflicts, and were thus not able to help Lucy assume the necessary attitudes and tasks for effective executive functioning in the family; the team viewed the prevailing systems involved in the case as divisive and inconsistent in their efforts to promote structure within this chaotic family life. The team was also concerned that Lucy was continuing to "act out" unresolved issues in her marriage, and considered recommending couple counseling.

In case conferences among the various workers and teams involved, discussion centered on Lucy's problems in being a responsible, consistent parent, and on her immature, narcissistic, disorganized behaviors. Lucy often appeared harassed, was critical of the help she was receiving, and missed appointments or was late for them; at home, she was careless about meals, smoked too much, and sometimes dated when she should have been at home. The court-appointed worker, a woman, was concerned about Joe's allegations and worried about Lucy's attitude. She wondered whether Lucy could provide a fit home for *any* of the children. Her history of divorce and remarriage, "out-of-wedlock" births, and origins in a "dysfunctional" family with an alcoholic father and "codependent" mother were reviewed in assessing her current functioning and in treatment planning. In this context, Lucy and her children were referred to us for family therapy.

The systematic inequity imposed on this mother and her children by a series of bureaucratic structures, social expectations, professional assumptions, legalities, double binds, and inadequate resources seemed lost in the maze of service delivery prerogatives and imperatives. Lucy had to provide for her children, but like many (if not most) women in our society, she was untrained and poorly paid. Moreover, as in many families of divorcing or divorced parents, the father's child support payments (when they came at all) were insufficient. Lucy had to work, but also had to provide adequate supervision for her children. However, public day care facilities had long waiting lists, and private ones were far too expensive. Her children needed care, support, and nurturing at the same time that her own life and support systems were falling apart. She had two children with special needs, but could not afford health insurance and was not eligible for Medicaid. She was expected to begin to restructure her own life, but in attempting to do so she was in danger of neglecting her children. She needed to demonstrate that she could protect the daughter who had been abused, but did not herself have legal protection from the harassment of the abuser. Lucy had become the locus of concern and the focus of intervention by the service delivery system. If she was critical, inconsistent, or late for appointments, she would be seen as uncooperative; if she was compliant, she might seem to lack initiative.

The perpetrator of the sexual abuse, Joe, had become accountable primarily to himself in the journey of restraint, treatment, and recovery. The victim of the abuse, Rose, was separated from her family and positioned in conflict with her primary systems of support. And a new problematic, in the person of the mother, is being constructed.

GENDER AND POWER
IN SERVICE DELIVERY SYSTEMS

Service delivery systems mirror gender-defined roles in the larger society: The direct service providers, caretakers, gatekeepers, and primary care workers are mostly women; the decision makers, executives, and power brokers are mostly men. Although there are, of course, significant exceptions to this rule—exceptions that are on the increase (particularly with the affirmative action initiatives of the Clinton administration under Secretary of Health and Human Services Donna Shalala)—it is well to remember that these remain exceptions to the prevailing order of things across the country. Women have made inroads into executive positions, but service delivery agencies and institutions still tend to be structured in a gender pyramid: women in front-line positions; men and women in middle management; men in upper management, executive, and policy-making positions. The vast majority of both public and private health and welfare systems are directed by men. Although this situation, of course, is no different from that in other institutions in our society, it is a particularly striking inequity in systems that currently serve, and historically have served, a largely female population (child welfare, foster care, programs for the elderly, Aid to Dependent Children, protective services, etc.). In fact, there is a certain irony in the concerted effort of these systems to recruit men into the field, thus helping to create a male hierarchy in a system dominated by women at both "ends"—as the recipients of care and the primary caregivers. Whether this will also serve to increase the image and status of human service systems is dubious. Direct service occupations, largely peopled by women, continue to be viewed by the larger community as low in status, and wages are commensurate with this view.

Social welfare and service delivery systems, both public and private, have become huge, bureaucratic operations with complex infrastructures, multiple funding sources, diverse programs and staffing patterns, special-interest groups, and competitive turf battles. In other words, much of what transpires in corporate and entrepreneurial life. Often the delivery of service is lost, bifurcated, or fragmented in a maze of priorities and hierarchies: The grant writer has greater status than the case worker; the administrator makes more money than the case supervisor; record keeping consumes as much time as the consumer; support staff and better offices belong to those in executive positions; public relations take precedence over staff relations; and in-service training is a perk instead of a priority.

The Making of Conflict

In this context, it becomes extremely difficult for direct service providers to experience themselves as valued or even as competent. Primary care workers—whether nurses, social workers, home care aides, day care workers, or school aides—often find themselves in positions of responsibility with a minimum of power. They must make decisions without adequate authority, perform multiple tasks with inadequate resources, and deal with crises without sufficient systems of support. Although these conditions are not uncommon in institutional life, they are particularly destructive in systems that exist to provide services to people, the vast majority of whom have little power, limited access to resources, and few systems of support. The result is a culture that structures conflictual transactions, thus maintaining a divisive process *between* and *among* women.

The case of Lucy's family is not an isolated, unusual, or even extreme example. It represents the daily fallout from service delivery systems structured by a social context that holds women responsible for the emotional welfare, the domestic tranquility, and often the fiscal viability of the family, and yet withholds from many women the means with which to be effective and successful in accomplishing this life task. In this way, service delivery systems often serve to maintain the very inequities they are designed to redress. What transpires, less explicitly and perhaps almost on the "meta" level, is that women caught in this system, either as providers or as recipients, do what people who feel powerless often do: They struggle and experience conflict with *one another.* Systems that mandate responsibility without authority and expectations without resources tend not only to create victims, but to position them in adversarial relation to one another.

Any system or institution in our society that is primarily identified with the needs of women is devalued in a number of ways: The staff is poorly paid, resources are limited, fiscal policy determines program priorities, social status is marginal and there is never enough to meet the need. Unless one considers the cosmetics industry as a system serving the basic human needs of women, these conditions have few exceptions! Certainly the exceptions do not exist in the areas of day care for children, welfare for single parents, prenatal and well-baby services, after-school programs, maternal health programs, teen mother programs, immunization programs for children, job training for homemakers, home care for the elderly, parent education programs, and so on and on. Although women are expected to rear the children and manage domestic life, activities related to these functions do not receive the kind of public support that would identify them as socially valuable and significant: fiscal priority on the federal level; statewide program development; access to public resources; and well-compensated, well-trained, well-respected staff.

The unfortunate fact is that child rearing and the management of domestic life are not directly income-producing; thus, while nominally revered in our society, they are largely relegated to individual initiatives. We all claim to love the family and care about the children, but their welfare is largely left to the exigencies of their connection to an individual who can provide for them, often in the person of a male wage earner. Single mothers and their children are rapidly becoming part of what economists have labeled the "feminization" of poverty. When the effects of racial discrimination, ethnic divisions, and social and educational disadvantage are factored in, the results are a series of conditions that create a strange culture within human service delivery systems. The system itself, which is devalued, employs people who are devalued, whose purpose it is to provide services to people who are devalued—and the majority of people struggling to achieve their ends within this system are women. This is not a good or healthy situation. It positions powerless people against one another and divides them both functionally and emotionally. The system becomes itself part of the process that maintains the disadvantage of the disadvantaged.

Reflections on Global Gender Inequality

On a global scale, we know that women do one-third of the world's work, earn one-tenth of the world's income, and own one-hundredth of the world's land; that two-thirds of the women of the world over 18 years of age are illiterate; and that if women did not take care of the children, governments would need to appropriate 30% of their national budgets to child care (UNESCO, 1991). In the United States, although the transformations in family life and in women's roles have created a truly revolutionary change in women's work, 70% of all women employed full-time in 1986 were still working in occupations in which over three-quarters of the employees were female, and part-time workers were even more heavily concentrated in female-dominated occupations. Over a third of all employed U.S. women work in clerical jobs, 70% of which are occupied by women. Female-dominated occupations (including those in the human services) are generally low-paying, with poor benefits and career ladders, and have considerably lower status than male-dominated occupations. Women have made only modest inroads into the high-paying sectors of the economy; even where they have been successful in penetrating nontraditional occupations, they are often ghettoized into lower-paying enclaves.[1]

Moreover, though well over 50% of married women with children work, the vaunted "new man" who shares household tasks and child rearing equally with his working wife has remained more myth than reality (Hochschild, 1989); he is seen much more often on film and in advertisements than in the kitchens, laundries, and living rooms of American households. With the rate of divorce only slightly declining in recent years, and the rates of out-of-wedlock pregnancies and births increasing, there has been a sharp decline in the standard of living of women and their children. After divorce, the income of women and their children suffers a significant drop, while that of their former husbands shows a considerable increase (Faludi, 1991). Over half of all children living in poverty are in households headed by women.

Reflections on Gender-Linked Values and Attitudes

Within service delivery systems, the values and attitudes of the larger society often get played out despite our very best intentions. The determination of the locus of pathology—the assessment of the psychosocial roots of the behavioral, emotional, or familial problem that comes before us—is, in fact, constructed within a culture that for centuries has assumed the measure of *man*kind to be the measure, the standard, even the model of *human*kind, thus locating *woman*kind as "other." So womankind, despite the promising gains of the past two decades of the woman's movement and of a feminist awakening, remains a population at risk.

Although women are positioned as the primary source of all that is nurturing and all that is destructive in the rearing of children, the socialization of these children functions to support dichotomies between dependence and independence, between other-determined and self-determined, between the relational and the rational. These dichotomies are reinforced by gendered roles and expectations. Women are expected to seek help; men are not. Women are expected to be expressive; men are expected to be instrumental. And service delivery systems become part of these social constructs.

Since women are seen as the gatekeepers of their families, it is they who are largely responsible for seeking the services attendant to the families' general welfare when these may be missing, lacking, or unavailable within the families themselves. When seeking these services, women both become dependent upon other women and are placed in opposition to them. As the caretakers of their children, they may begin to vie with service providers for recognition and status in various ways. For example, when a mother's child care provider reports a problem with the child and suggests ways of dealing with it, the mother may feel failed, deskilled. On the other hand, the mother may disapprove of the worker's way of mediating disputes or feel that the worker favors another child over hers, but is afraid to voice her fears, since she needs the worker's goodwill in leaving the child in her care. So her disapproval may be displaced by behaviors that undermine the worker's efficiency. And both women are caught in a system that is underfunded and devalued—whose services are much needed and always in short supply.

Or let us take the case of a grade school teacher and a troubled boy. His classroom behavior is disruptive and his grades are dropping. He seems to show no interest in school or in his peers. The parents are asked to come in for a consultation. The mother comes in alone because the father is at work. She works too, but only part-time, so is able to manage the appointment. As the teacher describes the problem, the mother begins to feel failed, responsible, and overwhelmed. She has two more kids at home—a younger daughter who has temper tantrums, and a teenage daughter who has always been well behaved and responsible but has begun to act out lately. As the teacher inquires about aspects of family life that might be affecting the boy's behavior in school, the mother begins to get the message that she may be causing the problem. She gets defensive and perhaps indulges in some denial. She's afraid that her son may be labeled as a troublemaker or misfit. She defends him and feels protective.

The teacher has 30 other kids in her classroom, and is a mother herself. She knows what this mother is going through, but she has her work to do and her job to protect. She begins to experience the child's mother as overprotective, defensive, and maybe resistant. The teacher recommends that the family seek help at the local family service agency.

The mother makes the call to the agency. The intake worker suggests that she bring her husband with her on their first visit. He refuses; he doesn't believe in all that psychology stuff, and anyway he has to work. The mother, son, and older daughter arrive for the first session at the agency feeling harassed and more than a little irritated with one another—not even quite sure why they are there. The social worker sees the overload on this mother, but when they begin to talk she experiences her as resistant to change and blaming others for her problems with her son: her husband, the school, her own mother, finances. As the worker tries to help the mother to take more responsibility for her part in the problem and to suggest or indicate pathways for change, they are both caught in a system that, despite the intention or consciousness of either, reinforces those conditions and ideas that assign the mother primary responsibility for the production of the problems of her children or family, as well as primary responsibility for their solution. And both have, in a sense, become "products" within institutional structures that reproduce social constructs and thus help to maintain sexist power arrangements within our culture.

MAKING A DIFFERENCE

How can we begin to make this different? Perhaps, to begin with, we need a deepening of consciousness about the ways in which the systems within which we work create divisions, competition, and conflict between and among women. We need to become increasingly vigilant in identifying attitudes and expectations on our part that play into maintaining these deadly cycles of failure. And we need to take a hard look at our own professional concepts, assumptions, and interventions in order to measure them against sex-role stereotyping, the blaming of mothers, gender-defined expectations, and existing developmental theories. We need ideas and techniques that are designed to empower women in every aspect of our work.

There is a need for the development of both theory and methodology in our field that is explicitly designed to validate the role and function of mothering. From *A Generation of Vipers* (Wylie, 1942) to *My Mother, Myself* (Friday, 1977), from "schizophrenogenic mothers" (Bateson, 1972) to the idea of "loving and letting go," mothers have been both reified and demonized. And throughout our own psychosocial theories of growth and development are ideas, formulas, and attitudes that tend to pathologize the mother–child relationship. Mothers must bond with their children at birth, yet this bond must be broken at the appropriate time in order to allow their children to individuate. They are expected to be involved in the lives of their children, and are expected to protect them, but are always in danger of becoming overinvolved and overprotective. They give double messages, especially about love, which in the extreme are said to cause mental illness. They are dependent and create dependency in their children. Their emotionality can be overwhelming to their families. They get depressed when their children leave home, and covertly try to hold on to them. Lacking an identity other than that of "mother," they live through their children or try to run their lives. Not only does our theory associate the symptomatology of children (and more recently even of so-called "adult children") with inadequate, problematic mothering; such formulations have become part of the common wisdom of our culture.

In order to counter some of these ideas, it is important for us to understand the social context in which mothers seek to operationalize their role and their functions. We need to seek ways to validate their efforts and expand their repertoire of behaviors in the rearing of their children. In doing this, we must search for *existing* competencies with which to build expertise, and must help mothers contextualize and find commonality with others in identifying the conflicts and problems of family life. We need to look for successes and endorse their significance, and to help mothers own their strengths both within and outside the family. Most important, we need to avoid "mother bashing." We must not get caught in blaming the very person whom society holds responsible for bringing about change in the family.

We need to develop systems of support and networks both within and among our agencies of practice—not only for ourselves, but in order to decrease the likelihood that our clients will fall between the cracks or get caught in our own turf battles. We need to encourage an atmosphere of respect for clients. Most importantly, we need to demystify the process of change, the practices of our trade. Professionalism does not require distance from our clients, but rather a relationship framed in the expertise of a clear methodology of practice. Hidden agendas serve to create a "we" and a "they." In case conferences and supervisory sessions, classrooms and counseling rooms, professional presentations and staff meetings, we need to challenge psychological and developmental theories and constructs that pathologize, blame, or devalue women, and to work on developing new initiatives for practice that are gender-sensitive.

Service delivery systems are seldom structured in ways that encourage and support their clients to be informed consumers, or that facilitate access to resources. Institutionalized hierarchies, boundaried levels of communication, professional privacy, and administrative privilege hinder the possibilities of making common cause either among ourselves or with clients. We need access to one another's work, critique of our methodology, and open discussion of our theoretical concepts. If we demystify what we do and why we do it, we can begin to break down a process that has discouraged informed consumerism and self-determinism on the part of the recipients of our services. When a client asks how we work or what our theoretical orientation is, we should be pleased to describe it; when a client inquires about the way an agency is structured, we should be prepared to delineate it clearly. We can share an awareness of the "double binds" implicit in some of our legalisms, lines of authority, divisions of labor, and regulations and explore ways to access power within these constraints. Although it is difficult to challenge the internal organization of an institution or agency, we can monitor the structures that tend to reproduce oppressive social and professional roles and relationships.

Whereas Jung developed the concept of the "collective unconscious," I prefer to think of a "collective consciousness." In our practice, we can carry with us a consciousness of the collective experience of women, or of any minority group or ethnic group that is in any way devalued or discriminated against in our society. So, for instance, a woman does not have to be the victim of an explicit sexist act to have shared that experience with other women, any more than a black person needs to have been the victim of a particular racist act to share the experience of racism in a white-dominated society. There are many ways in which such a consciousness can inform us in our work. We will feel more familiar and "knowing" with the people with whom we work when we presume some commonality of experience. When we differentiate these experiences by gender, we will be more aware, for instance, of the different meanings of our language as applied to men versus women. Adjectives such as "competitive" and "aggressive" conjure up very different images when they are used to refer to a man than when they refer to a woman. Even nouns such as "bachelor" and "spinster" have different implied meanings. If men tend toward problem solving and women toward processing, these characteristics, when translated within a domestic dispute, often emerge as his being "reasonable" and her being "emotional," usually accompanied by that prefix we so often apply to women, "over-" (as in "overemotional," "overinvolved," etc.). Since in our culture reason is the more valued characteristic, and emotion is a thing to be employed with caution, such words will be "heard" very differently by men and women, and our interventions will convey metamessages that our words do not intend.

Deconstructing Our Work: An Exercise

Recently at our training center, a peer group of family therapists met with the task of deconstructing clinical interventions for any messages (or metamessages) they might convey (implicitly or explicitly) that could reinforce sexist cultural norms or gender stereotypes. One of the therapists presented her work with a single parent she was seeing whose son was having school problems, both academically and with peers. The clinical impasse centered on the mother's repeated efforts to involve her ex-husband in seeking a solution to the problem. She called him regularly to discuss the problem, get his advice, and try to come to some agreement on what needed to be done. She felt frustrated in her dealings with the school, and angry at her ex-husband for giving advice but refusing to become involved. She would get almost daily calls from the school counselor about her son's behavior, as well as poor reports from the teacher. She would call the boy's father; he would make suggestions; she would argue with him because he "didn't really know what was going on" and "couldn't understand since he wasn't there"; he would tell her, "Then go ahead and do it your way"; and she was left "holding the bag" and feeling failed with the school, her son, and her ex-husband.

Seeking to empower the mother, the therapist had chosen the following course of action: She encouraged the mother to stop asking her ex-husband for advice and to turn over to him sole responsibility for negotiations with the school. She was advised to instruct the school to contact the ex-husband with regard to any future complaints or issues regarding their son. The therapist worked with the mother on her dependent behaviors and encouraged her to take a clear, independent position of her own with both the school and her ex-husband regarding her son's problem. The therapist used a formulation of complementarity in framing the intervention: "To the degree that you pursue, he distances; to the degree that he distances, you pursue." To break this dysfunctional cycle, she suggested that the mother should back off from the pursuit and take a stand on how she would "be there" in relation to the problem, when, and under what circumstances. This would allow her ex-husband to operate in a less reactive way.

The other members of the group considered a range of therapeutic options. One suggested that the mother could be directed to pretend that she was totally unable to manage the school problem, had no ideas about what to do, and couldn't even think about it any more—in other words, to feign total dependence when discussing the issues with her ex-husband or seeking his advice. This would "go with" his resistance and help restore his sense of authority, enabling him to become more involved. A second member of the group suggested using a "counterpoint." The original therapist could deliver the message that the son's symptom was functioning to keep his parents engaged with each other, and that if he behaved or got better grades, the mother would lose a critical pathway for contact with her ex-husband (however conflictual) and would be in danger of becoming depressed. The consulting therapist could insist that the mother would not get depressed and that she should disengage so that her ex-husband could take more responsibility. A third group member suggested that the hierarchy in this family needed to be restored. The mother needed to establish clear expectations with her son in regard to school performance, to set rules, and to enforce appropriate sanctions. The therapist could help her set goals and organize family management tasks more effectively. Since her interactions with her ex-husband were undermining, both for herself and for her son, more appropriate boundaries should be structured between the parents (with the mother taking the initiative to establish rules for telephone contacts, etc.). A fourth therapist in the group suggested that the mother was perhaps repeating dysfunctional patterns of dependence from her family of origin, and needed to take a look at what she had brought into her marital situation that was continuing to operate and disempower her within the interactions following the dissolution of her marriage. An overly close relationship with her own mother might be explored for ways in which she could learn to be more autonomous.

Clearly, all of these interventions could "work." The discussion in the group focused on an exploration of the potential for "mother-blaming," gender-biased messages in the suggested interventions, especially with respect to working with a female-head-of-household family.

In the intervention that the client's therapist had actually employed, the mother was advised to turn the management of their son's school problem over to her ex-husband. The danger was that the mother would "hear" in this intervention not the empowerment and self-determination intended by the therapist, but the message that if left to his own devices, her ex-husband could "do it better." Would she really be empowered by delegating or relegating authority to her ex-husband in an arena in which she felt both responsible and failed? In critiquing the "pursuer–distancer" concept, the group cautioned on the need for sensitivity to a social context in which a man's "distance" is more acceptable than a woman's "pursuit," so that despite its reciprocal formulation, the impact of such a message is more pejorative for women than for men. Furthermore, the intervention constructed the father's advice-giving, noninvolved role with his son as a position taken in response to the mother's pursuit, rather than as a position of his own making, or one that is socially constructed.

The first intervention suggested by a member of the group would encourage the mother to do what women have been counseled to do for ages—"Fake it," "Pretend you can't do it in order to get him to do it," or, more crudely, "Act dumb so he'll feel smart." The group agreed that other than serving to improve the mother's acting skills, this intervention would subvert her self-esteem and convey the gender-stereotyped message that "artful" manipulation of a relationship is what is expected of women. It would further impart the idea that getting her own act together was of secondary importance to finding a way to improve his.

The group found the second suggested intervention to be congruent with societal assumptions that attribute a child's behavior directly to the dynamics of parental interaction—in this instance, the divorce and continuing conflict over authority. Although the message contained in the "function" of the symptom clearly indicted both parents in a causal link between their marital woes and their son's problems, in this instance the sense of blame, with the mother in therapy, would land more solidly on her shoulders. Although each therapist in the "counterpoint" would take a different position, the message conveyed by both would reinforce the idea that a woman's primary sense of well-being is to be found in her relationship with her spouse or children, without reference to other sources of self-esteem.

The third intervention suggested by one of the participants, which focused on structures, rules, and sanctions in confronting the child's problem behaviors, was seen as reinforcing a standard of hierarchy based on power and being "in charge." It would convey the message that the mother's way of parenting, which included the need "to understand" and "to be connected," was not as valuable a mode of executive functioning as that associated with clear lines of authority, rules, consequences, and so forth. For a female single parent, such a standard of hierarchical authority, especially with a teenager, may simply be impossible to achieve—if only because of the child's size and strength.

Embedded in the fourth suggested intervention would be the message that dependency and autonomy are oppositional frameworks of behavior, and that whereas dependency is problematic, autonomy is a characteristic of maturity. The intervention would do little to locate these two frameworks as two parts of an integrated whole. Since the concepts of "dependency" and "autonomy" are also sex-linked—for instance, "tied to his mother's apron string" is "bad," whereas "following in his father's footsteps" is "good"—the message might serve to define the mother's behaviors with her ex-husband in pejorative terms.

Having addressed the potential of gender bias in these interventions, the group members struggled with alternatives that would not convey sex-role-stereotyped messages, and that might even go *counter* to cultural biases. With this in mind, they developed the following course of action.

The therapist would suggest to this mother that her efforts to engage her ex-husband in their son's school problem, however well-meaning and surely worthwhile, were just not going to work at this time—for whatever reason. Probably the reasons were too loaded with past history to sort out at this juncture. What *was* important was that in trying so hard to get her ex-husband involved, the mother was depleting the very energy she needed to manage the problem herself. So her efforts had become self-defeating and kept her in a position that was either oppositional (with her ex-husband) or protective (with her child). Both positions restricted her ability to utilize her own knowledge and skills as a parent. Moreover, they generated feelings of failure and alienation from her son, so that she was forgetting what she knew—and perhaps even what she liked—about her son.

Within this framework, the therapist would redirect the mother's attention to what she knew about her son and herself, what worked well for them both in difficult times, and what worked during those times that they enjoyed together. The therapist would reference and rereference their sources of connection. She would create a context within which interactions between them during sessions would be experienced as competent, playful, comforting, and/or supportive. She would then suggest ways in which such transactions could be expanded on, both at home and in relation to school.

At the same time, the therapist would coach the mother on ways of dealing more effectively with the school, using role plays and strategizing on "what if's." The therapist would offer to participate in a joint conference with the school if the mother felt that one was needed. She would help the mother to gather information from school and other sources (testing, etc.) about what was contributing to her son's poor school performance, so that she would feel better prepared to be "in charge" when necessary, and to "get tougher" with her son if that should prove to be appropriate.

The therapist would also encourage the mother to reassure her ex-husband that she was "on the case" if he should inquire about his son's schooling. And the therapist would explicitly assure the mother that her son's behaviors were not "her fault" and had nothing to do with a "broken home." At the same time, she would assure her that informed and comfortable interventions on her part could indeed alter the situation for her son.

None of us should accept the idea that "It works" is a sufficient criterion for the use of any intervention. Change-producing interventions should always be measured against a yardstick of values that takes into account the social construction of the behaviors, interactions, feelings, or belief systems not only of our clients but of ourselves, particularly as this construction contains messages that disempower, devalue, or disadvantage a group of people in our society.

Working with Lucy and Her Family

In our first session with Lucy, after she had aired her "side" of the story, we quickly turned to the belligerent, angry, irritated attitudes with which she had introduced herself to us, both in entering the agency and in beginning the session. We remarked on her energy, her ability to articulate her perceived needs, and her "*chutzpah.*" (Lucy is not Jewish, but in using an ethnic expression we could, while translating it, describe a range of behaviors, feelings, and attitudes with which Lucy was familiar.) We wondered about this way of being, the way she positioned herself in relation to others, and the strength and sense of purpose she projected. We then expressed concern that such competent behaviors were "spent" on rather inconsequential issues (such as decaffeinated coffee) when she had such major issues to confront in her life.

Much of the first session was devoted to developing a theme that was employed in different ways throughout our contact with Lucy: that people who feel powerless to effect change in the major, significant areas of their lives tend to assume "negative," oppositional behaviors in regard to minor issues as a way of constructing some sense of choice and self-determination. Although there is nothing inherently wrong with this, it does tend to impede the energy needed for larger life issues or crises. It also has the side effect of turning people off, so that persons who do this get into double binds with some of the very people whose job it is to be on their side. In subsequent sessions, we would expand on this theme, identify Lucy's strengths, reframe self-defeating behaviors (such as missing appointments made to visit Rose) as choices made in a powerless context, and work together to prioritize the use of her energy and self-determination. We would also consistently explore the sources of Lucy's feistiness and resourcefulness. This theme was attached to an ongoing discourse centered around the dangers of behaviors that tend to maintain the "victim" position of a person who experiences victimization, and the difficulty of *not* acting in "victim-like" ways. We would offer alternative behaviors by coaching, scripting, creating stories and "as-if" situations, and of course maintaining an awareness of the dynamics of our own interaction and reactions in therapy sessions.

In addition to working directly with Lucy, we employed three other options: regular meetings with all of the workers from the various agencies involved with Lucy and her family; a series of sessions with Lucy and Rose, two of which included the foster mother; and several sessions with Lucy and all of her children, including Rose. In our meetings with the other workers, the goals were to identify areas of cooperation, lines of authority, common goals, and time expectations, and to clarify and agree upon our own agendas. A system for regular communication was set up; we also agreed to constitute ourselves as an interdisciplinary "team," with the family therapist taking responsibility for continued leadership of the team.

The sessions with Lucy and Rose were very volatile at first, so triangulated were they with regard to the abuse Rose had suffered. Although Rose's anger at Lucy for not protecting her was part of the discourse during our sessions, we struggled to help Lucy respond in comforting ways rather than becoming defensive. What helped Lucy most in these encounters were (1) the interpretation of Rose's silence about the abuse as an act intended to protect her; and (2) the interpretation of Lucy's "not knowing" as a loss of faith in herself and in her ability to make a difference, particularly with someone whose life was so important to her and whose safety was so much a measure of her sense of competence as a mother. Session after session was spent in designing interactions between Lucy and her daughter that were competent, comforting, aware, and open to criticism, and that both validated and helped them to experience their deep attachment to each other.

The sessions with Lucy and all of her children occurred during the final phase of treatment, when Lucy and Rose were preparing for Rose's return home. They were organized around ways in which this family could begin to operate as a system of support, with the children feeling as much providers of family life as consumers of it. We dismissed any effort to provide marital counseling; we also helped Lucy in her efforts to obtain good legal help and in her arrangements for custody of the children (including considerations related to visitation, child support, etc.).

There were three follow-up sessions, each a month apart, and a final session 6 months later. One session was with the whole family, and the others exclusively with Lucy and Rose. During these meetings, attention was paid to the process by which plans were made in the family; to financial issues; and particularly to employment and educational opportunities for Lucy and Rose. Lucy entered a food management training course, and Rose and Lucy together worked on getting Rose a scholarship to the local junior college. Rose had been on her high school newspaper staff and aspired to a career in journalism. It was agreed that Rose would not work her first year, until she felt more secure in her ability to "concentrate," but would probably do so later on. Rose was referred to an incest survivors' group, which she attended for about 8 months. Lucy never lost her "attitude." The last time we saw her, she complained about our having only regular coffee—noting that caffeine was not healthy! I guess that is also progress!

NOTE

1. Unless otherwise indicated, all statistics on this page were obtained from the research notes of the Institute for Women's Policy Research in Washington, DC.

REFERENCES

Bateson, G. (1972). *Schizophrenogenic mothers*. San Francisco: Chandler.
Faludi, S. (1991). *Backlash: The undeclared war against American women*. New York: Crown.
Friday, N. (1977). *My mother, myself*. New York: Delacorte Press.
Hochschild, A. (1989). *The second shift*. New York: Viking Press.
Institute for Women's Policy Research. (1990–1993). *Research notes*. Washington, DC: Author.
UNESCO. (1991). *The world's women: Trends and statistics, 1970–1990*. New York: Author.
Wylie, P. (1942). *A generation of vipers*. New York: Rinehart.

2

The Interweaving of Gender, Class, and Race in Family Therapy

JODIE KLIMAN

As a new stepmother, I was delighted with my young stepson's creative ideas, one of which was to build a space ark to rescue thousands of people should Earth become lethally polluted. Intrigued with his thinking and eager to carry on the Jewish tradition of adults' nurturing children's intellectual and critical skills, I peppered him with questions about the social implications of his plans. I expected an enthusiastic response, but he seemed sullen and bored until other interests called him away. Months later, I was horrified to learn that our exchange had left him believing I thought he was stupid. Fourteen years with his African-American/Native American, high school graduate mother had not prepared him for his Jewish stepmother's attempt to affirm his intelligence by challenging it. We had not recognized the gulf of culture, class, and gender, and had yet to build a bridge.

I invite you to join me in building such a bridge by exploring how gender, class, and culture combine to shape family experience. Each of these central organizing principles of family life has been addressed (to different extents, and mostly separately from each other) in the family therapy literature. But these treatments often underestimate each variable's contribution to the social contexts in which the others are experienced and defined. Because these principles shape family life *in dynamic relation to one another,* their implications for family therapy theory and practice are best understood in their shared context. This argument is familiar to family systems therapists, as it recalls the mutual, recursive, and collective shaping of family experience and behavior. Here, however, I emphasize the over-arching or meta-level principles of gender, class, race, and ethnicity's interactions with one another, in relation to family life. A synthetic analysis of dynamic interaction among the organizing principles of gender, class, and race requires addressing them simultaneously.

Writing about these principles in relation to one another *and* in relation to particular clinical issues reflects our collective difficulty in thinking and communicating simultaneously about multiple processes and structures. When, for the purposes of a particular argument, I address one or two principles apart from the others, I return the discussion to how the effects of one principle (e.g., the experience of being male or female) shapes and is shaped by the effects of the other principles (e.g., experiences of being working-poor, middle-class, or wealthy, and of being Chinese-American, Irish-American, African-American, or a Salvadoran refugee), in relation to a particular topic (e.g., boundaries between family and environment or hierarchical arrangements by gender and generation).

Toward this goal, we can construct a three-dimensional matrix of culture × class × gender, with one axis for race and ethnicity, another for class, and each cell divided by gender. Within this matrix, we can compare what effective therapy would be like for a problem such as truancy in the families of a middle-class Puerto Rican girl, a poor Puerto Rican boy, a wealthy African-American boy, and a working-class Irish-American girl. These therapeutic differences reflect the intersecting contexts of gender, class, and cultural norms and values; the ways in which social institutions (e.g., schools) respond differentially to members of each gender × class × culture subgroup; and the consequences of truancy for each cell.

Each discussion in this chapter informs and shapes all the others. Each is limited by my own understanding and by the linear language required to render that understanding. I ask you, the reader, to provide the perspective(s) of any principle not being addressed at any given moment (including other important variables, such as sexual orientation and age). This endeavor is similar to our attempt in family therapy to respond to each family member's experience in the context of what we learn about the others' experiences, relating each member's constructions to the others.

GRINDING A PARADIGMATIC LENS: MY OWN FAMILY

My view of families in their social context is shaped through the prism of my own gender, class position, and cultural experience. I am a woman. My relationship to class is less clear, and is interwoven with my Jewish identity. My father's grandparents were all working-poor Ukrainian Jewish immigrants. His mother's parents were socialists and suffragists, who were also pious. His father's father, a union organizer and a founder of the Jewish–socialist Workman's Circle, rejected orthodox Judaism. My paternal grandparents left the working class when my grandfather became a business executive. Before my generation, women worked only before having children or if married to underemployed men. My father, a psychiatrist, was the first in his family to go to college.

My mother's maternal grandmother, educated and wealthy until she lost her parents and left Lithuania, worked from adolescence to support her siblings. She married a working-class Lithuanian immigrant. Her children, including my grandmother, went to college on scholarships; the boys earned Ph.D.'s. My mother's father, a German immigrant and doctor, left her family when my mother was 3. My grandmother supported her children before remarrying, later working with her second husband's successful business for some years.

My parents married as students; my mother did not finish college and graduate school until my teens, but started working in psychology when I was little. In the 1950s, it was, of course, her career and not my father's that child rearing interrupted. My husband and I, in contrast, met as professionals and shared the assumptions of equal partnership in both economic and domestic spheres (thanks largely to our working mothers' examples).

My mother's intergenerational legacy of economic yo-yoing left feelings of deprivation in the midst of comfort; the members of my father's family celebrated their recent escape from poverty. My own class identity necessarily differs from each parent's, as well as from my younger brothers', who do not remember life on a tight budget. My family conveyed a clearer, very positive message about our ethnic (if not religious) identity, particularly through my maternal grandmother's Zionist leadership and my father's family's commitment to economic and social justice and to the extended family.

Add to the mix my marriage to a psychologist whose mother, from a Yankee family with a long memory of economic decline, was a librarian with two master's degrees. My father-in-law is of English, Scottish, and Irish ancestry; he was a minister's son, and is himself a minister and sociologist. Stir the mix, adding my two stepchildren, whose mother was of African-American and Native American (Nipmuk and Narragansett) descent; she was a high school graduate and executive secretary, 11th of 13 in a poor family. Finally, our son, a white child, became Jewish when his Jewish mother, his WASP father living as a Jew, and his multiracial, gentile siblings adopted him at birth.

Each race, ethnicity, religion, and class in any family brings its own cultural norms about family life. Knowing about my parents' contrasting class backgrounds, my husband's complex class background, and the less privileged circumstances of my stepchildren's mother compared to our own would help a therapist understand us. At the winter holidays, it helps to know that my father's Ukrainian grandmother kept kosher; my mother's German grandmother had a Christmas tree; I had Hanukkah at home but

Christmas carols at school; my husband gave up his Christian traditions to raise his third child as a Jew; and Christmas is a gala affair for our older children and their mother.

MARGINALIZATION AND GHETTOIZATION

Gender is finally gaining recognition as central to family organization. This change is indicated by the birth of publications such as the *Journal of Feminist Family Therapy;* the fact that major family therapy journals (Braverman, 1987; Simon, 1984, 1985) and conferences now devote significant attention to gender; and the publication of this book and others (Ault-Riche, 1986; Goodrich, Rampage, Ellman, & Halstead, 1988; Luepnitz, 1988; McGoldrick, Anderson, & Walsh, 1989; Walters, Carter, Papp, & Silverstein, 1988). Much has changed since the first neglected articles on the gendered nature of families and family therapy (Caust, Libow, & Raskin, 1981; Goldner, 1985; Hare-Mustin, 1978). Family therapy still ignores patriarchy more than challenging it, but more family therapists now recognize gender as fundamental. Increasingly, feminist family therapists are changing the field and holding it accountable.

Class, race, and ethnicity are less recognized than gender as organizing principles of family life and family therapy. Class and race interpenetrate each other in American society, and so are introduced together; however, as I argue below, they must not be confounded.

The present discussion draws on historical materialist definitions of class (Bernal & Alvarez, 1983; Poster, 1978), based on one's relationship to the means of production (not social status or income level)—the economic structure of capital, labor, and services. In this model, the classes include (1) the ruling class (or wealthiest households), (2) the petit bourgeoisie (or "upper-middle-income" and "middle-income" households), (3) the proletariat or working class (including "lower-middle-income" and "working-poor" households), and (4) the poor. Inclan and Ferran (1990) have divided the poor into these subgroups: (recently) unemployed; chronically unemployed (at least 5 years in 7), who hold mainstream values about work and education; and the underclass or "lumpenproletariat," who make their livings illegally or otherwise on the fringes of society.

Family therapists, like most Americans, think more in terms of socioeconomic status (SES) than of class. Although the two have some relationship, they are not equivalent. SES is estimated through a weighted index using head *(sic)* of household's educational level and occupational category; it does not account for more profoundly formative aspects of family members' relationships to the economy. A class perspective allows for a clearer and more precise understanding of family experience than an SES perspective can. Nevertheless, in some instances, I use SES terms as a kind of shorthand to simplify narratives that otherwise would be overly cumbersome.

Not only is race generally more obvious than ethnicity, but in the United States it affects experience far more powerfully. "Race" refers to membership in a biological human grouping, (usually) distinguishable by such features as skin color, hair texture, facial structure, and so on. "Ethnicity" refers to a social grouping sharing national origin and linguistic and cultural traditions, with which members may or may not actively identify.

Since the publication of *Families of the Slums* (Minuchin, Montalvo, Guerney, Rosman, & Schumer, 1967), family therapists have addressed class, race, and ethnicity in books (Boyd-Franklin, 1989; Carter & McGoldrick, 1988; Combrinck-Graham, 1989; Elkaïm, 1987; Falicov, 1983; Ho, 1987; McAdoo, 1981; McGoldrick, Pearce, & Giordano, 1982; Mirkin, 1990; Papajohn & Spiegel, 1974; Schwartzman, 1985; Tseng & Hsu, 1991), articles and chapters (Aponte, 1976; Fulmer, 1988; Inclan & Ferran, 1990; Pinderhughes, 1986; Schwartzman, 1982), and the occasional special journal issue (Saba, Karrer, & Hardy, 1989; Simon, 1986, 1987). But this rich body of work is all too often marginalized—ignored or else pigeonholed as an interesting afterthought—in most family therapy training and writing. It is as if we could understand "*the* [monolithic] family" without addressing the economic and cultural realities that (differentially) affect *all* families.

The Myth of Middle-Class Membership

Our culture cherishes a dual myth: We are all middle-class and have an equal opportunity to be middle-class. National Public Radio once reported a poll in which 90% of the respondents identified themselves as middle-class. Yet over 14% of all Americans live below the (artificially low) poverty line (U.S. Bureau of the Census, 1992); many more live just above it. Edelman (1985) reported that 20% of all children and 50% of all black children live in poverty. A very few Americans live way beyond middle-class means. Accepting this myth means that if everyone except me (or "them") is middle-class, it is my fault (or "theirs"). Denying the reality of differential access to resources and power (allocated differentially by gender and culture within each class) allows us to blame the victim instead of social stratification itself (Ryan, 1971).

Afterthought Status

Class and race are often presented as afterthoughts (e.g., accorded separate "special-population" chapters in books), as if they were only relevant to people outside the mainstream. We read, without elaboration, that an author's foregoing description of "the" family life cycle, "the" family structure, "the" family politics of gender, and so forth, may not apply to diverse (i.e., "not the dominant") classes and cultures. (I apologize if this chapter does the same regarding sexual orientation.) These caveats acknowledge class and cultural diversity in the abstract, without weaving a critical awareness of difference into the particulars of a given theory or practice. The dominant group provides the "real" norm(s), from which poor, dark, gay, or otherwise disenfranchised groups differ—and suffer by comparison.

Thus, the effects of class position and cultural experience—not only on poor, but also on bourgeois and ruling-class families; and not only on multicultural families, but also on the cultural mainstream of the descendants of British and Western or Northern European immigrants—are obscured. Oppression and dominant culture follow multicultural people of all classes and poor people of all races home, affecting their relationships, possibilities, and perceptions. Racial privilege also follows white people home, more discreetly affecting their relationships and world views. They need not notice or acknowledge their privilege or any other experiential differences from nondominant groups. Family and network relations, access to resources and power, responses to family crises, and sense of self are just as culturally determined for self-defined "nonethnics" as for Vietnamese refugees, Puerto Rican migrants, African-Americans, and Italian-Americans. Members of the dominant group may misperceive others as just like them or as deviant, rather than as embedded in different contexts. Finally, privilege follows the wealthy into their homes, which often include servants, employees, and advisers from other classes.

The greater our privilege, the less we are likely to notice how fundamentally shaped we all are by our cultural and class contexts, values, world views, and privileges or oppressions, as exemplified below. A white middle-class colleague was concerned about an inner-city-raised African-American job applicant who gratefully acknowledged a preacher and a couple of relatives and teachers who had urged him on to college and beyond. How could we hire someone who had "needed help every step of the way"? Embedded in her class and racial privilege, she did not perceive the seamless web of support holding her safely and discreetly, letting her perceive her successes as hers alone. Through her privileged lens, she saw the morsel of help given this man, not all the support that she (but not he) could take for granted—nutritious breakfasts, parents who helped with homework and paid tuition, well-funded schools, and teachers who expected her to do well.

Cross-cultural families exemplify how cultural differences can be overlooked or pathologized. Those with racial and/or class privilege may view partners' or relatives' situational appraisals, grounded in painful personal and collective racial and/or class experience, as paranoid. Conversely, people of color and/or from a lower class may view as entitlement white and/or higher-class partners' or relatives' assumptions that people get what they need, want, or work for. (The similarity to the differing experiences of men and women in couples is inescapable.)

An Italian-American may interpret her Vermont Yankee husband's and in-laws' (unsolicited) respect for her privacy as cold and unloving; he may respond to his wife's and in-laws' (unsolicited) advice and emotional displays as incursions into his privacy. My WASP husband used to wonder why I phoned my brothers without news to relate; it broke my Jewish heart how rarely he called his sister. Even family members with similar backgrounds may need help in distinguishing assumptions based on culture, class, or family idiosyncracy. They may interpret similar cultural norms differently, or expect partners and in-laws to share beliefs unique to their own families of origin.

Confounding Class and Race

Glossing together race and class also relegates both to the margins of family therapy. Being African-American is often equated with being poor, and being white is equated with being middle-class (Boyd-Franklin, 1989). African-Americans and other people of color are disproportionately represented among the poor, but this equation obscures the experiences of middle-class and wealthy people of color; the white majority of the nation's poor; and the tiny, virtually exclusively white ruling class. Like others, family therapists may stereotype African-Americans as poor (and on welfare), Jews as rich, Southeast Asians as workaholic small merchants, and the generic middle-class person as a white Protestant. In fact, each cultural group has class divisions; each class is culturally diverse; and the experience of each culture × class group is unique. Furthermore, the experiences of women and men within each subgroup differ from each other's and from those of the same sex in other subgroups.

Ignoring Racial Groups

Discussions of race encompassing only whites (as the dominant group) and blacks (as "the" minority group) render nonblack families of color invisible. Even discussions that acknowledge Latinos, Asians, and Native Americans often ignore their enormous ethnic, economic, and political intraethnic differences. Latinos come from Puerto Rico, the Dominican Republic, Cuba, countries throughout South and Central America, and Mexico; others' ancestors settled what is now the U.S. Southwest centuries ago. Some Latino cultures have primarily European roots; others are a *mestizo* blend of Native American and European cultures. Others also have a small Asian and major African presence, and so their members experience more racism on arriving here. Yet many Latinos who identify with one race or many are seen simply as "Latino."

Asians and Asian-Americans, also frequently described in homogenized terms, include descendents, immigrants, and refugees (of many religions) from China, Japan, Southeast Asia, Korea, India, Pakistan, several former Soviet republics, and the Pacific islands. Growing numbers hail from the culturally diverse nations of the Middle East. Recent immigrants from the many nations and cultures of Africa are mistakenly categorized with Caribbean islanders and Americans whose ancestors arrived in chains centuries ago. The families and descendents of immigrants from Eastern and Southern Europe are often lumped together with those from Western and Northern Europe. And finally, scores of Native American cultures are ignored.

Each race embraces an array of ethnicities, cultural norms (including gender roles), urban and agrarian backgrounds (and their related class divisions), and politics. For instance, Jorge (1983) reported that in 1976, 34% of Puerto Rican women and 42% of Mexican-American women were employed; by contrast, 33% of Puerto Rican families, but only 14% of Mexican-American families, were female-headed. In other words, Puerto Rican women are less likely than Chicanas to be employed and more likely to be single parents, both of which have enormous economic consequences. Jorge ascribed these disparities to two factors. First, urban renewal and long-distance migration have culturally uprooted Puerto Ricans, whereas Mexican-Americans migrate a much shorter cultural and geographical distance (or no distance at all, as many Chicanos' families were living in the Southwest before it joined the United States). Second, Puerto Ricans, who are often of mixed Spanish, Native American, and African ancestries, are more victimized by racism than are lighter-complected Mexican-Americans.

Ignoring "Other" Religions and Philosophies

Non-Christian religions and philosophies are almost invisible in U.S. society, although they provide the medium in which millions of us develop family structures, ethics, and patterns. When politicians and pundits invoke "our Judeo-Christian values," what do they mean? Being Jewish, I understand them to mean: "Christian values, which we assume Jews hold, or should hold, too." Such overinclusiveness silences and disqualifies the minority group subsumed by the majority culture. It culturally eradicates those groups *not* appropriated by the majority culture. Family therapists, too, can be blind to spiritual systems outside the mainstream. Can Caribbean or Mexican families speak openly about the approaches of *Espiritismo,* Voodoo, or *Santeria* (including practices proscribed by the dominant culture) to their problems, while therapists probe intergenerational triangles, communication, or behavioral sequences? Can family therapists who focus on the nuclear family be helpful to Buddhists, whose moral responsibility extends to *all* relatives, past, present, and future; or to Native Americans, who are responsible to nature, rather than to immediate family alone or to a Christian conception of God?

The path toward answering these questions is fairly clear, although it can be challenging to put our answers into practice. Answers are harder to come by when we encounter families whose religious and spiritual practices seem profoundly to contradict feminist (and humanist) commitment to universal dignity and safety. How do we balance respect for a given culture with our feminist concern that its patriarchal forms are particularly crippling?

I suggest that the balance must shift toward feminist concerns as we move from more subtle to more violent forms of patriarchy. Inequitable division of labor and decision making between spouses, women's exclusion from religious rituals and positions of power, and a double standard for sons and daughters, however unacceptable to American feminists, cannot compare with clitoridectomy or female infanticide. Therapists must take a liberational stance in the latter cases. But what of patriarchal forms that oppress without killing or maiming? Can we openly oppose polygamy, which the fathers of some of our African and Middle Eastern clients may have practiced, or the wearing of the veil, without disrespecting and losing our clients? How do our female and male clients experience such practices? Some Muslim women have argued, for instance, that the veil frees them from the sexual predation that Western women endure; others protest that it renders them invisible.

How can feminist therapists challenge and subvert oppressive family arrangements without being psychological colonialists? It may be best to ask questions that help a therapist and family move together toward understanding current gender arrangements for the family members and the cultures they straddle. Such questioning may allow all or some family members to recognize and reject patriarchal arrangements; it may help the therapist to understand arrangements in a more complex and inclusive way; it may do both.

MULTIPLE CONTEXTS, OVERLAYS, AND CONTRADICTIONS

It becomes increasingly challenging to embrace and transcend contradiction and avoid single-lens reductionism as we move toward reconciling feminist, cultural, and class analyses. Goldner (1989) has argued that "gender and gendering are not secondary mediating variables *affecting* family life; they construct family life in the deepest sense" (p. 56). All households—comprising one, two, three, or four generations, identifying with immediate or extended family, and including heterosexual or homosexual couples or single parents—are shaped by gender. Its form varies with members' class, race, ethnicity, and sexual orientation, but the gendering remains central: Goldner (1989) has described gender and generation as family life's two most fundamental organizing principles.

This argument is fundamental to my own thinking. But analyzing the interplay of gender, class, and race reveals contradictions between—and potential syntheses of—compelling arguments by scholars of race and class and by feminist theorists. Students of family therapy with members of racial minorities (Boyd-Franklin, 1989; De la Cancela, 1991; Greene, 1990, 1992; Pinderhughes, 1986) have made a powerful two-part argument, presented below.

First, gender roles and expectations, and the dynamics of patriarchy for oppressed and dominant cultural groups, differ in ways easily misperceived by members of the dominant culture (including white feminists using ethnocentric paradigms). For instance, job discrimination against black men has historically required black women to work more and to depend financially on (and therefore marry) men less than do white women. This adaptation to racism has been described pejoratively as "matriarchal." Greene (1990) has argued that black women are thereby blamed for the familial consequences of institutional racism (such as black men's systematic exclusion from the work force). The pejorative use of "matriarchal" is itself sexist, implying that women should not be breadwinners. Black women are seen as "too" powerful; their male counterparts, when they do not overcome multiple obstacles to leading productive lives as parents and workers, are stereotyped as "shiftless."

Second, people of color are generally more oppressed on the basis of race than of gender. Race therefore tends to be more salient to family members than gender, even when there is tension or even hatred between the sexes. This prioritization has important implications for family therapy. The women's movement has long been divided over the fact that many women of color put their oppression by men (of all races) second to all multicultural people's oppression by whites (of both sexes). Black women in particular have argued that black men's oppression is even more malignant than their own double oppression as women of color. They cite the devastating rates at which African-American men are unemployed, incarcerated, addicted, assaulted, murdered, and otherwise likely to die younger than white men or African-American women, as well as the ratio of one black man to every four black women in higher education (U.S. Bureau of the Census, 1989). Many black women argue that it is more important to support sons, brothers, and partners who are being undermined and destroyed by a racist social structure than it is to challenge gender-based domination, including domination by black men (Boyd-Franklin, 1989).

This support does not condone sexism, but aims to ensure the survival of a community under siege. Because black women are at least as oppressed on the basis of gender as white women, this support exacts a high price. The 1991 U.S. Supreme Court confirmation hearings for Clarence Thomas shook and divided many black women (and men), crystallizing the powerful and contradictory realities of gender-based and racial discrimination (N. Boyd-Franklin, personal communication, November 1991). Race and gender competed in this microcosmic struggle. Some black women chose race, supporting Thomas. Others chose gender, and supported Anita Hill. Still others rejected "either–or" in favor of "both–and," wedding the struggle for racial equality to the struggle for gender equality; they, too, supported Hill.

It has been argued that one's relationship to the economy is the primary social determinant of experience (Poster, 1978) or at least coequal with gender or race (Bernal & Alvarez, 1983; Desmarais, Lavigueur, Roy, & Blanchet, 1987; Elkaïm, 1987; Inclan & Ferran, 1990; Patchesky, 1983). De la Cancela (1991) has pointed to an ironic confluence of discriminations: Latina and black women are more employable than their husbands and brothers, because sexism facilitates and excuses hiring women at lower wages. Women of color get work but exploitation, while the men get less work (and are faulted for it). De la Cancela has asserted that *machismo*, often characterized as a noxious Latino male characteristic, actually reflects a positive sense of responsibility for family welfare, distorted by the economic oppression that prevents men from supporting their families adequately. Unable to provide for their families as expected, they compensate in maladaptive and sexist ways.

The apparent contradictions between viewing race and viewing gender as the primary basis of oppression underscore profound differences among women, who share gender-based oppression but whose racial (or class) oppression or privilege divides them. When several white college athletes were accused of gang-raping an African-American student in March 1990, her supporters kept vigil at their trial. Angry denunciations soon threatened their alliance: The white feminists defined the crime as male violence against women; the African-Americans defined it as white racist violence. Each group accused the other of denying the obvious for ideological purposes. Some of the white feminists could not expand their focus to include the race hatred fueling this young African-American's brutalization, regardless of gender. Some African-Americans (female and male) could not expand theirs to include the misogyny required to rape any woman regardless of race. Most white feminists are as racist as nonfeminist whites, and most African-Americans are as sexist as most whites. It is safest for all of us to keep to our familiar lenses, which leave our assumptions, fears, and hatreds unchallenged. Each group in this case had one useful and necessary lens and one distorted beyond utility; neither could use the other's good lens to develop the perspective that binocular vision provides.

All other things being equal, gender is primary, and families of all cultures and classes are equally (if differently) gendered. *But all things are not equal.*

We must focus on race first when it presents more danger and discrimination than gender, which does not mean that we can afford to relinquish our focus on gender. Pogrebin (1991), a founding editor of *Ms.* magazine, has similarly argued that because most Jews are as sexist as most gentiles, and most gentile feminists are as anti-Semitic as other non-Jews, a Jewish feminist must be a feminist first among Jews at the same time that she is a Jew first among gentiles.

Unlike women of color, whose racial features are usually obvious, many American Jewish feminists can choose the comfort of white privilege—up to a point, so long as they are not "too Jewish." They need not feel bound by Pogrebin's imperative; their assimilation to dominant culture allows them not to be "Jews first." However, Orthodox, Hassidic, and other unassimilated Jews today, like European Jews of earlier generations, are easily identifiable targets of discrimination and hatred. Memories of my great-grandmother, raised in the undeniably sexist *shtetl* (Jewish ghetto), sometimes challenge my sense of personal comfort as an assimilated Jew. Years before she could march for American women's suffrage, her first concern was survival. She matter-of-factly reported, "When the Christian children beat us, we never complained. If we did, the villagers would find out and kill us." Most of her family did die, in *pogroms* (massacres of Jews), after she had fled with one brother, her husband, and their child to the United States and started saving—too late—to pay their passage.

TOWARD TRANSCENDING CONTRADICTIONS IN CLINICAL PRACTICE

Let us return to the thesis that the politics and experiences of gender, class, and culture are best understood in the contexts they provide one another. De la Cancela (1991) has proposed a dialectical model that accounts for cultural and economic realities as well as those of gender domination. He criticizes much of feminist family theory and practice as emphasizing

> the influence of gendered world views while addressing masculinity in universal terms that neglect racial and ethnic variations. Even efforts to include cultural sensitivity or minority issues often lack socio-political contextualization, leading at times to the creation of new negative stereotypes about men of color. (p. 195)

This critique speaks to clinical, ethical, and political concerns. How can we maintain a feminist analysis *and* be sensitive to the exigencies of race and class? How can we respect the different realities of men and women whose tapestries of behaviors and beliefs based on cultural, class, and gender positions differ radically from our own or even disturb us, *and* maintain our personal and professional integrity? These questions apply to a Jewish therapist feeling confused (and perhaps judgmental) about a working-class Dominican mother who resents but does not protest her husband's living part-time with the second family he started while married to her, *or* his forbidding their teenage daughter to date. They apply equally to a Puerto Rican therapist feeling confused (and perhaps judgmental) about a British-American husband and wife who consult neither family members nor each other on major decisions; who derive self-worth from professional accomplishments rather than from loyal, respectful, and helpful relations with kin; and who define maturity as independence from, not interdependence with, family members.

Embedded in our own matrix of gender, class, and racial circumstances, we therapists may easily misperceive and respond inappropriately to the members of families whose experiences are embedded in a unique multiplicity of unfamiliar contexts. We therefore must strive with our clients to distinguish conflicts and differences (both intrafamilial and between a family and therapist) based on (1) idiosyncratic patterns; (2) cultural × class × gender patterns that, however unfamiliar, are adaptive in their context; and (3) a family's (and perhaps a therapist's own) problematic adaptations to oppression, minority status, and gender-, class-, and culture-based intrafamilial differences.

Exploring Family Arrangements: Culture × Class × Gender

Consider our three-dimensional matrix, which categorizes households along three axes: culture × class × gender. Such a matrix reveals enormous variations in (1) communicational patterns; (2) boundary maintenance, at home and with the social network; and (3) the allocation of power, resources, and leisure, as well as child care, housework, financial support, and planning responsibilities. For instance, if a mother is too ill to care for her children, how is their care arranged? Does the father take over her tasks, alone or with network or paid help? If he is unavailable or unwilling, do relatives or friends take the children (and perhaps the mother) in, or do various part-time helpers come to them? Does she pay for home care? Do protective services place the children in foster care or assign a home health aide? If they are separated, do the children and mother stay in frequent contact? How openly are needs and feelings communicated, and how does the network respond? How would things differ if the father, a child, or a grandparent were ill instead? Finally, how does the family's situation affect relatives' and friends' lives, and what obligation (if any) do they feel?

The answers depend on many factors. In the United States, the dominant ethnic and class cultures both value independence and privacy; middle-class families from the dominant culture, or fairly well assimilated into it, rely mostly on themselves or on paid help. Imber-Black (1990) has described such families as easily preventing unwanted intrusions by social agencies. In contrast, many poor families, as well as most traditional families from African-American, Latino, Asian, Jewish, and Southern European cultures (which value interdependence and reciprocal obligation), turn to their networks, although they differ over exactly whom in the network to involve. Social agencies easily break through the household–environment boundaries of these less powerful families' private spaces.

These class × culture generalizations break down when we consider poor families from the dominant white culture and middle-class families from cultures valuing interdependence. Poor families of British or Northern European origin must occasionally use interdependent strategies to survive, but their cultural imperatives militate against asking for help; they do so much less than poor blacks, Latinos, or Jews, for whom mutual help is culturally syntonic. Although middle-class blacks rely less than poor blacks on the reciprocal obligations to kin and friends that are so strongly rooted in many African cultures, they share network resources far more than mainstream middle-class whites do. Poor whites from individualistic cultural backgrounds take in needy relatives far less often than do either poor or middle-class African-Americans, Latinos, Asians, Jews, or Southern Europeans.

Each approach has benefits and costs. Families that emphasize collectivism can pool inadequate resources, buffering the otherwise catastrophic consequences of unexpected expenses, unemployment, illness, or the like. Participating in this resource pool literally keeps families fed, clothed, and housed in hard times, although it does so less effectively when a bad economy stretches inadequate resources even further. Households from independence-oriented culture × class backgrounds can be ill prepared for unemployment, major illness, or single parenthood; neither they nor their networks think of sharing resources (Roberge, 1990). A working-class British-American family is more likely to become homeless with job loss than a working-class Vietnamese family, who can join relatives in a crowded apartment. On the other hand, collective obligations can make personal upward mobility virtually impossible: For example, a person cannot save money for college or an interview outfit when a poorer relative needs it for food or rent (Stack, 1974).

Gender permeates these arrangements. In individualistic class × culture groups, men more than women set the norms for independence. Most American women do much more network maintenance than men—making contact and social arrangements, as well as exchanging child care, errands, household items, and small sums of money (Trimble & Kliman, in press). As gender and collectivist culture intersect, however, these differences often diminish. The sexes in many collectivist groups are fairly equally committed to the cultural norm of interdependence: Mexican-American men initiate caregiving contact with relatives more than Norwegian-American women, and not much less than Mexican-American women.

Asking gender-, culture-, and class-sensitive questions about how domestic life is organized can be transformational, challenging old epistemologies and structures and allowing new ones to develop. We can ask families of all classes and cultures who ensures that bills are paid; dentist appointments are made and kept; homework is done; hems are mended; child care is arranged; taxes are prepared; milk is in the fridge; and birthday presents are bought, wrapped, and mailed. Who leaves work for a sick child, or responds to children's fears and teenagers' late-night calls for rides home? Who buys the car and who the sneakers? How do these arrangements evolve? For whom do they work best and worst? Do relatives and friends approve? (This question distinguishes arrangements syntonic to culture and class from idiosyncratic ones.)

Specific Examples

Focusing on the details of domestic structure was revelational for a Jewish professional couple from working-class (Mark) and bourgeois (Sandy) backgrounds. Despite their egalitarian beliefs, Sandy alone responded to the frequent nightmares of their daughter, Leah, ostensibly because Mark was too depressed to soothe her. Off the hook, Mark settled into domestic incompetence. (Who says learned helplessness is a woman's problem?) Sandy's resulting exhaustion and resentment occasionally exploded into what she overdramatically called "abusive tantrums," which cowed Mark into rising (angrily) to the occasion—until she calmed down again.

Instead of the classic intervention—defining Sandy as overinvolved and suggesting that Mark could do better than Sandy—we (the couple and I) explored the minute details of their competent–guilty–overworked (*not* overinvolved!) spouse versus incompetent–guilty–overwhelmed spouse two-step dance. We agreed that Mark was quite competent in other realms and parented effectively in Sandy's absence. Puzzling over these findings put the situation into bold relief for Mark; Sandy already knew something was wrong, but had not quite put her finger on it. They readily concluded that it was equitable and do-able for Mark to take the initiative to get up with Leah half the time, even when it *felt* impossible. They felt closer and more effective, and Leah learned to depend on both parents.

This intellectual approach was well suited to this particular couple. Metaphorical, directive, or joking approaches might be better for couples from other cultural and class groups. The question might not even come up for those African-American parents who have responded to decades of high rates of black male unemployment with flexible gender roles—or for those mothers who can expect no contribution at all from absent fathers. Perhaps no approach would work for some traditional couples from ethnic groups in which child care is non-negotiably the woman's responsibility.

How does one help a family with less class privilege in such a situation? What of the woman whose husband cannot afford to get up because he works the 6:00 A.M. shift before picking up the children at school, or whose husband has been drinking since his layoff and cannot be roused at night? What of the single mother, who must function at work the next morning, every morning?

Patchesky (1983) has asserted that discrimination in the workplace and in domestic responsibilities means that the sexes' productive and reproductive lives shape each other differently. Men and women in the same household, with similar class *backgrounds,* may have markedly different current *individual* class positions. These differences become clear when, for instance, the economic paths of a part-time secretary and her executive husband, the parents of three children, diverge when they divorce.

Not only does class play out differently for the sexes, but gender and class play out differently among cultures. Comparing the reasonably well-functioning families of three hypothetical mothers—one German-American, one African-American, and one Puerto Rican, all employed in "pink-collar" jobs, and newly separated from husbands ethnically similar to themselves who pay little child support—illustrates these points. The German-American woman's ex-husband makes much more money and is the accepted authority and disciplinarian. The family may have difficulty letting a previously subordinate mother become the primary authority. She may have some accumulated assets, but her income has plummeted. Unlikely to turn to her network for financial or child care help, she goes through her reserves of money and energy quickly. Her social life, organized around couples and nuclear families, is sharply curtailed. Family therapy would focus on legitimating the mother's authority; questioning the cultural belief that needing help means failure; and affirming, strengthening, and utilizing network ties.

The African-American woman probably earns more than her ex-husband, who may be unemployed, so her income loss is not so pronounced. On the other hand, she has much less to start with and fewer, if any, assets. Because many (though not all) black couples share flexible gender roles, she loses the father's domestic labor, but easily exerts (already established) authority. Network members of both sexes help with material needs and child care, sometimes taking in children; collectivist communities support single-parent families. In many cities, decreased supervision may leave her children (especially her sons) more vulnerable to the many dangers of the street. Therapy might focus on safety issues and on ensuring that the mother neither becomes overly central nor relies on an older child at the expense of that child's developmental needs.

The Puerto Rican-born woman's ex-husband, if employed, earns somewhat more than she; employed or not, he is the undisputed head of the family. If her roots are in one of Puerto Rico's more patriarchal agricultural communities, she is especially expected to sacrifice for, but not to lead, her family. In her husband's absence, a male relative (often her father or, in time, a new partner) takes leadership, while she remains the "heart" of the family. She can expect a great deal of instrumental help; relatives and *compadres y comadres* (her children's godparents, who have significant coparenting responsibilities) may take her children for extended periods. However, there is little money to share. She is also subject to criticism for not meeting the requirements of *marianismo*—that is, she did not sacrifice or endure enough to keep her family together. Being employed, she has a more bicultural network than a homemaker might; coworkers may help less but more readily accept her new marital status. Family therapy would focus on legitimating the mother's authority in ways that are compatible with cultural values of *respeto* (respect, particularly for older generations); renegotiating relations with judgmental relatives; and clarifying boundaries between the mother–relatives–children and father–relatives–children sub-systems.

FAMILY THERAPY ACROSS CONTEXTS

In some of my own cross-cultural family therapy encounters, I am un-ambiguously more privileged than poor and working-class clients of color. With lower-class white Christian families, I have more class privilege but less ethnic privilege. When my clients have an equal or higher class position and we are ethnically different, my Jewishness is more salient to me—particularly when I notice any form of prejudice on their parts. (In one network intervention, I was uncharacteristically paralyzed by the long and rambling monologues of the Boston Brahmins assembled. A Yankee colleague, immune to stereotyping as a pushy Jew, freed me by insisting that I interrupt and get some work done.)

An African-American middle-class colleague described his work with a white middle-class man, whose romantic relationships were mostly with African-American men. My colleague, perplexed at first by confusing transference dynamics, soon noticed that his client seemed to view him as more privileged and powerful in the world than himself. This view con-tradicted my colleague's own perceptions and his experience with other white clients. He then realized that they were both in oppressed minor-ities—he as an African-American in a racist society, his client as gay in a homophobic society. As such, neither had expected to be seen as the more privileged of the two. Addressing the dual realities of their respective privilege and oppression on the basis of both race and sexual orientation broke the therapeutic impasse.

A couple embroiled in vitriolic arguments over extended family and domestic responsibilities demonstrates the importance of balancing multiple lenses and analyses:

> Elise was a Scottish-American from a working-class family; Olu, from a professional Yoruba family in Cameroon, had immigrated here for college. They had three school-age children, and both worked as middle-level professionals. Olu maintained close family ties, here and abroad; most of Elise's family had cut her off when she married an African.
>
> Elise resented Olu's welcoming relatives who came uninvited from Cameroon for college or medical care and stayed with them for months or years without her consent. She was outraged that Olu made such major decisions without consulting her. Her friends condemned Olu as a sexist, whose unilateral decisions were especially intolerable because his work hours put primary responsibility for the visitors on Elise. Viewing the situation through my feminist lens alone, I might have joined the condemnation, moved Olu toward collaboration with Elise, and encouraged her to be more assertive. But I had to respect and utilize Olu's Yoruba lens to understand this family more fully.
>
> Olu's father was polygamous; his two wives had raised their many children together. Like members of many traditional societies, the Yoruba do not distinguish the immediate from the extended family, and their bonds of mutual obligation go deep. Olu's older siblings had paid for his education, assuring him of a career after their father's death. It would be unthinkable to turn away their children and grand-children when they needed help. (In Cameroon, reciprocal obligations ensured Olu's financial stability; here, they slowed his nuclear family's upward mobility.) Olu's relatives viewed Elise's position as racist, uncaring, ungrateful, selfish, and irresponsible. For them, concerns about relatives' impact on household finances, upward mobility, self-determination, and privacy were insignificant, compared to collective responsibility and well-being.
>
> Who was right? Elise and her friends, and Olu and his relatives, were all justified within their respective cultural frameworks—and dead wrong in each other's. In an old story, a quarreling couple approached the rabbi (the judge and family therapist of Eastern European *shtetls*) to resolve their dispute. He listened carefully to the husband's argument, nodded wisely, and intoned, "You are right." The wife protested his deciding without hearing her side of the story, which she then told. The rabbi listened carefully and nodded, "You are right," sending the confused couple on their way. The rabbi's wife, who had been eavesdropping in the kitchen (where else?), strode in to upbraid her husband: How could he say both were right when they were in such obvious disagreement with each other? He listened thoughtfully to his wife's criticism and nodded, "*You* are right!"
>
> Like the rabbi, I had to affirm each spouse's culture- and gender-based experience; I also had to help each respect and understand the

other's. Falicov (1986) has described well-functioning cross-cultural couples as operating within a balanced framework that acknowledges and respects cultural (I would add gender and class) similarities and differences. In contrast, she suggests, minimizing or maximizing cultural differences keeps couples and families stuck and unbalanced. Olu and Elise condemned each other on the basis of unspoken and contradictory rules of family relations and individual rights. Treatment helped them clarify their frames of reference, detoxify their ethnocentric interpretations, and address their contradictory values and needs collaboratively and respectfully.

This case reveals another facet of our kaleidoscopic exploration of gender × class × race/ethnicity in family life. Our view of family politics through the lens of gender is crucial, but incomplete and even distorting without cultural and class lenses. *These multiple lenses must shape our fundamental understandings and assumptions about male and female psychology.*

For instance, it is widely accepted in American feminist psychology that women are more relationally oriented than men in their identity formation (Chodorow, 1978) and moral reasoning (Gilligan, 1982). However, mainstream North American women may look downright individualistic (masculine, in our ethnocentric terms) compared to many traditional male Africans, Asians, Latinos, and Pacific islanders. Olu did use (Yoruba *and* American) male privileges to make major decisions without his wife. But he was not egocentrically trying to meet his own needs, as some American men might. He was placing his culturally determined responsibility (equally, if differently, powerful for both genders) toward kin above (American-nurtured) sharply delineated boundaries or upward mobility. Although both partners were operating within their respective culturally determined gender roles, Olu was more profoundly Yoruba (collectivist and relational) than what Americans consider to be masculine (individualistic). Elise was also operating within a relational framework, but hers was profoundly American, focusing on the relational needs and family obligations of the immediate family. Olu's family had woven a tapestry of mutual caring and responsibility. Elise's domestic labor was needed for Olu to continue his part of the weaving, but she was not welcomed by in-laws into a true reciprocity (as an American sister-in-law might require before helping out too much); nor was she a Yoruba woman willing to meet her husband's familial obligations.

TOWARD LIBERATIONAL APPROACHES TO FAMILY THERAPY

Patriarchy takes profoundly different forms across cultures. Viewing women generically as relational and men generically as individualistic confounds patriarchy (which is on a meta level to culture) with its culture-specific manifestations in dominant American culture. A truly liberational family therapy respects the multiple realities of multicultural families embedded in two unequally influential layers of patriarchy—one constructed in their original culture and class positions, the other constructed in relation to dominant North American culture and present class positions.

I began this chapter with an account of the difficulties and limitations of pursuing such a complex liberational approach. I end it hopefully, having elucidated theoretical efforts moving us toward the synthesis we require. My optimism grows with the development around the world of technical approaches informed by the kaleidoscopic lenses of gender, class, and race, and by the need to extend our work beyond the family to the structure of society.

Three developments are particularly exciting. A Brussels community team, La Gerbe, uses network, multiple-family therapy, and ecological approaches to help disenfranchised poor and immigrant clients recognize and challenge the economic and racial oppression contributing to their emotional difficulties (Elkaïm, 1987; Trimble & Kliman, in press). A Montreal team has synthesized La Gerbe's model with feminist analysis and techniques (Desmarais et al., 1987; Trimble & Kliman, in press).

In Lower Hutt, New Zealand, the Family Centre's team of Samoans, Maori, and whites uses the Just Therapy approach to heal families and to rectify gender-, culture-, and class-based power differentials (Waldegrave, Laban, & Tuhaka, 1991). The team is accountable to oppressed people, as the best judges of how well therapy addresses their issues. Male therapists must answer to the concerns of female clients and staff (including nonprofessionals). The same holds for the non-Maori and non-Samoan therapists of Maori and Samoan families. The Family Centre community functions as an action-reflection team, with moral authority, ensuring that therapists do not impose dominant values and realities.

Just Therapy seeks to clarify and transform family dynamics, including power relations based on culture, class, and gender, and to affirm what Samoans call the "sacred space between" people, between people and the environment, and between people and the spiritual world. Just Therapy calls for each family and therapist to collaborate in developing a critical understanding of how patriarchy, racism, and class oppression are reproduced in the problematic dynamics (including domestic violence) that the family brings to treatment. At the same time, it requires a humanizing respect for the reality of each family member, oppressor and oppressed.

My own dream is that the field of family therapy will develop theoretically, technically, and morally to the point that just such a collaborative and liberational approach is commonplace. That dream is a long way from fulfillment, but it draws closer with the recognition that each strand of oppression, strength, perspective, and hope that gender, class, and race have woven into the fabric of our lives has its own reality, its own urgency, and its own potential for transformation.

ACKNOWLEDGMENTS

Much of this chapter was inspired by the ideas and example of Nancy Boyd-Franklin, Virginia Goldner, and colleagues and teachers in the old Group for a Radical Human Science. My students and my colleagues on the curriculum transformation project at the Massachusetts School of Professional Psychology have stretched my thinking about multiple levels of diversity. My friends, especially Sylvia and David Hammerman, have been most supportive. My immediate and extended families have been loving, encouraging, patient, and forgiving. Most of all, I thank my husband, David Trimble, for his helpful ideas and generous critiques, for his partnership, and for all that extra domestic labor.

REFERENCES

Aponte, H. (1976). Underorganization in the poor family. In P. Guerin (Ed.), *Family therapy* (pp. 432–448). New York: Gardner Press.

Ault-Riche, M. (Ed.). (1986). *Women and family therapy*. Rockville, MD: Aspen.

Bernal, G., & Alvarez, A. (1983). Culture and class in the study of families. In C. Falicov (Ed.), *Cultural perspectives in family therapy* (pp. 33–50). Rockville, MD: Aspen.

Boyd-Franklin, N. (1989). *Black families in therapy*. New York: Guilford Press.

Braverman, L. (Ed.). (1987). Women, feminism, and family therapy [Special issue]. *Journal of Psychotherapy and the Family, 3*(4).

Carter, B., & McGoldrick, M. (Eds.). (1988). *The changing family life cycle: A framework for family therapy* (2nd ed.). New York: Gardner Press.

Caust, B., Libow, J., & Raskin, P. (1981). Challenges and promises of training women as family systems therapists. *Family Process, 20*(4), 439–447.

Chodorow, N. (1978). *The reproduction of mothering: Psychoanalysis and the sociology of gender*. Berkeley: University of California Press.

Combrinck-Graham, L. (Ed.). (1989). *Children in family contexts: Perspectives on treatment*. New York: Guilford Press.

De la Cancela, V. (1991). Working affirmatively with Puerto Rican men: Professional and personal reflections. *Journal of Feminist Family Therapy, 2*(3–4), 195–212.

Desmarais, D., Lavigueur, H., Roy, L., & Blanchet, L. (1987). Patient identifié, réseau primaire et idéologie dominante. In M. Elkaïm (Ed.), *Les pratiques de réseaux: Santé mentale et contexte sociale* (pp. 41–74). Paris: Les Editions ESF.

Edelman, M. W. (1985). The sea is so wide and my boat is so small: Problems facing black children today. In H. McAdoo & J. McAdoo (Eds.), *Black children* (pp. 79–82). Beverly Hills, CA: Sage.

Elkaïm, M. (Ed.). (1987). *Les pratiques de réseaux: Santé mentale et contexte sociale*. Paris: Les Editions ESF.

Falicov, C. (Ed.). (1983). *Cultural perspectives in family therapy*. Rockville, MD: Aspen.

Falicov, C. (1986). Cross-cultural marriages. In N. Jacobson & A. Gurman (Eds.), *Clinical handbook of marital therapy* (pp. 429–450). New York: Guilford Press.

Fulmer, R. (1988). Lower-income and professional families: A comparison of structure and life cycle process. In B. Carter & M. McGoldrick (Eds.), *The changing family life cycle: A framework for family therapy* (2nd ed., pp. 545–578). New York: Gardner Press.

Gilligan, C. (1982). *In a different voice: Psychological theory and women's development*. Cambridge, MA: Harvard University Press.

Goldner, V. (1985). Feminism and family therapy. *Family Process, 24*(1), 31–48.

Goldner, V. (1989). Generation and gender: Normative and covert hierarchies. In M. McGoldrick, C. Anderson, & F. Walsh (Eds.), *Women in families: A framework for family therapy* (pp. 42–60). New York: Norton.

Goodrich, T., Rampage, C., Ellman, B., & Halstead, K. (Eds.). (1988). *Feminist family therapy: A casebook*. New York: Norton.

Greene, B. (1990). What has gone before: The legacy of racism and sexism in the lives of black mothers and daughters. *Women and Therapy, 9*(1–2), 207–230.

Greene, B. (1992). Black feminist psychotherapy. In E. Wright (Ed.), *Psychoanalysis and feminism: A critical dictionary*. Oxford: Blackwell.

Hare-Mustin, R. (1978). A feminist approach to family therapy. *Family Process, 17*, 181–194.

Ho, M. (1987). *Family therapy with ethnic minorities*. Newbury Park, CA: Sage.

Imber-Black, E. (1990). Multiple embedded systems. In M. P. Mirkin (Ed.), *The social and political contexts of family therapy* (pp. 3–18). Boston: Allyn & Bacon.

Inclan, J., & Ferran, E. (1990). Poverty, politics, and family therapy: A role for systems theory. In M. P. Mirkin (Ed.), *The social and political contexts of family therapy* (pp. 193–213). Boston: Allyn & Bacon.

Jorge, A. (1983). Issues of race and class in women's studies: A Puerto Rican woman's thoughts. In A. Swerdlow & H. Lessinger (Eds.), *Class, race and sex: The dynamics of control* (pp. 216–220). New York: G. K. Hall.

Luepnitz, D. (1988). *The family interpreted: Feminist theory in clinical practice*. New York: Basic Books.

McAdoo, H. (1981). *Black families*. Beverly Hills, CA: Sage.

McGoldrick, M., Anderson, C., & Walsh, F. (Eds.). (1989). *Women in families: A framework for family therapy*. New York: Norton.

McGoldrick, M., Pearce, J., & Giordano, J. (Eds.). (1982). *Ethnicity and family therapy*. New York: Guilford Press.

Minuchin, S., Montalvo, B., Guerney, B., Rosman, B., & Schumer, F. (1967). *Families of the slums: An exploration of their structure and treatment*. New York: Basic Books.

Mirkin, M. P. (Ed.). (1990). *The social and political contexts of family therapy*. Boston: Allyn & Bacon.

Papajohn, J., & Spiegel, J. (1974). *Transactions in families*. San Francisco: Jossey-Bass.

Patchesky, R. (1983). Reproduction and class divisions among women. In A. Swerdlow & H. Lessinger (Eds.), *Class, race and sex: The dynamics of control* (pp. 221–241). New York: G. K. Hall.

Pinderhughes, E. (1986). Minority women: A nodal point in the functioning of the social system. In M. Ault-Riche (Ed.), *Women and family therapy* (pp. 51–63). Rockville, MD: Aspen.

Pogrebin, L. C. (1991). *Deborah, Golda and me: Being Jewish and female in America.* New York: Crown.

Poster, M. (1978). *Critical theory of the family.* New York: Seabury Press.

Roberge, C. (1990). *Single mothers' experiences of their social networks: A phenomenological study of separated women's relations.* Unpublished doctoral dissertation, Massachusetts School of Professional Psychology, Boston, MA.

Ryan, W. (1971). *Blaming the victim.* New York: Random House.

Saba, G., Karrer, B., & Hardy, K. (Eds.). (1989). Minorities and family therapy [Special issue]. *Journal of Psychotherapy and the Family, 6*(1–2).

Schwartzman, J. (1982). Normality from a cross-cultural perspective. In F. Walsh (Ed.), *Normal family processes* (pp. 383–398). New York: Guilford Press.

Schwartzman, J. (Ed.). (1985). *Families and other systems.* New York: Guilford Press.

Simon, R. (Ed.). (1984, May–June). Family therapy: Putting women in their place? [Special issue]. *The Family Therapy Networker, 8*(3).

Simon, R. (Ed.). (1985, November–December). Feminism: Shedding new light on the family [Special issue]. *The Family Therapy Networker, 9*(6).

Simon, R. (Ed.). (1986, January–February). Another country: The family therapy of the urban poor [Special issue]. *The Family Therapy Networker, 10*(1).

Simon, R. (Ed.). (1987, November–December). When the bough breaks: Homelessness in America [Special issue]. *The Family Therapy Networker, 11*(6).

Stack, C. (1974). *All our kin: Strategies for survival in a black community.* New York: Harper Colophon Books.

Trimble, D., & Kliman, J. (in press). Network intervention. In M. Elkaïm (Ed.), *Panorama des thérapies familiales.* Paris: Les Editions du Seuil.

Tseng, W.-S., & Hsu, J. (1991). *Culture and family: Problems and therapy.* Binghamton, NY: Haworth Press.

U.S. Bureau of the Census. (1989). *Statistical abstract of the United States* (109th ed.). Washington, DC: U.S. Government Printing Office.

U.S. Bureau of the Census. (1992). *Poverty in the United States 1991: Current population report on consumer income* (Current Population Report, Series P-60, No. 181). Washington, DC: U.S. Government Printing Office.

Waldegrave, C., Laban, W., & Tuhaka, F. (1991, November). *Just therapy.* Paper presented at the Just Therapy Conference of the Cambridge Family Institute, Cambridge, MA.

Walters, M., Carter, B., Papp, P., & Silverstein, O. (1988). *The invisible web: Gender patterns in family relationships.* New York: Guilford Press.

3

The Impact of Misogyny and Homophobia on Therapy with Women

PRISCILLA ELLIS
BIANCA CODY MURPHY

Our culture divides people into categories of gender and sexual orientation. One is either male or female, heterosexual or homosexual (or, more recently, bisexual). Most people think and act as if there were fundamental, enduring differences between men and women and between heterosexuals and homosexuals. Many of the perceived characteristics by which women are differentiated from men and homosexuals are differentiated from heterosexuals are devalued and stigmatized. These perceived differences are used to justify discrimination against, and oppression of, one group of people (women, homosexuals) by another (men, heterosexuals). The creation and exaggeration of difference provide an opportunity to increase the value of one group at the expense of others. Difference is used to create and maintain power (Scott, 1988).

Our society, then, is organized around the subordination and devaluation of women and of those perceived to be nonheterosexual—in other words, around misogynist, sexist, heterosexist, and homophobic beliefs and practices. Some clinicians have written about the effects of sexism and misogyny on women in therapy (Chesler, 1972; Showalter, 1985; Ussher, 1992). Others, mostly gay and lesbian therapists, have written about the effects of homophobia and heterosexism on lesbian and, recently, bisexual women (Falco, 1991; Murphy, 1992; Nichols, 1988; Roth, 1989; Vargo, 1987). We believe that misogyny, sexism, heterosexism, and homophobia affect *all women, regardless of sexual orientation,* and shape the context within which therapeutic work with women takes place.

THE POLITICAL CONTEXT

Misogyny and Sexism

"Misogyny" is hatred of women. "Sexism" is the valuing of one gender over the other, most often the valuing of male over female. The dominant culture in the United States (and most of the world) is sexist and misogynist. Misogyny and sexism are so embedded in our culture and our individual psyches that many of us take for granted their myriad manifestations in everyday experience. Misogyny and sexism permeate the social, political, economic, educational, and personal fabric of our lives. Our daily experience as women tells us this; the statistics prove it.

Until 1920, women in this country could not vote. Although women in the United States have had the right to vote longer than women in most Western nations, U.S. women are least represented among Western nations in political offices at every level of government. Of the 100 senators in the 1993 Congress, only 6 are women, and this is after what was called the "Year of the Woman" in electoral politics. The proposed Equal Rights Amendment to the U.S. Constitution, a simple statement that "Equality of rights under the law shall not be denied or abridged by the United States or by any states on account of sex," remains unpassed since it was first introduced over 70 years ago. Women are discriminated against economically, educationally, and vocationally, and that discrimination is still legal in many states.

Throughout the world, women do approximately 75% of the work, receive 10% of the pay, and own 1% of the property, according to official U.N. statistics (cited by Brock-Utne, 1989, p. 63). In the United States, women earn, on average, 59 cents to every dollar men earn, a ratio essentially unchanged since 1955 (Faludi, 1991). When women divorce, their economic status declines by 33%, while that of their ex-husbands increases (U.S. Bureau of the Census, 1991). The vast proportion of households below the poverty line are headed by single female parents (Edelman, 1987).

Women are the targets of sexual exploitation and violence in the media, on the job, and in their homes. Scantily clothed female bodies are used to sell everything from cars to detergent (Kilbourn, Vitagliano, & Stallone, 1979). Cable television and dial-a-porn movies bring pornography into the living rooms of homes and motels. *Playboy* and *Penthouse* combined sell more copies than *Newsweek* and *Time* together (Henaut, Shannon, & Klein, 1991). Pornography is increasingly violent, with depictions of women being beaten, mutilated, and murdered (Malamuth & Donnerstein, 1984). Sexual exploitation at the workplace gained public attention when Anita Hill's charges of sexual harassment against U.S. Supreme Court nominee (now Justice) Clarence Thomas unleashed a torrent of similar stories from women in all walks of life. It is estimated that as many as 90% of women have been sexually harassed at work (Hamilton, Alagna, King, & Lloyd, 1987). Girls and women are frequently victims of sexual abuse and violence. One in three adult women has been sexually abused in childhood (Russell, 1984). There is a 26% chance that a woman will be raped in her lifetime (Russell & Howell, 1983). If a woman is a victim of violence, it is often perpetrated in her own home and by someone she knows. If a woman is lucky enough to escape the personal experience of violence, she lives with fear and the threat of violence every day of her life. These crimes against women are perpetrated almost exclusively by men.

For women of color, women with disabilities, women of lower socio-economic status, old women, and women who are perceived to be nonheterosexual, the discrimination, oppression, and violence are multi-plied.

Heterosexism and Homophobia

"Heterosexism" has been defined as "a world-view, a value system that prizes heterosexuality, assumes it is the only appropriate manifestation of love and sexuality, and devalues homosexuality and all that is not hetero-sexual" (Herek, 1986, p. 925). Heterosexism manifests itself in innumerable ways. Our society assumes heterosexuality in its unvarying belief that little girls will grow up to marry men. The primacy of heterosexuality is deeply embedded in popular culture—movies, advertisements, magazines, books. We seldom see lesbian relationships portrayed by the media, and the few times that they are, the relationships usually end in death, suicide, or betrayal (Murphy, 1991a). "Family" in the United States usually means a heterosexual family consisting of a mother, father, and children. A woman partnered with another woman will often be treated by her family of origin as single, and invited alone to family functions and celebrations. The assumption of heterosexuality that pervades our discourse, our transactions, and our attitudes is an irritant and sometimes a humiliation for the person who does not have or does not want a partner of the other gender.

In addition to the assumptions of heterosexuality, there are laws and regulations that maintain heterosexuality as the only sanctioned mode of intimate relationships. Persons of the same sex cannot legally marry. In-surance companies do not provide benefits to "nonfamily" members, ruling out partners of the same sex. Rights that automatically accrue to a legally designated spouse (inheritance, bereavement leave, property ownership, hospital visitation, etc.) have to be specially requested and granted, and are often denied, to a nonheterosexual (and therefore nonlegal) partner. These practices are shaped by heterosexism and hardened by homophobia.

"Homophobia" is the prejudice, discrimination, and hostility directed at gay men and lesbian women because of their sexual orientation (Herek, 1986). The majority of people in the United States perceive gay men and lesbian women as sick, immoral, or criminal (*Newsweek*, 1983; *San Francisco Chronicle*, 1982). In a Roper Center national survey, 73% of the respondents agreed that sexual relations between two adults of the same sex are always wrong (Davis & Smith, 1984). These negative attitudes and misinformation contribute to discrimination against lesbian and bisexual women (and of course gay and bisexual men) in many areas, including jobs, housing, and child custody.

The civil rights of gay men and lesbian women are legally protected in only eight states and a few municipalities such as New York City, San Francisco, and Chicago. In the other 42 states and in most cities and towns, gay men and lesbian women have no legal recourse when they are fired, evicted, or lose custody of their children solely because of their sexual orientation. In fact, in almost half of the states they would be considered criminals. In a recent U.S. Supreme Court decision (*Bowers v. Hardwick*, 1986), the Court upheld the right of states to prosecute adults for engaging in consensual sexual acts with each other in the privacy of their own homes.

For every effort to increase protections for gay and lesbian civil rights, there have been countermoves to take them away. A recent Vatican statement to U.S. bishops supports discrimination against gay men and lesbian women, and urges Catholics to oppose the passage of civil rights legislation for these groups. In 1992, the state of Colorado passed a referendum prohibiting the state and all its agencies from acting on any claim of discrimination by a lesbian woman or gay man. That same year, a stronger initiative in Oregon stating that public institutions (including the schools) "shall assist in setting a standard for Oregon's youth that recognizes homosexuality . . . *as abnormal, wrong, unnatural and perverse and . . . to be discouraged and avoided* [emphasis added]" was defeated, but received support from 44% of the voters.

In their most severe form, prejudice and hostility produce violence that ranges from verbal harassment to murder. Crimes committed against individuals because of their membership in a minority group are called "hate crimes." Like African-Americans, Jews, Latinos, and Asians, gay men and lesbian women are frequent targets of hate crimes. According to a report to the National Institute of Justice, "homosexuals are probably the most frequent victims of hate violence" (Finn & McNeil, 1987, p. 2). The violence directed at gay men and lesbian women can be horrendous. The director of victim services at Bellevue Hospital in New York has stated that "attacks against gay men were the most heinous and brutal I encountered. They frequently involved torture, cutting, mutilation, and beating, and showed the absolute intent to rub out the human being because of his sexual preference" (M. Mertz, cited in Berrill, 1990, p. 280).

Herek (1989) reports that in recent surveys, as many as 92% of lesbians and gay men responded that they have been the targets of antigay verbal abuse or threats, and as many as 24% reported physical attacks because of their sexual orientation. It should be noted that many gay men and lesbian women do not report verbal harassment or physical violence against them to the authorities, because they fear that they will be subjected to secondary victimization at the hands of police or others, who may learn of their sexual orientation as a result of their having reported the original attack. Although much of this violence is directed at gay men, lesbian women are also victims. For example, in 1985 in Los Angeles, a man yelling "sick mother-fucker" threw a beaker of acid in the face of a lesbian employee of the local Gay and Lesbian Community Service Center (National Gay and Lesbian Task Force, 1986). Lesbian women are assaulted, raped, and murdered because they are lesbian. Lesbian women are victims of violence, both as women in a sexist society and as lesbians in a homophobic society.

The Lesbian Threat

Heterosexism and homophobia operate in the service of misogyny and sexism (Pharr, 1988). Heterosexist attitudes and institutions keep women in subordinate relation to men, preserving male dominance and female dependence. Heterosexism maintains the view that women need men to function properly, to be fulfilled and secure. It rejects the possibility that women can do things independently, or, even more unthinkable, with other women. Women bonding in any way that threatens male dominance and control—political, economic, or sexual—are at serious risk of retaliation. Homophobia is a primary means of retaliation, the ultimate weapon against women's empowerment. Thus, the effects of homophobia are not limited to lesbian women.

Homophobia affects *all* women through the lesbian threat. As lesbianism is a threat *to* the patriarchy, so "lesbian" becomes the threat *of* the patriarchy: Any woman can be threatened with the label "lesbian" if she rejects male domination and control. An example of lesbian baiting is television evangelist Pat Robertson's argument against the passage of the Equal Rights Amendment: "It [the Equal Rights Amendment] is about a socialist, antifamily political movement that encourages women to leave their husbands, kill their children, practice witchcraft, destroy capitalism *and become lesbians*" (cited in the *New York Times,* 1992, p. A-16; emphasis added). To be labeled "lesbian" puts women at risk of greater discrimination and violence than they would be subjected to just for being female. The attacks against lesbian women remind all women what could happen to them if they do not submit to the prescriptions of the patriarchy. The purpose of lesbian baiting, Pharr (1988) maintains, is "to hurt lesbians, to control all women, and *to stop women's social change work*" (p. 34; emphasis Pharr's).

THE THERAPEUTIC CONTEXT

The damaging effects of misogyny, heterosexism, and homophobia pervade every major sphere of a woman's inner and interpersonal life: her identity and self-esteem, her sexuality and sexual identity, her relationships with intimate partners and family, her attitudes and feelings about men, and her sense of safety. These effects will vary according to an individual woman's personal history, age, class, race, disability, and sexual orientation, but the common denominator is the same: She is separated, subordinated, and devalued because of her gender; kept "in her place" by homophobia; and will encounter resistance and retaliation if she challenges, threatens, or departs from patriarchal rules and paradigms.

Therapy can be a context in which women confront the effects of misogyny, sexism, heterosexism, and homophobia on their lives, or it can reinforce and perpetuate these effects. As therapists, we should be aware that the perspective we take, as well as our own biases and blind spots, will determine the extent to which therapy serves to challenge or reinforce the consequences of misogyny, sexism, heterosexism, and homophobia. We are contaminated by the same forces as our clients, so we would do well to examine our own assumptions, ignorance, and confusion about these issues. Many times there will be no single or simple answer or approach; indeed, when we try to include an understanding of the impact of the larger context on our clients' struggles, we find that questions and paradoxes proliferate. Sometimes the best we can do is try to hold these questions in our minds, and include our clients in the effort to make sense of them.

Katherine's story illustrates some of the ways in which misogyny, sexism, heterosexism, and homophobia shape a woman's experience.

> Katherine was a 34-year-old white woman from a working-class background who worked as a firefighter and was studying environmental science in a community college at night. Lately, she was being subjected to sexual harassment by a superior whose support she needed to get the promotion she sought at work. Her work situation was becoming increasingly unpleasant, even though she got along well with several of her coworkers.
>
> Katherine had a 17-year-old son who had lived with his father and stepmother since Katherine's divorce 15 years ago. Until recently Katherine did not want much contact with her son, for which she felt enormously guilty: "I'm not a normal mother." She had been involved off and on for the last 7 years with a man whom she described as both caring and occasionally physically abusive. She had also had several short-lived sexual/romantic relationships with women over the last 10 years.
>
> Katherine's relationship with her elderly parents was strained. She

felt guilty and ashamed that she did not turn out to be the type of daughter they wanted; she also resented her father's seeming lack of interest in her as she was growing up, and her mother's criticism and judgments. She always felt her older sister to be the favored child. This sister was "feminine" and popular with boys as an adolescent, and was now married to a successful insurance agent and the mother of two children. Katherine wondered whether an uncle who lived with them when she was young did something to her to "screw me up sexually." She had no specific memories of abuse, only vague uncomfortable feelings whenever she thought of this man.

Katherine came into therapy to work on her long-standing depression and self-esteem problems (as she defined them) and her desire to be able to have a satisfactory intimate relationship.

The Personal and the Political: A Dynamic Interplay

We can see in Katherine's story elements of many women's experience: the struggle of growing up with expectations about what it means to be "female," and to be acceptable to parents, peers, and community. Katherine's youthful inclinations and interests did not conform to the conventional expectations in her community: She was physically active (too aggressive and competitive); she was bright and rebellious (provoking many teachers and getting indifferent grades); and she had little interest in clothes, makeup, and the dating scene (not "feminine"). She felt odd, confused, and unhappy about whether she was ever going to find a place where she could be herself and feel at home.

As Katherine told her therapist the beginning of her story and her reasons for seeking therapy, the therapist tried to listen carefully to Katherine's rendering of her experience, at the same time as she was framing it according to her own schemata. There would be a constant interplay, at times tension, between Katherine's understanding and the therapist's. The personal meanings of her struggles were also interwoven with the political. How the therapist moved back and forth between these levels would be delicate matters of timing and emphasis. Deciding where to place emphasis, or how to make an observation or interpretation, would sometimes be exceedingly difficult. Too narrow a focus on the "dysfunction" of her family of origin and the injury to her psychic functioning might leave Katherine feeling more despairing and helpless than before. She might blame herself and her family without seeing that forces beyond the family contributed to the family's difficulty. Too broad a view of the sociocultural forces that had warped her ability to be and do her best in the world might seem to her a misreading or inattention on the therapist's part, irrelevant and unhelpful—too much, perhaps, like the inattention of her father or the judgments of her mother. Too broad a view might also leave her feeling helpless, powerless to change the larger context, and unable to find effective ways of responding. The therapist had to strive to maintain a balance, however precarious, between the "personal" and the "political."

Traditionally, the psychological perspective has ignored or minimized the impact of the external world on the development of people's psychological or "inner" problems. Psychotherapy's focus on the intrapsychic tends to pathologize and privatize. There is a long history of blaming women (i.e., labeling them "sick" or "crazy") for symptoms that are in large part responses to oppression and victimization (Chesler, 1972; Showalter, 1985; Ussher, 1992).

The tendency to pathologize women's experiences can be seen in the following excerpt from the diagnostic evaluation Katherine received when she was hospitalized for depression and suicidality at one point:

> Katherine is an individual who at times may be quite hyperemotional and impulsive in either a narcissistic or hysterical manner . . . and appears quite aloof, withholding, and even frankly paranoid. . . . There is a considerable sense of deprivation about this patient upon which much of her anger appears based. . . . She is apt to be asocial/antisocial or rebellious, and act without sufficient thought. . . . She appears dissatisfied with her life situation and may be withdrawn. Family problems are likely. At times she may appear demanding, self-centered, and immature, lacking in insight.

Alternatives to this kind of psychological blaming reframe women's behavior and symptomatology in the larger social context. Kaplan (1983) has suggested that female depression be redefined as a response to the depressing and oppressing realities of women's lives. Pharr (1988) suggests redefining women's ubiquitous "self-esteem" problems as "internalized sexism." Some of these redefinitions proved useful in understanding Katherine's depression and low self-esteem. Although they did not explain them fully, of course, they provided a context in which Katherine and her therapist could make sense out of the long-standing and persistent nature of these problems: They were not simply attributable to Katherine's deficient mothering or her characterological vulnerabilities. Katherine's feelings of isolation, of not fitting in, of being flawed or deficient were in some ways accurate or at least natural responses to her social and cultural environment and the messages she received about what it meant to be an acceptable, "normal" female. (See Lewis, Chapter 8, this volume.)

At various times during her hospitalization, Katherine was described as manifesting "inappropriate" behavior—for example, when she expressed anger at those in authority, or reported having engaged in sexual relationships with women. The term "inappropriate" is a favorite one among mental health professionals. Literally, it means "not proper" or "ill-fitting" (i.e., not conforming to the accepted norms or standards). Katherine's behavior or feelings might well be considered "inappropriate" if measured against traditional definitions of what is "proper" and "fitting" for a female.

Katherine received the diagnosis of borderline personality disorder at the day hospital she attended after her discharge from the inpatient hospital. This label has also been re-examined and reinterpreted by feminists. The diagnostic category of borderline personality disorder, in which women are vastly overrepresented, has been found to be highly correlated with a history of child abuse (Herman, 1992). Viewing a woman's "borderline symptomatology" as the result of traumatic childhood experiences can be liberating for both client and therapist. It frees the client of a therapeutic stigma ("borderline" is often synonymous with "difficult") and may enable the therapist to join more empathically with her client, rather than dreading and resenting her troublesome behavior and powerful feelings. This broader understanding of the origins of "borderline symptomatology" can lay the foundation for a collaborative relationship between therapist and client, which is essential for the healing and empowerment of effective therapy.

There are numerous examples of how we as therapists need to keep in mind the political context. There is a widespread tendency in the culture to hold mothers responsible for everything from sexual dysfunction to low self-esteem. Keeping daughters (and sons) enraged at mothers is a powerful means of perpetuating misogyny and sexism. Blaming mothers allows clients and therapists to avoid looking at the parenting patterns and power relationships between men and women that create the conditions keeping many mothers overinvolved and fathers distant. By helping Katherine to consider the context in which her mother raised her—the constraints on her mother's freedom and autonomy, the distance or absence of her father—the therapist helped her to refocus some of her anger and disappointment on other important people in her life in addition to her mother, as well as to understand the conditions that fostered her mother's own depression and need to control and disparage her daughter.

Another illustration of the personal–political interplay can be found when a young woman in her 20s seeks therapy because of extreme feelings of loneliness. She feels worthless and empty because she has not met an eligible man, and she wonders what is wrong with her. The therapist working with her attempts to understand her experience along several dimensions: Although the feelings are deeply personal, they are linked to the larger cultural assumptions that a woman should be paired with a man; that there is something wrong with her if she cannot find one; that friends are not as valuable as a male lover or husband; and that this deficiency *in her* will persist unless she works hard to make herself available and attractive to men. Possibly this situation has been influenced by her own personal history of feeling like an unwanted or unacceptable child in her family. And that personal history is itself related to a larger context: Her mother received little emotional support from her husband, and he did not share in household responsibilities. She was her mother's fourth child, and by the time she was born, her mother was too exhausted to give her the kind of nurturance she had given the older three.

Yet another example of the need to attend to the larger context occurs when a therapist works with a closeted lesbian woman. If the therapist presses her to examine only her internalized homophobia, and challenges her about her decision to remain closeted, she may be ignoring or minimizing the external homophobia that influences her choices. If her job or physical safety is at risk, choosing the discomfort and distortion of secrecy may be preferable to the economic and/or physical dangers of disclosure. By acknowledging the pervasive effects of homophobia on a woman's daily experience at work, on the street, and in her relationships, the therapist can validate the psychic toll she suffers and the complex, difficult considerations that go into her decision making. Such validation must be part of the process of sorting out her own internalized homophobic attitudes that contribute to her low self-esteem, guilt, secrecy, and difficulty in asserting herself and taking action.

> Some of the isolation and paralysis Katherine experienced at work was connected to her being female in a largely antifemale environment, and being bisexual in a traditionally homophobic culture—in this case, the fire department. She worried that if she "came out" at work, she would risk further isolation, ostracism, and harassment. Her therapist validated the reality of some of these fears, and explored with her other ways in which she might be more assertive at work to counteract her feelings of impotence and passivity. Katherine eventually decided to be more open about her sexual orientation in work settings as she developed a greater overall sense of professional confidence and competence. These two aspects of her sense of self—her sexual identity and her work identity—began to shift from the negative cycle ("I'm bad, incompetent, deviant; people look down on and revile me; I can't afford to take risks") to a positive one ("I'm good at my work; people respect me; they'll take me as the good firefighter that I am, even if they know I'm 'queer'").

The stories are endless. Each client's story is unique, affected by her distinctive personal experiences, which are mediated by age, race, class, and disability. However, each woman's story is woven from some of the same sociopolitical threads. Our task as therapists is to try to understand and join with our clients in untangling the interwoven threads of the personal and political.

Sex and Sexuality: Shame and Silence

Silence and shame surround sexuality for many women. They stem in large part from the misinformation and distorted paradigms of sexuality women

have absorbed about what it means to be female, and what are "appropriate" and "healthy" expressions of their sexuality. These paradigms have
largely been the creation of men.

When she was growing up, Katherine received a number of messages
about her sexuality. A woman must be sexy but not sexual, and
certainly not autonomous in her sexuality; women's bodies and
women's sexuality are for male pleasure and for reproduction (the
offspring, in many instances, will also be under male control);
women's bodies are dirty and shameful; a woman is a madonna or a
whore—pure, holy, motherly, and therefore nonsexual, or hypersex-
ual, ravenous, and promiscuous. Finally, sex can be dangerous; to be
sexual risks not only condemnation but exploitation and abuse.
Katherine's possible sexual abuse at the hands of her uncle might have
led her to fear sexual feelings. Even if she had not experienced sexual
trauma herself, she did so vicariously through other women's experiences; every woman is a potential trauma victim.

Women therapists share this sexual legacy. We may ourselves be
trauma victims; we may be uncomfortable discussing sexual issues because
of the internalization of the messages we have received about women's
sexuality; we may assume that the emotional is more important than the
sexual for women. For these and other reasons, women therapists may shy
away from sexual matters; avoid explicit exploration of sexual practices,
fantasies, and desires; or translate conversations about sex into the language
of emotional as opposed to sensual/physical feeling.

Therapy offers a woman an opportunity to reclaim her sexuality. It
may begin with the most rudimentary need to discover the capacity for
sexual pleasure and/or to free it from the kinds of shame and guilt many
women experience. The experience of breaking the silence about sexuality
with a trusted therapist may be the woman's first experience of exploring
the forbidden, the shameful, and the dangerous. Talking about masturbation, lubrication, vibrators, and anal stimulation may take some effort on
the part of the therapist at first, but practice makes it easier. The therapist
can become an affirming "good mother," sister, or ally who supports and
even celebrates the client's discovery of her own sexuality.

In addition to discomfort and shame, therapists may also carry some of
the dominant culture's heterosexist and homophobic beliefs about sexuality:
Heterosexual intercourse is the apogee of sexual expression; orgasm
through intercourse is the primary sexual goal; women should not require
manual stimulation during intercourse to reach orgasm; lesbian women
who have heterosexual fantasies are not "real" lesbians (and the converse for
heterosexual women); women should be careful not to frustrate their male
partners by "denying" them sex, or anger or frighten them by being "too"
aggressive; sex between women consists mainly of holding and caressing;

women's erotic feelings toward men are "healthier" than those toward women; and so on. We need to question and challenge our assumptions if we are to enable our clients to free themselves from some of these straitjackets. We need a vision of sexual behavior that is freer of normative goals, and is shaped more by the particular needs and desires of the participants.

Sexual feelings may emerge in the therapeutic relationship itself. Therapists may avoid discussing these feelings because of their discomfort talking about sex or their belief that erotic feelings do not belong in the therapeutic setting. Furthermore, internalized homophobia may cause a female therapist to deny, minimize, or misinterpret the erotic feelings that she or her female clients experience in what is a highly intimate and intense relationship. Some therapists translate their clients' erotic feelings toward them into a yearning for the maternal breast. Others may become anxious or surprised by some of their own responses to clients. When the therapeutic relationship becomes an arena for erotic feelings, it can feel dangerous to both therapist and client. But therein lie opportunities for deep exploration. The discovery that sexual feelings can be experienced without damaging consequences can be one of the greatest gifts of the therapeutic experience.

> Katherine struggled with the sense that there was something wrong with her sexually. She had sexual feelings about people she "should not" (women, a man who made her feel inadequate and stupid, her therapist). She did not have sexual feelings for people she "should" (her former husband, other "appropriate" men). The ways she enjoyed being sexual (masturbating, making love *to* a woman—not being made love to *by* a woman) were not entirely acceptable. With considerable discomfort and embarrassment, she began to voice some of these concerns in her therapy. The therapist tried to frame them in part as consequences of the rigid sexual norms and prescriptions of the culture. She also validated the naturalness of Katherine's having erotic feelings for her therapist—someone with whom she had shared so much—and assured her that talking about such feelings would not lead to acting on them.
>
> For her part, because of her own work in supervision, the therapist was not alarmed by the emergence of erotic feelings toward Katherine. She understood them as a natural response to the intimate links between client and therapist: they did not become a distraction from the therapy work.

Discussions about sexuality in our sexually phobic and conflicted culture are almost always charged and weighed down with misinformation, judgment, bias, and distortion. Therapists need to address their own ignorance, confusion, conflicts, and biases in the area of sexuality with special care and attention. Training, their own therapy, supervision, and consultation in this area are essential.

Sexual Orientation Identity: Ignorance and Bias

If sexuality in general is an area fraught with misinformation and overlaid with religious, social, cultural, and political bias, the question of sexual orientation is even more so. The concept of "sexual orientation" is largely a product of the late 19th- and early 20th-century Western European tradition of the "scientific" study of sex or sexology. This tradition created the dichotomous categories of "homosexual" and "heterosexual." The scientific construction of sex replaced sin and immorality with sickness and abnormality (Duberman, Vicinus, & Chauncey, 1989). Both legacies—the dichotomization and the pathologizing of sexuality—have become firmly rooted in our cultural and psychic lives.

Kinsey's pioneering work in the study of human sexual behavior (Kinsey, Pomeroy, & Martin, 1948; Kinsey, Pomeroy, Martin, & Gebhard, 1953) rejected the dichotomous view of sexual orientation and demonstrated that sexual behavior is much more fluid and varied than was formerly thought. The Kinsey Scale, describing a range of sexual behavior from 0 (exclusive heterosexual behavior) to 6 (exclusive homosexual behavior), attempted to represent more accurately the continuum of human sexual behavior. Kinsey's work has sometimes been used to substantiate the creation of yet another category, that of the "bisexual." Thus, the continuum view of sexual orientation has been replaced with a tripartite categorization of "heterosexual–bisexual–homosexual" or the binary distinction "heterosexual–nonheterosexual."

Despite Kinsey's work and more recent challenges to the traditional views of sexual orientation (see McWhirter, Sanders, & Reinisch, 1990), the popular view of sexual orientation continues to be a unidimensional categorical system. Recent studies in neuroanatomy, psychoendocrinology, and genetics have suggested that there may be biological factors in the development of sexual orientation (Bailey & Pillard, 1991; LeVay, 1991; for a current overview of these issues, see Burr, 1993). The findings suggest that biological differences can be used to support beliefs that sexual orientation, like gender, is fixed and enduring, and that there are significant differences between "heterosexuals" and "homosexuals."

Other research has amply demonstrated that the similarities among so-called heterosexuals, homosexuals, and bisexuals on psychological as well as other dimensions far outweigh the differences. Exaggerating the distinctions *between* groups, and minimizing the diversity *within* groups, serve political purposes: They keep "homosexual" (or "nonheterosexual") individuals and relationships in the category "other"—different, abnormal, inferior.

An alternative view of human sexuality maintains that the meaning of sexuality, above all, is a social and cultural construction reflecting the dominant paradigms and power arrangements of the time (Foucault, 1984;

Kitzinger, 1987; Sedgewick, 1990). This view challenges some of the core heterosexist and homophobic beliefs and structures of our culture: the norm of the "traditional" family; the dominance of men over women; the essential normality and supremacy of heterosexuality; and the superiority of genital sexuality (and its major purposes, male orgasm and reproduction). A social-constructionist view holds that human sexual behavior and its meanings are varied, complex, and variable (i.e., the same sexual act can mean different things to different people, and different things to the same person at different moments), and that change is possible in sexual behavior and its meanings over a person's lifetime (i.e., sexual orientation identity is not fixed, but capable of more variation than is acknowledged or allowed in our culture). The recent emergence of the concept of "the bisexual" supports the constructionist view of sexuality: People had been engaging in "bisexual" behavior for generations before the category or the social identity (and community) were created.

> Katherine's affectional and sexual struggles reflected, in part, the domi-
> nant culture's expectations about "appropriate" or "healthy" gender
> roles and sexual behavior. From an early age, Katherine felt yearnings
> for closeness with women (in particular a camp counselor), about
> which she felt embarrassed, guilty, and confused. As she entered
> adolescence, she worried that she was a lesbian because she found
> herself drawn emotionally more to females than to males. This fear of
> being "abnormal" helped to plunge her into the sexual encounter that
> resulted in her pregnancy. Her sexual life in her marriage was un-
> pleasant, causing her further distress and confusion about what was
> "wrong" with her sexually. When she became sexually active with
> women in her 20s, she found it very difficult to experience sexual
> pleasure. She was beginning to feel that she was "neither fish nor
> fowl"—in other words, that she did not fit either of the prescribed
> sexual orientation categories—and she despaired of ever having a satis-
> fying sexual relationship. "I guess I'm bisexual," she said in her initial
> interview.

The hospital evaluation mentioned earlier said, "Katherine presents with numerous identity issues and sexual confusion." The confusion and identity issues about so-called sexual orientation reside more in the de-finitions and judgments of our culture than in individuals like Katherine.

There are still large gaps and subtle biases in therapists' understanding of the complex issues of sexual orientation. Therapists often get caught in the trap of viewing sexual orientation identity as a fixed and unchangeable category. A therapist may assume that a woman who leaves a 20-year heterosexual marriage for a relationship with another woman was "really" a lesbian all along and has only just now discovered her "true" sexual orienta-tion. Another may believe that a woman who feels erotically and emotionally drawn to both men and women is in a "transitional phase" until she settles on a permanent, more cohesive identity. A therapist may struggle to find a response to an adolescent girl who is terrified of her "homosexual" longings. The therapist can reframe (and thereby trivialize) them as a normal adolescent "crush"; can encourage her to affirm her lesbian identity, perhaps before the girl is ready to assign herself a label; or can support her exploration and provide her with information about the variability and diversity of sexual feelings, behavior, and identities.

Sometimes clients will want to know the sexual orientation of their therapists, or at least their therapists' attitudes and beliefs on the subject of sexual orientation. Usually the question comes from clients who have suffered the impact of homophobia in their lives, or who are struggling with questions about their own sexual orientation. In effect, they may be asking: "Are you homophobic? Will you see me as sick, or define all my problems as related to my sexual orientation? Can you understand my experiences and struggles?" These questions are pertinent, since numerous studies have demonstrated that therapists may be biased and unqualified to work with gay men and lesbian women (Casas, Brady, & Ponterotto, 1983; Committee on Lesbian and Gay Concerns, 1990; Graham, Rawlings, Halpern, & Hermes, 1984; Wisniewski & Toomey, 1987).

> At the beginning of therapy, Katherine asked her therapist directly whether she considered homosexual relationships (and therefore, presumably, herself) "sick." The therapist said that she did not believe that homosexual relationships are sick, and that she affirmed and supported women who were in lesbian relationships. The therapist also stated her belief in the variability of human sexuality, and her rejection of the devaluing and overvaluing of different kinds of sexual behavior. The therapist invited Katherine to bring these issues up whenever they occurred to her, and suggested that they look at the ways Katherine's feelings about herself and her relationships had been colored by the dominant cultural views about sexuality, as well as by her own personal history.

Even if clients do not raise issues of sexual orientation, therapists need to consider why issues of sexual orientation are not being discussed, and what might be the implications of not bringing up the subject. Many therapists assume that talking about sexual orientation (especially the question of their own) is not salient or important unless the issue is brought up directly by their clients or is implicit in the material. But in a culture in which some people are categorized, oppressed, and even murdered because of their supposed sexual orientation, and others are assumed to be normal or even superior because of theirs, it can be argued that the issue of sexual orientation is always relevant. Heterosexual therapists may collude with the heterosexism of the culture if they think that issues of sexual orientation are only relevant to those who are nonheterosexual. Those who suffer the oppression know that the definition by which they are oppressed is always an issue. It is the privilege of those who do not suffer the discrimination that they do not have to pay attention to it; they can take for granted that they are white, able-bodied, or heterosexual (McIntosh, 1988).

There are various ways therapists can indicate to clients that they do not assume heterosexuality as the only, primary, or preferred orientation, and that they recognize and affirm same-sex relationships. Therapists can explicitly include the term "heterosexual" when referring to a heterosexual couple; they can use gender-nonspecific terms, such as "partner," "lover," or "spouse," rather than "husband" or "boyfriend"; and, when exploring sexual history, they should always explicitly ask about same-sex relationships.

The question of therapists' self-disclosure of their own sexual orientation puts their clinical judgment and political consciousness to the test. It may even put them at some professional risk. As with most such questions, there are no easy or simple answers. One's clinical belief system may collide with one's political values. For those therapists who believe in the therapist-as-blank-screen paradigm, self-disclosure will probably be ruled out. For therapists who subscribe to therapy-as-a-coequal-partnership model, self-disclosure may be routinely practiced. Most therapists fall somewhere in between and probably do different things at different times with different clients. Trying to be clinically responsible and true to one's political values can be a complex and difficult balancing effort. How we as therapists make these moment-to-moment decisions bears examination, for our unwitting behavior may perpetuate heterosexist and homophobic attitudes we have internalized from the culture.

Relationships and Family: Norms and Asymmetries

Models of intimate relationships, and women's experiences in them, have been warped by heterosexism and homophobia. The heterosexual couple has been the norm against which all other kinds of couples have been measured and judged deviant. Indeed, a woman's identity and psychological "health" have often depended on, and been defined by, her capacity for intimacy with a man. A woman who chooses not to be partnered may be labeled as psychologically damaged in some way, ranging from schizoid to fearful of intimacy. A woman who chooses to be with another woman may be perceived as a man-hater, as looking for her mother, or as "going through a phase" (i.e., in some state of psychological arrest or disarray).

> Katherine's pregnancy when she was 17 resulted in part from the enormous pressure she felt to have a relationship that would legitimize her and make her acceptable. In addition were the pressures of her own

sexual curiosity and attraction to boys. Her guilt and shame caused her to hide her pregnancy until it was too late to abort, and she felt that her only choice was to marry the boy who had impregnated her, whom she knew she did not love.

The marriage was brief and unhappy. Leaving the marriage made her feel like a failure, and choosing not to have custody of her child made her feel like a monster. Not only had she failed at the most important roles for a woman, marriage and motherhood; she had *chosen* to "abandon" her most important female responsibility (even though she maintained contact with her son through occasional visits and letters). Her choice came out of fear that she could not provide economically or emotionally for her son; her terror (only dimly perceived at the time) that she would repeat the injuries with her son that she had suffered in her family while growing up; and her resentment about the interference that a child posed to her need to figure out who she was and what she wanted to do with her life ("selfishness"). There was no need for Katherine to wear a scarlet letter on her breast; she carried that badge of shame and guilt in her own heart.

Katherine's story illustrates another prescription for women in our culture. Marriage and motherhood are glorified—the *sine qua non* of female fulfillment. Women who do not marry and become mothers, or who are not successful in those roles, are stigmatized and penalized (Weinreb & Murphy, 1988). The bias against women who choose not to mother or who "abandon" their children through adoption may invade the therapeutic relationship. A therapist may look for pathology in the client's relationship with her mother, for a defect in the woman's character structure ("narcissistic personality"), or for an arrest in her psychological development that prevents her from carrying out her psychologically "natural" or "healthy" roles and responsibilities. There may indeed be individual psychological and historical reasons for such actions, which need to be understood and explored in therapy. It is necessary to examine the complexity of motives and circumstances that may lead a woman to choose not to mother. The therapist needs to acknowledge the enormous pressures and impossible expectations placed on women in our culture to be the primary—and exemplary—caretakers in traditional families.

As Katherine developed greater confidence in herself, and became less depressed and self-critical, she began to increase her contacts with her son, who was by now an adolescent. Feeling on firmer ground emotionally and financially, she decided to request that he live with her. This was a watershed in Katherine's life, opening the way for increased responsibilities, self-esteem, and emotional contact with someone about whom she had previously felt guilty, resentful, and insecure for years. Although there were many problems in having her teenage son living with her, Katherine faced them and demonstrated new capacities for taking responsible action and being realistic about how much she could do for him. Her sense of herself as a responsible, caring person—and mother—took root and grew.

Therapists' assumptions about the significance of women's relationships and the meaning of "family" have been shaped by the views of the dominant culture. The traditional family (father, mother, children) is the cornerstone of patriarchy, in which male power and domination over women and children are protected and enshrined. As the normative model of the family, it is a bastion of heterosexism and homophobia. Therapists reinforce its power every time they assume that a woman needs to create a family in order to be whole, legitimate, or fully "actualized"; when they draw a genogram and fail to accord comparable importance to nonrelatives or nontraditional family members; when they give workshops on "marital therapy"; when they form professional associations called the American Association of *Marital* and Family Therapy; or when they avoid or minimize the importance of women's friendships and associations with other women in their emotional development and functioning.

Challenges and alternatives to traditional views about "appropriate" gender roles and "normal" relationships are increasing in practice and theory. But despite these challenges and the growing accumulation of data about the psychological similarities among different types of couples (Kurdek, 1991; Kurdek & Schmitt, 1986), the view that same-sex couples are significantly different from and inferior to heterosexual couples still prevails in the general culture, and to some extent in the mental health profession (Murphy, 1991b). It is important that therapists working with clients like Katherine interpret some of their experiences as understandable responses to gender stereotyping and bias, heterosexist pressures, homophobic attitudes, and discrimination and oppression of women. This is especially true for those women who forgo traditional roles and rules about marriage and motherhood.

Although Katherine's therapist validated the pressures and double binds Katherine experienced, she also began to challenge Katherine to look at the ways she personally contributed to, or remained stuck in, some of those binds. Her erotic relationships with women tended to be superficial and short-lived, suggesting that she needed to look more deeply into her yearnings for and fears of intimacy, whether with a woman or a man. In some of her relationships with men, Katherine seemed to want both a protective, nurturing parent figure, and someone she felt equal to. She tended either to idealize or to demonize men. Both positions prevented her from achieving a more mutual relationship with a man. In therapy Katherine tried to disentangle her sense of herself as a relational being, and her struggles with intimacy, from the cultural meanings and expectations that boxed her in.

Feelings about Men: Misogyny's Legacy

Katherine had rejected a particular marriage and was wary of entering such an arrangement again. Nevertheless, as noted earlier, she had been deeply involved with a man for the past 7 years. Her feelings for this man were complex: She admired his intelligence and savvy about the world, but was sometimes angry and fearful about the way he used them and his physical power to intimidate and humiliate her. She worried that she was too dependent on him, at the same time that she resented his apparent difficulty in tolerating her independence from him. She felt that in certain ways it was not an equal partnership, but was unsure how or whether she could achieve that equality in a relationship with a man.

In her work life, Katherine was surrounded by men. Indeed, she prided herself in being able to be "one of the boys." She could take on the same physical challenges as they; she handled crises better than some of her male coworkers; and she had developed some real friendships with a couple of them. Yet (again as noted earlier) she was being sexually harassed by her boss, toward whom she had come to feel rage, contempt, and fear. When Katherine despaired of men or of decent relationships with them, she would say she wished she could just be a "dyke" and be done with the struggle.

Women's feelings about men will invariably arise in the context of therapy. At some point, almost every woman client will bring in her feelings about men. Addressing the anger, fear, contempt, distrust, and rage that many women experience and express about men in general—and, most troubling, the particular men in their lives—is a challenge for women therapists. A therapist may be tempted to join with her client in the perception that men are hopeless, or to support the client's anger at "men in general." The therapist confronts her own biases and beliefs as she attempts to help her client make decisions about whether or when to accommodate, challenge, or separate from a male partner, coworker, or friend. It is important to underscore that these feelings are natural, direct, and inevitable responses to the personal experience of misogyny, heterosexism, and homophobia.

Katherine was able to see that many of her feelings about men grew out of her own experiences: a child ignored by her father and quite possibly molested by her uncle; a teenager in a boy-crazy/girl-devaluing culture; and a young adult involved with men who exploited and sometimes abused her. Her fear, anger, and disgust were rooted in real life. Affirmation of the roots of these feelings allowed Katherine to look at how they had become entangled with her inner and interpersonal life in ways that kept her isolated and at times immobilized.

A woman who is assertive or angry is often dismissed with the accusation that she is just a "castrating bitch"—next in line to a "dyke"—trying to usurp male power. Indeed, she may be legitimately angry about the gendered power inequities and abuses, and the personal indignities, humiliations, and violence, that she encounters daily. A popular stereotype is that lesbians are the ultimate man-haters, that their hatred of men explains their being with women. Katherine herself resorted to this image when she despaired of relations with men. This view is quintessentially heterosexist; it assumes that women would never choose women in their own right, but only as a reaction against men. Furthermore, it diverts attention from the arena where "man-hating" may be the most troublesome and disturbing: in intimate relations between women and men. How does a woman live and deal with her rage at men in the context of her relationship with a particular man? Women partnered with men have to struggle with this rage on a daily basis—over the dishes, at the day care center, in the bedroom. The struggle may take the form of an internal battle the woman wages with herself about the legitimacy of her anger and demands for more autonomy and power; it may be about what she is willing to give up—some of her freedom and power, or perhaps the relationship; it may involve exploration of the reasons she stays in a relationship that is abusive, perhaps dangerous.

Sometimes women choose to wrestle with these issues only in the company of other women. In individual therapy with a woman therapist, and in women-only therapy groups, women find support and validation for their experiences with and feelings about men. In these forums they can examine specific situations and issues and the possible choices open to them. Whether and when to assert, to compromise, to divert, to separate—these may be moment-to-moment or major life-changing decisions. Women's groups and support networks are often critical alternatives or adjuncts to therapy in addressing these issues.

At other times, women and their therapists may choose to address these issues in heterosexual couples therapy. Here the personal meanings and daily experience of political reality enter the office, truly challenging therapists' clinical skill and political consciousness. Many of the issues are deeply divisive and frequently explosive. Domestic disputes about who takes time off from work to care for a sick child or who folds the laundry are not trivial, nor are they necessarily resolved by chore assignment. These disputes often reflect real asymmetries in gender roles and power arrangements, and are among the most intractable and inflammatory for heterosexual couples (Bograd, 1990). The chronic resentment and anger of many wives toward their husbands about unequal participation in domestic responsibilities threaten the stability and certainly the satisfaction of many marriages (Hochschild, 1989).

Although these larger issues cannot be resolved in therapists' offices, they can at least be acknowledged and examined. In working with hetero-sexual couples, we must be alert to two dangers: first, minimizing the real divisions and imbalances in an effort to reach accord; and second, becoming immobilized in our own rage and despair about relations between men and women. We need to acknowledge the larger realities and couples' personal experiences of them, but we must also try to help them negotiate, in specific, concrete ways, some kind of common ground.

Violence and Abuse: Trauma and Revictimization

The traditional family is the primary arena of sexual and physical violence against women and children. For too long, therapists carried on the tradi-tion of Freud by denying or reframing the abuse into something else (such as the seductive fantasies and wishes of the child). By now most mental health professionals are well aware of the prevalence of family violence and abuse, especially that directed toward girls and women. However, the examination and interpretation of the abuse often focus on the pathology of the family, as opposed to the pathological social conditions that foster and maintain the abusive behavior (Herman, 1992; see Pressman, Chapter 16, this volume). It is only recently that mental health professionals have begun to view domestic abuse and psychological trauma in their larger sociopoli-tical context. "Trauma," as Judith Herman asserts, "is an affliction of the powerless" (1992, p. 33). Among the most powerless in our culture are children.

> Katherine discovered after some time in therapy that her uncle had indeed sexually molested her from the ages of 5 to 11. Some of her sexual hangups began to make sense to her. She now understood some of the reasons for her desire to remain in control in sexual relationships and the difficulty she had in allowing herself to receive pleasure.
>   At times Katherine wondered whether it was her fault that her uncle had molested her. She blamed herself for not doing something to stop him. With her therapist's support and prodding, she came to recognize the power imbalance that exists between a child and an adult male, and saw that her uncle had exploited her need for special atten-tion. Coming to this realization involved not only intellectual recogni-tion of these facts, but the painful emotional work of grieving and raging about the people who and circumstances that had betrayed her.

The legacy of childhood abuse persists in a woman's views of herself and her capacities for intimate relationships.

> Katherine felt that she was "damaged goods." She wondered whether she had stayed in the abusive relationship with her boyfriend because of

something perverse in her. She questioned whether she "liked" being put down—that is, whether she fit the image of the "masochistic" female. Part of the therapy involved educating Katherine about how common these responses are as the aftermath of childhood sexual abuse.

We need to ask ourselves a number of questions when working with families or couples in which there is abuse or battering. To what extent do we apply the old paradigms of the "collusive" mother or the "masochistic" wife in trying to understand the abuse? How much do we look at the power inequities, as opposed to the psychological pathology, in the family structure and its social context? With a wife who stays in an abusive marriage, do we consider the economic and social forces, as well as the psychological ones, that keep her with her husband? Fear alone keeps many women with battering partners. Women who leave batterers are at greater risk of physical retaliation, often murder. These are complex, multilayered issues that have particularly challenged couple and family therapists. For too long, many family therapists subscribed to a value-neutral systemic approach that failed to address power issues in the family. The efforts of feminist family therapists have begun to alter this position (e.g., see Goldner, Penn, Sheinberg & Walker, 1990).

Some therapists may assume that violence and abuse do not occur, or are not significant, in lesbian couples and families because of the common belief that "women are not violent." However, battering among lesbian couples exists and needs to be addressed directly and specifically with such couples (Lobel, 1986; Morrow & Hawxhurst, 1989).

Clients may come to therapy because of the abuse they experienced in their lives before therapy. Unfortunately, clients may suffer abuse and trauma in the therapeutic office. Therapist sexual abuse of clients is the ultimate perpetuation of misogyny and sexism. As in the wider society, the vast majority of therapist perpetrators are men, and the vast majority of client victims are women—frequently women who have a history of childhood sexual abuse. In this way, therapy becomes a microcosm of the culture, where the cycle of female oppression and victimization continues. It is not only male therapists who abuse, however. An uncomfortable truth is that some (not many) women therapists also abuse their clients, men and women. We cannot pretend that because we are women, we are incapable of the kinds of violations men commit far more often and in far greater numbers. Nor must we try to protect the image and solidarity of the women's therapy community by failing to bring these violations to the attention of other professionals. Denial and avoidance of the abuses within our own system perpetuate the disorders of the larger system.

CONCLUSION

All women are affected by sexism, heterosexism, misogyny, and homophobia, just as they are affected by the other large social dimensions of racism, classism, ableism, ageism, and economic difference. When as therapists we fail to acknowledge the impact of these forces on women's psychological experience, we fall into the old traps of blaming and pathologizing the victims. When we allow the political to enter the therapy room, we run another risk: If we overemphasize the inequities and abuses perpetrated against women, we may fail to appreciate and examine the complex personal meanings of our clients' struggles. We must always explore with our clients how much their struggles are related to being women in a misogynist, heterosexist, homophobic culture; how much they feel like inner, personal struggles; and how and where the issues interact. We must be able to move back and forth between generalities and particularities. Navigating the therapeutic relationship requires an understanding of the cross-currents of the personal and the political. The therapist must have both a vision of the ocean and a chart of the bay.

REFERENCES

Bailey, J., & Pillard, R. C. (1991). A genetic study of male sexual orientation. *Archives of Psychiatry, 48,* 1089–1086.

Berrill, K. (1990). Anti-gay violence and victimization in the United States. *Journal of Interpersonal Violence, 5,* 274–294.

Bograd, M. (1990). To love, honor and obfuscate. *Readings: A Journal of Reviews and Commentary in Mental Health, 5*(2), 4–8.

Bowers v. Hardwick, 478 U.S. 186 (1986).

Brock-Utne, B. (1989). *Feminist perspectives on peace and peace education.* Elmsford, NY: Pergamon Press.

Burr, C. (1993, March). Homosexuality and biology. *The Atlantic Monthly,* pp. 47–65.

Casas, J. M., Brady, S., & Ponterotto, J. G. (1983). Sexual preference biases in counseling: An information processing approach. *Journal of Counseling Psychology, 30*(2), 139–145.

Chesler, P. (1972). *Women and madness.* Garden City, NY: Doubleday.

Committee on Lesbian and Gay Concerns. (1990). *Final report of the task force on bias in psychotherapy with lesbians and gay men.* Washington, DC: American Psychological Association.

Davis, J. A., & Smith, T. (1984). *General social surveys 1972–1983: Cumulative data.* New Haven, CT: Yale University, Roper Center for Public Opinion Research.

Duberman, M., Vicinus, M., & Chauncey, G. (1989). *Hidden from history: Reclaiming the gay and lesbian past.* New York: Meridian.

Edelman, M. W. (1987). *Families in peril.* Cambridge, MA: Harvard University Press.

Falco, K. (1991). *Psychotherapy with lesbian clients: Theory into practice.* New York: Brunner/Mazel.

Faludi, S. (1991). *Backlash: The undeclared war against American women.* New York: Crown.

Finn, P., & McNeil, T. (1987). *The response of the criminal justice system to bias crime: An explanatory review.* (Available from Abt Associates, 55 Wheeler Street, Cambridge, MA 02138)

Foucault, M. (1984). *The history of sexuality.* New York: Random House.

Goldner, V., Penn, P., Sheinberg, M., & Walker, G. (1990). Love and violence: Gender paradoxes in volatile attachments. *Family Process, 29*(4), 343–364.

Graham, D. L. R., Rawlings, E. I., Halpern, H. S., & Hermes, J. (1984). Therapists' need for training in counseling lesbians and gay men. *Professsional Psychology: Research and Practice, 15*(4), 492–496.

Hamilton, J., Alagna, S., King, L., & Lloyd, C. (1987). The emotional consequences of gender based abuse in the workplace: New counseling programs for sex discrimination. *Women and Therapy, 6*(12), 155–182.

Henaut, D. T., Shannon, K. (Producers), & Klein, B. S. (Director). *Not a love story: A film about pornography.* Québec City, Québec: National Film Board of Canada.

Herman, J. (1992). *Trauma and recovery: The aftermath of violence from domestic abuse to political terror.* New York: Basic Books.

Herek, G. (1986). The social psychology of homophobia: Toward a practical theory. *Review of Law and Social Change, 14*(4), 923–934.

Herek, G. (1989). Hate crimes against lesbians and gay men. *American Psychologist, 44,* 948–955.

Hochschild, A. (1989). *The second shift.* New York: Avon Books.

Kaplan, M. (1983). A woman's view of the DSM-III. *American Psychologist, 38,* 786–792.

Kinsey, A., Pomeroy, W., & Martin, C. (1948). *Sexual behavior in the human male.* Philadelphia: Saunders.

Kinsey, A., Pomeroy, W., Martin, C., & Gebhard, P. (1953). *Sexual behavior in the human female.* Philadelphia: Saunders.

Kilbourn, J., Vitagliano, J., & Stallone, P. (Producers). (1979). *Killing us softly.* Cambridge, MA: Cambridge Documentary Films.

Kitzinger, S. (1987). *The social contruction of lesbianism.* London: Sage.

Kurdek, L.A. (1991). The dissolution of gay and lesbian couples. *Journal of Social and Personal Relationships, 8,* 265–278.

Kurdek, L. A., & Schmitt, J. P. (1986). Relationship quality of partners in heterosexual married, heterosexual cohabitating, and gay and lesbian relationships. *Journal of Personality and Social Psychology, 51*(4), 711–720.

LeVay, S. (1991). A difference in hypothalamic structures between heterosexual and homosexual men. *Science, 253,* 1034–1037.

Lobel, K. (Ed.). (1986). *Naming the violence: Speaking out about lesbian battering.* Seattle: Seal Press.

Malamuth, N., & Donnerstein, E. (Eds.). (1984). *Pornography and sexual aggression.* New York: Academic Press.

McIntosh, P. (1988). *White privilege and male privilege: A personal account of coming to see correspondences through work on women's studies* (Work in progress, No. 189). Wellesley, MA: Stone Center, Wellesley College.

McWhirter, D. P., Sanders, S. A., & Reinisch, J. M. (Eds.). (1990). *Homosexuality/ heterosexuality: Concepts of sexual orientation.* New York: Oxford University Press.

Morrow, S. L., & Hawxhurst, D. M. (1989). Lesbian partner abuse: Implications for therapists. *Journal of Counseling and Development, 68*(1), 58–62.

Murphy, B. C. (1991a, August). *The portrayal of lesbians in film: Reflections of lesbian relationships.* Paper presented at the annual meeting of the American Psychological Association, San Francisco.

Murphy, B. C. (1991b). Educating mental health professionals about gay and lesbian issues. *Journal of Homosexuality, 22*(3–4), 229–246.

Murphy, B. C. (1992). Counseling lesbian couples: Sexism, heterosexism and homophobia. In S.H. Dworkin & F. Guitierrez (Eds.), *Counseling gay men and lesbians: Journey to the end of the rainbow* (pp. 63–79). Alexandria, VA: American Association for Counseling and Development Press.

National Gay and Lesbian Task Force. (1986). *Task force report.* (Available from the National Gay and Lesbian Task Force, 1517 U Street, N.W., Washington, DC 20009)

Newsweek. (1983, August 8). *Newsweek* poll on homosexuality, p. 33.

New York Times. (1992, August 26). Robertson letter attacks feminists, p. A-16.

Nichols, M. (1988). Bisexuality in women: Myths, realities and implications for therapy. *Women and Therapy, 7*(2/3), 235–252.

Pharr, S. (1988). *Homophobia: A weapon of sexism.* (Available from The Women's Project, 2224 Main, Little Rock, AR 72206)

Roth, S. A. (1989). Psychotherapy with lesbian couples: Individual issues, female socialization and the social context. In M. McGoldrick, C. Anderson, & F. Walsh (Eds.), *Women in families: A framework for family therapy* (pp. 286–307). New York: Norton.

Russell, D.E.H. (1984). *Sexual exploitation: Rape, child sexual abuse and sexual harassment.* Beverly Hills, CA: Sage.

Russell, D. E. H., & Howell, N. (1983). The prevalence of rape in the United States. *Signs, 8,* 688–695.

San Francisco Chronicle. (1982, November 9). Gallup poll on attitudes about gays, p. 7.

Scott, J.W. (1988). *Gender and the politics of history.* New York: Columbia University Press.

Sedgewick, E. K. (1990). *Epistemology of the closet.* Berkeley: University of California Press.

Showalter, E. (1985). *The female malady.* New York: Viking Penguin.

U.S. Bureau of the Census. (1991). *Family disruption and economic hardship: Survey of income and program participation* (Current Population Reports, Series P–70, No. 20). Washington, DC: U.S. Government Printing Office.

Ussher, J. (1992). *Women's madness: Misogyny or mental illness?* Amherst: University of Massachusetts Press.

Vargo, S. (1987). The effects of women's socialization on lesbian couples. In Boston

Lesbian Psychologies Collective (Ed.), *Lesbian psychologies* (pp. 161–173). Urbana: University of Illinois Press.

Weinreb, M., & Murphy, B. C. (1988). The birth mother: A feminist perspective for the helping professional. *Women and Therapy, 7*(1), 23–36.

Wisniewski, J. J., & Toomey, B. G. (1987). Are social workers homophobic? *Social Work, 32,* 454–455.

II

WOMEN IN CONTEXT
THROUGH THE
LIFE CYCLE

4

Female Adolescence Revisited: Understanding Girls in Their Sociocultural Contexts

MARSHA PRAVDER MIRKIN

On the surface, the adolescent girls who enter my office could not look more different. There are the angry girls, virtually dragged in by their parents; the polite, fading-away ones who agreeably sit there and starve themselves; the talkative ones who grope for words to explain their last suicide attempt. As they each, in their own ways, allow me to enter their worlds, what becomes clear is that their differences dull in their common struggle to become women in a patriarchal society.

These are the girls who until quite recently (Gilligan, 1982; Gilligan, Lyons, & Hamner, 1990) were ignored in traditional theories of individual psychology, and even in more contemporary theories of family therapy. Most of the early work on individual adolescents was done by men and about boys (see, e.g., Kohlberg, 1976; Erikson, 1968). When the world of girls was examined at all, this was most often done as an afterthought (Erikson, 1968), and at times it was suggested that girls are not up to par with boys (Kohlberg, 1976). In the transition from individual to family therapy, the concept of gender was often ignored; power and hierarchy were discussed as if men and women were treated equally, as if we were dealing with a neutered population. Early family therapy theory continued to be developed by men and about boys. Minuchin, Montalvo, Guerney, Rosman, and Schumer's (1967) important, ground-breaking work was done at Wiltwyck, a school for boys, and the theory, without gender-based change, was later taken as a model for treating anorexic girls (Minuchin, Rosman, & Baker, 1978).

The purpose of this chapter is to revisit the issues surrounding female

development within and beyond the family context. Just as family therapists once discovered that understanding the intrapsychic workings of
clients is not sufficient for an appreciation of their experience, so we must
now look beyond the family to understand the development of adolescent
girls. To do this, we must widen our lens to take in the view that girls have
a particular socialization in a particular society at a particular time. As we
construct meaning from the experience of adolescent girls, their context is a
central part of that construction. Since it is beyond the scope of this chapter
to examine every aspect of female development, I have chosen to explore
separation/individuation, sexuality/body image, and identity development.
I recognize that these are traditional male categorizations of development,
but they provide fertile ground for a critique and reconstruction of our
understanding of female adolescents.

SEPARATION AND INDIVIDUATION

Most readers probably share my experience of learning that separation and
individuation are the primary tasks of adolescence. The jargon—"breaking
away," "breaking free," "cutting the umbilical cord"—implies a jolting
disconnection. In my experience as a trainee, and even my early experience
as a trainer, words like "separation," "autonomy," and "individuation" all
had positive connotations; words like "dependence," "fusion," and
"enmeshment" had negative connotations; words like "mutuality" and
"interdependence" were not even mentioned. We would reseat family
members to provide an experience of distance between mothers and
daughters. The message that I believe we were giving to these families was
that we valued separation and shunned connectedness.

    With the publication of Miller's *Toward a New Psychology of Women*
(1976), followed by the works of her colleagues at the Stone Center (e.g.,
Surrey, 1984), and Carol Gilligan (1982; Gilligan et al., 1990), a new
perspective on womanhood emerged. These theorists argue that females
develop best within the context of mutually enhancing relationships. It is
connection, not separation, that is central to female development; autonomy and self-direction for females occur within the context of relationships.
Pollak and Gilligan (1982), in a study using Thematic Apperception Test
(TAT) cards, found that men reported more violent images when people
were brought closer together in TAT pictures, whereas women's violent
stories increased as people were set further apart. Closeness and relatedness
form the context in which girls can develop; exclusion and isolation are
avoided at all costs. A primary goal of this chapter is to examine the
importance of connection in relationships when therapy deals with the
problems presented by adolescent girls.

    The language of separation continues to be used in the treatment of girls, even in those problem areas (e.g., eating disorders) where girls are more markedly affected than boys. In their pioneering work dealing with anorexic girls and their families, Minuchin et al. (1978) stated that the goal of treatment is to support individuation while maintaining family connectedness. This goal is compatible with the relationships necessary in female adolescent development. However, as they described it, the work of therapy itself ended up focusing on separation to the exclusion of connection. The therapists in their study defined their goals as developing independence, and chose to work with older adolescents separately from their parents in order to promote disengagement. When separation is the goal, then attempts at connection are often pathologized.

What are the implications of a separation model for family therapy with adolescent girls? The focus on separation as the goal of mature development leads to blaming mothers and daughters for the same behaviors that are socially mandated for women. Girls and women are the caretakers in our society; yet in the course of therapy, caretaking is labeled derogatorily as "codependency" (see Krestan & Bepko, 1990), connection is reframed as "enmeshment," providing for safety is called "overprotection," and relationship maintenance is termed "conflict avoidance." These labels pathologize and shame girls and their mothers.

Furthermore, if girls are taught that distance and disengagement are signs of growing maturity, whereas their internal experience is that isolation is intolerable, then one message is that they can never truly grow up. A girl will move from childhood to being a woman-child, still viewing her connection needs as immature and childlike. The perspective of women as "grown-up children" is supported in a society where rules are made by men to be followed by women; where those in power are men, while women and children are disempowered; and where violence is used against women and children to maintain the power structure.

Still another implication is that adolescent girls, who need relationships and are coached to become disengaged, feel disconnected. Since their direct appeal for connection has been thwarted, these girls can then feel depressed, rebel, or starve themselves in desperate attempts to connect with and engage the adults around them.

Understanding the importance of connection can also help us to understand how frightening conflict is for adolescent girls, and to appreciate their efforts to resolve conflict in a way that is satisfactory to all involved. However, this often means that girls will not voice conflict, disagreement, or anger for fear of losing a relationship (Miller, 1985). It also means that girls often care for others to the exclusion of themselves.

The expectation of limitless female giving and self-denial is woven into the fabric of our culture. In the best-selling children's book *The Giving Tree* (Silverstein, 1964), the female's growth is literally stunted by the selfless giving expected from her. In this story, a boy asks a female tree for all her apples, branches, and trunk so that he can sell those items and finance his life's wishes. At the end, all that is left is the female tree's stump, and the boy sits on her. The book remains beloved by many who see it as the ultimate expression of mother–son or female–male loving relationships. It can instead be used therapeutically as an example of societally mandated expectations: The female gives all with no limits, and the male takes all with no reciprocity. When I share this book in therapy or training, I often ask, "How would this story change if the tree included herself among those for whom she gave care?" The expectation of the all-giving and selfless woman, the male abusiveness disguised as ideal love, and the emptiness experienced by both the male and female characters make the story an excellent metaphor for families and trainees, and highlight how important it is for girls to include themselves in the caregiving equation.

Therapy provides an opportunity to support these young women as they attempt to articulate what they want for themselves—not in disconnection with the needs of others, but as a way of including themselves as they grapple with the issues of what and how much to give to others. Sharon's case demonstrates this.

Quiet in the Dorms[1]

Sharon became bulimic during her freshman year of college. Traditional psychological wisdom would indicate that she was having a hard time separating from her parents, and that the bulimia was a way to return home. However, as I worked with Sharon, it became clear that she was having difficulty with her roommates, and that at first she was unaware of having any feelings about their behavior. Later, she recognized that she and her mother shared the belief that a woman needed to be polite and not express anger or conflict. Her roommates' behavior had gotten so impossible that Sharon was "bursting" with anger, which she believed she could not express. Individual and family therapy focused on both her lack of connection with her feelings and the prohibition against direct confrontation. When Sharon experimented with sharing her feelings with her roommates, and as she joined with her mother in working on their mutual discomfort with conflict, her bulimia diminished. Our work did not focus on separation from her mother, but rather on identifying and expressing feelings, thus making connections more intimate and honest. Doing this, of course, involves risking the other person's leaving the relationship.

A crisis manifests itself as girls reach adolescence with a need for connection coupled with a sensitivity toward social nuances in a society that orders girls to be "nice"—even if that means denying their knowledge of themselves and others. This denial of self in adolescence is eloquently described in Gilligan's recent work (Gilligan et al., 1990), in which she and her colleagues examined the crisis that emerges when girls gain knowledge in adolescence: They see that women "keep quiet and notice the absence of women and say nothing" (p. 26). If a chasm is created between their self-knowledge and what they speak, their relationships become less honest and therefore less connected; if, instead, they choose to speak their knowledge, they may lose relationships altogether. Therefore, it is Gilligan's thesis that adolescent girls learn to think in a way that is different from what they really feel, and that Western culture teaches these girls to lose their knowledge—a profound observation of the social world that could be articulated with fervor prior to adolescence. This piercing knowledge is disclaimed by adolescent girls, whose use of the phrase "I don't know" increases dramatically as they become disconnected from their own thoughts and feelings. As Gilligan et al. (1990) write, adolescence is a time when "girls are in danger of losing their voices and thus losing their connection with others, and also a time when girls, gaining voice and knowledge, are in danger of knowing the unseen and speaking the unspoken and thus losing connection with what is commonly taken to be 'reality' " (p. 25). The passage concludes with the statement that girls are more likely to speak in relationships where "nobody will leave and someone will listen" (p. 27).

Therefore, even as we therapists validate and respect adolescent girls' desire for relationships, it is important for us to help the adolescents voice their knowledge. This is risky for both the adolescents and their families. Many girls and women are afraid of losing relationships, of being abandoned; at a more basic level, they may not even be in touch with what they want or need. The challenge of therapy is to weave together common experiences within a family—experiences that on the surface may seem disparate—while at the same time creating an atmosphere in which differences are tolerated and ultimately valued. This takes place within a context that recognizes gender inequalities and their impact on each family member, as the case of Diana illustrates

If Not an Art Gallery, Then What?
I first met Diana and her parents when Diana was an emaciated, silent 17-year-old hospitalized with anorexia. Diana's father, Mr. C., was a famous artist who frequently traveled to international exhibits. Her mother, Mrs. C., also a painter, gave art lessons and taught an occasional seminar at a local college. Diana's 20-year-old sister, Regina, was away at college with plans to be a lawyer—a career that her father had considered pursuing.

Diana confided that she had neither Regina's academic interests nor the artistic talents of her parents, and that she therefore found no way of connecting with her parents. In particular, she wished to feel closer to and accepted by her mother. Diana expressed concern that her mother was depressed, though Mrs. C. adamantly denied feeling depressed.

Diana claimed to hate art, yet almost every weekend for a year

82 WOMEN IN CONTEXT THROUGH THE LIFE CYCLE

prior to her hospitalization, she had accompanied her mother to museums and art galleries—an activity that had been shared by Regina and Mrs. C. prior to Regina's leaving for college. Diana had decided to accompany her mother to exhibits in part because she was concerned that her mother would be unhappy if she had to go alone to the museums, and in part because she assumed that appreciating art was a prerequisite for acceptance in the family and for connecting with her mother.

I encouraged Diana to share with her mother her reasons for going to museums and galleries, and Diana told her parents that she was concerned that her mother would be alone if Diana refused to go with her. Mr. C.'s offer to accompany his wife to the museums was met with stony silence on her part, which then opened up concerns Mrs. C. had about her husband's availability and quick temper. Several sessions later, this discussion of their relationship and Mrs. C.'s isolation led to her acknowledging that she often felt depressed, but did not want to admit it aloud because it was inappropriate for a parent to burden children with her problems. Diana, however, was relieved: Her mother's admission had confirmed her own reality, and also gave permission for Diana to talk about her own sadness. Diana felt that she now had a chance to get closer to her mother—that her mother's emotional honesty made her a real person and gave them something they could have in common.

In individual sessions, Diana professed that her mother had failed both at being a traditional mother and at becoming a successful artist, and Diana had her own doubts about whether she herself could succeed as a mother (which was very important to her) and still have a career. In judging her mother, Diana had never thought that it might be unrealistic to expect anyone always to be available to her children, let alone whether it was possible to do that and still concentrate, uninterrupted, on painting. As family therapy progressed, Mrs. C. revealed that she had once had great promise as an artist. When she married, she was expected by her family of origin, her husband, and her own internalized view of her role to make her career secondary to her job as a mother and housekeeper. By the time the girls were old enough for her to feel comfortable pursuing her career, she had missed too much ever to become a "great" artist.

As her mother discussed these issues, Diana became more animated. She realized that she didn't need to be an artist or a scholar to have a relationship with her mother. They could connect over a range of feelings they experienced, and their struggle to find a place in the personal and public worlds.

At first, Diana's wish not to attend college and to be an at-home mother appeared to be in stark opposition to the feelings of her mother, who valued her career. However, Diana's experience was actually a mirror image of Mrs. C.'s: Mrs. C. had wanted a career desperately, but had no hope that her traditional mother would ever understand those cravings. Diana and her mother connected over their common experience of having to make choices that felt like losses, and wondering whether anyone could truly understand their struggle and offer support.

These discussions helped Diana to create another story about her mother. Mrs. C. was no longer a woman who had attempted to juggle career and family, and failed at both. Instead, she was a woman who had broken with her family's tradition and pioneered new ground—a legacy that Diana could feel comfortable carrying on. Instead of viewing her mother as a cold, depressed woman, she experienced her mother as a woman full of feelings, who did experience great sadness (if not depression), and whose sadness resonated with her own. Instead of viewing her mother as defective, she could understand and grapple with the gender conditions that place all women in a common struggle. In connection rather than isolation, with a better understanding of herself and her relationships, Diana was able to let go of her symptoms, gain weight, and maintain the gain.

In summary, rather than viewing separation as the goal of therapy with adolescent girls, we need to find ways of helping families in their attempts to form developmentally appropriate connections and become "mutually interdependent."[2] We need to value the female experience of relationships, and help girls include themselves in their expressions of concern.

SEXUALITY AND BODY IMAGE

A second major group of issues with which adolescents grapple has to do with sexuality and body image. Yet, once again, the experiences of boys and girls differ tremendously within the sociopolitical context in which they participate. Becoming comfortable with sexuality and body image involves feeling at ease with and in charge of one's body and making choices concerning one's body. Yet the ownership of one's own female body is challenged by living in a patriarchal society. Judith Herman (1987) has stated that for women in the United States, the risk of being raped is about one in four, and for girls, the risk of sexual abuse by an adult is greater than one in three. According to the Fund for a Feminist Majority (personal communication, 1991), every 6 minutes a woman is raped in the United States, and every 15 seconds a woman is beaten by her husband or partner. How can an adolescent girl get the message that she is in charge of her body when all that surrounds her indicates that she is not?

The structures which are in place in our society have not been protective of girls or women, nor have they given women the message that they are in charge of their bodies. In the course of therapy, a young woman reported to me that when she was a college student, someone had tried to rape her and slashed her with a knife as she escaped. She reported that her college infirmary refused to believe her story, stating instead that they felt she had sliced her leg and was suicidal. This statement was made without any knowledge of the girl's history or mental status prior to the rape. According to my client, they would not let her leave the infirmary because, ironically, of their concern for her safety. It was only after a male relative intervened that she was transferred to a hospital with a rape crisis team, whose members believed and supported her. Therapy focused not only on the trauma of a rape attempt, but on the assault this young woman experienced within the health system.

Although this might appear to be a unique case, I would argue that the message that subtly encourages violence against women, and then denies women's experiences of violence, is woven into our society's tapestry and experienced by adolescent girls. It happens at the domestic level when girls see their mothers beaten, and then their reality testing is questioned as all agree that the mothers fell down the stairs accidentally. It was seen in the judicial and legislative systems when, for example, a Canadian judge recently allowed a rapist to go free because the judge assumed that the 3-year-old rape victim had been seductive, or when the U.S. Senate chose to confirm a Supreme Court nominee accused of sexual harassment, thus dismissing the painful story of a female lawyer. Tragically, the Supreme Court has made decisions which can restrict a woman's right to choose an abortion, thus sending the message that women do not own their own bodies. (See Chapter 12 of this volume for a more complete discussion of abortion.) The situation was further exacerbated, until President Clinton mandated otherwise, by banning the discussion of abortion in Title X-funded clinics—clinics that serve the most disenfranchised and voiceless girls and women.[3] The Court has thus sent the message that the men who have power in government can tell women what to do or not to do with their bodies, and thus that men control women's bodies. This message, that men, and not women, can control a woman's body can be taken, at an extreme, as a license to beat, rape, and otherwise intimidate women. Adolescent girls witness the violence perpetrated against women, and often fear their emerging womanhood.

A girl is directly affected with the message that she may not make decisions about her own body when she is forbidden to get an abortion without parental consent. This not only denies ownership of her body, but also denies the abuse she may have experienced within her family. This ruling assumes that girls would receive support and guidance if they spoke to their parents. It ignores how many girls are physically abused by their parents; how often incest is the cause of teenage pregnancy; how open communication must be developed and nurtured, not forced; and how, ultimately, a girl must be able to make decisions about her own body.

A second issue related to adolescent sexuality is that our society assumes not only that girls belong to the boys, but also that all girls desire boys. This means that as girls struggle with their sexual orientation, they often struggle alone for fear of acknowledging that they may be, or are, lesbians. As sex education courses are more routinely incorporated into school curricula, they continue to leave out a significant number of girls, because they discuss heterosexuality and rarely mention homosexuality. If homosexuality is mentioned, it is not discussed as an orientation that is as viable as heterosexuality; it is not given the same space in the texts or the same credibility. When curricula include units on the family, lesbian and gay families are rarely mentioned. Adolescent girls, who often feel on the fringe because of sexism, feel even more isolated because of heterosexism. In our own offices, we therapists need to be vigilant about heterosexist assumptions and language. If we assume heterosexuality, we are closing the door on any discussions about sexual orientation and further alienating lesbian adolescents.

Third, girls are confronted not only by male-dominated sexuality, but also by male-dominated body images. The message about female appearance as the gift wrap to attract men is seen in fairy tales. Girls have read about Cinderella, who needs a beautiful dress in order to go to the ball or attract the prince—she simply cannot go in her rags. Furthermore, the Prince searches after the ball for the girl with the smallest foot in the land; a big, fat foot would never win a Prince! Finally, the Prince is Cinderella's only road to happiness—without him, life would be lonely and gloomy. She cannot count on female friendships; her stepsisters make her life miserable. Only a man can save her, and a rich white man at that. Fairy tales, with Cinderella as a prototype, can convey destructive messages for all girls,[4] and can pack a double whammy for economically deprived girls, lesbians, and girls of color.

In the society of adolescent girls, the glass slipper is not simply a metaphor; it is a concrete example of the society's obsession with thinness. Adolescent girls receive the message to be thin at all costs, to deny their needs and appetites to achieve this goal, and to deny themselves and their bodies to please others (Mirkin, 1990a). The simple pleasure of biting into a morsel of chocolate and savoring it is made impossible by the fear of appearing piggish, getting fat, and not being attractive. Eighty percent of women surveyed by *Glamour* magazine (*Glamour,* 1984) felt that they had to be thin to attract men. Women have even lost their ability to assess their bodies realistically (Cash, Winstead, & Janda, 1986). In one study (Thompson, 1986), over 90% of women studied overestimated their body size.

Left unchallenged, female rites of passage involve the implicit acknowledgment that a woman's body is not perceived as her own. Treatment needs to make these issues explicit, so that girls can deal with the shame they have experienced at being violated, so that they can own and accept their anger, and so that they can be helped to find their voices and reclaim their bodies. The case of Susan demonstrates this.

Taking Off the Rose-Colored Glasses

Sixteen-year-old Susan J. entered a psychiatric hospital after making a suicide attempt. Her mother, a divorced working-class white woman in her early 40s, reported that Susan had been drinking and had gotten involved in a number of brief, intense sexual relationships that always left her feeling unhappy. When I asked Susan for her understanding of the suicide attempt, she said that she "didn't know," but that she had been very upset because her former therapist had been sexually involved with her. She told another therapist, who she felt dismissed it. Susan's understanding was that the counselor thought she was "fantasizing" the entire episode, or that it was too "unimportant" to require further consideration. Susan said that her mother also did not believe her, which was extremely painful to Susan.

Because of Mrs. J.'s own traumatic history, she had learned to protect herself by assuming things were not as bad as they appeared, and she looked for the brighter and more benevolent side of each issue. We called this tendency "putting on her rose-colored glasses." When Susan told her mother how deeply pained she was that her mother did not believe her about the sexual abuse, Mrs. J. responded, "Don't worry about this so much, dear. It's time to move on with your life." Enraged, Susan lapsed into silence. I asked Mrs. J. what she would see if she took off her rose-colored glasses for a moment, and responded to Susan without them. Susan immediately shouted, "She would say that I'm lying."

"Not at all," responded Mrs. J., very seriously. "You've already been hurt, Susan. I just don't want to see you hurt any more." When I pursued this with Mrs. J., she said that given Susan's history of drinking and sexual activity, she did not think the courts would believe her; she did not want her daughter dragged through the mud, only to see the man who did this to her vindicated. Susan lit up at her mother's response: "You mean you believe me?" was her reaction. Her mother replied that at first she did not, but that when she "took off the rose-colored glasses," she did believe Susan and did not want to see her hurt further by the judicial process.

The combination of Mrs. J.'s and my belief in Susan empowered her to begin to decide how she wanted to deal with the situation. Her mother firmly maintained that she did not want Susan pressing charges, given how fragile she had been feeling and how difficult the process was. Susan reluctantly agreed. Much of therapy focused on how guilty Susan felt, because she was attracted to her therapist and was pleased that he was attracted to her. As she could see more clearly that it was his responsibility not to touch her, no matter how provocative she might have been, she was able not only to become angrier and less depressed, but also to set clearer limits with some of the boys she dated. Six years later, an adult Susan returned to therapy saying that she had decided to press charges, and needed support through the process.

IDENTITY

I asked a 20-year-old client, Julia, to write to me about her memories of adolescence:

> "I think of the beginning of my adolescence as when my body started to change and I developed breasts. It was a shameful time. I wanted to deny it was happening to me. . . . I didn't want to become a woman. Maybe I didn't have the greatest role model—my mother was not a happy woman. . . . At puberty, I felt that being a woman was the short end of the stick—I didn't see all the lovely things about being female. I had a lot of fear."

Julia poignantly told me that she felt safer as a child, and that as an early adolescent she viewed womanhood as a risk without payoff. It was only much later, after several years of therapy and other positive life experiences, that she began to see the beauty of womanhood. However, in spite of this insight, Julia still pointed to her mother as a poor role model, rather than looking beyond this to understand why womanhood felt like the "short end of the stick." In this regard, Julia was like many of the girls with whom I work.

Julia's mother had three young children when her husband left her. Financially and emotionally, she was in crisis, yet she found a job and was able to provide economically for her children. Julia felt abandoned and hated being poor, and she blamed her mother for their predicament. Yet statistics tell us that there is a much greater chance of females' experiencing poverty, and that these figures are more dramatic still for women of color (Jewish Fund for Justice, 1989). After a divorce, women's incomes drop by an average of 73%, while men's rise by 42% (Weitzman, 1985). Julia stated that she did not respect her mother's job and blamed her mother for the drop in income. Yet women simply do not earn as much as men. In 1987, four out of five women earned less than $19,000 per year; male secretaries earned 33% more than female secretaries, and female clerical workers earned a median income of $284, compared to the male income of $403 (*Boston Globe*, 1987a, 1987b).

When daughters personalize these situations, mothers are patholo-gized, and anger is turned toward them rather than toward the dis-criminatory society. Instead of feeling good about themselves as girls who could grow up like their mothers, female adolescents often devalue their mothers and are frightened of being like them. Many of the girls with whom I work are concerned about their mothers, feel protective of them, and want to maintain a relationship with them. Yet, paradoxically, each girl is simultaneously afraid of being like her mother. What an impact it must have on identity formation to be moving toward womanhood and seeing their primary role models in such contradictory terms!

For girls to feel better about their own possibilities, they need to confront their fears of becoming like their mothers (Mirkin, 1990b). In their search for role models, many girls turn to television mothers. The one I have heard about the most until recently is Claire Huxtable, the mother in "The Cosby Show." This television mom, representing societal ideals, has raised five children; has a high-powered, well-paid, and well-respected job; and is thin, heterosexual, beautiful, married, and energetic. Her home is clean; she is supportive of her spouse, available to all her children, and gets along strikingly well with her teenagers; and she does it all with ease and grace. If Claire expresses anger, it is over a behavioral issue that can be immediately corrected so that everyone is happy. If a problem involving racism or sexism is ever dealt with, it is superficially solved within the half-hour time frame.

Whose mother can measure up to this Superwoman? Yet the presence of this societally dictated message about the ideal woman takes its toll on the real-life relationships between women grappling with the problems of emotional and financial survival and their daughters, who look to them to be clones of the television moms and are bitterly disappointed. Being a Superwoman is such a formidable, impossible task that even while these girls are angry at their mothers for not achieving it, they doubt their own abilities to measure up to this standard, and anticipate failure "just like their moms."[5]

There is some hope that girls will begin to see the recognition of strong, smart women in our society, as evidenced by the election of four women to the U.S. Senate in 1992 (bringing the total number of women senators only to six). At the same time, however, there are also regressive pulls that are destructive to the identity development of adolescent girls. A recent article (Vivelo, 1992) notes that Nancy Drew stories have been revised and rewritten over the last 30 years, so that the proactive heroine is now little more than a Barbie doll. For example, in the original edition of one story, Nancy frees herself when she is bound and gagged; in the rewritten version, her male counterpart saves her. In the original version of another story, Nancy is saved and then accosts the suspect. In the revised version, Nancy is saved by a man, who then sweeps her up and carries her, exhausted, to the second floor. As women begin to challenge the old order, the order's supporters counter with messages advising adolescent girls to maintain their wilting-flower image.

Adolescent Girls in New Immigrant Families

It is not sufficient to simply explore gender as we attempt to understand adolescent girls. Race, class, ethnicity, religion, and sexual life style are also critical elements in the life of an adolescent and in her understanding of herself and her world. Feminist therapists are often criticized for not recognizing the overarching importance of, for example, racism in the lives of women of color, and assuming the same gender dynamics across racial and ethnic groups.

In an effort to begin to address this crucial issue, let me take the example of the experience of recent immigrants, and the impact of that cultural context on mother–daughter relationships and identity formation of girls. While it is beyond the scope of this chapter to explore the family's reasons for immigration, even immigrant families who have not witnessed and experienced trauma in their countries of origin may experience major disruption and change. Much of the conflict between newly immigrated parents and their children can be traced to their different rates of acculturation. (Lee, 1990; Szapocznik, Rio, Perez & Kurtines, 1986).[6] As parents try to maintain their cultural values and customs, their daughters often learn English more rapidly and have greater exposure to the norms of the new culture through school and friendships. This leads to several potential dilemmas. Without knowing English or dominant North American customs, parents may depend on the daughter to navigate their new living situation, which can result in her belief that her parent(s) are not as competent or skilled as those of her friends. A recent Russian immigrant told me that her daughter ridiculed her for the menial job that the mother had to take upon arrival in the United States. Both parents were working long hours in order to provide their daughter with social and academic opportunities. The daughter felt different than the other children and embarrassed by her parents' differences from her peers' parents; she heard little in the media, school, etc., that underlined the courage and talent of immigrant parents such as her's, and the incredible efforts needed to begin life anew. If anything, immigrant parents are faulted for not learning English quickly enough or for being different than the dominant culture, thus supporting her embarrassment.

The mother–daughter struggle often intensifies as the daughter tries to act like her peers, and mother interprets these behaviors as turning against the family and its values. While the mother may hold on to what she values of her old culture, her daughter often wants to join the new culture and is bombarded with the promise of what her life might become if she looks and acts like her new peers. Sides are drawn and positions become polarized: Mothers view their daughters as misbehaving and as disrespectful as the daughters experiment with the new culture, and daughters view their mothers as useless in guiding their development. This same Russian mother told me that in her small village women married young and were virgins until marriage. She was horrified that her daughter did not believe in either of those values.

Added to this are gender role expectations. Often, the girls are expected to become involved with household tasks and rituals that are in direct conflict with what they see in the families of their new peers. For example, one mother reported being very upset that her daughter was not attending school. The daughter was expected to attend school, care for her grandmother and younger siblings, and clean and cook while the mother worked two jobs and attended school. The mother felt that it would be inappropriate to ask her own brothers to help out since this was "woman's work." The daughter felt that she could not juggle so many tasks and still have time to spend with her friends, and she thought her mother was very unfair. The mother was angry at her daughter's lack of cooperation because when the mother was an adolescent, she too had these assigned responsibilities. The involved agencies identified the problem as the mother's lack of time at home with her daughter, taking into account neither the many challenges of immigration nor the strengths demonstrated by both the mother and the daughter.

Lack of culturally sensitive intervention, in addition to devaluation and denigration of their mothers, can leave daughters without a role model from which they can begin to shape their own identities. By rejecting their mothers and denying their cultures of origin, girls are left without that fertile soil from which identity blooms. With cultural and gender-sensitive psychotherapies, parent–child bonds can be supported, and progress can be made toward a family definition of biculturality.

For psychotherapy to be effective, we need to be sensitive to cultural transitions and the quest for biculturality (Lee, 1990; Szapocznik et al., 1986). We need to respect the position of both parents and adolescents, but rather than see it as a generational struggle, we need to frame the differences as a response to the two different cultures coming together in the family. Conflict can be framed in cultural terms, rather than in terms of a "disobedient" daughter and an "unreasonable" mother. Values from each culture can be found to ally with so that parents identify positive acculturated values, and children identify positive values from their culture-of-origin (Szapocznik et al., 1986). Through a process that looks at cultural strengths, families begin their journey toward biculturality, in which the culture-of-origin is not forsaken because of the new culture and the new culture is not ignored. By finding value in the culture-of-origin, as well as identifying family strengths, daughters can again identify with their mothers, and their identity development can be nourished within that relationship.

Restorying Women's Lives

How can we expect girls to want to move on to womanhood, given the misogyny that surrounds them? It is in the context of psychotherapy that we can acknowledge that while girls may have difficulty navigating adolescence, they can develop another story in which womanhood is seen in a far more positive light. In order to do so, I find that it is critical for these girls to begin to experience their mothers differently. Through therapy, mothers and daughters can form a new connection through which new stories are woven. Daughters can take pride in their mothers' skills as survivors, explorers, tradition breakers, and/or tradition keepers, and the daughters can begin to imagine which positions they will want to take as they become women. The case of Marie and her mother illustrates this.

We Keep It in the Family
    Fourteen-year-old Marie was hospitalized at a short-term state-contracted facility because of an alcohol and aspirin overdose, oppositional behavior at home and school, and polydrug abuse. Prior to hospitalization, Marie lived with her mother and three younger sisters in a low-income Portuguese community. In therapy at the hospital, Marie revealed that she had been sexually abused by her father, and that she had told her mother, who had called the police and insisted that the father leave the house. When the therapist, a white, middle-class male, asked Mrs. S. about the sexual abuse, she stared blankly and denied that it had occurred. When he shared Marie's story, Mrs. S. said that she "remembered," but said nothing more about the incident. Mrs. S. also insisted that her daughter was ready to come home from the hospital after a week, and Marie joined her in saying that she was ready to return home. The treatment team felt that nothing had changed, and called me in as a consultant with the goal of my finding a way to gain the mother's approval for a longer hospital stay.
    I met with Mrs. S., Marie, and their therapist in front of a one-way mirror with the other unit therapists observing. Mrs. S. was soft-spoken, polite, and anxious as she explained to me that she was told that the interview was to determine whether Marie should return home this week. Marie chimed in by saying that she would not use any more drugs, she would listen to her mother, and she would not try to kill herself. Mrs. S. used Marie's statement as proof that she was ready to return home, and did not appear to hear the opposing arguments presented by the team.
    I then asked Mrs. S. to explain to me how a Portuguese family would handle a teenager who had recently attempted suicide and was having difficulties like Marie's. Mrs. S. initially felt defensive and asked why I wanted to know about Portuguese families, stating that "we are just like everybody else." She appeared concerned that I would use whatever information she gave me to stereotype her family negatively.

When I shared that I needed to learn from her about her cultural background, so I would not err by assuming that our cultures dealt with everything the same way, she responded with absolute clarity: "We keep it in the family. We deal with it ourselves."

At that point, it was clear that the team and I were standing in stark opposition to Mrs. S.'s cultural values: We were intruders, yet she was taught to be subordinate and respectful, and therefore seemed to "tune out" the issues we raised rather than openly disagree with us. Recognizing that I needed to be more in sync with her values, I asked her about her plan for helping Marie with her problems, should Marie return home. Mrs. S. reported that there was a counseling center within walking distance of their home, and Marie would have appointments several times per week. She added that if Marie did not "listen" and stayed out late using drugs, Mrs. S. would support rehospitalization.

The rest of the session was spent recounting decisions that Mrs. S. had made throughout Marie's life that had been protective of Marie— decisions she had made in spite of ethnic pulls to keep family life private and to be subordinate to men. Mrs. S., the therapist, Marie, and I all agreed to her plan, and Marie went home several days later. Several weeks later, she returned with her mother, who said that Marie's behavior was out of control again. During the second hospitalization, mother and daughter spoke in detail about the sexual abuse.

In this case, Marie was receiving the message from many contexts that her mother was ineffectual and unable to take care of her. When Marie misbehaved in school, the message was that if Mrs. S. were a better mother, Marie would not be acting out. When Mrs. S. called the police, the subsequent investigation implied that she had known about the abuse and "denied" her knowledge. We almost replicated the blaming and disempowerment of Mrs. S. at the hospital. Had we kept Marie, both mother and daughter would have been told that Mrs. S. did not know what was best for her daughter, and that to protect Marie we had to intervene and remove her from her mother. The more ineffectual and unsupported the feisty Mrs. S. felt, the more Marie got the message that even women with spunk who defy traditional cultural roles are doomed to failure. Under these conditions, there was no good decision that Marie could make: She could act out (and have the larger system impose its will on her) or attempt to silence herself (through overdosing). She desperately needed to develop another story.

The central effort of the consultation was to begin to provide a means for Marie to change the story—for Marie to experience her mother as an effectual woman who dared to speak out to protect her child, and who was heard. By understanding their cultural background, we could see Mrs. S. in action as a protective mother who saw us as "outsiders" who could not be trusted, and therefore protected herself and Marie by keeping us out. By supporting Mrs. S.'s plan, we were helping to write the opening lines to a new story—one that would be important to Marie's development. Marie saw her mother, and by extension herself as an adult, as someone with no influence. That story was retold here: Marie's mother had the power to remove an abusive man from the household, and to develop a plan to help her daughter that the "experts" saw as valuable. Maybe Marie, too, could learn how to influence those around her without having to act out anti-socially. The new story formed a new image of womanhood, and paved the way for a more useful therapy.

CONCLUSION

In summary, by viewing female adolescent development within a sociopolitical context, we can begin to develop a new approach toward treating adolescent girls and their families. This approach validates an adolescent's need for connection and is sensitive to her fears of losing relationships, while simultaneously supporting her potential for becoming an assertive, challenging, and instrumental woman. Through this integration, it is my hope that the next generation of adolescent girls—and possibly even this one—will feel more empowered and able to experience the joy and wonder of emerging womanhood.

ACKNOWLEDGMENTS

This chapter is based on a paper presented at the annual convention of the American Association of Marital and Family Therapy, Washington, DC, 1990, and a previous version appeared in Mirkin (1992). Copyright 1992 by Haworth Press. Adapted by permission. I would like to acknowledge the work of Jean Baker Miller, Irene Stiver, Janet Surrey, Judith Jordan, Alexandra Kaplan, and Carol Gilligan, as well as the Women's Project in Family Therapy—Marianne Walters, Betty Carter, Olga Silverstein, and Peggy Papp. Their work has influenced my thinking, and has contributed greatly to this chapter.

NOTES

1. For more detailed descriptions of the case examples in this chapter see Mirkin (1990a).
2. Cathy Colman, Ed.D., introduced me to this expression.
3. It is my sincere hope that by the time this book is published, the Freedom of Choice Act will have passed and Title X funding will have been restored, signifying the beginning of a shift in government policy toward supporting a woman's control over her own body.

4. Recently, books such as *The Paper Bag Princess* (Munsch, 1980) have tried to deal with some (though not all) of these messages.
5. Steiner-Adair (1986) offers some interesting insights on the consequences for teenage girls of accepting or rejecting the Superwoman ideal.
6. This discussion will focus on mother–daughter relationships, although Lee and Szapocznik et al. write about fathers, sons, and extended family as well.

REFERENCES

Boston Globe. (1987a, May 10). Leaving mother behind, p. A-26.
Boston Globe. (1987b, August 21), U.S. news briefs, p. 6.
Cash, T., Winstead, B., & Janda, L. (1986). The great American shape-up. *Psychology Today*, pp. 30–37.
Erikson, E. H. (1968). *Identity, youth, and crisis.* New York: Norton.
Gilligan, C. (1982). *In a different voice.* Cambridge, MA: Harvard University Press.
Gilligan, C., Lyons, N. P., & Hamner, T. J. (1990). *Making connections: The relational worlds of adolescent girls at Emma Willard School.* Cambridge, MA: Harvard University Press.
Glamour. (1984, February). Feeling fat in a thin society, pp. 198–201.
Herman, J. (1987). *Sexual violence.* Paper presented at Learning from Women: Theory and Practice, a Harvard Medical School Department of Continuing Education conference, Boston.
Jewish Fund for Justice. (1989). *Seek justice: Women and poverty.* Washington, DC: Author.
Kohlberg, L. (1976). Moral stages and moralization: The cognitive-developmental approach. In T. Lickona (Ed.), *Moral development and behavior.* New York: Holt, Rinehart & Winston.
Krestan, J., & Bepko, C. (1990). *Too good for her own good.* New York: Harper & Row.
Lee, E. (1990). Family therapy with Southeast Asian families. In M. P. Mirkin (Ed.), *The social and political contexts of family therapy* (pp. 331–354). Needham, MA: Allyn & Bacon.
Miller, J. B. (1976). *Toward a new psychology of women.* Boston: Beacon Press.
Miller, J. B. (1985). *The construction of anger in women and men* (Work in Progress, No. 4). Wellesley, MA: Stone Center, Wellesley College.
Minuchin, S., Montalvo, B., Guerney, B., Rosman, B., & Schumer, F. (1967). *Families of the slums.* New York: Basic Books.
Minuchin, S., Rosman, B., & Baker, L. (1978). *Psychosomatic families: Anorexia nervosa in context.* Cambridge, MA: Harvard University Press.
Mirkin, M. P. (1990a). A feminist family therapy perspective on eating disorders. In M. P. Mirkin (Ed.), *The social and political contexts of family therapy* (pp. 89–119). Needham, MA: Allyn & Bacon.
Mirkin, M. P. (1990b, July–August). The new alliance. *Family Therapy Networker*, pp. 37–41.
Mirkin, M. P. (1992). Female adolescence revisited: Understanding girls in their sociocultural contexts. *Journal of Feminist Family Therapy, 4*(2), 43–60.

Munsch, R. N. (1980). *The paper bag princess.* Toronto, Canada: Annick Press.

Pollak, S., & Gilligan, C. (1982). Images of violence in TAT stories. *Journal of Personality and Social Psychology, 42*(1), 159–167.

Silverstein, S. (1964). *The giving tree.* New York: Harper & Row.

Steiner-Adair, C. (1986). The body politic: Normal female adolescent development and the development of eating disorders. *Journal of the American Academy of Psychoanalysis, 14*(1), 95–114.

Surrey, J. (1984). *The self-in-relation: A theory of women's development* (Work in Progress, No. 13). Wellesley, MA: Stone Center, Wellesley College.

Szapocznik, J., Rio, A., Perez, Z. A., & Kurtines, W. (1986). Bicultural effectiveness training (B.E.T.): An experimental test of an intervention modality for families experiencing intergenerational–intercultural conflict. *Hispanic Journal of Behavioral Sciences, 8*(4), 303–330.

Thompson, J. K. (1986, April). Larger than life. *Psychology Today,* pp. 39–44.

Vivelo, J. (1992, November–December). The mystery of Nancy Drew. *Ms.,* pp. 76–77.

Weitzman, L. J. (1985). *The divorce revolution: The unexpected social and economic consequences for women and children in America.* New York: Free Press.

5

Women Growing Older:
Partnerships for Change

SARAH GREENBERG
ALUMA KOPITO MOTENKO

As the number of older women in our society continues to increase dramatically, so does the need for practitioners to learn about this population in order to provide respectful and effective treatment. Older women face many challenges posed by the laws, policies, and programs of an ageist and sexist society.

For the purposes of this chapter, "older women" are those over the age of 65. Although many women lead vibrant, active lives until they become 75 or 85, 65 continues to be considered "old," 75 is considered "older," and the "old-old" are those over 85. "Ageism" is the term used to describe negative prejudices about and stereotypes of older people on the basis of their age alone (Butler, Lewis, & Sunderland, 1991). These negative attitudes are believed to stem from younger people's fear of aging and their reluctance to deal with the social and economic challenges related to the increasing number of older people. Ageist and sexist beliefs reflect society's emphasis on productivity, physical attractiveness, and sexual desirability. Our societal context both teaches and perpetuates the cultural denigration of older women, beginning with the portrayal of old women in classic fairy tales as scary old witches, mean hags, and generally ugly and evil people. Older women are frequently seen as having outlived their usefulness; that is, they have borne and raised their children, and often nursed their partners through terminal illness. Older women are universally mistreated and seen as burdensome. They are part of an invisible majority whose economic, emotional, and physical concerns remain, for the most part, ignored (Butler et al., 1991).

In this chapter, we discuss four areas that are of concern to all older people but have a differential impact on older women: loneliness, mental illness, physical illness/disability, and poverty. The treatment implications of the points raised in this discussion are then considered.

FEAR OF LONELINESS: MYTH AND REALITY

Older women fear that when they age they will be abandoned by loved ones. As women age, and lifelong friends, confidants, and other age peers die, do older women feel alone and lonely?

Being alone does not always mean that an older woman is lonely. Women's capacity for developing and maintaining friendships and relationships with family members, neighbors, and others is an important buffer to loneliness in later life. It can be an avenue for affirming a positive sense of identity, developing new roles, and giving and receiving help. We cannot ignore the fact, however, that living alone is a major transition for most older women. Losses of spouses and confidants are also major transitions, which often take considerable time to adjust to.

It is true that older women live longer than men and are more likely to live alone. Women 65 years of age and over now outnumber their male age peers in the United states by a ratio of 3:2—a considerable change from only 30 years ago, when the ratio was almost equal (6:5) (Markson, 1988). Women aged 85 and over represent 72% of the old-old population (U.S. Bureau of the Census, 1989a). Black women make up 60% of the total black aged population. There is a smaller proportion of elderly nonwhites than elderly whites. In 1989, 13% of whites, 8% of blacks, and 5% of Hispanics were 65 and older. These differences are expected to continue until the next century (U.S. Bureau of the Census, 1989b, 1990b).

These trends reflect the fact that women generally live longer than men, and are more likely to be widowed and less likely to remarry than men of the same age. Women, therefore, less frequently live with their spouses in late life than their male counterparts. By the age of 85, nearly 50% of men live with their spouses, compared to only 10% of women. The likelihood of a woman's living alone in old age increases with advancing age. More than half of all women who are 75 and older lived alone in 1990 (U.S. Bureau of the Census, 1990a). Many women have never lived alone until old age, making this a major transition for them to cope with.

The average American woman can anticipate 10 years of widowhood. Moreover, the current cohort of 80-year-old women has the lowest fertility rate in history, having been at the height of its childbearing years during the Depression. About one-fifth of the women in this age group had no children, one-fifth had only one child, and one-fifth had two children. The result is that today about 25% of these women have no children, and nearly

30% of African-American women of this age group are childless (Butler et al., 1991). With almost 20% of older women living with relatives, 2% with nonrelatives, and 5% in institutions, older women rely more heavily on age peers, siblings, and friends for assistance and support. As peers die and friends are not able to meet the needs of these women, social agencies become more important as sources of material and emotional support.

Widowed African-Americans and Latinas are more likely to live with other family members, whereas widowed white women are more likely to maintain separate households (U.S. Senate Special Committee on Aging, 1991, p. 187), a difference reflecting both cultural tradition and socioeconomic status. Older black women are much more likely to be the primary heads of their families (19%) than white women (7%) (Manuel & Reid, 1982). Black working-class older women are also the group most likely to have a related child under 18 living with them (Jackson, 1985).

The Importance of Friendship

For those who live alone, friends are often the primary and most enduring links with society, as well as the main sources of emotional support (Arber & Ginn, 1991). We cannot underestimate the importance of friends to older women. Older women's friendships have several distinctive features. Kahn and Antonucci (1980) suggest that friends in later life affirm a person's identity and self-worth through expressions of liking, respect, and agreement. Friendships develop voluntarily and are based on mutual gratification, emotional intimacy, and companionship (Crohan & Antonucci, 1989). Women's friends are often their closest confidants, with whom they share troubles and joys, anxieties, and hopes (Booth, 1972; Lowenthal & Haven, 1968).

Women's skills in developing and maintaining friendships, and their enjoyment of these relationships, are assets throughout life and especially into old age. Although older women may lose their friends as people die and relocate, they maintain continuity in their style of forming relationships, which they developed earlier in their lives (Crohan & Antonucci, 1989). For example, Taylor (1982) has shown that many elderly black women have a kin and friendship network that becomes an integral part of their ability to cope.

Social class influences the way in which friendships are made and maintained. Elderly middle-class women often make friends through membership in an association (Jerrome, 1981, 1989). The main basis of such friendships is the shared pursuit of the interests of the group and of goal-directed activities. Working-class friendships are more likely to be based on informal mutual aid than on more formal organizational involvement. In either case, formal or informal, friendship groups provide a valuable peer culture in which identity is affirmed and new roles can be developed.

Friendships are an important source of physical and mental health. The social support of close friends has been found to buffer the effects of stress on mental and physical health, and to encourage preventive health behaviors (Bankoff, 1983; Abella & Heslin, 1984; Langlie, 1977; Schaefer, Coyne, & Lazarus, 1981). Women who have supportive networks are more likely to have increased access to resources, to take better care of themselves, and to seek professional assistance when the need arrives. Friendship is an outlet through which women can both help others and receive help. It extends the caring role for women and provides them with an opportunity to feel needed (Atchley, 1980), combating the negative social stereotype of uselessness and incompetence in old age.

Despite the fact that many older women live alone, they are often not lonely because of their strong capacity for developing and maintaining mutually supportive relationships, particularly with friends. Since friendships tend to be egalitarian, they can become strained if the ability to reciprocate is impaired or appears to be so by the onset of chronic illness or other physiological limitations that can occur in old age. The effects of illness, impaired mobility, and physical decline need to be actively explored by clinicians in a way that helps older women maintain their connections as long as possible. This necessitates helping them to see what they can continue to offer to friends and family members, even in the face of physical changes. Clinicians should validate older women's need and desire for continued social activity by placing a high priority on this growth-enhancing sphere of their lives.

The Role of Family Members

Although friendships provide unique and valued support, studies show that family members remain the primary sources of assistance throughout the life course for individuals with families. Although the social support network of the majority of the urban elderly is comprised of core family members with peripheral friends and neighbors (Stoller & Pugliesi, 1988), this pattern of support should not be understood as the ideal or only model. Family relationships are different from, not substitutes for, friendships. Family relationships are based more on cultural kinship norms, prescribed roles, and formal obligations than are the more voluntary and informal friendship relationships.

Morgan (1989), in a study of transition to widowhood, found that the commitment of family members is counterbalanced by the flexibility of friendships. Older women work at preserving family relationships even if such relationships are not supportive. Societal belief in the importance of family connections can perpetuate family relationships with problematic obligations and dysfunctional behavior patterns. In friendships, there is an increase in positive relationships, because personal needs and values can be pursued in a friendship without sacrificing either member's well-being.

Although family relationships are complex, study after study has shown the persistence of family bonds (see, e.g., Cicirelli, 1983; Mutran, 1985; Shanas, 1980; Sussman & Burchinal, 1968). These bonds are demonstrated by frequent writing, phoning, and visiting; children's expressions of concern for their parents' well-being; and the family members' willingness and ability to provide help to older women when help is needed (Seccombe, 1988).

Older lesbians are reported to have the advantage of enjoying mutually supportive, long-lasting relationships with their partners (Butler et al., 1991). Most older lesbians report excellent health, positive acceptance of their own aging, and high levels of life satisfaction (Deevey, 1990; Quam & Whitford, 1992). Being active in the lesbian community supports positive attitudes.

Although mutually supportive partnerships are satisfying, relationships in the larger community can be problematic for lesbians. Life cycle issues such as bereavement, disability, problems of inheritance, and other legal and family issues can be difficult as homophobia, sexism, and ageism are encountered. For example, lesbians are frequently denied the recognized status of widows when their partners die. Families can prevent lesbian partners from participating in hospital visits, caregiving responsibilities, and funeral services by leaving them out of the arrangements. An example of this occurred when a client of ours who was a long-term lesbian partner was forbidden by family members to visit her lover in the hospital during a terminal illness; the family's homophobia prevented them from acknowledging or allowing for the lesbian relationship. These concerns need to be addressed by practitioners with older lesbian clients.

Black, Hispanic, and Native American women appear to have stronger ties to family members than do white American women. Studies caution, however, that clinicians should not simply assume the strength of families of color, but should assess the functioning of every older woman on an individual basis. Most studies do cite strong traditional and cultural values, including family commitment, as a strength in minority women's ability to adapt to old age. Gratton and Wilson (1988) caution against misinterpreting research findings showing that black and Hispanic families have stronger cultural norms of family obligation than do white families. They point out that although black and Hispanic family support systems play prominent roles in the lives of the elderly, the capacity of a family to provide assistance should not be exaggerated. Many black, Hispanic, and Native American elderly women give more assistance to their families than they receive. They often care for their grandchildren and provide financial assistance. Fifty percent of Native American older women and 29% of Hispanic older women provide child care, as compared to only 18% of white older women (Harris, Begay, & Page, 1989).

The complexity of older women's family relationships needs to be better understood by mental health professionals. Positive relationships can be encouraged, and difficulties can be approached with consideration of the autonomy of older women and the potential for mutuality between the generations.

FEAR OF MENTAL ILLNESS: MYTH AND REALITY

Researchers show that aging is accompanied by progressive increments in emotional and mental disorders. Yet the stereotype that aging inevitably leads to mental deterioration and "senility" is unsubstantiated and reflects ageist attitudes. Although there is an increased incidence of senile dementia with advancing age, elderly women with dementia can be helped with treatment. Since older women predominate in the 85+ group, they more frequently suffer from dementia in late life than men.

It is also a myth that older women are depressed—that depression is intrinsically part of the aging process. The current data show that the elderly have lower rates of major depression than do younger adults (Gurland, Dean, Cross, & Golden, 1990). As clinicians, we should not assume that the majority of older women are depressed, but we should be attentive to the signs and symptoms of major depression when they are evident. Butler et al. (1991) posit that the signs and symptoms of major depression in the elderly are not different from those of younger adults. Recent studies do show that less severely depressed groups of outpatients, however, exhibit different symptoms according to their age. In one study, older patients reported more physical symptoms and increased thoughts of death (Blazer, George, & Landerman, 1986).

A clinician's role in enhancing an older woman's continued growth and positive mental health is to help the client define her own goals and wishes for change. As practitioners, we need to utilize our listening skills to hear older women's stories, which are among the primary ways they communicate their feelings and concerns. Indirect communication is normative for this generation of older women and needs to be accepted, received, and interpreted by practitioners. We believe that older women continue to grow and develop in late life. Change *can* and *should* be expected. The transitions of old age may challenge family members' or practitioners' expectations of older women. A clinician needs to educate and help a client's family and social network adapt to this transition into old age.

An example of the need for a family and clinician to help an older woman define her goals for herself occurred in the case of an 80-year-old client who was encouraged to relocate to the West Coast from her lifelong home in the Northeast. This was assumed to be a good change for her, because she would be geographically nearer to her only son and his family, who wanted her closer to them. The move precipitated a severe depression for the woman, who, with help, was able to realize and state that though she liked being close to her son, she missed her community and the friendships she had created throughout her adult life. She moved back to her home in the Northeast, and her depression lifted.

Markides and Mindel's (1987) review of the literature on older people's depression and psychological distress indicates that the black and white elderly have similar levels of psychological distress. Epidemiological data are not available on the Hispanic, Asian-American, or Native American elderly. Although statistics report that minority elders use mental health centers infrequently, this may not be an accurate indication of the prevalence of mental illness among these elders. Cultural norms against traditional help seeking may work against their utilizing mental health services. Overuse of hospitals in minority communities may also affect these statistics.

Although we do not have evidence of racial differences in the mental health of older women, we do know of racial differences in institutionalization patterns. Blacks are underrepresented in nursing homes and overrepresented (along with other low-income groups) in public mental hospitals. The National Caucus and Center on Black Aged (1987) reports that 26% of white females over 85 are in nursing homes, compared to 14% of black women. Considerable evidence suggests that for older blacks and other ethnic elderly, the state mental hospital functions as a nursing home. With the closing of these facilities in many states as part of the deinstitutionalization movement, many of these patients have joined the ranks of the homeless. Although there are no known studies comparing rates of mental illness between aging minority women and white women, research suggests a higher degree of risk for those at lower incomes (Padgett, 1989).

FEAR OF PHYSICAL ILLNESS/DISABILITY: MYTH AND REALITY

Older women report both more acute chronic illness and more frequent rates of disability than older men. They often have multiple health problems, requiring coordination of care among providers. Because of the chronicity of older women's health problems and these women's longevity, they are more likely than men to spend time in a nursing home or to need home care services. About 75% of nursing home residents are females

(Lewis, 1987). The most prevalent chronic illnesses of older women are as follows, in rank order: arthritis, hypertension, hearing and visual impairments, heart disease, and chronic sinusitis.

Many older people do not report symptoms to health providers. Besdine (1985) reports that elders living in the community may be concealing as many as half of their symptoms. Treatable conditions that are not reported are often not diagnosed until it is too late to prevent disability. Therapists need to encourage older women to seek medical assistance, and should collaborate with their clients' doctors. Too often, older women may consider aches and pain to be parts of aging, when in fact they may have a treatable medical condition. Practitioners need to advocate on behalf of their clients to ensure that the medical profession takes older women's symptoms seriously and does not dismiss them as just part of "old age."

Sexual Relationships

Older women experience little biologically determined sexual impairment with age (Butler et al., 1991). In late life, many emotionally healthy older women have a growing capacity to develop sexually satisfying relationships. The realization that older people with chronic illness have sexual interests and capacities may be unsuspected and even unwelcomed by spouses, by other family members, and even by health and mental health professionals. Many heterosexual older women have limited opportunities to be involved in sexual relationships.

For example, a married woman was unable to continue a sexual relationship with her husband because of the effects of his Alzheimer's disease. The woman explained to a social worker that her husband still wanted to have sex with her, but she was unwilling because he was not able to keep himself clean and she did not want to be put at risk of infection. This was a major problem for her in caring for her husband, who was demented to the degree that he could not be left alone unsupervised.

Other difficulties are finding a sexual partner and a conducive environment. Elderly women are concerned with what other people will say about them, which can inhibit their having sexual relationships. Older women who have mobility difficulties may be restricted in their opportunities to socialize. And those in institutions have no privacy. A task of mental health professionals is to help older women deal with their personal feelings, fears, and possible misunderstandings about sex in old age. Clinicians should also recognize and support the need for privacy in all settings where older people are treated.

Perceptual Impairment

Perceptual impairments, especially hearing and vision loss, are of great importance to older people but are commonly overlooked by helping professionals. Attention to perceptual issues among older women is essential to maintaining their positive self-esteem and social interaction. Much vision loss (especially as a result of cataracts and glaucoma) is avoidable, either through prevention or treatment.

Practitioners must be aware of hearing- and vision-related issues, and help clients maintain conditions that maximize their perceptual capacities. For instance, therapists need to be aware that clients may need to be medically examined for hearing and vision losses. Clinicians also need to speak slowly and clearly while looking directly at their clients, keep down background noises, and have adequate lighting. Individual and group therapy can be very helpful for older women with hearing and vision loss, to improve their communication techniques and help them to overcome self-consciousness and embarrassment.

It is also important not to mistake a physical perceptual problem for a psychological one. For example, feeling dizzy or disoriented may be an inner-ear impairment, rather than a symptom of mental or other physical illness. As clinicians, we need to become aware of the common physical symptoms of eye and ear problems, in order to avoid mistaken psychiatric labeling.

POVERTY AMONG OLDER WOMEN: MYTH AND REALITY

Health Care Systems and Poverty

The greater longevity of women and the greater chronicity of their health problems put them at a disadvantage in the U.S. health care system, which focuses on acute health care needs to the exclusion of long-term care needs; this approach is more appropriate for older men (who have more acute health conditions and fewer chronic illnesses) than for older women. Medicare makes very little contribution to long-term care services in institutions or in the community. Thus, only 38% of the health expenses of older persons are met by Medicare; the rest must be paid out of pocket (Butler et al., 1991). At this writing, private insurance for long-term care is expensive and not available everywhere.

Many older women are forced to "spend down" their resources to the poverty level in order to be eligible for state-funded Medicaid help for long-term care. Many older couples are also required to "spend down" if one partner requires long-term care. The high costs of care can deplete the couple's financial resources very quickly (U.S. Senate Special Committee on Aging, 1991, p. 180). In such a situation, if the wife outlives her husband (which she is likely to do), she is left destitute.

Many older couples are reluctant to "spend down." Since they live on fixed budgets, many curtail social, nutritional, and housing expenditures to pay privately for home care services, in attempts to avoid costly institutional care and impoverishment. For this reason, many older women live in less than adequate circumstances.

Mental health professionals need to be aware of the limited options available to meet the long-term care needs of older women, and of the choices that often have to be made. They should encourage clients on limited budgets not to curtail important social activities or nutritional needs in favor of other expenses. Clinicians working with older women should also actively explore housing and nutritional options to make sure they are adequate in meeting the needs of their clients. These areas need to be explored delicately and respectfully, as older women will often deny these problems to cover up their shame about having them. Advocacy efforts among older women and mental health professionals to improve health policies must be an integral part of providing effective services.

Income

A small proportion of older women are financially secure, but the majority of older women are poor. Compared to older men, older women of every marital status and age group have lower income (U.S. Senate Special Committee on Aging, 1991, p. 47). This low-income status is primarily associated with widowhood in old age, with inequality in women's access to the work force and to equal pay, and with a pattern of lifelong economic dependency on men. In 1989, the median income of elderly women was $7,655—58% of the median income of elderly men ($13,107). One in five women aged 85+ was poor in 1989 (p. 46). Twenty-three percent of women living alone were poor, and 70% of black women living alone were poor (p. 55). Although older people represent 12% of the total population, they constitute 27% of the poor in the United States (p. 42).

Women receive less in Social Security benefits than men do, because of less pay for equal work, periods outside the work force because of caregiving responsibilities, and built-in inequities in the Social Security system. In 1989, the average monthly Social Security benefit was $458 for women, compared to $627 for men. African-American women received an average of only $369 per month in Social Security benefits in 1988 (Butler et al., 1991).

Displaced homemakers often become poor in old age. These women— 10 million of them over the age of 45 in 1989 (Butler et al., 1991)—have lost their primary source of income as a result of separation, divorce, widowhood, prolonged unemployment of spouses, disability, or loss of eligibility for public assistance.

Many older women are eligible to receive welfare supplements to their Social Security checks. The Supplemental Security Income (SSI) program is a joint federal–state welfare program designed to supply monthly cash payments to individuals whose income falls below the poverty level. The program only provides enough income to bring an individual to 70% of the poverty level. Many low-income and minority older women are unaware of the SSI program. As therapists working with older women clients, we need to become informed about the financial benefits available for older people and to share that information with our clients. Networking and phone calling in these circumstances are appropriate, as is advocating for changes in public policy. U.S. policy at the present time discriminates against older women and denies them minimum adequate resources after a lifetime of service to their families and in employment outside the home. This economic discrimination, in conjunction with a society that provides minimal resources for older women, is often the source of many of the emotional disturbances we see in our clinical practice with the elderly:

> The vulnerability of older women to mental health problems results not from longevity per se but from the fact that longevity can cause a woman to outlast her personal financial resources and to overwhelm current prevention, treatment, and rehabilitation capabilities in the community. (Lewis, 1987, p. 11)

TREATMENT IMPLICATIONS

Being old, being a woman, being disabled, being a woman of color, being a lesbian, and being poor are all positions that are marginalized in U.S. society. Moreover, these views are internalized by older women. A key role for us as practitioners working with older women clients is to use ourselves in the therapeutic relationship in ways that mirror the lived experience of older women, as opposed to the societal constructs that distort and devalue their lives. In order to provide effective treatment to older women, we must identify and confront our own feelings about and fears of aging, mortality, and older people. An exploration of our own ageist beliefs is necessary for the development of nurturing relationships with older women clients.

As therapists working with older women, we must function in some unique ways to create relationships that are reparative experiences. We have to provide and advocate for concrete services, participate in various aspects of the clients' lives, and be connected in a manner that entails personal sharing and genuine responsiveness to the clients. Relationships with older women challenge our traditional professional boundaries, often requiring that we share more of ourselves than we do with other populations, as well as receive the clients' wisdom, advice, food, gifts, and other offerings. This helps to establish the mutuality needed to develop a successful therapeutic alliance. Older women clients come from a generation in which women were socialized exclusively to give to and take care of others. The concept of receiving services and attention for themselves is often incompatible with their self-image or their vision of relationships. It is the mutuality of being able to give and receive in a therapeutic relationship that allows an older woman client to incorporate both sides of the nurturing equation.

The Volunteer Insured Timebanking Association (VITA) program, sponsored by the Kit Clark Senior House in Dorchester, Massachusetts, is a programmatic example of effective use of mutuality with the elderly. The VITA program encourages volunteers, who are often isolated elders themselves, to provide services to other isolated elderly people by daily telephoning, friendly visiting, going shopping, doing errands, and participating in leisure activities; in exchange, a volunteer receives credit for every hour of service delivered. Earned credits can be used to provide necessary services for the volunteers themselves or for someone else in need. The volunteers also participate in monthly training meetings and annual recognition functions, and receive a monthly newsletter. Their work is honored, recognized, and rewarded through the system of repayment. According to an administrator of the program, the phone calls and visits often serve as impetus to the provider as well as the receiver to get up in the morning, get dressed, and have some breakfast in order to be alert enough to make or receive the phone call or visit (S. K. Albright, personal communication, 1993). Phone calls, she says, often last many hours and serve as a personal connection for both people. The structure is set up to validate older women's need to be needed and provide help without diminishing the nature of their contribution. It also provides an important service to isolated elders. Another example of mutual aid for older women is the Widow to Widow program, which is run by widowed volunteers who reach out to support new widows. The use of volunteers in the same predicament fosters reciprocity by providing them with the opportunity to give in return for the services they receive.

This framework of mutuality supports a predominant theme of our chapter, which is the concept that women's development occurs in connection with others (Gilligan, 1982; Berzoff, 1989; Surrey, 1991; Miller, 1976, 1988). Scholars have proposed that a woman's growth occurs *within* relationships, rather than through a process of separation from her family of origin (Erikson, 1950; Mahler, 1968; Kohlberg, 1969, 1976, 1981; Vaillant, 1977; Levinson, 1978). We believe that older women can be empowered within relationships in an environment of reciprocity, connectedness, responsibility, and care. We suggest that practitioners encourage older women to creatively develop and maintain this context of connection, as they attempt to cope with some of the difficult life circumstances that can occur during the aging process. We also suggest an assessment of each older woman's social network, as it is essential to supporting women's capacity and desire to continue significant relationships throughout their lives.

Creative Use of Self in Treatment

As practitioners who provide treatment to older women, we need to use ourselves in more creative and active ways than we do with other populations. To create a trusting relationship with an older woman client, a clinician must be responsive in ways that correct society's treatment of older people. The relationship then serves as a model that enables the elderly woman to experience the strength and vitality of her life, rather than the constraints of the stereotyped vision of the dominant culture. Most importantly, the clinician needs to demonstrate belief in the older woman's value by showing concern for her history, validating her wisdom, helping her without infantilizing her, and understanding the older woman's current concerns in the context of her history. The clinician must include the older woman in a partnership in which the client and practitioner together address, understand, and resolve the issues of concern to the client.

As clinicians, how do we achieve these goals? Recent literature identifies a number of special principles in effective treatment of the elderly: increased activity, more frequent use of touch, greater use of reminiscence to help the elderly client recapture and reaffirm the self, and an awareness of the countertransference issues evoked in geriatric practice (Tobin & Gustafson, 1987).

In addition to these principles, we need to be more "real" with elderly clients—to share more of ourselves with them than we do with other populations. This serves many functions in providing effective treatment. It bridges the generation gap between an older client and a younger practitioner, affirming the commonalities between the generations; it helps the older person to feel connected to the clinician in a more familiar and egalitarian manner; and it provides the older client with an opportunity to share some of her wisdom while telling her story.

> For example, a social worker taking a history of an older woman in her 70s asked about her social network. The woman informed her that she had been divorced for many years. The social worker shared that she too was divorced, but more recently. She then asked the woman what she could tell her about being divorced; this provided an opening for the client to be helpful to her, and enabled the client and worker to learn from each other. A more traditional and neutral relationship rarely provides this type of opportunity for sharing, in which

the client is provided with the sense of self-esteem that comes from having something to offer the practitioner while receiving help at the same time.

The Importance of History Taking

The geriatric practitioner has to walk a fine line between respecting the tradition and history of the older women and continuing to affirm her capacity for change and adaptation. Taking a history on all older woman clients helps to achieve this goal by including their past as it affects their current adaptation. Gathering information from family, friends, neighbors, and other service providers can be helpful in doing this. An older woman's history provides a context in which to understand her current concerns. Interventions can then be designed to help the older woman adapt to or change her current circumstances, with respect for the continuity of personhood found to be characteristic of older people (Atchley, 1980).

An example of an intervention that considered and respectfully pushed on the client's historical behavior occurred in an interview between a social worker in a residential setting for the elderly and an 80-year-old client. In taking a history of the woman, the social worker learned that she came from an Irish Catholic background and that she was a person who had always obeyed the rules. Being assertive was difficult for her and did not fit into her picture of herself. She complained to the worker about how much she hated the food in the rehabilitation center—that it was tasteless and terrible. The worker told her that there was a barbecue for staff and residents on her floor that afternoon, where there was likely to be better food than usual. The client explained that she could not possibly go because she was on a salt-free diet. Considering the "good girl" history of this client, the social worker warmly challenged her acceptance of the rules by asking her whether she thought this one time would really hurt her. The client went and had a great time, smiling conspiratorially at the worker. In this case, breaking a rule allowed the woman to adapt her style in a way that better suited her current circumstances. This might have required a different intervention if the client had a different history.

Mutuality in the Therapeutic Relationship

Home visits as a regular or periodic way of meeting are important. Visiting an older woman in the context of her primary social environment—whether this is her own home, a nursing home, or a hospital—is often critical in establishing the mutuality needed for creating a good therapeutic relationship. It helps to confront the isolation of so many elderly women, and facilitates the management of mobility and transportation problems involved in getting to an office. It also provides a setting more conducive to sharing, in which an older woman is comfortable and can offer the worker something to drink or eat, and can share mementos from her past (e.g., photographs) that provide a natural opportunity for reminiscence. This enables the worker to be included in an important aspect of the client's life review, from which the worker might otherwise be excluded.

Of primary importance in this work is the emphasis on the mutuality of the client–worker team approach. As noted earlier, work with older women often requires that practitioners become involved in "doing things" for and with their clients. We clinicians must recognize and utilize the therapeutic potential available in the provision of concrete services to the elderly. Understanding the role of case management in treatment of older clients is central to the development of a trusting relationship. We must also be able to provide helping services in a manner that respects and incorporates our older clients' preferences (e.g., always arriving early for doctors' appointments). This generates a therapeutic atmosphere in which older woman clients can share their wisdom and knowledge with practitioners, who can, in turn, contribute their skills and energy in carrying out the mutually identified task.

> An example of this type of collaboration occurred when a social worker, in response to her client's expressed interest, wanted to involve the client's adult child in planning for his mother's care. A lifetime of protective mothering precluded the client from making the request directly. She agreed, however, to allow the social worker to call her son, and was able to advise her as to the best time to call and the best approach to use to form a successful alliance with her adult child. The process of mutual planning served to empower the older woman, even in this situation that involved the social worker asking for her client's son to help in his mother's care.

Filial Maturity

Although children are usually well intentioned, their efforts sometimes come across in a paternalistic or overprotective manner. Our practice experience shows that it is common for adult children to think that once their mothers are ill and need help, it is the children's responsibility to decide what type of care is best and how the care should be provided. We have found that this response serves to undermine the autonomy of older women. We believe that the elderly have the right to make decisions for themselves, and that aging or illness does not mean they are no longer competent to know what is best for them. Adult children can help by asking their mothers what the mothers' needs and wishes are, as well as by finding out about available resources. The treatment goal for adult children is to help them to act in partnership with their mothers. It is also important for helping professionals to preserve the autonomy and self-esteem of older women in their relationships with them (Motenko & Greenberg, in press).

In addition to being the care receiver, an older woman is frequently also the caregiver to other elderly family members, primarily her spouse, her siblings, or even her parents. The quality of the relationship between the caregiver and care receiver can influence the gratification, frustration and overall well-being of the older woman care provider. Motenko (1989) found that wives who provided care out of affection for and reciprocity with their husbands achieved more psychological well-being and satisfaction than wives whose primary motivation was a sense of duty or obligation. The caregiving role, although burdensome, can have gratifications if it is performed out of caring, desire, and mutuality. Wives reported that they enjoyed expressing their affection for their husbands through nurturing and were gratified by continuing a meaningful marital relationship. This was less true of wives who provided caregiving primarily out of a sense of obligation.

Another aspect of effective treatment for older women and their families necessitates that clinicians have a good understanding of the developmental tasks of late-life families. Margaret Blenkner (1965) describes the concept of "filial maturity" as a normal, desirable developmental task for adult children of aged parents. It is the shift that occurs for most individuals in their 40s or 50s when they can no longer look to their parents as a steady source of emotional and financial support. At this stage of life, older parents begin to depend on their offspring for support and comfort. Adult children need to incorporate responsibility toward their parents into their own developmental tasks, while the aging parents must begin to acknowledge and accept their increasing dependency (Greenberg, 1983). Blenkner (1965) affirms this shift as a normal stage of development, as opposed to the frequently described late-life role reversal, which she sees as a pathological development. The achievement of filial maturity is believed to facilitate a person's own transition into old age and to lead to a more successful aging process for the adult child. As clinicians, our ability to understand, convey, and translate the concept of normalized filial maturity into action is central to successful therapeutic intervention in late life.

To translate this concept into clinical practice, a practitioner must reframe a client's commitment to being a "good mother" to mean that she allows her children the opportunity to participate in her caretaking and active planning in her old age in mutually agreed-upon ways. By encouraging older women clients to involve their children *more* in their care rather than less, clinicians can confront their clients' fears of becoming a dependent burden on their adult children, and can educate older women and their families to accept that the moderate, respectful involvement of their adult children is acceptable and valuable to both generations. The filial crisis marks the end of childhood, but does not make the child a parent to the parent. Thus, the aging mother continues to be seen as a parent, regardless of her level of increased dependency. Filial maturity allows adult children to perceive their mother as a person in her own right, with her own needs, limitations, and life history. Achieving this perception is a rite of passage.

The Family Life Review

The family life review, in which family members look back on and come to understand and accept their history as a family together, depends on this filial transition for its successful therapeutic outcome. An effective meeting necessitates the generational shift that allows for the older woman to share her personal story, including her personal limits and conflicts in shaping earlier family history. The parent has often not previously revealed these experiences to the children, and the expanded discussion of earlier family crises facilitates a new understanding of the meaning of these life markers, which encourages acceptance and forgiveness between family members (Walsh, 1980).

There are, of course, exceptions to the use of this intervention. In a family with a history of violence, abuse, or neglect, the scars may be too deep to permit an adult child to connect positively with his or her mother. When the adult child is clear about not wanting to be involved in the care of his or her mother for this reason, the child's wish needs to be respected. The worker in this case may choose to do a life review with the client (Butler, 1968), in which the loss of this connection is identified and mourned. Frequently we clinicians can use ourselves in such situations to fill in some of the family gaps. For those older women who have no children or kin, we can become the providers of comfort, concern, and dependability. This process can, in turn, facilitate our own filial maturity (Greenberg, 1983). This process can also be used in a family in which the aged mother has a history of dependency. A clinician can help the adult children find acceptable limits and ways of continuing their contact with their mother, and can provide some relief in sharing the caretaking responsibility with them by providing transportation, making phone calls, advocating, and networking for the older client. This is a challenging task of the treatment, but one that must continue to be mutual.

When members of a family with a history of parent–child conflict choose to reconnect in a parent's old age, it can provide an opportunity for them to understand and redo *in vivo* the traumas they experienced in their earlier life together. Through inclusion in the separate inner life of the older parent, which includes the context in which family decisions took place long ago, adult children are given the opportunity to develop a more expansive understanding of parental behavior previously experienced only as painful or rejecting. This allows adult children the chance to recon-struct their view of their mother as a separate individual with a history of her own. Forgiveness becomes a possibility that allows for transformations in a family system previously stuck in old hurts and angers (Walsh, 1980).

An example of a therapeutic family life review occurred in Greenberg's work with a family in which the older working-class woman client was a recovering alcoholic, with a history of having disrupted each of her children's homes and families as she tried to live with them. At the idea of having to live alone, she presented her children with her suicidal depression. They were burnt out and tired of her complaints and demands, but also concerned. The mother was able to tell her story to the clinician with two of her children present as the participatory audience. She talked of having moved from her parents' house into her husband's house and then, when he became unemployed, moving back into her mother's house in order to provide her children with the shelter and care they needed. She tearfully shared the pain she had experienced about this decision. When her parents died, she had no place to live and began to live with her children, each in turn. Her panic about being on her own, at age 70, for the first time in her life was more than she felt she could handle. She had never learned the skills she needed to be able to cope with this challenge.

The mother's sharing enabled her children to understand her circumstances in a different historical context, and they were able to feel more empathic toward her dilemma. The difficulty of her life became more real and touched her children in a way that made them more willing to help her. They worked out a support system for staying in close contact with their mother, and Greenberg, in collaboration with the older woman, worked out a plan for her participation in a day program that expanded her network beyond her children. Being able to work as a team with her family and the social worker allowed the older woman client to feel more supported in her struggle and less alone; this helped her to manage her fears successfully and to cope with living on her own. The relationships with the two children who had been present at the meeting were strengthened. Her other two children continued to remain cut off from their mother, despite efforts to involve them in the treatment. They were kept informed of her adjustment by their siblings. There was some hope expressed by the family that, after a respite, the other children might rejoin the support system that had been set in place for their mother.

It is important for the clinician to deal with the family in a manner that continues to include the older woman. Frequently, family meetings in hospitals and nursing homes either ignore the older woman or exclude her from her own decision making. Interviewing the older woman is most effective when the worker is patient and allows the woman to tell her story in her own way at her own pace. It is only after a long while that the practitioner can make use of the story to help the older woman to develop her insight. Moving too quickly will interrupt the therapeutic alliance.

CONCLUSION

In summary, the issues of fear of loneliness, mental and physical illness, and poverty are both realities and myths in the lives of older women living in an ageist and sexist society. As clinicians, we must be aware of the concerns confronting older women in our society, so that we are prepared to hear them, to realize the impact of these circumstances on our older women clients, and to validate and correct the reality of these injustices and stresses. We can help counter some of the painful realities through the creation of trusting and enabling therapeutic relationships, and through advocacy with our clients to change the circumstances and societal responses that create and perpetuate the injustices. As practitioners working with older women, we are uniquely challenged to utilize all aspects of ourselves and our training to create genuine, active, and effective relationships with our older women clients. The reciprocity of such relationships is their most basic element. The satisfaction and fulfillment we experience as a result of the special bond created with our clients are older women's gifts to those of us in the helping professions who have chosen to work with these women.

ACKNOWLEDGMENTS

We would like to thank Joan W. Berlin and Sandra K. Albright for their significant contributions to this chapter.

REFERENCES

Abella, R., & Heslin, R. (1984). Health, locus of control, values and the behavior of family and friends: An integrated approach to understanding health behavior. *Basic and Applied Social Psychology, 5,* 21–25.
Arber, S., & Ginn, J. (1991). *Gender and later life: A sociological analysis of resources and constraints.* Newbury Park, CA: Sage.
Atchley, R. (1980). *The social focus in later life.* Belmont, CA: Wadsworth.
Bankoff, E. (1983). Social support and adaptation to widowhood. *Journal of Marriage and the Family, 45,* 235–240.
Berzoff, J. (1989). From separation to connection: Shifts in understanding women's development. *Affilia, 4,* p. 1.
Besdine, R. W. (1985). Rational and successful health care of tomorrow's elderly. In C. M. Gaitz & T. Samorajski (Eds.), *Aging 2000: Our health care destiny. Vol. 1. Biomedical issues* (pp. 12–19). New York: Springer-Verlag.

Blazer, D., George, L., & Landerman, R. (1986). The phenomenology of late life depression. In P. E. Bebbington & R. Jacoby (Eds.), *Psychiatric disorders in the elderly*. London: Mental Health Foundation.

Blenkner, M. (1965). Social work and family relationships in later life with some thought on filial maturity. In E. Shanas & G. Streib (Eds.), *Social structure and the family: Generational relations* (pp. 46–59). Englewood Cliffs, NJ: Prentice-Hall.

Booth, A. (1972). Sex and social participation. *American Sociological Review, 37,* 431–438.

Butler, R. N. (1968). The life review: An interpretation of reminiscence in the aged. In B. Neugarten (Ed.), *Middle age and aging: A reader in social psychology.* Chicago: University of Chicago Press.

Butler, R., Lewis, M. I., & Sunderland, T. (1991). *Aging and mental health: Positive psychosocial and biomedical approaches* (4th ed.). New York: Macmillan.

Cicirelli, V. (1983). A comparison of helping behavior to elderly parents of adult children with intact marriages. *The Gerontologist, 23*(6), 619–625.

Crohan, S., & Antonucci, T. (1989). Friends as a source of support in old age. In R. Adams & R. Blieszner (Eds.), *Older adult friendship* (pp. 62–71). London: Sage.

Deevey, S. (1990). Older lesbian women: An invisible minority. *Journal of Gerontological Nursing, 16,* 5.

Erikson, E. (1950). *Childhood and society.* New York: Norton.

Gilligan, C. (1982). *In a different voice: Psychological theory and women's development.* Cambridge, MA: Harvard University Press.

Gratton, B., & Wilson, V. (1988). Family support systems and the minority elderly: A cautionary analysis. *Journal of Gerontological Social Work, 13,* 62–70.

Greenberg, S. (1983). *The family in later life: A descriptive study.* Unpublished doctoral dissertation, Boston University.

Gurland, B. J., Dean, L., Cross, P., & Golden, R. (1990). The epidemiology of depression and dementia in the elderly: The use of multiple indicators of these conditions. In J. O. Cole Jr. & J. Barrett (Eds.), *Psychopathology in the aged.* New York: Raven Press.

Harris, M., Begay, C., & Page, P. (1989). Activities, family relationships and feelings about aging in a multicultural elderly sample. *International Journal of Aging and Human Development, 29*(2), pp. 104–110.

Jackson, J. L. (1985). Race, national origin, ethnicity and aging. In R. H. Binstock & E. Shanas (Eds.), *Handbook of aging and the social sciences* (2nd ed., pp. 361–369). New York: Van Nostrand Reinhold.

Jerrome, D. (1981). The significance of friendship for women in later life. *Aging and Society, 1*(2), 206–211.

Jerrome, D. (1989). Virtue and vicissitude: The role of old people's clubs. In M. Jeffreys (Ed.), *Growing old in the twentieth century* (pp. 401–412). London: Routledge & Kegan Paul.

Kahn, R., & Antonucci, T. (1980). Convoys over the life course: Attachment roles and social support. In P. Baltes & O. Brim (Eds.), *Life-span development and behavior* (Vol. 3, pp. 119–130). New York: Academic Press.

Kohlberg, L. (1969). Stage and sequence: The cognitive developmental approaches to socialization. In D. A. Goslin (Ed.), *Handbook of socialization theory and research.* Chicago: Rand McNally.

Kohlberg, L. (1976). Moral stages and moralization: The cognitive developmental approaches. In T. Lickona (Ed.), *Moral development and behavior: Theory research and social issues.* New York: Holt, Rinehart, and Winston.

Kohlberg, L. (1981). *The psychology of moral development* (Vol. 2). San Francisco: Jossey-Bass.

Langlie, J. (1977). Social networks, health beliefs and preventive health behavior. *Journal of Health and Social Behavior, 18,* 26–32.

Levinson, D. (1978). *Seasons of a man's life.* New York: Knopf.

Lewis, M. (1987). Sex bias dangerous to women's mental health. *Perspectives in Aging, 16,* 9–11.

Lowenthal, M., & Haven, C. (1968). Interaction and adaptation: Intimacy as a critical variable. In B. Neugarten (Ed.), *Middle age and aging: A reader in social psychology* (pp. 390–400). Chicago: University of Chicago Press.

Mahler, M. (1968). *On human symbiosis and the vicissitudes of individuations. Vol. 1. Infantile psychosis.* New York: International Universities Press.

Manuel, R. C., & Reid, J. (1982). A comparative demographic profile of the minority and nonminority aged. In R. C. Manuel (Ed.), *Minority aging: Sociological and social psychological issues* (pp. 121–141). Westport, CT: Greenwood Press.

Markides, K. S., & Mindel, C. H. (Eds.). (1987). Marital health and psychological well-being. In *Aging and ethnicity* (pp. 121–147). Beverly Hills: Sage.

Markson, E. (Ed.). (1988). Introduction to older women: Issues and prospects. In *Older women* (pp. 1–3). Lexington, MA: D.C. Heath.

Miller, J. B. (1976). *Toward a new psychology of women.* Boston: Beacon Press.

Miller, J. B. (1988). *Connections, disconnections, and violations* (Work in progress, No. 33). Wellesley, MA: Stone Center, Wellesley College.

Morgan, D. (1989). Adjusting to widowhood: Do social networks really make it easier? *The gerontologist, 29*(1), 78–85.

Motenko, A. K. (1989). The frustrations, gratifications and well-being of dementia caregivers. *The Gerontologist, 29*(2), 166–172.

Motenko, A., & Greenberg, S. (in press). Reframing dependence in old age: A positive transition for families. *Social Work.*

Mutran, E. (1985). Intergenerational family support among blacks and whites: Responses to culture or to socioeconomic differences. *Journal of Gerontology, 40*(3), 382–389.

National Caucus and Center on Black Aged. (1987). *The status of the black elderly in the United States.* Washington, DC: U.S. Government Printing Office.

Padgett, D. (1989). Aging minority women: Issues in research and health policy. *Women and Health, 14,* 213–225.

Quam, J. K., & Whitford, G. S. (1992). Adaptation and age-related expectations of older gay and lesbian adults. *The Gerontologist, 32*(3), 301–306.

Schaefer, C., Coyne, J., & Lazarus, R. (1981). The health related functions of social support. *Journal of Behavioral Medicine, 4,* 106–111.

Seccombe, K. (1988). Financial assistance from elderly retirement age sons to their aging parents. *Research on Aging, 10,* 26–32.

Shanas, E. (1980). Older people and their families: The new pioneers. *Journal of Marriage and the Family, 42,* 9–15.

Stoller, E., & Pugliesi, K. L. (1988). Informal networks of community-based elderly. *Research on aging, 10,* 301–307.

Surrey, J. L. (1991). The "self in relation": A theory of women's development. In J. V. Jordan, A. G. Kaplan, J. B. Miller, I. P. Stiver, & J. L. Surrey, *Women's growth in connection* (pp. 51–66). New York: Guilford Press.

Sussman, M., & Burchinal, L. (1968). Kin family network: Unheralded structure in current conceptualizations of family functioning. In B. Neugarten (Ed.), *Middle age and aging: A reader in social psychology* (pp. 247–254). Chicago: University of Chicago Press.

Taylor, S. (1982). Mental health and successful coping among aged black women. In R. C. Manuel (Ed.), *Minority aging: Sociological and social psychological issues* (pp. 95–100). Westport, CT: Greenwood Press.

Tobin, S., & Gustafson, J. (1987). What do we do differently with elderly clients? *Journal of Gerontological Social Work, 10,* 107–121.

U.S. Bureau of the Census. (1988). *Poverty in the United States: 1988* (Current Population Reports, Series P-60, No. 160). Washington, DC: U.S. Government Printing Office.

U.S. Bureau of the Census. (1989a). Current Population Reports, Series P-25, No. 1045. Washington, DC: U.S. Government Printing Office.

U.S. Bureau of the Census. (1989b). Current Population Reports, Series P-60, No. 161. Washington, DC: U.S. Government Printing Office.

U.S. Bureau of the Census (1990a). *Marital status and living arrangements* (Current Population Reports, Series P-20, No. 468). Washington, DC: U.S. Government Printing Office.

U.S. Bureau of the Census. (1990b). *U.S. population estimates by age, sex, race, and Hispanic origin: 1989* (Current Population Reports, Series P-25, No. 1057). Washington, DC: U.S. Government Printing Office.

U.S. Senate Special Committee on Aging. (1991). *Aging in America: Trends and projections.* Washington, DC: Author.

Vaillant, G. (1977). *Adaptation to life.* Boston: Little, Brown.

Walsh, F. (1980). The family in later life. In E. A. Carter & M. McGoldrick (Eds.), *The family life cycle: A framework for family therapy* (pp. 312–335). New York: Gardner Press.

6

Lesbian Families:
A Cultural Perspective

JOAN LAIRD

The very phrase "lesbian family" presents, for some, an enigma, a conceptual leap. Until recently, one rarely heard the word "lesbian" joined with the word "family," for the two ideas were viewed as mutually exclusive. However, not only does this family form appear to be on the increase (or at least more visible); it is fair to speculate that it may be one of the more viable family forms in this age of gender wars, high rates of divorce, and alarming levels of family violence, particularly husbands' violence against their wives.

Yet very little is known about lesbian families in their social contexts—where they live and how they go about their daily lives, how they fit well or do not fit well in their sociocultural surrounds, how they meet the expectations typically required of all families, and how they deal with the special stresses and challenges they face because of their "difference." There are many reasons for our current lack of information. Part of the problem is that the *sine qua non* of lesbian marginality is lesbian invisibility. Lesbians are doubly difficult to see: They are invisible and silenced as women in a patriarchal society, and invisible and silenced as women who choose to commit to other women in forming couples and families, thus violating the fundamental rule of patriarchy, compulsory heterosexuality (Rich, 1980).

In the world of the mental health professions, our knowledge about lesbian couple and family experience has been circumscribed in particular ways and for particular reasons, not the least of which has to do with the positivist, empirical, scientific paradigm that has dominated most research—a paradigm that some feminist scholars (e.g., Davis, 1985; Harding, 1986; Keller, 1984) have seen as better reflecting male than female ways of knowing. It is primarily an "essentialist" body of research, in the sense that lesbianism is viewed as a state of being, some kind of fundamental self that finally "comes out," rather than as an evolving and shifting narrative about self in a complex social context. This emphasis in some ways has been enormously valuable, helping to undermine some of the troublesome social and professional myths that have dominated the social discourse in relation to gays and lesbians. There are other ways in which the research emphasis to date has produced its own set of limitations and problems. Research on homosexuality, paralleling mainstream research, has been dominated by male researchers studying male subjects; this dominance has obscured and often failed to differentiate the experiences of lesbians. It is also a body of research largely dominated by psychological thinking and attention to the inner world of individual feeling and cognition, and at times to couple relationships. These are, of course, important dimensions of lesbian experience, but the overwhelming emphasis on the individual psyche has tended to obscure the social and cultural dimensions of lesbian life, hiding from view important questions that might enrich society's understanding of a large and important segment of its population and that might make it easier for clinicians to attend to the sociocultural contexts in which lesbian family life is shaped.

Moreover, clinicians are of course interested in problems, in troubles; their writing too often focuses on the problematic, the "dysfunctional," the deficits, contributing to an overall portrait of lesbian life that can mask its richness and complexity. Our psychodynamic, family systems, and other clinical theories, on the one hand, help us to organize and think about what we see; on the other hand, they also create what we see, forcing a blueprint, a plot structure, on a dense human mystery, and often blinding us to other possibilities. Clinicians often fail to take adequate account of the sociocultural contexts and power arrangements that potentiate and constrain the stories available for lesbian life, but at the same time they are in a unique position to illuminate those contexts and to testify to such experience in the larger clinical and social community.

I begin this chapter by reviewing the major themes in research on lesbians and teasing out some of the questions that remain largely unexplored. My vision is that of the ethnographer and of the clinician as ethnographer–practitioner—someone who approaches the strange, the other, as an eager and curious learner who asks to understand the culture of the other. She knows she cannot leave behind her own culture, her own narratives, but she does not try to hide or suppress them; she brings them into the dialogue so that both parties may examine their contributions to the coevolving conversation.

RESEARCH THEMES

What Causes Homosexuality?

In the years before the famous 1969 Stonewall rebellion in Greenwich Village and the 1973 decision of the American Psychiatric Association to discontinue its categorization of homosexuality as a disease, the prevailing theme in research on homosexuality was a search for etiology. Some researchers struggled to find the cause of homosexuality, which was seen variously as a biological defect, a mental illness, or a result of developmental arrest (e.g., of incomplete oedipal resolution). Explanations were sought in genetic endowment and in early childhood experiences, particularly in faulty mothering.[1] As family theory took hold, a later generation of researchers sought to define particular sets of family dynamics or faulty family structures that might produce homosexual children. (Interestingly, no researchers searched for the causes of heterosexuality.) In spite of efforts to blame certain stereotypical family constellations (e.g., the domineering, seductive mother and the passive, peripheral father), researchers were not able to link male or female homosexuality to any particular family form.[2] Nor have researchers been able to successfully link the choice of gay or lesbian identity to the sexual orientations of one or both parents; both heterosexual and gay or lesbian parents appear to produce about the same proportions of children who come to define themselves as straight, gay, or lesbian.

Gay and Lesbian Mental Health

As the interest in etiology gradually waned, a new trend took shape in the 1970s, one that continues into the 1990s—namely, a body of research dedicated to determining whether gay men or lesbians are as mentally healthy as heterosexuals. Again, the convergence of results suggests no consistent differences beween heterosexuals and homosexuals in degree of mental health or mental illness, in spite of the special environmental stresses experienced by gay men and lesbians.[3]

The Coming-Out Process

Related to the mental health theme is a large body of research on gay and lesbian "coming-out" or identity-making processes (Cass, 1979, 1984; Coleman, 1981–1982; Hencken & O'Dowd, 1977; Minton & McDonald, 1983–1984; Troiden, 1979). This third theme is grounded in the developmental metaphor of "stage," in which the life cycle (or, in this case, "coming out") is envisioned as a series of stages that the individual must master before some final stage of identity integration can occur. The stage model has also been applied to the process of gay and lesbian couple development (McWhirter & Mattison, 1984), the process that families who learn their children are gay or lesbian must go through (DeVine, 1984), and most recently by Slater and Mencher (1991) to the notion of the lesbian family life cycle.

Gay and Lesbian Couple Relationships

A fourth research theme, which continues to be central, concerns the nature and quality of gay and lesbian couple relationships. Bell and Weinberg (1978); Blumstein and Schwartz (1983); Harry (1984); Kurdek and Schmitt (1985, 1987); Peplau and Cochran (1981); Peplau, Cochran, Rook, and Padesky (1978); and Zacks, Green, and Marrow (1988) are among those who have examined relationship quality, social support systems, sources of stress, coping resources, and other dimensions of coupling patterns. Again, although there are certain kinds of important differences along various measures between homosexual and heterosexual couples as well as between gay and lesbian couples, my reading of the data suggests that the overall similarities among these various kinds of couples far outweigh the differences. Gay and lesbian couples, of course, face certain kinds of challenges that heterosexual couples typically do not; yet they are as "functional" in all of the many possible meanings of that conception as any other kind of couple. Interestingly, the most significant differences—in role divisions, in the uses of power and money, in the expressions of sexuality, and so on—seem more related to differences in gender socialization than to differences in sexual orientation.

Children of Lesbian Parents

In recent years, a new research theme has taken hold. Although gay men and lesbians have always parented, their children have usually been born in the context of heterosexual marriage. These children, then, are both the children of divorce and the children of lesbian or gay parents who may or may not be partnered. In a case in which the biological mother's lesbian partner (the "co-mother") is living in the household, the family then resembles the stepfamily headed by a heterosexual father and stepmother, in that the co-mother's position is at least as precarious and ambiguous as that of the stepmother.[4] The position of the co-mother, however, is further complicated by the fact that she may have no legal protections and may also lack various kinds of socially sanctioned rights or privileges in relation to her partner's children. Most recently, we are said to be experiencing a lesbian "baby boom"—a phenomenon in which single or partnered lesbians make the choice to bear, adopt, or foster children outside of heterosexual marriage.

The research on lesbian and gay families with children repeats the earlier themes of research on individuals and couples. Are the children of lesbian or gay parents as psychologically and socially healthy as other children? What special challenges do they face? Again, a dozen studies examining over 300 children of lesbian parents (e.g., Golombok, Spencer, & Rutter, 1983; Green, Mandel, Hotvedt, Gray, & Smith, 1978; Hoeffer, 1981; Kirkpatrick, Smith, & Roy, 1981) have produced no evidence that children of lesbian or gay parents are harmed or compromised, or even differ significantly along a host of psychosocial measures from children raised in heterosexual families.[5] In fact, there is some evidence to suggest that such children tend to be less rigid, more tolerant of differences in others, and more flexible in terms of their own gender identities.

To date, there have been very few studies of what might be called "chosen" children—that is, of children born or adopted in the context of lesbian relationships or to single lesbians. The results so far, however, suggest that these children also function and fare at least as well as children from heterosexual families (Patterson, 1994).

A Critique of the Literature

As important as the various research contributions have been in providing more insights into gay and lesbian experience and dispelling some of the prevailing destructive mythologies, in my view there are also some problems and some gaps in the research and clinical literature. Perhaps the most pervasive impression is that researchers on gay and lesbian themes have taken a basically defensive and to some extent a deficit-based stance. Few have attended to what might be characterized as the extraordinary strengths, courage, resiliences, and innovativeness found in the gay and lesbian population. Few if any have asked, "How can it be that in a world in which lesbians and gays are subjected to invisibility, silence, homophobia, and other forms of prejudice and discrimination, so many of these individuals, couples, families, and children seem to be doing as well as everyone else?"[6] Taken as a group, they seem in general to be doing as well, *in spite of* the actual or potential hostility they face every day. How can we understand these seemingly healthy couples and families, when we all know the devastating results on family life of secrets, silences, emotional cutoffs, and rejection? Could it be that lesbians and their families have special experiences and special strengths that give parents and children alike the courage to master adversity? How do they do it? Could it be, in the language of White and Epston (1990), that they have constructed alternative stories and in fact alternative families that, for them (many of whom have spent time in heterosexual marriage), better fit their lived experiences and may better fit the possibilities for family life today? How do they counter the silence or the pathology stories that are pervasive in their sociocultural surround? Most of these women and their children have not been broken by society's words about them; they have managed to construct stories for themselves and their relationships that open up new possibilities. They have, in fact, actively sought to liberate themselves from handicapping narratives—from a social discourse that can constrain the choices and possibilities for women and especially for lesbians. A strengths-based perspective, along with greater attention to the question of culture, can reshape clinical approaches to working with lesbian couples and families.

LESBIAN FAMILIES: A CULTURAL PERSPECTIVE

Anthropologist Gilbert Herdt (1992), critiquing existing research for its emphasis on identity making as an individual rather than a cultural process, argues that we have been asking the wrong questions. He believes that we should be asking the following:

1. What does a gay man (or lesbian) come out *to?*
2. What does a gay man (or lesbian) come out *to be?*

For Herdt, being gay is not merely adopting a sexual identity, a lifestyle, or an enclave, but becoming part of a gay cultural system. The gay liberation movement and the gradual rise of cultural symbols and institutions (gay pride marches; lesbian and gay music festivals, bookstores, newspapers, magazines, films, and plays; lesbian and gay community and social groups; etc.), Herdt believes, signal the rise not only of a sense of *communitas* or of *Gemeinschaft,* but also of a larger national culture, or *Gesellschaft.*

Certainly in many communities today, the person who is "coming out" can find a hospitable "culture" with which to connect and identify. Some large cities boast community centers for gay and lesbian youth, where young people can find recreational activities, support groups, and counseling opportunities. Again in larger cities, university towns, and other environments more hospitable to lesbians, the lesbian can rather easily build friendship networks, locating the self in a context where various community and cultural institutions may be identified as lesbian or at least as gay-friendly. Many lesbians, in their daily lives, walk relatively comfortably between contexts that may be largely heterosexual and heterosexist and contexts that may be gay- or lesbian-identified, using somewhat different languages and costumes in each, depending on their own degree of "outness." Certainly geography, the character of the larger community, class, ethnicity, gender, the power of more conservative political or religious institutions, and many other social forces influence the local discourse on homosexuality, the degree of integration, and the person's access to gay or lesbian cultural symbols and models.

But the state of our knowledge about lesbian culture is very thin. I have discovered no ethnographic studies of lesbian families—that is, "thickly described"[7] studies of individual families—and very few studies of lesbian communities or lesbian cultural life. We know very little, for example, about how lesbians are fashioning families and redefining notions of kinship. One exception is the work of Weston (1991), who concludes that lesbian notions of kinship are becoming an important force in the remaking of American culture.

Definitions of "culture" are at best amorphous, combining notions of ethnicity, common language, geographical location, heritage and traditions, symbols, mores and values, and so on. Not only is it difficult to articulate what we mean by "culture" in general; it is even less clear what we can point to as "lesbian culture." Thus, it is confusing to talk of lesbian culture on a national, community, or familial level. Furthermore, each lesbian will participate in the larger American culture and in lesbian culture to different degrees and in different ways. Lukes and Land (1990) argue that gays and lesbians are "bicultural"—that is, that they absorb and draw upon both the larger American culture and gay culture, just as an immigrant to these shores or a person of color merges particular ethnic customs with those from the surrounding culture.

In my own view, "culture," like "ethnicity," should not be viewed as a relatively stable combination of particular characteristics, behaviors, meanings, and beliefs, and even the term "bicultural" does not capture the experience. "Culture" is ephemeral, a moveable feast. It is best understood as always emerging, always changing, always improvisational—a social construction, but one always in a state of being reconstituted. For example, a woman may be proudly "Irish" on St. Patrick's Day, but disclaim any particular identity or affinity with "Irish" the rest of the year. Is this person someone essentially Irish? What makes her so? Country of origin? Customs? Appearance? Religious affiliation? Family and friends? Her own set of meanings and definitions? In this country, we decide that someone is essentially and culturally "black" even when that person, by bloodline, is predominantly white. Similarly, homosexuality can be socially and personally ascribed on the basis of one or two sexual acts—a "master status" (Goffman, 1963) applied to what may be only occasional behavior. Such people are often seen as "latently" homosexual.

Being "lesbian" means different things to different people at different times in their lives as well, and even from one hour to the next, as contexts and meanings shift. Much gay and lesbian research has pictured the making of a gay identity as a stage or life cycle process—the "normal" and "healthy" stages of identity consolidation conceptualized in a number of models. These models have received considerable criticism in recent years for a number of reasons, which I will not elaborate on here.[8] My own view is that stage models superimpose prior maps or blueprints on what is a much more complex, shifting, emergent, and individual process. Stage models cannot account for culture, for context, for shifting meanings over time, for cohort differences, for changing social and political meanings, and so on. It is a very different experience for a woman in her 50s with grown children, living in a rural Midwestern town, to embrace a lesbian identity than it is for an 18-year-old attending an Eastern women's college. One woman of 70 I interviewed, educated in English boarding schools before World War II, knew that she was attracted only to other females from her early teenage years on and has since the age of 18 lived a woman-identified life. But only during the women's movement of the 1970s and 1980s did she venture to use the word "gay" to describe and think about herself; she began to claim the identity "lesbian" for the first time during our interview in 1992, and later that year decorated her Christmas tree, for all to see, with women's and lesbian symbols. Another woman I interviewed has never had an intimate sexual relationship with another woman, only with men, but firmly defines herself as a "lesbian." For her, this self-definition has to do with feminist politics and a way of life. Currently, it is becoming fashionable on college campuses for young women who might in another year have identitified themselves as either "lesbian" or "straight" to describe themselves as "bisexual."

We "perform" and "improvise" our cultural meanings, depending on the surround—strengthening and claiming certain meanings in some contexts and times, and keeping silent about or eschewing those meanings in other contexts and times, rearranging the elements of our life stories as we enact them. People vary, of course, in terms of how firmly they hold on to particular sets of meanings. Some people welcome new information, new meanings; others hold on to their prior texts even when they are exposed to new contexts or new information that we would think might influence them to alter their story (Riess, 1980). We need to know more about how lesbian couples and families from diverse ethnic, racial, and social class backgrounds construct their cultural meanings; how they interact with their communities and neighborhoods; how they deal with enforced silences and invisibility; how they give language to themselves and their lives in varying contexts; how they buffer experiences of homophobia, how they strengthen their couple relationships; and how they help their children grow strong.

Students of lesbian and gay life have been fond of arguing that lesbians and gays in couple and family relationships have few or no cultural models for fashioning their own family cultures—no culturally sanctioned, widely supported rituals to draw upon (e.g., Roth, 1989; Slater & Mencher, 1991; Zitter, 1987). Such statements do certainly convey something important about the lack of legal and social supports for lesbian relationships. But the notions of "culture" and "cultural models" are used in misleading ways here. First of all, it is assumed that American culture *is* heterosexual—that its meanings are owned by heterosexuals and unavailable to gays or lesbians. Although it is the case that heterosexuality is assumed in our heterosexist society and that we have all been socialized to the notion of compulsory heterosexuality, this does not mean that American culture is "heterosexual"; it is much more complex than that. I would argue that gays and lesbians are multicultural beings, and that most of us firmly planted in the complexity of whatever we call American culture and our particular interpretations of it—reflecting, absorbing, and at times rejecting or refashioning its cultural traditions and meanings. At the same time, as lesbians, we may also be more or less identified with whatever lesbian and gay cultural symbols are available, reshaping, integrating, and inventing new meanings in an ethnogenic-like process. Furthermore, gays and lesbians do not belong to some monolithic collectivity to be contrasted with straight American culture. Such an effort, opposing two "cultures" in some sort of reductionistic or binary opposition stance, does an injustice to the enormous diversity within each group.

    Lesbian couples and families *do* have models to draw upon; they, like everyone else, must decide what parts of their family, community, and national values and customs they will carry into their newly formed families. What is different is, of course, that a lesbian couple consists of two women and that they will be designing their lives in a social surround that may not value their relationship and may even actively discriminate against it. They, like everyone else, will make certain kinds of compromises in their presentation of themselves as individuals and as a couple or family, depending on their "reading" of each context. And they will more or less imitate or more or less repudiate the coupling and family-making patterns feminists have labeled "patriarchal."

STORY AS A CULTURAL CATEGORY

The Social Discourse

In this era of postmodernism and social constructionism, the metaphors of "story," "text," and "narrative" are being used to provide fresh views of family therapy approaches and the role of the therapist. Therapy is seen as the writing of a new story (Laird, 1989)—the construction of an alternative narrative, one that is not problem-saturated (White & Epston, 1990). Therapy is reconceptualized as ongoing conversation or dialogue (Anderson & Goolishian, 1988, 1992) in which new ideas, new stories, and new interpretations of old, handicapping narratives can be generated. However, this conversation, in my view, must always take place with an acute sensitivity on the part of the therapist not just to the individual, couple, or family narrative, but to the social context of power relations in which both client and therapist are embedded and to the social discourses that have shaped the stories of all concerned.

One of the key goals of the women's movement and other civil rights movements has been to open up space for the voices of women and other oppressed groups to be heard. Women's words and women's speech genres have been ridiculed, discounted as "gossip," not taken seriously, and disallowed in the public forums where major social and political decisions are made. To "speak out," for many women, has been dangerous. Many have adopted the strategy of silence or secrecy—sometimes a frightened, passive silence, and sometimes a silence in the service of resistance (Laird, 1993, 1994).

Lesbians as women face at least double discrimination, and sometimes they must cope with additional statuses that mark them as "other," as is the case with lesbians of color. Oppressed in the larger society, they may be oppressed within their own ethnic groups as well, since such groups vary in the degree to which homosexuality is tolerated. Without belaboring the point, lesbians, then, face all of the discriminations women in general face, overlaid with a larger social discourse in which lesbians are variously storied as nonwomen, nonfeminine bitches, seducers of other women.

In the family therapy field, the lesbian story has also been suppressed. Lesbian family therapists are greatly underrepresented and virtually invisible in the family therapy field—in part, perhaps, because of the fact that conceptions of "lesbian" and "family" have been, until very recently, mutually exclusive ideas. Much if not most of the woman-centered, feminist scholarship in the family therapy field fails to mention lesbians, replicating some of the divisions and silences in the early women's movement. A token workshop or two on gay and lesbian themes may characterize family therapy conferences, reminding us all that lesbians are marked as "different" from the unmarked category of female—heterosexual.[9]

In other words, the "lesbian story," in the larger social discourse (which provides the cultural repertoire and materials from which we can select to construct our own narratives) is a "bad" one: It is largely a negative, "problem-saturated" story, and it is a silenced and punished story. Similarly, the dominant narratives in professional discourse have been "bad" or pathology-focused. Family therapists, whether straight or gay, come from a mental health–illness tradition in which homosexuality was defined as deviance, an illness, a developmental arrest; thus they are not immune from these kinds of larger social stories (see, e.g., Pittman & DeYoung, 1971).

Both psychodynamic and family systems theorists in the 1980s were repeatedly finding what was termed "fusion" or "merger" in lesbian couples—a phenomenon that Krestan and Bepko (1980), in their pioneering paper, attributed to the social isolation and difficult boundary maintenance issues these couples experience. Crawford (1987, 1988) and Roth (1989) have also sought understanding of lesbian couple fusion in the cultural milieus in which lesbians seek to define their relationships. Others (e.g.,

Burch, 1982, 1987), in keeping with feminist thinking in the tradition of Chodorow (1978) and others, have attributed the fusion phenomenon to the fact that lesbian couples consist of two women, and thus of two people oversocialized for emotional connectedness and undersocialized for differentiation. Most recently, Mencher (1990) argues that although mental health professionals, influenced by prevailing patriarchal norms for relationship and sexuality, tend to label fusion as problematic or pathological, lesbian couples themselves see this same emotional connectedness as a central strength and source of satisfaction in their relationships. It is clear that we do not know enough about women's relationships and women's sexuality; here, as is the case with much of what we think we know about women, male norms for relationship dominate the discourse.

Lesbians' Stories about Themselves as Individuals and as Couples/Families

To repeat a point made above, the social discourse surrounding lesbians and lesbianism, which is often a pathologizing discourse, provides the major cultural repertoire from which families can construct their own narratives to explain their children's lesbianism, as well as the major source of stories for lesbians and lesbian couples to explain themselves. Couples and families have troubles when they incorporate problematic stories into their own identity narratives—another way of describing what has been termed "internalized homophobia." Many parents whose daughters are lesbian construct a "failure in parenting" narrative, a self-blaming story. Others disown their daughters or build a "seduction" narrative, a version of the wicked witch or sorceress fairy tale, in which their innocent young daughters are bewitched and captured by evil creatures. And, of course, many families are concerned that they will somehow be contaminated by the lesbian connection—guilt by association.

In a context in which women's stories in general and lesbian stories in particular are constrained and devalued, lesbians face story-censoring decisions every day. Heterosexual couples live in contexts in which their couple relationships are part of ordinary conversation, a central part of their life narratives. For lesbians, every shifting conversational context represents a new decision: How do I define my life, my family, in this context? Do I use "I" or "we"? Do I act as if I am single? Do I invent a boyfriend, pretend the "we" is a heterosexual relationship? How will my descriptions and language affect my children, my parents? How will my language risk my job security, my future, my child's future? How will my "outness" (or "closetedness") affirm or invalidate the centrality of my partner in my life and in the parenting of my birth child? What costs do my silences exact? What does it do to me, to my partner, to our children not to share our joy on our 10th anniversary? Whom can I talk to about my pain and loss, now that we have separated?

Furthermore, when the specific nature of the relationship is not voiced, others in the social context are also more uncertain and constrained. Those who might be more accepting and inclusive also have to edit their conversations; they are sometimes unsure about the commitment in the relationship, sometimes concerned about offending. Others may treat each partner in the lesbian couple as single, calling the two of them the "girls" or the "ladies"—terms that are personally and politically offensive to many if not most lesbians. Still others may make blatantly heterosexist or homophobic remarks or tell lesbian jokes. And many lesbians are subjected to unwanted advances from men and even sexual harassment—open season on the "single" woman.

USING THE STORY METAPHOR IN PRACTICE WITH COUPLES AND FAMILIES

There are several ways in which the notion of "restorying" (Laird, 1989) or the constructing of "alternative narratives" (White & Epston, 1990) is a helpful one for guiding more collaborative, empowering practice with lesbians and their families. It should be noted that lesbians do not usually come for help for problems directly related to lesbian identity, but many of the problems and needs they do identify are related to the management of a stigmatized identity in a homophobic environment (de Monteflores, 1986). Three of the many possible "story management" roles for the therapist are discussed here: (1) helping lesbians recast negative self-stories; (2) helping lesbians "come out" to their families and in other important contexts; and (3) becoming an "ally"—bearing witness/restorying in the larger community. In the following case example and discussion, all three of these points are illustrated and then discussed.

Leslie, a 60-year-old accountant, and Mollie, a 48-year-old archivist, came for counseling after experiencing increasing conflict in their 16-year relationship. Mollie's son, Jim, from her 8-year marriage was aged 3 when the couple began living together. A number of issues particular to the lesbian definition of their couplehood seemed relevant to the current disturbance in a relationship both women described as having been "very special," loving, and companionable for many years. For one thing, Jim, now 19, seemed to have distanced himself from them and become more silent and secretive; he was also having difficulties in college. Mollie worried that he was drinking too much and smoking pot. Periodically threatened over the years by her ex-husband with a custody battle, Mollie had tried to ward off this threat by never giving language to her relationship with Leslie. The couple was always careful about any demonstration of intimacy in Jim's presence. In his adolescent years, Jim had gradually stopped bringing his friends over to the house. Mollie felt that it was time to name their relationship for him, while Leslie still thought he would ask "when he was ready." Mollie also said that she sometimes felt "suffocated" and "bored" and had distanced herself sexually, all of which was painful for Leslie. Although they never hid their "coupleness" or their commitment, neither woman had ever "come out" in her family of origin or in her work setting. They had a close relationship with one other closeted lesbian couple, and otherwise socialized occasionally with family members and with heterosexual friends from work, always carefully screening their presentations of themselves and their coupleness to exclude any references to their lesbian commitment.

They had no connections to any larger lesbian network or community, and knew very little about lesbian culture or history. In spite of her career as an archivist, Mollie knew nothing about lesbian literature. In fact, both women acknowledged their discomfort with using the term "lesbian."

Their "lesbian" stories were somewhat different. Leslie "knew" she was "different" from midadolescence, had never dated males, and had begun experimenting with lesbian sex in college. As a young woman during the McCarthy era, she had been arrested in a gay bar, and had had the excruciatingly painful experience of losing a job as a teacher after being accused of being a lesbian. As she matured, her major adaptive strategy became one of extreme caution concerning disclosure. Mollie, on the other hand, had dated many boys, had had several "serious" relationships with men, and had married immediately after college. She saw herself as oppressed in her marriage to a man she described as disloyal, irresponsible, and alcoholic. She met Leslie shortly after she left her husband, but even after 16 years together and a mutual lifetime commitment to the relationship, Mollie was not sure she would define herself as "lesbian."

Recasting Negative Self-Stories

It is the narrative or story, in my view—not some underlying structure or organization of personality or family system, some essential cluster of characteristics or patterns—that is constitutive of lives and relationships. And it is through storying or performing their narratives that people invest their lives with meaning, creating and recreating their identities. It is thus through "restorying," constructing new narratives, that people can reauthor or reconstitute their lives. In work with a lesbian couple, that frequently means deconstructing destructive and subjugating social stories, scrutinizing them, and freeing up the possibilities for reauthoring.

The clinician, whether lesbian or not, must try (insofar as possible) to divest herself of her own prior cultural assumptions about homosexuality or lesbian family culture. Her particular ideas about lesbianism are no more expert or privileged than those of any other party to the conversation. On the other hand, the therapist should be, as an ethnographer, something of an expert on the prevailing social discourses about homosexuality in general and lesbianism in particular, and on the ways such stories may be oppressive. In work with a lesbian couple, the ethnographically oriented therapist encourages the identification and deconstruction of the self-stories that seem to dominate couple or family discourse, examining them in relation to their cultural contexts of discourse, knowledge, and power. People are invited to map the influence of these stories (White & Epston, 1990), and whenever they are limiting or constraining, to generate new ideas, to create alternative narratives—that is, narratives that contradict the handicapping effects of the individual and social narratives by which they have lived. The clinician's role becomes instrumental in challenging any early return to the canonical.

Lesbian lives, like those of African-American and other oppressed groups of women, have been largely unsung throughout history; lesbians have been denied their cultural heroines. Famous women leaders in history, if they are portrayed at all, are almost never identified as lesbians in our educational systems; this denies young lesbians the opportunity to identify with strong and widely respected women, to see their own aspirations mirrored in the careers of outstanding women leaders. The underground lesbian network in my own profession, social work, suggests that many of social work's founders (and, indeed, contemporary leaders) were (are) women-identified women who, if not ever "named" as lesbians, spent (spend) their lives in committed relationships with other women. One lesbian friend, a fellow social worker, acknowledged, after I had "logged her on" to the network and claimed these women as ancestors/heroines, that she was "horrified" that these women she admired had probably been lesbian. Her images of them were somehow tarnished, she felt. This experience led her to re-examine her self-story and to reconfront her own homophobia. A teacher of social work, she recently "came out" in her classes for the first time; has been working with the campus lesbian, gay, and bisexual student alliance; and has been instrumental in promoting faculty and curriculum development on gay and lesbian issues.

Similarly, clients can be helped to explore the sources of their own stories about themselves and about their couple and family relationships. Lesbians can be helped to search out positive, heroic stories of lesbian women to counter the deviant stories. Art, film, biography/autobiography, music, and other repositories of cultural narratives can be drawn upon to locate both kinds of stories and to identify the interests behind the authoring of particular kinds of stories. For example, lesbians are rarely represented in movies; even when they are, they are often portrayed in stereotypical and even deadly ways. Most recently, the seducer/lesbian we have been taught to fear has become a killer, committed to a woman companion while she exploits male sexuality and desire and then murders her victims *(Basic Instinct)*. What larger social purposes and whose interests, we might ask, do such narratives serve?

To return to the case of Leslie and Mollie, it became clear in the therapeutic dialogue that they were largely unaware of the negative self-stories they were performing (Bauman, 1977), let alone the possible influences of these stories on their lives. As the therapist encouraged them to identify and examine both the stories themselves and the contexts in which their lesbian self-stories had been shaped, Leslie remembered a time of such repression that silence seemed the only possibility, while Mollie described how she had never even heard the word "lesbian" spoken aloud before meeting Leslie, and since then had been terrified of losing Jim. She had internalized images of lesbians as male-like, leather-and-chains-wearing "dykes," and could not find herself in that picture.

Self-defined feminists, but isolated from any wider supportive network of lesbians, these women were afraid to risk their connections to Jim, their families of origin, or their work. As therapist and couple together examined the influences of the larger social discourses that had in turn shaped their self-stories, they identified many ways in which the partners' rather passive acceptance of negative stories and images was exacting costs in their relationship. For example, they were cutting themselves off from a community of women with whom they might have a great deal in common, and they were unable to fully "tell" their lives within their families or in other important contexts, which both of them felt made them inauthentic and brought unnecessary distance into the relationships. The fact that they had to monitor their behavior and their language so rigorously with everyone in their surround meant that over the years they had become increasingly unable to be openly affectionate with each other. This constraint had become so pervasive that it characterized their daily lives even when Jim was away. The only time they were able to be demonstrative at all with each other was when they were away on vacation and unlikely to see anyone they knew.

This bright, intellectual couple, challenged by the therapist to invent other possible stories for themselves, began to read lesbian literature recommended by the therapist, as well as history and poetry—all modes of storying in keeping with their ways of knowing. As they began to search out and challenge common stereotypes of lesbian life in popular culture, they began to take more charge of what their own new lesbian narrative might be like and what possibilities it might open up. For example, as Mollie began to realize that being lesbian was not just a matter of (deviant) sexuality but of social and political commitment, of being woman-identified and woman-centered, she began to claim a clearer story of herself as a lesbian. Leslie, who had always secretly feared that Mollie might leave her for a man (as a former lover had done), began to see that the self-protective strategies she had used in one era were not necessarily adaptive in the 1990s.

Coming Out

Only when lesbians are free to make their stories public, when they can emerge from the deadly realms of secrecy and silence, will there be a culture for the next generations of women to come out *to* and proudly held role models to come out *as*—women to emulate, women whose stories serve as inspiration to others.

The issue of "coming out," to oneself and to others, is frequently relevant to the therapeutic conversation. Do the partner's ways of constructing their narratives in shifting contexts, to use White and Epston's (1990) phrase, fit their "lived experiences"?

"Coming out," typically understood as a developmental "stage" phenomenon, may also be thought of as the reconstruction of a lesbian self-story or couple narrative. It is a lifetime restorying process, in which the past is recast to explain the present and present narratives help shape future outcomes. Although I believe that many lesbians who do remain silent and secretive in certain contexts have unique ways of buffering and countering what we have seen as the insidious effects of secrecy (Laird, 1993), "coming out" can clearly be a freeing, enriching, pride-making experience that can have enormous impact on both individual and couple narratives, as well as on the couple relationship.

For example, if a couple relationship can be claimed by the partners themselves in the wider family and community, it creates a context in which others may be freer to discriminate, but also a context in which others are not free *not* to at least recognize the couplehood, with all that this might imply. It can actually mean that some are not quite so free to oppress, either covertly or overtly, because the larger discourse has changed in such a way that such behavior will not be tolerated. The claiming/storying process, once initiated, can affect every aspect of a couple's family life, opening up new possibilities both inside and outside the family. The partners do not have to monitor their language and their behavior so carefully; even more importantly, their own language and behavior can reflect back to them a new sense of pride in their identities and relationships.

Family-of-origin work can become a powerful location for change in the lesbian story. Here too, the issue of self-disclosure, behaviorally and/or linguistically, is crucial to the individual–family relationship; it is a powerful issue that will need to be addressed in many situations. Lesbians and lesbian couples vary on a continuum from maintaining total secrecy to being fully open with their families. A not uncommon situation is one in which the relationship is behaviorally enacted in more or less open ways, but not languaged; that is, each partner simply assumes that the other will be included in family affairs, and family members accept the importance and quality of the relationship. In a sense, everyone seems to agree to accept the relationship as long as it is not talked about—the current strategy of choice for our joint chiefs of staff and other military leaders regarding gays in the military. Although lesbians often accommodate to these subtle rules and manage to counter their potentially harmful effects, the partners' sense of their own integrity, authenticity, and agency is threatened, and the intimacy possible in relationships with the families of origin is limited. Furthermore, the couple must maintain a hypervigilant stance against revealing language and overtly affectionate behavior, which lessens comfort and often adds stress to the couple relationship.

A clinician can help a couple protect and strengthen the integrity of the relationship, even though one or both partners may not wish to come out to family members. For example, the partners may develop special signals to communicate with each other and to establish a connection in the face of enforced distance; may carve out times when they can be alone together to resolidify their coupleness; and so on.

A therapist can also help a couple examine the "lesbian" family-of-origin narratives. The partners can openly identify and can consider challenging each family's language rules around what can be said and what must be left unsaid—the rules for having conversations about the partners' lesbian identity or lesbian couplehood. Lesbian clients can be helped to explore the social and cultural contexts that surround their families, so that they can better interpret their families's reactions and develop ideas about how to work on changing the discourse. Frequently, the "lesbian issue" is a red herring for other unresolved issues in families. For example, some families are reluctant to allow their daughters to leave home in ways that are both independent and connected; the fact that a daughter has disclosed her lesbian identity or choice can become the symbol over which the battle for differentiation is fought. Some young women, hurt, rejected, and resentful when their parents do not respond positively to self-disclosure, cut off completely from their families of origin and further isolate themselves; others keep that part of their lives silent and secret, in order (they think) to maintain their family connections. And some make serious compromises in their own couple relationships in order to maintain some more or less peaceful connection with their families of origin.

Any of these adaptations can, of course, add to the burdens of the lesbian couple or family. One partner, who is "out" and accepted in her own family, may feel like a dirty secret in her partner's family, while the partner who believes she cannot be "out" in her family may envy and resent the "out" partner's connectedness. Children of lesbians, particularly adolescents, can be both protective of their mothers and concerned about how their mothers' lesbianism will affect their relationships with peers. Some children, questioning their own sexuality and/or angry at and embarrassed by their mothers' orientation, are fearful of taunting and ostracism by peers. Such children may isolate themselves from others, which, of course, can lead to other kinds of problems.

The families and children of lesbian couples themselves may need help not only in accepting the news, dealing with the complexity of feelings it generates, and mourning the losses that may be experienced, but also in "coming out" themselves. Many families feel that the family story must be kept secret from the rest of the world, which will not understand and will somehow taint them as well. Families, it should be remembered, do not usually have access to the gay-affirming communities of peers and supports that many lesbians enjoy. In addition to including extended family members and children in the therapeutic conversation, in many communities today the clinician can help to connect parents with Parents and Friends of Lesbian and Gays (P-FLAG), a self-help organization that has been most helpful for families. Some agencies may sponsor groups for children of gays and lesbians; if not, the clinician can consider starting one. The family members, too, need to revise their own narratives in ways that help them retain their pride in "familyness," and that help them recast their past, present, and future stories in empowering ways.

In the case of Mollie and Leslie, as they began to revise their self-narratives, they also began to believe that coming out might enrich their lives as well as free up some of the constraints in their relationship. The therapist helped them consider the costs of not being out and the risks they might be taking to come out in varying contexts. The women felt that they must begin with Jim. He was perhaps the most difficult to tell, and their relationship with him was the one they were least willing to risk, but he was also the most important other person in their lives. Jim's reactions at first were anger and a sense of betrayal, but a week after the first conversation he confided that he thought he had, at least on some level, known for a long time, and he asked Mollie whether she thought Leslie really knew how much he loved and respected her. Several months later, he suggested to Leslie that he would like it if she could call him her son; Leslie, for her part, although always deeply committed to parenting Jim, began to claim her role as co-mother in a more assured, open way. He began to ask questions about gay and lesbian culture and to share his new knowledge with his closest friends, who began to appear at the house more often. At present, he is very supportive. The opening up of this formerly forbidden conversation has unlocked the doors to other silences in the various family relationships.

After coming out to Jim, coming out to others has seemed less threatening, as both Leslie and Mollie have gradually been experimenting with "telling" their lives. Mollie recently shared the news with her father and with an old friend from her married days, while Leslie talked about "my son" with a colleague—positive experiences all. Both women describe the sense of well-being, and indeed the feelings of liberation, associated with these actions. As others accept and even endorse the relationship, and as both partners edit their old, limiting stories, they are gradually reapproaching each other with less anxiety. At this writing, Mollie and Leslie have made new connections with several other lesbians in the community, and are beginning to widen their social networks.

Bearing Witness

It is not enough, as a mental health professional, to draw one's professional boundaries around the individual case. The clinician–ethnographer, as a student of culture, is in a unique position to serve as an expert witness in the larger community, to challenge oppressive and constraining narratives, to influence the adoption of more "just" stories, and to work toward a more "just" society (Waldegrave, 1990). As therapists become familiar with the strengths and unique possibilities in lesbian families, they have the responsibility to help educate others.

  Griffin (1993) describes the role of the heterosexual "ally"—that is, a person who, having moved beyond a stage of "acceptance" of homosexuality to a stage of active resistance to oppression, challenges expressions of heterosexism and homophobia in self and others. The "ally" is someone who marches with her lesbian sisters, who may wear a button that says "Straight But Not Narrow!," who may testify on behalf of lesbian causes. She (or he) is someone willing to challenge subjugating mythologies in the media, the courtroom, the school, the church—indeed, in any context in which lesbians risk oppression. An "ally" is someone who brings lesbianism into mainstream conversation.

RITUAL AS A CULTURAL CATEGORY

Ritual is one of the major vehicles our culture provides for the expression of our most cherished and deeply held values, meanings, traditions, and beliefs. In that sense, it is a conservative force, one that works for cohesion and continuity. At the same time, however, in ritual we not only express such meanings but create them anew, in the process continually recreating ourselves. Rituals, then, are vital for marking and resolving important life transitions as they help us separate from the old and incorporate the new; for celebrating our achievements and healing from our losses; for resolving, or at least tolerating, life's paradoxes; and for connecting us as individuals to our families and to the larger community. They are both culture-preserving and culture-making, preserving coherence and continuity as well as ushering in change. Ritual is also multivocal; much of its power lies in the fact that its language, its metaphors and symbols, speak to us on many levels at once. Thus, as many several family therapists have argued, it is a powerful medium for change (see, e.g., Imber-Black, 1988, 1989; Laird, 1988).

Students of lesbian life tend to believe that lesbians are often culturally adrift, with few or any rituals available to them to mark their important transitions or to connect them with family or community. It has been said that our culture provides few meaningful ingredients from which lesbians can draw to express and create meaning in their own lives. But to argue that lesbian lives are not marked by ritual or are underritualized, without familial or cultural models to follow, is, I think, to oversimplify the complexities of lesbian lives and the meanings of culture. It is to make the "alpha" error (Hare-Mustin, 1987)—that is, to exaggerate the differences between lesbian and heterosexual family life. To repeat points made earlier, lesbians are multicultural; although it is the case that they are denied certain cultural rituals, such as that of legal marriage or church recognition, they are like everyone else in making more or less conscious choices about which cultural meanings, values, and symbols they will incorporate and preserve and which they wish to leave behind. Although some lesbians may walk through ritual lives that have lost their relevance or meanings, and may be caught up in the routinizing and mindless power of some traditional rituals, I would argue that because lesbians stand at the margins of society, they are forced to take more conscious charge of their ritual lives, and a certain kind of strength emerges from that process. The marginal position provokes certain kinds of questioning, a heightening of certain kinds of consciousness. When one knows that the dominant social discourse is wrong about oneself and one's community, one is more likely to question other powerful social narratives that shape one's life. As Collins (1989) writes, "Black women cannot afford to be fools of any type, for their devalued status denies them the protections that white skin, maleness, and wealth confer" (p. 759). Similarly, as Davis (1994) points out, the lesbian—oppressed as woman, as homosexual, and perhaps also as a woman of color—must have at least dual and perhaps multiple vision. She must always be looking through her own lenses as well as those of her oppressors. This can give her an acute sense of sight.

In terms of ritual, lesbians cannot afford to be thoughtless or habitual in their choices of symbolic representation. Consequently, many lesbians today are consciously building rituals that are complex blends of the old and the new, incorporating values and meanings that may connect them in varying degrees with the largest sociocultural levels in this society, with their families of origin, with the lesbian community, and with the larger gay and lesbian subculture as well. Sullivan (1991) found, in her study of lesbian couple commitment ceremonies, that many lesbians were borrow-

ing symbols and images from the traditional, heterosexual marriage cere-
mony; others "avoided identification with mainstream culture at all costs"
(p. 107). Both groups, she believes, are engaging in "an extremely radical
act" (p. 108).

The following examples illustrate this blend of the traditional and the
innovative. The first describes my own changing Christmas holiday; the
second a birthday party I attended recently; and the third a ritual reported
to me by a lesbian couple I interviewed as part of a research work in
progress.

A Christmas Ritual in Transition

For several years after my divorce, I, my young son, and my
partner would spend most Christmas holidays at my parents' home in
Florida; the family collected as it had done in my childhood years at the
home of my maternal grandparents. As a lesbian, I never thought in
those years that I could host the Christmas holiday—that I could
perhaps be the "grandmother" for my own or the next generation. I
was, after all, divorced, a lesbian, and never certain about whether
family members had given a name to my relationship with my life
partner. I had, I felt, little in common with my sisters-in-law—
politically conservative, Southern, traditional women bound to home
and children. I listened to endless stories of their daily routines, their
children's lives, and my brothers' work, but no one asked about my
career or my domestic life. Perhaps for me to say, or them to ask,
anything might threaten the agreed-upon secrecy.

There were parts of those holidays I greatly valued: the connections to family, the links with those who had come before in the
many memories and artifacts from Christmas past, the visits from
neighbors, the cherished tree ornaments, the holiday dishes handed
down the generations, the stockings, the gift exchange, the traditional
meal. There were other parts that angered me, holdovers from childhood resentments—some of which had to do with what I perceived to
be powerful labor inequities between the men and the women in the
work of the ritual, and others with the endless and sometimes hurtful
conflicts and arguments between various family members, part of
long-standing and seemingly unresolvable family patterns. I also suppressed any resentment I may have had about the fact that I could not
openly talk about my relationship with my partner, although everyone
seemed to accept the permanence of our life commitment. After 5 years
or so, no one asked any longer whether I had a boyfriend.

At some point, many years ago, my partner and I made the
decision to spend Christmas in our own home, gradually constructing
a holiday ritual that better met our family and emergent cultural
definitions. A full deconstruction of this ritual would reveal many
practices, symbols, and possessions that connect each of us with our
family traditions, preserving valued memories and providing a sense of
coherence in our individual lives. Other parts of this celebration are

marked by symbols that reflect our own "nuclear family" culture: favored dishes, the decorations and ornaments that we as a family have given each other and rediscover with delight each year, our special heirlooms, music both old and new. In all of this, the symbols and meanings that were present in our families of origin and are available in the larger American culture enter our home—sometimes transformed, but in ways that connect us to the world outside of our home. In that sense, at those moments, we are as "American," as "traditional," as anyone else.

In other ways, however, this Christmas celebration separates us from old, unsatisfying patterns that had become rigidified. For example, roles are no longer allocated by tradition or by sex, but by interest and talent; most tasks are shared. There is no "head" of the table; everyone takes a turn at playing Santa Claus. For several years, we have shared our holiday with another lesbian couple, sometimes at their home, sometimes at ours; we have become a family of choice, an extended family in addition to our families of origin. Often our 29-year-old son, my birth child, who will soon marry, is with us; these are times he greatly cherishes. He will be bringing many of these customs developed in his "lesbian family" to his newly formed heterosexual family. And, as in most families, Christmas is a time for visiting back and forth and exchanging good wishes and gifts with many friends, for marking our membership in a larger community; for us this means, for the most part, our lesbian friends.

This ritual is "culturally" very much modeled on our family-of-origin rituals; we have continued many of the central traditions. What is different? It is not that we have had no role models and have had to invent a culture anew because we are two women, lesbians. As many heterosexual couples are doing, we've taken familiar roles and symbols and shaken them up a bit—reallocated them to fit our shared conceptions of couplehood and family, of how we want things to work. This is not a process unique to lesbians or gays; many families do this. In fact, there is very little about this particular ritual that connects to any larger gay or lesbian cultural symbolism, except for a pink triangle on the tree, except for the cast of characters—and, yes, except for the conversation. That, indeed, is quite different. Lesbianism is not hidden; it is celebrated.

A New Year's Birthday Party

This year my beloved friend Lois decided to give a party in honor of her own 45th birthday, on New Year's Day. She invited 14 friends, half of whom are Jewish (like her), half of whom are not—and all of whom are lesbian. Lois, who has a 10-year-old birth daughter conceived in the context of a long-term lesbian committed relationship, is currently not seriously involved with anyone. Two former lovers, now important friends, attended.

What is a lesbian birthday party? Does the larger culture offer any help? This party proved to be a truly original creation, a *bricolage*, a veritable patchwork quilt with its patterns pulled from many cultural directions and sewn together in what became a unique and beautiful piece of art. Lois invited one of her closest friends to serve as the shaman, the ritual specialist, but she also consulted each friend about various details as the day drew near. Jyl, our leader and shaman, plunged into this challenge with great enthusiasm. Together, she and Lois designed an event intended to incorporate and blend together those parts of Lois's life that would have the most meaning for her on this special day: friends from her lesbian community/family of choice; symbols and meanings from her strong identity and beliefs as a Jewish woman (which connect her to her heritage and her family of origin, as well as to part of her lesbian community); and finally, playing at least a small part, familiar cultural birthday symbols—the cake with its birthday candles, the gift exchange, the cards.

The celebration began with each guest quietly lighting a candle (much as in the Sabbath ritual), saying a few words, and circling the candles, which were themselves placed in a circle—enacting, perhaps not consciously, the female symbol. Then began a very long, at times solemn, at times hilarious, and at times very moving ode to Lois. Each guest had brought something special, something that marked her particular connection to or ideas about Lois. One sang a lovely song, several read poems by women about women, some brought pictures, and several shared stories of Lois. Some celebrated her lesbian identity, her sexuality; others her special gift for friendship, for mothering; all toasted her womanhood. One friend and former lover told a grandmother story, and soon the entire group became engaged in grandmother stories, connecting everyone there to the generations of women who had come before. Until now, Jewish culture had predominated; now the group's multicultural heritages entered the shared experience. Lois worried that the ritual was "too Jewish"; the non-Jews felt privileged to have been allowed to participate. Halfway through we ate, and this time Lois lit a candelabra that had belonged to her grandmother, linking family traditions with ethnic and religious identity.

Then followed more stories and many gifts—all of them thoughtful, all connected to Lois in some personal way, for this is a woman with many interests and many connections. And, finally, the birthday cake reminded us that it was, after all, Lois's birthday that had spawned this extraordinary occasion. Lois, as is typical of her, gave, even on her own birthday.

Here we see again how a lesbian need not relinquish her familial or cultural models and symbols. In this case, Lois used a good deal of ritual license to borrow and to blend cultural material that was meaningful to her, to shape and bend it in ways that would express what she wanted to express. For her, the symbols and meanings of New Year's Day, Sabbath, and her birthday, as well as cultural representations from the lesbian world (e.g., lesbian music and poetry), could be joined to create a new kind of ritual to mark the beginning of a new year for her. We see here in action the emergent, improvisational qualities characteristic of ethnic identity—the social construction of the lesbian as a cultural being.

A Breast Ritual

I was told about this third ritual during an interview with a lesbian couple, Carol and Janet. The two women had been living for some years in a small rural village that has attracted, over the last 10 years, a large number of lesbians. Many of these women have built their own homes, live simply, and have strong feminist and environmentalist convictions. The night before my visit, said Carol and Janet, they had attended a celebration for a friend, a woman who was entering the hospital on this day for a mastectomy. A goodly portion of the community—some 100 women—had gathered at her house to help mark her transition from home to hospital, to mourn with her the impending loss of her breast, and to join together in wishing her Godspeed. The women reminisced, told breast stories and jokes, and sang songs of brave women who had overcome losses. I had the sense, as Carol and Janet described this event, that this illness belonged to the "tribe," to the community; if they could join solidly enough together, perhaps they could exorcise the cancer demon.

Some people are fortunate enough to have strong, supportive extended families, or have created networks of friends who offer mutual support at times of crisis; that is said to be what families (or friends) are for. The lesbian community can and does serve as a very powerful natural helping network for many women fortunate enough to live in communities with a critical mass of lesbians. The above-described event, reminiscent of Native American tribal healing rites, was more consciously organized as a ritual than the kinds of spontaneous support frequently offered by family, friends, and neighbors. Perhaps this says that lesbians, oppressed for both their sex and their sexual orientation, must work more creatively to define community, to work at cohesiveness, to find strength in solidarity.

On another level of ritual, one question that emerges is how lesbians can be a part of the larger rituals that are not organized around the lesbian couple or family, but that nevertheless constitute an important part of their connections to the world. For example, how will a lesbian daughter (alone or with her partner, or the partners with their children) participate in larger family and community rituals—a son's wedding, a niece's bat mitzvah, her parents' anniversary celebration, the annual office party, the neighborhood July 4th barbecue, parents' night at the local school, the death of her own partner/lover?

The levels and meaningfulness of the participation will, of course, depend directly on whether and how openly the lesbian partners have defined their relationship in larger family and community contexts, as well as on the ways in which family and community have responded. Some lesbians, whether single or in coupled or family relationships, are parts of extended families in which the family members themselves have also "come out"—perhaps the ideal situation. Such an extended family may include a lesbian couple/family in all of its important rituals, publicly and openly accepting, naming, and recognizing the couple's relationship. Thus the couple may dance at a brother's wedding, the lesbian coparent will be included on the announcement of her partner's daughter's wedding invitation, and so on.

In a situation where the couple is cut off from one or both families, the couple's ritual life may be more impoverished, depending on whether the couple is part of a larger chosen family, a church community, a ritual-conscious lesbian community, or some other extended support system, as well as on whether the partners have invested effort in constructing meaningful couple and family rituals of their own.

USING RITUAL IN PRACTICE

Ritual, in work with anyone, offers a window into a family's cultural (and psychological) life, its system of meanings and beliefs. The clinician, if it is related to the request for help, should explore how the lesbian partners or family members mark and celebrate their lives; how much thought and care they have given to this dimension of human life; and whether they are satisfied with this part of their life. Lack of meaningful rituals or connectedness to a wider family or community can intensify the burden on a couple relationship to meet needs that are typically in part met in the context of a larger network, and can add to the partners' sense of delegitimization. (As we know, the ritual of therapy itself can become the substitute for other rituals of connection.) The therapist can serve here as a ritual consultant, giving the partners/family members permission and encouragement to acknowledge and celebrate themselves. Such conversations provide an opportunity for heightened consciousness of and attention to the ways they do or do not allow themselves definitional time and space.

Some of the opportunities for ritual intervention may have little to do with the fact that the family constellation is defined as lesbian. The same kinds of situations that suggest ritual interventions in work with any families may be equally appropriate in work with lesbian couples or families. For example, members of a lesbian family may need better marking of life transitions, particularly the marking and celebrating of turning points in their own commitment; the family may be underritualized for a range of reasons not particularly related to the lesbian theme; the family may be rigidly ritualized; or the family members may be carrying forward stories—

unresolved events from the past, losses that are still raw and painful—that constrain their lives in the present and that can be reauthored through the healing power of ritual.

In other situations, the need for more careful attention to a couple's or family's ritual life springs directly from its lesbian status. A couple's life may be underritualized, for example, for any number of reasons:

1. The wider culture may not offer easily accessible opportunity for lesbian-centered rituals.
2. The partners themselves may have internalized society's negative messages, so that they do not entitle or empower themselves to take more positive charge of their ritual life.
3. One or both families of origin may not recognize or accept their children's lesbian identity, or recognize their "familyness." This in turn may mean that any rituals the couple designs are carried out in ways that are disconnected from the extended families, or the partners may separate during important ritual times to remain connected to their families of origin.
4. The couple may not have formed a new or "chosen" extended friendship family or become connected to community institutions that can offer opportunities for shared ritual life.

In addition to bearing witness to the legitimacy of the couple's relationship and giving the partners permission (i.e., acknowledging their right) to celebrate their lives and to develop as full a ritual life as they choose, the therapist can also serve as a ritual consultant. By this I mean that the therapist can help the partners think through and plan how they will enhance their ritual lives, and how they can strengthen their connections to both the straight and lesbian worlds. It is important to fully explore the nature and quality of the relationship with both families of origin and the potential for growth and change. The therapist—as ethnographer, as cultural consultant, as conversational artist, as family coach—needs to create a context in which new possibilities can be generated. Clients can be helped to examine whether their ritual lives and family relationships are meeting their needs, and can collaborate in redesigning their ritual lives in ways that are more fulfilling.

CONCLUSION

In this chapter I have argued for a cultural perspective and an ethnographic stance in work with lesbian couples and families. "Story" and "ritual" are suggested as examples of two of the many possible cultural lenses that can be useful in such practice, and illustrations of how these cultural lenses can be worn in the therapeutic conversation are offered. A cultural perspective makes easy the alliance with postmodern thinking and the notion of the deprivileging of "expert" knowledge, as long as we are not ethnocentric (or, in this case, heterocentric).

One caution is in order. The heterosexual therapist, or the lesbian therapist who may enjoy an open and rich sense of connection with her own family, may not fully appreciate the pain and difficulty or the levels of rejection some lesbians experience. The lesbian therapist who is "out" may underestimate the potential hostility and homophobia a "closeted" couple in a different family or community context may face. This work must be slow, careful, and always extraordinarily sensitive to social context. Finally, as therapists, we must be prepared to move from private conversation to public dialogue if we are to seriously challenge both the said and the unsaid in the dominant social story.

NOTES

1. Browning (1984) offers a comprehensive review of these themes. See also Morin (1977).
2. See Bell, Weinberg, and Hammersmith (1981) for a review and analysis of the research on family constellation in families with gay children.
3. Morin (1977) examines heterosexual bias in this body of research. See also Bell and Weinberg (1978) and Bell, Weinberg, and Hammersmith (1981).
4. Muzio (1993) examines the position of the (invisible) lesbian co-mother.
5. See Patterson (1992) for an excellent and thorough review of the research on the mental health and social adaptation of children of lesbian parents.
6. In spite of these positive trends and my emphasis here on strengths, it is important not to minimize the very real problems faced by gays and lesbians. Most tragic are the very high rates of suicide among gay and lesbian adolescents (Herdt, 1992) and the disproportionately higher rates of alcoholism among gays and lesbians.
7. "Thick description," a term coined by Geertz (1973), I take to mean in-depth, enriched, full description of the particular, of the one (individual, family, society), as opposed to the kind of partializing accounts of the many that we find in, for example, survey research. Geertz describes the role of anthropological interpretation as the "tracing the curve of a social discourse; fixing it into an inspectable form" (p. 19). The anthropologist approaches "broader interpretations and more abstract analyses from the direction of exceedingly extended acquaintances with extremely small matters" (p. 21).
8. Faderman (1984–1985) and Sophie (1985–1986) are among those who have been critical of "stage" research models, arguing that the models, developed from observations of gay males, do not fit lesbian processes of coming out and identity making. Anthropologist Andrew Boxer and psycholologist Bertram Cohler (Boxer & Cohler, 1989) bring a postmodern narrative perspective to their critique of stage models, arguing that one's gay identity can be seen as a self-story or

narrative that is constantly reshaped and recast to fit present experiences. Lillian Faderman, a historian, stresses the importance of shifting historical contexts in shaping lesbian experiences of coming out. Her 1991 book, *Odd Girls and Twilight Lovers: A History of Lesbian Life in Twentieth-Century America,* is a compelling account of how changing social climates and sociocultural discourses have shifted the possibilities for lesbian identity.

9. There are, of course, some exceptions to this state of things. The American Family Therapy Academy devoted one of its three 1992 plenaries to gay and lesbian issues, and gay and lesbian themes were featured in a recent issue of *The Family Therapy Networker* (1991). These are important advances, to be sure. In the long run, however, the experiences of other than traditional, heterosexual families must become part of ordinary professional conversation—sometimes at the center, sometimes at the periphery.

REFERENCES

Anderson, H., & Goolishian, H. (1988). Human systems as linguistic systems; Evolving ideas about the implications for theory and practice. *Family Process, 27,* 371–393.

Anderson, H., & Goolishian, H. (1992). The client is the expert: A not-knowing approach to therapy. In S. McNamee & K. J. Gergen (Eds.), *Therapy as social construction* (pp. 25–39). Newbury Park, CA: Sage.

Bauman, R. (1977). *Verbal art as performance.* Prospect Heights, IL: Waveland Press.

Bell, A. P., & Weinberg, M. S. (1978). *Homosexualities: A study of diversity among men and women.* New York: Simon & Schuster.

Bell, A. P., Weinberg, M. S., & Hammersmith, S. K. (1981). *Sexual preference.* Bloomington: Indiana University Press.

Blumstein, P., & Schwartz, P. (1983). *American couples: Money, work, sex.* New York: William Morrow.

Boxer, A. M., & Cohler, B. J. (1989). The life course of gay and lesbian youth: An immodest proposal for the study of lives. *Journal of Homosexuality, 17*(3–4), 315–355.

Browning, C. (1984). Changing theories of lesbianism: Challenging the stereotypes. In T. Darty & S. Potter (Eds.), *Women identified women* (pp. 11–28). Palo Alto, CA: Mayfield.

Burch, B. (1982). Psychological merger in lesbian couples: A joint ego psychological and systems approach. *Family Therapy, 9*(3), 201–277.

Burch, B. (1987). Barriers to intimacy: Conflicts over power, dependence, and nurturing in lesbian relationships. In Boston Lesbian Psychologies Collective (Ed.), *Lesbian psychologies: Explorations and challenges* (pp. 126–141). Urbana: University of Illinois Press.

Cass, V. (1979). Homosexual identity formation: A theoretical model. *Journal of Homosexuality, 4*(3), 219–237.

Cass, V. (1984). Homosexual identity formation: Testing a theoretical model. *Journal of Sex Research, 20*(2), 143–167.

Chodorow, N. (1978). *The reproduction of mothering.* Berkeley: University of California Press.

Coleman, E. (1981–1982). Developmental stages of the coming out process. *Journal of Homosexuality, 7*(2–3), 31–43.

Collins, P. H. (1989). The social construction of black feminist thought. *Signs, 14,* 745–773.

Crawford, S. (1987). Lesbian families: Psychosocial stress and the family-building process. In Boston Lesbian Psychologies Collective (Ed.), *Lesbian psychologies: Explorations and challenges* (pp. 195–214). Urbana: University of Illinois Press.

Crawford, S. (1988). Cultural context as a factor in the expansion of therapeutic conversation with lesbian families. *Journal of Strategic and Systemic Therapies, 7*(3), 2–10.

Davis, L. V. (1985). Female and male voices in social work. *Social Work, 30,* 106–113.

Davis, L. V. (1994). Feminism and constructivism: Teaching social work practice with women. In J. Laird (Ed.), *Revisioning social work education: A social constructionist approach.* New York: Haworth Press.

de Monteflores, C. (1986). Notes on the management of difference. In T. S. Stein & C. J. Cohen (Eds.), *Contemporary perspectives on psychotherapy with lesbians and gay men* (pp. 73–101). New York: Plenum.

DeVine, J. L. (1984). A systemic inspection of affectional preference orientation and the family of origin. *Journal of Social Work and Human Sexuality, 2,* 9–17.

Faderman, L. (1984–1985). The new "gay" lesbians. *Journal of Homosexuality, 10*(3–4), 85–95.

Faderman, L. (1991). *Odd girls and twilight lovers: A history of lesbian life in twentieth-century America.* New York: Columbia University Press.

The Family Therapy Networker. (1991, January/February). Gays and lesbians are out of the closet. Are therapists still in the dark? [Special issue], *1,* 26–60.

Geertz, C. (1973). Thick description: Toward an interpretive theory of culture. In C. Geertz (Ed.), *The interpretation of cultures* (pp. 3–30). New York: Basic Books.

Goffman, E. (1963). *Stigma: Notes on the management of spoiled identity.* Englewood Cliffs, NJ: Prentice-Hall.

Golombok, S., Spencer, A., & Rutter, M. (1983). Children in lesbian and single-parent households: Psychosexual and psychiatric appraisal. *Journal of Child Psychology and Psychiatry, 24,* 551–572.

Green, R., Mandel, J. B., Hotvedt, M. E., Gray, J., & Smith, L. (1986). Lesbian mothers and their children: A comparison with solo parent heterosexual mothers and their children. *Archives of Sexual Behavior, 15*(2), 167–183.

Griffin, P. (1993, April 28). *Gay and lesbian issues in social work education.* Workshop/consultation presented at the Smith College School of Social Work, Northampton, MA.

Harding, S. (1986). *The science question in feminism.* Ithaca, NY: Cornell University Press.

Hare-Mustin, R. (1987). The problem of gender in family therapy theory. *Family Process, 26,* 15–33.

Harry, J. (1984). *Gay couples.* New York: Praeger.

Hencken, J. D., & O'Dowd, W. T. (1977). Coming out as an aspect of identity formation. *Gay Academic Union Journal: Gay Saber, 1,* 18–26.

Herdt, G., & Boxer, A. (1992). Introduction: Culture, history, and life course of gay men. In G. Herdt (Ed.), *Gay culture in America: Essays from the field* (pp. 1–28). Boston: Beacon Press.

Hoeffer, B. (1981). Children's acquisition of sex-role behavior in lesbian-mother families. *American Journal of Orthopsychiatry, 5,* 536–544.

Imber-Black, E. (1988). Idiosyncratic life cycle transitions and therapeutic rituals. In B. Carter & M. McGoldrick (Eds.), *The changing family life cycle* (pp. 149–163). New York: Gardner Press.

Imber-Black, E. (1989). Rituals of stabilization and change in women's lives. In M. McGoldrick, C. M. Anderson, & F. Walsh (Eds.), *Women in families: A framework for family therapy* (pp. 451–469). New York: Norton.

Keller, E. F. (1984). *Reflections on gender and science.* New Haven, CT: Yale University Press.

Kirkpatrick, M., Smith, C., & Roy, R. (1981). Lesbian mothers and their children: A comparative survey. *American Journal of Orthopsychiatry, 5,* 545–551.

Krestan, J., & Bepko, C. S. (1980). The problem of fusion in the lesbian relationship. *Family Process, 19*(3), 277–289.

Kurdek, L. A., & Schmitt, J. P. (1985). Relationship quality of gay men in closed or open relationships. *Journal of Homosexuality, 12*(2), 85–99.

Kurdek, L. A., & Schmitt, J. P. (1987). Perceived emotional support from family and friends in members of homosexual, married, and heterosexual cohabiting couples. *Journal of Homosexuality, 14*(3–4), 57–68.

Laird, J. (1988). Women and ritual. In E. Imber-Black, J. Roberts, & R. Whiting (Eds.), *Rituals in families and family therapy* (pp. 331–362). New York: Norton.

Laird, J. (1989). Women and stories: Restorying women's self-constructions. In M. McGoldrick, C. M. Anderson, & F. Walsh (Eds.), *Women in families: A framework for family therapy* (pp. 427–450). New York: Norton.

Laird, J. (1993). Women's secrets—women's silences. In E. Imber-Black (Ed.), *Secrets in families and family therapy* (pp. 243–267). New York: Norton.

Laird, J. (1994). Changing women's narratives: Taking back the discourse. In L. V. Davis (Ed.), *Building on women's strengths: A social work agenda for the 21st century.* New York: Haworth Press.

Lukes, C. A., & Land, H. (1990). Biculturality and homosexuality. *Social Work, 35,* 155–161.

McWhirter, D. P., & Mattison, A. M. (1984). *The male couple: How relationships develop.* Englewood Cliffs, NJ: Prentice-Hall.

Mencher, J. (1990). *Intimacy in lesbian relationships: A critical re-examination of fusion* (Work in Progress, No. 42). Wellesley, MA: Stone Center, Wellesley College.

Minton, H. L., & McDonald, G. J. (1983–1984). Homosexual identity formation as a developmental process. *Journal of Homosexuality, 9*(2–3), 65–77.

Morin, S. F. (1977). Heterosexual bias in psychological research on lesbianism and male homosexuality. *American Psychologist, 32,* 629–637.

Muzio, C. (1993). Lesbian co-parenting: On being/being with the invisible (m)other. *Smith College Studies in Social Work, 63*(3), 215–229.

Patterson, C. J. (1992). Children of lesbian and gay parents. *Child Development, 63,* 1025–1042.

Patterson, C. J. (1994). Children of the lesbian baby boom: Behavioral adjustment, self-concepts, and sex-role identity. In B. Greene & G. Herek (Eds.),

Contemporary perspectives on gay and lesbian psychology: Theory, research, and applications (pp. 156–175). Newbury Park, CA: Sage.

Peplau, L. A., & Cochran, S. (1981). Value orientations in the intimate relationships of gay men. *Journal of Homosexuality, 6*(3), 1–19.

Peplau, L. A., Cochran, S., Rook, K., & Padesky, C. (1978). Loving women: Attachment and autonomy in lesbian relationships. *Journal of Social Issues, 34,* 7–27.

Pittman, F., & DeYoung, C. D. (1971). The treatment of homosexuality in hetero-geneous groups. *International Journal of Group Psychotherapy, 21,* 62–73.

Rich, A. (1980). Compulsory heterosexuality and lesbian existence. *Signs, 5*(4), 631–660.

Riess, D. (1980). *The family's construction of reality.* Cambridge, MA: Harvard University Press.

Roth, S. (1989). Psychotherapy with lesbian couples: Individual issues, female socialization, and the social context. In M. McGoldrick, C. Anderson, & F. Walsh (Eds.), *Women in families: A framework for family therapy* (pp. 286–307). New York: Norton.

Slater, S., & Mencher, J. (1991). The lesbian family life cycle: A contextual approach. *American Journal of Orthopsychiatry, 61,* 372–382.

Sophie, J. (1985–1986). A critical examination of stage theories of lesbian identity development. *Journal of Homosexuality, 12*(2), 39–51.

Sullivan, E. (1991). *Lesbian commitment ceremonies: A contextual understanding.* Un-published master's thesis, Smith College School of Social Work.

Troiden, R. R. (1979). Becoming homosexual: A model for gay identity acquisition. *Psychiatry, 42,* 362–373.

Waldegrave, C. (1990). Social justice and family therapy. *Dulwich Family Centre Newsletter* (South Adelaide, Australia), No. 1.

Weston, K. (1991). *Families we choose: Lesbians, gays, kinship.* New York: Columbia University Press.

White, M., & Epston, D. (1990). *Narrative means to therapeutic ends.* New York: Norton.

Zacks, E., Green, R.-J., & Marrow, J. (1988). Comparing lesbian and heterosexual couples on the circumplex model: An initial investigation. *Family Process, 27,* 471–484.

Zitter, S. (1987). Coming out to Mom: Theoretical aspects of the mother–daughter process. In Boston Lesbian Psychologies Collective (Ed.), *Lesbian psychologies: Explorations and challenges* (pp. 177–194). Urbana: University of Illinois Press.

7

Therapy with Bisexual Women: Working on the Edge of Emerging Cultural and Personal Identities

MARGARET NICHOLS

The anthropologist Herdt (1990) has described our culture as one in which changes in sexual values and practices occur so rapidly that new forms replace in a few years old ones that may have lasted for decades or even centuries before, and even newer ones evolve in less than one generation. No area of sexuality has changed more quickly than our thinking about sexual identity. This chapter attempts to help the struggling, conscious, and conscientious feminist therapist keep close to the current cutting edge of thought on sexual identity through an examination of the theory and research on bisexuality in women. As a veteran of the feminist movement of the 1960s, I learned early to believe fully that "the personal is political," so I have parted somewhat from scholarly tradition in infusing this chapter with my own story as a case example. I hope to convey more questions than answers on this subject, because I see bisexuality as a symbolic issue that represents the intersection of many other sexual concepts, and as a vehicle to stimulate thought on how and in what ways our diverse sexual desires are shaped.

The last 25 years have seen two revolutionary changes in the way we view sexual identity and sexual orientation. The first change started culturally, with the feminist movement of the 1960s and its expansion of female sexuality, and with Stonewall and the gay liberation movement of the early 1970s. The scientific watersheds of this first revolution included the convincing body of research started by Dr. Evelyn Hooker that disproved the pathology theory of homosexuality, and the 1973 American Psychiatric Association nomenclature change that removed homosexuality from the list of recognized mental disorders.

Where sexual identity was concerned, this first phase accomplished a staggering goal, at least within the fields of psychology and mental health: the normalization of homosexuality. To be sure, this goal has not been entirely attained (even among professionals who should know better), but gains have been considerable. By and large, the "homosexuality as 'madness' or 'badness' " paradigm has been replaced by the "homosexuality as alternative sexuality" paradigm. A significant number of therapists and counselors practicing today probably now accept a gay or lesbian lifestyle/identity as a legitimate alternative to heterosexuality, even though the culture at large still lags far behind.

CHALLENGING THE CONFLICT MODEL

What has not yet been accepted is the shift that has accompanied the second stage of the revolution in sexual identity. This second stage, more radical than the first, calls into question a basic assumption underlying our notions of sexuality—what Zinik (1985) calls the "conflict model" of sexual orientation:

> Underlying the conflict model . . . is the notion that sexuality is a dichotomy: one is either heterosexual or homosexual. This dichotomous notion derives from the following logic. Since men and women are viewed as opposite sexes, it appears contradictory that anyone could eroticize two opposite things at the same time. Attraction to one sex would logically rule out attraction to the other, or else lead to psychological dissonance and conflict. It follows that people claiming to be bisexual are: 1) experiencing identity conflict or confusion; 2) living in an inherently temporary or transitional stage which masks the person's true underlying sexual orientation (presumably homosexual); and 3) employing the label as a method of either consciously denying or unconsciously defending against one's true homosexual preference. (p. 9)

Inherent in the conflict model are several ancillary assumptions: sexual attraction is dichotomous; gender is dichotomous and oppositional; sexuality is static within a lifetime, rather than fluid; and sexual attraction is essential—that is, an inborn part of one's genetic/biological nature.

In the last decade, all of these assumptions have begun to be challenged, primarily on a cultural level but also on scientific grounds. The first wave of the cultural sexual revolution, for all its progressiveness about gay and lesbian issues, still perpetuated the conflict model of sexuality. The standard gay liberation "line" has been something like this: "There are two kinds of people, gay and straight; homosexuality is inborn and essential, not a choice; gays are just as good as straights; sexual orientation has nothing whatsoever to do with gender identity." Interestingly, the first revolt against this view has come from within the lesbian feminist subculture, specifically the lesbian sex radical movement, which has come to see this view as narrow and confining.

Although a full discussion of this phenomenon is beyond the scope of this chapter, it is useful to know something of the "sex revolt" that came from within the lesbian feminist community, starting in the late 1970s and pioneered by women such as Pat Califia, Gayle Rubin, and Joan Nestle, who might be termed "lesbian sex radicals." The lesbian sex radicals (Nichols, 1987) espoused a simple but startling premise: Any form of sexuality practiced by two consenting adult women is by definition nonpatriarchal and deserving of feminist support. Within this value-free framework, the sex radicals felt free to explore various forms of power-polarized sex games (colloquially called "sadomasochism" or "S/M"). Lesbians who experimented with S/M often experienced these roles as at the least accentuations of the tension found within all erotic exchanges, and at the most near-mystical encounters in which power was in fact equalized by being dichotomized. And within the S/M community some women found, for example, that their primary "orientation" did not even relate to gender, but rather to dominant versus submissive sexual status or to specific sexual acts (Califia, 1983a). In other words, desire might transcend gender and be "bisexual" but power-role-specific.

Other women played with "gender bending," the deliberate juxtaposition of strongly feminine and strongly masculine characteristics within one individual, epitomized most graphically by the full-breasted woman wearing a strap-on dildo. Many of these women found historical precedent for gender bending within the lesbian community in the "butch–femme" tradition, "a lesbian-specific way of deconstructing gender that radically reclaims women's erotic energy . . . gender pioneers with a knack for alchemy" (Nestle, 1992, p. 14). Lesbian sex radicals exploring butch–femme relationships saw gender as yin and yang, not biological male–biological female, and as ranging along a continuum not restricted by our two-gender system.

Almost inevitably, this deconstruction of sexuality and gender coming from the lesbian sex radical movement helped set the stage for a new analysis of bisexuality in feminist terms (Weise, 1992). Again, much of the impetus for this has come from the lesbian feminist community, particularly from women who identified themselves as bisexual after first openly embracing lesbianism. In Boston, for example, a support group for such women (who call themselves the "hasbians") fosters discussions of such topics as the impact of a lesbian identity upon relationships with men. Some of the precepts of the body of theory emerging from the bisexual feminist community are that sexual identity is not necessarily predetermined; that there is an element of choice involved in sexual orientation, at least for some people; and that identity can be fluid rather than static.

Scientifically, paradigms are shifting as well. Among sexologists, the dichotomous model of sexual identity was ostensibly replaced several decades ago by the Kinsey model, a 7-point unidimensional scale suggesting that sexual orientation ranges along a continuum from exclusive heterosexuality to exclusive homosexuality. But in reality, "Kinsey's work tended to dichotomize people into the more or mostly 'heterosexual' or 'homosexual,' with bisexuality a residual category" (Herdt, 1990, p. 224). More recently, the scientific community has been considering multiple dimensions of sexuality and concepts of fluid versus static identity, just as the lesbian feminist subculture has been doing. For example, the most recent Kinsey Institute volume on this subject, *Homosexuality/Heterosexuality: Concepts of Sexual Orientation* (McWhirter, Sanders, & Reinisch, 1990) concludes that

> sexual orientation cannot be understood in terms of simple dichotomies or unidimensional models. Sexual orientation is multidimensional in its essence. . . . The fact that sexual behavior patterns and sexual self-labeling can change dramatically and sometimes several times (e.g., from heterosexual to homosexual and back to heterosexual) within an individual over time challenges the view that sexual orientation is fixed or determined early in life and remains constant. (pp. xxiv, xxvi)

For professionals, this cannot help being confusing. Just when we think we have finally "got it"—we come to agree that "gay is okay," and accept the gay liberation perspective that homosexuality is the alternative to heterosexuality and an inborn predetermined characteristic—this second revolution in paradigm proposes that sexual orientation may be fluid, changeable over a lifetime, and not only bisexual but perhaps gender-irrelevant (i.e., unrelated to one's biological sex). This newer perspective is a more threatening one for both heterosexuals and the gay community. Indeed, it is threatening to the gay community precisely because it is so terrifying to "straights." The comfort of the conflict model of sexual orientation is that it still allows us to divide the world into "us" and "them"—even if we espouse a "separate but equal" liberality. This newer model of orientation is as threatening as race mixing, for it means that no one can be certain of his or her "intrinsic" identity. "Heterosexual" merely means "primarily attracted to the opposite sex at the present time." Our mainstream culture is simply not ready for this view of sexuality, and the gay community senses this and intuitively rejects this view as well, for the most part. A committed clinician, however, cannot afford to be threatened. We feminist therapists have frequently been the first to "see" accurately what the culture at large is reluctant to admit; for example, our uncovering of the prevalence of domestic violence and incest far preceded the acceptance of these phenomena by the mainstream. We are in a similar position regarding bisexuality and its implications for our understanding of sexual identity.

BISEXUALITY IN WOMEN: THE PROBLEMS WITH DATA

Up until the first stage of the revolution in thought about sexual orientation, scientific data came from pathology-oriented research that is now considered worthless by any reputable sexologist. Since Kinsey, research has reflected the tendency to see orientation as dichotomous or, at best, continuous but unidimensional. The contradictory and confusing results of this research are the inevitable products of imposing a one-dimensional model upon a multidimensional phenomenon.

For example, most research has concentrated upon sexual behavior, and even a moment's personal reflection tells us that sexuality involves, at the least, attractions and fantasies as well as behavior. Kinsey's original data (Kinsey, Pomeroy, Martin, & Gebhard, 1950) represented sexual outlets: behavioral acts culminating in orgasm, or behavioral responses without orgasm. When simple "counts" of behavior have been used, the incidence of bisexuality among women has always been quite high, just slightly lower than that for men. Sanders, Reinisch, and McWhirter (1990) summarize the Kinsey statistics: "28% of . . . white women between the ages of 12 and 45 reported they had responded erotically to women, and 13% had engaged in sexual activity with a female to the point of orgasm." Fewer than 1% reported exclusive homosexuality. Hyde (1982) has reviewed research since Kinsey and reported a rate of 15% of women engaging in bisexual behavior and 1% exclusively gay. Clearly, from a behavioral standpoint, exclusive heterosexuality among women is most frequent; bisexuality rates are quite high, and exclusive homosexuality is rather rare. The very low rates of exclusive lesbianism are to an extent a product of social homophobia; as Bell and Weinberg (1978) have reported, nearly all gay-identified women have "behaved" heterosexually at some point in their lives, often to hide or avoid coming to terms with their own lesbianism. However, as we shall see later, not all heterosexual contacts among lesbians are "faked."

If one looks at research on fantasy or attraction, the rates of bisexuality among women are even higher. Masters and Johnson (1979), for example, found that what they termed "cross-preference encounters" constituted the third most frequent category of sexual fantasy for both homosexual males and homosexual females, the fourth most frequent category for heterosexual males, and the fifth most frequent category for heterosexual females. Bell and Weinberg (1978) have reported that only about half of gay men and lesbians rate their sexual attractions as exclusively gay.

To complicate matters further, many individuals seem to change sexual orientations within one lifetime, although this has been less systematically studied. In the 1990 Kinsey Institute report (McWhirter et al., 1990), nearly one-third of the contributions address intraindividual changes that seem to contradict a static theory of sexual orientation.

Given these data—high frequencies of bisexual fantasy, attractions, and behavior; incidences of change in orientation within one individual—one would expect to find many self-identified bisexuals in our culture. In fact, the opposite is true. Self-labeling as bisexual seems to be very infrequent indeed, so infrequent that it is rarely even studied. Few studies or surveys have even bothered to address the issue of self-labeling; the *Playboy* (1983) sex survey, one of the few that has, reported 1% of females identifying themselves as bisexual—lower than the rate of self-identified lesbians. The implications are clear: Although rates of bisexual fantasy, attractions, and even behavior are rather high, extremely few people (male or female) call themselves bisexual.

Conclusions from the Data

What conclusions can we draw from the data? First, it is clear that dichotomous or unidimensional models of sexual orientation simply do not fit reality. A more appropriate model might be that of Klein (1990), who has devised the Klein Sexual Orientation Grid—an instrument that measures sexual orientation across seven dimensions ranging from sexual attraction to self-identification to lifestyle, and that takes into account changes within one individual over one lifespan.

Second, it appears quite problematic that self-labeling matches so poorly with other measures, especially since self-identification is the type of data most accessible to the average clinician. Let us take a closer look at this issue. Individuals who behave bisexually tend to label themselves as either heterosexual or homosexual, and this discrepancy seems to be greater for self-identified gays. Nearly all lesbians, in particular, have had heterosexual contact, whereas perhaps only 10% of self-identified heterosexual women have behaved bisexually. Why is this so? Probably much of the tendency of self-identified heterosexual women to avoid a bisexual label can be attributed to homophobia. And much heterosexual behavior among lesbians was conducted before their "coming out" and was the result of attempts to "act straight" rather than reflections of genuine desire, so for these lesbians the bisexual label would not feel genuine. But this does not account for all heterosexual behavior among lesbians. Reinisch, Ziemba-Davis, and Sanders (1990) studied lesbians who had identified themselves as such since age

18, and found that 45% had had sex with men since "coming out." I found (Nichols, 1985) that measures of various dimensions of sexual orientation (fantasy, romantic attraction, past and current behavior, etc.) were more discrepant with self-labeled identity for self-identified lesbians than for self-identified heterosexual women. In fact, self-labeling correlated significantly among lesbians only with sexual behavior in the last year. And within the lesbian community, disclosures of this kind of discrepancy are becoming more and more common (Hutchins & Kaahumanu, 1991). Pat Califia writes:

> I have no way of knowing how many lesbians and gay men are less than exclusively homosexual. But I know I am not the only one. . . . I live with my woman lover of five years. I have lots of casual sex with women. Once in a while I have casual sex with gay men. I have a three year relationship with a homosexual male who doesn't use the term gay. And I call myself a lesbian. (1983b, pp. 24–25)

One way of explaining this data is to understand the impact of homophobia upon self-labeling. In the last two and a half decades, the strongest force counteracting homophobia has been the emergence of a proud, visible, active gay and lesbian community. Individuals who experience a significant degree of same-sex attraction find it hard to come to terms with these attractions without identifying with and obtaining the support of this subcultural community. And this community has had a historic mistrust of the term "bisexual," assuming that it represents a lack of commitment to a homosexual lifestyle. So, ironically, the label "gay" has become a residual category in contemporary culture—one that might more accurately be seen to represent "not primarily heterosexual."

Multiple Meanings of Bisexuality

If the label "gay" represents a residual category, what does the self-identification as "bisexual" mean? Unfortunately, research on self-identified bisexuals is minimal (Klein & Wolf, 1985). Moreover, just as the labels of "gay" and "straight" do not always mean what they seem to, the label "bisexual" may mean many different things. Some women who label themselves as bisexual are undoubtedly describing the transition from a heterosexual to a homosexual lifestyle, particularly since the modal bisexual woman identifies her heterosexuality first (Zinik, 1985). For these women, bisexuality may indeed be a temporary identity on the way to lesbianism. Some of these women can truly be considered to have "chosen" lesbianism—what used to be called "political lesbianism."

Other bisexual women may be describing their capacity for sexual attractions but not the desirability of emotional relationships. For example, female bisexuals report similar levels of erotic attractions to men and women, but more frequent limerance toward women and more satisfying relationships (Zinik, 1985).

Some bisexual women experience a need for relationships with both men and women at the same time; others consider themselves monogamous and are simply describing an inherent capacity to be attracted to both sexes. Some experience their attractions as gender-irrelevant—that is, transcending gender ("I'm just attracted to a person; it doesn't matter whether it is a male or female person")—while other women feel they "get different things" from relationships with men versus women. Most recently, some women come to a bisexual identity after a long period of identifying themselves as lesbian, and these women may have clinical issues that are qualitatively different from those of other bisexual women. They have generally worked through their own internalized homophobia and are more likely to be grappling with the perceived loss of support from the lesbian community, for example.

Summary of the Data

In summary, the little we know from the scientific data on bisexuality does not confirm the popular view that women are more bisexual than men. In fact, the behavioral rates of bisexuality are slightly lower among women, but this probably reflects the fact that even postfeminist women are less likely to actualize any aspects of their sexuality than are men.

Second, bisexual fantasies and attractions are extremely common among women; bisexual behavior is less common, but still more frequent than exclusive homosexuality; bisexual self-labeling is quite rare.

Third, many self-identified heterosexual women will in fact experience same-sex attractions, fantasies, and behavior during their adult life. Even more self-identified lesbians will experience some heterosexuality, not simply before "coming out," but quite possibly simultaneously with their lesbian identification. In short, labels are misleading.

Finally, the self-identified label "bisexual" may represent many meanings for many women, ranging from those for whom the label is a temporary transition on the way to lesbianism to those who endorse nonmonogamy to those who feel that their sexual orientation transcends gender.

THE FUTURE OF BISEXUALITY: SOCIAL TRENDS

It should be clear by now that the term "bisexuality," like the label "heterosexual" or "lesbian," covers a very diverse and only partially understood group of phenomena. Moreover, it is also clear that it is impossible to divorce these terms and their various elements—behavior, attractions, identity—from their social and political underpinnings. In terms of bisexuality, the emergence of the gay/lesbian community has been a double-edged sword. On one hand, it has helped liberate millions from the personal oppression of the homophobic mainstream; on the other hand, it has tended to perpetuate a dichotomous, static view of sexual identity that is probably appropriate for only a minority even of the community's own people. The heterosexist bias and strong homophobic messages of our culture act to prevent many people from actualizing any homosexual component of their identity, and the gay liberation movement counteracts these forces. But the gay/lesbian community, in helping people express the homosexual component, has at the same time tended to encourage repression of bisexuality:

> When gay and lesbian activists claim bisexuality to be fraudulent or as no more than denied homosexuality, when they denounce self-identified bisexuals as traitors to the community, or when they rush to claim every women who has experienced same-sex feelings or a same-sex affair as "really" a lesbian (e.g., Joan Baez, Margaret Mead, Eleanor Roosevelt), they perpetrate upon women the exact mirror of the oppression women experience from the heterosexual mainstream. Under these circumstances, it is not surprising that many women suppress their bisexuality, cloak it in secrecy, or experience personal conflict. To claim an identity as bisexual in our current culture is to isolate oneself in a grey area where little sense of community or support exists. It is not surprising that, despite data that consistently suggest that bisexuality is more prevalent than exclusive homosexuality, there are far fewer self-labeled bisexuals than homosexuals or heterosexuals. One would predict that, if cultural sanction for bisexuality increases, the numbers of identified bisexuals will also increase, with a substantial proportion of these individuals coming from within the gay and lesbian communities. (Nichols, 1988, pp. 242–243)

Since I wrote those words, much of what I predicted has already come true. The gay and especially the lesbian community is embracing bisexuality as never before: Bisexual groups march in gay pride celebrations all over the country; the Gay and Lesbian Community Center in New York has three different bisexual support groups; where I live in New Jersey, most gay organizations have changed their names to incorporate "bisexual" in their titles; and some specifically bisexual organizations have sprung up. In 1989, when I did a workshop on bisexuality at the annual New Jersey statewide gay conference, fewer than a dozen participants showed up; in 1993 there were nearly 50, and the conference itself had three workshops on bisexuality. And women—particularly bisexual women who formerly identified themselves as lesbian—tend to be at the forefront of this movement. Younger women in particular seem to reject the label "lesbian" in preference to "bisexual," while at the same time being "out" and "proud" about their choices. As this trend toward a more supportive environment not only for bisexuality, but for fluidity, change, and choice in sexual identity continues, we can expect to see in our offices not only more self-identified bisexual women, but also more women who want to seriously examine all aspects of their sexual identity.

One benefit we will undoubtedly gain from the more visible emergence of a bisexual community will be a deeper understanding of the social construction of gender. Why does research suggest, for example, that both male and female bisexuals report better relationships with women than with men (Zinik, 1985)? Perhaps it is the result of the socialization of women toward intimacy and valuing intimate relationships; perhaps women put more energy into relationships, or have less need to dominate in a partnership. When bisexuals report viewing their relationships with men and women as different in nature, how are they different? That is, how has the different socialization of men and women in regard to intimacy manifested itself, from the perspective of individuals who have experienced both? A bisexual male friend once observed to me that in his experience, men and women resolved conflict in relationships differently: Women, he said, tended to verbalize and discuss conflict, while men tended to acknowledge conflict tacitly by rearranging their postures or stances. Bisexuals who have experienced both male and female sexual relations and intimacy may teach us a great deal about gender and closeness. For now, the best source of such learning will not be research, which at its present level of sophistication cannot hope to capture the subtleties of the bisexual experience. Probably the best of all sources will be bisexual feminist women, as evidenced by the interesting thinking of many different writers in *Closer to Home: Bisexuality and Feminism* (Weise, 1992).

A PERSONAL CASE VIGNETTE

My own personal evolution may illustrate some of the concepts discussed in this chapter; it certainly has been the source of my interest in bisexuality. Inspired by the lessons learned in consciousness-raising groups of the 1960s and 1970s, as continued in the manner of *Closer to Home,* here are the lessons I have learned from my own story.

As a child, my earliest memories of being "different" had to do with my rejection of the role of my mother. Although I was not a tomboy (I was too much of a "loner" ever to play team sports), I hated dolls; loved the outdoors, woods, and climbing trees; and always played the male role in fantasy play with other little girls. I knew from the time I was 6 that I did not want to be like my mother—I saw her life as a housewife and mother as boring and subservient. My earliest sexual experiences began at about age

10 and were with other little girls. I remember them as quite energetic and joyful contacts. They ended abruptly when I was about 12 years old: The mother of one of my partners caught us in the act; I was banished from the house; and for the first time in my life I heard the word "lesbian." I was not sure what it meant, but I knew that it was bad and that it had to do with my sexual activities with girls. My response, almost overnight, was to repress not only my behavior but my conscious sexual desire for girls/women. I was not conscious again of these desires until I was 20.

During my adolescence, however, I became quite sexual with boys, surprisingly so for that era (the early 1960s). I fantasized about males, had crushes on them, and was aroused sexually by them. I now believe that my obviously bisexual potential, evidenced at about age 12 or 13, made it easier to eliminate same-sex sexual desires. The only time these desires ever came close to "breaking through" in these years was when I developed an infatuation with my college roommate. At the time, I did not experience it as more than an intense closeness with Amy, even though during summer vacations I wrote her joking letters about how we should marry each other rather than men because we got along so well. In college I developed a serious drug abuse problem, and my drug use may have helped keep my homoerotic desires in check.

When I was 20, in 1967, I entered a drug rehabilitation program that had what was at the time a rather progressive stance toward sexuality. The belief system of this program, which influenced me greatly since my life revolved around it for several years, included the idea that all humans have bisexual impulses. In this supportive environment, within a year my attractions to women re-emerged, and for the first time I identified myself as bisexual. Since my peer group did not, however, support homosexuality as a primary lifestyle, I confined my bisexuality to sporadic sexual encounters with women, while I married a male member of the program. Looking back now, I see my bisexual identity at that time as a transitional one, because I had not yet fully come to terms with my own internalized homophobia. Over a period of several years I gravitated more and more toward friendships with self-identified lesbians, and my husband and I started a commune with, among other people, two lesbian women. We had an "open marriage," so I was free to experiment sexually while maintaining a heterosexual appearance. I was the kind of bisexual the gay community mistrusts: willing to partake of the advantages of same-sex relationships, but too afraid to commit to a woman. During these years I became involved with the feminist movement, but my contact with that community did not include a great number of lesbians.

That changed for me in 1975. My marriage was breaking up, and I joined a new group—a chapter of the National Organization for Women known for its strong lesbian presence and militant lesbian stance. With the support and approval of this group, I catapulted into lesbianism. I experienced this total transition as remarkably easy. Within a year I was living with a woman I had fallen in love with and was directing a feminist women's counseling center/battered women's shelter. I identified myself openly as a lesbian in every forum—professionally and personally—and viewed myself as bisexual from the point of view of sexual arousal, lesbian by political/personal choice. I lived in this way for 11 years, during which time I was extremely active in the lesbian feminist community and the larger gay community. I became the first openly gay psychologist in New Jersey; started first a private practice and then a counseling center catering to the gay community; became involved in gay politics, made speeches, appeared on television, and wrote papers; and, finally, founded the largest AIDS social service agency in New Jersey. My lover and I joined the emerging ranks of "lesbians choosing motherhood" when I gave birth to my son, Cory, in 1983 after becoming pregnant through donor insemination. All three of us were public as a family, appearing nationwide on public television as well as in various print media. Certainly no one could claim I was hiding from a homosexual identity.

During those years, I gave lip service to my bisexuality in speeches in which I talked about myself. In fact, it was not much of an issue for me. Like many monogamously married women of any sexual orientation, I seemed unconsciously to close a door on most outside attractions to anyone other than my lover. I did continue to have both heterosexual and homosexual sexual fantasies, and one clear attraction to a man; however, I compartmentalized those fantasies and the attraction in much the same way I had compartmentalized my homosexual attractions and even behavior during my prelesbian years. My life excluded men to a large degree. During the latter part of this period, I began to incorporate more and more gay men into my social and professional life (especially once I became involved with AIDS in the early 1980s), but I rarely had more than superficial contact with heterosexual men. I basically regarded men as subhuman, making exceptions for some gay men.

I actually think I might have gone on like that forever—many lesbians do—except for one thing. I mark the beginning of the end of that phase of my life from the day my amniocentesis results came back and I discovered I was carrying a male child. After a period of profound shock and grieving, I began to come to terms with what it would mean to raise a son. Most particularly, I admitted to myself that I had dismissed men as less than human, and that I could not continue to do that and mother a boy morally and conscientiously. I set about privately to accept men; to do that, I had to start to take them seriously, learn about them, and see them as valuable and equal to women. I cannot really explain how this process developed, but as it developed it was as if the door to my sexual and romantic desires for men was reopened.

In 1986 my relationship with my long-term lover broke up; to this day

I cannot ascertain how much of my desire to leave that relationship came from my emerging bisexuality, and how much came from other dissatisfactions with the relationship. As my relationship dissolved, I found that I had fallen in love with a gay man with whom I had been friends for several years.

It is difficult to describe how distressing this all was. My identification as a lesbian had been, by contrast, easy: I simply shifted allegiance from one community to another, felt that I belonged in the lesbian world, and felt accepted. My re-emergence as a bisexual woman was lonely and fearful. For a long time I could not imagine how I would do it; not only my personal life but even my professional life revolved around being a lesbian, and I anticipated complete rejection within both realms. The option of "returning" to heterosexuality was never real to me; my experiences as a lesbian had convinced me that rejecting my homosexual part would never work, just as I realized belatedly that rejecting my heterosexual part had not really worked. This is an important point for the clinician working with any client who has a significant bisexual component (i.e., more than a fleeting fantasy or desire). Many of us bisexuals have learned that it is personally dangerous to repudiate either orientation, even though there is an overwhelming temptation to label oneself on the basis of the gender of one's current partner. Such self-labeling as gay or heterosexual when one is genuinely bisexual can be a form of self-hatred, and surely is a splintering and partial denial of one's own core identity.

Of great help to me was my membership in the Lesbian Sex Mafia (LSM), the New York-based group of lesbian and bisexual sex radicals who characterize themselves as eschewing "politically correct sex." Within this group I could get some support, although it never was as large a part of my life as lesbian feminist groups had been previously. Over time, I learned a very useful lesson: how to forge one's identity without the support of a group—indeed, as a social outcast and pariah. My fears of rejection from the lesbian and gay community were largely realistic at first; I lost many friends, some of whom had been very close, and was widely regarded as a traitor and turncoat. But I stubbornly refused to leave the gay community. Although I have come to see myself as living largely outside any community, I find the gay community a much more comfortable place than the heterosexual one, despite the fact that after several years of being single and dating both men and women I have now settled down into a monogamous relationship with a man. For me, the gay community is still more open and flexible, more richly diverse, and more creative and interesting than the "straight" world. Although I am with a man, my consciousness is more gay than straight. I call myself a bisexual lesbian mother.

What have I learned about relationships and sex with men versus women? Personally, I experience men and women differently, although I notice that I tend to be attracted to "butch" people regardless of their gender. I find sex with women sweeter and slower, like a fire that builds slowly to a peak; sex with men is more like firecrackers to me. My experiences as a lesbian transformed my relationships with men. By and large, I consider same-sex relationships to be more naturally and easily egalitarian than mixed-sex pairings. After 11 years of exclusive lesbianism, I found that I approached men differently: I had been completely divested of whatever socialization within me had inclined me, in prelesbian years, to accept my female role unconsciously. I no longer have to fight subtle internal messages to assume a subservient role; these messages simply no longer exist. Moreover, my years as a lesbian helped me overcome any vestiges of the belief most women hold that having a male partner is necessary for social approval, strength, or protection. I experience relationships with women as closer and more intimate than relationships with men, but I also find the increased intimacy a bit cloying. Interestingly, I like the differences and the separateness of a mixed-sex relationship. My partner and I do not assume that we are much like each other, and this suits me fine. Sometimes I feel that my childhood persona, the "loner," is expressing itself more and more in my middle age, and that this has helped determine my partner choice.

What direction will my future take? I feel that I am and always have been bisexual, but my current priority is maintaining the relationship I have now. Were I single now, I have no idea whether I would end up with a man or a woman. But with a bisexual identity, it also does not feel like a burning issue.

CLINICAL ISSUES IN WORKING WITH BISEXUAL WOMEN

Clinically, the issue of bisexuality is potentially important with three types of clients: (1) women who label themselves as bisexual; (2) women who are unsure about their sexual orientation; and (3) women who identify themselves as lesbian or heterosexual, but for whom bisexual fantasies, attractions, or behavior may be distressing or ego-dystonic.

Successful therapy, even with women who identify themselves as bisexual, must begin with an examination of whether the bisexuality is indeed a clinical issue. Just as there has often been a tendency for heterosexually biased therapists to assume that homosexuality is a therapeutic issue for all gay and lesbian clients, many therapists may assume that bisexuality is an issue for all clients who exhibit bisexual behavior, attractions, or self-identity. Many such clients enter treatment with no internal conflict about their orientation; the first order of business for the therapist is to determine whether the client herself considers her sexual orientation in any way worthy of discussion. For example, I have experienced both heterosexually identified clients with significant lesbian experiences and lesbian clients with significant heterosexual contact whose behavior did not apparently cause them to experience personal conflict. It is not my business to start to create conflict for them.

Sexual and Romantic History

For those women who report a need to work on issues of sexual identity, a detailed sexual and romantic relationship history is essential. This should include a history of the emergence and expression of both heterosexual and homoerotic fantasy, attractions, and behavior, including masturbation fantasies.

In addition, the clinician should obtain a relative weighting of the power of heteroerotic versus homoerotic attractions. Does one type of attraction seem primary (i.e., more satisfying, more romantically compelling, or more erotically charged)? How much variation is there over time? Probably most important are the recent experiences of the client, as they are most likely to predict a future direction.

Next, the therapist should assess the degree to which these experiences are ego-dystonic or ego-syntonic, and the likelihood that the client could compartmentalize the ego-dystonic component of her sexuality should she desire to do so. Notice that this is an acceptable alternative for me, if it appears practical. I do not take the political or therapeutic stance that all bisexuals must identify themselves as such; I help many lesbians compartmentalize their bisexuality if it seems practical and that is what they want to do, just as I have helped some heterosexual women compartmentalize theirs.

The clinician must also ascertain the social supports a client has for bisexuality and her potential ability to maintain a bisexual identity without support, or the social supports she has for maintaining a lesbian identity if that is how she labels herself or if she decides to do so.

Next, the therapist needs to help the client explore her self-identity and what this means to her. It can be especially revealing to determine how she labels herself in different situations. Some such labels, if they are discrepant with her personal identity, may reveal internalized biphobia or homophobia. For example, the client may consider herself bisexual, but may identify herself as lesbian with lesbians and heterosexual with heterosexuals.

Finally, it is important to understand the degree to which, in general, the client is motivated and prepared to deal with upheavals in her life that would be created by a change either in personal self-identity or in self-disclosure to others. It is also important to explore specific issues and difficulties that may realistically be expected. For example, a previously heterosexually identified mother who is grappling with potential bisexuality may make choices in behavior or disclosure according to their possible repercussions for child custody.

Identity Formation

Probably the single most common issue the clinician will encounter in work with potentially bisexual clients is the very issue of identity formation: "Am I bisexual, lesbian, or straight? If so, what does this mean? How do I figure it out? How do I handle it if I am?" Clinicians not experienced in dealing with gay and lesbian clients might consult the writings of gay and lesbian therapists on identity formation, as many of the same principles hold for bisexual identity formation (Cass, 1979, 1990). In a culture that repudiates both homosexuality and bisexuality, most individuals will find it both imperative to come to terms with the despised and denigrated elements of identity and exceedingly difficult to do so. The journey to self-integration will be time-consuming and conflict-laden for most, and will include information-seeking, behavioral exploration, the need for social supports, and some degree of self-disclosure to others. Moreover, this odyssey invariably includes periods of defensive strategies that seek to deny, compartmentalize, or repress certain aspects of self. It is most important that this journey be self-determined. In clinical issues, the policy of "outing" is destructive; the therapist's most useful role may be to support partial denial of identity, while planting the idea that continued evolution of identity may take place in the future.

In transposing the model of gay and lesbian identity formation to bisexual identity, the picture gets more complicated because many more variations are possible. Some women move from a heterosexual to a bisexual identity and comfortably remain there, whereas for others bisexuality is a way station toward lesbianism. Still others perceive themselves as lesbian and then as bisexual. When a woman is undergoing a second major transformation of sexual identity, it is advantageous for her to build upon the strengths gained during the first transformation, and it may be clinically helpful for the therapist to point this out to the client. A woman who has previously identified herself as a lesbian and is currently struggling to come to terms with attractions to men can be reminded of the process she went through in "coming out" as a lesbian. As she notices the similarities in process, she can access past experiences and skills to help her with her current situation.

Therapeutic Validation

I find it very useful to help women make clear distinctions among the following: aspects of internal experience (feelings, fantasies, attractions) behavior, self-labeling, and self-disclosure. I validate apparent dissonance among these elements if the dissonance is comfortable for the client, at the same time as I point out possible disadvantages of maintaining this dissonance. In effect, I do recognize an "essential" nature of sexual orientation, at least as determined by internal experience, but make that separate from all other elements. For example, I may say to a client,

"You may indeed be bisexual internally—be capable of attractions to some degree or another to both men and women. But you may choose whether to act upon these feelings. Moreover, you can choose what you want to call yourself and to whom you want to reveal any of these aspects of yourself. You can be internally bisexual and call yourself a lesbian (or heterosexual). You can "come out" as a lesbian to others, or you can choose not to disclose anything. This is perfectly okay, but there is some potential for problems. You may eventually find that you feel a need to act upon both sets of feelings, and you may feel phony or superficial with others if you do not disclose your bisexuality. You can do whatever is comfortable for you now, recognizing that you may or may not decide differently in the future."

Perhaps the single most important thing a therapist can do for female clients who have any degree of bisexuality is to validate the concept of bisexuality and give information. This can be important even for women whose bisexual component seems insignificant at the time. Validating lesbian fantasies in a presumably heterosexual woman, for example, may not seem important at the time it is done; however, given the fluidity of sexual orientation, it can have great future significance. The "heterosexual" woman of today may choose to actualize her lesbian fantasies tomorrow. And for the woman whose bisexuality is more than incidental, validation and information from the therapist are even more important. The therapist may be the only person in the client's social system who even corroborates the existence of bisexuality, so the therapist must be able to provide unwavering support, as well as information that includes reading material and (most importantly) referrals to bisexual organizations and support groups. Fortunately, these days such literature and support groups can usually be accessed through local lesbian and gay hotlines, organizations, and bookstores.

Although identity is the most common issue the clinician will confront regarding bisexuality, other problems may present themselves. The book by Klein and Wolf (1985) includes a chapter on counseling bisexuals that describes many of these issues (Lourea, 1985). Some of the problems bisexuals may encounter include the following: dealing with partners who cannot handle their bisexuality; grappling with the issue of monogamy-nonmonogamy; and coping with the reactions of others to whom they have disclosed their bisexuality. Women who have previously identified themselves as heterosexual face many of the same issues confronted by lesbians in "coming out." Women who have previously identified themselves as lesbians have additional conflicts. They may include guilt and a sense of betraying their community, as well as "culture shock" when they find themselves relating to men again and having to confront sexism, which they thought they had left behind forever.

Case Vignettes

It may be useful to conclude this section with several vignettes of my own clients in recent clinical practice.

> Lee is a 33-year-old self-identified bisexual married woman. She lives with her husband and her female lover, both of whom accept her dual relationships, but who are not romantically or sexually involved with each other. She entered therapy on the premise that these relationships would not be challenged. Although some of her clinical issues involve the complexities that managing these relationships entail, her situation has remained stable for several years, as has her identity. She feels no need to participate in the bisexual community, although she does not conceal her identity from others.

> Marion was a middle-aged suburban housewife with three children at the time she entered treatment for what she reported as sexual identity confusion. Although her behavior was bisexual, her attractions since adolescence had been exclusively lesbian, and her marriage was strictly a pretense. Her primary clinical issue was considerable internalized homophobia, reinforced by a lifetime of being a "good girl" who lived the lifestyle her parents chose for her. This was complicated by the losses she feared she would suffer should she actualize her lesbian potential: the loss of child custody, and the loss of substantial income from her husband. Marion eventually left her husband and has been a self-identified lesbian for a number of years. She learned to cope with the altered lifestyle necessitated by an income decrease. While she did not lose custody of her children, the two older boys were troubled by her lesbian lifestyle and one eventually left to live with his father.

> Lily is a 28-year-old self-identified lesbian who sometimes sleeps with men but considers these encounters purely sexual. Although she accepts the term "bisexual" as a behavioral description, she rejects it as an identity and experiences no conflict over the discontinuity between her label and her behavior.

> Diane is 28 and thinks she may be lesbian. She is behaviorally and romantically bisexual, but has recognized her lesbian attractions only recently. She has never sustained a long relationship with anyone of either sex. For now, a bisexual self-identity is the most comfortable alternative for her, as she continues to explore in therapy her in-

ternalized homophobia and her attractions to women. It is unclear both to her and to me whether her inability to sustain relationships is the result of a primary lesbian orientation or simply a conflict about commitment and intimacy.

Ann is 41, has been living for 6 years with a man, and is trying to have her first child. Eight years ago I helped her make the transition from a 12-year politically active lesbian identity and relationship to a bisexual identity. She came back to deal with her grief over miscarrying two pregnancies. She still considers herself bisexual and is very active within the bisexual movement and community.

Joanne is 39 and in the process of divorce. One of her clinical issues was potential bisexuality; she had several lesbian experiences during her marriage. During the course of treatment, however, she decided that these were not emotionally significant to her, and she maintains a heterosexual identity. She recently fell in love with a man.

Terri is a 30-year-old postoperative male-to-female transsexual. Before surgery, she did not think much about her sexual orientation. Even though, as a male, she had been attracted to and married a woman, she had also had sexual fantasies about being a woman and having sex with a man. After surgery, her first sexual experiences were with men, and she found them satisfying. However, she was still attracted to her ex-wife, and this led her to question her orientation. Eventually she made contact with a bisexual S/M group through a computer bulletin board and became active with these men and women. She found that S/M was only of mild interest to her, but that she was clearly attracted to women at least as much as to men. She is now in a lesbian relationship. Affirming her bisexual identity was extraordinarily easy for her; in actualizing her female identity, she had lost so much in her life that the orientation change seemed minimal by contrast.

CONCLUSION

In our rapidly changing contemporary culture, we are in the midst of a second revolution in our paradigm of sexual orientation. The most recent paradigm recognizes that sexual orientation is multidimensional; this conception not only includes attraction, behavior, and identity, but also allows for fluid identity over the life cycle. At the forefront of these changes are bisexual women, especially those working within the lesbian community, so it is appropriate that a book on feminist reconstruction of psychotherapy with women includes a chapter on bisexuality.

For clinicians working with sexual identity in female clients, it is no longer sufficient that they be comfortable and supportive of lesbianism. They must support and understand bisexuality as well, or they will do a disservice to all their female clients, including those who currently identify themselves as heterosexual or lesbian but may have within them a potentially significant bisexual component of their identity. In a culture that at worst allows women only a heterosexual option, and at best acknowledges two options (heterosexual or lesbian), clinicians must be a source of information and help regarding bisexuality, because the most important function they may fulfill is that of validating its existence.

REFERENCES

Bell, A. P., & Weinberg, M. S. (1978). *Homosexualities: A study of diversity among men and women.* New York: Simon & Schuster.

Califia, P. (1983a). A secret side of lesbian sexuality. In T. Weinberg & G. W. Levi-Kamel (Eds.), *S and M: Studies in sadomasochism.* Buffalo, NY: Prometheus Books.

Califia, P. (1983b, July). Gay men, lesbians, and sex: Doing it together. *The Advocate,* pp. 24–27.

Cass, V. (1979). Homosexual identity formation: A theoretical model. *Journal of Homosexuality, 4,* 219–233.

Cass, V. (1990). The implications of homosexual identity formation for the Kinsey model and scale of sexual preference. In D. P. McWhirter, S. A. Sanders, & J. M. Reinisch (Eds.), *Homosexuality/heterosexuality: Concepts of sexual orientation* (pp. 239–266). New York: Oxford University Press.

Herdt, G. (1990). Developmental discontinuities and sexual orientation across cultures. In D. P. McWhirter, S. A. Sanders, & J. M. Reinisch (Eds.), *Homosexuality/heterosexuality: Concepts of sexual orientation* (pp. 208–236). New York: Oxford University Press.

Hyde, J. S. (1982). *Understanding human sexuality.* New York: McGraw-Hill.

Hutchins, L., & Kaahumanu, L. (1991). *Bi any other name: Bisexual people speak out.* Boston: Alyson.

Kinsey, A., Pomeroy, W., Martin, C., & Gebhard, P. (1950). *Sexual behavior in the human female.* Philadelphia: Saunders.

Klein, F. (1990). The need to view sexual orientation as a multivariable dynamic process: A theoretical perspective. In D. P. McWhirter, S. A. Sanders, & J. M. Reinisch (Eds.), *Homosexuality/heterosexuality: Concepts of sexual orientation* (pp. 277–282). New York: Oxford University Press.

Klein, F., & Wolf, T. J. (Eds.). (1985). *Two lives to lead: Bisexuality in men and women.* New York: Harrington Park Press.

Lourea, D. N. (1985). Psychosocial issues related to counseling bisexuals. *Journal of Homosexuality, 11*(1/2), 35–50.

Masters, W. H., & Johnson, V. E. (1979). *Homosexuality in perspective.* Boston: Little, Brown.

McWhirter, D. P., Sanders, S. A., & Reinisch, J. M. (Eds.). (1990). *Homosexuality/heterosexuality: Concepts of sexual orientation.* New York: Oxford University Press.

Nestle, J. (1992). *The persistent desire: A femme–butch reader.* Boston: Alyson.

Nichols, M. (1985, September). *Relationships between sexual behavior, erotic arousal, romantic attraction, and self-labeled sexual orientation.* Paper presented at the Society for the Scientific Study of Sex Conference, San Diego.

Nichols, M. (1987). What feminists can learn from the lesbian sex radicals. *Conditions, 4,* 152–163.

Nichols, M. (1988). Bisexuality in women: Myths, realities, and implications for therapy. In E. Cole & E. D. Rothblum (Eds.), *Women and sex therapy* (pp. 235–252). New York: Harrington Park Press.

Playboy. (1983). *Playboy sex survey.*

Reinisch, J. M. (1990). *The Kinsey Institute's new report on sex.* New York: St. Martin's Press.

Reinisch, J. M., Ziemba-Davis, M., & Sanders, S. (1990). Sexual behavior and AIDS. In B. Voeller, J. M. Reinisch, & M. Gottlieb (Eds.), *AIDS and sex.* New York: Oxford University Press.

Sanders, S. A., Reinisch, J. M., & McWhirter, D. P. (1990). An overview. In D. P. McWhirter, S. A. Sanders, & J. M. Reinisch (Eds.), *Homosexuality/ heterosexuality: Concepts of sexual orientation* (pp. xix–xxvii). New York: Oxford University Press.

Weise, E. R. (Ed.). (1992). *Closer to home: Bisexuality and feminism.* Seattle: Seal Press.

Zinik, G. (1985). Identity conflict of adaptive flexibility? Bisexuality reconsidered. *Journal of Homosexuality, 11*(1–2), 7–20.

8

Single Heterosexual Women through the Life Cycle

KAREN GAIL LEWIS

What is wrong with the title of this chapter? Look carefully. These seven words contain two possible oxymorons. For many single women, there is no cycling of their lives; without children, their lives end at their deaths. Second, if the title said "single . . . females," their lives would start at conception or at birth, depending on one's beliefs. But it says "single . . . women." When does a woman *become* single?

Although single women are perhaps the biggest consumers of therapy, there is no theoretical framework for understanding adult singlehood. Based on a study of single women (Lewis, 1992a), this chapter looks at the definition, onset, and dual mythology of adult female singlehood and some relevant clinical issues.

WHO IS THE SINGLE WOMAN?

The literature on single women, offers no consensual definition of the words "single woman." There are no distinctions among the three main categories—always single, divorced, and widowed—even though these are very different types of singles. "Single" is also used for women in long-term committed relationships; women dating or not dating but who hope to marry; women who hope to find a partner but have no intentions of being legally wed; confirmed singles who have no intentions of ever dating; and nuns and others with a religious mandate to remain celibate. Single and coupled lesbians are often both seen as "single," as are single parents (whether previously married or not). Furthermore, many women have

170

fallen into several of these categories at different periods of their lives, and being any of these singles at 22 is different from being one at 52.

Therefore, for the purposes of this chapter, the term "single" is used to identify "always-single" (AS) and "single-again" (SA) heterosexual women over the age of 30, who are not currently in a committed relationship, and who are not adverse to being married.[1] The term "always-single" (AS) was chosen in order to avoid the deficit label of "never-married" or "un-married."

DUAL MYTHOLOGIES OF THE SINGLE WOMAN

Single women born more than 30 years ago may be living under two conflicting mythologies of singlehood—the stigmatization and the glamorization.

The Old Myth—Stigmatization of Singlehood

Prior to the 1960s, marriage was seen as a women's primary goal in life; "spinsters" and "old maids" were pitied for not having "caught a man." Today, some people would say this is outdated. However, there are many indications that the stigma of singlehood is alive and well, albeit sometimes subtly dressed.

The novel *Sheila Levine Is Dead and Living in New York* (Parent, 1972) resonates for many single women. In the following passage, Sheila is describing her parents' conversation at her birth:

> "My what a beautiful baby. . . . So, it's a girl, Manny? You know what that means; you have to pay for a wedding." One day old! One day old, and they're talking about weddings! (p. 9)

Today, the message to "find a man" is still pervasive, albeit less overt. The preferability of couplehood emanates through our daily lives: Advertisements and songs capitalize on romance; hotel rooms are more expensive for singles; public dropoff lanes for transportation are nicknamed "kiss and ride" lanes; and so forth.

A professional woman in her late 40s complained,

> "My mother says I am looking for too perfect a man. She thinks I should have lowered my standards; then I could 'catch a man.' She also thinks I should have acted dumber, and that would have helped me attract a man."

Even while most women consciously reject these messages, they have spent their lives making themselves "right" for a man. There are many stories about girls giving up dancing because it made them too muscular; adolescents pretending to be less capable because boys would not like them if they were smarter or more athletic; young women forfeiting or choosing careers on the basis of their wish to meet a man and marry. And, if after all this, they still remain single, they take full responsibility and blame.

The New Myth—Glamorization of Singlehood

Superimposed over the stigmatizing myth is the glamorizing myth of the single career woman. She has independence, freedom to do as she pleases, passionate romance, and money to travel to exotic places. Television and movies have fueled this image with shows such as "thirtysomething" and "Designing Women." Hovering in the wings, though, is always the man—the one she has or the one she still must meet.

To some extent, child-free single women do have more freedom to be selfish and self-indulgent. However, few single women are free from responsibility and burden. Many family members may turn to them because they are single, assuming that they have more time and energy to help. Yet most single women have the same daily responsibilities as married couples: shopping, cooking, cleaning, running errands, making major decisions.

A Bit of Both: Advantages and Drawbacks

Most single women say that neither of these myths fits them; they are not so polarized in their view of singlehood. They seem well aware of both the advantages and drawbacks of being single in today's world. The primary advantages have to do with freedom from caretaking (for the child-free); the freedom to do as they want, when they want, how they want; and not having to answer to others in terms of time, decisions, and behaviors. The primary drawbacks have to do with the absence of being special to a man, the absence of touch, and (for the child-free) the absence of children; the lack of spontaneous companionship and someone to share interests; and the sadness about growing old alone. Ironically, many of the advantages are also listed as drawbacks, as explained by this AS woman in her mid-30s:

> "I'm free to do a lot of self-disclosure. I'm free to work on me; I have energy to figure out who I am, where I'm going, without also having to work on a relationship. . . . The drawbacks, though, are that . . . part of me will only grow and develop within a relationship; that part of me will never be developed."

Talking with Single Women

How do single women incorporate these two images? In this section and throughout the chapter, I report on some of the major themes that evolved from a study I conducted with 77 single women (Lewis, 1992a).[2] These single women were not "losers" or "wallflowers." They had worked very hard at their lives and careers. For the most part, they had active lives and were fairly content, with the exception of being single. They certainly had tried many creative ways to meet men, but they felt they either met men who were not appropriate for them or did not meet men at all. In both situations, they consistently blamed themselves for not trying hard enough or for not giving a man a chance.

Contradictions in Explanations of Singleness

Most of these women saw their singleness as a result of their being emotionally unhealthy and having problems, even though some had tried to get their former partners into therapy, and many had left lousy relationships. Their explanations for why they were single fell primarily into four categories: physical (big bust, overweight, fainting spells); personality-related (shyness, independence, lack of social skills, competence); psychological (selfishness, low self-esteem, demandingness, vulnerability, childhood sexual abuse, codependency); and cognitive (lack of intelligence, intelligence, learning disability). They did not notice the various contradictions among these.

When asked whether they knew married women who had their same problems, they explained that those women must have had less serious problems or must have been more patient, less choosy, or more willing to compromise. Most of the women in the study said that they felt blamed, ashamed, and embarrassed when others asked whether they were married; in addition, however they answered the question, they felt that their responses sounded defensive, apologetic, or sarcastic. When the women were asked, "Are you single by choice?", whether they said yes or no, their written comments were basically the same: "I am single because I don't like my choices."

The major surprise from the study was the inordinate number of contradictions in these women's views, as demonstrated by this interview:

INTERVIEWER: Why and how do you understand your being single?
KARA: That's a tough one. Well, I'm single because I'm not finding anyone
   I want to marry. But that's just a surface answer.
I: Not necessarily.

K: Well, it is for me; well, it's partly true, but the question is "Why aren't
you finding anyone?" I'm single because I don't believe that any man that
I want to marry would want to stay in a relationship with me, and I don't
want to go through the pain of leaving.

I: That's interesting; you think in terms of his not wanting to stay in a
relationship with you, not of your not wanting to stay in a relationship
with him.

K: I don't think in terms of that except when I'm trying to get out. Then I
wonder if I could ever really stay with him or not; I do everything I can to
make it work, and then I decide it won't work, and then once I get out, I
wonder, "Oh God, what if I had married him? I couldn't have made a
commitment to him anyway."

I: You identify your being single as it's your problem—you can't stay in a
relationship with men, despite you just got through saying you stay with
them until you decide it won't work, and then you leave. You've made
the choice that you've worked hard to make it work, and yet something
is wrong with him in the relationship, and you can no longer try to work
to make it better. Yet, when I asked you why you are single, you said—

K: 'Cause no man will stay with me. I guess it's because there's a twisted
thinking he wouldn't become or be the asshole he becomes or bes [sic]
that makes me leave.

I: So, the assumption is that if a man really [loved you], he'd behave better.
It doesn't occur to you that he's behaving as best he can?

K: After I'm out.

I: Is there a contradiction there?

K: (Silence) I can see why you would see there is. It makes sense (laughs) to
me—because if he really wanted to be in this relationship, he wouldn't
behave the way he behaved.

I: But you also say that once you're out of a relationship, you no longer see
that. How do you put these together?

K: Once I'm out of it, I say, "Gosh, he did the best he could do and I
shouldn't have been there," and then he's absolved and I'm absolved from
failing.

I: But then when you go back to the first question, "How do you understand your being single?", that seems to contradict "He doesn't want
to be with me."

K: (Softly) That is what I said, and I almost think I probably would say it
again, even though we just had this conversation.

    It is important to understand contradictions such as these. I speculate
that they are efforts to consolidate the old and new myths. Some of the
women in the study seemed to say what they thought they believed, yet
others knew they were giving socially acceptable answers. For instance,
many women said, "I don't monitor my competence and assertive qualities

when I'm with a man," unaware that their behaviors showed otherwise. Other women said that they loved being single, while knowing
that this was only partly true. They also felt lonely for a relationship,
hungry for a loving touch, and guilty and responsible for being single.
Whether they were aware or not of the contradictions, almost all the
women wanted to avoid the most dreaded image of all, "the desperate
single."

Few Differences across Class and Race

Much to my surprise, this study did not show significant differences among
single women across class and race. The study gathered financial information about family of origin and current income. Most women were raised in
working-class or middle- to low-income families for at least part of their
growing-up years. At the time of the study, many were middle- to lower-
middle-income; all had more than a high school education, most had more
than 2 years of college, and many had postgraduate education. The study
did not assess with which class these women now identified.

For all of these women, with one exception, the message they received
when they were growing up was that it is better to be married. However,
class and race were related to the differences in the reasons for that message.
Working-class parents may have encouraged marriage, believing that their
daughters needed the respectability and financial security it brings. Middle-
class parents may have had the same beliefs, but with perhaps less emphasis
on the financial security.

White, African-Americans, and Asian-Americans were the three races
identified in the study.[3] One AS Asian-American woman recited her culture's mandate: "A responsible adult is married with children." It was
expected that she would be both professionally and financially successful,
but that she would defer appropriately to her husband. White and African-
American women from two-parent families received the same message that
it is better to be married. White and African-American divorced mothers
sent their daughters a dual message: They should not count on men, yet
they needed to be married.

ADULT SINGLEHOOD

When does singlehood start and end? Everyone has been single—at birth,
through childhood and adolescence. There are two paths through adulthood: singlehood and committed couplehood. Many people move back and
forth several times before they die. The majority of women end their lives
single, since men tend to die younger (Saluter, 1992).

Lack of Distinction between Young and Adult Singles

There has never been a distribution between young singles (adolescents and young adults) and adult singles. Historically, rituals such as the engagement party and the wedding marked the passage from childhood to adulthood, regardless of age. Since women now are marrying at later ages, and some not at all, the absence of this distinction has become problematic.

There are no rituals for moving from young singlehood to adult singlehood.[4] Without protocols for being an adult single, many AS women have difficulty forming an adult inner identity (Mason, 1991). An AS woman in her late 30s said, "I feel like I'm getting older and older, but why am I still an adolescent?"

When women return to singlehood, they use the only rules they know, the ones they last used—as young singles. Six years after her divorce, Lynn reflected,

> "I find myself waiting until I hear from [the man I'm dating] before making my own plans. I know I should just go ahead and do what I want, and if he calls and I'm already busy, well, that's too bad. I can't believe I am still doing this."

This lack of distinction becomes even more apparent when one listens to single women in their 60s and 70s. SAs feel great pressure remembering how they used to act as "singles." In one group I met, they complained about meeting dull men who "are only after sex." One AS woman was studiously reading the personal ads, as she had done for almost 40 years. These women were angry at feeling inadequate and childish in not knowing how to be adult singles.

No Road Maps

There are no guidelines for adult singlehood. Neither self-help books for single women nor professional texts offer a developmental model for the life stage of adult singlehood. The theories that come closest are those of Erikson (1950), Carter and McGoldrick (1988), Levinson (1978), and Mason (1991).

Erikson's (1950) historical work on life stages posits the existence of three adult stages: "intimacy" (emotional and orgasmically physical heterosexual commitment to another without ego loss); "generativity" (productivity and creativity, used for guiding the next generation); and "integrity" (in old age, "a postnarcissistic love of the human ego" and acceptance of one's life). Although dated, some of these ideas are still significant for single women.

Single women do need intimacy, but it needs to be understood in sexual and nonsexual terms. For child-free singles, generativity needs a broader definition; such women need to feel that they are producing something meaningful by their existence (whether the production is work, creative art, friendship, volunteer work, etc.). Integrity, the stage in which one looks back and accepts one's life, is crucial for single women, so they can see that their lives have significance—with or without a man.

A more recent developmental life stage model for adults comes from Daniel Levinson (1978). He states that for young men (ages 17–33) the sequential tasks are to form a dream, a mentor relationship, an occupation, and a love relationship leading to marriage and children. In Dederick and Miller's preliminary study (1992), they found that women go through the same age-linked stages of development as men. However, they question whether there are some gender-related differences in the stage transitions. In my clinical practice and research, the major difference I see is the order of the tasks. Forming relationships is primary and often part of women's dreams. Many women cannot move on to the other tasks until they do marry. In addition, most single women do not have mentors guiding them through adult singlehood.

The Changing Family Life Cycle (Carter & McGoldrick, 1988) was significant as the first attempt to see life from a cyclical perspective in which one generation affects the others. However, there is still no place for those adults who do not move from "Leaving home: Single young adults" to "Joining of families through marriage: The new couple." The model does not account for single parents who do not join families through marriage, nor for child-free SA women who do not recycle life into another generation.

Marilyn Mason (1991) has recently identified six challenges women must meet to achieve their personal growth: "leaving home," "facing shame," "forging an identity," "integrating sexuality," "claiming personal power," and "tapping into their creative spirit." As a model for adult female development, it comes the closest to being meaningful for single women because it is focused specifically on women. However, the developmental tasks unique for singles are not addressed.

Developmental Tasks for Adult Singles

Many tasks for adult development are similar for married and single men and women. However, there are some tasks for a healthy adjustment to adult singlehood—for however long a woman is there. These are spelled out in more detail elsewhere (Lewis, 1992b, 1992c). Although some of these tasks are also applicable for women in other life positions, they have a special significance for women who are not in a committed relationship.

Grounding

Whether a single woman rents an apartment or owns a home, or lives by herself, with her parents, or with others, she feels grounded. Her living space reflects her tastes and personality. She feels a part of her neighborhood and community. She prepares herself for her financial future while spending her days at a gratifying job with a work family that offers personal satisfaction. She has a satisfying social life with different levels of friendships.

Emotional Intimacy

The single woman has close female friends with whom she shares emotional intimacy.[5] She has assessed her long-term friends for those who can provide that degree of intimacy, moving some out of her inner circle and others in. As some friends become less consistent with her current life, she reaches out to meet others. She may develop a peer family—a cohesive group of friends who get together at some point each year.

Basic Daily Needs

The single woman protects herself and feels as secure as a woman can in today's world. She is aware of the hazards of "touch deprivation" (Spitz, 1945, 1946), and ensures that she has appropriate outlets for physical contact and/or life-enhancing means for redirecting those needs. She develops rituals that enrich her daily life and that highlight the special events of her life. She uses her free time in ways that enhance her self-esteem.

Mutual Empowerment and Nurturance

The single woman is aware of the importance of mutual nurturance and limits unilateral caretaking. She is aware of the benefit of mutual empowerment (Surrey, 1991), nurturing and allowing herself to be nurtured. She makes her own decision about having children—whether, when, or under what circumstances. She has developed aspects of her life that provide a sense of fulfillment and meaningfulness.

Sexual Feelings

The single woman is aware that she has sexual feelings, whether or not she is involved with a man. She develops means of expressing these feelings, and knows when she wants to acknowledge them and when she wants to numb or deny them. She is aware of and prepared for the emotional difficulties in making the transition between having and not having a sexual partner.

Grieving

The single woman accepts the ambiguity of being single and grieves for her lost childhood dreams. She does not absorb others' grieving for her singleness. She owns her sadness at not having a loving partner; she owns the pain of what she does not have and recognizes what she does have.

Making Peace with Parents

The single woman teaches her parents how to treat her like an adult single, coaching them when they slip into seeing her as a child or young woman. She resolves old family issues whenever possible, and accepts the limitations of her parents. She avoids absorbing negative family injunctions. She tries to find some positive messages she has learned from each parent.

Old Age

The single woman develops a positive image of herself as an older single woman. She maintains her friendships and perhaps even considers living with friends. She financially prepares for old age. She takes charge of planning for her death. She looks back over her life, content with what she has done with what she had.

DEVELOPMENT OF SYMPTOMS

By the time a woman reaches her mid-30s, even if she is not worried about marriage, she probably has begun hearing "You're not getting any younger," or "You should hurry up and get a husband," as if a spouse were something she could order at the store. Resorting to self-blame, a woman frequently answers, "I must have a problem." She may then identify her "symptom." As so many women in my study said, "If only I [were thinner, were less depressed over my childhood, were not fearful of intimacy, had more self-esteem, etc.], I would then be ready for a relationship."

If she can identify a problem within herself, she has a "fixable" problem; she can feel in control of an otherwise out-of-control situation. This means that once she loses weight, is less depressed, or the like, she will be ready for a man. A 40-year-old SA woman said, "Well, I'd rather think [I'm single because of] my weight than [because of] my personality! Then I can do something about it." She may then embark on a self-improvement plan (e.g., diet, therapy, self-help support groups), which lasts until she meets a man. If she does not meet one, she can continue telling herself she is not yet healthy enough. If she finds a man, she can say, "You see, all that work paid off; I'm [not afraid of intimacy, etc.]." If that relationship does not last, she has a built-in self-blaming explanation that she was not healthy enough, after all.

Another form of self-blame is "I'm not trying hard enough."

> Jane entered therapy concerned she was a quitter. After three or four tennis lessons, she always quit. In discussing this, she said that she hated athletic sports of any kind. I asked the obvious question: If she hated sports, why was she trying so hard to learn tennis? She quickly replied, "Playing tennis is a good way to meet men." Jane forced herself to take classes, hated it, dropped out, and then berated herself for being a quitter.

The costs of women internalizing responsibility for not being married are low self-esteem and poor self-image. This often leads women to reshaping their personalities to please a man and to "de-pressing" their competence and professional potential. At the risk of over-statement, women's self-identified problems (which were supposed to be a solution to the problem of their singleness) may end up giving rise to much more pervasive and subtle concerns. Therapists need to be aware of possible links between these issues.

THERAPEUTIC ISSUES IN WORKING WITH SINGLE WOMEN

Certainly, many single women have familial, interpsychic, and intrapsychic problems that are totally unrelated to their singleness. Certainly, many women have intimacy problems. (In fact, most people probably have intimacy problems.) For single women, though, therapists also need to consider the extent to which their being single is related to their problems.

There are at least six areas that need careful attention in working with single women: the duality of women's feelings about singleness; ambiguous loss; other meanings of a symptom; fear of the image of the "desperate single"; problems in transitioning between being partnered and being unpartnered; and the use of the developmental tasks described earlier as assessment guidelines.

Duality of Feelings about Singleness

Therapists may inadvertently participate in single women's self-blame. They may perpetuate the stigmatizing myth by seeing singleness only as a sign of women's inability to establish intimacy; they may look for (and find) "personal neurosis" in the women's childhoods and psyches (Papp, 1988, p. 377). Although a woman may have problems with intimacy, talking *first* about the pathology reinforces what she is already saying to herself: It is her fault.

On the other hand, therapists may perpetuate the glamorizing myth by reiterating the advantages of being single and the reality that a woman can live a successful, productive life without a man. Feminist therapists, in particular, need to be wary of this as they react against the traditional pathologizing of women. It is important not to ignore the biased reality women face today: Being heterosexual without a man *is* difficult and lonely for those wanting marriage.[6] It is important not to ignore the effects of touch deprivation, or the pain these women feel of not having someone specially theirs. Appreciating the duality will help therapists recognize that statements like "I love being single" may have many levels of meaning (perhaps simultaneously), including a strong wish to be partnered or married.

Ambiguous Loss

For women who are "not adverse to being married," singlehood may cause a perpetual grieving, like an ambiguous loss (Boss, 1991). At no point do single women know for sure that they will never marry. The ambiguity always leaves room for hope: Maybe the right man will come along during the next week or next month, on the next vacation, at the next business meeting, during the next walk with the dog. And as long as there is hope, there is the pain of the ambiguity. Many women say, "It'd be easier if I just knew for sure; then I could adjust fine." They could grieve for the loss of their dreams and move on. Without this clarity, though, there is no closure; without closure, it is harder to mourn and move on.

Many women in therapy talk about their longing for a man and grieve for a lifestyle from which they are excluded. They complain about the pervasive pain, asking whether it will ever end. Therapists may help these women mourn the absence of a man, or point out that they are spending more energy on finding one than on enhancing their lives—for however long they are single. But neither tactic usually makes much impact. Out of their own frustration and helplessness, therapists may then react with more questions about the women's childhoods, more suggestions for finding a partner, or more advantages of the single life.

It is more than likely, though, that these women have already asked the questions, have tried the suggestions, know the advantages. Perhaps what is needed first is to clarify why they are grieving. They may have sufficiently mourned the lack of a man, but not the lack of clarity in the situation. If they understand that the protracted grief is about the ambiguity, not their singleness, they may be able to stop the self-blame and personalization of being single and to focus more clearly on how to live their lives while living with the ambiguity.

These women may need to assess whether they are carrying the grief for others as well as for themselves. For example, a woman's parents may be mourning the loss of their next developmental stage of grandparenting. Her father may be mourning the loss of a namesake. Her mother's "nagging" may be related to the responsibility she feels for her daughter's singleness. Helping the woman talk with her parents, siblings, grandparents, and other significant relatives about *their* feelings about her singleness will help her distinguish her own grief and return the rest to them.

Other Meanings of a Symptom

Therapists who accept a woman's definition of her symptom may be missing other, sometimes more relevant issues:

1. The symptom may be a result of the woman's effort to solve what she sees as the real problem—her singleness.
2. The symptom may be masking her depression about her internalized sense of failure by not marrying.
3. The symptom may be her effort to take control, to have something she can *do*, so she does not feel so helpless.
4. The symptom may be a result of her being or feeling treated as a young single, not as an adult.

As with all clients, the presenting symptom may be a smoke screen. For example, a single woman may enter therapy saying that her fear of intimacy interferes with her meeting a man. Rather than talking about her intimacy problem, it may be more useful (depending on the woman and her situation) to help her look first at why she is accepting responsibility for not having a man. The therapist can remind her that there are no indications that married women have fewer problems with intimacy than single women.

Therapists need to assess whether single women are pushing men away or just not meeting them. If the former is true, are the men they are pushing away appropriate for them, or have they seen that they are not? If these women are not meeting men, is it because they avoid them or because they have appropriately limited the men they bother meeting? Being discriminating may well save women time and emotional energy; they need to understand, though, that being more appropriately selective may limit the number of men they meet. The fact is, there may not be anything in particular a woman can do to assure her finding an *emotionally available* man. In hearing this, some women are disturbed; others are relieved.

For women who stay in bad relationships, therapists need to assess how much this can be attributed to the women's personal pathology, how much to their repeating historical family patterns, and how much to their attempting to meet society's expectations for women. As Goodrich, Rampage, Ellman, and Halstead (1988) point out, tolerance, patience, loyalty, and commitment are highly valued qualities on the job. However, when a woman applies them to what has been seen as her primary job of relationship maintenance, she may be called "pathological" and "co-dependent."

In working with single women, it is important to consider possible connections between any presenting problem and their singleness; however, therapists must not *assume* that such connections exist.

Fear of the Image of the "Desperate Single"

The fear of sounding desperate is a driving force for many women. After a 3-hour group interview, an AS professional wrote thanking me for the opportunity to be heard and commenting on a dilemma that had occurred to her after the meeting:

"It's hard for me to hear a woman talk about how much she wants to get married and not hear her as desperate or whiny—cardinal sins in our society, you know. So, it's just as hard to hear me say those words myself. [Especially since I consider] myself a feminist—[that is,] a woman doesn't need a man to be complete."

Because of the dreaded image of the "desperate single," many women deny the part of themselves that feels deprived while overstating their satisfaction with being single. The dual myth forces women to rigidly dichotomize a complex issue: How does a woman acknowledge her longing for a man without being heard as sounding desperate? How does she acknowledge her satisfaction with the autonomy of singlehood without sounding as if she is not interested in marriage? Therapists need to help such women discuss the full range of their feelings about being single.

Problems in Transitioning between Partnered and Unpartnered States

The study I conducted (Lewis, 1992a) supported what many therapists have observed: When not partnered, many single women feel they are most powerful, productive, creative, and in control of their lives; when partnered, they feel loved, complete, and satisfied. These are very different feelings, yet with both, women feel good about themselves. This suggests that the most difficulty comes when women are making transitions between being partnered and not being partnered. As one woman said, "Going back and forth drives me screwy."

Therapists can help women normalize, prepare for, and understand the extra pain they feel when moving from one state to the other. They can remind women how strong they felt before they had a particular relationship, and reassure them that the unsettling feelings will soon pass.

The Use of Developmental Tasks as Assessment Guidelines

The developmental tasks described earlier can be used as guidelines for healthy adult functioning for single women.[7] It is more than likely that a woman will find she is stuck in only some tasks. Going through the tasks is validating and offers her future direction. The tasks can also be used by a therapist who feels stuck when a woman focuses only on her lack of a man, as in the example of Maria.

> Maria, a 31-year-old AS stockbroker, entered therapy after breaking up with Ron. She spent the next few months mourning the loss of this 6-year relationship. Despite the work she did on her grief and anger, and even despite her knowledge that Ron was not good for her, Maria remained depressed.
>   I had Maria assess the parts of her life that felt satisfactory and the parts that needed attention. The guidelines validated when she felt comfortable in her singleness and acted as a spur for her to take more steps. During the next few months, she decided to move to a larger apartment and decorate it in her own taste (not with her mother's hand-me-downs). She asked for and got a promotion at work. She began talking more personally with her friends. She started going to church more regularly, singing in the choir, and volunteering in the nursery program. She became more straightforward with men. She stood up to her parents' unrealistic demands and set appropriate limits on their requests for her time and attention. (She had already financially prepared for her old age.) Despite these changes, she was still depressed about not having a partner. She said, "I'd give up all this progress, I'd even hide my smartness, if it would help me find a man."
>   There was only one developmental task in which Maria had not shown much progress. One day, I asked her to draw a circle showing the size of her grief about being single, and then to divide it up showing how much was hers and how much was others. When she said it was all hers, I said, "Try it, anyway." After sitting for a few minutes with her very large circle, she started making divisions. When she was finished, she was surprised to see how much of the circle belonged to others—in decreasing order, her mother, her grandmother, her sister, herself, her father, her brother, an old college professor, and a small section labeled "others."
>   The week after she made the circle drawing, Maria reported a discussion with her first-generation Italian parents regarding their feel-

ings about her being single. Her mother cried, sharing the loss it was to her; her father also joined in. Maria felt freer by seeing how little of the circle consisted of her own grief. Six months later (after therapy had ended), Maria was still single and still not in a committed relationship, but she was no longer depressed. "I am still very sad about it, thinking what I will miss, but I don't feel depressed all the time now."

MESSAGES FROM SINGLE WOMEN TO THERAPISTS

Each woman in my study (Lewis, 1992a) was asked what she would like to tell therapists working with single women. Here are some of their responses:

1. Do not blame women for being single. It is not always a question of fault. There is not always a deep-seated psychoanalytic reason for being single.

2. Being single is very painful for most people. It is usually not a lifestyle of choice, but [a result of] circumstances and bad luck. I do not want to hear, "Well, you could be in a really bad marriage, instead."

3. Do not project the "singlehood" of your past to today's situation. Remember, when you were single, you probably were younger than I am now; you may have had less experience in being single than I do now.

4. Help your single clients have a positive attitude about themselves. Society puts a high value on "mating," so those who do not feel like they have failed, somehow.

5. Be aware that a woman's unhappiness may be related to . . . parental pressure.

CONCLUSION

There is some indication that single women are physically and emotionally healthier than married women, single men, and married men (Bernard, 1972; Johnson & Elkund, 1984). Although this may be true, most heterosexual women do not make a free choice to remain single (unpartnered or unmarried). They carry within them a deep longing for a relationship with an emotionally available man.

Single women need validation that they are not failures because they are without a man; that their longing is normal; that the emptiness is real; and that although these feelings may always be there, they may not always be so intense. They need validation that the ambiguity of their loss does make it more difficult to find a nonintrusive place for grief in their lives, and that their self-identified personal problems may not be the causes of their being single.

Therapists need to appreciate how painful it can be for women to want marriage and children but feel they cannot talk about it, as well as how painful it can be for them *not* to want marriage and children when others assume that they should. Either way, their need for a protective front and their need to juggle the dual myths are what make it difficult for single women themselves and those talking with them to know what they are really saying. Are they saying what they *really* believe, what they *believe* they believe, or what they believe others want to hear? When therapists' own biases (of any type) infuse the therapy, it is even less possible for women to understand the full range of their feelings about being single.

A nonjudgmental life stage model that acknowledges the two possible paths through adulthood—singlehood and committed couplehood—would be most helpful in normalizing singlehood. Rituals for moving through singlehood, marking both significant life events and daily situations, would also help. If the stigma, pathology, and glamorization of being single were removed, it would be easier for women to deal with their lost dreams and to accept the reality that married is not necessarily better than single, nor is single better than married. A healthy adjustment to singlehood allows many heterosexual women to own their wish to be married, while also owning that they are satisfied if they are to remain single.

NOTES

1. Although this chapter is about heterosexual women, many of the issues are also relevant for single lesbians, a nearly forgotten group. They feel many of the same pressures from society about being without a male partner; they have many of the same feelings of being uncoupled. Pam Evans, from Coon Rapids, Minnesota, is currently engaged in research on single lesbians.
2. Similar research on single lesbians is in process (see note 1), which will then be compared with these results.
3. The sample of women of color (African-Americans and Asian-Americans) was not large enough to permit definitive statements about the effects of race.
4. Books on rituals make no mention of passage into adulthood, and there are none specifically for singles (Imber-Black, Roberts, & Whiting, 1988; Imber-Black & Roberts, 1992).
5. Research suggests that women, whether married or not, tend to rely on other females for their emotional intimacy (Hite, 1987; Lewis, 1989).
6. It is not clear whether this is also true of single lesbians looking for a partner. I hope that the research mentioned in note 1 will shed some light on that.
7. These developmental tasks may also be appropriate, with adaptations, for single and married men and for married women. I am in the process of undertaking a similar study for single men, which may indicate what if any tasks might be different.

REFERENCES

Bernard, J. (1972). *The future of marriage.* New York: Bantam.

Boss, P. (1991). Ambiguous loss. In F. Walsh & M. McGoldrick (Eds.), *Living beyond loss: Death in the family.* New York: Norton.

Carter, E., & McGoldrick, M. (Eds.). (1988). *The changing family life cycle: A framework for family therapy* (2nd ed.). New York: Gardner Press.

Dederick, J., & Miller, H. (1992). Transitions in adulthood: Are they the same for women and for men? In B. R. Wainrib (Ed.), *Gender issues across the life cycle.* New York: Springer.

Erikson, E. (1950). *Childhood and society.* New York: Norton.

Goodrich, T. J., Rampage, C., Ellman, B., & Halstead, K. (1988). *Feminist family therapy: A casebook.* New York: Norton.

Hite, S. (1987). *The Hite report: Women and love: A cultural revolution in progress.* New York: Knopf.

Imber-Black, E., & Roberts, J. (1992). *Rituals for our times.* New York: HarperCollins.

Imber-Black, E., Roberts, J., & Whiting, R. (Eds.). (1988). *Rituals in families and family therapy.* New York: Norton.

Johnson, M., & Elkund, S. (1984). Life adjustment of the never married: A review with implications for counseling. *Journal of Counseling and Development, 63,* 230–236.

Levinson, D. (1978). *The seasons of a man's life.* New York: Ballantine Books.

Lewis, K. G. (1989). *Women's friendships: Asset or deterrent to professional growth?* Unpublished manuscript.

Lewis, K. G. (1992a). *A study of adult singlehood: Talking with always single and single again women.* Manuscript submitted for publication.

Lewis, K. G. (1992b). *Life stage of singlehood: An addition to family therapy theory.* Manuscript submitted for publication.

Lewis, K. G. (1992c). *Life beneath the stereotypes: Traveling through adult singlehood— for however long you are there.* Manuscript submitted for publication.

Mason, M. (1991). *Making our lives our own: A woman's guide to the six challenges of personal change.* New York: HarperCollins.

Papp, P. (1988). Single women: Early and middle years. In M. Walters, B. Carter, P. Papp, & O. Silverstein, *The invisible web: Gender patterns in family relationships.* New York: Guilford Press.

Parent, G. (1972). *Sheila Levine is dead and living in New York.* New York: Putnam.

Saluter, A. (1992, March). *Marital status and living arrangements* (Current Population Reports, Series P-20, No. 468). Washington, DC: U.S. Government Printing Office.

Spitz, R. (1945). Hospitalism. *Psychoanalytic Study of the Child, 1,* 53–74.

Spitz, R. (1946). Hospitalism: A follow-up report. *Psychoanalytic Study of the Child, 2,* 113–117.

Surrey, I. P. (1991). Relationship and empowerment. In J. V. Jordan, A. G. Kaplan, J. B. Miller, I. P. Stiver, & J. L. Surrey, *Women's growth in connection: Writings from the Stone Center.* New York: Guilford Press.

9

Women in Stepfamilies: The Fairy Godmother, the Wicked Witch, and Cinderella Reconstructed

ANNE C. BERNSTEIN

The two Barbaras were sitting at either end of the couch in my office. Both are bright, engaging, caring women. Although they would not be mistaken for sisters, they are of the same physical "type": tall, brunette, and robust. They are mother and stepmother to the same child.

It was early in my work with stepfamilies, and I had foolishly decided—after meeting with mother and child, with father and child, with the child alone, with mother and father, and with father and stepmother—that a meeting between these two smart, personable women would be an opportunity to dispel mutual suspicion. The mother was convinced that the stepmother was childishly competitive with her daughter for the father's attention; the stepmother believed that the mother was instigating her daughter to cold-shoulder her, leaving her feeling like an unwelcome guest in her own home. How could they fail to see their mutual interest in the welfare of a 10-year-old girl they both loved? "I want to make Susan's time with us happier for her," the stepmother ventured in one way after another throughout the session. And each time the mother's response was, in variation, "Susan's interest is in her father, not you." The stepmother called me that evening in tears, distraught that once again her role in the girl's life was dismissed as inconsequential. Although my intention was to dispel myths of ill will and incompetence—a goal accomplished in prior cases by meeting with ex-spouses and their new partners—I wondered whether I had failed to account adequately for how gender is a key player in the stepfamily scenario.

In proposing to recontextualize the stepfamily, I must first contextualize myself: I became active in the feminist movement in the late 1960s, a family psychologist in the early 1970s, and a stepmother and mother in the early 1980s. In this chapter, I explore how and why women's experience of stepfamily life differs from men's, thus introducing gender into the clinical discourse. I first consider the stepfamily in its evolving societal context, highlighting how stepfamily stories—those we are told and those we tell ourselves—inform our experience and shape our relationships.

THE STEPFAMILY IN CONTEXT

Much of the dissatisfaction for all participants in stepfamilies comes from their employing a user-unfriendly yardstick—the "Ozzie and Harriet," "Father Knows Best" version of American family life. A "nuclear" family, comprised of a breadwinner father, homemaker mother, and their dependent children, has been both the implicit and explicit frame of reference in assessing stepfamily experience. This results in a "deficit comparison" model, whereby the stepfamily is seen as a less effective constellation. It is important to remember here, as with the reports of stepfamily outcome research that follow, that significant differences between groups can overshadow the most important finding of all: that majorities of parents and stepparents of both sexes are both involved in and satisfied with stepfamily life.

Clinical thinking about working with stepfamilies often begins with addressing the ways in which stepfamilies differ from first-marriage families. We are repeatedly reminded how important it is to underline the differences between nuclear families and stepfamilies in thinking about what is functional or dysfunctional, normal or abnormal; family members themselves are urged to accept that their relationships with stepkin cannot and should not be forced into the nuclear mold. As welcome antidotes to the handicapping expectation that stepfamilies can be "just the same" as those formed from first marriages, these psychoeducational efforts have helped stepfamily members avoid the misery that comes with falling short of impossible goals. But while we have been busily encouraging stepkin to hold themselves to a different measure, the basis for comparison has itself been transformed: The deviant has become the norm, and what we have long held to be normal is itself aberrant.

Demographic Shifts

By the early 1990s, residential married-couple stepfamilies outnumbered "traditional nuclear families" with provider husbands and homemaker wives, and projections for the year 2000 are that stepfamilies will outnumber any other single family type (Furstenberg & Cherlin, 1991). Americans born in the 1980s have a probability of one in two that they will be members of stepfamilies, either in their childhood or as adults (Furstenberg, 1980). Moreover, official statistics do not include part-time stepfamilies; remarried families with younger children, in which the older stepchildren have already left home; or *de facto* stepfamilies not involving remarriage (e.g., the first marriage of a formerly unmarried parent, or the long-term cohabitation of parents with heterosexual or lesbian/gay partners). Taken together, we are talking about more families having stepkin than not.

Traditional, Modern, or Old-Fashioned?

Contemporary socioeconomic issues, combined with these demographic trends, show that the "traditional nuclear family" that forms the basis for the deficit comparison model has outlived its historical moment. In fact, it is not traditional at all. It is a "modern" form that developed in conjunction with the industrialization of society, not achieving predominance until the post-World War II period.

In *Brave New Families,* Judith Stacey (1990) describes the decline of the modern family as a response to postindustrial economic conditions, including the shift away from productive employment and the failure of most jobs to pay a family-supporting wage, without which the gendered roles that are the linchpins of the modern family cannot be sustained. Feminist criticism of the family views women's economic dependency as disempowering, and the narrowing definition of women's realm as housework, consumption, and raising fewer and fewer children as exploitative and constricting. This critique has provided ideological support for women's entering the labor market, accelerating postindustrial economic trends. Entry into the work world has given women both the ability to envision other possibilities and the economic wherewithal to make leaving unsatisfying marriages feasible, contributing to the divorce rate, leading to the proliferation of female-headed households, and rendering the "modern" family "old-fashioned."

The "postmodern" family, viewed by Stacey (1990) as "a normless gender order, one in which parenting arrangements, sexuality, and the distribution of work, responsibility, and resources are all negotiable and constantly renegotiable, can also invite considerable conflict and insecurity" (p. 258). The postmodern perspective embraces uncertainty and doubt; old patterns or ideas are implicitly discarded or radically transformed, while the shape and significance of what is to follow remain unfathomable. In employing this concept to characterize changing family and gender arrangements, Stacey's ethnography illustrates that "no longer is there a single culturally dominant family pattern to which the majority of Americans conform and most of the rest aspire" (p. 17).

Thinking about stepfamilies can follow a similar course. The "traditional" stepfamily, epitomized by a remarriage following bereavement, was a variant of the "modern" family, with the stepparent as a replacement for the dead parent in an attempt to recreate the original family. The division of parental labor was gender-specific, following the Parsonian model of a partnership between an "instrumental" male and an "expressive" female (Stacey, 1990, p. 10). The "modern" family map was superimposed on the stepfamily terrain, with roles and rules that conspired to make stepfamily members feel deprived and dysfunctional. But in their variety and complexity, in the ambiguity of both membership and family roles, and in the prevalence of experiential uncertainty, insecurity, and doubt, stepfamilies constitute a prototype of the "postmodern" family.

Considerations of Class, Race, and Sexual Preference

Most of the stepfamily literature describes white middle-class stepfamilies that seek psychotherapy or participate in research. About the "white" part of it, there is little ambiguity, but "middle-class" is increasingly a catch-all term claimed by all but the indigent and the superrich. One household may contain blue-, white-, and pink-collar workers; family income may depend more on how many members are bringing home paychecks than on the occupational or educational standing of any individual. Although definitive statements about the impact of social class on stepfamily process may be impossible given this ambiguity, this blurring of class boundaries seems to point to a greater generalizability of findings than might otherwise be expected.

Racial differences are another story. There is a dramatic dearth of information about African-American and other minority stepfamilies. As psychologist Nancy Boyd-Franklin (personal communication, February 29, 1992) has said, pointing to how social science has pathologized black experience, "whites are described as having stepfamilies, African-Americans as coming from 'broken homes.' " Demographers tell us that African-Americans are more likely than whites to experience marital disruption in both first and second marriages, and, women especially, are less likely to remarry following divorce (Fine, McKenry, Donnelly, & Voydanoff, 1992). The percentage of all families that are stepfamilies is higher for whites than for blacks, indicating that African-Americans who remarry constitute a smaller segment of the black community. When nonmarital or "boyfriend" stepfamilies are taken into account, the proportion of African-American stepfamilies increases, but their numbers are still limited by the greater numbers of eligible women relative to men.

In one of the few empirical studies, Fine et al. (1992) concluded that African-American stepfather families were generally similar in parent and child adjustment to both white stepfather families and African-American first-marriage families, although they differed from each comparison group in some ways. A fuller discussion of the interaction of race and stepfamily dynamics awaits more data, but there is evidence that demographic family patterns among blacks are being replicated among whites at a slower rate (Walker, 1988).

Other underexplored groups, usually not included in the ranks of stepfamilies by demographers, are gay and lesbian stepfamilies.[1] Although reliable demographic data are difficult to locate, estimates are that 10% of gays and 20% of lesbians have children, typically from prior heterosexual partnerships. Patterson (1992) estimates that in the United States there are between 1 and 5 million lesbian mothers, between 1 and 3 million gay fathers, and between 6 and 14 million children of either. Any subsequent residential partnership creates a stepfamily.

Although a comprehensive discussion of this subject is beyond the scope of this chapter, lesbian and gay stepfamilies are both like and unlike their heterosexual counterparts. In the therapist's office, many of their experiences will be similar to the referring stories of male–female stepfamilies. There are, however, important differences. These stepfamilies are even less "institutionalized" than those formed by remarriage, and often are closeted to avoid discrimination. Ambiguous to begin with, the "stepparent" role is still more improvisational in lesbian and gay families, where parenthood is less likely to be part of a partner's expectations for relationships. Studies comparing gay and lesbian couples with heterosexual couples report that what differences do exist are mostly reflective of differences in gender socialization (Blumstein & Schwartz, 1983). In looking at stepcouples who are lesbian or gay, we might expect that most of the differences from their heterosexual counterparts stem from being households headed by two women or by two men, and/or from the added stress of confronting societal homophobia.

WOMEN'S EXPERIENCE OF STEPFAMILY LIFE[2]

In the past decade, researchers (Pasley & Ihinger-Tallman, 1987; Hetherington, 1987; Zaslow, 1988, 1989) have confirmed what clinicians (Visher & Visher, 1979; Keshet, 1987) who work with remarried families have noted for years: that females in stepfamilies—be they mothers, stepmothers, or stepdaughters—experience more stress, less satisfaction, and more symptoms than their male counterparts.

What is so hard for females living in stepfamilies? Is it really more difficult to be a stepmother than a stepfather? A stepdaughter than a stepson? A remarried mother than a remarried father? And if these findings accurately reflect the experience of those who occupy those roles, why?

Differences among Stepfamilies

In talking about stepfamilies, we are considering not a single family type but an array of possible kinship systems. A parent, who has been widowed, divorced, or previously unmarried, creates a household with another adult who has been widowed, divorced, or never before married. The new mate may or may not already be a parent, and they may or may not go on to have a child together. Children from prior unions may reside with the new couple, may visit on alternate weekends or during vacations, or may divide their time nearly equally between two households. A stepparent and stepchild may become acquainted any time between the child's infancy and adulthood, or even beyond. All these factors create important differences in the experience of all family members in the process of stepfamily formation and integration.

Both because mothers retain custody of their children in 90% of contemporary divorces and because many stepfather families include a previously single mother, residential stepmother families are far less prevalent than those families in which children live with their mothers and stepfathers (Furstenberg & Cherlin, 1991). As a result, residential stepmother families face a greater number of risk factors. The stepchildren are more likely to have experienced profound disruptions in their relationships with their parents: loss of their mothers through death; being the objects of custody battles; separations from their siblings in what is called "split custody"; and changes in custody. In many cases, they have moved in with their fathers because their single mothers could not manage their behavior problems (Greif, 1985; Glick, 1980; Spanier & Glick, 1980; Risman, 1986). As a result of greater disruption, conflict, and loss, these children are more likely to have problems that precede stepfamily formation. In addition, because they do not live with their mothers, they are more apt to see themselves as deviant at a time of life when being "like everyone else" is highly valued.

Another way that stepmother families differ structurally from stepfather families is in greater boundary ambiguity within the "binuclear family" (Ahrons & Rodgers, 1987). Because a stepmother family is usually not the primary residence for the father's children, their membership in the household and status as family "insiders" can be ambiguous. Nor is the separation between households as clearly bounded as that between a stepfather family and a father's home. Mothers are more of a presence in stepmother households, calling to keep contact with their children and to make arrangments for the myriad activities for which they typically take responsibility. Even when the children live with their fathers and stepmothers, mothers remain more involved with their children than do noncustodial fathers (Furstenberg, Nord, Peterson, & Zill, 1983). Because the relationship between parents more often deteriorates with remarriage, especially if only the fathers have remarried, this greater contact will result in more prolonged conflict and stress between parents and stepparents in stepmother families, complicating children's relationship with their stepmothers (Ahrons & Rodgers, 1987; Furstenberg & Nord, 1985; Ihinger-Tallman & Pasley, 1987).

Women's and Men's Experience of Stepparenthood

In summarizing the greater stress and negative outcome for children in stepmother families, Pasley and Ihinger-Tallman (1987) concluded:

> . . . stepmothers are less satisfied with their relationship to their stepchildren, feel that their marital relationship is negatively affected by their husband's children, are more dissatisfied with their role, and feel that the relationship between them and the biological mother is more difficult. Stepmothers also report themselves to be less involved with their stepchildren and have more conflictual relationships with them. (p. 310)

Stepfathers, who have been far more extensively studied, have traditionally been described as "detached" in their relationships with their stepchildren (Duberman, 1975; Hetherington, 1987). Yet those few studies that compare stepmothers with stepfathers show that stepmothers feel still less involved than stepfathers (Ahrons & Wallisch, 1987; Ahrons & Rodgers, 1987). But are they?

Why these grey-tinted glasses on the part of the women? I suggest that one answer may be that stepmothers hold themselves to a higher standard and care more about the quality of relationships than do stepfathers. In trying to meet their own and others' relational needs, all stepfamily members struggle with role ambiguity and the almost inevitable mismatch in what members expect of one another, making reciprocity a significant challenge. Females may be more sensitive to the quality of relationship within each family dyad; their emotional seismographs identify problems earlier, when the difficulties are more subtle, and their dissatisfaction with family relationships matters more in reckoning their general life satisfaction.

The character Joanie Caucus in the comic strip *Doonesbury,* a congressional aide and remarried mother of a mutual child, sits up one night in bed and asks her husband: "Rick, I know you love Jeff as much as I do. So why don't you seem as torn up about not being able to spend time with him?" Not even opening his eyes, he replies: "Well, it may be because I'm spending a whole lot more time on family than my father did, and you're spending far less time than your mother did. Consequently," he goes on in the next frame, "you feel incredibly guilty, while I naturally feel pretty proud of myself. I think that's all it really amounts to, don't you?" Still not fully roused, he tells her to try and get some sleep, oblivious to the lamp she is hurling in his direction (Trudeau, 1985).

This example suggests how women expect more of themselves as parents, and, I propose, as stepparents. When stepfathers measure their involvement with their stepchildren, their basis of comparison is how involved they think fathers are with their children, whereas stepmothers compare their own involvement with what they think mothers would do or feel. When stepfathers report that they are "very" involved with their stepchildren in greater numbers than do stepmothers, what we may be witnessing is their employing very different standards.

Stepfathers are more like fathers because their roles are essentially similar. Despite a great deal of media attention to fathers' more active participation in child care, the trend toward shared parenting is still a limited phenomenon (Ehrensaft, 1987); women are still primarily responsible for the care of children. The mother–child relationship may be the most monogamous of all. The expression "a face only a mother could love" says it all. Stepmothers do not offer that level of acceptance—nor, we must remember, do all mothers—but neither fathers nor stepfathers are expected to provide unconditional acceptance. Less than unconditional love is thus felt as more of a deficit in a stepmother than in a stepfather.

Children in stepmother families appear to underestimate their stepmothers' involvement even as they overestimate their mothers' involvement in their lives; this may testify to children's need to preserve the image of a mother who is always there. In a study of full-time stepmothers who were sharing many child-rearing activities with their husbands and struggling to establish good relationships with their stepchildren, Santrock and Sitterle (1987) found that

> despite the stepmothers' persistent efforts to become involved, their step-
> children tenaciously held onto the view of them as somewhat detached,
> unsupportive and uninvolved in their lives. Not surprisingly, stepmothers
> seemed to have reached a similar conclusion about their role in the family
> system. (p. 291)

Although few, if any, little girls go to bed at night hugging their pillows and dreaming that "someday I'll be a stepmother," part of what it means to grow up female is to try on—even if only to later discard—the role of mother as a core component of feminine identity. In thinking of herself as a mother, every woman confronts powerful cultural imperatives: to be always available, to be all-giving, to do it all. It is the very impossibility of measuring up to this societal ideal, reflected in the splitting of "good mother/fairy godmother" and "bad mother/wicked stepmother" in the fairy tales, that introduced us all to what stepfamily life might be expected to be. Faulting themselves for not feeling or doing all that they assume *real* mothers feel or do, stepmothers often do not realize that being a mother forces every woman to accept her limitations. Women who are stepmothers without first being mothers base their maternal self-esteem on experience with stepchildren and have a harder time gaining a sense of themselves as "good enough" mothers.

Although custodial remarried fathers are more actively involved in their children's daily lives than are fathers in general, they leave more "mothering" tasks undone than do their female counterparts (Santrock & Sitterle, 1987; Guisinger, Cowan, & Schuldberg, 1989). In her study of shared parenting, Ehrensaft (1987) found that women care more about how the children's appearance reflects on them, worry more, and do more of the psychological management, keeping track of what needs to be done for the children and when. Similarly, stepmothers compare the parenting that fathers provide with their own internalized templates of what needs to be done, and find that there is "mothering" work left undone. Because "mothering" means more contact between stepparent and stepchild, and because more contact (especially when it entails the traditional tasks of socialization) makes for more opportunities for conflict, the results are greater stress, anxiety, depression, and anger in stepmother families.

When stepmothers withdraw, it is more reactive than disengaged, more of a cutoff than a modest backing away. Stepmothers who describe having been actively involved with their stepchildren at the beginning of a remarriage and later retreating in frustration, hurt, anger, and disappointment, date an improvement in the stepparent–stepchild relationship to the time of their retreat from "trying too hard." Children, however, do not always agree, registering the loss of a prior level of involvement they did not seem to appreciate at the time (Bernstein, 1989b). The question remains, however, as to whether those stepmothers who see themselves as less involved with their stepchildren, using as their referent an earlier unrealistic or unworkable model, are actually any less involved than the stepfathers who did not demand as much of themselves to begin with.

The more disengaged masculine style of relating may be an asset for a stepparent in the early stages of a remarriage, during which time clinicians generally advise that stepparents not directly offer guidance or discipline (Visher & Visher, 1988; Bray, 1990). Traditionally more involved in the external world of work and achievement, men invest less of their identities in family role status than women do. Men are thus better able to remain "relatively pleasant in spite of the aversive behavior they encounter" with stepchildren (Hetherington, 1987, p. 196). Stepmothers, however, consistently report to clinicians their pain in feeling peripheral to family emotional life; they complain of feeling exploited by stepchildren who eat their meals and leave towels on their bathroom floors while remaining personally disengaged, if not hostile.

Mothers in the Middle

Even remarried mothers who are not stepmothers are less satisfied with both their marriages and life in general than are remarried fathers (Hetherington, 1987). As is true of stepmothers and women in general, their experience of one relationship within the household is contingent on their satisfaction with each of the others.

Unlike stepmothers, however, mothers in stepfather families have more influence with the children; they have both more power and more responsibility. Socialized to see the maintenance of relational quality as their job, mothers feel the need to satisfy everyone's needs, even when competing demands make that impossible. A mother may shuttle between faulting her partner for not fulfilling her dream of giving her children a full-time Daddy, and not wanting to put too many demands on her new husband for fear of making the "package deal" so onerous that he takes flight. Seeking relief from the responsibilities of single parenting, a mother can be torn between wanting her new partner to take over and shutting him (or her) out, protecting her children from the discipline of someone she cannot trust to love them as she does. Wanting the children to be well cared for, she nonetheless can be impatient as their needs seem to preclude couple time and resentful that they are an issue of contention with a new partner.

Marie, the lesbian mother of 19-year-old Debbie, described the stress she feels in being the person to whom all family members turn:

> "There is this push–pull thing between your partner and your child. It feels like you're trying to mother two people—sibling rivalry, in a way. I feel I have to make decisions where Sally will perceive that I'm taking Debbie's side, and Debbie will perceive that I'm taking Sally's side, based on Debbie's feeling not included and Sally's feeling that it's probably not the appropriate way for a parent to act. I feel constantly in the middle and always have. It doesn't seem like it ever goes away."

Because it is less obvious to the community that they are in stepfamilies, mothers may attempt to pass their families off as first-marriage families. In a consultation about problems with her 11-year-old son, for example, Marge began to see the ill effects of her insistence on always being in the middle between the boy and his stepfather, as well as her elation when a fight at his father's house led to Sam's being with her full-time, making her feel as if she had won the "best parent" award. In a follow-up interview, she told me:

> "I feel that I denied for a long time that we were a stepfamily, and that Sam's place in it was any different than that of our two younger children. Even though Sam can be a real pain in the neck—on an

outing, for instance, he'll complain, whine, and fall down more often than you would expect—I still wanted him there because this was my family. And if someone said, 'Oh, you have two kids,' I'd correct them, 'No, I have three kids.' I pretended that we were a nuclear family, and if we made believe that that other out there didn't exist, it would go away and we could put up our white picket fence and be fine. But it didn't work that way."

Stepdaughters at Risk

Stepdaughters, too, fare less well in remarried families than do stepsons. A review of the literature by Zaslow (1988, 1989) concluded that girls with remarried mothers showed more externalized symptoms (behavior problems, hostility, acting out) and internalized symptoms (anxiety, depression, withdrawal, dependence) than did boys in the same family configuration—a reversal of the pre-remarriage picture of boys' more negative responses to parental divorce. Although there is less information available about remarried fathers, this differential outcome by stepchild gender seems to apply to these families as well: Stepmothers and stepdaughters reported abiding conflict (Furstenberg, 1987), and stepmother–stepdaughter relationships were more detached and negative than stepmother–stepson relationships (Clingempeel, Brand, & Ievoli, 1984).

A daughter typically experiences more of a sense of loss when a parent enters a new partnership than does a son. Daughters have more often been close confidants of their single mothers. The greater the intimacy in a mother's new partnership, the less access a daughter feels to her mother, and the more she misses the exclusivity she enjoyed earlier. Talking with Debbie, the teenage daughter in the lesbian family above, conveys this sense of loss:

"You really feel like your mother's gone, that the person takes your mother. Sally spends more time with my mother; my mother sleeps with her. We used to spend time watching TV together, and now she spends time with Sally, alone in the room, and she goes out more."

When it is a father who remarries, a stepdaughter's loss may be still more bitter. Not only are single fathers more indulgent and more permissive with their daughters than with their sons, but daughters of single fathers are more apt than their brothers to cast themselves in a partnership role in their fathers' households, making the entry of stepmothers more of a usurpation (Santrock & Sitterle, 1987).

Just as stepmother–mother relations are more intense and conflictual than stepfather–father relations, stepmother–stepdaughter relationships may be more difficult than stepmother–stepson relationships because they include at least two people in ambiguous roles with a heightened sensitivity to the relational context. Their relationships may be rated as more problematic because they are subjecting the quality of the relationship to greater scrutiny and have higher expectations to begin with. It is possible that there may be a continuum of stepparent–stepchild relationships, with both the positive and negative extremes of the continuum occupied by stepmother–stepdaughter pairs. In other words, stepmother–stepdaughter relationships may be both worse and better than stepmother–stepson relationships, which may be both more affable and more disengaged.

Stepmothers, Stepdaughters, and Mothers

Having been a girl herself, the childless stepmother is more confident of her ability to parent stepdaughters than stepsons—a confidence that has its underside, however, in trying too hard too soon to make a difference in the girls' lives. As females, both stepmothers and stepdaughters may have a harder time defining boundaries. Stepmothers are more likely to see their stepdaughters as extensions of themselves than their stepsons, whom they expect, by reason of gender, to be different. And a stepdaughter, more than a stepson, in developing a sense of her own identity, will be more judgmental of her stepmother's personal traits, seeing in the older woman's characteristics a model that must be adopted or discarded. Looking for and not finding in the other a reflection of the self can lead to estrangement or conflict.

Identity issues as part of stepmother–stepdaughter conflicts may not, however, be obvious to the participants. A stepmother who complains about her stepdaughter's appropriating her belongings is usually not thinking that in wearing the woman's clothes, the girl is trying to feel closer to her. Helen Coale (1993) describes how she defused a stepmother's anger at her stepdaughter's going through her drawers and helping herself to lingerie and cosmetics: By hiding little gifts and notes in her drawers, the stepmother could playfully take control of what had felt out of control, making explicit the stepdaughter's indirect attempts at contact, changing her own response, and thereby changing the girl's behavior.

Intimately connected with the stepmother–stepdaughter relationship is a third female: the girl's mother, whose role, though not so ambiguous as the stepmother's, becomes less clear when her children are (at least in part) in the care of another woman. Typically, it is no small adjustment for a mother to feel, for example, that her child is sick and she has no access to the child's bedside, when everything she knows and feels about being a mother dictates that she should be there for her child. Access to children can be an explosive issue in separating and separated families, and the entry of another

200 WOMEN IN CONTEXT THROUGH THE LIFE CYCLE

woman into the parental field can intensify feelings of being displaced in mothers who do not see fathers as real competition or as standards for comparison.

Children, especially girls, need their mothers' permission to accept their stepmothers; otherwise, to welcome the stepmother is disloyally to abandon the mother. When a stepmother has been "the other woman" in a triangle that preceded the dissolution of the marriage, a mother faces a formidable obstacle to releasing her children to form an independent relationship with the father's new partner. When a mother has initiated the marital separation, or is happily settled in her own life, the blessing comes more easily.

Each woman, mother and stepmother, brings different challenges and vulnerabilities to the task of working out how they will acknowledge and respect each other's role in the lives of the children who travel between them. For the most part, mothers need to be less intrusive and stepmothers less territorial. Centrality in their children's lives is one of the few areas in which women generally feel empowered; for a mother who is already disempowered by the loss of a spouse, to relinquish any more power can be unbearable. To learn to be a divorced mother means to unlearn the idea that "wherever my children are is my space." Only when a stepmother can be consistently clear that she is not out to replace the mother's centrality in the children's affection can their mother find the resources to honor the boundaries of the stepfamily household. Conversely, a stepmother can only be inclusive when she feels that her needs count too.

In thinking about her evolving relationship with her stepchildren's mother, one stepmother recalled:

> "In the early days I was with my husband, we would be in bed, and we'd hear her walk down the hall and into the bathroom on the other side of the wall, because she'd forgotten to brush the boys' hair and let herself into the house they used to share to use a hairbrush. Even after we'd moved, she'd stop by in the morning to pick up a child, and before we knew it she'd be in the bathroom, talking to my husband while he took a shower. In those first few years, I felt like I had to be a sentry and meet her at the door before she could get up the stairs, or ask her to leave when I'd come home to what I thought would be an empty house and find her sitting there helping Carl with his homework. As those intrusions lessened and essentially disappeared, I find myself much readier to consult with her about decisions on 'my watch' and to insist that she participate when we're making plans for the boys."

This anecdote demonstrates how the children's needs are more likely to be met when the mother's need for access to her children is balanced with the stepmother's need for privacy and predictability.

THERAPY WITH STEPFAMILIES

Stepfamily therapy is not so much a question of technique as a way of engaging with the discourse about family life that "disrupt[s]" or "relax[es] . . . [the] complex network of presuppositions" (James & McIntyre, 1989, p. 18) that create distress and foreclose possibilities. I am using the language of social construction (Gergen, 1985) and narrative approaches to therapy (Laird, 1989; White & Epston, 1990) to propose that therapy be grounded in the cocreation of new stepfamily stories—stories that enable family members to discover ways of thinking, feeling, and behaving that are both more personally satisfying and more congruent with the changed context of family life. By recontextualizing stepfamily life, the therapist invites the family to create inclusive and democratic solutions to family membership, to build empowering alliances, and to redistribute the emotional division of labor, both within a stepfamily household and between households linked in the remarriage chain.

Deconstructing Stepfamily Myths

A postmodern approach to therapy with stepfamilies calls for a radical deconstruction of the disabling family stories of failure, insufficiency, and neglect that have made 'stepchild' the popular image for any "person, organization, project, etc. that is not properly treated, supported or appreciated" (*Webster's College Dictionary*, 1991, p. 1311). By actively constructing stories that liberate our relationships from the legacy of the Brothers Grimm, and by redefining the meanings of "family" and "kinship" to create nurturing and empowering contexts for contemporary social life, we ease the pain for those whose life stories take place in the transition between the modern family and its successors.

Recent research has validated clinicians' long-held belief that teaching stepfamilies about normal and expectable differences from first-marriage families produces immediate relief and can generate changes that resound throughout the family system (Elion, 1990). Psychoeducation is the point of departure for effective therapy with stepfamily members. This involves dispelling myths, normalizing client's experiences, and locating them in a developmental framework that looks beyond the impasses of the present and provides strategies that have proven effective to others similarly situated.

I have discussed earlier how women's narratives of stepfamily life are more disappointed than men's. In storying their lives as stepfamily members, women can be encouraged to examine what they expect of themselves, what the men and children in their lives expect of them, and what cultural expectations they have absorbed. Are they facing demands and asking of themselves feelings and behaviors that are more appropriate to first-marriage families? How do these expectations fit current opportunities and inclinations? Which beliefs are remnants from ill-fitting hand-me-down fashions, and what might they design to fit their lives as they are living them?

Beyond Categories, Toward Connection

Workable stepfamily narratives need to entertain the possibility that the relationship between two people is not totally circumscribed by social categories. Using stepkin labels as an explanatory frame may be reducing reality to its barest outlines, obscuring the influence of developmental factors, and serving as a shield against a more personal connection.

Hare-Mustin (1987) has proposed two ways to err in creating therapeutic models: "Alpha prejudice" exaggerates differences between groups of people, while "beta prejudice" ignores differences when they do exist. In thinking about stepfamilies, most writers have attacked the beta prejudice of a stepfamily's pretending to be a family formed from a first marriage, and it is in countering this set of distortions that psychoeducation is most helpful. But there is another side to the situation—the alpha prejudice of making too much of the differences that do exist. Although differentiations from the nuclear model must be made in both descriptive and prescriptive conceptualizations about stepfamilies, overuse of the "step-" qualifier in relationships in remarried families can also be problematic.

Delia, for example, attributed feeling estranged as a teenager to Irene's being her stepmother. Had she entertained the possibility that they could be close, albeit stepkin, she could have approached Irene and said, "I know you're busy, but I'd really like to go shopping and have lunch with you, like my friends do with their mothers." Irene, too, held back, feeling that she did not have the legitimacy to push too hard for her stepchildren to adopt her values. Delia recounts,

> "Irene would say to Dad, 'Go tell your daughter.' Later, I asked her, 'Why?' She said, 'I felt that I couldn't do that with you kids, because I wasn't your mother.' But I think it would have been better if she had. I really wanted a mother."

In the same vein, conflicts within stepfamilies can be too easily diverted to stepfamily status (e.g., "You wouldn't treat me like this if you were my real parent/child"). If what is undesirable (e.g., a particular behavior) is a necessary function of what is immutable (i.e., being a stepparent/stepchild), change, by definition, cannot occur. Commenting on his wife's calling his then 16-year-old daughter "the Ice Princess" and attributing her teenage uncooperativeness to their not being mother and daughter, one father I interviewed philosophized,

"Part of having a good blended family is having a good myth: that it's possible; that the kids will be okay, you'll be okay, and that it will all work out reasonably well. Everyone has problems, and theirs may not be substantially worse than anybody else's."

In hearing the family story, the therapist listens for superimpositions of paragraphs or even chapters that have been cut and pasted, out of context, from other families' stories; normalizes the emotional discrepancy created by the mismatch; explores possibilities for moving beyond the current impasse; and then helps family members to work through the transition, both interpersonally by renegotiating relationships and intrapersonally by understanding how echoes of old scripts intrude on the current scene.

For example, a stepmother struggling with feeling excluded by her husband's relationship with his children is validated in her pain at being the outsider to an intimacy that precedes her entry into the family. She is helped to understand that stepfamily integration is a process that takes time. She and the children's father then are assisted in negotiating ways to make her feel that she matters, creating "both–and" solutions to what appeared to be an "either–or" choice of attending to wife or children. She may also need to explore how family-of-origin issues have made belonging and exclusion particularly salient issues for her in a more personal way. (See the case example of Nell, Ken, and Darla, below.)

Differentiating between which aspects of the presenting problem pertain to stepfamily status and which are particular to the individuals involved is the initial challenge of the therapy. The effects of stepfamily dynamics are not always obvious to participants, who may either overplay or underplay such issues in the initial contact. Emotionally and logistically central to their families, mothers who are not themselves in steprelationships may not think of theirs as stepfamilies. In contrast to stepmothers and stepdaughters, who tend to overuse stepkin status as an explanatory frame for family problems, mothers may neglect to mention being part of stepfamilies, simply reporting children's symptoms. For example, a mother calling for help in managing her pubescent son may not consider that the family dynamics of his being the only mutual child of her remarriage play a part in the problem and have some bearing on the solution.

Recreating Roles: Toward Inclusivity and Empowerment

Role ambiguity is another source of distress that brings stepfamily members to therapy, either because stepparents are unsure and uneasy about how to relate to their stepchildren or because their preferences are rejected by partners and/or children. The consulting room is an arena in which all parties can compare and contrast their expectations of what appropriate and comfortable roles might be, working toward agreement.

Although lack of role clarity is normal in stepfamilies, and clarification among family members can decrease conflict and improve relationships, there is virtual consensus that new stepparents should go slowly in being "parental" to their partners' children. With stepfamily integration, the evolution of parental authority is usually toward shared responsibility: Parents and stepparents will never be equals in this regard, but they usually become more balanced.

Some styles of stepparenting yield better results than others, especially in the first few years of remarriage. Bray (1990) and his colleagues found that "parental monitoring" by stepfathers—being aware of where and what the children were doing and upholding the rules set by the parents, much like babysitters or child care providers—was associated with fewer behavior problems in stepchildren. Such monitoring requires parents to let children know clearly what their expectations are and that they have deputized stepparents to see to it that these are met in the parents' absence.

One approach in working with stepfamilies is to advocate drastic revisions of traditional family gender roles, so that stepmothers do not end up "wicked" and depressed from failed attempts to make up to the children for their family losses, and so that stepfathers do not become depressed "ogres" from taking on all the responsibility for providing discipline and financial stability. Instead, parents are asked to "own a full range of parenting tasks for the children: so that 'moms' are not needed to nurture and 'dads' are not needed to discipline" (Webb, 1990, p. 21).

There is much to be said for this approach, and for efforts to redistribute the division of labor (both physical and emotional) within stepfamilies, as within other households. Caution must be taken, however, to ensure that it not be used to disempower women further. Mothers left with the sole responsibility for nurturing and discipline may be overburdened, functioning as virtual single parents despite the presence of their partners. And stepmothers, relieved of the "traditional" female child-rearing tasks, may be left relationally underemployed and tangential, helplessly sidelined as their stepchildren are underparented. This does not mean that stepmothers want to take over primary responsibility for the children. When the division of labor is along traditional gender lines, they become increasingly dissatisfied with their marriages and are most content when both child care and household tasks are shared (Guisinger et al., 1989).

Accomplishing a shift in gender roles can also be a therapeutic challenge. Telling people to do things differently is generally insufficient, as gender roles are deeply structured and cannot be casually rearranged. Partners frequently take issue with each other's attempts at assuming nontraditional parental functions. Stepmothers, like women in general, see men as not covering the bases when the "mothering" is left to them (Ehrensaft, 1987), and stepfathers chide mothers for "letting the kids walk all over them." Anticipating that there will be difficulties in making the transition, as men assume primary responsibility for nurturing and women for limit setting, helps prevent precipitous interventions by stepparents who see partners avoiding or struggling with tasks that they feel they could do better. Both for men and for women, the temptation in such a position is to jump in to fill the void—or, conversely, to withdraw from the field, cutting off either physically or emotionally.

Preparing a couple to work out a system of consultation, so that the "expertise" of one gender is seen as a resource that can be shared with the other without fear of being put down, can accomplish this shift while keeping the couple connected and attending to the children's needs. "Consultation" implies imparting information and experience to a less experienced but respected colleague. The challenge, to paraphrase Keshet (1989), is to work out a role division within a stepfamily that respects and challenges both the biological ties of the parent and children and the gender roles for which men and women have been socialized. It is not enough to tell stepparents what not to do; in order for them to feel connected to their stepchildren, they must be helped to discover how they can make a significant contribution to family relatedness.

Extending Inclusivity and Democracy between Households

In working with stepfamilies, clinicians who can extend the strategy of inclusivity to relations between households help create the basis for a parental coalition among all the adults that reduces conflict and improves child outcome (Visher & Visher, 1989). Addressing issues of power and control, therapy can help in working out flexible yet protective boundaries, with mother respecting the integrity of the new marriage and stepmother honoring the irreplaceable precedence of the mother. Each sees the other as more powerful than either experiences herself. A mother feels diminished by not being able to live out her culturally created expectations of centrality and control. And a stepmother is hungry for acknowledgment as a contributor to the children's welfare. Both women need to learn that they occupy different spaces in the children's lives and that taking care of children is not a zero-sum game: What one is able to give does not diminish what the other can contribute.

To appreciate what their stepmother does for her children, a mother needs to feel that she does not have to compete for primacy in the children's affection; to be able to reassure the mother that a stepmother is not taking over her role, the stepmother needs to feel that the mother values her participation. Women in stepfamilies learn earlier than most that even a mother's control or possession of her children is limited, that it is shared with the larger social context.

One difficulty in reassuring mothers that stepmothers are not out to replace them is fathers' dramatic devaluation of their former wives (Schuld-berg & Guisinger, 1991), so that a mother often correctly perceives that a father fantasizes that his remarriage can recreate a family in which the mother plays no part. He complains to his new wife, who gets angry both at his ex-wife on his behalf and at him for the passive resignation that frequently accompanies his extreme negativity. By focusing on the "out-rageousness" of an ex-wife, a stepmother misdirects her energy and atten-tion from the unresolved issues within the new marriage. Similarly, a mother who targets her ex-husband's new wife as responsible for his uncooperativeness or for her disappointment in how her children are cared for in his home is diverting accountability from where it belongs: with the children's father. Frequently, both women find it less dangerous to scapegoat each other than to risk an open confrontation with the man who occasions their participation in each other's lives.

Building empathy between a mother and stepmother can be a chal-lenge, but the payoff more than rewards the cost. The higher the regard in which a stepmother and her husband hold his ex-wife, the happier both are with the current marriage (Guisinger et al., 1989). And the more respect a mother has for her children's stepmother, the easier it is for the stepmother to be open-hearted and open-handed to her stepchildren. Most mothers would be astonished by how much their children's stepmothers long for the mothers' acceptance and approval, and how moved they are when these are forthcoming.

Detriangulating

Another important component of the therapeutic work with stepfamilies is sorting out and working through conflicts by proxy, whereby family members take on others' emotional work. Women are typically more expressive of men's unvoiced issues, and children typically carry their parents' pain, resentment, and guilt.

> Ten-year-old Susan was referred to me by her pediatrician for headaches that were making her miss school. Her parents had been divorced for more than 7 years, but her kinetic family drawing de-picted herself, her mother, Barbara, and her father, Eric, who is remarried: They are the family in the case example with which I opened this chapter. Susan frequently called Eric to intercede on her behalf in arguments between mother and daughter, but she was loath to tell Eric directly when she was angry at or hurt by him, complaining to her mother instead. When she was at Eric's house, she wanted his exclusive attention; on alternate weekends, her stepmother felt like the maid. Eric wanted to please everyone and ended up with everyone angry at him.
>
> The initial therapy, conducted in ones, twos, and threes, resolved

Susan's somatic symptoms and began the process of disengagement in this incomplete divorce. The mother's life had been centered around Susan; as her roles narrowed from wife and mother to simply mother, she became determined to be the best one possible. When Barbara shifted her approach to respond only minimally to Susan's symptoms, they diminished in frequency and severity and no longer interfered with her school attendance. We then worked on redefining boundaries between the two households. Instead of giving herself permission to consult Eric as Susan's coparent about whether their daughter was old enough to walk to school, Barbara felt compelled to raise with him their daughter's complaints about events at his house. When Mom told Susan that she could not do anything about things that happened at Dad's house, suggesting that Susan speak directly to Eric, Susan mustered the courage to talk with her father about her own needs, both in my office and at home. In an individual therapy that resumed 2 years later to deal with her own depression, Barbara told me that the earlier sessions had been the first time that she had crossed the line to not wanting Eric back. From that time forward, they were able to collaborate as parents to make decisions together in their daughter's best interests. And as Barbara began to feel better about herself, she was able to have pleasant, casual contact with the other Barbara, Susan's stepmother, as well.

Presented with any stepfamily dyad experiencing conflict, it is important to look at whether another twosome is avoiding conflict. The stepparent can be a free-fire zone in families, diverting children's anger from the parent. For example, one 13-year-old boy made it clear that he enjoyed getting his stepmother worked up; it was obviously safer to provoke her than his father, who was stricter with him and whom he both loved and feared. Even as adults, stepchildren may focus on the stepparent as the cause of either childhood or continued unhappiness, diverting their gaze from their parent's complicity in the process. For example, a young adult stepdaughter saw her stepmother's hand in everything her father did, picturing him as a pushover to a manipulative and demanding woman, and underestimating his ability to make his own choices.

Redistributing the Division of Emotional Labor

Another therapeutic task is redistributing the emotional division of labor. This involves getting men to do their own emotional work, instead of drafting their often all-too-willing partners into acting as their proxies. In such situations, husbands and fathers emerge unscathed as feelings fly fast and furious, only to complain how irrational women are. Whether the two women in question are past and present wives or wife and daughter, a man who is slow to know his own feelings and unaccustomed to emotional expression may unwittingly orchestrate a real-life psychodrama in which his female kin play out his own angers or fears.

Nell and Ken were referred for marital issues after she pummeled him awake, so furious was she at feeling an outsider in her own home. They had been married for several years; it was a second marriage for both. Ken got along fine with Nell's adult sons, while she had more trouble with his daughter, Darla, then a college student. Ken reported great anguish in feeling he could not make his daughter welcome in his home.

For years Darla had made a point of letting Nell know she was not her friend—grunting in response to questions and refusing invitations to join them at table, only to re-enter noisily to prepare her own meal 10 minutes later. Nell felt exploited when her resources were used and she was excluded. But what compounded her hurt was how much she was also left out by Ken's style of responding to conflict with paralysis; feeling mortified and helpless, he did nothing when Darla was rude or Nell distraught, leaving Nell feeling abandoned and enraged.

We worked out ways for the couple to respond to Darla's provocations, so that whether or not these were designed to divide them (as Nell suspected), Darla could not get between them. Ken had dismissed efforts to request change of Darla as doomed to failure, feeling that his directives would foment her rebellion. Asked whether he could instead frame a request for change as a consideration he would appreciate as a loving father, Ken shared a long history of difficulty in talking about feelings. The son of a father who did not appear to have any feelings and a mother who appeared to use hers only to manipulate him, he was suspicious of feelings in general and scared of his own "shadow feelings," discounting them whenever possible: "It's nothing really, only my reaction."

A few weeks into the therapy, Nell told her story of the difficult night that led them to seek help, recounting her experience of loneliness and abandonment. Recalling how scared he had been of her anger, needing to walk away in order not to respond in kind, Ken pictured Nell as a raging maniac, running down the street trying to kill him. I invited him to think of her as running after him to get him to see and hear and understand her. We talked about how when one member of a couple overreacts it can mean that the other is underreacting, and Ken recognized himself in that formulation. His strategy—of keeping his fear a secret and trying to distract her—had not worked.

It was not easy for him, but Ken made an effort to talk to Nell and was pleased by her response. More confident that Ken loved her and was dedicated to working things out with her, Nell offered to wipe the slate clean and start over with Darla. She surprised Ken by not being upset that Darla had taken pillows from the house without asking, or that they had to drive home separately from a meeting so that he could do a favor for his daughter. She did not know why, she reported; it just was not an issue for her.

Instead of brooding about the possibility, Ken mustered the courage to discuss his worry that Darla would interrupt a dinner party by enlisting him to move her belongings during the only inconvenient evening that week. Nell appreciated hearing of his concern, and they negotiated a plan for him both to help his daughter and to protect their social time. Six weeks into the therapy, Darla departed for school, after giving a gift she made a point of saying was for both of them and hugging her stepmother as the older woman left for work. At the next session, Ken announced that he had his own issues with Darla. Brokering between the two women had been an unpleasant but "safer" option. The distraction of stepmother–stepdaughter conflict had abated, and he was faced with having to look into himself in ways that left him "shivering."

This pattern of diverting a family's emotional tasks to its female members can occur across households in the remarriage chain, so that stepmother and mother can redirect their dissatisfactions with their present/ past partner toward each other, and he can avoid responsibility for his own actions and desires by enlisting one (or, less frequently, both) as his agent(s). The mother may blame the stepmother for the father's unavailability to his children; the stepmother may blame the mother for turning her life upside down with capricious changes in plans. Each sees the other as controlling her ex- or present spouse, who "neglects my needs and gives in to hers," rescuing him from having to come to terms with himself and assert on his own behalf.

CONCLUSION

In reading about the stepfamilies discussed in this chapter, some of us see our own family stories played in variation; others see "the decline of western civilization." It is important to recognize that family change is not the result of its members' devaluing the family. The dramatic and far-reaching changes in how people organize their family lives is neither a matter of personal depravity nor of ideological agenda; families exist in a cultural context. Some families continue to approximate "traditional" models. Other families work hard to bring about deliberate changes in a structure experienced as oppressive. Perhaps the majority, to paraphrase Shakespeare, have change thrust upon them.

Working through the pain and discovering the promise of change in our family possibilities constitute the special province of therapy—our contribution to the discourse on families in transition. Finding acceptable narratives for stepfamilies in therapy may depend on developing a new appreciation for both ambiguity and ambivalence; neither can be found in the psychological and cultural stepfamily legacy that stepchildren are mistreated Cinderellas, stepmothers are wicked witches, and mothers should be fairy godmothers who can make things all better with the touch of a wand. There is much to be ambivalent about in postmodern family life. People in stepfamilies are tyrannized by a demand to embrace an unambivalent narrative—a demand that they make of themselves and of each other. Allowing for an ambivalent story enables family members to move beyond begrudging how current realities are discrepant with past expectations and to discover new ways to nurture caring and connection.

ACKNOWLEDGMENTS

I would like to thank Jane Ariel, Hendon Chubb, Diane Ehrensaft, Conn Hallinan, Casi Kushel, Marsha Pravder Mirkin, Phyllis Nauts, Roz Spafford, and Mary Whiteside for their thoughtful suggestions on earlier drafts of this chapter.

NOTES

1. In talking about homosexual stepfamilies, I am not referring to the families of the "lesbian baby boom." When homosexual partners choose to have a baby together, although only one can be the biological parent, this is not considered a stepfamily because the couple relationship precedes the birth.
2. An expanded form of this section can be found in Bernstein (1989a).

REFERENCES

Ahrons, C. R., & Rodgers, R. H. (1987). *Divorced families: A multidisciplinary developmental view*. New York: Norton.
Ahrons, C. R., & Wallisch, L. (1987). Parenting in the binuclear family: Relationships between biological and stepparents. In K. Pasley & M. Ihinger-Tallman (Eds.), *Remarriage and stepparenting: Current research and theory* (pp. 225–256). New York: Guilford Press.
Bernstein, A. C. (1989a). Gender and stepfamily life: A review. *Journal of Feminist Family Therapy, 1*(4), 1–27.
Bernstein, A. C. (1989b) *Yours, mine and ours: How families change when remarried parents have a child together*. New York: Scribner's.
Blumstein, P., & Schwartz, P. (1983). *American couples: Money, work, sex*. New York: William Morrow.
Bray, J. H. (1990). Overview of the developmental issues in stepfamilies research project. *INSTEP: Newsletter from the StepFamily Research Project* (Baylor College of Medicine, Houston, TX), *1*(1), 1–7.

Clingempeel, W. G., Brand, E., & Ievoli, R. (1984). Stepparent–stepchild relationships in stepmother and stepfather families: A multimethod study. *Family Relations, 33,* 465–474.

Coale, H. (1993, January) Use of humor in stepfamily therapy. *Stepfamilies: The Bulletin of the Stepfamily Association of America,* pp. 10–11.

Duberman, L. (1975). *The reconstituted family : A study of remarried couples and their children.* Chicago: Nelson-Hall.

Ehrensaft, D. (1987). *Parenting together: Men and women sharing the care of their children.* New York: Free Press.

Elion, D. (1990). *Therapy with remarriage families with children: Positive interventions from the client perspective.* Unpublished master's thesis, University of Wisconsin–Stout.

Fine, M. A., McKenry, P. C., Donnelly, B. W., & Voydanoff, P. (1992). Perceived adjustment of parents and children: Variations by family structure, race, and gender. *Journal of Marriage and the Family, 54,* 118–127.

Furstenberg, F. F. (1980). Reflections of remarriage. *Journal of Family Issues, 1,* 443–453.

Furstenberg, F. F. (1987). The new extended family: The experience of parents and children after remarriage. In K. Pasley & M. Ihinger-Tallman (Eds.), *Remarriage and stepparenting: Current research and theory* (pp. 19–41). New York: Guilford Press.

Furstenberg, F. F., & Cherlin, A. J. (1991). *Divided families: What happens to children when parents part.* Cambridge, MA: Harvard University Press.

Furstenberg, F. F., & Nord, C. W. (1985). Parenting apart: Patterns of childrearing after divorce. *Journal of Marriage and the Family, 47,* 893–904.

Furstenberg, F. F., Nord, C. W., Peterson, J. L., & Zill, N. (1983). The life course of children of divorce: Marital disruption and parental contact. *American Sociological Review, 48,* pp. 656–668.

Gergen, K. J. (1985). The social constructionist movement in psychology. *American Psychologist, 40,* 266–275.

Glick, P. C. (1980) Remarriage: Some recent changes and variations. *Journal of Family Issues, 1,* 455–478.

Greif, G. L. (1985). Single fathers rearing children. *Journal of Marriage and the Family, 47,* 185–191.

Guisinger, S., Cowan, P. A., & Schuldberg, D. (1989). Changing parent and spouse relations in the first years of remarriage of divorced fathers. *Journal of Marriage and the Family, 51*(2), 445–456.

Hare-Mustin, R. T. (1987). The problem of gender in family therapy theory. *Family Process, 26,* 15–27.

Hetherington, E. M. (1987). Family relations six years after divorce. In K. Pasley & M. Ihinger-Tallman (Eds.), *Remarriage and stepparenting: Current research and theory* (pp. 185–205). New York: Guilford Press.

Ihinger-Tallman, M., & Pasley, K. (1987). *Remarriage.* Newbury Park, CA: Sage.

James, K., & McIntyre, D. (1989). A momentary gleam of enlightenment: Towards a model of feminist family therapy. *Journal of Feminist Family Therapy, 1*(3), 3–24.

Keshet, J. K. (1987). *Love and power in the stepfamily: A practical guide.* New York: McGraw-Hill.

Keshet, J. K. (1989). Gender and biological models of role division in stepmother families. *Journal of Feminist Family Therapy, 1*(4), 29–50.

Laird, J. (1989). Women and stories: Restorying women's self-constructions. In M. McGoldrick, C. Anderson, & F. Walsh (Eds.), *Women in families* (pp. 427–450). New York: Norton.

Pasley, K., & Ihinger-Tallman, M. (1987). The evolution of a field of investigation: Issues and concepts. In K. Pasley & M. Ihinger-Tallman (Eds.), *Remarriage and stepparenting: Current research and theory* (pp. 303–313). New York: Guilford Press.

Patterson, C. J. (1992). Children of lesbian and gay parents. *Child Development, 63,* 1025–1042.

Risman, B. L. (1986). Can men "mother"? Life as a single father. *Family Relations, 35,* 95–102.

Santrock, J. W., & Sitterle, K. A. (1987). Parent–child relationships in stepmother families. In K. Pasley & M. Ihinger-Tallman (Eds.), *Remarriage and stepparenting: Current research and theory* (pp. 273–299). New York: Guilford Press.

Schuldberg, D., & Guisinger, S. (1991). Divorced fathers describe their former wives: Devaluation and contrast. *Journal of Divorce and Remarriage, 14*(3–4), 61–87.

Spanier, G., & Glick, P. (1980). Paths to remarriage. *Journal of Divorce, 3,* 283–298.

Stacey, J. (1990). *Brave new families: Stories of domestic upheaval in late twentieth century America.* New York: Basic Books.

Trudeau, G. (1985, June 13). Doonesbury [Comic strip]. *San Francisco Chronicle.*

Visher, E. B., & Visher, J. S. (1979). *Stepfamilies: A guide to working with stepparents and stepchildren.* New York: Brunner/Mazel.

Visher, E. B., & Visher, J. S. (1988). *Old loyalties, new ties: Therapeutic strategies with stepfamilies.* New York: Brunner/Mazel.

Visher, E. B., & Visher, J. S. (1989). Parenting coalitions after remarriage: Dynamics and therapeutic guidelines. *Family Relations, 38*(1), 65–70.

Walker, H. A. (1988) Black–white differences in marriage and family patterns. In S. M. Dornbusch & M. H. Strober (Eds.), *Feminism, children, and the new families* (pp. 297–326). New York: Guilford Press.

Webb, C. (1990, May–June). Stepfamilies require special FT handling. *Family Therapy News,* pp. 21–22.

Webster's College Dictionary. (1991). New York: Random House.

White, M., & Epston, D. (1990). *Narrative means to therapeutic ends.* New York: Norton.

Zaslow, M. J. (1988). Sex differences in children's response to parental divorce: 1. Research methodology and postdivorce family forms. *American Journal of Orthopsychiatry, 58*(3), 355–378.

Zaslow, M. J. (1989). Sex differences in children's response to parental divorce: 2. Samples, variables, ages, and sources. *American Journal of Orthopsychiatry, 59*(1), 118–141.

SUGGESTED READINGS

Ariel, J., & Stearns, S. M. (1992). Challenges facing gay and lesbian families. In S. Dworkin & F. Gutierrez (Eds.), *Counseling gay men and lesbians* (pp. 95–114). Alexandria, VA: American Association for Counseling and Development.

Baptiste, J. A. (1987). Psychotherapy with gay/lesbian couples and their children in "stepfamilies": A challenge for marriage and family therapists. *Journal of Homosexuality, 14*(1–2), 223–238.

Bernstein, A. C. (1988). Unravelling the tangles: Children's understanding of stepfamily kinship. In W. Beer (Ed.), *Relative strangers: Studies of stepfamily processes* (pp. 83–111). Totowa, NJ: Rowman & Littlefield.

Crosbie-Burnett, M., Skyles, A., & Becker-Haven, J. (1988). Exploring stepfamilies from a feminist perspective. In S. M. Dornbusch & M. H. Strober (Eds.), *Feminism, children, and the new families* (pp. 297–326). New York: Guilford Press.

Keshet, J., & Mirkin, M. P. (1985). Troubled adolescents in divorced and remarried families. In M. P. Mirkin & S. L. Koman (Eds.), *Handbook of adolescent and family therapy* (pp. 273–293). Boston: Allyn & Bacon.

Maglin, N. B., & Schniedewind, N. (1989). (Eds.). *Women and stepfamilies: Voices of love and anger.* Philadelphia: Temple University press.

Whiteside, M., & Campbell, P. (1993, Summer). Stepparenting in gay and lesbian families: Integrity, safety, and the real world out there. *Stepfamilies: The Bulletin of the Stepfamily Association of America,* pp. 13–14.

Whiteside, M. (1988). Creation of family identity through ritual performance in early remarriage. In E. Imber-Black, J. Roberts, & R. Whiting (Eds.), *Rituals in families and family therapy* (pp. 276–304). New York: Norton.

III
WOMEN AND HEALTH

10

Keep Abreast:
Women and Breast Cancer
in Context

ROBERTA J. APFEL
SUSAN M. LOVE
BARBARA HANSEN KALINOWSKI

The "Keep Abreast—Get a Second Opinion" button is an emblem of the breast cancer situation in the 1990s. The message encompasses the importance of the breast, the mobilization of political awareness about this deadly disease of women, and a message about choices in medical care. The breast has special meanings for women and in our culture; disease in this intimate maternal and sexual area affects many dimensions of a woman's being. Everyone knows someone—a mother, sister, or friend—who has been afflicted with this disease. The incidence is also increasing, and there has been no change in the mortality from breast cancer for several decades. Gone are the days when women were blamed for having personalities that caused breast cancer; going is the paternalism of a medical view that gives the illusion of simple, and secret, surgical solutions to the illness (Rowland & Holland, 1991). The appalling statistics, together with the women's movement and the impact of AIDS activism, have stimulated recent politicization of the cause of breast cancer (Marshall, 1993). Breast cancer confronts us as women with the need for taking care of our bodies and ourselves as no other single disease has done.

THE BREAST AND ITS SYMBOLISM

For women in our culture and many others, the breast is endowed with special significance, greater than other body parts. Breasts are what develop first as we bud into womanhood; breasts are what we measure and compare with our peers in prepubescence. It is with a sense of urgency, as if our whole self-esteem depends on it, that we chant "We must, we must, we must increase the bust" when we first realize the way our breasts may be seen by others as an emblem of our value. The breast is the external badge of femininity. We look at the breasts of strangers to determine which gender they are. Women who are "flat-chested" feel unattractive and wish they were "better endowed," as if the breasts are a particular inheritance gained from the previous generation or denied by parents (usually mothers) who have withheld a birthright, perhaps from meanness or retaliation for some imagined wrongdoing. Those who develop "too large" breasts may feel uncomfortable and freakish, also cheated of the imagined normal breasts; they may even seek out breast reduction surgery. We live in a culture that has expended inordinate amounts of plastic surgery time on helping women to achieve their ideal breast shape and size—a surgery that women request with the implicit belief that they will become more comfortable in their bodies and with themselves once their breasts are transformed. Furthermore, the ideal of the perfectly sexual breast has changed with styles, just as hemlines change: in the 1930s, it was the firm, small breast shape of Jean Harlow; in the 1950s, it was the voluptuous size of Marilyn Monroe; in the late 1960s, it was the braless look (Love with Lindsey, 1990).

Importance of the Breast

Why this importance of one part of the body? How did this extraordinary meaning become attached to breasts? The biological/physiological purpose of breasts is their function as mammary glands, for lactation and the feeding of the newborn dependent infant. Breast feeding has had its ups and downs in popularity in this century in this country; this topic is of great interest and relevance in itself, but is beyond the scope of this chapter. Suffice it to say that probably because of the unique role of the breasts as the literal feeding part of a woman, breasts are associated with nurturance. Enormous power is contained in this part of the body that fulfills our most primitive oral needs for food and nourishment. The power of the breast is so great that it is both revered and resented in our culture. Women with breasts that become affected by cancer buy into these myths, as do their families and society.

One way that men in our society have dealt with the reverence and resentment about "tit power" (a crude but revealing term) is to eroticize breasts, and thus to put them more in the control of the male-dominated culture. The eroticization is clear in popular sex symbols—magazine and calendar pin-ups, models with their exposed cleavages.

Yet there is another, and contradictory, message: that breasts should not be exposed in public. Breast feeding in public places has not been generally accepted. Topless bathing is a novelty for American women to find on European beaches, not a freedom or pleasure they can expect at home. Whereas *Playboy* and its clones exhibit bare-breasted women on magazine covers, a woman sunning herself for her own pleasure violates a social taboo (and even risks breaking the law). These inconsistent and punitive messages help to produce ignorance about the breast and inhibitions about examining the breast; they also contribute to the negative experience of the woman with breast cancer.

Since the breast is functionally important in reality only for the breast-feeding function, the additional value placed on the breast is a result of societally accepted and personally developed myths. If a woman's breasts embody many of her feelings about her attractiveness and worth, she will be devastated to lose one. If the breasts are felt to be only part of a well-functioning, attractive body and self, their relative value decreases, and the meaning of a potential or actual mastectomy is less. The feelings associated to breasts are very culture-bound: For example, the Amazons, mythic creatures who were masculine women, routinely performed mastectomy on one side so as to be able to shoot a bow and arrow without interference! In our culture, there is much less attention paid to loss of the uterus (and to the high rate of unnecessary hysterectomy)—not because the uterus is any less precious, but because it is less visible and less sexualized. Mastectomy is a more dreaded surgery than hysterectomy, even though the surgery itself and the resulting disability may be much less. This is because mastectomy changes appearance on the outside, and something central about the lifelong definition of womanhood on the inside.

Loss of the Breast

The experience of breast cancer thus forces a woman to confront her core definition of who she is as a woman. Given our culture, and the baggage carried by the breast as a symbol of sex and sustenance, it is understandable that the finding of cancer in the breast represents a significant blow. At some level, cancer of the breast reinforces all the worst, most ashamed feelings about "inadequate" and "wrong" breasts that have been harbored since adolescence. The threat of losing a valued breast is replete with fears of losing sexuality, bodily integrity, acceptability, belonging, and being like other women, and these are very profound losses (Bloom, 1987).

Unfortunately, the diagnosis of cancer may be only the start of many losses and bodily insults that follow from having this disease (Cella & Holland, 1988). Of all the losses during the treatment of the disease, women report hair loss with chemotherapy to be the worst, perhaps because it is another feature of appearance and another external sign to the world about how much is being lost and changed inside (Morrison, 1990).

In fact, in view of all that is represented by the breast, it is remarkable how quickly almost every woman who has breast cancer is ready to lose a breast in order to get rid of the cancer. The expedience with which some women choose to proceed with radical surgery may bespeak their wish to choose life and to dissociate themselves from the more metaphorically cancerous feelings about themselves. A woman may even prematurely and unnecessarily have a mastectomy, even a bilateral mastectomy, in order to rid herself of the dreaded disease. Women with a strong family history of breast cancer may prophylactically elect to have their breasts removed, so as not to repeat the untimely disease history and death of their mothers. Such extreme action ought to be preceded by considerable thinking about options and consequences. Unfortunately, this difficult path has been encouraged and even presented lightly by some surgeons, who see the breasts as superfluous and extraneous parts that can be shed.

As women who understand the deep meanings of the breast to women, we believe in treating breasts (and women) with more respect. These days, most women who get breast cancer do not lose their breasts. Most do not die of breast cancer right away. Women can and do live for many years with breast cancer as a chronic illness. The psychological task of living with breast cancer over time presents different challenges and opportunities, from the initial impact of the diagnosis throughout the lifespan.

FACTS ABOUT BREAST CANCER[1]

Breast cancer is occurring in epidemic proportions. It is most common in Caucasian women of high socioeconomic status. It is significantly less common in women of color, and geographically less common in Asia and developing countries. These facts have led many to look for an environmental link. Indeed, women in Japan have a low incidence of breast cancer, which increases when they move to Hawaii or San Francisco. This increase is even more marked in their daughters. Some have blamed dietary fat for this increase. Although there is some evidence to support this hypothesis, it is probably more complicated; contaminants of the fat, such as pesticides and hormones, are probably just as causal as the fat itself. Other environmental factors have yet to be identified (Harris, Lippmann, Veronesi, & Willett, 1992).

There are also personal factors that lead to increased risk of breast cancer. Age is the most critical factor: Breast cancer becomes more common with age. By age 25, only 1 in 19,608 women has developed breast cancer. This incidence increases to 1 in 50 by age 50, and to 1 in 9 by age 85 (Marshall, 1993). This message is often lost amidst the ageism in our society. Articles about breast cancer and television stories typically present a young woman's story or a young woman's body as illustrative of breast cancer. This subtle message has 20-year-olds worrying about the disease and requesting mammograms, while 65-year-olds may not seek the detection of breast cancer they require.

Family history is well known and significant as a risk factor for breast cancer, but its actual importance is often exaggerated (Marshall, 1993). Eighty percent of women who get breast cancer have no family history. Most of those who do have a relative with breast cancer have inherited a tendency for the disease rather than a surety. Only about 5% of breast cancer cases are truly hereditary. These are families with several first-degree relatives (mother, sister, or daughter) with breast cancer, where the risk can be very high. One of the genes for this type of cancer will soon be identified; this will allow for testing and will give some women the knowledge that they are indeed at very high risk (50% by age 50). Some women with this very high risk have chosen prophylactic bilateral mastectomy to avoid developing the disease. Unfortunately, this gives no guarantee; it is impossible to surgically remove all the breast tissue, and removing 95% of the breast tissue does not remove 95% of the risk. It leaves 5% of the breast tissue at full risk. Moreover, there are no good prevention modalities at this time, and early detection is not fully reliable. In this very difficult situation, women may actively choose preventive mastectomies as the only choice that helps them feel that, psychologically, they have done something toward averting the tragic fate of their relatives. When the genetic factor is discovered, the possibility exists in the future for genetic manipulation of generations of granddaughters, to avoid the familial susceptibility to breast cancer. Women with a strong family history of breast cancer, when they are aware and vigilant, tend to get detected earlier and therefore to have a better chance of survival than the average patient (Biesecker et al., 1993; King, Rowell, & Love, 1993).

Reproductive history also affects risk. Early menarche and late menopause increase risk, whereas early first pregnancy decreases it. The theory is that breast tissue does not go through full development and differentiation until the first pregnancy. Less mature and differentiated cells are more sensitive to carcinogens than more mature cells. A late pregnancy, however, acts as a promoter, increasing breast cancer risk. More complicated is the effect of exogenous hormones. Birth control pills have not been shown to increase breast cancer risk. The synthetic estrogen DES, given to some women during pregnancy from the 1940s through the 1960s, has increased their risk of later breast cancer. Postmenopausal hormones are still an unknown quantity. Estrogen alone seems to have a small effect on breast cancer risk, which relates to dosage and duration of therapy. Adding progesterone may increase subsequent breast cancer risk, although definitive long-term research has yet to be done. Anyone deciding to take estrogen (with or without progesterone) postmenopausally must weigh her individual risk of breast cancer against her other risk factors, such as osteoporosis (Colditz et al., 1990).

There is some thought that lesbians have an increased risk of breast cancer. This comes from analyzing limited, and perhaps flawed data indicating that lesbians usually have not had children, are often overweight, and have a higher-than-average rate of alcohol use. Although these assumptions may or may not be true, it is true that lesbians are less likely to avail themselves of medical care. Other women with less or no access to care also have a higher rate of death from breast cancer. Poor women have a 30% higher mortality rate from the disease than women with means; this is apart from race or ethnicity (Love with Lindsey, 1990).

Early detection of breast cancer is an additional problem. Most breast cancers have been present for a long time before a lump is palpable or anything can be seen on a mammogram. Most estimates are 10 years to be able to feel a lump and 8 years for an abnormal mammogram. Cancer cells have access to the bloodstream at year 1 or 2. Therefore, by the time they are detected, many cancers have already spread to other parts of the body. Sometimes the immune system will have taken care of these escaped cells, and sometimes they will have established themselves in other organs. Self-examination can reveal a lump, but will only be life-saving if there has been no metastatic spread in the years during which the lump was developing.

Mammographic detection finds tumors earlier than physical examination. In women over 50, mammographic screening will reduce the mortality of breast cancer by 30% (Davis & Love, 1994). Mammography is the single most important factor in reducing death from breast cancer. However, it is not perfect. Not all tumors will show up on a mammogram before they have spread. Thirty percent of nonpalpable tumors demonstrate positive lymph nodes at the time of detection. Also randomized controlled trials have not demonstrated that mammography in women under 50 reduces death from breast cancer.

Unfortunately, the mass media and the medical profession have given a false impression to the public about the efficacy of early detection of breast cancer. The impression conveyed is that breast self-examination and mammography can find tumors at an early stage, when they are 95% curable. Although it is true that earlier detection significantly improves mortality, it is certainly not true that mammography screening can find all tumors when they are 95% curable. Newer techniques being developed will improve mammography for earlier detectability of breast cancers; it will take some time for these techniques to develop and to be disseminated to the general population of women at risk.

The problem is that what can be seen on a mammogram, or felt by examination, is the reaction of the body around the cancer cells, not the cancer cells themselves. Until a cancer has enough reaction around it, it will not be palpable or visible. The reason why cancers are usually found at 2 centimeters is that this is when they can be felt by the human hand. If a woman is lucky enough to have a tumor with a lot of reaction around it, it will be found early; a tumor with little reaction around it will not be found early. Oversimplification has led to confusion and anger on the part of many women. A woman who has been conscientious about regular mammograms, and then is diagnosed with breast cancer that has already spread, feels betrayed and angry, and looks for who made the mistake in her case.

This understanding of the natural history of the disease has an impact on the way we view breast cancer treatment. First, the diagnosis of breast cancer is not an emergency. By the time a cancer of the breast is diagnosed, it has been locally present for many years, and has also had access to blood vessels that might have transported cancerous cells elsewhere in the body. We assume that some cells escape in everyone, and thus an attempt is made to find micrometastasis whenever there is a breast cancer diagnosis. Unfortunately, there is not yet a single reliable test or scan that can tell whether the cancer has spread. Lymph nodes under the arm near the affected breast are removed as one method of determining the likelihood of spread. Since blood vessels rather than lymphatic vessels are the major route of spread in breast cancer, the lymph node analysis is not terribly accurate. About 60% of women with lymph nodes that are positive for breast cancer will have microscopic cells elsewhere; retrospectively, we learn that 20–30% of women with negative nodes also probably had micrometastasis. If there is sufficient evidence of spread, systemic therapy is used to attempt to eradicate it—chemotherapy, or hormone therapy such as tamoxifen. These adjunctive treatments will increase survival overall, but do not work for everyone.

The secondary aspect of treatment is what is done to the breast itself. This is of much less importance. No one dies from cancer in the breast. Breast cancer kills women because breast cancer cells travel to, and compromise the function of, more vital organs (especially lungs, liver, bones). All treatment of the breast can do is decrease the chance that cancer will recur in the breast. This can be done equally well with either of two methods: mastectomy, or lumpectomy with radiation. Mastectomy removes most of the breast tissue, but still has a possible recurrence rate (averaging 8%) in the scar or chest wall. Lumpectomy removes the lump, and is followed by radiation therapy to the rest of the breast for 6 weeks; this technique also has about an 8% recurrence rate. Many women feel that removing the breast is more aggressive, since it is more mutilating. In fact, lumpectomy and radiation is the more aggressive approach, since it is easier to radiate all the breast tissue than to attempt to remove it surgically.

This new paradigm of breast cancer treatment can be confusing, because it is contrary to what many women have heard in the past. There is no urgency to get surgery; there is no advantage to aggressive surgery. There may be an advantage to aggressive chemotherapy, but this is still being studied. Our absence of certitude regarding prognosis and treatment can be very stressful for those women who yearn for the days when a doctor did a mastectomy and proclaimed, "We got it all; there is nothing more to worry about." Although some doctors, and some women as patients, still prefer that style, we believe it is more honest to acknowledge that not all the answers are in, that life is capricious, and that breast cancer is not usually cured by the knife and proclamations.

In our experience, it is best to start with a respectful, informative discussion, and to establish a relationship. We start by using the word "cancer" and by talking about it in a matter-of-fact but not too nonchalant way. We try to demonstrate that we are not afraid to say the "C word" and to talk openly and honestly about the most feared things. This is useful to do even before there is a biopsy or actual diagnosis of cancer. At surgery, the patient is groggy, supine, and relatively defenseless; it is appropriate to be kind, hand-holding, and present for the patient, all of which can be done without being patronizing. Surgery is not the time to give any information, because the patient cannot optimally absorb information and because findings are still inconclusive at that time. Rather, we provide news to the woman in a way that will permit her to assimilate it and choose how she will proceed further. Dr. Love lets each of her patients know after a biopsy that she will give a diagnosis based on the pathology report on the phone between 4 and 5 P.M.; then she sets up an appointment with the woman to see her in person for a long consultation within 24 hours of the news. That way, the woman who is the patient can control where she will be to receive the call and whom she will bring to the appointment; can think about herself with cancer in the relative safety and control of her own home or workplace; and can prepare herself for the meeting and for the gathering of further information. She has time to start to grieve and to gather herself for the next phase of treatment.

Ultimately, it is a balance between the tumor and the woman's immune system that determines her mortality. Surgery and radiation can address the local disease, and chemotherapy can address the micrometastases. We are only now learning more about how to enhance the immune system. Psychological interventions are thought to work via this mechanism. When a woman's sense of well-being, social relatedness (Broadhead & Kaplan, 1991), and optimism about pursuing further treatments are strengthened, she may be able to shift the balance of forces so that she is not so readily overcome by cancer (Ganz, 1988; Ganz, Coscarelli, Schag, & Cheng, 1990). Women can and do live for many years with microscopic and even major spread of breast cancer to other organs (Cassileth, Lusk, Miller, Brown, & Miller, 1985).

PSYCHOLOGY: WOMEN AFFIRMING THEIR RIGHTS TO THEIR BREASTS—AND THEMSELVES

The diagnosis of breast cancer is always a crisis, which means that it is both a traumatic time and, ideally, an opportunity to grow. Many women see it as a time to rethink their priorities, lifestyles, and relationships. Our hope is that ultimately each woman diagnosed with breast cancer will see an oncologist, a surgeon, and a psychiatrist; the psychiatric evaluation will provide her with an opportunity to acknowledge the enormity of the diagnosis, to explore its meaning for herself and her life situation, and to evaluate what type of additional support will best help her bolster her personal resources for coping and growing. Relatively few women will need to be referred to individual mental health professionals for crisis therapy, which may extend to overdue longer-term individual psychotherapy. Almost every woman, however, can profit from at least a short-term support group. Group therapy has been demonstrated to increase the participants' morale and sense of well-being, and even to enhance immune functioning and longevity (Spiegel, Bloom, & Yalom, 1981; Spiegel, Bloom, Kraemer, & Gottheil, 1989; Goleman, 1990).

Group Therapy

We start group therapy with the belief that cancer of the breast is not the worst thing that can happen. The worst thing is ignorance about one's body and choices; we thus believe in providing information, as well as time to discuss and to make choices about treatment. This approach minimizes the losses of having breast cancer, and may (sometimes for the first time in her life) empower a woman to make crucial decisions about herself and her body, thus giving her more of a sense of self than she had before the diagnosis. In this way, breast cancer presents an opportunity for growth as well as a challenge to overcome.

Having a life-threatening illness—a diagnosis of cancer—naturally induces anxiety, and can make some women look to a hierarchical power to decide for them what is best and what to do. This is understandable, but it can further diminish the woman's self-esteem, self-respect, and sense of control and mastery in life. At the very time when a critical diagnosis is made, a woman may want to regress and may need most to progress in terms of her ability to care for herself in a different way. Rapidly succumbing to a quick treatment is a style that may produce the illusion that the disease can be cut out and cured. However, once breast cancer develops, a woman needs to be even more vigilant about recurrence over time. Establishing a way of dealing with the illness and shopping for a relationship with a team of professionals with whom she can work over time is essential for the long haul of breast cancer. This can take some weeks, and the process itself can be quite educational. It is a chance to observe different styles and disagreements, to compare opinions, and to find a team whose members seem personally compatible with the woman's own style. This shopping phase is something that experienced group members can advise newcomers about, giving specific suggestions and support based on full knowledge of how anxiety-provoking this period is and how much everyone wishes to short-circuit the uncertainty and obtain resolutions.

The presence of health care professionals and other women who have undergone the treatments themselves is most essential to minimize despair and to maximize growth. Beyond the decision-making phase, even with a team of professionals who are well chosen, the treatments are grueling, lonely, and frightening; it helps to have others who know the path and the journey and can share it. Our experience is that the group is a place to share practical information about who and what helps, to talk over options in treatment, and to sort out confusions. This is all done in the presence of informed professionals who are not afraid of hearing group members' worst fears and fantasies or talking about the "C word" or the "D word" ("death"). The women show a great deal of altruism toward one another; they watch out for one another. It is a place to vent frustration, sadness, and rage, and thus helps members not to overburden loved ones at home. It is a chance to compare scars and deformities, which cannot be done so easily with friends who are unaffected and unmutilated by breast cancer. It is an opportunity to take advantage of women's best affiliative, relational capacities, and to affirm this core identity as women—based on connections between people, rather than on the shape of the breast or body.

In a first-diagnosis support group, the intention is to get past the treatment, to move on with life. The fantasy/wish is that the group will not have to deal with breast cancer in the present tense again. There is often a shared group illusion that breast cancer will all be over soon, and that everything should be fine afterward. If a woman in the group does have a recurrence, the group leader can help the participants to shift the focus to include a conversation about breast cancer as a chronic illness. The women can look at the recurrence and their responses to it without having experienced it directly themselves. In a group that starts as a mixed first-diagnosis and recurrence group, the long-term perspective can be valuable. When a woman has a recurrence while in a first-diagnosis group, the group may react with tremendous upset. Members may leave the group temporarily or permanently if they feel too sad or threatened; or there may be intolerance for, and extrusion of, the woman with the recurrence.

A Recurrence Group

We formed a group specifically for women who had had recurrences and had lost their original support groups. This group has proven to have all of the benefits described above, but also an added realistic anxiety about mortality. Choices inevitably become fewer as the disease progresses. The sense of sadness and loss is profound. One older woman started the group with news of her latest metastasis, "a lump over the heart where there's nothing else left but a little skin." Soon it became clear that she had a great deal of heart—and humor—left, despite the lump: She was able to be present for a younger woman who was mourning the loss of her menstrual periods and never having borne children.

We elected to combine in one "recurrence group" women who had local recurrences at the site of the breast and those who had distant spread. We did this knowing that those with local spread had a better prognosis than those with bone metastases. However, we wanted a group to start simultaneously for a number of women who were dealing with the shock of recurrence. For almost 2 years, the similarities outweighed the differences: chemotherapy, ostracism, fear. It took that long for two divergent subgroups to become apparent. This happened at a time when the group was considering adding new members (to increase from 8 to 10 participants). It became apparent that several of the women were looking younger and stronger, and they reported more optimism and zest for life and for new endeavors, having survived another round of chemotherapy. Others were failing—running out of treatments to have, making plans for a last dreamed-of trip, talking more openly of their fears of suffering and dying. The weaker women seemed genuinely cheered by their friends who had gotten a reprieve and had a new lease on life; they were amazingly unenvious, and seemed to derive vicarious enjoyment from the renewal of energy they observed. The rejuvenated women were interested to know the details of their sicker friends' conditions. They made helpful suggestions about how to be comfortable, providing reminders of their continuing support. We concluded that this was not a time to add anyone new to the group, as the members were undergoing such intense emotional feeling, based on a long time of getting to know and trust one another. They now needed time as a group to celebrate these friendships, to say goodbye to some members who were dying, and to rejoice for those who were living.

Psychological Tasks of Living with Breast Cancer

Women who are empowered with medical information ask more questions and read and learn more. Some of this information inspires hope; for example, many women are hopeful that taxol will be available as a possible new treatment when their lifetime limit of radiation and/or chemotherapy has been reached. Other news intensifies the sadness. For instance, the silicone implant side effects in the news stirred rage and grief among many women who had had breast implants as part of breast reconstruction after mastectomy; some of them had been urged to get implants against their first impulses. When they asked to have them removed, they were told that they would die soon anyway, so priority for removal of implants would be given to women with nonmalignant illness.

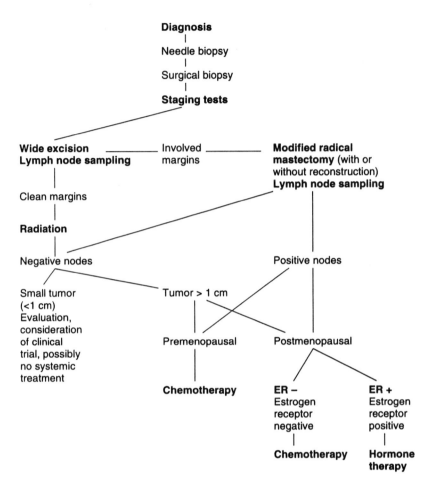

FIGURE 10.1. Options for treatment of early-stage breast cancer.

Definition of terms:

Diagnosis. Needle biopsy: Can be either fine-needle aspiration or a core biopsy. Usually done in the office, using local anesthesia. Surgical biopsy: Usually done as outpatient surgery, using local anesthesia.

Staging tests. Tests done after a positive biopsy to determine whether there is any spread of breast cancer to other parts of the body. Usually includes bone scan, liver tests, and chest X-ray.

Wide excision. Removal of the area of concern (can be mass or microcalcifications) with a rim of normal tissue. Also called a "partial mastectomy" or "breast-conserving surgery."

Lymph node sampling. Removal of lymph nodes under the arm. Usually 5–15 lymph nodes are removed to determine the likelihood of microscopic spread of the breast cancer cells. Done with a different incision if wide excision is done.

Modified radical mastectomy. Removal of all of the breast tissue of the involved breast. Does not remove muscles; does not usually require skin graft. Reconstruction can be done at the same time or at a later time. Lymph node sampling can be done using the same incision. Incision is usually horizontal across the chest wall.

While dealing with the horrific discomfort from treatments and the disruption to their lives, women report the hope that their latest treatment will be the successful one in at least arresting the spread of the disease and buying them more time. They are disappointed when their blood counts fall too low and they have to postpone chemotherapy, even though the chemotherapy is so nauseating and weakening. They realize with some pathos that nothing has only one meaning. The estrogens their peers are taking to alleviate hot flashes and menopausal symptoms are deadly for the breast cancer patient with estrogen receptors on her tumor. Tamoxifen, first greeted as a panacea, can be uncomfortable and ineffective. Hot flashes and sudden menopause are disturbing, especially when there is no warning, but they are also greeted with gratitude because they are evidence of a diminution of estrogen. There is no one answer for everyone with the disease, either. The best that can be done is to find a place that, and people who, will administer the treatments in a friendly and respectful way. And the sharing of information by professionals helps provide mastery and decreases passivity. (Figure 10.1 depicts an algorithm developed by the Faulkner Breast Centre as an educational aid.)

The daily dealing with treatments and side effects is more debilitating than is often appreciated by medical professionals (Kaplan, 1992). Hair loss is sad even when anticipated and prepared for with wigs and scarves; much discussion follows from learning about Gilda Radner's icing her head to prevent fallout of hair (Radner, 1989). Associations with concentration camp victims and shaven heads express many women's feelings of victimization when undergoing therapy. When self-pity continues unabated and humor and self-awareness are not present, there may be real clinical depression, which needs to be treated with medication and psychotherapy. There can be great value in individual therapy at a time of such life crisis, and therapy should not be overlooked for someone because she is physically ill.

Women who come from different religious and cultural traditions can share their ways of using their own traditions to enhance healing for themselves and their fellow group members. With slight embarrassment,

---

Radiation. Daily radiation treatments to the whole breast for about 5 weeks, with boost treatments to the tumor site for about 1 week.

Chemotherapy. Intravenous medicine and sometimes oral medicine, given in cycles, usually once or twice a month for 6 months. Most common medicines are CMF (cytoxan, methotrexate, and 5-FU) and CAF (cytoxan, adriamycin, and 5-FU).

ER (estrogen receptor). A test done to determine whether the tumor is sensitive to estrogen. If the tumor is ER+, then an estrogen-blocking drug (usually tamoxifen) can be used. If the tumor if ER−, then hormonal manipulation usually has little effect.

Hormone therapy. Oral medicine, usually tamoxifen, which blocks estrogen from entering the cell.

they may admit to going to alternative healing ceremonies. Meditation, bibliotherapy (Pennebaker, 1988), and guided imagery have been used by women with breast cancer, with moderate success. The staple of most group experiences, though, is talking and sharing. When there is someone failing, the group tends to talk less, and then a proscribed guided exercise can be useful to uncover more of the true feeling. Alternatives are best received when suggested or provided by a group member, rather than by a leader who is identified as a "medical person." One welcomed example occurred when a group member combined a wine-tasting trip in France with a detour to Lourdes and returned with gifts of plastic Virgin Marys containing holy water.

Women with breast cancer are involved in the balancing act of continuing to live life with an accelerated intensity because of their disease. Everyday questions take on new meaning: For example, should a woman diet, or should she eat all the hot fudge sundaes she can now while there is still life? The passion to affirm life and to ignore the minor disturbances is great; the self-criticism at being irritable and totally focused on minor concerns of comfort is also considerable. In microcosm, these are dilemmas that many women feel and that are emblematic of women's psychology: how giving to be and how selfish; how altruistic and how hedonistic. Women with breast cancer grapple with how the disease taxes intimate relationships, how much to expect, how to get needed support without overtaxing loved ones. Although most women respond according to their individual lifelong personality styles, breast cancer can shift a woman's balance either way—toward more entitlement and permission for long-denied self-care, or toward the realization that her days are numbered and a redoubling of effort to provide for her loved ones. Creating a balance is a challenge for every woman, one that is put into sharp focus when seen through the lens of breast cancer.

WOMEN GROWING IN THE CONTEXT OF THE FAMILY

Breast cancer is a crisis for the entire family. A woman with the illness is not going to be as available in the same way, and presents the family with the ultimate threat of losing her altogether. The woman may feel isolated within her own family and unable to share her worries and needs. She may move to protect the other family members at her own expense, or she may feel resentful about the lack of support and thus insert another barrier in intimate relationships. Family members will of course range in their responses to breast cancer, from quite available to quite removed. Communication can become difficult. The burden of worry over the future of the family adds considerably to the weight that the woman with breast cancer carries. The American Cancer Society has arranged helpful family retreats to try to increase awareness among family members (Lewis, 1990; Lieberman, 1988).

The following case from a group will illustrate the centrality of family concerns, and the ways in which a group can serve as a surrogate family for problem solving:

> Diane had spoken several times about her worries about her children's response to her metastatic breast cancer. She wanted to be honest with them, and to permit them in turn to tell her their feelings and fears. In one group session, Diane asked to talk about family concerns. Specifically, she felt excited that her daughter had started college and was away from home at the school of her choice, embarked on her life away from the family. However, by the middle of freshman year, soon after learning that Diane had bone metastasis, her daughter had started having difficulties that were not satisfactorily discussed by phone. Diane did not know to what extent these were expectable freshman adjustment problems and to what extent they had to do with news of the spread of Diane's breast cancer. On visits home, the daughter behaved differently than she had in high school; she was less social, stayed around the house, and was not interested in seeing old friends. The college had been informed of the mother's disease, and provision was made for a counselor to meet with the daughter. Diane felt guilty and sad that she had messed up her daughter's first year at college, burdening her with preoccupation about her mother's illness in addition to all the usual adjustments.
>
> Group members empathized with Diane's sadness—the expectable sadness of having a teenager grow and move on, and the profound sadness of anticipating that she might not live to see her daughter graduate 4 years hence. They constructively discussed alternative plans that might alleviate the suffering of both Diane and her daughter: transferring to a local college, taking a leave of absence, or getting through the year until summer break would provide a chance to talk over changes at length. No one suggested that the daughter had to stay where she was. Others articulated Diane's options and helped her express her wish to be closer to the daughter at this time.
>
> At another level, there was commentary on our culture as not family-oriented, too often pushing children out of the home when this is not necessarily warranted by the circumstances. One woman leaned over and said to Diane: "You know it's okay for you to let your daughter love you, and for you to love your daughter enough for her to come home and be with you now. In fact, it is probably more of a gift to her to let her be with you than to keep her at a dis-

tance at school, worried as she is about you and not able to see you daily." The group came to a consensus that Diane was a wonderful mother to want what was best for her daughter, and allowed her to see that "best" in this circumstance could be allowing the daughter to come home. This would give something special to her daughter, not be a deprivation.

Not all family members feel such ease about staying close to a woman with breast cancer. Mythology about cancer in general is prevalent (e.g., "Is it contagious? What did she do wrong to get it?"). One young mother with the illness described how her child care provider left precipitously when told about the breast cancer for fear of "catching it," thus leaving the patient who needed extra child care without coverage, and adding to the shock and loss for the young child and mother. When others blame the woman with breast cancer for the disease, this adds to whatever self-blame there inevitably is: Did I do enough breast self-examination (a common worry, since few women do regular self-exams, the invention of a man!)? Did I get enough mammograms? Did I get enough checkups? Did I eat the right foods? Young children will blame their mothers for getting sick, since they believe mothers are supposed to be omnipotent and know how to stay well. This adds to the young child within each of us that blames and thinks "What if?" and that gives the illusion that we might have prevented the disaster from occurring.

Women with breast cancer feel betrayed by their bodies, and often also by their doctors and their medical treatment, which is never clear and consistent and easy. They fear pushing others away with their anger, as most women do; feeling very frightened and sad, they also feel very angry, and fear that they will antagonize everyone in proportion to the anger they feel. They do not want to overburden others with their problems, and yet they resent not having the support they need, especially from partners. (By contrast, it is easier to talk with and trust members of a breast cancer support group—people who are nonjudgmental and truly know what it is like to live with breast cancer.)

Family members and histories are also drawn upon and become heroes/heroines and heroic stories for a woman with breast cancer. Stories of hope are especially valued: For example, one woman's father was terminally ill with tuberculosis when sulfa drugs became available, and he lived for decades after that timely cure. A sense of family and community can be enlarged by experience with this illness, even as the losses are threatening and mounting. In no way is this enhancement more apparent than in the political arena and the activities of the National Breast Cancer Coalition (NBCC). As one woman phrased it, "The rallies make me feel bigger and embraced."

WOMEN GROWING IN POLITICAL AWARENESS
AND EMPOWERMENT

Women helping women, with women professionals, is in itself a political statement and experience of empowerment. Coming together for the explicit additional purpose of political change has been a recent development in the area of breast cancer. Inspired by AIDS activism, and its apparent effect on public awareness and legislative appropriations, women with breast cancer have organized themselves to have a similar effect. Diagnoses of breast cancer in themselves or loved ones, and especially recurrences of breast cancer, have outraged women who were never before politically active. The private outrage is being translated into public outcry, and is increasingly moving to political education and effectiveness. Some of the protest is fueled by the fact that research on this disease, which primarily affects women, has been underfunded; that is, women in our society have been undervalued, and women's concerns have been relatively ignored.

For example, in 1991, the NBCC made a goal of sending a letter to Congress for each of the 175,000 newly diagnosed cases. This bipartisan effort was designed to flood congresspeople with letters from constituents and to raise awareness of the need for research into the causes and cures for breast cancer. Amazingly, over 600,000 letters were written in response to this request, thus necessitating congressional review of the paltry appropriations for this disease. By 1992, a year after this letter campaign, the NBCC had lobbied Congress so effectively that appropriations for breast cancer research doubled. Furthermore, breast cancer activists are now demanding participation in decision making about how the money will be spent, emphasizing prevention and basic science research. The personal experience and passion of these women are being combined with technical know-how and harnessed (Marshall, 1993).

Some women have objected to the imagery of war (e.g., the American Cancer Society's sword on its insignia) and fighting in "battling" breast cancer. They have preferred to think of the current situation as an unconscionable state of affairs, wherein daughters may have a higher risk of developing breast cancers than their mothers and grandmothers did (A. L. Morrison, personal communication, 1993). This intergenerational and related approach is much more consonant with women's ways of thinking. It may herald a new era of political thinking as women in government and women's issues come more to the fore. Breast cancer is one of the main issues to become a rallying point. Across the country, more and more people are becoming interested in women's health, because more people than ever are affected in their personal relationships. There has been a general rise in political consciousness across the country, and many more women are aware and active politically.

It has been important not to make breast cancer appropriations compete with AIDS budget items. Women in general have been sensitive to the need to avoid gaining dollars by mobilizing reactionary anti-AIDS support. Rather, the dollars should come from excessive defense expenditures. In fact, this has happened: $210 million of breast cancer money in 1993 is being administered by the U.S. Army, $197 million by the National Cancer Institute (Marshall, 1993).

Breast cancer coalition activities have mobilized a range of supporters from a whole range of political and personal persuasions. Women have combined efforts across sexual preference (breast cancer kills gay and straight women alike) and political ideology. It was the Komen Foundation for Breast Cancer in Dallas, a group of rich and prominent Republican women, who supported legislation in Texas (the first of 25 states) to require that mammograms be paid for by insurance for all women over 35, and that doctors tell women about all alternative treatments for breast cancer.

To focus public attention on breast cancer, there is now a national Mother's Day March, as well as associated local events in many cities in the United States. Choosing Mother's Day emphasizes the poignant intergenerational aspect of this disease. It also empowers mothers who have breast cancer by giving them and their offspring a relevant and meaningful way to mark the day. Children who have not talked explicitly about their mothers' illnesses have felt better for their participation in a public event that makes the private pain more legitimate and less lonely. To see so many others similarly affected by breast cancer can make mothers feel less alone with their guilt and shame for having the disease, and somewhat less sad at the prospect of leaving their children. The internal terror is diminished by the group sense of being with others who really know equivalent agony. The moment of asking all the women with breast cancer to stand within a circle at the rally seems to stand out as an "Aha!" time of realizing how many others like themselves are around (Morrison, 1993). To see the circle overflow with people impresses everyone that there are absolutely too many cases of this disease. At the 1993 National Mother's Day March in Washington, DC, legislative lobbying training was added to the demonstration events. Women are learning to translate their experiences and concerns into further action—legislation, appropriations, research, treatments.

Such political activism is psychologically therapeutic. Although it is not something we as clinicians might think to prescribe, it is consistent with what we know about subjectively feeling better when the passive, helpless state is transformed into the active, effective one (Vernon & Jackson, 1989; Taylor, Lichtman, & Wood, 1984). It is just this transformation, with its healing power, that makes work with women with breast cancer so moving. Those of us who work with these women are often asked, "How can you do it?" or "Isn't it depressing?" Our experience is that it is quite life-affirming; the women who have a potentially fatal illness focus on living and the quality of life more than others, who seem to have all the time in the world to wait and wonder about what is important. The work is difficult and emotionally draining, to be sure. However, it is also inspiring to work with women who have had to receive a "wake-up call" about life through facing a life crisis, often at a young age. As a result, they usually develop relationships with themselves, their bodies, and their significant others in a way that unaffected women do not have to do as focally or as early. It is a privilege to be present when this transformative personal work occurs. We all hope we are the better for it.

NOTE

1. Much of the statistical information presented in this section is from a personal communication with Dr. Susan Love (1993).

REFERENCES

Biesecker, B., Boehnke, M., Calzone, K., Markel, D., Garber, J., Collins, F., & Weber, B. (1993). Genetic counseling for families with inherited susceptibility to breast and ovarian cancer. *Journal of the American Medical Association, 269*(15), 1970–1974.

Bloom, J. R. (1987). Psychological response to mastectomy. *Cancer, 59,* 189–196.

Broadhead, W. E., & Kaplan, B. H. (1991). Social support and the cancer patient. *Cancer, 67*(Suppl. 1), 794–799.

Cassileth, B. R., Lusk, E. J., Miller, D. S., Brown, L. L., & Miller, C. (1985). Psychosocial correlates of survival in advanced malignant disease. *New England Journal of Medicine, 312,* 1551–1555.

Cella, D. F., & Holland, J. C. (1988). Methodological considerations in studying the stress–illness connection in women with breast cancer. In C. L. Cooper (Ed.), *Stress and breast cancer* (pp. 197–214). New York: Wiley.

Colditz, G., Stampfer, M., Willett, W., Hennekens, C., Rosner, B., & Speizer, F. (1990). Prospective study of estrogen replacement therapy and risk of breast cancer in postmenopausal women. *Journal of the American Medical Association, 264,* 2648–2653.

Davis, D. L., & Love, S. M. (1994). Mammographic screening [Editorial]. *Journal of the American Medical Association, 271*(2), 152–153.

Ganz, P. A. (1988). Patient education as a moderator of psychological distress. *Journal of Psychosocial Oncology, 6*(1–2), 181–197.

Ganz, P. A., Coscarelli Schag, C. A., & Cheng, H. (1990). Assessing the quality of life—a study in newly-diagnosed breast cancer patients. *Journal of Clinical Epidemiology, 43,* 75–86.

Goleman, D. (1990, October 18). Support groups do more in cancer than relieve the mind. *New York Times,* p. B12.

Harris, J. R., Lippman, M. E., Veronesi, U., & Willett, W. (1992). Medical progress: Breast cancer review article in 3 parts. *New England Journal of Medicine*, *327*(5), 319–328; *327*(6), 390–398; *327*(7), 473–480.

Kaplan, H. S. (1992). A neglected issue: The sexual side effects of current treatments for breast cancer. *Journal of Sex and Marital Therapy, 18*(1), 3–19.

King, M., Rowell, S., & Love, S. M. (1993). Inherited breast and ovarian cancer. *Journal of the American Medical Association, 269*(15), 1975–1980.

Lewis, F. M. (1990). Strengthening family supports: Cancer and the family. *Cancer, 65,* 752–759.

Lieberman, M. A. (1988). The role of self-help groups in helping patients and families cope with cancer. *Cancer, 38,* 162–168.

Love, S. M., with Lindsey, K. (1990). *Dr. Susan Love's breast book.* Reading, MA: Addison-Wesley.

Marshall, E. (1993). The politics of breast cancer. *Science, 259,* 616–621.

Morrison, A. L. (1990). Doing psychotherapy while living with a life-threatening illness. In H. J. Schwartz & A.-L. S. Silver (Eds.), *Illness in the analyst* (pp. 227–250). Madison, CT: International Universities Press.

Pennebaker, J. (1988). Disclosure of traumas and immune function. *Journal of Consulting and Clinical Psychology, 56,* 239–245.

Radner, G. (1989). *It's always something.* New York: Simon & Schuster.

Rowland, J. H., & Holland, J. C. (1991). Psychological reactions to breast cancer and its treatment. In J. R. Harris, S. Hellman, I. C. Henderson, & D. W. Kinne (Eds.), *Breast diseases* (2nd ed., pp. 849–866). Philadelphia: J. B. Lippincott.

Spiegel, D., Bloom, J. R., Kraemer, H. C., & Gottheil, E. (1989). Effect of psychosocial treatment on survival of patients with metastatic breast cancer. *Lancet,* 888–891.

Spiegel, D., Bloom, J. R., & Yalom, I. (1981). Group support for patients with metastatic cancer. *Archives of General Psychiatry, 38,* 527–533.

Taylor, S. E., Lichtman, R. R., & Wood, J. V. (1984). Attribution, beliefs about control, and adjustment to breast cancer. *Journal of Personality and Social Psychology, 46,* 489–502.

Vernon, S. W., & Jackson, G. L. (1989). Social support, prognosis, and adjustment to breast cancer. In K. S. Markides & C. L. Cooper (Eds.), *Aging, stress, health* (pp. 165–198). New York: Wiley.

11

Working with Communities of Women at Risk for AIDS: A Chronicle

HELEN LETTLOW GASCH
MINDY THOMPSON FULLILOVE

Being HIV-positive brings another new task with it, and that is learning a new language. We have all had the experience of going to a doctor, having the doctor tell us what is wrong with our bodies, and then not knowing or understanding, when the conversation is over, exactly what the problem is.

When I come to see you I am dependent on you for your creativity in helping me decide what is best for my situation. . . . I can take in only so much information at a time. You may have to explain issues to me several times before I really understand [them]. You may have to interpret—perhaps simplify—your language for me.

I am one of the women you may be working with. We are all individuals, all engaged in the struggle to live. We need your respect, not your pity. We need your professional judgments, not your personal judgments. We need your expertise to help guide us through this maze we must journey alone.

—ANONYMOUS

There is a poster that reads, "We all have AIDS."

The bodies of our leaders, friends, and sisters have become home to HIV. Unable to reach into their cells and strip away viral particles, we watch and grieve and daily learn to rejoice in minutes we once took for granted.

We—women of color who have been working for years in the fight against AIDS—have AIDS in our world. Our dreams of escaping AIDS are dreams of reinventing the world without this plague—the tragic epidemic is our reality—that marks the contours of our lives. We must become the triumphant face of the epidemic, that face that has a story and a name and a proud tradition.

Catastrophe and recreation are the subjects of our text, a text that must reach across cultures and through masks, veils, stereotypes. We have chosen to place this text within a diary of our own lives as women affected by this epidemic. It is our hope that, by linking the personal and the academic, we can reach across barriers and convey some of the reality of poor and minority inner-city communities in the United States attempting to respond to AIDS.

On the streets of the inner city it is common for people to ask of strangers, "Who is you?" This interrogation is a request for credentials and allegiances. The residents of the community want to know, "Is you wit me or is you agin me?" (Thompson & Thompson, 1976). Sociologists, among others, share a concern that social allegiances shape research. They point out that researchers with commitments (often concealed) to dominant social norms tend to view subordinate people as troubled, defective, or pathological. Adam (1992, p. 4) notes, "The resulting scientific images come to be used to invalidate the experiences of the oppressed and to legitimate state domination or professional control, ultimately feeding back into ideologies that blame the victim."

We believe, therefore, that it is helpful to tell the reader something about our work and, more important, about our commitments. We are coworkers at the HIV Center for Clinical and Behavioral Studies, a research group based at the Columbia–Presbyterian Medical Center in New York City. With grant support from the National Institute of Mental Health and the National Institute on Drug Abuse, the center conducts studies of HIV disease, disseminates information on HIV/AIDS, and builds links between the community and the university. It is this last task that is our focus through our work with the Community/Substance Abuse Core. The Core maintains a resource room for the community, offers educational activities, provides technical advice to community agencies, and conducts research, primarily on the relationship between drug abuse and HIV/AIDS. As black women working to understand and prevent the spread of AIDS in communities of color, we see our mission as twofold: first, to provide information to the community about the AIDS epidemic, and second, to ask questions that will deepen our understanding of the epidemic. In each of these roles, we are advocates for people with AIDS. Furthermore, we are advocates for community survival.

March 1986

After a tense week of work, Mindy is planning a quiet Saturday. The phone rings at 8 A.M. Sala Udin, a leader in the fight against AIDS in San Francisco, wants to know if Mindy will head the minority component of an AIDS research unit to be formed at the University of California, San Francisco (UCSF). This seems like a preposterous idea, especially on a Saturday morning. "Come talk," says Sala, who is a persuasive man. The plan is powerful. Because of the support of the San Francisco Department of Health, the university researchers have actually accepted, at least in principle, the idea that a portion of a major center grant would be under "minority control." It remains to resolve who will be the minorities and how will they exercise control. Mindy, with a modest track record in research, joins the team. The negotiations are delicate. At one point, Sala slams down his briefcase and threatens to leave the table, a moment that seems to arrive freeze-dried from the 1960s, but the act sways the balance in the right direction. Minorities are recognized and accepted, provided wholehearted support.

In fact, the model that is developed will be a unique and powerful one for AIDS research, a model of true collaboration between university-based and community-based researchers studying AIDS. An important battle has been won, one that has shifted the fulcrum ever so slightly in the right direction, affording critical leverage to a trusted community-based organization and away from traditional (white) research centers. At least now there is the promise of sensitive, respectful observation and study of community health problems. To be able to provide the leadership, to pose research questions freely, to own the means of producing "knowledge" for and about communities of color—these are the cherished spoils of war on AIDS in urban communities of color. Perhaps it happens because it is time for it to happen.

In *AIDS and Its Metaphors* Susan Sontag (1988) noted that AIDS is a global phenomenon: "Like the effects of industrial pollution and the new system of global financial markets, the AIDS crisis is evidence of a world in which nothing important is regional, local, limited; in which everything that can circulate does, and every problem is, or is destined to become, worldwide. Goods circulate (including images and sounds and documents, which circulate fastest of all, electronically). Garbage circulates: the poisonous industrial waste of St. Etienne, Hanover, Mestre and Bristol [is] being dumped in the coastal towns of West Africa. People circulate, in greater numbers than ever. And diseases" (p. 92).

Though it is a global phenomenon, AIDS is not randomly distributed. Particularly in the United States, HIV disease is concentrated in "high-risk" communities. These AIDS epicenters share a recent history of social upheaval that radically affected conventions surrounding sexuality and the use of drugs. War, gay liberation, and "urban renewal"—seemingly disparate processes—have as a common outcome vulnerability to HIV infection. Zwi and Cabral (1991, pp. 1527–1528) point out the commonalities of these social contexts:

Many of these situations occur where there is diminished concern about health, increased risk taking, and reduced social concern about casual sexual relationships. In some circumstances, such as refugee populations and street children, those affected may be struggling to feed themselves, and even if they were aware of HIV it would be considered relatively unimportant. A high turnover of sexual partners, often in exchange for money or goods, may be present. The ability to practice safer sex may be impaired by the use of alcohol and other addictive drugs as well as a lack of information, resources, and power. Those aware of the necessity to protect their health, such as commercial sex workers in many parts of the world, may be unable to ensure that their paying (and even less their nonpaying) partners use condoms. All these social contexts will be exacerbated by homelessness, landlessness, unemployment, rapid periurban settlement, migration, population relocation, and poverty, ensuring fertile ground for sexually transmitted diseases and HIV.

We would argue that these conditions are all unstable processes that are change factors, altering central social behaviors and reshaping the cultures in which the behaviors occur.

Various definitions emphasize that culture is an enduring set of concepts governing individual and group behavior. But in communities affected by AIDS, the received culture has been refined by social change and further reshaped by the epidemic itself. For any group, the culture that existed before the epidemic has become the progenitor of the culture that exists now. Sontag (1988) describes the changes in the culture of gay men in this way: "The view that sexually transmitted diseases are not serious reached its apogee in the 1970s, which was also when many male homosexuals reconstituted themselves as something like an ethnic group, one whose distinctive folkloric custom was sexual voracity, and the institutions of urban homosexual life became a sexual delivery system of unprecedented speed, efficiency, and volume. Fear of AIDS enforces a much more moderate exercise of appetite and not just among homosexual men. . . . After two decades of sexual spending, of sexual speculation, of sexual inflation, we are in the early stages of a sexual depression" (p. 76).

It is the process of social change and its impact on culture that is of concern to us in attempting to understand women's lives in communities affected by AIDS. In particular, it is the process of community disintegration that has been most important in placing women at risk for AIDS.

April 1988

Crack. San Francisco is convulsed by the epidemic. The *Chronicle,* San Francisco's major morning paper, reports that the epidemic may bankrupt the city through the costs of arresting, trying, and retaining drug dealers; the costs of foster care for neglected children; the costs of medical care for crack users. The Centers for Disease Control notes that crack is connected to a rise in sexually transmitted diseases in major cities. Community leaders tell Mindy and her research colleagues that crack—not AIDS—is *the* issue for minority communities in the Bay Area. "We have to study crack," Mindy says. The team is hesitant. "You know, they shoot strangers in those neighborhoods," a member points out. How to do research safely? Bob Fullilove, Mindy's husband and coworker, meets a community leader who offers to take them. "Just tell me what you need, how many kids you want to talk to, I'll get 'em for you." It is a new world. This drug, this intensely addictive, euphorogenic drug, requires a whole new vocabulary: tossin', tweakin', rocks, pipes. The words are important. They are not just new words for familiar things, they are new words for new things, things not seen before. In 1992 the *Village Voice* will say that the crack epidemic was the most significant cultural event of the 1980s. In 1988, we want to know if it will speed the spread of AIDS. The answer, sadly, is yes.

For all of the communities affected by AIDS, the equilibrium between community growth and death is linked to the community's ability to control the spread of HIV. The social response to epidemics requires resources and energy. Where these are available, communities can mount a vigorous and effective campaign in reaction to a threatening epidemic. Where they are absent, the response will be correspondingly diminished.

Communities of color affected by the AIDS epidemic are disintegrating communities that are already suffering economic and social crisis of massive proportions. The response to AIDS has been slow and painful, limited at every turn by the many problems competing for resources. Minority community leaders have struggled to "add AIDS to the list" of problems, which includes drug abuse, homelessness, teen pregnancy, inadequate education, and unemployment (Weinstein, 1991). Yet all of these problems have a common source: social disintegration of poor communities.

Because social disintegration is the underlying cause of multiple epidemics, we propose that community building must be the central response. It is not a short-term activity designed to keep us occupied until the arrival of a medical cure; rather, community building *is* the cure. We hope to show that the forces driving the AIDS epidemic in this country are the processes of social disintegration in the inner city.

In terms of economic and political developments in the United States, several forces played out over two decades or more have undermined the quality of life in inner-city communities. For example, as the country's economic base (as indicated by the gross national product) shifts from an agricultural and industrial economy toward a service economy, individuals

lacking higher education and marketable job skills are displaced and marginalized. The recession that followed the Reagan era—an era characterized
by extraordinary growth in private wealth and deep cuts to social and health
programs for low- to moderate-income citizens—has hit the have-nots the
hardest of all. Urban communities have fallen into a marked physical decay
brought on by reductions in investment in infrastructure, in preservation of
housing, in delivery of social and health services, and in enforcement of
public safety and sanitation services.

The South Bronx "burnout phenomenon" is in various stages of re-
enactment in minority areas of large cities around the country. The scenario
roughly sketched describes the milestones of urban decay, beginning with
the physical demise of housing and leading to the forced migration of
residents to surrounding areas, homelessness for many, and finally to the
splintering of social networks and a clustering of disease prevalence in
affected neighborhoods. In addition, underfunding of social programs and
community organizations has weakened or eliminated the ability of poor
communities to proactively fight the rapid increase in crime, drug use, and
the spread of AIDS. The virus that is spreading most rapidly of all in these
communities is one of marginality. Efforts to stimulate involvement of
ethnic minorities in the political process, economic viability of minority-
run establishments, and government resources directed to preserving social
structures can mitigate against the destructive force of the current epidemic.

The real control for the spread of HIV lies in rebuilding damaged
communities so that they can function in a health-promoting manner.
Without such broad-based, programmatic interventions, the continued deterioration of the inner city will promote the spread of AIDS and other
diseases, like tuberculosis, drug addiction, and violence.

As with drug addiction, which knows no socioeconomic bounds, this
spread of disease is not likely to be confined to the inner city alone. As
Wallace, Thompson, Thompson, and Gould (1992, p. 1) have argued, HIV
infection, "like any other contagious phenomenon, will inevitably diffuse
both spatially and socially from present urban epicenters into other communities and social strata at a rate dependent on the prevalence of the disease
within the epicenters." Thus, attention to the social foundations of health in
the inner city—this process of community building—is a critical step in
protecting the health of the nation as a whole.

February 1989

The Center for AIDS Prevention Studies (CAPS), Mindy's research group at UCSF, has established a home at 74 New Montgomery
Street. For more than a year the minority scientists of CAPS have been
working on the question, "Why is there excess risk for AIDS in the
minority community?" It is clear that blacks and Latins are 20%

of the U.S. population, but they constitute 40% of the people with AIDS. Why? Simple answers don't work. Minorities are not more promiscuous. It can't simply be drug use. There are more drugs in minority communities, but even among drug users minorities are more likely to be infected. "We must continue to search," Mindy tells the audience at the open house. Soon, Dooley Worth will send a copy of an obscure article entitled "A Synergism of Plagues" (Wallace, 1988). That article will provide insight. But it hasn't come yet.

COMMUNITY DISINTEGRATION

Although the modern process of community disintegration varies slightly from city to city, the abandonment of urban centers has occurred throughout human history. Wallace and Wallace (1990, p. 259) note:

> Significant contributions in archaeology have traced the rise and fall of several large centers of civilization: Mayan cities, Pella in Greece, Tihuanaco in Peru, Chaco in [the] Southwestern United States, and Ain Ghazal in Jordan. These centers featured populations in the tens of thousands to hundreds of thousands and high cultures. . . . These fell when environmental changes overwhelmed or outflanked the technology and imposed new limiting factors on the enlarged population. For Tihuanaco and Chaco, changes in rainfall and water supply disrupted agriculture over the entire hinterland. For Pella, the closing off of the bay sedimentation created a malarial swamp which eroded public health. In Ain Ghazal, the soil became exhausted by too intense agriculture and ceased producing quantities of crops needed to sustain the population.

Concurrent with the processes of depopulation was a devolution of those ancient cultures, characterized by alcohol abuse, routine cheating by merchants, and official corruption. The Wallaces suggest that observations of the destruction of modern cities shed light on the cultural decline of cities in antiquity. Dear, working in Philadelphia in the 1970s, described a process that he called "contagious housing abandonment" (1976, p. 30). In this process, the burning of a single building increased the risk for destruction of adjacent buildings. Through the deterioration of neighboring houses, whole blocks—and eventually whole neighborhoods—could be destroyed.

Wallace (1988, 1990) extended Dear's work to examine the destruction of the South Bronx, a part of New York City almost destroyed by fire between 1970 and 1980. The most vulnerable houses were those in overcrowded neighborhoods. When occupancy was noted to rise above 1.51 persons per room—a level considered "badly overcrowded" by the U.S. Census—the number of fires increased. Vulnerability to fire was also directly tied to fire services. With adequate resources for fire extinguishment, fires could be contained to a single room or single apartment, and the building could be saved. Without that protection, the building as a whole would be threatened, accelerating the process of "contagious housing destruction," which has serious health consequences. People who are burned out of their homes are forced to move to adjacent neighborhoods, disrupting their social ties and networks.

The mechanism by which social support protects individuals from disease and illness has long been debated. But a substantial body of literature provides evidence that social support is consistently associated with preventive health practices and positive health outcomes for a variety of acute and chronic disorders (see, e.g., Hamburg, 1982; House, Robins, et al., 1982; Broadhead, Kaplan, et al., 1983; Berkman, 1984; Berkman & Breslow, 1983; Berkman & Syme, 1979; Seitz, Rosenbaum, & Apfel, 1985). The vehicle for acceleration of HIV spread in damaged communities could take a number of forms. One possible means is through individuals' increased risk behavior owing to substance abuse and the absence of the protective influences of family, friends, and concerned others. Intact social networks, including family relationships and membership in a church, peer group, or other social organization, can help assure the well-being of its members by facilitating the sharing of information, advice, moral support, material goods, and favors. In the case of preventing AIDS, network connections can also mitigate the influence of such destructive elements as crime and drug use, as well as pass along information about risk factors and available health services. Families displaced by loss of affordable housing are often bereft of the social insulation that might protect them from high morbidity.

The growth in the number of AIDS cases in these areas is perhaps largely accounted for by migration patterns of drug users and their subsequent risk behaviors. Formerly stable drug-using networks also re-establish themselves in neighboring communities as they are displaced by burnout. Rates of HIV seroprevalence among injection drug users who had entered drug treatment programs in New York City from 1984 to 1987 averaged 57% (DesJarlais et al., 1989). The spread of HIV is facilitated as infected drug users find new needle-sharing partners or engage in unsafe sexual activity with previously uninfected individuals. The increase in heterosexually transmitted cases of AIDS in inner-city areas has been primarily linked to drug use—smokable cocaine (crack), as well as injection drugs.

The spread of HIV disease throughout the Bronx probably was augmented by the destruction of housing in the poorest sections. Curtailment of this spread was made more difficult by the same processes that rent the social fabric of the Bronx. Levels of HIV infection in the Bronx are now among the highest in the nation—a blinded seroprevalence study of U.S. hospitals observed that one in five young men there is infected with HIV. We learn from the story of the South Bronx that not just infectious disease, but homelessness, infant mortality, violence, and substance abuse are unleashed in the wake of urban decay.

The link between fire services and contagious housing destruction is probably Wallace's most important finding, as it allows us to observe the role of the body politic in the maintenance of the integrity of the urban environment. Maintaining populations at relatively high density requires adequate supplies of pure water, removal of waste, and maintenance of housing, among other services. Without these essential services, city residents will suffer from many kinds of discomfort, including rampant spread of such infectious diseases as AIDS. Yet the control of urban service delivery usually lies outside the minority neighborhoods, and often outside the city itself.

For example, New York—like several other major cities—has over the past decade experienced an increased concentration of poverty, particularly among the young, according to new Census Bureau data (Barringer, 1992). By 1990 the number of unemployed teenage dropouts, teenage pregnancies, and female-headed single-parent families had all increased in states like New York, where economies have shifted from resource-based industries to technology- and service-based ones, thereby eliminating jobs in the unskilled labor market. Census figures also point out the redistribution of poverty among population groups. From 1979 to 1989 the largest proportion of the 4.3 million increase in people living below the poverty line consisted of children. "One in four of new entrants into the ranks of the poor in the 1980s was under 18 years of age; one in twenty-five was 65 or older" (Barringer, 1992, p. A14); an analyst quoted in the article implied that the federally financed safety net is kept intact for politically vocal constituencies, such as the elderly. A hefty portion of the cost of programs and services for the poor has been transferred in the past decade from the federal government to state and local levels of government and to the private sector. Apparently, federal trickle-down economic policies (flawed in conception) have been stymied by recessions, deficits, and other factors. As AIDS becomes more and more a disease borne by environmental and social conditions inherent to poverty, the questions of who shall pay and what shall be paid for become more urgent.

The disenfranchisement of poor communities—their lack of political clout—underlies their vulnerability when decisions are made to cut services to local areas. Though an isolated, impoverished neighborhood can't pay for all of the costs of sewage, fire extinguishment, police protection, and health care, these services are not out of reach for us as a nation. If cities are to survive, the larger elements of the body politic must be pesuaded to commit resources to the task. The development of a larger political agenda that includes the have-nots is a responsibility at both local and national levels.

Coleman A. Young, then mayor of Detroit, said that "the only way we can repel those who would repress the Black people, in my opinion, is to consolidate our ranks and reach out to our potential allies" (Thompson & Thompson, 1976, p. iii). Coalition with allies outside of the minority community, he proposed in 1971, was the path to survival in the years to come.

Meanwhile, internal divisions can continue to threaten community integrity. A community mobilization in New Haven, Connecticut, designed to drive prostitutes off the streets made headlines by covering trees and telephone poles with "John of the Week" posters, listing the names of men arrested for soliciting (Associated Press, 1992a). That community protest against "outsiders"—described as drug users, prostitutes, pimps, johns—mirrors attempts around the country. Where such protests are successful, the community is able to continue to function; elsewhere, the introduction of drug use and sales into a neighborhood can initiate or accelerate its decline.

The presence of drugs and drug users poses a significant threat to community life; hence the intensity of the efforts to repel them. The repulsion is fueled by the connection between drug use and AIDS. A resident active in the New Haven protests made this connection, saying, "It is a tragedy [to publicize the names of the johns]. It's also tragic for little schoolgirls to have to wait for the school bus next to hookers. It's a tragedy to find used condoms in the sandbox and in the grass where the kids play outside. These are IV-drug users, and the highest risk category for AIDS" (Associated Press, 1992a, p. B8). The association with AIDS appears to underscore the danger these "interlopers" pose to respectable people and their children. On the other hand, it is an example of people pitted against each other: the insiders (mainstream members) attempting to protect their property from dangerous outsiders (subculture members). Such scenarios offer little hope for the solution to urban problems.

CHANGING CULTURE IN CHANGING TIMES

In 1971 Joyce Ladner published *Tomorrow's Tomorrow: The Black Woman*, a book that describes the circumstances governing girls' development to womanhood in an inner-city community. The girls were all poor and from families struggling to survive in spite of their limited opportunities. As described by Ladner, the complex social structure of the family and the community was critical to survival. Families, for the most part, were made up of three generations, and all members of the family, including very young children, contributed to the survival of the family unit. Families also helped each other. Sharing across families occurred within kinship and pseudokinship networks. Despite the ever-present stress of poverty and racial oppression, women had hopes that their children would have a better life than they had.

In the culture described by Ladner, girls were socialized in two primary settings: the extended family and the peer group. Because of economic stress on adults in the networks, the peer group often took on more significance than would have been observed in a more middle-class setting. Peers offered comfort, support, advice, and companionship. The influence of peers began at a very early age and increased in significance throughout the preadolescent and adolescent years. From these two sources girls were trained in self-sufficiency as well as interdependence, hostility as well as tolerance. In sum, they were prepared to survive in a world that had little concern for their well-being.

These survival skills have been sorely tested in the intervening 20 years. The social connections that Ladner described depended, in large measure, on the physical cohesiveness of the community. In the context of massive physical destruction owing to burnout of large segments of the housing stock, unenforced public safety measures, and widespread crime and drug use, residents have been forced out or have moved voluntarily. As a result, whole communities have disorganized and dispersed, their members no longer able to interact as they once had.

Two forces in the community Ladner described have emerged with particular salience under these new conditions. First, increasing violence is more and more an important part of women's daily lives. Second, Ladner emphasizes the role and importance of the peer group in the socialization of girls.

In our own research we have observed the impact on women of their involvement in crack cocaine abuse and of the violence and trauma that ravage their lives. The chaos and uncertainty created by cyclical experiences with drug use, violence, and disruption of family life are depicted in the story of "Stephanie," a participant in our Women and Crack study. Following is an excerpted narration to illustrate:

> Stephanie's home life was chaotic and abusive, and her adult relationships followed a similar pattern. For example, the father of her fourth child was a man she met through church. As the relationship progressed, he began to beat her:
>
> "Then he started getting viler and started hitting me and stabbing me, and he broke my ribs with a pipe, and he broke my jaw. . . . He used to drink too. He used to be in a methadone program. And after that . . . my kids [were] taken away, we had a fight, and drugs and all that."
>
> During her fifth pregnancy, she learned of the death by overdose of the father of her first two children. Drug dealers took over her apartment and converted it into a "crack spot" (a place where crack is smoked) with strangers coming and going at all hours of the day and night. Her fifth

child, now one year old, was exhausted and frightened by this chaotic situation. When Stephanie asked the dealers to leave, they beat her. "They started hitting me, punching me in my jaw. The other one would slap me. They had turned the light off, and my son was crying . . . After [pause] they kept coming back. . . . He threatened to kill me and my son. So I left." (Fullilove, Lown, & Fullilove, 1992, p. 280)

The emotional scarring is apparent among the women and children caught up in the cycle of urban decay and the deluge of drugs and violence. Ladner reported that "most" of the children she interviewed could relate directly to some form of violence. She was impressed that the children, who were exposed to violence at an early age, had learned some techniques for managing potentially violent situations.

In the 1990s both of these aspects of girls' lives have been reshaped. By most common measures, violence has increased dramatically in the past two decades. Statistics from the Justice Department's National Crime Survey for 1991 reported estimates of 2.6 million completed violent crimes, an increase of 7.9% from the level reported in 1990 (Associated Press, 1992b). Including attempted violent crimes, the total was 6.4 million for 1991, up 7% from 6 million in 1990. Young children are exposed to gunfire at school, in their neighborhoods, and at home. Carol Beck, a high school principal in New York City, reported in 1992 that half of the students in her school had suffered from puncture wounds. Three murders took place in that school during the 1991–1992 school year, raising the level of fear and terror to unprecedented heights (testimony at hearings on Violence and Youth, New York State Assembly, January 15, 1992). In the wake of those murders, city and state officials joined forces to declare April 4, 1992 Domestic Disarmament Day.

December 1989
    At an HIV Center colloquium, one of the senior researchers—a white man—cautions the group about providing condom education to poor black women who are sexual partners of drug users. "Many of these women have partners who are violent," he says, "and the women may be at risk for violence if they demand that men use condoms. One can only take assertiveness training so far, and then you risk placing these women at real risk of getting beat up." Helen is outraged. "I think you are perpetuating stereotypes in a careless manner," she tells the speaker. It is not true that all black men are violent. But it is true that some are brutal, some are rapists, some are murderers. That they were victimized and now injure others provides no solace to the women injured by them. Like many black women, Helen will continue to ponder the awful tension created by evoking the victimization of black men as a rationale for the victimization of black women. Since

the colloquium, Helen has had to rethink her position several times as more and more women encountered in women's shelters and elsewhere in the community have made her realize that the problem of violence against women, though not "owned" by black men, cannot be ignored. Preventing victimization is integral to the strategy for preventing AIDS in women. The struggle against racism ought not to be fought at the cost of sexism.

The peer group, which was always an important socializing force, has taken on even greater importance as orphans reappear on the American scene. Parents' deaths from AIDS have contributed to the burgeoning number of orphans, and the crack epidemic has disabled many mothers and fathers so severely that they are unable to provide adequate care for their young. The peer group is no longer simply an adjunct for parents who cannot provide enough support or guidance; it has become the mainstay of social support for children with no parents at all.

Attitudes and beliefs about life are reshaped by these extreme changes. Violence, some forms of which were always tolerated by the community—physical discipline of children, for example—has now become a major force distorting daily life. In 1991 a young man shot another who bumped into him on a subway, signaling that violence had become, at least for some, a solution for every imaginable problem. As violence escalates, its fallout spreads throughout the community. Violence leaves a mark, in the form of mental disorders, physical wounds, bereavement, fear, and more violence. The violence affects everyone.

January 1990
Mindy and Bob arrive at the HIV Center, and Mindy continues to study the crack epidemic. But the Columbia University they both knew as doctoral students is not the same. "You can never step into the same river twice." The medical center is drastically different. People get shot in broad daylight in Washington Heights, which some call Cocaine Central. Guards bar every door to the hospital. The armory that once housed track meets now shelters hundreds of homeless men on cold nights. The Audubon Ballroom, formerly the scene of union meetings and salsa dancing, is boarded up. The streets are littered, the buildings have deteriorated. No chance to say goodbye.

BUILDING COMMUNITY

On behalf of the U.S. Public Health Service Panel on Women, Adolescents and Children with HIV Infection and AIDS, then Surgeon General Antonia Novello presented a poster at the Seventh International Conference on

AIDS in which she called for the development of "family-centered, community-based, comprehensive care" to meet the needs of children with AIDS and their families. The panel's full report described the developmental, psychosocial, and psychiatric manifestations of HIV infection and AIDS in infants and children, noting that

> many HIV-infected children belong to single-parent families headed by HIV-infected mothers, women who may have limited social support and poor self-esteem, and who may be too ill to care for the child. If no one can assume the parental role, the child may face multiple disruptions in foster homes or institutional settings. Poverty, homelessness, drug abuse, and unemployment often exacerbate the problems associated with caring for seropositive children and their families. Further, the emotional impact of HIV infection and AIDS affects not only the children who are infected with HIV, but also their noninfected siblings. Additional threats to the family structure include multiple deaths, dissolution of the extended family, incarceration, additional illness, abandonment, court removal of children from home, and hospitalization of children or their parents. (Novello & Allen, 1991, p. 11)

Such a range of medical and social problems obviously cannot be addressed by isolated or simplistic solutions. Under Novello's and now Joycelyn Elders's leadership, vital policy and funding decisions have been made to support this comprehensive new approach to treatment. What is colloquially referred to as the "Four Cs"—family-centered, community-based, comprehensive care—has been introduced into many programs for people with AIDS and for the prevention of AIDS. These programs are essentially community-building interventions. Within the walls of clinics, day care centers, hospitals, or drug treatment clinics, staff members and clients rebuild the links that allow survival in difficult times and through life-threatening illness. Successful Four Cs projects are now under way in several major cities across the country, including Atlanta, New York, New Orleans, and Seattle. These projects have been federally funded in recent years by the Health Resources and Services Administration (HRSA) through Pediatric AIDS Demonstration Projects.

This model of health care succeeds not just because it integrates multiple services for affected families, but particularly because it builds connections between the disenfranchised and the health care providers. The impersonal clinic system, through which a woman might see a different provider on every visit, is replaced by a "personal physician." The hours of waiting, during which women form transient social connections, are replaced by support groups and classes of all kinds. As one provider observed, "Women may not spend less time getting care, but they get more care for the time they spend" (Dr. C. Healton, personal communication, October

1991). The women's own peer networks offer advice, guidance, and solace.

From these networks emerge natural leaders who have, in many instances, joined clinic staff as peer counselors or outreach workers. Their first-hand experience and their ability to lead strengthen the link between those who want to serve and those who want service. Instead of hostile and alienating encounters with a seemingly uncaring system, women find friends, support, and useful information in these new settings. Although it may seem that this is little more than reinventing the family doctor, successful family-centered, community-based, comprehensive care in fact accomplishes a task at which the health care system has rarely been effective: delivering care across divides of class, race, and culture.

> *March 1990*
>
> Helen is writing an article, to be published in the *Journal of Negro Education,* on AIDS prevention in the black community. She is writing about years of health education throughout the black and Latin communities of New York City. Yet it is easier to do than to describe. How do you put into words what happens in a group of women—the sudden laughter when you say what everyone is thinking but won't say; the feeling when women share the pain of fighting for relationships that don't seem to work; and all the feelings brought up around condoms? She struggles to describe her belief that these discussions can make women feel strong and can help women do what they have to do to make their relationships safe. But transforming years of experience into a few principles—how is this to be done?

Social and cultural issues must be resolved in delivering the Four Cs. Staff and clients must develop an effective common language, a set of traditions and rituals, a common history, and a shared hope for the future. In fact, within the context of the center, they must develop a common culture. This view of cross-cultural health care may be at odds with the view of some who believe that the care must be offered in the culture of the client. That would require a level of acculturation that is difficult for most people to make. It is improbable that health care professionals would be able to make that level of adaptation. Therefore, the development of a common culture—which is neither that of the clients nor that of the care providers, but something they invent together—is a more efficient solution to the problem of cross-cultural care delivery.

In the development of this common culture, the key actors on the clients' side are women who can verbalize the wants, needs, and desires of the clients to the provider community. On the provider side, the key actors are those who can listen. Through a slow and arduous process, these "translators" help all of those who are engaged in the setting to develop the shared culture.

What does this look like? At the Bayview–Hunter's Point Foundation in San Francisco, the acupuncture clinic offered services for people addicted to crack. As the project developed, it included more family members. One young mother was eagerly awaiting the birth of her baby. The acupuncture staff worked closely with her to support her efforts to maintain her sobriety. The other clients organized a shower, collecting much-needed baby clothes, diapers, and bottles. After the baby was born—drug-free and healthy—the clinic celebrated with a welcome-home party for the newborn.

April 1991

Helen has hired two community health educators to provide AIDS prevention information in Washington Heights, a New York community composed mostly of immigrants from the Dominican Republic. The two educators prepare for a presentation in the women's health clinic across the street. One is a Puerto Rican New Yorker who speaks almost no Spanish, and the other is a newly arrived Dominican woman who speaks virtually no English. Helen goes along to observe the presentation. Has she gone too far with this attempt at cultural appropriateness? The presentation is given in "Spanglish" (one has to be of two worlds to fully understand it). The women work together well, with humor and lots of visuals. The women in the waiting area are indispensable as translators for the others, supplying the elusive phrases that just don't translate well. Collective education blurs the lines between the educator and the educatee.

In a methadone program in the Bronx, the Four Cs approach has meant the development of a Women's Center. One of the activities of the center is a weekly support group. After about a year of meeting, the women in the group began to discuss HIV. One women tenatively revealed that she was HIV-positive, afraid that she would be rejected by the group. Her disclosure emboldened others to reveal their status, and the group members shared grief and hope. Through a video of the group's meetings, the women have been able to share their experience with others around the country.

November 1991

Helen is planning an AIDS seminar for women in a New York City prison. "I'm concerned about helping the women who have women lovers to talk in this session," she tells Mindy. "Why not start there? Be aggressive, put it up front." "The women will understand," Mindy says. When Helen checks her plan with the supervisor of the prison, the supervisor agrees. At the session, some of the women are sitting with their lovers. Helen's opening remarks are unexpected. Most people act "as if" (i.e., arrogant, superior) when they come to the prison. By opening the dialogue with remarks that validate love relationships between women and place these women's concerns about their risk for HIV foremost, Helen is warmly received. Women are eager to talk about sex—sex with men, with women, pleasures, fears, condoms, rubber dams. Whatever—it's important. But Helen violates a prison rule. She attempts to give the women personal "safer sex kits." The women reach for them rapaciously. The guard moves in. "No personal property here," the guard says, and takes them back.

CONCLUSION

Communities at risk for HIV are those that experienced rapid social change that altered sexual practices or drug use. The social changes parallel cultural changes. In many instances we have witnessed a disintegration of both social and cultural organization. AIDS services cannot solve all of the problems of disintegrating communities. But the services can play a part in rebuilding community through the development of "family-centered, community-based, comprehensive care." Such services help women suffering from HIV disease to connect to each other and to care providers. These connections replace many social connections that are lost or ruptured in the process of community decline.

These links, fostered by the health care system, provide a model for the rebuilding of community that must take place outside of the treatment setting as well. The effective development of such services will depend on the ability of the care providers to welcome and respect the clients who come to their center. Across barriers erected by class, race, and culture, it is difficult to create an atmosphere that conveys a message of acceptance. Yet those centers that succeed are able to offer healing. They become a model for other centers to emulate. We can and must begin to implement the cure—community building—as we deliver care.

ACKNOWLEDGMENT

This chapter originally appeared in Kurth (1993). Copyright 1993 by Yale University Press. Reprinted by permission, with minor modifications.

REFERENCES

Adam, B. D. (1992). Sociology and people living with AIDS. In *The social context of AIDS*. Newbury Park, CA: Sage.

Associated Press. (1992a). Curbing prostitution on demand side. *New York Times*, p. B8.

Associated Press. (1992b). Survey of victims shows increase in violent crime. *New York Times*, p. B12.

Barringer, F. (1992, May 29). New census data reveal redistribution of poverty. *New York Times*, p. A14.

Beck, C. (1992, January 15). Testimony at hearings on Violence and Youth, New York State Assembly.

Berkman, L. F. (1984). Assessing the physical health effects of social networks and social support. *Annual Review of Public Health, 5,* 413–432.

Berkman, L. F., & Breslow, L. (1983). Social networks and mortality risk. In *Health and ways of living: The Alameda County study.* New York: Oxford University Press.

Berkman, L. F., & Syme, S. L. (1979). Social networks, host resistance, and mortality: A nine-year follow-up study of Alameda County residents. *American Journal of Epidemiology, 109*(2), 186–204.

Broadhead, E., Kaplan, B. H., et al. (1983). The epidemiological evidence for a relationship between social support and health. *Americal Journal of Epidemiology, 117*(5).

Dear, M. J. (1976). Abandoned housing. In J. Adams (Ed.), *Urban policy making and metropolitan development.* Cambridge, MA: Ballinger.

DesJarlais, D. C., Friedman, S. R., et al. (1989). HIV-1 infection among in-travenous drug users in Manhattan, New York City, from 1977 through 1987. *Journal of the American Medical Association, 261,* 1008–1012.

Fullilove, M. T., Lown, E. A., & Fullilove, R. E. (1992). Crack 'hos and skeezers: Traumatic experiences of women crack users. *Journal of Sex Research, 29*(2), 275–287.

Hamburg, D. A. (1982). Human society, family, social support and health. In *Health and behavior.* Washington, DC: U.S. Government Printing Office.

House, J. S., Robins C., et al. (1982). The association of social relationships and activities with mortality: Prospective evidence from the Tecumseh Community Health Study. *American Journal of Epidemiology, 116,* 123–140.

Kurth, A. (1993). *Until the cure: Care giving for women with HIV.* New Haven, CT: Yale University Press.

Ladner, J. (1971). *Tomorrow's tomorrow: The black woman.* Garden City, NY: Doubleday/Anchor.

Novello, A. C., & Allen, J. R. (1991). *Report of the U.S. Public Health Service Panel on Women, Infants and Children with HIV Infection and AIDS.* Washington, DC: U.S. Government Printing Office.

Seitz, V., Rosenbaum, L., & Apfel, N. (1985). Effects of family support interven-tion: A ten year follow-up. *Child Development, 56,* 376–391.

Sontag, S. (1988). *AIDS and its metaphors.* New York: Farrar, Straus, Giroux.

Thompson, E., & Thompson, M. (1976). *Homeboy came to Orange: A story of people's power.* Newark, NJ: Bridgebuilder Press.

Wallace, D., & Wallace, R. (1990). The burning down of New York City: Its causes and its impacts. *Anthropos, 12,* 256–272.

Wallace, R. (1988). A synergism of plagues: "Planned shrinkage," contagious hous-ing destruction, and AIDS in the Bronx. *Environmental Research, 47,* 1–33.

Wallace, R. (1990). Urban desertification, public health and public order: "Planned shrinkage," violent death, substance abuse and AIDS in the Bronx. *Social Science and Medicine, 31*(7), 801–813.

Wallace, R., Thompson, M., Thompson, R., & Gould, P. (1992). *The U.S. urban crisis and diffusion of HIV into affluent heterosexual populations.* Manuscript submitted for publication.

Weinstein, M. (1991). *Add AIDS to the list: AIDS prevention in the black community.* Unpublished manuscript, San Francisco State University.

Zwi, A. B., & Cabral, A. J. R. (1991). Identifying "high risk situations" for preventing AIDS. *British Medical Journal, 303,* 1597–1599.

12

The Sociopolitical Context of Abortion

MARSHA PRAVDER MIRKIN
BARBARA OKUN

We began to write this chapter on July 1, 1992. The irony of this timing is not lost on us, since it is 2 days after the Supreme Court restricted women's access to abortion (*Planned Parenthood of South Eastern Pennsylvania v. Casey,* 1992), and 3 days before this country celebrates Independence Day. Those two events are intricately woven together, because the premise of this chapter is that no woman can ever hope to be free until, at the very least, she has control over decisions concerning her own body.

In this chapter, we examine conceptual and treatment issues related to abortion. Paradoxically, we argue that the issue of reproductive freedom is not really about abortion at all, but rather about how power is defined, interpreted, and used in a partriarchal society. Power is considered in political, economic, psychological, and family contexts. The struggle over reproductive freedom[1] is the struggle of the disenfranchised—women in general, low-income women, women of color—to claim ourselves and plan our futures. As we therapists support and empower women to make decisions concerning pregnancy and childbirth, we do not want to lose sight of the complexity of this decision and the impact of this decision on women.

Though abortion rights are being openly and hotly contested at this point in time, abortions have always been performed in the United States; Koop (1989) estimates that from 200,000 to 1.2 million illegal abortions were performed annually in the United States prior to the *Roe v. Wade* (1973) decision to legalize abortion. Koop (1989) also estimates that 1.5 million abortions have been performed yearly since *Roe v. Wade* in the

United States, and that 90% of these have been in the first trimester. Women who seek abortions cut across reproductively capable ages, class, ethnic groups, and religious groups.

POWER AND REPRODUCTIVE FREEDOM

In a ground-breaking chapter, Goodrich (1991) has defined "power" as "the capacity to gain whatever resources are necessary to remove oneself from a condition of oppression, to guarantee one's ability to perform, and to affect not only one's own circumstances but also more general circumstances outside one's intimate surroundings" (p. 10). According to this definition, freedom to choose when or whether to have children is a power base: It enables a woman to move from the oppressive situation of having others determine what takes place in her body, when that takes place, when and whether she can join the work force, whether she can have continuity within the work force, whether she is compelled to stay in an unhappy or abusive relationship, and so on.

A woman's decision to have children at a particular time in her life and not at another time, or not to have children at all, has economic, social, and political ramifications. Economically, the timing means that she can choose to finish high school, college, or graduate school; that she can return to work after raising children or return to work while raising children; that she does not have to interrupt her career; that she can decide when having children would be an economic hardship and choose to avoid that hardship. It can also mean that a woman chooses to have children in spite of her economic situation, which may be restricted by race and gender discrimination. The social and political issues are tied to the economics: If a woman has economic stability, she is more capable of leaving a poor relationship, choosing not to enter a relationship, or choosing a more mutually satisfying relationship. Furthermore, she is less likely to be influenced by regressive stances aimed at keeping low-income women from bearing children. Politically, this is an explosive statement. Reproductive freedom can undermine patriarchy by giving women the choice of saying "no" to male domination in this, the most personal domain in their lives.

Patriarchal power has been "power over"—domination of others, rather than the use of power to support and enhance in a mutually satisfying manner. Patriarchal power is hierarchical, whereas the power described by Goodrich (1991) is collaborative. When power is hierarchical, a leading motivator is maintaining that power. In patriarchy, men have power over women; more specifically, white, wealthy, Christian men have power over women, women of color, low-income women, and non-Christian women. One way of maintaining this power is ensuring economic and social dependence. In this way, reproductive freedom challenges male power, and one response of those who hold power is to ensure that men maintain control over women's reproductive functions.

The argument about abortion therefore becomes an argument about "power over" versus "power to." It is not surprising that the most violent countries in the world are the ones that either force women to remain pregnant or force women to have abortions. Nor is it surprising that during a time when efforts are being made to limit abortion in this country, violence against women has reached epidemic proportions. In the United States, every 15 seconds a woman is beaten by her husband or partner, and every 6 minutes a woman is raped (Fund for a Feminist Majority, personal communication, 1991). The connection is frightening: Once a man is given the right (sanctioned by the state) to impose himself on a woman's body against her will, then the boundary is violated and the imposition can be expressed through rape, beating, forced pregnancy, forced abortion, stalking, or verbal intimidation. In each of these cases, the woman's body is "owned" by another, subject to the whims of the other, and dissociated from the woman herself. In a case highlighting this connection, the Illinois House of Representatives approved a bill that allows a man who states he is the biological father and is willing to support the child to get a court order forbidding an abortion, "even if the father is a rapist and the pregnant woman is his victim" (Hayler, 1979, p. 309).

Any effort to intervene in this epidemic of violence must include the effort to define a woman's body as strictly her own, free of government regulation, but protected against violation by the law. Without that, the government is implicitly colluding with violence against women.

"Power over" Disguised as "Caring for"

How do we know, however, that the primary issue is about maintaining control over women and not about protecting life? Historically, prior to the 1880s, only abortion and infanticide were considered crimes against children in France (Fuchs, 1982); child abandonment was an acceptable alternative to abortion, and malnourishment and neglect were not crimes. Before we dismiss that information as antiquated, we should note that in the United States today there is a judicial move to limit abortion, while at the same time record numbers of children are malnourished, abused, or neglected. Keeping children healthy is not the focus of either government regulation or pro-life lobbying—once the children are born, the state no longer maintains its commitment to these children. Funding for social services has been cut to the point that there are not enough caseworkers to investigate abuse, or enough treatment providers to help children who have been abused or neglected. Private contributors desperately try to ease the hunger of children, but without federal organization of the task, children still go hungry. Shelters do not have the capacity to provide for all the homeless and battered women and their children. Schools are underfunded, and high-quality day care is unavailable to low-income families. It is only while the children are in their mothers' wombs that anti-choice advocates and many legislatures express interest in their well-being.

Nowhere is the issue of power over women disguised as caring for children more compelling than in the analysis of fetal protection laws. Under these regulations, a woman of childbearing age cannot be employed at certain jobs because of the harm that may ensue to the fetus should she get pregnant. However, in a stunning indictment of these regulations, Faludi (1991) argues that women are banned from higher-paying, traditionally male jobs because of alleged concern for fetuses, but at the same time are kept in lower-paying, traditionally female jobs that are clearly risky to fetuses. She cites the Reagan administration policy of encouraging fetal protection policies for the 1.4 million women who worked in traditional "men's industries," while thwarting investigations into the threat that video display terminals (VDTs) might pose to 11 million women. When a probe began on the higher rates of reproductive problems among Southern Bell VDT operators, the Office of Management and Budget, according to Faludi, insisted that the probe drop all survey questions on fertility. Finally, she argues, the same industries that have banned women from jobs to protect fetuses, *should they get pregnant,* allow men to work at those jobs in spite of the known harm to sperm. Few companies have endeavored to make the work environment safer for the women and men who are there day after day; safety becomes an issue only in terms of the control men have over women of childbearing age. The sad conclusion is that, rather than protecting fetuses, these laws serve to maintain the economic system of male patriarchy.

Faludi (1991) cites case after case in which fetuses have been used as the means to control and maintain power over women:

> In California, a young woman was brought up on fetal neglect charges . . . [for] failing to heed a doctor's advice . . ., not getting to the hospital with due haste, and having sex with her husband. The husband, a batterer whose brutal outbursts had summoned the police to their apartment more than a dozen times in one year alone, was not charged—or even investigated. . . . In Michigan, another husband hauled his wife into court to accuse her of taking tetracycline during pregnancy; the drug prescribed by her physician, allegedly discolored her son's teeth. . . . The court ruled that the husband did indeed have the right to sue for this "prenatal negligence." (p. 425)

Race, Class, and Gender

Nowhere is the power issue of reproductive freedom played out more poignantly than in the issues surrounding the interaction of race, class, and gender. The power of the state in its relationship to low-income women, many of whom are women of color, is appalling in its multilooped Catch-22.

One could argue that the dominant culture wants to limit the number of poor people in this country, not by redistributing the wealth, but by limiting their number of offspring. The racist undertone is that this limitation on pregnancy would reduce the number of nonwhite citizens. There is outrage expressed at low-income women who continue to get pregnant, and a resultant moral indignation at spending tax dollars to underwrite their abortions. And, finally, this outrage persists once the children are born, with the idea that the state should not "make it easy" for these mothers to keep getting pregnant; thus, aid to dependent children is cut significantly, and there are those arguing to refuse aid to any woman who has more than one or two children.

What has resulted is a war of encouraged sterilization, forced pregnancy, and poverty against poor women. Statistics reveal greater encouragement for sterilization among poor and nonwhite women (Glen, 1978). Herman (1977) reports the appalling statistic that most physicians favor compulsory sterilization for a welfare mother with three or more children born out of wedlock. The *Relf v. Weinberger* (1974) court decision noted that there was "uncontroverted evidence [that] an indefinite number of poor people have been improperly coerced into accepting a sterilization operation under the threat that . . . benefits would be withdrawn" (quoted in Hayler, 1979, p. 320). Hayler continues by citing evidence that many physicians and hospitals will not provide abortions to poor women unless they also agree to be sterilized. In a poignant illustration of how extreme this policy can be, Hayler cites research indicating that in Puerto Rico, 35% of women between ages 20 and 49 were sterilized by the end of the 1970s.

At the same time that sterilization is encouraged, roadblocks are set up to make it difficult or impossible for indigent women to obtain an abortion. Abortion is not available in 83% of America's counties, where nearly one-third of American women of childbearing age reside (Lacayo, 1992). The same article notes that just one doctor provides abortions in South Dakota. Without financial resources, traveling to other states or distant counties for an abortion is equivalent to banning legal abortions for many poor women. Furthermore, 31 states will not provide Medicaid funding for abortions unless the woman's life is in danger (Lacayo, 1992), making abortion a financially impossible option. Add to this the ban on federally funded clinic counselors (upheld by the U.S. Supreme Court), which prohibits them from giving abortion information or referrals, and the right to an abortion has become an illusion for the indigent women of this country.

When abortions were restricted prior to *Roe v. Wade,* the vast majority of therapeutic abortions were performed on private hospital patients who were predominantly white and affluent (Hayler, 1979)—the same group who also had access to clandestine illegal abortions performed by physicians. Given that Hayler cites statistics indicating that abortion mortality is higher for women of color than for white women, then the present limitations on abortion for the indigent may be placing poor and nonwhite women at higher risk if they do obtain abortions, with the alternatives being the risk from forced continuation of pregnancy.

When abortions are legal, available, and affordable, terminating a pregnancy may be, but is not necessarily, the choice of women of color. For poor women of color, the struggle for reproductive rights may mean the right *to* reproduce (B. Greene, personal communication, 1992), and "the notion of a 'woman's right to choose' to bear children has always been mediated by a coercive, racist state" (Mohanty, Russo, & Torres, 1991, p. 12). In communities ravaged by high infant mortality, cocaine-addicted and fetal alcohol syndrome babies, and early violent deaths, the decision to abort a healthy baby can be seen as genocide—as yet another way for white Americans to support the decimation of a race. Although the pregnant woman must still be the one to make the decision, and although affordable abortion is often chosen by low-income women (Kramer, 1975), an understanding of these issues is critical to a more inclusive pro-choice movement. The issue for many members of the African-American and Native American communities is receiving support and even permission (given the high rates of sterilization and out-of-home placements) to have and raise their children.[2]

A full commitment to reproductive rights therefore includes advocating for a broad range of affordable, high-quality reproductive services. As stated by Luz Alvarez Martinez (1992), cofounder of the National Latina Health Organization,

> . . . choice is meaningless to many women if they don't first have access to quality health care. This means a national health plan; it means information and education on sexuality that is culturally relevant and in their language; and birth control that is affordable. It means having prenatal care so we can have healthy babies. It means being able to make knowledgeable, healthful choices so that we are not left with abortion as our only choice. It means access to fertility services, something that is never considered as a need for poor women and women of color. It very much means freedom from sterilization abuse and other reproductive abuses. . . . The traditionally recognized reproductive rights movement must join the broader women of color reproductive rights movement. Only together, sisters, will we survive. (p. 4)

Patriarchy and Unwanted Children

A "power over" system victimizes the children born from forced pregnancies as well as their mothers. In spite of all the lip service paid to the unborn child, there are relatively few treatment programs for pregnant drug abusers, and prenatal care is not readily available to uninsured, non-Medicaid women. Although anti-abortion advocates argue for the alternative of adoption, racism and class inequalities lead to easy adoption of healthy white babies, whereas many children of color, children with special needs, and abandoned older children live out their childhood in institutions or in a series of foster homes.

The research, limited as it is, also points to the toll that being unwanted takes on children. Russo (1992b) reports that unwanted children, regardless of the economic circumstances of their parents, are at higher risk for psychological and social problems, abuse, and neglect. She suggests that unwanted children perform more poorly in school, exhibit delinquent behavior, and require psychiatric treatment; as adults, they are more likely to engage in criminal activity and to be welfare recipients. A study done in Prague (Dytrych, Matejcek, Schuller, David, & Friedman, 1975) with families whose mothers were twice denied abortion suggested that while many families were able to make positive adjustments, there were small, consistent disadvantages affecting the unwanted children (especially boys). These included poorer social skills, lower social status among peers, less stable families, poorer family relationships, and to some extent poorer school performance. A Scandinavian study done that same year (Prescott, 1975) showed that unwanted children were more than twice as likely to suffer social, emotional, and educational disadvantages. Furthermore, this study reported other indicting evidence of the trauma of forced pregnancy: These children were more likely to be abused, neglected, or even killed.

Although more research needs to be done in this area, it is hard to imagine that unwanted children are *not* at risk for abuse and neglect, given the lack of societal supports for women and children in general, and for the children resulting from forced pregnancies in particular. If we have a dual system of abortion availability, then the most disenfranchised women are the ones who will be denied abortions—the women who are most unable to economically care for children, and to whom these births represent yet another way in which their voice has been denied. Given that the United States has the poorest system of day care among industrialized nations (*Boston Globe,* 1987), and medical insurance is beyond the reach of many low-income families, then this societal structure alone requires that children be neglected when parents go to work, and that their health needs are unattended. The right to have a child as well as to terminate a pregnancy must be protected by mandating that resources be made available to mothers and children.

DEBUNKING THE MADONNA AND THE WHORE: REASONS FOR ABORTIONS

Ours is a society that idealizes and denigrates mothers at the same time. There is an ideal Madonna-like mother—all-giving, self-sacrificing, chaste.

Few if any women can match that ideal, and as they attempt to, they do so at the expense of self. Yet, when a woman wants to get an abortion, she is depicted as the whore: She has sexual appetites; she does not want to sacrifice her well-being for this particular fetus; she is saying "no" to a belief system that nothing is more important for a woman than having a child. In short, she is sending patriarchy into a tailspin.

Deven (1976) has suggested that the socially constructed mystique surrounding motherhood and femininity leads researchers to assume that abortion is traumatic for women, since it goes against their "true nature." Once this sociopolitical assumption is challenged, then abortion may not be as traumatic as assumed. In fact, it may be that the more a woman buys into the societal idea of femininity, the more difficult an experience abortion could be for her. In a study of 120 women who had undergone first-trimester abortions, Alter (1984) reported that androgyny and masculinity were related to a more positive abortion outcome, especially when there was congruence between one's self-image and one's image of a career woman. Our objection to that study is its labeling strong, positive traits as "masculine," rather than redefining self-confidence, interdependence, strong sense of self, and so forth as "feminine" or "human." However, the critical concept is that the more a woman buys into the socially accepted definition of "feminine," the more she accepts her role as an all-sacrificing mother, and the harder it may be for her to deal with an abortion.

In order to understand a woman's decision to have or not to have an abortion, and in order not to victimize her by colluding with the patriarchal model of blaming or pitying the woman, we need to examine some of the sociopolitical factors that most often contribute to the decision to have an abortion.[3] This exploration is not meant to diminish the decision to have an abortion in a case where a woman in an economically stable, loving relationship did not use birth control, but rather to recognize that there are often sociocultural factors contributing to the decision to have or not to have an abortion.

Economic Reasons for Abortion

Many women who choose abortion have concerns about whether they can economically support a child (Hare & Heywood, 1981). The traditional American myth is that if a woman works hard enough, saves enough, is less selfish in what she buys for herself, is able to be emotionally supportive of a man so that she can get married, does not get divorced, and so on and on, then she will be in a better financial situation. If not, she is blamed for her economic deprivation, and then for having an abortion for economic reasons.

Even as more women get to the lower rungs of the corporate ladder (the upper rungs remain off limits), the idea that most women have achieved economic parity with men is a myth. Women are trying to support themselves, and often children, while earning between 54¢ and 59¢ to the white man's dollar (U.S. Bureau of Census, quoted in Faludi, 1991). Faludi cites a number of references indicating that as much as 45% of the pay gap is caused by sex segregation in the work force. To summarize, Faludi reports that the higher-paying jobs are traditionally male, women are discriminated against in that job market, and the majority of women work poverty-level jobs. The economic burden felt by women is a direct result of discrimination.

In addition, the medical crisis in this country takes a huge toll on women and children. If a woman is unable to afford health care, the decision to have a child may be at the expense of being able to provide medical services for herself and, if she is already a parent, for her other children.

This economic climate is even more bleak, given that half of women seeking abortions are already mothers, and nearly 10% of unmarried minors seeking abortions are already mothers (Russo, 1992a). Women are in the position of having to choose between caring for their existing children or giving birth to another child, recognizing the toll that this will take on the children already born.

The primary responsibility of raising children falls most often on women. Women may work, but then they also have the jobs of housekeeping and child rearing (Hochschild, 1989). With the defeat of the Family and Medical Leave Act[4] and the lack of availability of affordable day care, a woman may choose not to have a(nother) child because there is no support in caring for that child while she is working; no job security during maternity leave; no support for her to take a break from the child(ren) (which we know is important for the emotional well-being of mothers and children); and no relief from the cycle of work and child care/housework. In a male model of development, this independent, do–it–alone form of child rearing might be glorified. However, women thrive on mutually enhancing relationships and focus on cooperative efforts (Miller, 1976; Gilligan, 1982). Thus, to support families, the government needs to provide adequate day care, maternity leave, and medical benefits. Women need help in articulating the issues that contribute to their decisions about whether and when to have children, in order to help depersonalize the arguments made by groups who feel that abortion is the choice of "unnatural" women.

Heterosexual Relationships and Abortion

Although the popular myth may be that having an abortion leads to the destruction of the relationship between the adult partners, some studies (Robbins, 1984; Rossi, Bassi, & Delfino, 1988) indicate that difficult relationships precede the abortion, and thus may be a factor in the decision. In one study, single women who had abortions were less tied to their partners before pregnancy than women who chose to have babies (Robbins, 1984). An abortion did not necessarily trigger the decision to end a relationship. Interestingly, however, those women who had strong relationships had more of an emotional reaction to their abortions than did women with weaker relationships. This study would argue that a woman may be more likely to choose to have a baby within the context of a loving relationship, and less willing to have a baby in a nonsupportive relationship. In a French study, Pierre, Jourdain, and Lecorps (1981) found that 33% of their sample chose abortion because of romantic or social problems. As discussed in the preceding section on economics, it is economically difficult for many women to raise children alone, and women with the weaker relationships may not trust or choose to have the relationship continue. Furthermore, if a woman develops best in mutually enhancing relationships (Jordan, Kaplan, Miller, Stiver, & Surrey, 1990), then she may recognize that a weak relationship will not be useful to her development; she may decide that if she wants a child, she should wait until she is either in a more satisfying relationship or on her own.

Another largely unexplored issue is the relationship between wife battering and the decision to have an abortion. In the United States, 25% of families have a history of woman abuse (Pagelow, 1981), and more than half of all homeless women are fleeing domestic violence (Fund for a Feminist Majority, personal communication, 1991). Conventional wisdom is that the more children a woman has, the harder it is for her to leave her partner. A battered woman is often fearful that if she leaves, her partner will beat or kill her. Furthermore, many batterers are particularly abusive to pregnant women, and the abuse often gets worse as a woman becomes more focused on her pregnancy and the coming of a new baby. The decision to share with her partner that she is pregnant thus puts the battered woman at further risk. Another consideration is the welfare of the child, whom the mother may feel she cannot protect if she has to escape from her partner. The *Planned Parenthood of South Eastern Pennsylvania v. Casey* (1992) U.S. Supreme Court ruling places battered women in Pennsylvania at particular risk by allowing abortions to be on public record, and thus accessible to their battering partners, who may not have been informed about the pregnancy.

Rape

When we speak of rape, we are including rape within families, as well as rape by men known and unknown to the women. Statistics indicate that one out of three women will be forced to have sex without consent during her lifetime, meaning that women are as likely to be raped as to be divorced (Boston Women's Health Book Collective, 1984). We also know that only 1 in 10 rapes is ever reported to authorities (Fund for a Feminist Majority, personal communication, 1991). Add to this that there is a 90% chance of pregnancy without use of birth control (Boston Women's Health Book Collective, 1984), and we can assume that there are many women, most who remain silent about the cause, who are seeking abortions because their pregnancies resulted from rape.

The trauma of rape, the restrictions placed on abortion, and the lack of support women receive in the legal system when they decide to prosecute can all contribute to the silence that may exacerbate the trauma. Only 1% of women in a French study (Pierre et al., 1981) acknowledged rape as their reason for abortion, whereas the Planned Parenthood League of Massachusetts (1991) reports that 5.4% of all reported rapes end in pregnancy. And yet, if we take the lower statistic and extrapolate to Koop's (1989) data, we would end up with 15,000 abortions per year as a result of rape.

Failure of Birth Control

In spite of statements to the contrary, there are no safe and effective forms of birth control available in the United States today. Each form of birth control has its drawbacks, and actual failure rates are higher than the reported theoretical failure rates (see Boston Women's Health Book Collective, 1984, for details). Although any method of birth control is better than no method, many women become pregnant in spite of using birth control. By extrapolating from Koop's statistics, we can conclude that although 12% of women do not use contraceptives, 54% of births are unintended, which supports the idea that many women become pregnant even when using contraception. As with other women's health issues, little research is being undertaken on safe, inexpensive forms of birth control.[5]

PSYCHOLOGICAL EFFECTS OF ABORTION

Up in Pennsylvania, I met a little man,
not Rumpelstiltskin, at all, at all . . .
he took the fullness that love began.

Returning north, even the sky grew thin
Like a high window looking nowhere.
The road was as flat as a sheet of tin.

Somebody who should have been born is gone.

Yes, woman, such logic will lead
to loss without death. Or say what you meant,
You coward . . . this baby that I bleed.
—From "The Abortion," by Anne Sexton[6]

The purpose of a discussion of reproductive rights and of male power and dominance is to highlight that the responsibility for maintaining or terminating pregnancy needs to rest with the woman. It does not, however, address the issues that arise for that woman once she takes on the responsibility of choice. The issue of abortion is a complex moral dilemma, pitting a woman's own needs and understanding of her life against the possibility of the life she holds within her. The word "fetus," rather than "baby" or "unborn baby," is used by most pro-choice advocates as a political statement emphasizing the lack of viability of this being. However, the terminology chosen is connected to its context. Most women who have experienced a wanted pregnancy, regardless of their belief in reproductive rights, think of that fetus as a baby. A miscarriage is experienced and grieved for as the loss of a baby. A pregnant woman and her significant others feel for "the baby's" kick, for the stirring of the unborn child. An expectant mother often delights in hearing the heartbeat of her "baby." When the experience of fetus as baby is denied for some women, because of the political implications, much of the complexity of the abortion decision is lost.

The issue of pregnancy and abortion is unique, unparalleled by any other situation that we are aware of. Inside of a woman's body, another person is growing, taking in food, releasing waste, supporting a heartbeat, sucking a thumb. Yet this new life exists within another life, a life that is necessary to sustain the other. If one respects the boundaries of women, refuses to violate women, and sees a woman's body as her own and not governed by men or the state, then the woman's life takes precedence over the new life, and she alone must make the decision about whether to continue or terminate the pregnancy. Many women make this decision with the awareness that they believe in this choice, opt for abortion, and also believe that the life of a baby is involved. A client, who is a staunch pro-choice activist, was horrified when her partner discussed aborting if the fetus was male, saying, "How can you kill a baby just because it's a boy?" Although this statement appears to be a contradiction, it probably is not: Her world incorporates the inherent contradictions and complexities of "life within a life" with full respect for the choice belonging to the woman.

The argument that a woman should not have an abortion because it can be emotionally difficult for her is the patronizing arm of patriarchy. But even if there were evidence that abortions are traumatic, the assumption that women have to be protected against their feelings by laws that would disallow abortions is disrespectful of women's adult decision-making capabilities, resilience, and responsibility both to make decisions and to deal with the consequences. Women's emotions, particularly those representing ambivalence or conflict, have customarily been viewed as "pathological" in our patriarchal society, which values rationality over emotion. In our pro-natalist culture, reproduction is considered a woman's obligation.

In the United States, the politicization of abortion has focused on power dynamics for at least two centuries. Legislation in the latter half of the 19th century placed the power for authorizing abortions strictly in the hands of a woman's personal physician (who was almost always male). It was not until the 1950s that this became a mental health issue. At this time, psychiatric authorization was required for legalized abortion; in order to have a safe, legal abortion, it was necessary to present oneself as being "at risk" psychologically. Women with money have always been able to choose for themselves, circumventing this humiliating process by traveling abroad. Women without such means were forced to pretend to be psychologically distraught. Many, then, became confused by the prevailing dominant view that obvious sexual behavior and resulting pregnancy could only lead to emotional conflicts, and that such emotional conflicts are signs of serious psychological distress. And then there certainly have been women with valid medical and/or psychological disorders who would be harmed by continuing their pregnancies. The point is that all women without the personal financial means to take matters in their own hands were lumped in the same "psychologically at-risk" group in order to obtain this authorization. As the power to make an abortion decision passed from the private domain of the woman and her physician (still a one-down position for the patient) to the public domain of hospital review boards and federal and state legislatures, women were at the mercy of not one, but several "authorities" with institutionalized power and status. In this nondominant position, women's feelings as well as their behaviors were judged to be "dangerous," needing legal control and protection.

The conflicting feelings, including relief, guilt, and grief, that many women experience in regard to abortion are rarely pathological. (By "pathological," we mean of lasting intensity and duration, with harmful impact on a woman's subsequent functioning and relationships.) They comprise the normal, psychological-growth-producing ambivalence or suffering that any adult experiences throughout the lifespan when dealing with moral dilemmas. Women, who have been socialized to acknowledge and tolerate their emotions to a greater degree than males, may be less defended than males against both the experience and the expression of emotional conflicts. For women, then, experiencing and expressing conflicted feelings and ambivalence can be more a sign of health than of pathology.

Because of the politicization of abortion, women are in a bind about acknowledging their normal ambivalence. Should they support a woman's right to choose and still talk about their experience of a life inside of them, they may feel as if they are betraying their connection with abortion rights; at the same time, they may fear being misinterpreted, as their statements may be seen as supportive of the anti-choice groups. If they have expressed anti-choice sentiments, they may fear that contemplating abortion will alienate them from their support group. This politicization can silence women, leaving their ambivalence buried and unresolved.

Physical and Psychological Difficulties Following Abortion[7]

A review of the literature on both physical and mental health sequelae of abortion indicates relatively benign, short-term effects for the vast majority of women (Lemkau, 1991; Turell, Armsworth, & Gaa, 1990; Hittner, 1987; Adler et al., 1992; Russo, 1992a). Koop (1989) has noted that infertility, miscarriage, premature birth, and psychological trauma are no more frequent among women who have abortions than among women in the general population. Importantly, the risk of death from abortion has decreased more than fivefold since abortion was legalized (Gold, 1990). Gold reports that the risk of death from legal abortion is now less than 1 death per 100,000, making it less of a risk than death from an injection of penicillin.

The literature on the psychological effects of abortion is both vast and scanty. In any examination of this research, it is important to consider the research design. As reported by Koop (1989) and Haber (1991), many of the studies lack representative samples, focus only on clinical populations and short-term effects, and lack control groups of women who chose not to have abortions. Thus, we must be careful not to generalize the conclusions of these studies to all women. In an attempt to differentiate valid research findings from political rhetoric, an American Psychological Association panel reviewed the methodologically soundest studies of women's responses to legal abortion. This review shows that

> . . . the legal termination of an unwanted pregnancy does not have severe or lasting negative effects on most women undergoing the procedure, especially when performed in the first trimester of pregnancy. Studies of women's psychological responses before and after an abortion show that distress levels drop immediately after an abortion and are lower several weeks later than they were before the abortion. (Public Interest Directorate, 1987)

In a more recent review and study by Lemkau (1991), the response most strongly reported was that of relief, although the respondents noted some mild distress—experienced as small to moderate degrees of guilt, anger, anxiety, and depression, and small levels of concern about future relationships and pregnancies—in the first 3 months after their abortions. Russo (1992a) tracked the emotional health and reproductive lives of 5,295 women of childbearing age over an 8-year span and found the "post-abortion syndrome to be just a myth" (p. 1). She reports that the women with the poorest self-esteem were those who had unwanted births, not the ones who chose to have children or sought abortions. There was no link between abortion and mental health, but there was a link between unwanted children and mental health.

This is not to say that abortion is psychologically risk-free. As clinicians, we know that some women do come to therapy because of difficulties following an abortion. We see other women and couples years later, and only then can relate some of the issues they present to the previous abortion experience. Current research estimates the range of adverse psychological reactions to abortion to be anywhere from 0.5% to 15% over time spans of 1 week to 10 years after abortion (Public Interest Directorate, 1987). Psychological studies have found that those women who do experience psychological distress after abortion often have a history of emotional and relationship problems. They may have felt coerced by family or life circumstances to abort, received little support from significant others, or held strong religious convictions prohibiting abortion. These findings confirm Koop's (1989) report that strongly held personal values, ambivalence about abortion, excessive pressure from others, termination of an originally desired pregnancy, health issues, a late second-trimester decision, and lack of personal support are the primary issues related to negative psychological sequelae of abortion.

Considerations for Adolescents

There has been particular attention in the press to the psychological impact of abortion on adolescents. Over one-quarter of the abortions performed in this country are performed on adolescents (*New York Times,* 1989). The issue of legislated parental notification is a major component of anti-abortion legislation efforts. Indeed, there are special issues associated with adolescent pregnancy, primarily regarding adolescents' physical, economic, and emotional dependency on others for caretaking and survival. Rickel (1989), for example, observed that teen mothers were repeatedly surprised at how much their babies restricted their lifestyle—an indication of adolescent naiveté about what parenting entails. After reviewing the literature, Haber (1991) reports that the psychological risks concomitant with an adolescent's completion of a pregnancy are substantially greater than the risks of adolescent abortion, and that there is no evidence to indicate that adolescents are not able to make mature and reasoned decisions regarding abortion.

Given what we now know about cognitive development, adolescents may require different decision-making models than adults. Gordon (1990) proposes that adolescents who are able to engage in formal reasoning can benefit from abstract discussions, whereas those who are unable to engage in formal reasoning can profit from concrete decision-making tasks (such as actual role playing, babysitting, etc.). How paradoxical it is that the same adolescents who are viewed as too immature to make an abortion decision are considered mature enough to be parents!

CLINICAL IMPLICATIONS OF ABORTION ISSUES

The clinical implications of abortion issues are considered in two different contexts: (1) helping women with their decision making during pregnancy, and (2) consideration and incorporation of abortion issues into therapy when the abortion happened years earlier.

Abortion Counseling

The premise of any psychotherapy approach is to facilitate and empower clients to consider multifaceted perspectives, so that they can make decisions that feel right to them and can live with the consequences of their decisions. Responsible self-determination is a major priority. The most important task for the therapist is to advocate for and support the rights of clients to make their own decisions about abortion. The literature indicates that in addition to preparing women for the actual abortion procedure and for the short-term emotional bereavement that may follow the procedure, addressing issues of ambivalence, excessive pressure from others, and religious beliefs is critical (Lemkau, 1991).

The context of the pregnancy is a major factor for abortion counseling. Is the pregnancy an accident in a long-term relationship? The result of a casual fling? The result of rape or incest? Is abortion being considered because of economic or political or medical factors? Is this the woman's first abortion? What is the developmental life stage of the woman? In other words, what does this *mean* to the woman? The exploration of the meaning of the conception, the pregnancy, and the consideration of abortion to the woman calls for paying particular attention to her ingrained beliefs and values, as well as to the effects of her socioeconomic class, her ethnicity, the region of the country or world from which she comes, and her family system. And yet time is critical, so this exploration of meanings must be intense and focused. Moreover, it is important that the therapist be open to supporting the client's views about abortion while exposing her to (not indoctrinating her in) broader perspectives and the connections among her personal well-being, her abortion dilemma, and relationship and sociocultural power issues. Techniques that may help clients organize their thoughts within these time limits may include discussion, role playing, guided imagery, genograms, informational interviewing, brainstorming, and the like.

The pressure of time may either help or hinder the process of therapy. Some women find this pressure intolerable, and they are not able to work through these kinds of issues fully until *after* they have obtained abortions. Their decision may appear precipitous to others, but time usually proves their intuitive actions to be right for them. There is no real evidence that these women suffer any differently from those who used more reflection and care in their decision making. Again, this may be a reflection of a lesser degree of underlying ambivalence; a woman may intuitively know that she must have an abortion, without processing the reasons and possible outcomes, and she may need to act before she can attend to this processing. Some other women with more ambivalence freeze and want to rely on others to guide them into decision making. These women may benefit from intense, short-term multimodalities of counseling—group, individual, and family. Still others are able to tolerate their ambivalence and want to use whatever time is available to consider and reflect upon all the related issues.

When a woman wants her baby, but an abortion is being considered because of possible birth defects, the health issues of the mother, marital difficulties, or economic factors, the decision-making process may be more heart-wrenching. If she really wants to have the baby but feels that she cannot for "practical" or "reality-based" reasons, all alternatives must be thoroughly explored. The important focus must be on her getting in touch with her own true feelings and wishes, so that she can make a decision in accordance with these rather than succumbing to others' pressure. She must choose for herself, but for a woman, this means exploring and including the impact of her decision on others. After responsible processing—which most likely includes consideration of, for example, religious influences, financial factors, all possible consequences of abortion or having a baby, adoption, and perhaps talking to others—the woman's choice must still be supported, even if the therapist does not agree with it. However, within the context of a trusting, empathic relationship, the therapist often has the opportunity to suggest broader perspectives and alternatives for a client's consideration. Literature on the therapeutic relationship suggests that a powerful working alliance begins from the first moment of contact (including the setting up of an initial appointment), and that even though the scope and context of contact may be limited, the influence process is already in place (Okun, 1990, 1992).

There is a fine line between appropriate and inappropriate influencing within the context of a therapeutic relationship. Joffe (1986) has analyzed three ideologies competing for therapists' loyalties: (1) the family planning establishment, emphasizing the medicalization of contraception; (2) feminism, insisting on reproductive self-determination; and (3) the "pro-family" faction of the New Right, reasserting parental control over adolescent sexuality and patriarchal control over adult women. Observing clients and counselors in a variety of agencies, Joffe noted that there could be a great deal of strain for counselors if there was a discrepancy between their personal views and the cardinal therapeutic rule of supportive but neutral and respectful decision-making facilitation. Because as therapists we are human beings, we are never really neutral. But we can own our views and respect others' differing views. We can express our views and perspectives as our own personal ones, and not expect others to share or own them too.

One woman in her early 40s who had married late and was then delighted with her pregnancy was devastated when she lost her baby during the amniocentesis procedure. She subsequently became pregnant, did not have amniocentesis, and then delivered a baby with severe Down's syndrome. In her third pregnancy she had amniocentesis, which indicated birth defects, and she agonized over whether to have an abortion. Her husband did not want to have another handicapped child, and her parents and siblings also put pressure on her to have the abortion. However, it was not easy for her to find a doctor who would perform an abortion in the second trimester. After much going back and forth about her yearning for another baby, her guilt about wanting a healthy baby and not "loving enough" a handicapped baby, and her religious views, this woman chose to have an abortion. Her therapist was as conflicted as she was, and could only be of help by joining with her in her agonizing and attempting to help her by clarifying the emerging and underlying thoughts and feelings. There was no clear-cut answer for this client, and she indeed ended up making a decision that she felt was best for the others (her husband, the child she already had, her parents, and her friends and other supporters), even though she was not sure it was best for her personally. Much later, she reported that she felt living with the pain of bereavement was better for both her and these others than the alternative of having two handicapped children. What was important to her was that she took responsibility for her choice. She told her therapist that what she benefited from in the therapy was the empowerment to make a choice. This process of choosing within an effective helping relationship was more important to her own growth and well-being than the content of her choice.

Some of the issues that often come up during the preabortion counseling involve boundaries: whom to tell and whom to avoid telling. Should the sexual partner be a part of the decision making? Lemkau (1991) was surprised to learn from her sample of 73 women students in the health care professions who had had abortions that those who either had not consulted their sexual partners or had pursued abortion in spite of partner opposition had a more favorable postabortion adjustment than those who had consulted and received support for their abortion decision from their sexual partners. Perhaps this finding indicates that those women who assume that any choice about themselves and their lives is their responsibility fare better than those who are unsure as to whose responsibility this type of choice is. The finding may be more indicative of a woman's self-esteem and self-responsibility than of a woman's feelings about the specific issue of abortion. Lemkau (1991) suggests that those women who are less ambivalent about abortion require less "permission" from significant others, although everyone benefits from others' support.

A therapist needs to consider the short- and long-term implications of pregnancy and possible abortion for a woman's relationship, particularly if it is ongoing. What are the advantages and disadvantages to the client for telling her family and peers? From whom is she likely to receive support? If she is married with children, does she want to share this with these children? If so, when and how? The focus in therapy must be on the process of decision-making and support of choice, not on the advocacy of a particular outcome. As therapists, we need to be sure that we support our clients who choose not to have abortions, who decide to parent themselves, or who decide to give their babies up for adoption.

A distraught 40-year-old woman recently consulted one of us about her 23-year-old cocaine-addicted daughter with a psychiatric history, who had become pregnant by her drug dealer. The first trimester was ending, and the daughter refused to have an abortion. She lived with her mother, was not working, and expected her mother to support her financially and to help raise the baby. The grandmother-to-be, having raised this daughter as a struggling single parent, had already recognized her own enabling proclivities and was not about to engage in further enabling. She was also very concerned about her daughter's substance abuse, lifestyle, and physical and mental health. Her daughter's therapist seemed to be inducted into this mother–daughter system, in that she too expected the mother both to financially support the daughter and to agree to raise the grandchild. In fact, the therapist phoned the mother daily to demand payment for daily sessions, insisting that the pregnant daughter was "suicidal" but refusing any outside consultation or hospitalization. The consultation focused on disentangling the involved parties so that each could look at her own expectations and participation. An immediate psychiatric evaluation was obtained for the pregnant daughter; community services were arranged in the form of group counseling for both the prospective mother and grandmother; and the daughter's individual therapist was urged to seek her own supervisory consultation. The consulting therapist served as a coordinator, case manager, and advocate for both the daughter and the mother. Although she personally thought that this young woman would be unable to take the responsibility for raising a child, and that the mother would be better off taking care of herself for a change rather than adding another caretaking responsibility, she was careful to focus first on a fact-finding exploration of all the elements in this situation and then on what decisions each person could make for herself. As of this writing, it appears that the daughter will continue her pregnancy with close medical supervision in a community-based independent living situation. Whether she will choose to raise the baby or give it up for adoption is not yet known. The grandmother is working through her anxiety, guilt, and anger, but also learning how to be emotionally supportive of her daughter while not taking responsibility for her life decisions.

Adolescent clients seem to benefit from individual sessions as well as family sessions. In the individual sessions, it is helpful to use strategies that allow them to foresee possible immediate, intermediate, and long-term consequences of their choice. This affords the therapist the opportunity to educate clients about possible consequences, as well as to teach effective decision-making strategies. As mentioned earlier, awareness of adolescent styles of decision-making based on their cognitive development is important, as is caution about the possibility of an adult therapist's having undue influence on a young adolescent. One helpful strategy might be to ask the adolescent client to visualize herself at a crossroads, and walk her down the road of abortion as well as the road of childbirth (including, then, the road of parenting and the road of adoption), elucidating all of the possible happenings and ramifications. This may elicit distortions based on the adolescent's unmet needs or her insistence on denying needs and difficulties (i.e., there is "no problem"). If time allows, talking to other teenage women who are of the same race and class but who have made various choices can be helpful. Often, visits can be arranged to teenage mother groups or facilities for pregnant teens.

A more recent issue that women have to contend with is the aggressive anti-abortion picketing around abortion clinics.

One client, who felt very sure about her decision to have an abortion, reported afterwards that the most traumatic aspect for her were the jeers and name calling she experienced after her abortion. Although her companion tried to protect her, she found herself feeling ill and faint as she tried to break through the crowds. Although we had talked about this possibility prior to her abortion, the actual experience was more devastating than she could have anticipated. It took several sessions relating the feelings of being scapegoated and pilloried to her similar experience of being the "bad girl" in her family of origin before she was able to understand and accept her vulnerability to this particular type of situation.

Postabortion Counseling

Immediately after the abortion, women may need some acknowledgment and support for their bereavement. If a woman is in ongoing therapy when the pregnancy occurs or enters therapy after the abortion, it is indeed likely that much of the immediate postabortion work may pertain to the emotional aftermath. If the woman has consulted a therapist for help with the abortion decision, she may choose to return for some follow-up work, or she may feel that she does not want or need to do so. Sometimes a telephone inquiry from the therapist will suffice. The door can be left open for further work, whether it involves the abortion, the relationship within which the pregnancy occurred, or other issues.

One area that is rarely mentioned, and that to our knowledge has never been researched, is the impact of the abortion on issues presented years later in therapy. A previous abortion may become a presenting issue years later if difficulties with conception, pregnancy, or power struggles in relationships ensue. The client may assume a link between a previous abortion and subsequent conception and pregnancy difficulties; however, since the legalization of abortions, this is unlikely. Women who have not worked through their ambivalence or guilt about an abortion or who underwent an earlier illegal abortion may associate later difficulties with previous abortion experiences. When abortion issues are unfinished business for a woman, one must consider the developmental and contextual circumstances.

> For example, one client who had had a secret, back-room abortion in the late 1960s, just before abortion was legalized, married in her late 30s and was distraught over her inability to conceive. Raised a Roman Catholic, she had harbored guilt for over 20 years and had never discussed her abortion with anyone other than one sister, who had supported her through this ordeal. When she was referred to a therapist by her fertility specialist, her "terrible secret" was revealed. Although her scar tissue could have been caused by the abortion, this was not necessarily so, and it took her quite some time to work through her guilt and shame so that she could share this secret with her husband and reduce her anxiety. Bereavement work included writing a letter to the unborn baby, reading this letter to the grave of an unknown infant in a local cemetery, reliving her abortion decision via role plays and guided imagery, and engaging in cognitive restructuring of unexplored assumptions and beliefs. This gave her a space to get in touch with her anger at the *illegality* of the abortion, rather than the abortion itself. This same woman became enraged when the Supreme Court began to deliberate the repeal of the *Roe v. Wade* decision, as she got in touch with her anger at having been forced to have an illegal procedure that could have jeopardized her health and life. She became quite an activist for the pro-choice movement! Her impassioned concern was for the right to safe abortion.

Although a previous abortion may not be spontaneously discussed in the beginning of therapy, a genogram or careful history taking is likely to reveal whether or not there have been pregnancies, miscarriages, stillbirths, and abortions. We feel that it is important for therapists to encourage women to tell their stories when these past events are uncovered, to hear these stories in a supportive way, and to help women to understand their pregnancies and abortion choices in a broader as well as an intrapersonal context. Was abortion a woman's choice? What were the pressures she experienced? What were the circumstances and relationships, as well as family system variables, involved? How does she feel the effects of this decision?

Often, when previous abortion issues have current salience, there are significant underlying relationship power struggles.

One couple with a 4-year-old son came in for couples counseling. They both engaged in serious verbal fighting, and the major issues were their roles and responsibilities. It eventually became clear that the husband resented being "tied down" with a wife and son; he felt "trapped" and not ready for all of this responsibility. Later, the wife mentioned that she had become pregnant by him prior to their marriage and had had an abortion. She had felt so guilty and upset about this that she had insisted they get married and have a baby. Although he advocated for her to have the abortion, he also experienced guilt, which led him to marry before he felt he was ready. When the spouses were helped to rewrite their narratives about the early pregnancy, and thus to understand that the wife too was "trapped" and that they had both participated in the abortion choice, they were able to define their relationship roles and rules and to attain a different, more egalitarian level of collaboration. The therapist nonjudgmentally helped them to understand the religious and cultural pressures they had experienced, and to mourn their loss (of the earlier baby as well as of their freer lifestyle), so they could stop blaming each other and let go of their past resentments.

In another case, a professional couple in their late 40s came for divorce counseling after the husband's son from his first marriage died of cancer. The wife, was devastated by her husband's blame and abandonment, and wanted desperately to be of support. He was adamant that their marital problems had nothing to do with his son's death, and maintained that the relationship difficulties had always been there. In the third couples session, he accused her of having had two abortions against his wishes—one prior to their marriage, and one right after his son died, when he had already left her. They each told different versions of the decisions to abort. As the wife listened to her husband's version, it became painfully clear to her that her husband had, even prior to his son's death, no consideration or concern for her health and needs, and that his tacit agenda for this marriage really had been to have another child. She had experienced no ambivalence about either abortion decision, although she would have liked to have a child with him in better circumstances. The first time, she had had an abortion because they had not yet decided to marry and she already was raising two youngsters from a previous marriage. The second time, more recently, she had had an abortion because he had emotionally and physically left the marriage without any discussion or processing. Focusing on these abortion issues enabled this wife to feel stronger about her own perceptions and perspectives, as well as to see the enormity of her marital relationship power struggles (over her career and earnings, child rearing, and lifestyle). As a result, she could begin to let go of him and to mourn the loss of her dream about him, her marriage, and any possible children of this marriage. She c_____ had made the right choice, even though, again, _____ have another child in a strong marriage. She was indeed compassionate and sensitive to her husband's pain, but she was secure in taking responsibility for her body and decisions about what was best for her health, for her life, and for her existing children.

Whereas many of our female clients chose to have abortions and are dealing with their partners' anger about the decision, some of our clients feel that they were required, without their consent, to have abortions.

One client recalled that when she was a teenager, her mother, a single parent, did not discuss alternatives to abortion with her. Instead, she took her out of state to get a legal abortion. Her mother's fury over her pregnancy silenced her, so that she never told medical personnel about her indecision. Only 22 years later, in therapy, did she begin to connect that experience with her present problems. The issues surrounding her abortion were manifested by her resignation to her husband's wish not to have children, without ever examining her own desire to bear children. Her rationale was that her abortion, and subsequent unrelated medical problems, meant that she was not supposed to be a mother. In her marriage, she replayed the initial powerlessness that she experienced during the abortion, and found herself feeling depressed and angry with no context for her feelings. Therapy helped her both to revisit that traumatic time, and to use the voice that she could not have then to renegotiate her present relationship.

Although the examples above focus on couples therapy, there has also been some excellent work in group therapy with postabortion women (J. Tyndall, personal communication, July, 1992). In a setting where women can empathically connect with one another's experience, the group provides acknowledgment of what a woman's circumstances were at the time she made the choice to have an abortion, and affirms along with her that she made the best choice available for her at that time in her life.

As with any milestone event in a relationship, individual history, or family history, we can listen carefully, nonjudgmentally, and empathically to clients' abortion stories, in order to help them to understand and connect the emotional ramifications of the event with what is going on currently.

THE THERAPIST IN THE LARGER SOCIETY

We all have our own personal biases. Some of us who are therapists believe that abortion is not an acceptable alternative; others believe that it is. Whatever these personal biases, as therapists we must support our clients' choices on this issue. There are times when our own personal values, attitudes, and beliefs interfere with our ability to support clients' choices that are antithetical to our own views. When do we refer such clients to someone else? When do we acknowledge to our clients that we are experiencing conflicts and cannot be genuinely supportive of their choices, or even their rights to make their own choices? And how do we respect our clients' autonomy, so that we do not even subtly use the power of the therapeutic relationship to impose our values on them?

One supervisee reported that she could not accept her client's desire to have an abortion. This clinician believed this was an immoral act, and that it would be "wrong" for her even to support the discussion of the issue. When it was pointed out to the supervisee that this was a true clinical ethical dilemma, she and the supervisor became very troubled. They finally agreed that the therapist needed to tell the client about her personal feelings and discomforts, and to encourage the client strongly to consult a colleague who was able to deal comfortably with the issue of abortion. The difficulty was helping this clinician to communicate this message in a genuinely caring, respectful manner, allowing the client the freedom to differ and offering them both the opportunity to continue their therapy together, with these acknowledged differing views. Another supervisee in this seminar group pointed out that she also believes that abortion is murder, but that she has struggled to come to the point where she can support the rights of women to make their own choices about their bodies and reproductive rights. The point is that while we need to be supportive of women's choices even if they differ from our own views, we are never neutral. In other issues, such as violence, we take an ethical stance that the choice to be violent is not acceptable.

Feminist psychotherapy has heightened our consciousness: "The personal is political." Some therapists choose to intervene in the larger society,[8] through professional associations, demonstrations, political campaigning, letter writing, and so forth. Others choose to be active by providing volunteer work, educational opportunities, mentoring, and supervising. As therapists, we have personal, professional, and political power; we need to monitor ourselves, our colleagues, and our professions continuously to ensure that our clients receive treatment characterized by fairness, integrity, and ethical responsibility. The bottom line is to recognize the use and abuses of power at the individual, couple, family, and larger system levels, and to acknowledge, support, and empower our clients to value themselves and to be supported in their endeavors to be in charge of their own bodies and lives.

Herman (1992) argues that political movements provide necessary support for therapists who engage in the front-line struggles for human rights. As advocates for women's sexual and reproductive self-determination, we need the love, understanding, and support of our own families, friends, peers, professional associations, and political movements to fuel our commitment to liberation and human rights. Thus, it is our responsibility to support these movements actively in whatever ways are congruent with our selves.

NOTES

1. Reproductive rights involve a much broader spectrum of freedom than abortion rights. As we discuss in the section on race, class, and gender, reproductive rights include the freedom to raise one's children, as well as to determine whether to remain pregnant and bear children.
2. We's like to thank Dr. Beverly Greene for sharing these ideas with Marsha Pravder Mirkin.
3. Teenage pregnancy is not included in this chapter, as it is covered elsewhere in this volume (see Lappin, Chapter 21).
4. Since this chapter was written, the Family and Medical Leave Act was passed by the Clinton administration.
5. The November–December 1992 issue of *Network News: National Women's Health Network* includes a critique of the use of Norplant to force women to use birth control without their informed consent.
6. From Sexton (1962). Copyright 1962 by Anne Sexton, renewed 1990 by Linda G. Sexton. Reprinted by permission of Houghton Mifflin Co. All rights reserved.
7. This section does not cover studies of RU–486, a chemical abortion technique illegal in the United States and targeted in this country by anti-abortion groups, but available in Europe. Callum, Klein, Dumble, and Raymond (1992) provide an excellent discussion of the benefits and risks associated with RU–486.
8. In recent years, several groups of family therapists have attempted to intervene in the larger system concerning the issue of abortion. The Public Conversations Project (Becker, Chasin, Chasin, Herzig, & Roth, 1992) is an attempt by family therapists to foster dialogue on abortion, and thus find common ground among people who have identified themselves as pro-choice or pro-life. The American Association of Marital and Family Therapy (AAMFT) ad hoc committee on reproductive rights, chaired by Elana Katz, was an effort to advocate for

AAMFT's taking a pro-choice policy stance. The Women's Institute and Family Policy Committee at the American Family Therapy Academy encouraged members to have the organization's pro-choice statement published in local newspapers.

REFERENCES

Adler, N., David, H., Major, B., Roth, S., Russo, N. F., & Wyatt, J. E. (1992). Psychological factors in abortion. *American Psychologist, 47*(10), 1194–1204.

Alter, R. (1984). Abortion outcome as a function of sex role identification. *Psychology of Women Quarterly, 8*(3), 211–233.

Boston Globe. (1987, May 10). Leaving mother behind, p. A26.

Boston Women's Health Book Collective. (1984). *The new our bodies, ourselves.* New York: Simon & Schuster.

Callum, J., Klein, R., Dumble, L., & Raymond, J. (1992, September–October). RU-486: A dialogue. *Network News: National Women's Health Network,* p. 1.

Chasin, L., Chasin, R., Herzig, M., Roth, S., & Becker, C. (1991, Winter). The citizen clinician: The family therapist in the public forum. *American Family Therapy Academy Newsletter,* pp. 36–42.

Deven, F. (1976). Sociopsychological aspects of induced abortion. *Tijdschrift voor Sociale Wetenschappen, 21*(3), 241–264.

Dytrych, Z., Matejcek, Z., Schuller, V., David, H., & Friedman, H. (1975). Children born to women denied abortion. *Family Planning Perspectives, 7*(3), 165–171.

Faludi, S. (1991). *Backlash: The undeclared war against American women.* New York: Crown.

Fuchs, R. G. (1982). Crimes against children in 19th-century France. *Law and Human Behavior, 6*(3–4), 237–259.

Gilligan, C. (1982). *In a different voice.* Cambridge, MA: Harvard University Press.

Glen, K. B. (1978). Abortion in the courts: A laywoman's historical guide to the new disaster area. *Feminist Studies, 4*(1), 1–26.

Gold, R. B. (1990). *Abortion and women's health: A turning point for America.* New York: Alan Guttmacher Institute.

Goodrich, T. J. (1991). *Women and power: Perspectives for family therapy.* New York: Norton.

Gordon, D. E. (1990). Decision-making about pregnancy and contraception. *American Journal of Orthopsychiatry, 60*(3), 346–357.

Haber, S. (1991, Winter). Psychology and reproductive choice: A model speech. *Psychology of Women Newsletter,* pp. 6–9.

Hare, M. J., & Heywood, J. (1981). Counseling needs of women seeking abortions. *Journal of Biosocial Science, 13*(3), 269–273.

Hayler, B. (1979). Abortion. *Signs, 5*(2), 307–323.

Herman, J. (1977, January–February). Fighting sterilization abuse. *Science for the People,* pp. 17–19.

Herman, J. (1992). *Trauma and recovery.* New York: Basic Books.

Hittner, A. (1987). Feelings of well-being before and after an abortion. *American Mental Health Counselors Association Journal, 9*(2), 98–104.

Hochschild, A. (1989). *The second shift*. New York: Viking Press.

Joffe, C. (1986). What abortion counselors want from their clients. *Social Problems, 26*(1), 112–121.

Jordan, J. V., Kaplan, A. G., Miller, J. B., Stiver, I. P., & Surrey, J. L. (1991). *Women's growth in connection: Writings from the Stone Center*. New York: Guilford Press.

Koop, C. E. (1989, December 11). *The federal role in determining the medical and psychological impact of abortions on women* (HRNO1013). Testimony given to the Committee on Government Operations, U.S. House of Representatives, 101st Congress, 2nd Session.

Kramer, M. (1975). Legal abortion among New York City residents: An analysis according to socioeconomic and demographic characteristics. *Family Planning Perspectives, 7*(3), 128–137.

Lacayo, R. (1992, May 4). Abortion: The future is already here. *Time*, pp. 27–32.

Lazarus, A. (1985). Psychiatric sequelae of legalized elective first trimester abortion. *Journal of Psychosomatic Obstetrics and Gynecology, 4*(3), 141–150.

Lemkau, J. P. (1991). Post-abortion adjustment of health care professionals in training. *American Journal of Orthopsychiatry, 61*(1), 92–102.

Martinez, L. A. (1992, November–December). Caramba, our Anglo sisters just didn't get it. *Network News: National Women's Health Network*, pp. 1–5.

Miller, J. B. (1976). *Toward a new psychology of women*. Boston: Beacon Press.

Mohanty, C. T., Russo, A., & Torres, L. (1991). Introduction. In C. T. Mohanty, A. Russo, & L. Torres (Eds.), *Third World women and the politics of feminism*. Bloomington: Indiana University Press.

New York Times. (1989, July 16). p. 1.

Okun, B. F. (1990). *Seeking connections in psychotherapy*. San Francisco: Jossey-Bass.

Okun, B. F. (1992). *Effective helping: Interviewing and counseling techniques* (4th ed.). Pacific Grove, CA: Brooks/Cole.

Pagelow, M. (1981). *Women battering: Victims and their experiences*. Newbury Park, CA: Sage.

Pierre, M. T., Jourdain, A., & Lecorps, P. (1981). Voluntary termination of pregnancy. *Revue Française des Affaires Sociales, 35*(2), 7–54.

Planned Parenthood League of Massachusetts. (1991). *Questions and answers about abortion*. Boston: Author.

Planned Parenthood of South Eastern Pennsylvania v. Casey, 91-744, 91-902 (1992).

Prescott, J. (1975). Abortion or the unwanted child: A choice for a humanistic society. *Humanist, 35*(2), 11–15.

Public Interest Directorate, American Psychological Association. (1987, December 2). *The psychological sequelae of abortion*. Testimony presented to the Office of the U.S. Surgeon General.

Relf v. Weinberger, 372 F. Supp. 1196 (D.D.C. 1974), at 1199.

Rickel, A. U. (1989). *Teen pregnancy and parenting*. New York: Hemisphere.

Robbins, J. (1984). Out of wedlock abortion and delivery: The importance of the male partner. *Social Problems, 31*(3), 334–350.

Roe v. Wade, 410 U.S. 113 (1973).

Rossi, N., Bassi, L., & Delfino, M. (1988). Voluntary interruption of pregnancy and the problem of repeated abortion. *Archivo di Psicologia, Neurologia, e Psichiatria, 49*(4), 429–450.

Russo, N. F. (1992a, September 15). Post-abortion trauma disputed. *USA Today,* Section D, p. 1.

Russo, N. F. (1992b). Abortion and unwanted childbearing: The impact of *Casey. Psychology of Women, 19*(4), 1–2.

Sexton, A. (1962). The abortion. In *All my pretty ones* (pp. 20–21). Boston: Houghton Mifflin.

Turell, S., Armsworth, M., & Gaa, J. (1990). Emotional response to abortion: A critical review of the literature. *Women and Therapy, 9*(4), 49–68.

13

The Counterrevolution: Sex, Politics, and the New Reproductive Technologies

JILL BETZ BLOOM

The body is like an actor on stage, ready to take on the role assigned it by culture.

—Thomas Laqueur (1990)

In this era of sexual epidemics—AIDS, herpes, teenage pregnancy—women have been increasingly confronted by medical studies and media reports of the ominous threat of infertility. By 1985, one infertility specialist had already referred to infertility as a growing public health problem of epidemic proportions (Sandelowski, 1990). "Ticking biological clocks" have entered into the jargon of the day, and have progressively worked their way into women's consciousnesses. The "infertility epidemic" has led many women to question and reconsider their choices—a questioning that is loudly echoed in the media.

In 1982, a study that received wide media coverage reported that a woman's chances of conceiving dropped suddenly after age 30. Women between the ages of 31 and 35, the study suggested, stood nearly a 40% chance of being infertile. This was unprecedented news, for virtually every study up until then had found that women's fertility did not decrease until their late 30s.[1] Widespread criticism of the researchers' methods and inferences ensued. A senior associate at the Population Council's Center for Policy Studies, for example, called the study "a poor basis for assessing the risk of female sterility," and statisticians from Princeton University's Office of Population Research warned that the study could "lead to needless anxiety and costly medical treatments" (Faludi, 1991, p. 28). Even the original researchers backed away from their own findings, stating "that they never meant their findings to apply to all women" (Faludi, 1991, p. 29). Nevertheless, neither the authors' retreat nor their peers' disparaging assessments attracted press attention.

Nor did a study conducted 3 years later by the U.S. National Center for Health Statistics, which surveyed 8,000 women and found that American women between the ages of 30 and 34 faced a 13.6%, not 40%, chance of being infertile, make the news. Indeed, women in their early 30s had only a 3% higher risk of infertility than did women in their early 20s. Since 1965, infertility had declined slightly among women in their early to mid-30s—and even among women in their 40s. Overall, the percentage of women unable to have babies had actually fallen—from 11.2% in 1965 to 8.5% in 1982 (Faludi, 1991). Time, it was found, is the greatest and certainly the cheapest cure for infertility. In a British longitudinal survey of more than 17,000 women, one of the largest fertility studies ever conducted, 91% of the women eventually became pregnant after 39 months, falling outside of the newly defined 1-year definition (Faludi, 1991). Women made anxious about their biological timing, as well as the national press and government officials, took little notice of this contradictory evidence. Women's choices for liberation over maternity were decried. Feminism was portrayed as the "great experiment that failed"; from this point of view, women, duped by the women's movement, had lost ground instead of gaining it (Faludi, 1991).

As in other historical periods—the late 19th century, and the postwar years of the 1950s—a declining birth rate, specifically among white middle- and upper-middle-class Americans, has led to an intense and widespread endorsement of pronatalism with a rhetoric and ideology to support it. Because of the fear that women might be inclined to shirk their maternal role—to the nation's detriment as well as to their own—an idealization of motherhood and a concern for "family values" has emerged in each period. Fueling the current "baby hunger" are accusations of selfishness and inverted priorities; the specter of "glass ceilings" and infertility; and declamations that feminism is dead—all culminating in today's "mini-baby boom."

This chapter argues that the contemporary baby boom is not just a demographic phenomenon; rather, like the baby boom of the 1950s, it is the result of a fully articulated ideology that finds expression in the political culture, in the popular culture, in medical literature and in the thoughts and desires of women and men. The first section examines the current explanations of what constitutes the "infertility crisis" to which reproductive technologies are seemingly a solution. Next, the entire issue of infertility is contextualized in a broader historical and political framework; infertility and the medicalized reproductive technologies are examined alongside other

contemporary sexual/social epidemics. Such an analysis reveals how political and ideological interests have entered into the content of scientific and
medical claims, and accordingly, "inside" women's bodies. Finally, I argue
that what is revealed and called into question by the current "epidemic of
infertility" is the entire manner in which our culture constructs and values
sexuality and motherhood.

It is clear that neither all individual women nor all feminists agree on
the benefits and dangers of reproductive technologies. Medical technology
has historically been both responsive and unresponsive to women's needs.
The issues to be explored here cannot simply be reduced to the question of
whether reproductive technologies are bad or good; rather, can women use
these technologies to their benefit and not be used by them? What underlies
the controversy, and what is at stake, is as complex and contradictory as it is
political and personal.

Historians of science and feminists concur that medical science in
general, and the medical treatment of women in particular, reflect the
political and social forces of a culture. Historian Linda Gordon (1990) points
out that birth control, has always been socially regulated in some way. This
is because birth control has consequences that are central to two critical
issues for societal development: sexual activity and population control.
Birth control is also related to a third phenomenon, the role of women.
Systems of sexual control change as women's status changes. They both
affect and reflect one another. Since the 1980s, a shift has occured in the
reproductive control controversies. Prior to the 1980s the controversy
centered exclusively around abortion and birth control, or attempts *not* to
reproduce. In the last decade the controversy has expanded to include the
new reproductive technologies, or strategies *for* reproduction. Linking the
two are common anxieties and concerns surrounding the separation of
reproduction from heterosexual sex, marriage, and patriarchal family law,
as well as the increasing experience of parenthood as choice (Gordon, 1990).

The condition that drives the new reproductive technologies—
infertility—is filled with cultural meaning. The infertile blame themselves
or are blamed for attempts to defy the "natural" life cycle, sex roles, and
gender behavior. In one respect, reproductive technologies are a way out;
they enable choice and a second chance. *In vitro* fertilization (IVF) and
gamete intrafallopian tube transfer (GIFT) are commonly represented as the
gifts of advanced technology. At the same time, there is opposition to this
turn to technology (which will be explored more fully later)—an opposition
that is waged by both the right and the left and by conservative and
progressive movements.

In this era of reproductive politics, Ann Snitow (1991) poses a cautionary analogy. In the 19th century, she explains, feminism's *idée fixe* was the
vote. Once the vote was won, it was hard to make it mean something

larger, to extend it into a source of public authority for women. In our day, the *idée fixe* has become the right to an abortion. Choice and control over our bodies and over childbearing have become hotly contested political issues. With hard work this too may be won, but Snitow warns that there will be much resistance to allowing the right of abortion to expand into its' larger meaning.

By focusing attention upon reproductive technologies, my intent is twofold. First, I wish to expand and provide a way to rethink what confronts us today in women's struggles over reproductive rights; second, I wish to examine how these technologies enter into the contemporary debate and discourse on women's rights and women's nature. Potentially, what women stand to gain by acquiring access to abortion and attaining reproductive control and reproductive freedom is far-reaching. It is the possibility for new identities, in which reproductive capacity or motherhood is no longer *the* defining characteristic of every woman.

In a specific consideration of the impact of the new reproductive technologies upon contemporary women's lives, questions arise: Who is being served or disserved by these technologies? Is technology the outgrowth of advanced knowledge, the solution and treatment to societal ills, as some argue; or is technology the problem? And what is propelling the rapid advance of procedures that produce such complex opposition and reactions? In attempting to respond to these questions and considering, as many social historians do, that there is no technology separate from its historical context, I begin by undertaking a closer examination of the history of infertility. What will follow explores shifting views of infertility and reproductive control; historical, economic, and social changes; and the ideologies and technologies that have surfaced in reaction. It is only when the issues embedded in these struggles over reproductive rights have been teased apart that the liberatory possibilities can be realized.

HISTORY OF INFERTILITY

"Infertility" is an ambiguous condition whose etiology and progress lack any precise definition. Infertility has been variously described as a syndrome of multiple origins, a consequence or manifestation of disease rather than a disease entity itself, a biological impairment, a psychosomatic disorder, a condition characterizing a couple rather than an individual, a failure to conform to cultural prescriptions to reproduce, and a failure to fulfill the personal desire to beget a child (Sandelowski, 1990). Currently, the conventional medical definition of infertility is an inability or failure to conceive after 1 year of regular, unprotected intercourse; the regularity of intercourse and the lack of contraceptive protection document the desire to conceive

(Sandelowski, 1990). Parenthetically, the 1-year rule is a recent development; formerly, the determination of infertility was set at 5 years (Faludi, 1991).

Although such a linkage is typically secondary to strictly scientific discussions of infertility, women's emancipation has been linked with the loss of their fertility since the 19th century. Medical literature has consistently constructed infertility as a social disease—a disorder of civilization and modern living, involving culpable, largely female acts of omission and commission. One hears in current discussions of the causes of infertility the echoes of 19th-century physicians' and social critics' concerns about women's health and their new activism, and the relationship of these factors to national growth and prosperity.

Prior to 1856, when Augustus Gardner published *The Causes and Curative Treatment of Sterility,* there were very few English-language books or papers on sterility. In the 18th and early 19th centuries, physicians were not interested in infertility or birth control, because the inability to have children was not thought to place lives in danger (Sandelowski, 1990). By the late 19th century, however, infertility and sterility had become topics of great concern in medical literature. It was then a way of life that was believed to be endangered.

Historians note that sexual relationships, fertility rates, and the use of birth control are extremely sensitive to social and economic changes (Tilly, Scott, & Cohen, 1978; Gordon, 1990). The attempt to control fertility through the use of birth control methods and the use of methods to increase fertility, although seemingly opposed to each other, are in many ways closely interconnected. Historically, strategies to control and/or regulate fertility have varied with the social and economic needs of the times. Religious ideologies about sex and motherhood—specifically, early Christian ideologies that sanctioned sex for procreation only and procreation as the only justification for women's existence—were powerful ideological weapons that were, and remain, central to reproductive control.

The Ideology of Motherhood

By the late 18th century, as an ideology of separate spheres emerged—the domestic world for women and the public world for men—it consolidated gender roles in particular ways and produced a cult of true womanhood in which motherhood had a primary place.

In many cultures, ideologies about motherhood are seen as central to the justification of patriarchy. Motherhood, Gordon (1990) explains, has three components: a biological one, comprised of pregnancy and childbirth; a social one, consisting of child rearing; and an ideological one. The first two became conflated when women's biological relationship to children led to the "natural" social and legal requirement for women to assume responsibility for child rearing, and to the systematic devision of labor that assigned women to domestic work and to the private sphere of housework and service. Furthermore, male-dominated culture institutionalized women's mothering through an ideology that declared the separation of childbearing from child raising immoral (or, today, psychologically harmful). The ideology made the biological processes of motherhood symbolic: "Women were the universal nourishers, givers of milk, love and the rules of the society to a new generation" (Gordon, 1990, p. 10).

This ideology served preindustrial society's economic need for large families well, and remained largely unchallenged until industrialization created a new economic system with new problems, as industrial capitalism became increasingly dependent upon a growing labor force for production (Ehrenreich & English, 1979; Weltner, 1978; Gordon, 1990). Industrial production brought about profound changes in family structure. As men moved out of the home to socialized workplaces, the economic basis of family unity dissolved; this led to an increased separation of husbands and wives, and to an attention to different problems and concerns for men and women. Women became functionally independent of their husbands while remaining financially dependent, and women's work became increasingly degraded to activities outside of the economy: cleaning, consuming, and child rearing (Gordon, 1990).

It is argued that it was precisely because male authority was being weakened within the home that the stability—indeed, viability—of the traditional family required the imposition of a repressive ideology. The "Victorian prudery" referred to by some, and the "cult of true womanhood" defined by others, served this end (Smith-Rosenberg, 1985; Weltner, 1978; Ehrenreich & English, 1979; Tilly et al., 1978; Gordon, 1990). The notion that women were profoundly different from men, as it re-emerged in the late 18th century, was, as these women's historians explain, a male-imposed doctrine to keep women from escaping from their homes.

A Changed Consciousness for Women versus the Cult of True Womanhood

The new industrial economy that reordered the old unity of home also opened up the possibility of choice for women, however remote this possibility may have been or seemed. It was during the late 19th century that the "woman question" emerged, both as a subjective dilemma for women, and as a public "issue" for scholars, statesmen, and scientists (Ehrenreich & English, 1979). What were women to do with these new possibilities; what was best or most "natural" for women to do; and what was to be done with women?

The "new masculinism" that was emerging in the market economy helped shape the answers to these questions. The "cult of true womanhood" meshed neatly with the needs of a maturing economy, for it defined woman as the antithesis of the economic man. The 19th-century man, a busy builder of railroads and bridges, had little time to observe and practice the religious values of his forebears. But as historian Barbara Weltner (1978) has observed, he could salve his conscience by rationalizing that he left behind a hostage, not only to fortune, but to all the values he felt dearly. Woman, as the "cult of true womanhood" was to define, was the hostage in the home.

> In a society where values changed frequently, where fortunes rose and fell with frightening rapidity, where social and economic mobility provided instability as well hope, one thing at least remained the same—a true woman was a true woman wherever she was found. . . . It was a fearful obligation, a solemn responsibility, which the nineteenth century American woman had—to uphold the pillars of the temple with her frail white hand. (Weltner, 1978, p. 313)

The "true woman's" place was unquestionably at home, as daughter or sister, but most of all as wife and mother. Women who, like Mary Wollstonecraft, Frances Wright, or Harriet Martineau, responded to the possibility of choice and a changed consciousness and asked for a wider scope, were condemned and "read out of the sex"; they were viewed as "semi-women" and "mental hermaphrodites" (Weltner, 1978, p. 326). This viewpoint was elaborated into an ideology that considered women intellectually, artistically, and physically inferior to men. Women were told that they were morally superior, however, and that their greatest holiness came from their innate capacity for motherhood.

Sexual morality for 19th-century women was being defined not only by the clergy and political philosophers, as in earlier centuries; it was now reinforced by the newly emerging medical profession, a powerful source of control over women's lives. "Woman's reproductive organs are pre-eminent," one mid-19th-century physician explained. "They exercise a controlling influence upon her entire system, and entail upon her many painful and dangerous diseases. . . . Everything that is peculiar to her, springs from her sexual organization" (quoted in Smith-Rosenberg, 1985, p. 184).

Such views were not new. Since classical antiquity, views of women's anatomical and physiological inferiority have been graphically detailed (Smith-Rosenberg, 1985; Laqueur, 1990).[2] The second half of the 19th century, however, witnessed a growing physiological sophistication in medicine generally, and an increasing (although circumstantial) knowledge of the female reproductive system specifically, enabling a far more elaborate explanation of femininity and a firmer rationale for woman's role as wife and mother.

Reproduction as a concern, and pronatalism as its expression, emerged, not coincidentally, at the same time that modernization had begun to shift the emphasis to the quality of life and the desire for fewer children. Clearly related to this pronatalist movement was the decrease in the total white fertility rates by 50% between the years 1800 and 1900—a decrease, for the most part, attributable to a reduction in childbearing among the middle and upper middle classes (Sandelowski, 1990).

Nineteenth-century industrial production had begun profound changes in family structure by dissolving the economic basis of family unity. On the one hand, the family remained, until the first half of the 20th century, the primary means of socialization of children into adults with personalities appropriate to the demands of industrial capitalism. On the other hand, the family was now required to absorb the strains that the economy placed upon individuals. The gendered division of labor within the family meant that women had to carry the bulk of the new psychological burden (Gordon, 1990).

Both of these family functions led to an intensification of the cult of motherhood—that is, the extension of motherliness to the very definition of femininity. It was the 19th-century family, Freud's "oedipal family," that acquired a new centrality as both metaphor and regulator of the carefully circumscribed maternal and paternal roles. And as Michel Foucault (1978) and others (Bordo, 1989; Bartkey, 1988; Poovey, 1992) have argued, it was during this time that the female body was constituted as a maternal body— that maternity now became a social practice over and above simple reproduction. What was to follow included not only the notion of maternal instinct, but also the idea that the desire to be a mother lies at the heart of all female desire.

Not surprisingly, marital infertility became increasingly important to 19th-century physicians. A constant theme in 19th-century medical literature on women's health and fertility was that expanded education and ambitions perverted women's biological destiny. "Although most women might want eventually to become mothers, their involvement in intellectual pursuits that diverted energy away from the reproductive organs to the brain would lead to conditions that lowered fertility" (Haller & Haller, 1984, p. 73). In 1883, Horatio Bigelow—who believed, like his medical colleagues, that civilization was harder on women's health than on men's— advocated a system of education that taught women the importance of maternity (Sandelowski, 1990).

The focus in 19th-century medical literature was on intellectual rather than on physical labor as the cause for sterility, since physicians were almost exclusively concerned with the declining birth rate among classes of women who were most likely because of privilege to pursue intellecutual careers: namely, white middle- and upper-middle-class women. This was despite the fact that the incidence of infertility was at least as great in the economically poorer classes, and among women engaged in strenuous physical labor. Physicians rationalized their concern about upper-income women by theorizing, incorrectly, that physical labor and poverty were conducive to fertility, whereas indolence and wealth were associated with decreased fertility.

It was the "depreciating habits of civilized life that predisposed the 'civilized woman,' in contrast to the 'North American squaw' and the 'Southern negress,' to sterility." These "civilized and problematic habits" included "neglect of proper nutrition and outdoor exercise, brain fatigue, improprities in dress, imprudence during menstruation and the prevention or termination of pregnancy" (quoted in Sandelowski, 1990).

Infertility in the 20th Century

Similar views and arguments continued to be expressed by medical experts well into the 20th century. In 1931 medical experts discussed the preventable causes of sterility, pointing admonishing fingers at "modern women who transgressed the laws of nature" (Sandelowski, 1990). C. G. Child attacked American women, including "fat women, academicians, public women, detached women and social corsairs," whom he held ultimately responsible for the American population crisis (quoted in Sandelowski, 1990, p. 488).

The conjoining of female agency with infertility assumed a new and more subtle form in the 1940s, with the increasing interest in psychosomatic medicine, Freudian concepts of disease causation, and the psychological linkage of women's "maternal nature" (Sandelowski, 1990). The Great Depression and the need for women's labor in World War II had led women to opt for childlessness or to delay childbearing, while at the same time exposing women to lifestyles and opportunities previously available only to men. As in other historical moments when women have gained opportunities outside of the home, this heralded a pronatalist national sentiment and a nostalgic desire for tradition and family harmony (or, in today's terminology, "family values"). One cannot help wondering, then and now, whether the zeal with which the popular press, political figures, and the medical community have concerned themselves with a nostalgia for the "traditional family" betrays an awareness that domestic tranquility does not fully satisfy women.

Recasting women's "moral failures," as 19th-century experts called them, as "psychological aberrations" in postwar America mandated a new, even more subjective scientific diagnosis and cure. Infertility now became a symptom of a complex psychic chain of events that was hidden even from the infertile spouses themselves (Sandelowski, 1990). Infertility was depicted as a maladaptive disguise for and defense against hostility or fear of reproducing. Hostility to men and reproduction were included as causes of structural organic changes, altered reproductive physiology, and aberrant sexual behavior that reduced the chances of conception. The Freudian concept of unconscious motivation was appropriated to diagnose unconscious rather than conscious desire or failure. Clinicians "easily and unerringly proved the presence of unconscious factors by assuming that true desire for children in almost all cases would lead to children, while the true lack of desire would lead to infertility" (Sandelowski, 1990, p. 491). Here, the *desire* to reproduce became an important determinant of the *ability* to reproduce, and cast doubts on the existence of both accidental pregnancy and involuntary childlessness.

The 1940s through the 1960s gave rise to notions of "hypofeminity" and "female masculinity." Miscarriages were due to "habitual abortions" and "hostile mucus." Even douching indicated "an ambivalence toward conceiving, since an overemphasis on cleanliness and body integrity was [thought to be] incompatible with sharing the body with husband or fetus" (Sandelowski, 1990, p. 492). During this period, medical treatment for infertility was sometimes delayed until the patient was evaluated psychologically and motivationally. Finding out why, and whether, women wanted to become pregnant assumed great importance. Childless women of this era constituted a discarded group, and were accused of selfishness and shamed, bringing both their character and their womanhood into question.[3] Infertility, in other instances, was theorized to be a protection of vulnerable, sick women against pregnancy; the rationalization was that immature women would lead to neurotic children (Sandelowski, 1990).

The 1970s and 1980s, following the women's movement, witnessed a renewed concern about the reproductive price of women's expanded freedoms. This has reached a fevered pitch in recent political discourse, with the "year of the woman" colliding with the rhetoric of "family values." Contrasts are drawn between stay-at-home cookie bakers and ambitious working women, and between what is "natural" for women and what is "perverted"—in short, between the possibility for a changed consciousness for women and "true womanhood."

In summary, despite all that has changed since the 19th century, assumptions about female nature have persisted and become institutionalized into a whole range of contemporary social practices. A cardinal feature of individualism (and the laws that were developed to define and protect the individual), as elaborated in the 17th century and institutionalized in the 18th and 19th centuries, was the constitution of maternity as the essence of the female subject. From this, it has seemed to follow not only that mother love emanates from the body in the form of maternal instinct, but also that desire to be a mother is central to all female desire. This assumption about female nature persists today, and its institutionalization into contemporary social practices reinforces the notion that the laws that were developed alongside it (i.e., the legal definitions of "personhood" and individual rights) are outside of history—simply natural and right. Behind this assumption lie dramatic implications for women and men. In the same way that the cult of true womanhood meshed neatly with 19th-century masculinism, each constituting the other, so too does today's normative woman as mother—that is, the maternal nature of woman—constitute a sexed identity for women, and by oppositional logic a masculinist identity for men. If women are allowed to question or reject their maternity, then not only is the natural (sexed) basis of rights in jeopardy, but so is the natural basis of female identity, and by implication the basis of male identity as well. Moreover, what we come to see is that what stands as medical science—that is, scientific knowledge about fertility—has a much broader role and impact in organizing social practices and social relationships.

THE NEW REPRODUCTIVE TECHNOLOGIES

Thomas Laqueur (1990) argues in *Making Sex: Body and Gender from the Greeks to Freud* that from the ancients to contemporary thinkers, much of the medical debate over male and female biology, and over fertility and infertility, has less to do with bodies than with power, legitimacy, and fatherhood. Conception is in a sense, he writes, the male's having an idea in the woman's body. Reproductive technologies are the result and accumulation of many ideas, and can be understood, in part, as a reassertion of male hegemony and a reaffirmation of the father.[4] Leon Kass has raised this possibility in *Making Babies: The New Biology and the Old Morality,* warning that the advent of these new powers for human engineering means that some men may be destined to play God, to recreate other men in their own image (quoted in Rowland, 1987, p. 528).

It is empirically true that the male is necessary for conception. Yet it was not until the 19th century that it was discovered that the union of two different germ cells—egg and sperm—constituted conception.[5] The elaborate theorizing about male and female potency perhaps hides the more pressing but unaskable question (which remained so until the 19th century) of whether there needs to be a male. It was perfectly possible until that time to hold that fathers mattered very little. The discovery of physiological paternity marked the first historical change and transformation in male reproductive consciousness (O'Brien, 1981). The second and more recent change in reproductive praxis, O'Brien claims, has been brought about by contraceptive technology: "The freedom for women to choose parenthood is a historical development as significant as the discovery of physiological paternity" (p. 22). Both developments, O'Brien contends, have created a transformation in human consciousness of human relations with the natural world, which must be renegotiated (or, in the language of dialectical analysis, must be mediated).

Types of Reproductive Technologies

Reproductive technologies, for the sake of definition, can be roughly devided into two types—the "old" and the "new." These represent the various biomedical interventions aimed at either producing a child or preventing/terminating a pregnancy. "Old" technologies include mechanical means of contraception (e.g., the intrauterine device [IUD], diaphragm, sponge, condom, and spermicide), as well as the various forms of hormonal contraception (e.g., the Pill and the hormonal implant). They also include female and male sterilization, abortion, and such birth interventions as episiotomies and Caesarian sections. The "new" technologies, which are the subject of this chapter, include preconception sex selection and postconception sex determination techniques, artificial insemination, and the whole range of "test tube" techniques: IVF; GIFT; embryo replacement, transfer, and flushing (surrogacy); embryo freezing; and (still being developed) the artificial womb. Also included are a number of tests during pregnancy: amniocentesis, fetal monitoring, sonogram/ultrasound, and various tests at birth (Klein, 1987).

IVF is considered the basis for all the new technologies. Once the egg and sperm are placed in a Petri dish, the embryo can then be frozen, or transferred from one woman to another; the sex can be determined; and the embryo can be used for experimentation and genetic manipulation. These procedures are costly and tend not to be federally funded in the United States. Rather, they are funded by individual patients, pharmaceutical companies, hospitals, and private organizations. Although costs vary, a conservative estimate is approximately $8,000 per IVF cycle, with many women returning for multiple procedures. Currently France and Australia lead the United States in this industry, but U.S. doctors are quickly joining the ranks. One American IVF center alone estimates that IVF could be a $6 million annual business (Raymond, 1991). As discussed in the previous section, the "infertility epidemic" is the price many contemporary critics insist liberated women have paid for their reproductive freedom. It is perhaps more accurate to say that the last decade has witnessed an epidemic of reproductive technologies and infertility specialists.

As these technologies reportedly flourish, their rates of success remain less clear. Raymond (1991) reports that half of the clinics reporting success have never had a live birth, and that the Wyden congressional subcommittee (one of few assessment reviews) found a 9% "take-home baby" success rate in 1989.

Clearly, reproductive technologies pose liberatory possibilities for women. The ability to conceive outside of intercourse and a heterosexual relationship become possible, as do many useful medical interventions. My attention, however, is directed toward critiquing and analyzing how these liberatory possibilites are blurred by the medical practice of reproductive technologies, which are too often utilized in the service of a particular ideology that singularly extols women's maternal nature, inciting women to crave babies above and beyond their own physical and emotional needs and lives.

The Politics of Reproductive Technologies

Feminist analyses of reproductive politics and maternity in general, and of reproductive technologies in particular, are numerous, varied, and at times contradictory. There are those, for example, who argue that women's realm of authority and control consists of childbearing and child rearing. This is an essentialist or "gynocentric" position, one that views reproductive technologies as useful in enabling maternity outside of patriarchal control and/or outside of heterosexual relationships (Snitow, 1991; Ferguson, 1989). An alternative position, most prominently held by Shulamith Firestone (1970), can be used to support reproductive technologies as a way to liberate women from the shackles of childbearing and maternity. Viewing pregnancy as "barbaric," Firestone sees freeing women from the tyranny of reproduction as an avenue to sexual equality and parity.[6]

Other feminists who write about the new reproductive technologies include an international group of women theorists and activists who in 1984 formed the Feminist International Network on the New Reproductive Technologies (FINNRET). Concerned about the potential for women to be reduced to living laboratories—"test tube women"—they locate the new reproductive technologies in the age-old tradition of the patriarchial domination of women and their bodies, and encourage women to question these so-called benevolent and therapeutic technologies (Corea et al., 1987).

In *Woman in the Body*, anthropologist Emily Martin (1987), too, warns of the potential dangers reproductive technologies pose in the current medical climate. Increasingly, she writes, childbirth is presented in this medical discourse as commodity production; eggs, sperm, womb, embryos, and even babies are being bought and sold. Drawing parallels between the labor of birth and the labor of the marketplace, Martin presents childbirth through metaphors of the baby as "product," the woman as "laborer," the uterus as "machine," and the doctors as the "management team" responsible for efficient production. Moreover, she warns that these technologies allow new standards, regulations, and legal sanctions to protect the fetus, and that these give a woman no choice in sacrificing her rights to those of the fetus.

Similarly, feminist scientists Ruth Hubbard (see Hubbard, Henifin, & Fried, 1982), Rita Arditti (1976), and Evelyn Fox Keller (1985) among others, caution that a largely male-controlled science raises questions as to who benefits from these technologies, particularly when the proliferation of reproductive technologies takes place in a climate in which scientists, for the most part, are unwilling to consider the social implications. Importantly, anthropologist Rayna Rapp (1991) argues that it is necessary to bring the impact on women and society into the foreground when we consider how reproductive technologies are changing the experiences of pregnancy, of becoming a parent, and of family life. Rapp contends that, covertly, these technologies validate white middle-class definitions of the perfect baby, as well as the culturally specific notion that infertility and imperfection are unacceptable.[7]

Clearly, feminism offers no single position or perspective from which to critique and assess the role of reproductive technologies in women's lives; rather, feminist discourse reflects the divergent views and theoretical tensions within feminism itself. Nor does the more consensual feminist position on reproductive choice—the right to choose abortion and contraception—necessarily extend to a unified position on reproductive technologies. Instead, what is revealed, I believe, is (1) feminism's failure to question the basic tenets of liberal individualism that inform the feminist positions on reproductive choice (the right to privacy and equal rights), and (2) the way in which the too-facile and underexamined extension of these legal notions of the individual to the abortion debate leads to the reductionistic construction of pro-choice versus pro-life.

Mary Poovey (1992) deftly speaks to the first point, arguing that unless feminists who support reproductive choice begin to rethink the gendered assumptions to which choice, privacy, and equal rights are historically and metaphysically wed, "we will inadvertently reinforce the discriminatory legal conceptualizations to which anti-abortionists so effectively appeal" (p. 239). In other words, the privacy argument, as used in support of legal abortions, argues that women, like men, should have the right to govern their own bodies. The problem in postulating a realm of the private and an autonomous individual, Poovey points out, is that such thinking ignores the extent to which social life permeates the home and sexual activity. In postulating a person capable of free choice, the privacy argument also ignores the extent to which women have been subjected to violence, especially in relation to their sexuality. What may be ascribed as free choice is not always free.

The primary difficulty with the equality argument, Poovey explains, is the flip side of the gender blindness of the privacy argument. In focusing upon women's reproductive capacity as that which unfairly subjects women to systematic oppression, the equality defense makes reproductive capacity the defining characteristic of all women.

When the whole issue of choice is problematized and extended to reproductive technologies, one may wonder, as Robyn Rowland (1987) does, whether the need or want for choice has no limits: "What of a choice that closes opportunities for the majority of women and places our futures at risk?" (Rowland, 1987, p. 527). Are there choices that tell us more than we want to know, that endanger women's bodies and emotions, or that position one class of women in the service of another? Are some choices made available according to race and class distinctions? Are choices for those who "qualify" narrowly defined, privileging biological childbearing over the choice of adoption, with little consideration of the choice of childlessness?[8] What we observe, in Susan Bordo's nomenclature, is a distinction between those who are embodied and those who are mere bodies. This leads into my second point.

Because abortion rights remain central to women's struggles for reproductive control, we remain locked in a pro-choice versus pro-life rhetoric that fails to situate the struggle within the broader context of reproductive control. The terms of the debate, as defined by law and medicine, reveal two different traditions concerning individual rights—in effect, a double standard. One tradition is for embodied subjects, the other for those treated as mere bodies. Definitions of women as fetal incubators, as well as definitions of fetal rights and fathers' rights, are emerging legally; reproductive technologies are susceptible to these definitions and can be used in the assistance of them. For example, amniocentesis, ultrasound, and fetal microsurgery render the fetus visible in a new way defining it as a subject; this serves to define the mother as a mere body and temporary container. We are increasingly witnessing cases of forced fetal interventions; instances where a pregnant woman is legally charged for drug use endangering the fetus; and a recent incident where a woman was publicly refused service and reprimanded for ordering an alcoholic beverage during the latter stages of pregnancy (Bordo, 1993). We begin to see how the present abortion debate, articulated in terms of women's right to choose versus fetal rights or fathers' rights, is limited and misleading.

Moreover, we begin to see how reproductive technologies are slippery issues for feminists, much as body building and cosmetic surgery are. Defenders argue that each is about taking one's life into one's own hands, having the ability to choose; those opposed contend that each amounts to giving oneself over to the hands of another, in many instances to men and medicine. In the case of reproductive technologies, the fear is that women will drop out of sight as "technodocs" focus on producing the perfect baby, the perfect product.

Although the oppression and domination of women have historical precedence and convincingly inform the debate over the benefits and dangers of reproductive technologies, we need a different analysis—a more comprehensive one that extends our understanding of the sexual politics of the body. In Bordo's words, we need "an effective political discourse about the female body, an adequate one to analyze the insidious, paradoxical pathways of social control" (1989, p. 15). If one staple of sexist ideology is the notion that it is women themselves who are responsible for their suffering because of their "female nature," the feminist defense that insists that women are the "done to," the oppressed, requires a critique. (All the while, of course, we need to be sensitive to how such a critique can be used by the backlash against feminism—for example, the recent attacks on feminists in the controversies over false memory and date rape.[9])

In short, we need to expand the "old" feminist discourse beyond the oppressor–oppressed model. Such distinctions were useful and instrumental in historically describing women's experience and in raising women's consciousness and voice; nevertheless, this discourse has proved inadequate to the social and historical complexities of the situations of men and women, as feminist and social criticism has evolved in the 1980s and 1990s. In current thinking, it has become increasingly necessary to account for the racial, economic, and class differences among women. Elizabeth Spelman (1988), Jana Sawicki (1991), Susan Bordo (1989, 1993), Linda Singer (1989), and Sandra Bartkey (1988) are among many who critique feminist theory as well as theorize about the body. So, too, a critique of women depicted as passive, without agency, has emerged (Benjamin, 1988); similarly, a critique of the essentializing, reductionistic portrayal of men as the enemy has been called for (Bordo, 1993). Also needed is a fuller analysis of women's collusion with patriarchal culture. Finally, as deconstructionists point out, the "old" feminism has directed insufficient attention to the multiplicity of meaning that can be read in every cultural act and practice (Diamond & Quinby, 1988; Sawicki, 1991; Singer, 1989). In general, the "old" feminism is seen as having constructed an insufficiently nuanced, binary view of power and of the politics of the body.[10]

A NEW POLITICS OF THE BODY

Historically, we have seen how women have been associated with the body and have been largely confined to a life centered on the body. Through the bodily processes of reproduction, motherhood can be understood as an identity, an ideology, and an institution.

A growing number of feminist theorists have turned their inquiry to the politics of the body.[11] To varying degrees, each has posed questions concerning the intersection of culture and the body—that is, how the body is a medium of culture, a "text" of culture, and in the grip of culture. This is not the craving, instinctual body imagined by Plato, Augustine, or Freud, but the docile, culturally regulated, disciplined body theorized by Michel Foucault (Bordo, 1993). Inevitably these theorists have turned to Foucault, whose work on a genealogy of sexuality[12] has usefully informed and provided a framework for a "political" understanding of female bodily practices (e.g., eating disorders, body building, cosmetic surgery), as well as of the social conditions of sexual violence and sexual epidemics. Increasingly, in acknowledging the subtle forms of social control and power—Foucault's "biopower"—feminism has come to imagine the body as itself a politically inscribed entity, shaped by histories and practices of containment and control (Bordo, 1993).

Biopower

In this final section, I concentrate on what Foucault refers to as "biopower", or the disciplinary model of power as a more culturally systematic method for critiquing and analyzing the impact of reproductive technologies on women's lives. As Foucault (1980) explains, disciplinary technologies control the body through techniques that simultaneously render it more useful, more powerful, and more docile. This form of power is different from the idea of power as something possessed by one group and used against another. Power for Foucault is not repressive but constitutive, "bent on generating forces, making them grow, and ordering them, rather than one dedicated to impeding them, making them submit or destroying them" (1980, p. 136).

Foucault claims that biopower was an indispensable element in the development of capitalism in the 19th century: "[T]he latter would not have been possible without the controlled insertion of bodies into the machinery of production and the adjustment of the phenomena of population to economic processes" (1980, p. 141). Foucaudian feminists claim that biopower, must also have been indispensable to patriarchal power, in that it provided for the insertion of women's bodies into the machinery of reproduction (Sawicki, 1991).

The 19th century's construction of femininity as fragile and domestic—the construction of a true woman as one who upheld the pillars of the temple with her frail white hands—is a clear example of what Foucault means by a socially trained "docile body." Foucault theorizes modern power as nonauthoritarian, "working from below"; yet it nevertheless produces and normalizes bodies to serve prevailing relationships of domination and subordination. If patriarchal power operates primarily through violence, objectification, and repression, we might wonder why women subject themselves to it. If, on the other hand, patriarchal power also operates by "inciting desire, attaching individuals to specific identities, and addressing real needs, then it is easier to understand how it has been so effective at getting a grip on us" (Sawicki, 1991, p. 85). When power works "from below" prevailing forms of selfhood, motherhood and subjectivity are maintained not through physical restraint and coercion, but through the individual's internalization of, for example, the cultural anxiety over infertility that creates the desire for motherhood. That is, they are maintained through internalization, self-regulation, self-surveillance, and self-correction to norms.

Within a Foucauldian framework, where culture itself is viewed as normalizing, it is simplistic to view men as the enemy and to ignore power differences of race, class, and sexual situation, as well as the fact that men and women are both embedded and implicated in institutions that they as individuals did not create and do not control. A Foucauldian framework requires the recognition of the degree to which women unwittingly collude in sustaining sexism and participate in cultural practices that objectify and sexualize women. This is not to say that men do not have a stake in maintaining institutions where they have dominance over women. Such a viewpoint of culture as normalizing does not prescribe rising above culture. Rather, as Bordo, (1993) suggests, our goal is to move toward understanding, toward an enhanced consciousness of the power, complexity, and systematic nature of culture. Our culture continually pulls us away from such an understanding, and leads us toward constructions that emphasize individual freedom, choice, power, and ability.

The Disciplinary Practices of Reproductive Technologies

The new reproductive technologies clearly fit the model of disciplinary power. For example, they involve sophisticated techniques of surveillance and examination such as ultrasound, fetal monitors, and amniocentesis, which make both female bodies and fetuses visible to anonymous agents and vulnerable to medical, legal, and state interventions (Sawicki, 1991).

Moreover, these technologies create new individuals—infertile mothers, surrogate mothers, genetically impaired mothers, unfit mothers—and thus in effect construct new norms of healthy and responsibile motherhood. When the problem is located within the individual, infertility is depoliticized because attention is shifted away from other (e.g., environmental) causes of infertility (Sawicki, 1991). Similarly, locating the problem within the individual constructs women as culpable for choices they have made or failed to make. Like the 19th-century bourgeoisie's preoccupation with the "cultivation" of its body and the improvement of its lineage, the new reproductive technologies, too, reveal a contemporary concern for the strength, endurance, and proliferation of a particular "class body." Presently, for example, IVF is available mainly to married, white, middle- and upper-middle-class women who perceive biological motherhood as desirable and who convince practitioners that they desire a child enough to withstand treatment. Sawicki (1991) points out that the criteria for eligibility reinforce a traditional classist, racist, and heterosexist ideology of fit motherhood.

The new reproductive technologies correspond, as well, to contemporary notions of body management and body building. The well-managed body of the 1980s and 1990s, Linda Singer (1989) aptly notes, "is a body that can be used for wage, labor, sex, reproduction, mothering, spectacle, exercise, or even invisibility, as the situation demands" (p. 57). As Singer persuasively argues, the very language of "body building" defines a body that is assumed to be rebuildable, divisible, fine-tuned, and in need of perpetual maintenance and surveillance. So, too, with the advent of reproductive technologies can women's bodies be disassembled, reassembled, managed, and disiciplined so as to be capable of conceiving and producing children on demand, or delaying that process until the time is right. Many of the innovations in both reproductive ideology and technology have sought to render women's bodies more easily mobilizable in response to shifting needs, which most often concern the production and coordination of populations (Singer, 1989).

Clearly, serving these objectives is what Singer refers to as the "marketing of motherhood." Varied strategies and interventions that differ by race and class are deployed, often through advertising campaigns. For example, in one advertising campaign, successful, attractive, white celebrity women pose proudly with their babies and extol the pleasures of motherhood, thus encouraging white, educated, middle-class women who have deferred or delayed childbearing to "have it all." In another campaign, young women of color are discouraged from reproducing through an emphasis on the burdens of motherhood. In this second example, a poster of a young African-American woman holding a baby and staring deadpan bears the inscription: "It's like being grounded for 18 years" (quoted in Singer, 1989, p. 59). Such tactics are useful, Singer (1989) maintains, either from the standpoint of maintaining race and class dominance, or as a strategy for inducing women's defection from the workplace.

As reproductive issues are increasingly taken up as cultural and not simply biological issues, more space is opened up for politicizing them. As disciplinary technologies, reproductive technologies represent an insidious potential form of social control, because they operate by inciting the desires of those who seek them out. But the question of whether they offer liberatory possibilities depends upon the extent to which mechanisms for resisting their pernicious disciplinary implications are devised. For example, lesbians, single women, and nonwhite, non-middle-class women can challenge these norms by demanding access to these technologies. The question is not whether women are victims of false consciousness in desiring to be biological mothers; rather, it is one of devising feminist strategies in struggles over who defines women's needs and how they are satisfied (Sawicki, 1991).

As history reveals, technological developments are many-edged. Rather than rejecting newly emerging technologies outright, "Feminists can meet multiple-edged developments with multiple-edged responses" Sawicki proclaims (1991, p. 91). She concludes that we can resist the dangerous trends, toward depoliticization, privatization, and lessened autonomy, ensuring that women are not treated solely as bodies, but as subjects with desires, fears, and varying needs.

In utilizing a Foucaudian analysis, therefore, we are able to critique the problems and desires the new reproductive technologies produce, as well as to consider the liberatory possibilities they may hold for women. At the same time, by viewing reproductive technologies as disciplinary technologies, and by emphasizing their more subtle control (attained not through oppression or violence, but through the creation of new norms of motherhood and identities as mothers), we are able to disrupt the notion of motherhood as synonymous with women's essential nature and to envision new identities for women. Moreover, such a perspective does not suggest that we were better off before these technologies were developed; rather, it allows us to view reproductive technologies as a contemporary extension of the medicalization and "biologization" of power.

Epidemics and Biopower

Finally, a critique of the logic and language of "sexual epidemics" adds yet another important layer to this analysis. The determination that a situation is epidemic is always, according to Foucault, a political determination, since the epidemic provides an occasion and rationale for interventions into the lives of bodies and populations (Singer, 1989). The construction of an epidemic situation, as infertility, AIDS, and teenage pregnancy are currently designated, has a strategic value in determining the configurations of biopower. For this reason, Singer argues, epidemics are always historically specific in a way that diseases are not: "When any phenomenon is represented as 'epidemic,' it has, by definition, reached a threshold that is quantitatively unacceptable" (1989, p. 50).

It is not surprising, therefore, that the emergence of an epidemic unleashes anxieties that are not limited to concerns about disease; rather, it prompts a renewed concern about the production of life itself—about reproduction, fertility, and the family, which are seen as threatened by current conditions. At a time when sexual freedom is under attack as unsafe, there is a felt need to construct a new, more prudent sexuality. As a result, there is a renewed emphasis on domestication for women. The sexual revolution, centered on a "politics of ecstasy," is revised under epidemic conditions to a "politics of sexual prudence and body management." The epidemic of infertility and other contemporary health crises become political strategies to revivify authority. The epidemic, consequently, is interpreted by cultural conservatives either as a retributive consequence of past transgressions, or as a call to revivify and intensify that authority. The failure to heed that authority, it is argued, has produced the crisis in which we now find ourselves (Singer, 1989).

CONCLUSIONS AND CLINICAL IMPLICATIONS

Throughout this chapter, I have sought out a fuller understanding of the impact of reproductive techniques upon women's lives without resorting to "better" explanatory models. Rather, I have attempted to construct what Foucault has called a "polyhedron of intelligibility" (i.e., an explanation of facets and intersections): cultural representations of reproduction and motherhood; the role of consumer culture; philosophical and religious attitudes toward women, sexuality, fertility, and motherhood; and what is considered "normal" female experience in our culture (Bordo, 1993).[13] Such a perspective appreciates the intersection of culture with family, with economic and historical developments, and with psychological constructions of gender and gender roles. Implicit, too, is a shift from the view of the body as static, natural, and biological, to imagining the body as a historical arena—shaped and often manipulated and contorted by social and economic forces, and importantly, differently shaped depending upon the gender, race, class, and sexual orientation of the body in question.

My intent has not been simply to criticize and condemn the use of reproductive technologies. Rather, it has been to underscore and bring to the surface a discourse that defines the body as malleable and able to be shaped to the meanings one chooses—for example, the claim that any woman can have a baby, regardless of age or medical problem. Such a discourse is gradually changing our conception and experience of our bodies, encouraging us "to imagine the possibilities" and to ignore limits and consequences. Bordo (1993) calls this a "postmodern intoxication with possibilities" (p. 41).

Infertility, although real, is also a social condition, the seriousness of which depends upon the social evaluation attached to childlessness, motherhood, and women's autonomy. As Stanworth (1990) notes, the very existence of reproductive technologies—which, like all technologies, bear the hallmark of the cultural context in which they emerge—makes it difficult for women to reconcile themselves to childlessness.

Short of simply opposing these new technologies, it is important to consider ways to protect women who seek out these services. Better research is called for; a fuller disclosure of information is also needed, as are more stringent conditions of consent and a means of access for poorer women. A broader, perhaps better, range of treatments for infertility for both women and men is required, with more funds allocated for research into the causes of infertility.

The implications for psychology are many. It is important to continue the feminist goal of extricating women and their bodies from the singular and narrow confines of the traditional patriarchal family and from compulsory reproductivity. But it is also essential to remove women from the psychological theories that confine them there. Psychological theories, including those of recent feminist revisionists such as Nancy Chodorow (1978) and Jessica Benjamin (1988), assume a heterosexual reproductive imperative. The infant–parent dyad remains the cornerstone of psychological development, and is as stolidly present in feminist psychological theories as in Freud's family romance.[14] In this respect, feminist psychology must challenge what has become a naturalized story of identity formation, which conflates female identity with motherhood—in spite of, the deeply felt need by feminists for a unified female identity around which to rally, as Doane and Hodges (1992) warn. Judith Butler (1990) points out that it is precisely the mission of feminism, and I would add specifically the mission of feminist psychology, to re-examine gender categories that have been made to seem natural, foundational unities. In Teresa Brennan's words in *Between Feminism and Psychoanalysis,* we must "scrutinize the history of such naturalized identities" (1989, p. 12).[15]

Clinically, therapists must be alert to, and help women to distinguish their intrapsychic issues from, culturally constructed notions of motherhood and reproductivity. Destigmatizing nonreproductivity and infertility through the unlinking of women's identity with biological motherhood is an important aspect of this work. It is important, too, that clinicians become aware of and consider their own countertranference issues, so as not to impose their own constructions of motherhood or infertility on the women and men with whom they work.

As therapists, we are confronted with myriad examples of women's struggles with and conflicts over reproductive issues—ranging from our clients' questions about the intersection of sexual identity and motherhood, to choices between biological and adoptive motherhood, to anxieties about conforming with or not conforming to medical proscriptions. What I have attempted to convey throughout this chapter, however, and what informs my own clinical work, is the importance not only of what we do in our clinical work, but of how we think.

ACKNOWLEDGMENT

I want to thank Ann-Louise Shapiro for her reading of and invaluable comments on this chapter.

NOTES

1. Susan Faludi (1991) has reported that this study, which received such wide and distorted coverage, was conducted by French researchers Daniel Schwartz and J. M. Mayaux. They studied 2,193 French women who were infertility patients at 11 artificial-insemination centers sponsored by a federation that stood to benefit, she writes, from heightened infertility fears. The patients, Faludi notes, were

hardly representative of the average woman—they were all married to sterile men and were trying to get pregnant through artificial insemination. Frozen sperm, which were used, are far less potent than "normally delivered" sperm. In fact, one of the researchers found in an earlier study that women were more than four times more likely to get pregnant by having sex regularly than by being artificially inseminated (Faludi, 1991, p. 28).

2. See especially two chapters in Thomas Lacqueur's (1990) *Making Sex: Body and Gender from the Greeks to Freud*—"Destiny Is Anatomy" and "Discovery of the Sexes" in which he shows on the basis of historical evidence that almost everything one wants to say about sex is situational. "Society haunts the body" from the ancient one-sex model through the 18th century's two-sex model, elaborated into distinctly gendered organs, natures and roles.

3. See the chapter "Baby Boom and Birth Control: The Reproductive Consenses in Elaine Tyler May's (1988) *Homeward Bound,* in which she reviews the potent ideology of the postwar years that defined parenthood as the route to happiness; and considered childlessness as deviant, selfish, and pitiful.

4. Thomas Lacqueur (1990, p. 57) presents Freud's views on the role of fatherhood from Freud's reading of the *Orestia.* Fatherhood, Freud concludes, "is a supposition" and, like belief in the Jewish God, is "based on an inference, a premise." Motherhood, like the old gods, is evident from the lowly senses alone. Fatherhood, too, has "proved to be a momentous step . . . a conquest of intellectuality over sensuality . . . it represents a victory of the more elevated, the more refined over the less refined, the sensory, the material."

5. See Emily Martin's (1991) "The Egg and the Sperm: How Science has Constructed a Romance Based on Stereotypical Male–Female Roles," in which she details the way that scientific as well as popular accounts of reproductive biology rely on stereotypes central to our cultural definitions of male and female, and are in effect "a scientific fairy tale" (p. 485).

6. Ann Snitow (1991), in "Motherhood: Reclaiming the Demon Texts," points out that everyone claims that Firestone's book *The Dialectic of Sex: The Case for Feminist Revolution* is mother-hating. However, Snitow argues that where the book is reactive and rhetorical, the point is always to smash patriarchy not, mothers (p. 34).

7. Rapp, in studying the use and refusal of a reproductive technology (amniocentesis) that is in the process of becoming routine medical practice, notes the cultural contradictions involved in the technological transformation of pregnancy. The reasons for refusing amniocentesis are many, she observes: "religious beliefs, nonscientific constructions of pregnancy and motherhood, distrust of the medical system, fear of miscarriage" (p. 392). Low-income African-American women, for example, often express a "homegrown" sense of statistics that varies radically from the sensibilities of middle-class couples who often have delayed childbearing and are experiencing a first or at most a second pregnancy, and to whom 1 in 300 sounds like a large and present risk. By contrast, for a low-income mother of four, the same number may appear very distant and small; it may seem at odds with her own experience and that of her sisters and neighbors with similar histories, as well as with her observation of scores of babies born without defects. For low-income and people of color, Rapp concludes, "chromosomes don't loom large as an explanatory force when com-

pared to ongoing prejudices and labels already present in the lives of [their] children" (1991, p. 392).

8. A recent op-ed piece by lawyer Elizabeth Bartholet ("Blood Parents vs. Real Parents," *New York Times,* July 13, 1993), in reaction to a court decision to award custody to biological parents over adoptive parents, argues that "children are paying a high price for the priority we place on blood ties." This same biological bias, she suggests, "results in the legal barriers to adoption that drives prospective parents away from those children who are free for placement." Bartholet concludes that "the law should stop defining parenting in terms of procreation and recognize that true family ties have little to do with blood."

9. For example, the date rape controversy was recently fueled by Katie Roiphe's article, "Date Rape's Other Victim" (*New York Times Magazine,* June 13, 1993). Roiphe states that in claiming a date rape epidemic on campuses, feminists are subverting their own cause. "Preoccupied with issues like date rape and sexual harassment", she argues, "campus feminists produce endless images of women as victims" (p. 20). Smacking of backlash, such thinking has aroused considerable opposition among feminists.

10. Susan Bordo (1989, 1993) refers to early feminist discourse as "old" versus "new." Others—Snitow (1991), for example—divide feminist discourse into chronological periods: 1963–1974, 1975–1979, and 1980–present. "Old-wave" and "new-wave" feminisms are other frequently used distinctions for American feminism, as are "feminist" and "postfeminist."

11. These include Sawicki (1991), Singer (1989), Bordo (1989, 1993), Jaggar and Bordo (1989), Diamond and Quinby (1988), Bartkey (1988), and Stanton (1992).

12. Foucault, as Diamond and Quinby (1988) explain, warns against the seduction of totalizing theory. In place of history's search for "origins", he proposes genealogy. Diamond and Quinby, quoting Foucault, note that genealogy with "patience and a knowledge of details, operates on a field of entangled and confused parchments, on documents that have been scratched over and recopied many times." What is at stake in replacing history with genealogy is nothing less than "the destruction of the subject who seeks knowledge in the endless deployment of the will to knowledge" (1988, p. xiii).

13. Foucault's term "polyhedron of intelligibility" is borrowed from Susan Bordo (1993) in her analysis of eating disorders, and aptly defines the approach and construct that have informed my work on reproductive technologies.

14. See Carolyn Stack's unpublished doctoral dissertation, *The Marginalization of the Body in Contemporary Psychoanalytic Theory* (1992), where this point is more fully elaborated.

15. *From Klein to Kristeva: Psychoanalytic Feminism and the Search for the "Good Enough" Mother* (Doane & Hodges, 1992) for an excellent critique of psychoanalytic theory's, and particularly object relations theory's, traditional notions about women and motherhood.

REFERENCES

Arditti, R. (1976). Women in science: Women drink water while men drink wine. *Science for the People, 8*(24), 72–94.

308   WOMEN AND HEALTH

Bartholet, E. (1993, July 13). Blood parents vs. real parents. *New York Times*, p. 22.
Bartkey, S. (1988). Foucault, femininity and the modernization of patriarchal power." In I. Diamond & L. Quinby (Eds.), *Feminism and Foucault: Reflections on resistance*. (pp. 61–86). Boston: Northeastern University Press.
Benjamin, J. (1988). *Bonds of love: Psychoanalysis, feminism and the problem of domination*. New York: Pantheon.
Bordo, S. (1989). The body and the reproduction of femininity: A feminist appropriation of Foucault. In A. Jaggar & S. Bordo (Eds.), *Gender/body/knowledge: Feminist reconstructions of being and knowing* (pp. 3–18). New Brunswick, NJ: Rutgers University Press.
Bordo, S. (1993). *Unbearable weight: Feminism, Western culture and the body*. Berkeley: University of California Press.
Brennan, T. (1989). *Between feminism and psychoanalysis*. New York: Routledge.
Butler, J. (1990). *Gender trouble: Feminism and the subversion of identity*. New York: Routledge.
Chodorow, N. (1978). *The reproduction of mothering*. Berkeley: University of California Press.
Corea, G., Hamner, J., Hoskins, B., Raymond, J., Klein, R., Holmes, H., Kishwar, M., Rowland, R., & Steinbacher, R. (1987). *Man made woman: How new reproductive technologies affect women*. Bloomington: Indiana University Press.
Diamond, I., & Quinby, L. (Eds.). (1988). *Feminism and Foucault: Reflections on resistance*. Boston: Northeastern University Press.
Doane, J., & Hodges, D. (1992). *From Klein to Kristeva: Psychoanalytic feminism and the search for the "good enough" mother*. Ann Arbor: University of Michigan Press.
Ehrenreich, B., & English, D. (1979). *For her own good: 150 of the experts' advice to women*. Garden City, NY: Doubleday/Anchor.
Faludi, S. (1991). *Backlash: The undeclared war against women*. New York: Crown.
Ferguson, A. (1989). *Blood at the root: Motherhood, sexuality and male dominance*. London: Pandora.
Firestone, S. (1970). *The dialectics of sex: The case for feminist revolution*. Garden City, NY: Doubleday/Anchor.
Foucault, M. (1978). *The history of sexuality* (Vol. 1). New York: Vintage.
Foucault, M. (1979). *Discipline and punishment*. New York: Vintage.
Gordon, L. (1990). *Women's bodies, women's rights: Birth control in America*. New York: Penguin.
Haller, J., & Haller, R. (1984). *The physician and sexuality in Victorian America*. New York: Norton.
Hubbard, R., Henifin, M., & Fried, S. (Eds.). (1982). *Biological woman and the convenient myth*. Cambridge, MA: Schenkman.
Jaggar, A., & Bordo, S. (Eds.). (1989). *Gender/body/knowledge: Feminist reconstructions of being and knowing*. New Brunswick, NJ: Rutgers University Press.
Keller, E. F. (1985). *Reflections on gender and science*. New Haven, CT: Yale Univerity Press.
Klein, R. (1987). What's "new" about the new reproductive technologies? In G. Corea, J. Hamner, B. Hoskins, J. Raymond, R. Klein, H. Holmes, M. Kishwar, R. Rowland, & R. Steinbacher (Eds.), *Man made woman: How new reproductive technologies affect women* (pp. 64–73). Bloomington: Indiana University Press.

Laqueur, T. (1990). *Making sex: Body and gender from the Greeks to Freud.* Cambridge, MA: Harvard University Press.

Martin, E. (1987). *Woman in the body: A cultural analysis of reproduction.* Boston: Beacon Press.

Martin, E. (1991). The egg and the sperm: How science has constructed a romance based on stereotypical male–female roles. *Signs, 16*(3), 485–501.

May, E. (1988). *Homeward bound: American families in the Cold War era.* New York: Basic Books.

O'Brien, M. (1981). *The politics of reproduction.* London: Routledge & Kegan Paul.

Poovey, M. (1992). The abortion question and the death of man. In J. Butler & J. Scott (Eds.), *Feminists theorize the political* (pp. 239–256). New York: Routledge.

Rapp, R. (1991). Moral pioneers: Women, men and fetuses on a frontier of reproductive technology. In M. diLeonardo (Ed.), *Gender at the crossroads of knowledge: Feminist anthropology in the postmodern era* (pp. 383–395). Berkeley: University of California Press.

Raymond, J. (1991, June). International traffic in reproduction. *Ms.,* pp. 38–41.

Roiphe, K. (1993, June 13). Date rape's other victim. *New York Times Magazine,* pp. 26–68.

Rowland, R. (1987). Technology and motherhood: Reproductive choice reconsidered. *Signs, 12*(3), 512–528.

Sandelowski, M. (1990). Failures of volition: Female agency and infertility in historical perspective. *Signs, 15*(3), 475–499.

Sawicki, J. (1991). *Disciplining Foucault: Feminism, power and the body.* New York: Routledge.

Singer, L. (1989, Winter). Bodies, pleasures, powers. *differences,* pp. 45–65.

Smith-Rosenberg, C. (1985). *Disorderly conduct.* Boston: Beacon Press.

Snitow, A. (1991, June). Motherhood: reclaiming the demon texts. *Ms.,* pp. 34–37.

Spelman, F. (1988). *Inessential woman: Problems of exclusion in feminist thought.* Boston: Beacon Press.

Stack, C. (1992). *The marginalization of the body in contemporary psychoanalytic theory.* Unpublished doctoral dissertation, Massachusetts School of Professional Psychology.

Stanton, D. (Ed.). (1992). *Discourses of sexuality: From Aristotle to AIDS.* Ann Arbor: University of Michigan Press.

Stanworth, M. (1990). Birth pangs: Conceptive technologies and the threat to motherhood. In M. Hirsch, & E. Keller (Eds.), *Conflicts in feminism.* New York: Routledge.

Tilly, L., Scott, J. & Cohen, M. (1978). Women's work and European fertility patterns. In M. Gordon (Ed.), *The American family in social–historical perspective* (pp. 332–348). New York: St. Martin's Press.

Weltner, B. (1978). The cult of true womanhood: 1820–1860. In M. Gordon (Ed.), *The American family in social–historical perspective* (pp. 349–364). New York: St. Martin's Press.

14

Over the Hill We Go: Women at Menopause

ELLEN COLE

There are more than 35 million women over age 50 in the United States today. That number is expected to top 50 million in the next two decades, causing *Newsweek* (1992) to call menopause "the woman's health topic of the 90's" (p. 71). Because each woman has a different story to tell, because these stories are the heart and soul of the journey through menopause, and because the task of the psychotherapist is to listen to these stories with the awe and respect they deserve, I begin this chapter with personal accounts I have collected from women from various ethnic and racial backgrounds, social classes, and sexual orientations. I then tell my own story as well—because I know it best, because it has been helpful for me to write it out, and because it provides you, the reader, with the context from which this chapter has been constructed.

FIVE WOMEN'S STORIES

Bea is a 56-year-old housewife, a former math and science teacher. She just started having her monthly periods again now that she has begun hormone replacement therapy (HRT). Her gynecologist recommended HRT because of her mother's severe osteoporosis and the results of Bea's own bone density test. Prior to HRT, according to Bea,

> "I really can't say I felt any different at menopause except for the fact that I didn't have my period any more. I thought that was a lot of fun."

Barbara is 50, an executive in the computer industry. She says she "got menopause" a year ago:

"At first it was an odd period or two, then I didn't have one for a few months, and I kinda knew it was menopause. Hot flashes and night sweats have been mildly bothersome, no big deal. I read the four books in my library about menopause and discovered other symptoms I had were probably related to menopause—like sleep disturbance, heart pounding, stress, and anxiety. Bouts of fatigue, I learned, can be related. I was exhausted, something I'm not used to. I had thought my job was wrecking my life. When I learned my symptoms were hormonal, I experienced an enormous feeling of comfort and relief. Because of a family history of breast cancer I've decided not to take HRT, but if my skin starts to look old, I might revisit that decision. I like looking pretty."

Kansas, age 47, is a secretary in New York City, and rides the subway to and from work each day. Her menopause has been petrifying. She says,

"I can deal with a flash if it's hot and wet. I get wet all over for a half an hour to an hour. I don't like it, but I can function with the wet ones. When the flashes are dry and all the heat is inside, I get nauseous and dizzy, and I feel as though I'll pass out if I don't lie down. This has been going on for the past 6 months, once or twice a week, usually in the morning. I've changed my whole work schedule for fear of passing out on the subway. Now I go to work late and stay late."

And Kansas is surprised by the loss of her sex drive:

"My husband used to think I was a nymphomaniac. These days, if I think he might be interested in sex I'll stay up late or do anything to avoid it. I never expected I'd ever feel this way."

Kansas takes Chinese herbs for her menopause, not wanting to put anything "unnatural" into her body. She says she has heard too many conflicting reports about HRT to take the chance.

Silvia, age 51, describes herself as a "health nut." She is an aerobics teacher, a bicycle racer, and a long-time vegetarian. She says that starting about 2 years ago, her body seemed to enter a period of decline. There were new aches and pains every day, dizzy spells, and extreme lethargy:

"I couldn't even wear the same clothing any more. My body became allergic to anything with wool, to turtlenecks, to any kind of tight-fitting clothes. I started to feel itchy all over, the kind of itchy that scratching doesn't reach, and my vagina became terribly dry and sore. It seemed like in one day I woke up looking and feeling old. My doctor recommended HRT, and it's made all the difference. I feel like myself again."

Polly is a 47-year-old physical therapist, and she and her female partner are experiencing menopause together. She says,

"My favorite part of menopause is the time and energy we put into our sexual encounters these days. Our breasts are losing elasticity, our joints are creaking a bit, and we've both found this process fascinating and a source of great tenderness. It's engendered fantasies about growing old together, something we never talked about before.

"But I haven't always felt so positively. When my doctor told me I was beginning menopause at age 45, I thought I would die. I thought it was a sign of shriveling up and fading away, and I thought 45 was too damned young for that. It wasn't until my partner became menopausal, too, that I felt okay about my own. I'm grateful in almost every way to have found this woman to share all aspects of my life with. Going through menopause with a man must be a real drag for both partners."

When I asked Polly whether she had considered HRT or alternative remedies, she looked at me blankly and asked, "Why?"

MY STORY

My story, too, has a flavor and character of its own. At this writing, I am nearly 52. The first change I noticed was in my late 30s, when I began to have occasional "night sweats." These have continued through the years, recently becoming more regular—perhaps one or two a night. I have learned to throw the covers off, keep the windows open on my side of the bed, and sponge down with cool water. My sleep is more intermittent now, but not to a very disturbing degree.

I noticed the first change in my periods when I was 47; that was the year I skipped the month of April. The following year my period arrived every month, but I noted in my diary that December's was "extra long." In the next year I skipped one month, as well; this time it was May.

I remember that first month without a period. I surprised myself by feeling intensely sad. In part, I was feeling, "Uh oh, here it is, I'm over the hill now, an aging woman"; but much more vividly, and unexpectedly, I missed that monthly ritual of blood and tampons, the pointed attention to my body I had experienced for 34 years. The rhythm of life had suddenly changed. I also remember the joy when my normal period returned the following month. Welcome back, old friend. I recall thinking how precipitous and jarring it must be for at least some women whose periods, through surgery, cease suddenly, women who do not have the luxury of time to say goodbye.

From the time I turned 50, the changes became more pronounced. That year I had my period only eight times, and for the past year and a half, I have been skipping every other month.

I had my first hot flash a couple of months before turning 51. I was sitting in my therapy office, quietly and intently listening to a male client talk about his marriage, when I felt a heat wave that was unmistakable. I had been expecting this event, of course, and had wondered if I would recognize it when it came. Let me tell you, there was no doubt. Nothing else feels like a hot flash—so aptly named. My attention veered from client to self. I was in a quandary. I wanted him to know; this moment deserved special recognition, or at least an announcement. "Yes," I thought. "This is it." (No grieving this time; I had been waiting with anticipation for years to see what *my* menopause would look like.) I wondered whether my client who was with me at the time could tell; I had no idea whether or not it showed (since then I have learned that people do not know unless I tell them). Well, the moment passed. I decided to celebrate a subsequent hot flash, and returned my attention to the room.

For the next 6 months I experienced hot flashes off and on throughout the day and evening, and then they stopped for a month and a half. Two weeks ago they began again, perhaps one or two a day, sometimes none at all. I have no idea, of course, how my hot flashes compare physiologically with those of other women, but I can tell you that I do not mind them. I can even say, although I hesitate for fear of sounding ridiculous, that hot flashes are fun. Sometimes I keep them secret; sometimes I announce their arrival to whomever I am with. Either way, I get a kick out of it. If I am alone with a hot flash, there is a special sense of self-communing that feels sacred, meditative. I feel as though I have been washed with a warm wind by an invisible hand. (One friend, a kindred spirit, describes her hot flashes as "an odd kind of sensuality.")

There is also a lot of opportunity for self-parody here, as I take off my sweater, put it back on, and take it off again. Finally, I am too hot! I have spent the greater part of my life feeling too cold. Last night I flew from New York to Phoenix, changing planes in Pittsburgh, and did not so much as ask for a blanket.

I have yet to experience vaginal dryness or a reduced interest in sex. Nor am I aware of depression or unusual mood swings, except for one day a couple of months ago: My husband and I went for a mountain-bike ride, and I could not do anything right. Every little rock and hill seemed insurmountable; I was a failure; I was hopelessly uncoordinated. I did not want to turn around and go home, and I did not want to proceed; I could not stop crying. I remember feeling at the time, "This is crazy. My emotions feel chemical; this isn't the real me." I was reminded of the onset of puberty at age 12, when I cried in the swimming pool at summer camp for no reason at all. "So that's what menopause feels like," I thought at the end of the day. A 1-day menopause. Well, we will see.

So that is my experience with the "big six" symptoms of the perimenopause: irregular periods, hot flashes, sleeplessness, vaginal dryness, changes in sexual desire, and mood swings. With the day-long exception on my mountain bike, my own experience has been limited to irregular periods and hot flashes—so far. But there have been other things, small but troublesome; perhaps these are related to the hormonal shifts of menopause, perhaps not.

On the one hand, I have never been more physically fit. I jog several times a week at least, play tennis, hike, eat reasonably well, look pretty good, and for the most part feel fine. But I have noticed a palpable shift since my 50th birthday. During my 20s, 30s, and 40s, I saw my dentist and my physician for yearly checkups and almost never inbetween. For the past few years, I have made considerably more frequent visits to my health care practitioners. I experienced dizzy spells for a month last fall; one of these was so severe that I canceled a class for the first time in my 27-year teaching career. I had root canal surgery on two teeth, several months apart. My right eyelid suddenly drooped several months ago, causing my first midlife panic—in part because I knew the cause could be serious (which it apparently, after a physical exam and an expensive imaging procedure, is not), but mostly because I prefer my old symmetrical face to my new asymmetrical one. I had a bout of borderline high blood pressure that lasted for a couple of weeks, and during that time experienced very scary and very loud heart pounding. After carrying around some heavy luggage on a recent trip, I developed a painful right wrist, diagnosed as tendonitis. And although physicians say these problems are unrelated to menopause, I know better. What I know is that no one really knows.

Let me use my own experiences to demonstrate some of the confusions experienced by women at menopause. Although night sweats, hot flashes, and dry vagina are the only conditions I have that are directly and certainly attributable to a reduction in estrogen production, consider my 2 weeks of heart pounding. The physician whom I consulted assured me that it was unrelated to menopause, and suggested that I keep track and report back. Since then, I have read that heart palpitations are frequently menopause-related, and I have been making it a point to ask my midlife friends whether they, too, have experienced them. Yes, yes, and yes. Here is another example: I was prescribed a painkiller/inflammation reducer for my wrist tendonitis. After the first few days of taking this medication, I began to experience insomnia. For four nights in a row I did not sleep at all. "So this is what menopausal sleep deprivation feels like!" And then it occurred to me that perhaps this was not menopausal at all, but induced by the medication. The day I stopped taking the anti-inflammatory drug I slept through the night. In the first example, a condition was not attributed to menopause that probably ought to have been; in the second, the condition was attributed to menopause incorrectly.

And adding to the confusion, perhaps topping the list, is the question of response. Do I make peace with my droopy eyelid, or do I opt for cosmetic surgery? At what point, with any of the symptoms I have experienced, do I seek professional help? And then will it be a traditionally trained physician (who is likely to prescribe HRT), or an alternative health care practitioner, such as a naturopath?

For many women, the main decision that needs to be made at the time of menopause, while we wait for research that is conclusive, is whether or not to begin HRT. I discuss this topic more fully later in the chapter, but for now let me say that this, at least, has not been a difficult decision for me. I am not in a high-risk category for osteoporosis; I exercise regularly; I have not had my uterus or ovaries surgically removed; I have actually (for the most part) been enjoying my menopause; and I am extremely curious about the course it will take on its own. I have a slight aversion to medicine of any kind, and a monumental suspicion of any tampering with women's bodies, especially our reproductive systems, by the medical establishment. I do not like what I have heard and read about the side effects of HRT, particularly progesterone; furthermore, my mother had uterine cancer in the early 1970s after taking unopposed estrogen at menopause. On the other side of the ledger, giving me some pause for reflection, is the protection HRT may provide against heart attack and stroke. Although scientific studies continue to produce conflicting results, the HRT decision must, for every woman, be a personal choice based on her medical history and her value system. The psychotherapist's job is to help her be informed and empowered to make her own choices, and then to support her in that choice. My own decision, for now, is to say "no, thank you" to HRT. Three months down the road, I, like Barbara, may revisit that decision.

Clinicians will be best able to encourage their clients to take charge of their own menopause if they have some information and guidelines of their own. My goal in the sections that follow is to provide psychotherapists with factual information about menopause and to place these facts in the context of history, culture, and intimate relationships. I then present a psychotherapeutic model for working with women at menopause and their families.

WHAT IS MENOPAUSE?

The Climacteric

Most women, unless they have had a surgically induced menopause, will begin to notice some physical changes in their late 30s or early 40s, as their production of estrogen and number of ova begin to decline. They may notice less monthly bleeding, or their periods do not last as long; there may be a cessation of or an increase in monthly cramps, premenstrual tension, or breast tenderness; and they may begin to have occasional night sweats. The climacteric is so gradual that many women do not notice the changes at all. According to Margot Joan Fromer (1985),

> The climacteric is the term (also applied to the male aging process) used to describe the gradual winding-down of the whole reproductive system. It lasts for about 15 years between the ages of 40 and 55. Menopause, on the other hand, is a specific event that takes place during the climacteric. (p. 7)

Perimenopause

The first indication that menopause is approaching is the beginning of anovulatory cycles, or irregular periods, generally experienced by women in their middle to late 40s. However, the range of individual differences is great, depending on each woman's general health, nutrition, and genetic makeup. Some women's periods do not become irregular at all—they just stop. Other women cycle regularly into their early 50s. Other early indications of approaching menopause are night sweats and hot flashes. These and other signs of the perimenopause typically last for 6 months to 3 years, but here too, there is much individual variation. The perimenopause begins officially when periods become irregular, and ends with the last menstrual flow.

Menopause

Actual menopause has occurred when a woman has not menstruated for an entire year, which means that she knows she has experienced menopause only in retrospect. I, for instance, had my last period 2 months ago. Since I have been on a bimonthly schedule for a while now, I expect it will arrive any day—but it may not. This is the suspenseful adventure of menopause. The average age of the last menstrual flow is 51.4 years; it is 2 years earlier for smokers (P. M. Sarrel, personal communication, February 9, 1985). However, it is entirely normal for menopause to occur any time between the ages of 45 and 55 (Fromer, 1985, p. 9).

The Phenomenology of Menopause

Although it is not entirely possible to separate the effects of aging from the effects of menopause, or to separate the physical aspects of both menopause and aging from their social and cultural contexts, it is clear that menopause is not an event in and of itself; it also contributes to and is part of other events. Nevertheless, there are conditions that are experienced by large numbers of perimenopausal and menopausal women. These conditions are usually called "symptoms" by physicians, researchers, and the public at large. Yet the word "symptom" connotes a disease, and menopause is not a disease. What follows is a description of the common conditions that women report experiencing at menopause.

Data from the Massachusetts Women's Health Study, the largest study to date based on a random sample of women, show little effect of menopause on women's mental health, and almost no impact on subsequent perceived physical health. In fact, the data suggest that the majority of women proceed through menopause with little discomfort (Avis & McKinlay, 1990; McKinlay, McKinlay, & Brambilla, 1987a, 1987b). However, some women do experience a very difficult time.

Perhaps the most unsettling aspect of menopause for many women (I, personally, like this part) is its unpredictability, frequently experienced as loss of control. "The change" is aptly named. Women most frequently report hot flashes and night sweats, sleeplessness, vaginal dryness and changes in sex response (discussed in more detail later), irritability, mood swings, short-term memory loss, headaches, urinary incontinence, weight gain, and a variety of other more idiosyncratic conditions, all of which are new experiences. It is common to hear a menopausal woman say, "I don't feel like myself."

In attempting to make sense of and adjust to these changes, and in order to assure optimal health for the rest of her life, each woman must decide whether or not to begin HRT. The next section provides a discussion of the historical context of HRT, as well as a brief discussion of its risks and benefits.

HORMONE REPLACEMENT THERAPY

Every psychotherapist who works with even one woman at menopause needs to know about HRT, because the decision to take or not to take HRT will be a prime issue for her. Ultimately, each woman must weigh the risks and the benefits and make her own individual decision, albeit with incomplete and contradictory information. Each woman must evaluate the possible advantages and the possible dangers as she considers her unique medical history, her levels of menopause-related discomfort, and her basic attitudes about drugs.

However, it is not easy for a woman to find an unbiased, unpoliticized source of information on HRT. Her physician is likely to treat menopause as a disease and urge her to take HRT to "cure" the disease, to prevent osteoporosis,[1] and to prevent heart attack and stroke. If she turns to a moderately pro-HRT book like Gail Sheehy's *The Silent Passage* (1992), she will get a supposedly balanced treatment of HRT's "risks" and "benefits." Sheehy's risk list, for instance, includes possible cancer of the uterus;

unknown associations with breast cancer; possibility of continued menstruation; breast swelling or pain; a premenstrual-like syndrome on progesterone; and the expense of doctors' visits and tests for screening. Sheehy's "benefits" include decrease in heart attacks; prevention of osteoporosis; no hot flashes; decrease in insomnia; improved energy; restoration of sexual interest and comfort; improved mood and sense of well-being; and possible improvement in concentration, memory, and longevity.

Yet several of the "benefits" that Sheehy lists are actively being questioned by current research. For instance, according to Andrea Eagen (1989), HRT may *not* decrease the risk of heart disease, and the National Women's Health Network (1989) provides a different and contradictory list of risks, benefits, and negative side effects of HRT.[2]

I encourage my menopausal clients to read at least one book about HRT. Because of her moderate and nonjudgmental stance, and her tone that respects all choices but puts diet and exercise first, I most frequently recommend Sadja Greenwood's *Menopause, Naturally* (1992).

The Historical Context: Medicine, Politics, and Choice

The 20th century's views on menopause fall into four distinct categories: pre-1966; 1966–1975; 1975–1980; and 1980 to the present.

Prior to 1966 menopause was viewed primarily as a time of loss and emotional difficulty, but not as a disease. Helene Deutsch (1944), for example, described it as a "partial death" and concluded that mastering one's reaction to menopause was surely "one of the most difficult tasks of a woman's life." Although the journey through menopause has not felt nearly so daunting or melodramatic to me or to the majority of women with whom I have consulted, I understand Deutsch's point. The loss of reproductive capabilities, an evident marker of aging, is in the words of Iris Murdoch (1987), an "august and indisputable pain," and in the words of Germaine Greer (1992), "unlike anything a woman can have experienced before" (p. 7). It would be a missed "existential moment" to be unconscious of its significance or to treat it too lightly.

A dramatic transformation in perspective began, however, with the increasingly strong alliance between the medical profession and the pharmaceutical industry. Menopause began to be less frequently considered a challenging and difficult time in a woman's life and more frequently considered a disease—in particular, an estrogen deficiency disease. This medicalization of a natural body process culminated in the 1966 publication of Robert A. Wilson's *Feminine Forever*.

Feminine Forever, a classic of modern misogynist writing, described menopausal women as "eunuchs" and "functional castrates" who suffer from "estrogen starvation." Wilson likened menopause to diabetes, calling them both "diseases" caused by a bodily "deficiency." He described meno-pausal women as "vapid" and "cowlike"; he called menopause a "living decay," characterized by "a loss of womanhood," "a loss of good health," and "the transformation of a formerly pleasant, energetic woman into a dull-minded but sharp-tongued caricature of her former self—one of the saddest of human spectacles."

Wilson admonished women to remain "feminine forever" through the use of estrogen replacement therapy (ERT), and urged them to begin an estrogen regimen even before the onset of menopause. He assured them of younger-looking skin, continuing sex appeal, and a youthful appearance, as well as the prevention of hot flashes, loss of memory, melancholia, nervousness, headache, indigestion, backache, and neurosis. He explicitly denied a link between ERT and cancer. The book sold over 100,000 copies and was serialized in *Look* and *Vogue*.

Other misogynists soon added their voices to the chorus. In 1969 David Reuben published *Everything You Always Wanted to Know about Sex But Were Afraid to Ask,* still in wide use on college campuses and in homes throughout the world as recently as the 1980s. Reuben said about the woman at menopause, "She's not really a man, but no longer a functional woman." And after menopause, "she will just be marking time until she follows her glands into oblivion." In 1971 the U.S. Government Printing Office published a pamphlet, *Menopause and Aging,* in which women at menopause were described as "a caricature of their younger selves at their emotional worst."

Given the pathologizing and blaming nature of the psychiatric model of menopause, the medical model must have been a great relief to many women, who could now identify a physiological condition correctable with drugs. Consequently and understandably, driven by fear and worry and also by relief, women rushed to purchase supplies of Premarin until it became the fourth most widely prescribed drug in the United States (Eagen, 1989), generating $70 million in annual sales (National Women's Health Network, 1989). In December 1975, however, the golden era of ERT crashed when two articles appeared in the *New England Journal of Medicine* (Smith, Prentice, Thompson, & Hermann, 1975; Ziel & Finkle, 1975) revealing that women on ERT faced a 5- to 14-fold increase in their risk of uterine cancer. Huge numbers of women were outraged, especially when it was demonstrated by Barbara Seaman in *Women and the Crisis in Sex Hormones* (1977) that Wilson's work had been amply funded by several drug companies, including Ayerst, the maker of Premarin.

By 1980 estrogen sales in the United States had dropped dramatically, from 4th place in 1975 to 25th in 1980, despite the advice of some physicians that women have their uteruses removed so they could take ERT with impunity, thereby supposedly getting the "best" of both worlds (Eagen, 1989). Other researchers more sensibly sought to find ways to nullify the carcinogenic side effects of ERT. In the late 1970s, the first studies on "progesterone opposing estrogen" were published (see Gambrell, 1977). Since that time, estrogen dosages have been lowered and estrogen is typically prescribed in conjunction with progestin, a synthetic progesterone. Whereas estrogen causes a buildup of the uterine lining, progestin causes it to shed. When these two hormones are administered together, the regimen is called "hormone replacement therapy" (HRT) in contrast with "estrogen replacement therapy" (ERT).

Hormone Replacement Therapy Today

Fortunately—for it is clear to me that the jury is still out—the debate about HRT continues. The "naturalists" are perhaps best represented by long-time feminist and menopause activist Rosetta Reitz, who in 1977 published the first popular book on menopause from a women's perspective, *Menopause: A Positive Approach*. More recently, Reitz (1990) has asked:

> Why, I still wonder, would women fool around with their endocrine systems by putting foreign hormones into themselves? Not only does it throw the system out of whack but adds the possibility of serious damage. It also creates a sluggishness in one's ability to make estrogen. Our body's capacity to supply us with estrogen doesn't shut off the day we become 50 years old. And when the ovaries slow down, the adrenals pick up some of that work and so does our fatty tissue.

Janine O'Leary Cobb, editor of the Canadian newsletter *A Friend Indeed: For Women in the Prime of Life*, takes a more moderate position, while still strongly adhering to the notion that in general, "nature knows best." However, there are some women for whom HRT may be warranted— specifically, those who experience extremely severe menopausal symptoms, as well as those who are at high risk for osteoporosis or have had an early total hysterectomy (i.e., have had their ovaries removed before the age of 40).

The mainstream medical community strongly promotes HRT, most commonly for relieving hot flashes and night sweats; counteracting the drying and thinning of the vagina; and preventing osteoporosis, heart disease, and stroke. Norman Beals, perhaps the most enthusiastic supporter of HRT (but not atypical among the medical establishment), has published an expanded list of the benefits of HRT in the newsletter of the HRT Women's Health Care Center in southern California:

> As a woman ages, her skin loses its luster . . . emotional and mental stability become difficult tasks and she experiences depression, anxiety, apprehension, insomnia, and periods of fearfulness. Embarrassing hot flashes, incontinence . . . fatigue . . . and more serious illnesses such as

osteoporosis, arteriosclerosis, and even cancer have been associated with unbalanaced or low levels of hormones. . . . Furthermore, given together, estrogen and progesterone are able to increase bone density, provide protection against breast and uterine cancer, significantly decrease the risk of heart disease, and help to create an overall sense of well-being. (quoted in Eagen, 1989, p. 4)

And lending an even more sobering note to the issue is the following excerpt from material that is handed out to patients who attend the gynecological clinic in my town:

> . . . estrogen replacement use is associated with lower death rates from acute myocardial infarction, ischemic heart disease, chronic forms of heart disease, stroke, and all forms of cancer. . . . In [one] study population, patients with a history of estrogen use had a 20% reduction in their overall death rate, and current estrogen replacement therapy was associated with a 40% reduction in mortality. (Biomedical Information Corporation, 1986)

Those who oppose the routine administration of HRT do not dispute the fact that it offers benefits and is certainly appropriate for some women at menopause. But at the same time they would caution that the research has produced contradictory findings, even as to the protective effect of HRT on osteoporosis and cardiac disease.

Perhaps the most confusing area is that of the relationship between HRT and breast cancer. Some studies suggest a higher risk of breast cancer among HRT users (Grady & Emster, 1991; Sillero-Arenas, Delgado-Rodriguez, Rodigues-Canteras, Bueno-Cavanillas, & Galvez-Vargas, 1992), while others conclude that HRT does not increase the incidence of breast cancer (Nachtigall, Smilen, Nachtigall, Nachtigall, & Nachtigall, 1992). A recently published article in a popular woman's magazine (Foreman, 1992) tells its readers quite accurately that "it's almost a fifty–fifty split in the medical community," and "researchers can't seem to agree" on whether or not HRT increases the risk of breast cancer (p. 66).

Germaine Greer (1992), after reviewing the scientific literature, concludes: "Estrogen is thought to confer some protection against diseases of the heart and blood vessels; the likelihood is that progestogens reverse this" (p. 192). According to the National Women's Health Network (1989), the side effects experienced by some women when progesterone is added to estrogen include nausea, weight gain, breast enlargement and tenderness, and depression (p. 17). Above all, the "naturalist" critics of HRT object to the routine prescribing of hormones to healthy women, when the data are incomplete about their short-term or long-term effects.

To summarize, since 1980 we have been once again in an era characterized by increased promotion and use of hormone replacement for women at menopause. However, I believe and hope, that we are entering into a time when the routine use of HRT is questioned by scientists and laypeople alike, and that alternative remedies are actively promoted by the medical profession when appropriate. Patricia Hynes (personal communication, August 29, 1992) draws an instructive analogy between agribusiness and HRT. In agribusiness the resources, research, time, and financial backing have gone into finding chemical and synthetic solutions to the industry's problems. Frequently these "solutions" have produced toxic side effects as bad as or worse than the problems themselves. Many small farmers and consumers have advocated for natural and safer solutions, such as organic fertilizers and the reduction of consumption, but these are not money makers for the industry. The same has been true of menopausal research.

I consider myself a moderate in the HRT debate, opting not to take HRT myself but remaining staunchly "pro-choice." Yet I wonder how many fewer physicians would recommend HRT and how many fewer women would be enticed in that direction if menopause were viewed as a natural time of life whose losses and discomforts could be accepted, even celebrated, rather than treated and avoided at who knows what cost. What stand in the way are our societally entrenched, adamantly negative views of the aging woman.

AGEISM, SEXISM, AND CULTURE

In some cultures, women's status is elevated as they age, whereas in other cultures (like ours), women are devalued with increasing age (Kaufman, 1967). Our society defines women as childbearers, making menopause the equivalent of retirement for many women in traditional households. Our culture also extols and glorifies youth and youthful bodies. These are some of the major social contexts for women at menopause.

Youth and youthful bodies are equated with beauty, excitement, and sex appeal; aging is equated with decay. A recent publication from even so naturalist a source as the Rodale Press (Tkac, 1990) is typical in its shame-inducing call to hide the evidence of aging:

> Gray hair, of course, can be touched up with a little dye. . . . Wrinkles, however, are an altogether different story. No, you can't iron them out. And you can't (like Peter Pan or Dorian Gray) simply wish them away. But . . . there are a number of strategies to keep you from looking old before your time. (p. 632)

Hand in hand with ageism for the woman at menopause is sexism. The "double whammy" is evidenced most clearly in the disservice done to women in the guise of medical assistance, and in society's views about women's weight.

Medicine's disservice to women has been amply demonstrated in its misunderstanding of female sexuality, the overmedicalization of childbirth, and unnecessary hysterectomies. It is, however, most clearly demonstrated in its treatment of menopause as a deficiency disease, instead of simply a natural aspect of life—in reality, much more akin to the onset of menses or to motherhood than it is to diabetes. The nature of medical language also keenly demonstrates the pathological, ageist, and sexist bias in the scientific literature about menopause. For example, the adjectives "senile" and "atrophic," connoting weakness, decay, and emaciation, are routinely used in the literature to describe menopausal vaginas. It is simply untrue that a woman decays as she ages, or that her vagina rots away (see Cole & Rothblum, 1990).

It is well established that ours is a culture that equates youth with beauty, and moreover that beauty for a woman means a thin body. How must a woman at menopause feel about herself, then, when she is likely to gain an average of 12 pounds if she has a natural menopause, or an average of 15 pounds if she has a hysterectomy (Wurtman, 1992)? Never mind that study after study suggests that heavier women have an easier time with menopause, because one of the primary sources of estrogen after menopause is fatty tissue (Gerson & Byme-Hunter, 1988).

We need a new standard of beauty, or at least a more flexible standard, so that a 50-year-old woman can be herself without the pressure to look like her daughter. We also need to stop assuming in our research and our popular literature that menopausal women are white, middle-class, and heterosexual. It is extremely likely that Margaret de Souza (1990) is correct when she speculates that "there is a difference in the needs and expectations of non-white women going through menopause" (p. 15). Finally, we need to put menopause in its place. Menopause is not an illness; it is an important marker of time and growth, a time of new opportunity, or as Gail Sheehy (1992) calls it, "the gateway to our Second Adulthood" (p. 143). We need to know this with certainty; so do our clients and the family members with whom they interact.

INTIMATE RELATIONSHIPS

The woman at menopause is not alone in the world. Even if she perceives her journey as sacred and full of promise, and even if the health care professionals with whom she may consult are supportive, she will be unable to sustain a positive and healthy attitude about aging and about herself without the cooperation of her intimates. The two areas in which support is most important are the domains of sexuality and communication.

In one study (Cole, 1988), 85% of women at menopause who attended a menopause clinic reported changes in their sexual response, including reduced sexual desire, pain with intercourse, increased arousal time, and changes in touch sensitivity (becoming either hyper- or hyposensitive), orgasmic response, and orgasmic frequency of intercourse. For the most part, women did not like these changes and described menopausal sex "essentially as an effort" (p. 165).

In another study, a colleague and I (Cole & Rothblum, 1991) surveyed lesbian women at menopause, and found in contrast that for 85% of these respondents menopausal sex was "as good [as] or better than ever." We concluded that although lesbian women are not as intercourse-focused, there may be a deeper reason for the differences between the two samples:

> Partner expectation may not be as much of an issue for lesbians. The social patterning of males gives rise to high levels of expectation and performance pressure, and women in heterosexual relationships may be prone to resultant feelings of not measuring up. (p. 192)

An important part of the psychotherapeutic process with menopausal women is discussing the level of support they receive from their partners or close friends. Actual inclusion of the partner, at least for a session or two, is ideal.

Because I am fortunate enough to have a partner willing to journey by my side through menopause, I have asked him to describe in writing the experience from his perspective, in order to demonstrate the importance of communication within a relationship and the advantages to a woman at menopause of having a cooperative partner.

> "My wife and I are going through her menopause together, and I think it is a very healthy process, both for me and for her. It is also a process, I would guess, that very few husbands get to experience fully. Since this chapter is addressed to counselors and family therapists, I would like to share a few reflections from the male (this male's, anyway) perspective.
>
> "Going through menopause together really means just one thing: We talk about it a lot. I am 52, my wife 51. For 2 years now, she has told me each time she has missed her period, each time she has had a hot flash, each time she has experienced a night sweat. I know what physical changes are likely to occur at menopause—wrinkles, less vaginal elasticity and lubrication—and why. We have talked about HRT and have agreed that taking life and its changes naturally is the path we want to follow. This feels not only physically healthier to me, but also psychologically healthier and emotionally deeper.
>
> "Doing menopause together feels akin to the way men are experiencing childbirth more fully and more realistically than they used to. When I fathered my children (1963 and 1966), fathers were kept out in the waiting room and presented with a glimpse of their children after

they had been all washed up. After that, the children could be seen behind glass. For decades I have envied fathers who were intimately involved in the birth of their children, who were really there, whereas I had been 'protected' and kept apart. A sanitized procedure had robbed me, my wife, and my children of one of life's deepest experiences. I am determined not to let that happen again.

"So I am a good candidate for doing menopause naturally and together. There is no question that all this talking is good for me: Life is richer and more present. After all, I am going through my own time of accepting middle age and its physical changes. Up to now, I always felt a little uncomfortable about mentioning my increasing aches and pains, expanding girth, decreasing sexual desire, and longer refractory periods. Now I have a partner in change.

"So much for me. What about heterosexual relationships in general? One of the first things I learned about menopause is that lesbians in committed relationships tend to have an easier time of it than do heterosexual women in committed relationships. I can see why. Menopause occurs at exactly that age when men are themselves experiencing a transition into the aged portion of their lives. It is a time when many men have, or think about having, affairs with younger women in order to prove to themselves that they are still young and sexually attractive.

"So I can see where men could put pressure on their wives, spoken or unspoken, to stay forever feminine at whatever cost to themselves, especially if we are so busy denying the reality of our own aging that we don't want to see it in our partners. At any rate, men can certainly play a role in making menopause less stressful."

IMPLICATIONS FOR PSYCHOTHERAPY

In 1976, Jack Annon proposed the "PLISSIT" model, which helped psychotherapists develop appropriate treatment strategies for working with couples who had sexual problems. I believe that the model is equally appropriate for working with women at menopause. I therefore conclude this chapter by describing the model and relating it to menopause.

The P in PLISSIT refers to "permission." The most important function a therapist can provide to the menopausal woman is permission to tell her story, in all its everyday detail. There is not a woman in the world experiencing "the change" who could not benefit from this opportunity. If clients do not offer up their stories, the therapist should ask them. Women at menopause also need permission to make independent decisions and choices—to take HRT or not; to see a traditionally trained physician or an alternative health care practitioner, or no one at all. Finally, a woman at menopause needs permission to be open or private about her age and her "condition." This is her experience, to experience in her own way.

The LI in PLISSIT stands for "limited information." For many women permission will be sufficient, but most women will benefit from the addition of certain kinds of information as well. A therapist may, for instance, recommend a particular book or article, or list for clients the common signs of menopause, or present some of the pros and cons of HRT. If a client is suffering from despair about her age, the therapist can inform her (while not discounting her feelings) that she has a third of her life yet to live, or one-half of her adult life. Philip Sarrel (personal communication, February 9, 1985), a menopause specialist from Yale, points out that menopause is the beginning of the next six stages of life: early midlife, middle midlife, late midlife, early aging, middle aging, and late aging. Gail Sheehy (1992) says that "the forties represent the old age of youth, while the fifties open up the youth of Second Adulthood" (p. 136). I, for one, find that an amusing and exhilarating concept.

If a client is worried about recent weight gain, the therapist can inform her that she has lots of company, and that in fact there is some benefit to extra weight at menopause. If a client is determined not to gain weight, the therapist can likewise reassure her that 25–35% of women do not gain weight, and "manage to hold the line" (Wurtman, 1992).

Information such as that presented in this chapter is often helpful to women at menopause for two reasons: Many of them will wonder whether their experiences are "normal," and they are likely to have heard a great deal of conflicting and confusing information about menopause. Even informing clients that the experts disagree, and that their confusion is perfectly understandable, can be important information for many women.

The SS in PLISSIT stands for "specific suggestions." Although all women will benefit from permission, and most from some degree of limited information, it will be a smaller number of menopausal women who can use specific suggestions, particularly since many of them will be seeing a health care (as opposed to mental health care) provider for that kind of assistance. Nevertheless, there is a time and place for specific suggestions.

For instance, a therapist might suggest to a client that she keep a wet washcloth by her bed if night sweats are keeping her awake. I learned this trick from the chapter on insomnia in *The Doctor's Book of Home Remedies* (Tkac, 1990), which asserts that "the body begins to get drowsy as its temperature drops." The woman with night sweats needs to reduce her body temperature so that her body realizes it is time to sleep.

Therapists might also suggest to clients that they join a menopause support group, or the therapists might want to start one themselves. In addition, a diary in which a woman keeps track of her menopause can be a good friend, helping her to regain some control and order.

Finally, therapists might want to offer clients advice about stress reduction as well as diet and exercise, which are proving crucial at menopause for comfort maintenance, general good health, and prevention of cancer and the serious later-life illnesses of osteoporosis and cardiac disease. For specifics, I recommend that both therapists and clients refer to Sadja Greenwood's *Menopause, Naturally* (1992); the newsletter *A Friend Indeed: For Women in the Prime of Life,* edited by Janine O'Leary Cobb; and material published by the National Women's Health Network, in Washington, D.C.

The IT in PLISSIT stands for "intensive therapy." The vast majority of women will neither want nor need intensive psychotherapy to address the problems of menopause. Permission, limited information, and specific suggestions will surely be sufficient for most. But some women (perhaps as many as 10%) will have severe or prolonged discomfort; will feel isolated and despairing; will have uncooperative, insensitive, or even hostile partners; or will suffer exceptionally from age or sex discrimination. For these women, menopause is but the top layer, and it will be time to use general psychotherapeutic skills.

Meanwhile, whatever her situation, the woman at menopause is, in the words of Germaine Greer (1991),

> climbing her own mountain, in search of her own horizon. . . . The way is hard, and she stumbles many times . . . the air grows thin, and she may often feel dizzy . . . but she knows that when she has scrambled up this last sheer obstacle, she will see how to handle the rest of her long life. (pp. 439–440)

This is the challenge and the adventure of menopause. Over the hill we go.

NOTES

1. According to Sadja Greenwood (1992, p. 66), women may be predisposed to osteoporosis if they fall into the following categories: (A) *Genetic or medical conditions*—being in a non-African-American ethnic group; previous fractures that occurred easily, without major trauma; female relatives with osteoporosis; being thin, and especially being both short and thin; early menopause, before age 40; chronic diarrhea or surgical removal of part of the stomach or small intestine; kidney disease with dialysis; daily use of cortisone; and daily use of thyroid (over 2 grains), Dilantin, or aluminum-containing antacids. (B) *Lifestyle factors*—high alcohol use; smoking; lack of exercise; low-calcium diet; lack of vitamin D from sun, diet, or pills; very-high-protein diet; high-salt diet; never having borne children; and high caffeine use (over 5 cups a day).

2. The National Women's Health Network (1989, p. 16) cautions women who are considering HRT to "*absolutely* avoid" its use (emphasis the Network's) if they have any of the following conditions: past history of stroke or heart attack; estrogen-dependent breast cancer or endometrial cancer; severe liver disease

or chronic impairment of liver function; unexplained vaginal bleeding; or chance of pregnancy.

REFERENCES

Annon, J. S. (1976). *Behavioral treatment of sexual problems: Brief therapy.* New York: Harper & Row.

Avis, N. E., & McKinlay, S. M. (1990). Health care utilization among mid-aged women. *Annals of the New York Academy of Sciences, 592,* 228–238.

Biomedical Information Corporation. (1986). *Estrogen replacement therapy: Compendium of patient information.* Author.

Cobb, J. O. (Ed.). *A Friend Indeed: For Women in the Prime of Life.* (Newsletter available from Box 1710, Champlain, NY 12919–1710)

Cole, E. (1988). Sex at menopause: Each in her own way. In E. Cole & E. Rothblum (Eds.), *Women and sex therapy: Closing the circle of sexual knowledge* (pp. 159–168). New York: Harrington Park Press.

Cole, E., & Rothblum, E. (1990). Commentary on "Sexuality and the midlife woman." *Psychology of Women Quarterly, 14,* 509–512.

Cole, E., & Rothblum, E. (1991). Lesbian sex at menopause: As good or better than ever. In B. Sang, J. Warshow, & A. J. Smith (Eds.), *Lesbians at midlife: The creative transition* (pp. 184–193). San Francisco: Spinsters.

de Souza, M. (1990). The coulours of menopause: Stories of women from different cultures. *Healthsharing, 11*(4), 14–17.

Deutsch, H. (1944). *The psychology of women.* Philadelphia: Grune & Stratton.

Eagen, A. B. (1989, May–June). Reconsidering hormone replacement therapy. *The Network News: National Women's Health Network,* pp. 3–5.

Foreman, J. (1992, August 11). The menopause dilemma. *Women's Day,* pp. 64–67.

Fromer, M. J. (1985). *Menopause.* New York: Pinnacle Books.

Gambrell, R. D. (1977). Estrogens, progestogens, and endometrial cancer. *Journal of Reproductive Medicine, 18,* 301–306.

Gerson, M., & Byme-Hunter, R. (1988). *A book about menopause.* Montreal: Montreal Health Press.

Grady, D., & Emster, V. (1991). Invited commentary: Does postmenopausal hormone therapy cause breast cancer? *American Journal of Epidemiology, 134,* 1396–1400.

Greenwood, S. (1992). *Menopause, naturally/updated: Preparing for the second half of life.* Volcano, CA: Volcano Press.

Greer, G. (1992). *The change: Women, aging and the menopause.* New York: Knopf.

Kaufman, S. (1967). *The ageless woman: Menopause, hormones, and the quest for youth.* Englewood Cliffs, NJ: Prentice-Hall.

McKinlay, J. B., McKinlay, S. M., & Brambilla, D. J. (1987a). Health status and utilization behavior associated with menopause. *American Journal of Epidemiology, 125,* 110–121.

McKinlay, J. B., McKinlay, S. M., & Brambilla, D. J. (1987b). The relative contributions of endocrine changes and social circumstances to depression in mid-aged women. *Journal of Health and Social Behavior, 28,* 345–363.

Murdoch, I. (1987). *Bruno's dream.* Harmondsworth, England: Penguin.

Nachtigall, M. J., Smilen, S. W., Nachtigall, R. D., Nachtigall, R. H., & Nachtigall, L. E. (1992). Incidence of breast cancer in a 22-year study of women receiving estrogen–progestin replacement therapy. *Obstetrics and Gynecology, 80,* 827–830.

National Women's Health Network. (1989). *Taking hormones and women's health: Choices, risks, benefits.* (Available from National Women's Health Network, 1325 G Street, N.W., Washington, DC 20005)

Newsweek. (1992, May 25). Menopause: The search for straight talk and safe treatment. pp. 71–82.

Reitz, R. (1977). *Menopause: A positive approach.* New York: Penguin Books.

Reitz, R. (1990). Foreword. In D. Taylor & A. C. Sumrall (Eds.), *Women of the 14th moon: Writings on menopause.* Freedom, CA: Crossing Press.

Reuben, D. (1969). *Everything you always wanted to know about sex but were afraid to ask.* New York: Bantam Books.

Seaman, B. (1977). *Women and the crisis in sex hormones.* New York: Bantam Books.

Sheehy, G. (1992). *The silent passage: Menopause.* New York: Random House.

Sillero-Arenas, M., Delgado-Rodriguez, M., Rodigues-Canteras, R., Bueno-Cavanillas, A., & Galvez-Vargas, R. (1992). Menopausal hormone replacement therapy and breast cancer: A meta-analysis. *Obstetrics and Gynecology, 79,* 286–294.

Smith, D. C., Prentice, R., Thompson, D. J., & Hermann, W. L. (1975). Association of exogenous estrogen and endometrial carcinoma. *New England Journal of Medicine, 293,* 1164–1167.

Tkac, D. (Ed.). (1990). *The doctor's book of home remedies.* Emmaus, PA: Rodale Press.

U.S. Government Printing Office. (1971). *Menopause and aging.* Washington, DC: Author.

Wilson, R. A. (1966). *Feminine forever.* Philadelphia: J. B. Lippincott.

Wurtman, J. (1992, September). Weight gain at menopause. *A Friend Indeed: For Women in the Prime of Life,* pp. 1–4.

Ziel, H. K., & Finkle, W. D. (1975). Increased risk of endometrial carcinoma among users of conjugated estrogens. *New England Journal of Medicine, 293,* 1167–1170.

IV

PROBLEMS PRESENTED IN THERAPY: THE IMPACT OF THE SOCIOCULTURAL CONTEXT

15

Diversity and Difference: The Issue of Race in Feminist Therapy

BEVERLY GREENE

Feminist therapy asserts that social inequities based on gender oppression represent a root cause of mental health problems in women, and it posits the understanding of those oppressive societal circumstances as a major focus of treatment. This process seems deceptively simple if we assume, as the preponderance of the feminist therapy literature does, that gender is the primary locus of oppression for all women. Such an assumption, however, does not realistically reflect the life circumstances and conditions of all women. The influence of race in African-American women's lives; its appropriate exploration; barriers leading to its exclusion in feminist therapy considerations, and the consequences of this exclusion; and an outline for culturally literate feminist therapy will serve as the topics for this discussion. Although this chapter focuses on African-American women, it proceeds with the assumption that it is important to understand the collective plight of all black women in the diaspora, and of all women of color as well. It is less clinically useful, however, to view all black women as if they or their socialization experiences are the same. While some of my comments are applicable to all black women, and indeed to all women of color, I caution the reader against simply transferring them to groups beyond women of African descent who have been raised and socialized in the United States.

FEMINIST THERAPY'S FAILURE TO CONSIDER RACE

Feminist therapy has its origins in the theories of feminist politics, philosophy, and ethics. The ideology of feminism has generally examined social systems characterized by male dominance and female subordination, and has questioned the relationship between sexism and other forms of discrimination and oppression (Lerman & Porter, 1990). An analysis of such systems has naturally extended itself to mental health institutions. A feminist therapy analysis has determined that gender-based inequities play a prominent role in creating and maintaining many of the problems presented by women in psychotherapy. It has further been determined that traditional mental health theories and approaches do not appropriately acknowledge the role of such factors in women's mental health and functioning. Traditional psychodiagnosis and psychological treatment are not regarded in feminist therapy as neutral or independent of the values of the dominant culture, which is patriarchal. Feminist therapy itself is no exception. Indeed, no psychotherapeutic approach is considered independent of some system of values, which serves as the context of the approach. In traditional systems, however, diagnosis is used as the means of stigmatizing women who do not conform to the dominant culture's gender-role stereotypes (Dutton-Douglas & Walker, 1988; Marecek & Hare-Mustin, 1991). Traditional treatment approaches are presumed to represent a means of getting women to conform or fit into the prevailing social order, regardless of its suitability for them (Dutton-Douglas & Walker, 1988; Greene, 1993). The tendency to stigmatize cultural norms and practices that deviate from white, Anglo-Saxon, Protestant, and middle-class norms reflects the use of the dominant culture as the standard or norm, against which all others are deemed either similar and normative or different and therefore deficient.

The resurgence of political feminism in the United States prompted closer scrutiny of the role of mental health institutions in perpetuating sex-role stereotyping and other practices deemed harmful to women. Specifically, this has included an examination of the role of mental health professionals in maintaining these stereotypes and practices. Feminist therapy approaches were developed in part in response to the male domination of mental health institutions and the conformity of those institutions to the patriarchal status quo (Cammaert & Larsen, 1988; Dutton-Douglas & Walker, 1988; Greene, 1993; Lerman & Porter, 1990). The core principles of feminist therapy assert that social inequality between men and women causes many of the problems that women present in psychotherapy. Hence, addressing those imbalances of power in society and their impact on the individuals being treated is an important focal point of feminist therapy.

In the practical application of feminist therapy principles, the feminist therapist is charged with validating clients' realistic perception of oppression and assisting clients in understanding the extent to which their problems are a function of social inequities and not simply their own internal deficiencies. Marecek and Hare-Mustin (1991) note that day-to-day life for most women is shaped by gender-based social inequality; this unequal social position can be a cause of psychological conflicts, frustration, and demoralization (Greene, 1993). I would suggest that the day-to-day lives of African-American women are shaped by social inequality that is a function of the convergence of gender, race, sexual orientation, and other variables, not simply gender alone. Although gender inequities are reflected in the overrepresentation of women in some diagnostic groups, differences in rates and patterns for those groups emerge when race or ethnicity is included as a variable (Greene, 1986, 1994b). Russo and Olmedo (1983) note that while depression is the leading diagnosis for all women, rates of depression for black women are 42% higher than those for white women. They further note that black women are more likely to receive drug therapy than white women (56% vs. 36%). Freudiger and Almquist (1983) and Bell and Weinberg (1978) provide extensive reviews of differences between black and white heterosexual and lesbian women on the dimensions of life satisfaction, characteristics, and preferences. Differences were found in a range of areas, including age, religious involvement, marriage, children, perceptions of physical and psychological health, and financial satisfaction. Although a detailed exploration of the differences found is beyond the scope of this chapter, they reinforce Russo's (1987) observation that gender should be viewed as a dynamic concept—one that varies across ethnic as well as socioeconomic groups.

For the feminist therapist, the task is not to make clients fit into oppressive, and by definition, unhealthy circumstances; rather, it is to assist clients in using their personal resources to challenge and alter their circumstances in ways that are consistent with their values. The commitment to recognizing the need for social change and making this consideration an explicit part of therapy is one feature that distinguishes feminist therapy from other traditional approaches (Greene, 1993). Other major components of feminist therapy include an explicit focus on the need for therapists to be clear about their own personal values, the values inherent in their treatment approaches, and the ways that those values are expressed, both for the clients' good and to their detriment in the therapy process (Cammaert & Larsen, 1988; Dutton-Douglas & Walker, 1988; Greene, 1993). It is deemed particularly important that therapists be aware of the manner in which their values may contribute to the maintenance of social inequalities, reflected in the perpetuation of gender-role stereotypes that maintain patterns of female subordination and male dominance. Another major theme in feminist therapy is that of identifying the common elements in the dilemmas of female clients and of women in general (Rothblum, Berman, Coffey, Shantinath, & Solomon, 1993). The problem that arises, however, is this: Which "women" are we referring to?

Despite the good intentions of the formulators, feminist formulations of psychotherapy have been assailed for their failure to reflect the full spectrum of diversity among women (Brown, 1990, 1991; Espin & Gawelek, 1992; Greene, 1993; Mays & Comas-Díaz, 1988). The founders of feminist therapy, like their political counterparts, have been primarily white middle- and upper-class women. These women have viewed women's problems within the feminist movement and feminist therapy through the lens of their own experience and condition. Feminist theoreticians have appropriately focused their attention on the imbalance of power between men and women, and its negative impact on women's mental health. They have, however, neglected to put forth a similar analysis of the imbalance of power that exists between white women and women of color, the absence of women of color in their ranks, and the effects of these factors on the mental health of women of color. Furthermore, the preponderance of clinical and empirical research on both heterosexual and lesbian women is conducted with groups in which the respondents are all white, or in which women of color are present in numbers that are statistically insignificant. Rarely is the limited generalizability of such findings reflected in titles of papers or discussions of serious limitations of the work. A body of knowledge that fails to acknowledge and correct these omissions cannot help giving rise to a biased and limited view of what women are or should be; how or what they define as their problems; how they should feel about or perceive themselves; what kinds of solutions they should seek for problems; and what they may even consider a problem that warrants seeking professional assistance.

A consistent and problematic theme throughout feminist therapy literature and a barrier to diversity within feminist therapy theory is the assumption that gender is the primary locus of oppression for all women. Such an assumption fails to recognize, or minimizes, the importance of race, sexual orientation, culture, socioeconomic class and other forms of oppression; the interactions of these factors with one another; and the impact of these interactions on the experiences, perceptions, and values held by women of color (Brown, 1991; Greene, 1993; Espin & Gawelek, 1992; Joseph & Lewis, 1981). A subtle but salient consequence of this assumption is that it overlooks the privileged status of being white, regardless of gender oppression, in white women (Joseph & Lewis, 1981; McIntosh, 1988). Brown (1991) and Espin and Gawelek (1992) note that white women, because they are white, are more likely than women of color to be found in positions of power, to engage in research, to publish that research and to have greater access to professional and academic institutions where that knowledge is generated and disseminated. Failing to acknowledge this locus of privilege may promote the avoidance of any inquiry into how it is used, for what purpose, and whom its use may in turn victimize. It may also promote other problematic behaviors. One is the tendency to minimize the lack of access of women of color to sources of institutional power and the resulting barriers to opportunities. Another, is the propensity to minimize the important connections to sources of institutional power that white women have traditionally enjoyed despite the barriers in those arenas to women of color (Espin & Gawelek, 1992). The expression of women's grievances from the perspective of white women as if that perspective were comprehensive and normative, is a core reflection of white privilege (Brown, 1991; Carraway, 1991; Espin & Gawelek, 1992).

The presumption of gender oppression as primary often leads to the assumption that there are stronger alliances and greater similarities between women of color and white women than between women of color and their male counterparts. Such notions have left many African-American women, for example, with a sense of estrangement and a perception that racial oppression and its attendant difficulties are not being addressed within the feminist community. In fact, women of color may perceive the exclusive focus on gender and gender oppression as a way that white women may avoid examining issues of race. These presumptions of similarities and presupposed unity between white women and women of color, under the banner of gender oppression, may often serve to avoid confronting antagonisms between them by obscuring the power differentials in their experiences. Avoiding the examination of race may allow women who benefit from the prevailing power structure to avoid an examination of their own participation in oppression, most specifically, the ways in which white women who are gender-oppressed may engage in oppressive behavior themselves (Espin & Gawelek, 1992; hooks, Steinem, Vaid, & Wolf, 1993; Joseph & Lewis, 1981). Membership in an oppressed group does not immunize against engaging in oppressive behavior toward others. Brown (1991) notes that confronting white skin privilege is a painful process for feminist therapists as it is at odds with their self concept.

For African-American women and other women of color as well, race and gender oppression cannot be neatly separated into distinct entities, which may then be addressed in isolation. Although sexism affects all women, the way it affects them may vary or be "colored" by the lens of race and other parameters. Hence, many women of color may understand gender oppression differently than white women, and may assign it a different priority in their lives. The extent of sexism within communities of color ought not to be underestimated; however, Mays and Comas-Díaz (1988) appropriately noted that it does not mitigate the strong links between and among persons of color, regardless of gender, forged by the common enemy of racial oppression. A psychotherapy analysis that fails to take the interaction of multiple, overlapping, and conflicting aspects of a woman's oppression into account can neither sensitively nor appropriately address her dilemma in treatment (Espin & Gawelek, 1992; Greene, 1993). A theoretical perspective that fails to do so cannot appropriately understand or contextualize the range of dilemmas confronting women as an oppressed but diverse group.

AFRICAN AMERICAN WOMEN AND FEMINISM:
HISTORICAL TENSIONS

Despite its astute focus on sexism, feminist theory and practice have historically displayed a level of obliviousness to the significance of factors other
than gender (particularly race) in women's lives, and to the diversity of
women as an oppressed group. Understanding the origins of this obliviousness warrants taking a brief look back at the history of feminism in the
United States. The women's rights movement of the 19th century had
many of its origins in the movement to abolish slavery in the United States.
It would be unrealistic to think that this movement was not affected by the
intense and overt racism that permeated U.S. society at that time. Indeed,
racism was reflected in the abolitionist movement and the women's rights
struggle as well (Carraway, 1991; Davis, 1981; Giddings, 1984). Although
the abolitionist and women's rights movements included many alliances
between blacks and whites, advocacy for the end of slavery was not synonymous with advocating a change in the basic racial hierarchies that
relegated blacks to positions in which they were subordinate to whites
(Carraway, 1991; Harley & Terborg-Penn, 1978; hooks, 1981; Greene,
1994c). The women's rights movement was no different: These patterns
were reflected in the preservation of racial hierarchies and segregation
within the movement, as well as the recorded protests of African-American
women against them (Carraway, 1991; Davis, 1981; Giddings, 1984; hooks,
1981).

    hooks (1981) and Carraway (1991) note that both Northern and South-
ern white women who participated in the women's rights struggles were
vigorous supporters of racial segregation across class lines. The demand for
racial segregation extended to participation within the women's rights
movement itself. Frederick Douglass, who was a supporter of women's
rights groups, frequently spoke at such gatherings. However, in 1890 Susan
B. Anthony requested that he not attend the National American Woman
Suffrage Association convention held in Atlanta, Georgia, that year. Southern white women objected to his presence, as well as to that of black
women as equals in their ranks in the women's clubs. Their objections were
presumed serious enough to create a concern that the heightened visibility
of blacks in the movement, particularly as integrated equals, would
jeopardize the wooing of Southern white women into the group's ranks
(Carraway, 1991; Giddings, 1984; Harley & Terborg-Penn, 1978; hooks,
1981; Hull, Bell-Scott, & Smith, 1982). Harley and Terborg-Penn (1978)
observe that Elizabeth Cady Stanton, in her plea for women's suffrage,
expressed indignation that "inferior niggers" (referring to black males)
would be granted the right to vote, while "superior" white women remained disenfranchised. This turmoil took place in the charged atmosphere
surrounding the introduction of the Fourteenth and Fifteenth Amendments

to the U.S. Constitution, in which the word "men" was first used in establishing who would be eligible to vote (Carraway, 1991). Despite the pleas of dissenters such as Abby Kelly and the Grimké sisters, both Stanton and Anthony adopted the most scathing racist rhetoric to express their opposition to the blatant sexism inherent in the amendments. Although their opposition to the sexist wording of the amendments was appropriate and shared by many black Americans at that time, the flagrant use of racism to attack sexism in an already segregated feminist/suffrage movement seriously undermined the credibility of feminism among black women. Furthermore, only the interests of the patriarchy and racism were served by the successful disruption of the uneasy but often crucial alliances that had developed between the abolitionist and suffrage movements.

A detailed discussion of racism within the various phases of the feminist movement is beyond the scope of this chapter: However, Carraway (1991), Collins (1990), Davis (1981), Giddings (1984), hooks (1981), and Joseph and Lewis (1981) provide extensive analyses. A central feature in Carraway's analysis is the observation that white racism has historically permeated feminist theory and practice, segregating black and white feminists and "silencing" black feminists. All too often, this leaves black women with the responsibility of educating white women about the realities and implications of racism within as well as outside of the movement. It also leaves black feminism with the challenge to deconstruct not only the images, identities, methodologies, and presumptions of androcentrism, but the racism within white feminism as well (Carraway, 1991; Collins, 1990).

SHAPING PSYCHOLOGICAL REALITIES: THE SIGNIFICANCE OF RACE

African-American women often consider race a primary locus of oppression—one that not only shapes but may also transcend other realities (Espin & Gawelek, 1992; Ladner, 1971). Despite the shared history of gender oppression, there are major differences in the social and psychological realities of African-American and white women (hooks, 1981). Contemporary African-American women, unlike their white counterparts, are descendants of perhaps the only group of American immigrants whose arrival was wholly involuntary and whose legal status on immigration was reduced to that of property. Without the legal status of human beings, black women were not viewed as female or as feminine in the ways that white women were defined. Rather, they were pieces of property whose purposes were to provide free labor, to be purchased and sold as any other commodity would be, and to produce offspring who would become saleable commodities as well. The buying and selling of slave children, with the brutal and often abrupt and lifelong separation of mothers from their children that this entailed, highlights the extent to which even the bonds between mother and child—traditionally regarded as important and sacred in American culture, did not apply to African-American women and their children (Fox-Genovese, 1988).

The roles of black women in American society were synonymous with work outside the "home" and with legalized sexual victimization from the outset (Greene, 1993). The latter was reflected in the practice of using female slaves for breeding purposes with other slaves and in the practice of forced sexual relations with slave masters (Fox-Genovese, 1988). Although all women were considered the originators of sexual sin, white women were elevated to a pedestal of sexual purity and virtue, whereas African-American women came to be depicted as the embodiment of sexual promiscuity and evil (Greene, 1986). By depicting their black female victims as morally loose, white males rationalized what had become their routine and accepted practice of rape. The distorted image of black men as uniformly hungry for and potential rapists of white women served as the companion to this image of sexually promiscuous black females (Davis, 1981). These distorted images clearly represented the projection of the attitudes and behaviors of the dominant culture's males onto black males and supported routine acts of capricious and lethal violence against black males. Having done this, the dominant culture's males could maintain an image of themselves as genteel men in a civilized and democratic society that was founded on Christian ideals; they could avoid confronting their own exploitive behavior, blatant hypocrisy, and the inherent contradictions in such practices. Hence, African-American women were blamed for their own sexual victimization; they served as repositories for the sexual propensities found in all persons and acted on with impunity primarily by the dominant culture's males, but deemed overtly negative in the sexually repressive context of that dominant culture. Little if any evidence would suggest that white women did not join in blaming them as well while maintaining their protected status as one of the privileges of the pedestal.

Gender-based divisions of labor, which made many forms of work considered appropriate for white males inappropriate for white females, were not observed for African-American women. For the most part, female slaves worked in the fields with their male counterparts and did not qualify for the special considerations traditionally bestowed on white women. Hence, many other traditional roles and courtesies extended to women were never extended to African-American women, even though many of these roles were ultimately used to limit and confine the scope of activities of all women. Simply put, female African slaves were not seen as women at all, but as beasts whose reproductive capacities were used to produce commodities just as their physical labor was used to produce commodities for someone else's benefit (Fox-Genovese, 1988).

The failure to establish gender-based dichotomies in the sphere of work made the dominant culture's norm of women remaining in the home while men worked outside the home one that was never really available to African-American women. Yet they shared the experience of discrimination in the workplace with African-American men. Black women's presence by necessity in the workplace was and is often used to pathologize them for their failure to achieve the dominant culture's norm, and for "castrating" African-American males. These assertions are made with the fallacious assumption that African-American women had a choice about entering the labor force, and that their doing so was and is the cause of discrimination against African-American men. Both assertions conceal the reality that neither African-American men or women had ultimate control over their respective roles in the workplace—roles designed to maintain their subordinate position to white men and women.

Another facet of the complex history of racism and sexism for African-American women is the extent to which African-American women are held accountable to standards of physical appearance based on the white female ideal (Neal & Wilson, 1989). Although conventional standards of beauty, based on idealized and unrealistic depictions of white women, may not be completely obtainable for many white women, they are unattainable for a majority of African-American women. The full spectrum of diversity in physical appearance among white women is not reflected in the mass media's depictions and images of women. African-American women, however, see reflections of themselves in drastically fewer numbers and with an even narrower range of diversity. Furthermore, many of the theatrical and cinema roles in which African-American women appear simply reinforce old and degrading stereotypes. It is noteworthy that the first of only two African-American actresses ever to receive the Oscar was Hattie McDaniel for her portrayal of the character Mammy in the 1939 motion picture *Gone with the Wind*. The second African-American actress to receive this award, Whoopi Goldberg, did so only recently for a role in the 1990 motion picture *Ghost*. The chief function of her character, Oda Mae—a bogus medium and con artist who stumbles onto her genuine clairvoyant powers—is to serve the interests of the film's leading characters, who are white. In many respects, this is a reprise of the Mammy role, with comedic aplomb. I do not suggest that such films do not have entertainment value or that black actresses should only agree to perform serious or political roles, however I do not believe that these appallingly few selections of black women in subservient roles for such honors, and the paucity of dramatic roles for black actresses is coincidental. Rather, I contend that black actresses in roles that maintain stereotypic rather than realistic images of black women are comforting to both the predominantly white motion picture academy and its audience. The need to believe that the stereotypes of black women are valid may explain some of the popularity of such film and television characters with the American public. The Mammy figure, who is stoic, strong, and aggressive in the defense of the "master's household" but has no needs of her own, and who is delighted to remain in her place as a subservient individual, is found symbolically in many contemporary television programs as well. She appears as the strong, burdened, but happy go lucky black woman who is everyone's caretaker. These degrading images over time can have devastating effects on the self image and self esteem of many black women who observe them.

Distorted ideas about the adequacy of their physical appearance continue to have a discernible effect on many African-American women. These may be reflected in a sense of shame, guilt, or anger about their physical characteristics, particularly variations in skin color, hair texture and length, and body shape and size (Boyd-Franklin, 1991; Greene, 1986, 1993, 1994a). The origins of these feelings and attitudes toward skin color variations may be found in the pervasive idealization of members of the dominant culture and physical features associated with them and the differential treatment accorded African-Americans based on skin color differences. Jenkins (1993) notes that skin color has been used by the dominant culture as the major indicator of the personal value or lack of value of African-Americans since the beginnings of slavery. For African-Americans who have internalized this insidious value, skin color becomes one of the indicators used to determine their own self-worth. Depending on the degree to which a client in psychotherapy has internalized such values and on the client's personal history, skin color can be a symbol of pride, honor, guilt, shame, or oppression (Jenkins, 1993). Such beliefs may be reinforced by family members, who are similarly preoccupied with the perception that approximating the physical characteristics of white women is synonymous with being "womanly" and attractive. Furthermore, variations in skin color within African-American families can intensify a normal range of intrafamilial and sibling rivalries (Greene, 1990).

An environment replete with negative images of African-American women gives rise to a range of stereotypes that many African-American women believe to be true about themselves and that are accepted in many quarters of the dominant culture without question (Greene, 1990, 1994a; Jenkins, 1993). Their failure to meet the dominant culture's gender stereotypes often leads to the conclusion that African-American women are neither as feminine nor as physically attractive as white women. Another fallacious assumption is that black women are always strong, can take care of everyone around them, and require virtually no care for themselves. At its core, this is a recapitulation of the Mammy image. There is, however, a high price to be paid for illusory, ubiquitous strength.

Strong women in American culture are often viewed as castrating, defective women. Thus, even the realistic levels of strength, tenacity, and resilience that African-American women possess are used to depict them negatively. The myth that characterizes African-American women as emasculating and sexually promiscuous promotes a view of them as women who provoke abuse and/or sexual victimization, and who therefore deserve it. This allows both the members of the dominant culture and African-American males who have internalized racist and patriarchal mythology to displace responsibility for their own rageful, abusive, and exploitative behavior onto the victims of such behavior. Such myths encourage African-American males to vent their impotent rage—a result of the oppressive discrimination that they too face on African-American women or themselves rather than on white males and the institutional racism which oppresses them. The latter are often the ones who control the institutions used to facilitate the exploitation of all African-Americans in contemporary environments, as they did when African-Americans were slaves.

When these myths are internalized without an awareness of who controls the institutions responsible for exploitation, and to what levels that control may descend, many African-American women hold themselves and other black women responsible for the oppressed condition of African-American males. In doing so, many unwittingly subscribe to patterns in relationships in which they unconsciously or covertly agree to support the dominance of males and the subordination of females—patterns that may extend to the extremes of emotional and physical abuse (Greene, 1993; Jenkins, 1993). Some women may express the notion that they are being "supportive" of their black brothers in the struggle, or that they must compensate their men for the racial abuse they encounter in the outside world. This is often accompanied by the assumption that as women, they have an easier time of it. Such behavior, however, does nothing to improve the status or condition of African-American males or females, as it was never intended to do so. Rather, it perpetuates a racist and patriarchal hierarchy in which not only are females subordinate to males, but African-Americans are perpetually subordinate to whites. Furthermore, the internalization of this component of racism may predispose the woman who has internalized it to disparage other African-American women and thus interferes with her ability to seek and sustain important support and validation. Addressing and correcting this legacy of distortion and myth, both in society and in the lives of the clients, should be an active part of therapeutic work when it is encountered.

Another pernicious myth that begins with some basis in reality, but is then exaggerated to serve racist and patriarchal interests, is that of the African-American woman as the glue holding her family together. Although African-American women have demonstrated great resilience in maintaining their families under adverse circumstances, this myth romanticizes their task and minimizes the difficulties inherent in successfully executing it—difficulties that many women are not able to overcome. Furthermore, placing the success and viability of the family on a woman's shoulders alone valorizes her when the outcome is positive, but holds her completely responsible when the outcome is problematic. This ignores the role of institutional racism in complicating the task of socializing helathy African-American children. Many African-American women believe the myth of the woman as the keeper of the family; it is reflected in the tendency for some clients to be greatly attuned to the internal needs and experiences of those close to them, but not to their own needs (Greene, 1994a, 1994b; Jenkins, 1993). Some clients may confuse the needs of family members and loved ones with their own needs, and may feel that others are more entitled to have their needs met even if this is done at the client's own expense. Assisting such clients in becoming more sensitive to their own needs, feeling entitled to address them, and seeking help in doing so is an active and important component of treatment.

When any or all of the stereotypes described above are internalized by African-American women, they can have a powerful negative effect on their psychological well-being. Internalized racism and realistic barriers of race, gender, and sexual orientation discrimination create a range of over-lapping and interrelated psychological realities. These realities may facilitate, challenge, or clearly undermine the optimal development of African-American women (Greene, 1993). Part of such development is the requirement to develop mechanisms for coping with and mastering the interrelated realities of race, gender, and sexual orientation oppression, in addition to all other life tasks, and to give appropriate priority to those tasks. Similarly, therapists' beliefs in such stereotypes will have a negative effect on the therapy process and inhibit their ability to fully appreciate the wide range of diversity within African-American women as a group.

CONSIDERING THE CONVERGENCE OF RACE AND GENDER IN FEMINIST THERAPY

Many African-American women enter the therapy process with many of the same feelings of discomfort found in clients from other ethnic groups. However, most white females who enter therapy may presume that their therapists, who are usually white, have some understanding of their cultural heritage and its effect on their lives. African-American women and other women of color may not presume that their therapists, even if the therapists are persons of color, are similarly familiar with their background. Most therapists, regardless of their own ethnicity, are trained in institutions that are a part of the dominant culture. Those institutions often have had an active role in reinforcing some of the stereotypes discussed here, rather than mitigating them. Scholarly institutions and literature have been selectively used throughout history to buttress patriarchal and racist political agendas. Hence, it cannot be assumed that formal training in such institutions represents the royal road to objectivity. Feminist therapy, despite its origins outside the mainstream of the mental health field, is no exception. Just as the feminist political movement has often presented the concerns of white women as if they were universal, feminist therapy has been guilty of this as well.

African-American women have not traditionally viewed psychotherapy as an appropriate place to seek assistance for themselves, and it is frequently not the first source to which they turn for help. Institutions of the dominant culture have rarely welcomed African-American women, and many such women have grown to distrust these institutions ubiquitously. Mental health research and its practitioners are included in this sphere of suspicion. Despite this history of wariness, increasing numbers of African-American women seek and utilize psychological services in both the public and private sectors.

Childs (1990) has noted that most African-American women enter therapy under great stress, often when all else has failed, and begin with little trust in the therapist. In my own clinical experience, an overwhelming majority of these women express fears with consistent themes about what it means to be in therapy. Commonly, they report feeling that they have somehow failed to attend appropriately to all of their burdens or solve all of their family members' problems. They rarely wonder whether their responsibilities are too extensive and that their expectations of themselves are unrealistic (Greene, 1994a). Others express the fear that coming to therapy means that they are "weak" or "couldn't take it"; that they are "indulgent" to spend time talking about their own personal concerns, or, even worse, that they will become "dependent" on therapy or the therapist. Many of these concerns have their origins in the internalization of racist and gender stereotypes. Such stereotypes must be appropriately labeled at the outset of therapy and addressed as a part of the therapeutic work. Similarly, African-American women have developed important resources, often as a result of the need to meet adversity on a routine basis. Many, however, are unaware of the special strengths and resilience that they may possess. Helping them to become more consciously aware of their assets and to use them consciously and selectively is an important part of the therapeutic work. Although such resources should not be romanticized, those that do exist should be utilized fully in the course of therapy.

Childs (1990) also notes that many African-American women begin to experience the depth of their anger early in therapy—an experience that they may have sought to avoid. She suggests that a therapist must expect this, and must reassure the client who is frightened by these feelings that they are a natural reaction to having spent many years either repressing her anger or directing it at herself. Such feelings may have their origins in the conflict between the desire to value herself and the need to deny herself an appropriate level of entitlement (Childs, 1990). It is appropriate in such cases that therapy assist a client in understanding what forces in her personal life, as well as in her social and political history, benefit from her silence and her self blaming (Childs, 1990; Greene, 1993). It is also important that the therapist accept the appropriate expressions of the client's anger—at times even being the target of the anger—without personalizing it. Personalizing such expressions may make therapists feel the need to defend themselves, avoid setting limits, or avoid the exploration of such material. Therapists who have internalized racist stereotypes of African-Americans as un-civilized, violent, and unable to modulate emotions may be predisposed to avoid exploring such material out of their own concerns about what the clients will do with their anger. This underscores the importance of thera-pists' understanding of their own feelings and motivations about working with African-American women.

CONCLUSION: CREATING CULTURALLY LITERATE FEMINIST THERAPY

Although feminism is theoretically opposed to social oppression and hence to racism, that philosophy does not automatically translate into practice. Therefore, it does not protect African-American women from the routine exploitation that is a function of racism. It is even more problematic that many feminist scholars reinforce the notion that a specific kind of oppres-sion is most salient for all women (i.e., gender oppression). Hence, the culturally literate therapist must first acknowledge the significance of race, ethnicity, sexual orientation, and other variables in addition to gender as variables that are critical to the accurate understanding of people (Chin, De La Cancela, & Jenkins, 1993; Greene, 1992, 1993; Guzman, 1993). Brown (1991) considers antiracism an ethical imperative of feminist therapy and presents a conceptual framework for viewing racist behaviors as unethical. Included in her framework is an analysis of the ways that ignoring racism perpetuates power imbalances between women, violates psychological and physical boundaries, and perpetuates a lack of mutuality and respect.

Consistent with the mandate of feminist therapy to acknowledge val-ues and biases, therapists must acknowledge the ways in which they may harbor biases in their attitudes toward clients (Howard, 1990; Kupers, 1981; Pinderhughes, 1989). Doing so requires that therapists not only understand the clients' racial and ethnic background and its effect on the clients' lives, but explicitly understand those aspects of their own background and the analogous effects (Kupers, 1981; Pinderhughes, 1989). Therapists who do not feel comfortable and competent or who feel guilty when treating African-American clients may be unconsciously predisposed to attempt to compensate the client by engaging in certain behaviors. For some, this behavior may be manifested in the tendency to patronize the client or presume to take care of needs that extend beyond the normal range of therapy. While there may be occasions when the therapist must depart from their usual role in therapy in order to be of maximum assistance to the client, the impulse to do so should always be scrutinized for these tendencies. There may be a reluctance to hold the client accountable to a mutually agreed upon contract, interpret acting out, or to set boundaries and limits. In such cases, the therapist may also harbor the fear that setting limits will result in the client's departure from therapy, confirming the therapist's fears of incompetence.

Therapists' cultural backgrounds and the ways in which these predispose them to respond to gender, race, sexual orientation, and other parameters should be explored in the therapists' own therapy or supervision. A client's therapy should not be used by a therapist as a forum for self-repair or self-exploration. The client should not be in the position of having to educate or take care of the therapist who is culturally illiterate. Feminist therapy principles would not expect a therapist to be blind to the effects of gender and what it means to be a woman in our society; rather, those principles directly challenge the therapist to attend to gender as a salient human variable and deems sexism an important area of scrutiny. Similarly, feminist therapy should neither expect nor support color or racial blindness in the therapist. To the contrary it must deem race, ethnicity, culture, and racial oppression equal in significance to gender issues and facilitate their exploration and expression.

It is particularly important that therapists be able to acknowledge and validate their clients' accurate perceptions of discrimination and oppression. The therapists cannot do this if they need, out of guilt, embarrassment, or ignorance, to avoid acknowledging the levels of their own privilege and its role in the oppression of others (McIntosh, 1988; Thompson, 1989). When a therapist from the dominant culture treats a client who is a member of an oppressed group, many of the social and political tensions which exist in conjunction with those dimensions do not disappear in the therapy process. This observation is valid even when both are members of the same group. Members of oppressed groups have feelings about one another as well as they do about dominant groups members—feelings the therapist may not presume that they know or understand without exploration. Each may experience their status and explain their discrimination differently.

Raising or responding to the issue of race in therapy is something which formal clinical training rarely addresses, nor does feminist therapy. In fact, feminist therapists may tend to overemphasize their shared gender status with the client and, for many reasons discussed previously, tend to minimize realistic differences between themselves and the client. In my clinical experience with therapists in training, and in supervision and consultation with experienced therapists, I have observed a reluctance on the part of the therapist to directly raise the issue of race when the client is African-American. This reluctance has been observed even when the client directly or obliquely raised concerns about racism in their lives, race in general, or the racial differences and similarities between the therapist and themselves. Such reluctance has also persisted even after it has been discussed in supervision and after the therapist has been directed to explore such material with the client. When their feelings about these matters are explored in supervision, most therapists reported experiences ranging from mild discomfort and moderate levels of anxiety to panic at the idea of exploring this material. At this juncture I request that the therapist consider the origins of such feelings and express their worst fear about what will happen if they openly explore the issue of race with the client. Frequent responses include, "I'm afraid if we talk about race, the client will be angry with me and we won't be able to work together," "There will just be anger, and the client won't want to work with me," "It's too painful . . . it's like I would be inflicting pain on the client by making them look at this." While such fears are understandable in a society tinged with ubiquitous racial tension, the therapist cannot, in being self protective, act on such fears and avoid the appropriate exploration of this material. Clients will often feel reluctant to raise or explore matters of race out of fear that they will make anxious or alienate the therapist. Indeed, some clients will deny having feelings about these issues even when the therapist inquires about them. This cannot be taken as a sign that the client has no feelings about these matters and may often reflect the level of danger many African-Americans experience around revealing their true feelings—particularly anger—about racial issues, even in the apparent safety and privacy of therapy. Furthermore, some therapists report that they do not think that racism has anything to do with the client's problems. While this is always a possibility, and all possibilities should be fully explored, therapists often make this assumption before they have even superficially explored it. This behavior may often reflect the therapist's difficulty tolerating their own anxiety when racial issues arise in therapy and their subsequent need to avoid, rather than explore, the material. With the mandate to be culturally literate and antiracist, feminist therapists are urged to raise the issue of race early in treatment, after appropriately prioritizing the presenting problems, in ways that leave clients feeling that they can explore feelings or attitudes about race fully and that they do not have to protect their therapists from their feelings about them (Greene, 1993, 1994a 1994b).

A culturally literate and antiracist therapist must begin with an understanding of the role of multiple identities and oppressions in clients' lives, and must have or be willing to acquire a familiarity with the clients' cultural and ethnic heritage and the role of institutional barriers in their lives. This includes the clients' varying experiences of their ethnic and cultural history. The therapist must also be willing to acknowledge each client's personal barriers and resources by exploring significant figures, relationships and their patterns, and events in their personal lives. Having done all of this, the therapist must avoid the temptation to reduce a client's dilemma to a series of dichotomized "either–ors." Rarely is institutional oppression the sole source of all of a client's difficulties. The struggle of negotiating discriminatory barriers may at times be less painful to address than troubled or conflicted personal histories with loved and trusted figures (Greene, 1993). It is essential to strike an appropriate balance between prematurely dismissing a client's realistic complaints about discrimination and focusing on such complaints exclusively. Similarly, exploring or exposing personal difficulties in a client's life should not be used to minimize problems that are a function of the client's oppressed status.

The therapist must also develop an analysis of where they are positioned with respect to the prevailing power structure and relative to the client's oppressed status. Requiring feminist therapists to be culturally literate does not require that they be of the same culture as their clients. Rather, it refers to an attitude of respect toward and a willingness to know a client's life context fully that is consistent with the principles of feminist therapy.

Finally, the obligation to educate and inform feminist scholarship and practice about the effects and dangers of racism and other forms of oppression is not the exclusive responsibility of African-American women or other women of color. Therapists and theoreticians who are women of color usually have far less access than white therapists to the venues that disseminate such information. These concerns must be elevated to the same level of legitimacy and made as explicit a locus of concern as gender. White feminists must take the responsibility of addressing these issues in their own communities, work, and writings and must challenge feminist practice to live up to its philosophical ideals.

REFERENCES

Bell, A. P., & Weinberg, M. S. (1978). *Homosexualities: A study of diversity among men and women.* New York: Simon & Schuster.

Boyd-Franklin, N. (1991). Recurrent themes in the treatment of African American women in group therapy. *Women and Therapy, 11*(2), 25–40.

Brown, L. S. (1990). The meaning of a multicultural perspective for theory building in feminist therapy. In L. Brown & M. Root (Eds.), *Diversity and complexity in feminist therapy* (pp. 1–21). New York: Haworth Press.

Brown, L. S. (1991). Antiracism as an ethical imperative: An example from feminist therapy. *Ethics and Behavior, 1*(2), 113–127.

Cammaert, L. P., & Larsen, C. (1988). Feminist frameworks of psychotherapy. In M. A. Dutton-Douglas & L. Walker (Eds.), *Feminist psychotherapies: Integration of therapeutic and feminist systems* (pp. 12–36). Norwood, NJ: Ablex.

Carraway, N. (1991). *Segregated sisterhood: Racism and the politics of American feminism.* Knoxville: University of Tennessee Press.

Childs, E. K. (1990). Therapy, feminist ethics, and the community of color with particular emphasis on the treatment of black women. In H. Lerman & N. Porter (Eds.), *Feminist ethics in psychotherapy* (pp. 195–203). New York: Springer.

Chin, J. L. De La Cancela, V., & Jenkins, Y. (1993). Themes in psychotherapy with diverse populations. In J. L. Chin, V. De La Cancela, & Y. Jenkins (Eds.), *Diversity in psychotherapy* (pp. 171–182). Westport, CT: Praeger.

Collins, P. H. (1990). *Black feminist thought.* Boston: Unwin Hyman.

Davis, A. (1981). *Women, race and class.* New York: Vintage.

Dutton-Douglas, M. A., & Walker, L. E. (1988). Introduction to feminist therapies. In M. Dutton-Douglas & L. Walker (Eds.), *Feminist psychotherapies: Integration of therapeutic and feminist systems* (pp. 3–11). Norwood, NJ: Ablex.

Espin, O., & Gawelek, M. A. (1992). Women's diversity: Ethnicity, race, class, and gender in theories of feminist psychology. In L. Brown & M. Ballou (Eds.), *Personality and psychopathology: Feminist reappraisals* (pp. 88–107). New York: Guilford Press.

Fox-Genovese, E. (1988). *Within the plantation household: Black and white women of the old South.* Chapel Hill: University of North Carolina Press.

Freudiger, P., & Almquist, E. M. (1983, April). *Sources of life satisfaction: The different worlds of black and white women.* Revised version of a paper presented at the annual meeting of the Southwestern Sociological Association, Houston, TX.

Giddings, P. (1984). *When and where I enter: The impact of black women on race and sex in America.* New York: Morrow.

Greene, B. (1986). When the therapist is white and the patient is black: Considerations for psychotherapy in the feminist heterosexual and lesbian communities. *Women and Therapy, 5*(2–3), 41–65.

Greene, B. (1990). What has gone before: The legacy of racism and sexism in the lives of black mothers and daughters. *Women and Therapy, 9*(1–2,3), 207–230.

Greene, B. (1992). Black feminist psychotherapy. In E. Wright (Ed.), *Feminism and psychoanalysis: A critical dictionary* (pp. 34–35). Oxford: Blackwell.

Greene, B. (1993). Psychotherapy with African American women: Integrating feminist and psychodynamic models. *Journal of Training and Practice in Professional Psychology, 7*(1), 49–66.

Greene, B. (1994a). African American women. In L. Comas-Díaz & B. Greene (Eds.), *Women of color: Integrating ethnic and gender identities in psychotherapy.* New York: Guilford Press.

Greene, B. (1994b). African American women: Derivatives of racism and sexism in psychotherapy. In B. Rosoff & E. Toback (Eds.), *Genes and gender series. Vol.7. Challenging racism and sexism: Alternatives to genetic determinism.* New York: Feminist Press.

Greene, B. (1994c). An African American perspective on racism and antisemitism within feminist organizations. In J. Adleman & G. Enguidanos (Eds.), *Racism in the lives of women: Testimony, theory and guides to practice* (pp. 499–518). New York: Haworth.

Guzman, L. P. (1993). Afterword. In J. Chin, V. De La Cancela, & Y. Jenkins (Eds.), *Diversity in psychotherapy* (pp. 183–188). Westport, CT: Praeger.

Harley, S., & Terborg-Penn, R. (1978). *The Afro-American woman: Struggles and images.* Port Washington, NY: Kennikat Press.

hooks, b. (1981). *Black women and feminism*. Boston: South End Press.

hooks, b., Steinem, G., Vaid, U., & Wolf, N. (1993, September–October). Let's get real about feminism: The backlash, the myths, the movement. *Ms.*, pp. 34–43.

Howard, D. (1990). Competence and professional self evaluation. In H. Lerman & N. Porter (Eds.), *Feminist ethics in psychotherapy* (pp. 131–136). New York: Springer.

Hull, G. T., Bell-Scott, P., & Smith, B. (Eds.). (1982). *All the women are white, all the blacks are men, but some of us are brave: Black women's struggles*. Old Westbury, NY: Feminist Press.

Jenkins, Y. (1993). African American women: Ethnocultural variables and dissonant expectations. In J. L. Chin, V. De La Cancela, & Y. Jenkins (Eds.), *Diversity in psychotherapy: The politics of race, ethnicity and gender* (pp. 117–136). Westport, CT: Praeger.

Joseph, G., & Lewis, J. (1981). *Common differences: Conflicts in black and white feminist perspectives*. Garden City, NY: Anchor.

Kupers, T. (1981). *Public therapy: The practice of psychotherapy in the public mental health clinic*. New York: Free Press.

Ladner, J. (1971). *Tomorrow's tomorrow: The black woman*. Garden City, NY: Doubleday.

Lerman, H., & Porter, N. (1990). The contribution of feminism to ethics in psychotherapy. In H. Lerman & N. Porter (Eds.), *Feminist ethics in psychotherapy* (pp. 5–13). New York: Springer.

Maracek, J., & Hare-Mustin, R. (1991). A short history of the future. *Psychology of Women Quarterly, 15*, 521–536.

Mays, V., & Comas-Díaz, L. (1988). Feminist therapy with ethnic minority populations: A closer look at blacks and Hispanics. In M. Dutton-Douglas & L. Walker (Eds.), *Feminist psychotherapies: Integration of therapeutic and feminist systems* (pp. 228–251). Norwood, NJ: Ablex.

McIntosh, P. (1988). *White privilege and male privilege: A personal account of coming to see correspondences through work in women's studies* (Working paper No. 189). Wellesley College. Wellesley, MA: Stone Center.

Neal, A., & Wilson, M. (1989). The role of skin color and features in the black community: Implications for black women and therapy. *Clinical Psychology Review, 9*(3), 323–333.

Pinderhughes, E. (1989). *Understanding race, ethnicity and power: The key to efficacy in clinical practice*. New York: Free Press.

Rothblum, E., Berman, J., Coffey, P., Shantinath, S., & Solomon, S. (1993). Feminist approaches to psychotherapy with depressed women: A discussion. *Journal of Training and Practice in Professional Psychology, 7*(1), 100–112.

Russo, N. F. (1987). Position paper. In A. E. Eichler & D. Parron (Eds.), *Women's mental health: Agenda for research*. Rockville, MD: National Institute of Mental Health.

Russo, N. F., & Olmedo, E. L. (1983). Women's utilization of outpatient psychiatric services: Some emerging priorities for rehabilitation psychologists. *Rehabilitation Psychology, 28*, 142–155.

Thompson, C. (1989). Psychoanalytic psychotherapy with inner city patients. *Journal of Contemporary Psychotherapy, 19*(2), 137–148.

16

Violence against Women: Ramifications of Gender, Class, and Race Inequality

BARBARA PRESSMAN

Writing this chapter has involved a personal inventory of my own connection and lack of connection with the people I am now writing about: women of color, minority ethnic women, aboriginal women (Native Canadians, in my practice), and immigrant women. With difficulty and pain, I acknowledge that the lack of connection has not been accidental and reflects my own origins and struggles.

The most important part of my being has until recently been carefully locked within me: my Jewishness. Although I openly declare I am Jewish, only other Jews have been allowed to know what this identity means to me and how my Jewish experiences and heritage have affected my life. Since kindergarten, the responses of others toward me because I am a Jew have deeply influenced my life; affected are my view of others, my view of the world, and my sense of personhood. Throughout grammar school, it was almost a daily occurrence that my Jewish friends and I would encounter taunts, threats, intimidating gestures, and verbal denigration by non-Jews. In my early teens, my Jewishness and understanding of the complexity of human behavior were molded by the most influential experience of my life: the beginning of my awareness of the Holocaust. This new learning was gleaned from books my parents brought into our home, which bore graphic images and photographs of the death camps. Imbued, then, since childhood with an ongoing sense of human violation and the isolation born of that degradation, I have focused during my adult years on bearing witness to the suffering of the Jewish people, conveying my deep and abiding concerns about Jewish survival to my children, and sharing with others my concerns about the devastation wrought by all forms of racism.

As immersed in my religious heritage as I have been, I have until recently compartmentalized this part of my life from public view. This part is so deeply personal and feels so unique that I believed I could share it only with other Jews. I believed that they alone could understand what it means to be Jewish—what it means to live in a world where thousands wish to annihilate us and view us as flawed, inferior, and responsible for the death of their savior or prophet. In recent years, I have come to realize that areas of many other people's lives are stored away as well. Most people do not talk of their ethnic experiences in hostile environments, their immigrant experiences in racist societies, or their oppression as aboriginal people except to their own. Violence in the family is also kept secret and apart from the awareness of others, even therapists. Unless we therapists encourage people to discuss these realms and express to them appreciation of the impact of racism, bigotry, and abuse, we shall be colluding in maintaining secrecy about the most significant experiences in people's lives.

Although keenly aware from an early age that I was female, I had no recognition at first of the comparable oppression that women experience simply because they are women. I did not appreciate the significance of the women's movement as relevant for me until 1980, when I was in my 40s. Since then, I have begun to grasp my own experiences of oppression as a function of being female. This awareness was the result of "discovering" battered women in my clinical practice. The "discovery" was the second most profoundly influencing event in my life, for I found that my training had not prepared me to understand why the violence was happening, how pervasive it was, or what its impact was on women's self-worth and functioning. Consequently, I began to study the issue, attend workshops, and consult a local shelter for information regarding wife abuse. This study awakened me to feminism and redefined my understanding of the world.

When I first confronted violence against women, my understanding regarding oppression focused on gender and unattended awareness of minority status within mainstream culture. Missing was concerted attention to class and race. In the last few years, as I began to allow myself to hear minority ethnic women speak out, I began as well to examine why I, someone who perceives herself as a sensitive, caring human being, had failed to attend to the experiences of millions of oppressed women: women of color, aboriginal women, immigrant women, and women seeking refuge from oppression and torture in their homelands. (I could include the physically challenged and lesbians as well; however, this chapter focuses on the groups just named.) The answer emerged with piercing clarity and alarming insight: With respect to these groups, I knew privilege and advantage as a consequence of their disadvantage. A few of the many examples of these privileges, cogently described by Peggy McIntosh (1988), are as follows: White children receive curricular materials that testify to the existence of their race; supermarkets routinely supply staple foods that fit white people's cultural traditions; a white woman can succeed without being called a credit to her race; if a white woman wishes to move, she can feel quite certain of renting or purchasing housing in an affordable area of her choice; on television and in the other mass media, she sees people of her race widely represented; if requesting to speak to a person in charge, she knows quite certainly that she will be facing a person of her race.

With this insight, I began to understand the huge difficulty that men have in acknowledging that they are accountable for male oppression and violence against women. Many of those who do not actively abuse women or perceive themselves as exerting power and control over women in their personal lives would still experience enormous discomfort, even shame, at knowing and acknowledging the many benefits they derive from disadvantages and discrimination against women, sanctioned by our societal institutions and social norms, and enacted by other men. By failing to acknowledge various ethnic and cultural groups and those who are visibly different, and failing to integrate their experiences into my writing and teaching, I was part of the denial of their suffering. Becoming aware of their suffering compels some form of action, advocacy, and involvement in redressing the injuries. To know without actively attempting to end injustice would be knowingly to participate in the injustices and in the maintenance of the inequitable status quo.

Assisting others in their healing from violence and oppression necessitates examining one's own experiences of abuse. I have discovered that perhaps even more significant than validating one's own abuse and oppression is the need to examine one's own experience as oppressor. As a white, Jewish woman, I have found it very easy to identify with "generic" women and other, vaguely defined minority women; I have not been so successful in identifying specifically with women of color, Native Canadian women, and immigrant women. It is my hope that in this chapter, I can in some small way bear witness to the racist experiences of ethnic women and of women from various cultural backgrounds, as well as to the pervasive and persistent subjection to violence in the oppression against them. My learning regarding these women has generated much self-exploration and a deep appreciation for the complexity of violence against women. There is no universal experience of oppression against women. Yet within the various forms that violence takes, there are significant similarities. The learning has significantly influenced my clinical practice and my view of therapy. The examples presented in this chapter are a means of highlighting the myriad issues for any one group, as well as the need for therapists to educate themselves regarding each ethnic or cultural group they are counseling.

DEFINING VIOLENCE AGAINST WOMEN AND
EXPOSING LAYERS OF OPPRESSION

For me, understanding violence against women and their oppression emerged from a highly involved analysis of human experience and behavior. It is most natural to approach a condition from the perspective of one's own experience. Consequently, that part of the women's movement inaugurated by white middle-class women, and my own initial analysis, tended to see women's oppression from this perspective and tended to define oppression in generic terms—for example, access to advanced education; access to high-status occupations; equal pay for work of equal value; representation in positions of influence and power, such as management and government; and access to high-quality, affordable day care. Illustrative of attention to conditions and programming that measure women's status but that, in fact, reflect "mainstream" women's experience is *The Unfinished Revolution* (Anderson, 1991). This outstanding work reviews the status of women in 12 European countries, Canada, Great Britain, and the United States by examining political representation, maternity leave, child care services, health benefits, and pay equity for many women. However, these elements will differ for women of color, aboriginal women, and immigrant women, because oppression is not uniform in nature and varies widely, depending upon the group to which a woman is affiliated. Exclusive attention to elements of generic oppression can obscure the further victimization, discrimination, and persecution of the women described above. Getting a job, any job, becomes focal for an immigrant, Native, or black woman, let alone securing a high-status position (Silvera, 1989).

Frequently, the literature that propelled wife abuse into therapeutic consciousness described wife abuse in the context of the global or generalized oppression of women (Davidson, 1980; Dobash & Dobash, 1979; Martin, 1983; Walker, 1979). Violence against wives was recognized as a means of controlling women and maintaining a power imbalance. Although these concepts are applicable to ethnic women, women of color, immigrant women, and aboriginal women, they do not fully describe the experience of intrafamilial abuse for these women, or indicate how wife abuse is an extension of the many forms of violence and oppression to which they are subjected. Moreover, differences in color, immigrant status, and ethnic affiliation greatly influence whether or not these women can gain access to professional supports and services, as well as the likelihood of their using these resources. Asian, Hispanic, and other immigrant women who do not speak English and/or are in the United States or Canada illegally can become virtual prisoners of abusive men (Schechter, 1982). To illustrate the specificity and uniqueness of experience for different ethnic peoples, the following sections describe the oppression experiences of several distinct ethnic groups; the consequent issues for those respective groups; factors that inhibit trust in therapists; and guidelines for counseling with these populations.

IMMIGRANT WOMEN

Conditions Spurring People to Immigrate

New Canadians migrate from their countries of origin for a variety of reasons: improved economic opportunities; political freedom; reunion with family members who came before them; and flight from political oppression and torture. Although many Third World countries are self-governing, large numbers of immigrants from these countries have experienced colonialization, oppression, racism, and the subsequent erosion of the spirit. The circumstances of their leaving will greatly affect how they perceive their new country. Those who have experienced political oppression fear and mistrust most authority figures, including even minor government officials, bureaucrats, and anyone in a position to make decisions. Authority figures also include social workers.

Conditions Influencing Resettlement

Despite the move to a democratic society, fear and mistrust are frequently deeply entrenched, and the losses inherent in immigration are enormous: loss of family and friends, loss of familiar surroundings, possible loss of a climate that was comfortable and warm, loss of access to traditional foods, and loss of a lifestyle that provided identity. As a colleague of mine who is an East Indian immigrant (Narayan, 1991) has stated, "For women, food is not a science but a relationship. Throwing away pumpkins is a horror to people for whom this is a staple food." She has also pointed out that "Nothing prepares you for the barrenness of fall." This is especially shocking and depressing for people from tropical lands that are constantly lush and green. Not only the color of the landscape, but also the stark clothing colors of winter—grey, black, and beige—further intensify the bleakness of winter and the cold. Consequent depression may be the most common response to the many and deeply penetrating losses.

Immigrants suffer many other hardships. Acculturation conflicts may develop as traditional ways collide with North American norms. Moreover, because of school experiences, children often adopt the host country's language and customs more rapidly than their parents do. As a result, previously unknown conflicts between parents and children may emerge, and an undermining of parental authority may ensue.

Because one's ethnic community shapes family values, roles, and rules, a common ethnic community is a critical source of support during resettlement. The existence of ready supports—either family members already established in the new country, or an established common ethnic community to whom the new family can turn—also determines whether or not the family experiences comfort, understanding, and guidance in the integration process.

Institutionalized Disadvantages for Immigrant Women

Canadian immigration policy in recent years has attempted to link immigration to economic and labor market needs. To effect this goal, in 1967 the government devised the "points system" criteria for immigration eligibility. Since that time, immigrants have gained admittance on the basis of points earned in a number of specific areas (e.g., education, language, and occupation). Immigrants who lack point status (i.e., are not "independent" immigrants) are classified as "family-class" immigrants because they lack qualification on the basis of education, work skills or occupation, and knowledge of English. They enter Canada by sponsorship and are dependent on others—usually immediate relatives who are either independent landed immigrants or Canadian citizens. In an immigrant family, only one member is generally the designated head of household. Because husbands are perceived to be heads of households, it is husbands who are granted this status. Wives are categorized as family-class immigrants along with their children. In essence, women and men are regarded as different and unequal.

This system ignores the fact that women may have education and work experience comparable to their husbands' and may have made essential contributions to family incomes before immigration. The immigration system "systematically structures sexual inequality within the family by rendering one spouse (usually the wife) to be legally dependent on the other" (Ng, 1988, p. 187). In general, family-class immigrants are ineligible for most forms of state assistance during the 5-year sponsorship period. They cannot obtain family benefits, welfare, or other benefits unless there is a break in the sponsorship. For immigrant women, this may necessitate proving that they are legally separated from their husbands, or that sponsors are unwilling or no longer able to support them and their children. The procedure of legally terminating sponsorship relationships is degrading and painful for both women and their families (Ng, 1988).

Free full-time training in one official language and employment training for the household head are the major statutory services for immigrants. The household head obtains an allowance from the federal department of employment and immigration while taking training. Since it is the husband who is usually designated the household head, most immigrant women are denied access to vital resources that could increase the possibilities for

skilled employment and further education. Exposed to educational opportunities not available to their wives, husbands acculturate more rapidly than
their partners. Women themselves, or their sponsors, must pay for language and job training programs. However, the high costs of these programs are frequently prohibitive. To qualify for job training programs, a
minimum of 8th-grade English or the equivalent is required. Most immigrant women from non-English-speaking countries are automatically excluded by this admission criterion. Lacking skills or language proficiency,
immigrant women are qualified only for low-skilled and low-paying
occupations.

Because Canadian institutions and employers are unwilling to recognize immigrant women's previous education and training, women with
professional degrees and extensive expertise in their respective fields are
barred from employment commensurate with their skills and experience.
Although elementary or secondary education is recognized, postgraduate
education or other vocational/professional training is not (Ng, 1988). Immigrant women holding managerial, administrative, and professional positions are from the United Kingdom and the United States and are not
viewed as "immigrant women" in everyday life. By contrast, women from
southern Europe, Asia, and other parts of the globe tend to work in service,
processing, fabricating, and assembly jobs, even those who were professionals and held highly skilled technical positions in their home countries
(Ng, 1988). Non-English-speaking and nonwhite immigrant women are
commonly recruited into the following kinds of services and industries:
private domestic and janitorial service; industrial home sewing; low strata
of the service industries, such as dishwashing, janitorial, and cleaning
services; and low levels of the manufacturing industries, such as the textile,
garment, and plastic trades. With the exception of those working in the
garment and textile industries, very few of these women are protected by
legislation setting labor standards or by union contracts. Consequently,
fringe benefits, such as medical and pension plans, are nonexistent.

In summary, institutionalized racist and sexist policies render immigrant women ineligible for programs that would allow them the possibility
of equal access to skilled labor, and legitimize highly discriminatory hiring
practices.

REFUGEE WOMEN

Violence against Women in Their Homelands

Compounding the difficult adjustment demands on immigrant women may
be a traumatic history in which they were forced to flee their homelands.
Refugees generally escape from torture, possible imprisonment, and dis-

sident status in their countries of origin. Trauma for refugee families frequently also involves the abduction of family members, not knowing the whereabouts of family members, and/or not knowing whether they are even alive. During flight, refugees may have suffered profoundly in holding camps that provided subsistence food rations and afforded overcrowded and disease-generating living accommodations. Women may have been subject to rape, starvation, and enormous survival uncertainty. Having endured the events of flight, these women are subject to further indignities in North America.

My self-immersion in the literature regarding refugee women's experiences has been a most difficult endeavor. The repeated and continuous subjection to sexual atrocities in their countries of origin defies comprehension and challenges one's faith in humanity. Their experiences epitomize the meaning of rape and sexual torture as the means by which men declare their control and domination over conquered peoples and over political dissidents (Brownmiller, 1976). Intensifying the experience of sexual violation for women is the value that a country places on female virginity and chastity. Women from countries that extol, glorify, and expect female chastity and virginity suffer increased degradation, shame, and worthlessness after sexual assault and sexual torture.

Not only is torturing women's bodies a weapon against them; threats to murder their children also become weapons against mothers if they do not "cooperate" during detention. Just as children are used as effective weapons to force compliance in women, the abuse of women by repressive force is also a very effective punishment and form of torture for men (Freire, 1989).

Even though some refugees do not suffer direct torture and the consequent effects of such psychological and/or physical torture, they suffer the effects of the violence committed against their loved ones. Some refugees have been threatened by arrest or mock executions without experiencing overt physical violence. Alternatively, they may have observed, and suffered from witnessing, the violence being perpetrated against friends or family members. These individuals have been referred to as "secondary victims" of political repression (Fornazzari & Freire, 1990).

Violence in the New Home

Following traumatic experiences leading to exile, women are again at risk of violence during the initial resettlement period. In her clinical practice, Freire (1991) has observed a heightened potential for domestic violence toward refugee women by their husbands. Although there is no excuse for violence against family members, it is important to understand the conditions that increase the likelihood of using violence, in order for therapists to address and try to ameliorate these conditions.

One condition is internalizing violence as a norm to cope with and solve problems, to express feelings, and to compensate for a sense of powerlessness. The internalizing occurs in men who have emigrated from countries where repressive regimes legitimize violence to maintain domination and control, and where, as in North America, controlling behavior toward women is the norm. McGoldrick, Garcia-Preto, Moore Hines, and Lee (1989) also note that one of the most common presenting problems for many recent immigrant groups is alcoholism or violence by husbands. They attribute this to shifts in marital styles and wives' wishing for change. Wives who were subservient in their countries of origin become more assertive than in the past as they take on values of the new country, where women experience increased freedom. Because many refugee men have been socialized to believe that maleness equates with feeling powerful and being in control, feeling powerless becomes especially intolerable for them. In my work with abusing men, I have observed them to resort then to the means that they believe will restore their sense of power: control over others. Stressful situations and situations over which men have no control exacerbate their sense of powerlessness—their sense of failure to protect loved ones from torture and government-sanctioned violation of their partners and children.

In North America, institutionalized racism makes men feel powerless when it precludes refugees and immigrants from acquiring work commensurate with their skills or experience. It is critical as well to recognize the particular impact of low-status work for people coming from class-structured societies, such as those of South America. In such societies, labor is not viewed as honorable and is, in fact, identified with poor, "inferior," native people. When forced to accept work deemed menial by themselves, educated immigrants who owned land or held high status in their countries of origin feel stripped of social status. As soon as they undertake the "menial" work, they feel shame derived from a cultural tradition in which patrician landlords did not work their own land. Native people were hired to do this. Those who aspired to European values and status sold the land rather than work it (P. Grunauer-Spinner, personal communication, February 1993).

Further accentuating stress and fueling a tendency toward violence are post-traumatic stress behaviors; massive losses; acute cultural translocation, leading to mild and even severe emotional disorganization; the demands of a new and threatening country; language difficulties; the need to renegotiate family roles; the need to redefine child-rearing practices and explore new ones; dealing continually with the uncertainty surrounding the fate of missing or detained family members; and concerns for those seeking refugee status. Most of these factors are present during the initial resettlement of refugees. Home may be the only place where men feel safe enough to release their frustrations, fears, anger, and other stressful feelings; however, they may lack the experience, tools, value orientation, and emotional well-being by which they can do this in nonhurtful and nondestructive ways.

Refugee women who experience abusive situations at home experience a powerful emotional trigger for reliving the violence inflicted while in detention or in transit. Furthermore, "private" violence—violence in the home—is experienced by women as more distressing than that by strangers, because it is enacted by those from whom women expect respect, love, nurturance, and protection. Most women who suffer physical violence at home experience psychological and sexual violence there as well. Frequently, when they attempt to leave their abusive partners, they encounter a barrage of verbal violence and intimidation: "If you leave, I will kill myself," "If you leave, I'll kill you and the children," "I will charge you with desertion," "I will have you deported," "I will denounce you because you have been working illegally," "I will not help you bring your relatives to Canada." Quite frequently, immigrant and refugee women alike are dispossessed of all financial support by abusive partners, as well as of all legal documentation. These become additional ways to immobilize them psychologically and keep them in abusive situations (Freire, 1991).

Implications for Treatment of Family Violence

Women who defy totalitarian regimes not only by speaking out, but also by seeking information about kidnapped and abducted children, husbands, siblings, and other family members, are at enormous risk of incarceration, torture, and murder themselves. As I read of the sexual perversions devised by their torturers, the feelings generated in me of horror, sadness, and wishing to obliterate awareness were overshadowed by an enormous sense of powerlessness. How do we as therapists meet the enormity of the suffering, the sacrifice, and the courage of these women? How do we comfort them and attend to the incomprehensible inhumanity and losses they have endured? Enormous attention must be given then to our own responses as we become exposed to suffering of the magnitude of survivors of torture.

As can be seen from the lengthy number of issues for immigrant and refugee women, a range of knowledge is required of us as therapists. We need knowledge of and training in the impact of trauma on emotional well-being and self-worth; the normal ways people cope with trauma, which are frequently misdiagnosed as pathological behaviors and affective disorders; and the specifics of abreactive and healing work. In addition, we need knowledge of the respective cultural backgrounds of these women, with particular emphasis on cultural pressures on them to remain with abusing husbands. Because of the enormous fear husbands can engender with their threats of deportation, we also need to be able to provide information regarding immigrant women's rights and access to welfare and subsidized housing. For example, in Canada, a woman who has achieved permanent resident status is eligible for welfare if her sponsorhip has been severed; in Ontario, if a woman leaves her partner because of violence, this is considered evidence that the sponsorship has been broken. Finally, we need knowledge regarding crisis counseling for women seeking help immediately after an assault, as well as knowledge regarding ongoing counseling for trauma victims (Riutort & Endicott Small, 1985).

NATIVE PEOPLE

Government policy in Canada reflects a systematic design at best to keep aboriginal people totally in subjugation and at worst to annihilate them. Since 1980, I have worked intensely with women who are abused in their homes and the men who abuse them. Abuse involves any behavior that demeans or denigrates; any behavior that physically or emotionally injures; intimidation or threatening gestures; and any act that reduces individuals' control over their own being or sense that they can take charge of their own lives. The very place where one would expect women and children to be most secure, safe, and protected becomes a prison in which they are continually endangered. Physical abuse is by no means the only mechanism for maintaining control. Abusing men maintain control over their partners by isolating them; by controlling the family income; by limiting women's mobility; by isolating them from contact with friends and even family members; by determining what their partners will or will not read; by verbally denigrating them, whereby women cease to view themselves as competent or worthwhile; by instructing them in appropriate attire; and by being ultimate decision makers in the home.

These very same mechanisms are practiced by the federal government to insure that aboriginal people will be subjugated, will be dependent, and will lack complete control over their own beings. Isolation, severe economic restrictions, limitation of mobility, determination by white society of what Native Canadians will think and believe, and extreme restraints over decision-making—all these characterize Canadian government policy.

Isolation

Reserves were an expedient solution to the potential conflict between whites and Native Canadians for land (Davis & Krauter, 1971). Although intended to protect aboriginal people from further encroachment by frontier exploration, the concentration of the bands allowed potential indoctrination into the modern world and erosion of traditional lifestyles. Ostensibly, the reserves were refuges to secure First Nation culture, heritage, and self-identification; however, a 1962 study concluded that "the social isolation of the reservations and the supervision by Indian agents may inhibit the resourcefulness, initiative, and individuality of the Indian people, and that however well intended, it could perpetuate the very situation which it is intended to alleviate" (quoted by Davis & Krauter, 1971, p. 11).

Denial of Self-Determination

Institutionalized denial of democratic freedom is evident in the denial of voting rights. Not until 1960 were all reserve Natives granted the federal vote, and even then many provinces still disqualified Native people from provincial voting (Davis & Krauter, 1971). Not until 1969 were all Native people granted provincial voting rights when Quebec became the last province to grant such rights (Ministry of Indian Affairs and Northern Development, 1980).

Land has always been central to the Native economy and the Native way of life; however, Native Canadians do not possess legal title to their land, and are thereby vulnerable to dislocation. Land claims are ignored, and expropriations for railway, expansion, water power, and minerals are treated with a white bias in the courts. Although the government provides reserve land to Native people for their use, the reserves are legally controlled by the federal government, which imposes severe restrictions on the political power of Native people in accordance with the Indian Act (York, 1990).

Restricted Education, Economic Development, and Religious Freedom

The potential for economic advancement through education and the establishment of self-esteem through pride in one's heritage were also destroyed by a government-imposed system of education. From 1860 to 1960, the federal government allowed churches to assume complete control of the education of aboriginal people on reserves from Nova Scotia to British Columbia. With government support and approval, the church educators conveyed religious ideologies, codes of behavior, and curricula consistent with white Christian mores, ideology, and history. The curriculum totally disregarded Native Canadian customs, values, history, religion, and culture. Native people's contributions to society and world thinking were rendered invisible and replaced with a view of them as barbaric, heathen, and inferior.

In 1920, amendments to the Indian Act made school attendance at residential schools mandatory rather than voluntary. At that time, Duncan Campbell Scott, deputy superintendent general of Indian Affairs, summarized the intent of these amendments: "Our object is to continue until there is not a single Indian in Canada that has not been absorbed into the body politic, and there is no Indian question, and no Indian department, and that is the whole object of this Bill" (quoted in York, 1990, p. 23). To ensure parental cooperation, parents were threatened with imprisonment; moreover, under the Indian Act of 1876, government officials could deny food rations to aboriginal families that did not comply with orders to send their children to residential schools. There children were stripped of dignity through contempt of their heritage. They were beaten for speaking their Native languages; depersonalized by uniforms; and forbidden to see their parents except under strict regulations. Not only were Native children inhumanely severed from their families and reservations, where they knew nurturing environments and adults who valued them; they also routinely experienced physical and sexual abuse in the residential schools (York, 1990). If a Native child desired education beyond high school, it was rarely possible.

Native Canadians are not allowed to mortgage land. In addition, before purchasing land, they need permission from Ottawa. Consequently, raising money for business ventures is extremely difficult, and Native people are severely hampered in their attempts at economic development and advancement.

To attract white professionals such as nurses and teachers, who would ordinarily be reluctant to adopt reserve living, the government assures them running water, indoor plumbing, and modern heating. These facilities are vastly different from the housing afforded aboriginal people, who live in substandard dwellings devoid of the amenities provided to the whites.

A defiled and dismissed culture, despair, total dependence on white society, and lack of housing are the most frequently cited elements underlying the alcoholism and other substance abuse common in Native communities.

Institutionalized Discrimination against Native Women

Because many Native Canadian tribes in the east were matrilineal, Native status was traced through the mother. However, in 1941, the definition was altered: Off the reserve, the father's ethnic status determined ethnicity of the children. On the reserve, both mother's and father's lineages determined membership (Ng, 1988). There was a further distinction between Indian and "mixed" origin. Under Section 12(1)(b) of the Indian Act, an Indian woman who married a non-Indian man automatically lost Indian status for herself and her children. On the other hand, if a Native man married a non-Native woman, she and her children legally became "Indians." If a Native woman married a non-Native man, she had to leave the reserve. Since Native people are under the administrative responsibility of the federal government, and since resources (such as transfer payments and education) are provided through the reserves to which they belong, a woman leaving her reserve was forced to give up her rights to these resources (Ng, 1988).

In lobbying to redress this discrimination against Native women, Native women proclaimed that the Indian Act grievously injured them in many ways: loss of nationality; loss of the right to reside where a woman was born; loss of close family ties; loss of a woman's culture and religion; loss of the right to family property and inheritance; loss of voting rights; loss of health services; loss of educational rights; and finally loss of the right to be buried on Native land. Through the determined efforts of Native women and the leadership of Jeannette Lavell and Sandra Lovelace (Lovelace took her case to the United Nations Human Rights Committee to argue that Canada had violated the International Covenant on Political Civil Rights on the grounds of sexual discrimination), Section 12(1)(b) of the Indian Act was suspended in 1981 (Ng, 1988).

Currently, the Native Women's Association of Canada is arguing publicly that federal money to aboriginal groups is directed almost entirely to male-dominated aboriginal organizations, rather than funded equitably to such organizations and Native women's associations. Consequently, men are granted the means to influence public and government opinion by this preferential funding, and women are denied a similar opportunity to advocate issues and concerns specific to Native women (*Herizons*, 1992).

Implications for Treatment of Family Violence

The years of degradation and inhumane treatment not only have profoundly affected each Native person individually, but also have eroded Native nationhood. Therapy for the individual alone, therefore, will not be sufficient. Only through reclaiming their roots, their past, their beliefs, and their culture; through celebrating that which they were told was bad, inferior, and flawed; and through exposing and validating the mammoth wrongs and illegal acts against them and challenging these in world courts, are Native people beginning to heal. Because this healing cannot be performed from outside of the self or by others, it must involve Native people healing themselves as individuals and as communities. White therapists can aid the healing of Native people, not by "therapizing" them but by sharing clinical tools helpful for them to do the work themselves, and by advocating for them. This advocacy can take the form of activism against policies allotting Native people reserve facilities that are shoddy and inadequate for human habitation and well-being, and that ultimately destroy human beings. This advocacy can declare the need for new policies that will ensure Native self-determination, and ultimately Native people's control over their own education, economic development, and religious practices—in short, control over their own lives.

Violence breeds violence. Oppression and experiences of abuse by white caregivers have generated both powerlessness and "education" in the specious ways of exhibiting power and feeling powerful: embracing of violence both inside and outside Native people's homes. "Native people are six times more likely to die violently than other Canadians" (Koptie, 1991, p. 44). A recent Ontario-wide study revealed that 8 out of 10 aboriginal women, and 4 out of 10 children have been abused or assaulted. In 84% of the cases, the batterers were identified as husbands. However, in 82% of the cases, it is the women who leave and lose their homes (Hare, 1991).

Although violence against women and children is a critical problem, many male leaders of Native communities have had difficulty in acknowledging and addressing it. Furthermore, there is an alarming lack of services within Native communities to meet the needs of women and children who are physically, sexually, and emotionally abused, and a severe lack of emergency shelters. Typically, also, in Native communities women live with their husbands and children in the homes of their parents-in-law or parents. Consequently, women and children must leave their homes and communities to secure their personal safety. This safety move doubly victimizes them, for they are then isolated and cut off from family supports (Hare, 1991; Subcommittee on the Status of Women, 1991).

Recommendations Regarding Services to End Violence in Native Communities

In both the United States and Canada, there must be financial commitment by federal, provincial, and state governments to provide adequate funding for services for aboriginal people. Healing lodges within Native communities must be established to offer refuge for battered women and their children. Treatment programs for abusing aboriginal men, battered women, and abused children must incorporate Native traditions, ceremonies, and customs, such as the smudge, prayer, Indian handshake, and sharing by passing the eagle feather or talking stick (Chapman & Nadeau, 1987–1990). Healing teams developed to treat family violence must exist in every aboriginal community, whether located on reserves, in rural areas, or in urban areas. To encourage Native communities to initiate their own healing programs, a system of educating these communities regarding the causes and nature of violence must be undertaken.

Further recommendations involve the development of an aboriginal justice system that will end discrimination against aboriginal women regarding property laws favoring men. In isolated areas, there must be vastly improved medical service and thorough training of medical personnel in identification of violence in the family and in culturally sensitive responses. Finally, there is the need for a toll-free province hotline specifically to provide victims of aboriginal family violence with information about local services (Hare, 1991).

PEOPLE OF AFRICAN DESCENT

Oppression of Black People: A Brief Glimpse

Although it is no exaggeration to say that all people of color in North American society experience and suffer from discrimination, demeaning epithets, and disdain, it is critical to recognize that each person of color will experience differences according to individual experiences: length of time in this country; immigrant status; first- or second-generation birth (Moore Hines & Boyd-Franklin, 1982); and whether or not parents have felt cultural and racial pride and have been able to convey this to their children. All too often, children of color begin to feel self-contempt and shame reflective of the way they are perceived, treated, and regarded by the mainstream population (Allport, 1958).

People of African descent constitute the largest minority group in the United States, and have endured a long-standing tradition of racism and a history of legalized maltreatment and enslavement in both the United States and Canada. How does one convey in a few lines the complete abandonment of humanity in the capture, uprooting, and treatment of black slaves? Initially, all slaves on board slave ships were branded and stripped of clothing. To destroy any possibility of defiance or rebellion, the men were shackled throughout the voyage from Africa to North America. Since complete power could be exerted over black women, they could move about freely. This specious "freedom" involved continual subjection to sexual harassment, intimidation, and rape. Nakedness, the threat of physical abuse, fear of torture, and the ongoing possibility of rape were terrifying deterrents to black women's recalcitrance. Commonly, African women arrived in North America impregnated by their white captors (hooks, 1981). How does one convey the inhumanity of forced impregnation of black women by white slave owners to expand the number of slaves? How can one appreciate the horror of being ripped from one's children or one's partner when family members were sold separately to other slave owners (hooks, 1981)? These events are imbedded in the collective memory of North Americans of African descent.

Less known, even to Canadians, than the apartheid that was legally practiced in the United States was that perpetrated in Canada. In addition to the racism practiced in housing and employment, blacks were frequently denied full use of provincial educational facilities and public accommodations such as movie houses and restaurants. The first schools for blacks in Nova Scotia and New Brunswick were operated by church groups. By 1850, blacks could also attend segregated public schools in both Nova Scotia and Ontario. Once such black facilities were established, they continued to exist alongside the all-white school system, and their existence could be cited as a reason for segregating blacks from the white educational

structure (Davis & Krauter, 1971). Segregated instruction was legalized in
Canada in 1849 by a statute that authorized municipal councils to establish
separate schools for blacks. Throughout the years of segregated schooling,
the separate education afforded blacks was inferior to that provided to
whites. Although black schools began to disappear in Ontario after 1910,
not until 1965 did the last black school in Ontario close. Not until 1963 did
legally segregated education end in Nova Scotia.

Implications for Treatment of Family Violence

Out of white clinicians' appreciation for black women's experiences of
oppression, or out of misinformation, there is the danger that the many
strengths of black women may be neglected. Ethnocentricity may preclude
recognizing strengths that differ greatly from those of traditional white
culture. For example, the extended family is a major source of support and
plays a significant role in family life, but could possibly be viewed as
enmeshed or intrusive (Hines & Boyd-Franklin, 1982). With respect to
appreciating black women's strengths, hooks (1981) warns that strength in
coping should not be confused with overcoming.

It is also important to recognize that oppression from without does not
immunize people from oppression within. However, "under both
sharecropping and slavery, the oppression of Black patriarchy paled beside
those of racism and classism" (Mann, 1988, p. 146). To this day, in literature about themselves, black women repeatedly stress the need to redress
the racism of all their people before or in conjunction with addressing
grievances regarding patriarchy (Davis, 1983; Bannerji, Brand, Gupta,
Khosia, & Silvera, 1989; hooks, 1981, 1989; McDougald, 1973). They are
keenly aware of the ongoing suffering of their fathers, husbands, and sons,
who experience persistent obstacles to education and employment.

When discussing male violence, writers of African descent invariably
refer to white images of black males as rapists and to the lynchings of black
men, which enabled white racists to maintain their supremacy over the life
and death of people they still deemed slaveworthy. These books refer as
well to white images of black women as sexually promiscuous and sexually
available, which enabled and justified the continuation of white men's
sexual exploitation of black women (Davis, 1983; Bannerji et al., 1989;
hooks, 1981; McDougald, 1973).

To address violence against black women in their homes would necessitate careful navigation through many clashing currents. Each black
male partner, like all men, is a complex human being with many endearing
attributes and much pain throughout his lifetime. Consequently, black
women's ambivalence and their gnawing recognition of all the outrages and
injustices against their partners are powerful forces to generate defensive-
ness, support, and protection rather than condemnation or even questioning

of the partners' behavior. Black women's concerns need to be fully appreciated and respected while they are helped to consider choices about their
immediate safety and their children's well-being. To hear that oppression is
no justification for any form of abuse may sound weak in the presence of
black men's suffering and their need in some way to feel powerful in a
society that renders them powerless.

Incest wounds may be soothed by several perpetrator actions:
acknowledgment of the wrongs against victims and their injuries; expressions of genuine remorse for victims' suffering; and significantly
changed behavior and attitudes on the part of the perpetrators. I believe that
similar acknowledgment and change must occur between races and nations.
As long as the present holds remnants of the collective past in the form of
discrimination, unequal opportunity, and contemptuous attitudes, there can
be no complete healing. Consequently, I believe that we therapists—
especially white therapists—need to advocate that public school education
require studying black people's history of oppression in North America as
well as their many contributions. Without this, we shall be invalidating
those of African descent, distorting their reality, and colluding in maintaining silence about the violent oppression against them. Moreover, we shall
be denying white society the opportunity to learn from history, and we
shall thus perpetuate the wrongs and injustices.

GUIDELINES FOR THERAPY WITH WOMEN WHO HAVE EXPERIENCED VIOLENCE

The sections above speak to the uniqueness of different women's experiences of violence. Although this uniqueness needs to be integrated into
clinical responses, principles of feminist therapy are especially useful when
dealing with violence against women of any cultural background (Pressman, 1989). An effective response to an abused woman depends upon
securing information of the woman's total life experiences: the sociopolitical context of her country of origin; her immigrant experiences; the experience of racism in her adopted country; the sociopolitical context of the
woman's life in North America; family history; and possible power imbalances and abuse in immediate relationships. Below are therapy guidelines
to help us as therapists—again, white therapists in particular—appreciate
diversity and the sociopolitical context as we work with abused women.

Challenging Our Own Biases

We need to be willing to examine, take responsibility for, and challenge our
own biases, prejudices, and stereotypical thinking regarding people different from ourselves. Before we try to address the problems and needs of

clients of different cultural and ethnic backgrounds from our own, it is critical that we examine our own biases and prejudices regarding these people. We must first ask, "What are my beliefs, attitudes, and knowledge regarding immigrants, people of color, ethnic populations, and aboriginal people?" We also need to know the answer to this question: "What are the proportions of ethnic members, immigrants, people of color, and aboriginal people in our communities?" Then we must ask, "Do our clients reflect these proportions in our respective agencies, and if not, why not?" We must also ask, "Do our agencies make a concerted effort to hire staff from these populations and to provide outreach, in order that the needs of these populations will be met?" A major consequence of racism and class barriers is a dismal shortage of services for the groups of women cited above. Moreover, these women may be reluctant to seek help from white "mainstream" therapists, who are viewed with suspicion and fear as part of the establishment that oppresses women of different ethnic and cultural backgrounds.

When educating ourselves to the contextual lives of clients from the populations discussed and their respective cultural values and customs, we should not impose our values when our values prove inconsistent with those of others. However, I feel the need to add a caution here. All too often, I hear white therapists expressing concern about imposing Western values of equality on women not accustomed to our "modern" ways, or suggesting that wife abuse is much more normative and accepted in other cultures than in our own. This thinking is potentially racist, because domination of women has been universal and has not been peculiar to certain ethnic groups. All the studies in North America regarding wife abuse and child sexual abuse, for example, consistently reveal that this violence is perpetrated by men and members from every ethnic group, every cultural group, every religious denomination, and every socioeconomic background (Pressman, 1984). White North Americans cannot claim that theirs is a less violent society than those of other countries. Those using services to treat violence in the family are not exclusively ethnic people and people of color. They are also white North Americans whose families have lived in Canada and the United States for generations. However, attitudes toward authority instilled in children in different countries of origin may render submission by women normative and the challenging of abusing behavior in husbands especially difficult.

Although it may no longer be fashionable to talk openly of "keeping one's wife in line" or speak of "being the boss," as did Ralph Kramden in *The Honeymooners* television series several decades ago, many men in North America, I believe, have become much more covert about control over their partners than in the past. This same phenomenon has been observed in abusing men's groups, which focus on physical abuse rather than on all the forms that control can take. In such groups, men readily agree that physical abuse is unacceptable, and then become much more adept than before they entered the groups at other forms of controlling behavior—that is, intimidation and emotional abuse (Dufresne, 1992). Susan Schechter (1982) makes a similar observation regarding white middle-class men, who may not resort to physical violence but readily resort to other controlling behaviors. Whether the type of domination is overt physical abuse or one of the more subtle forms of intimidation (e.g., control of finances, isolation of partners from friends and family, or protracted silences for days), the impact is the same: Women defer to partners out of fear or the desire to maintain tranquility in the home.

It is not disrespectful of people from other cultures to declare that we have learned the same values that they have learned; that these values are unacceptable wherever practiced; and that they need to be changed everywhere because they are so destructive to women and children. Ultimately, they are destructive as well for those who use them. Having worked with abusing men for well over a decade, I have observed consistently that the men employing controlling behaviors do not experience an increased sense of efficacy and power. On the contrary, they suffer increased low self-esteem, disconnectedness from their partners, and failure to get their needs met.

Assessing According to Race, Class, and Gender

The context of abused women's lives needs to be assessed according to race, class, and gender, and according to the impact of these on self-esteem and current functioning. In addition, when working with immigrant women (whatever the presenting problems), careful attention must be paid to exploration for violence as well as to the immigration experience, the reasons for leaving the country of origin, possible acculturation difficulties (Chambon, 1989), and exploration of experiences of racism and discrimination in the adopted country (Pinderhughes, 1989).

Violence is the best-kept secret in families (Pressman, 1984), and in my marriage and family therapy practice, rarely do I find a complete absence of power imbalance between partners. Frequently, too, people normalize, euphemize, romanticize, and minimize abusing behaviors in such a way that they distort or completely deny their existence. Jealousy that moves a husband to isolate his partner from female friends and even family members; long-protracted silences, which create enormous tension in the home and result in wives' capitulating to partners' demands to restore calm; denying wives decision-making power in money matters—all are controlling behaviors that husbands use toward their wives, and are therefore forms of abuse. Even pushing, shoving, and grabbing are not viewed by most as violence. Violence for most people means blackened eyes, visible bruising, or severe injury requiring medical attention. Consequently, verbal denigration, yelling, intimidation, throwing objects, and pounding walls, are not recognized by many as violence. Some therapists, too, fail to appreciate the impact and fear engendered by such acts (Pressman, 1989). It is incumbent, therefore, on us as therapists to ask questions to determine whether or not any form of violence or controlling behavior is occurring. These questions should reveal the dynamics of a wife-abusing couple and abuse by other family members, without necessarily even employing the term "abuse."

Because abused women are highly reluctant to risk evoking partners' wrath or displeasure by providing information or raising concerns that husbands may interpret as criticism, attack, or disagreement, I routinely interview partners separately. Assessment questions such as those suggested in Appendix A are asked of each partner. In the event that men minimize or deny altogether abusing behaviors exposed by partners, I also routinely ask women whether or not I may confront their partners with the discrepancies. When I confront, I do so nonjudgmentally by indicating how difficult it is for men to acknowledge behaviors about which they do not feel good, in view of the expectation that they should present a successful image to the world (and, in the case of immigrant men, in view of the expectation that they should not reflect ill on their people). I further suggest to such a husband that he may wish now to clarify or discuss again some of the information given initially. It is not uncommon for a man to begin to acknowledge some of the formerly denied abuse.

All the questions proposed in Appendix A are not necessarily asked in a sequential or structured way. They are carefully integrated into the session. I try to weave them in according to the material presented. If the material presented does not lead me to the questions, at an opportune and relevant time in the session I simply state,

> "I wish to know you better, in order that I best understand what you need in therapy and to understand what is happening in your life that may be influencing the things you are concerned about. Could you, therefore, tell me about your relationship?"

I begin with material that is probably not so stressful as abuse:

> "Do you have time together on a regular basis? What do you do as a couple? Is affection satisfactory? When you have differences or disagree, how are differences resolved? When you disagree, does anyone get upset or angry?"

I then move on to more specific details:

> "How is upset or anger expressed? Is anyone pushed or grabbed, or hair pulled, or objects thrown, or walls punched or kicked, or anyone called names?"

Because women normally minimize and deny abusing behavior toward them, naming specific forms of abuse is imperative to ensure that the interviewer learns whether or not such behavior is occurring. Appendix A provides the types of questions I wish to cover during the initial assessment phase. The questions are oriented toward wives and should be altered accordingly when they are used with husbands.

When abuse has been identified and becomes focal to therapy, a woman's coping abilities and choices to deal with the violence will depend upon ingrained values, available supports, earning potential, and (if applicable) degree of acculturation and comfort in a new community. Consequently, the questions in Appendix B will help the clinician and the client appreciate the pulls to seek or avoid help, and reasons to remain in an abusing relationship rather than leave. Reasons to stay may be far more compelling than any to leave. The questions also address the existence of trauma previous to wife abuse. A history of trauma will necessitate much longer therapy to restore self-esteem, self-confidence, and trust in others than will abuse experienced exclusively in the marriage or adult relationship.

If we focus exclusively on the problems of the respective groups from which women come, without gender sensitivity, we shall do women an enormous disservice. For example, the *Journal of Strategic and Systemic Therapies* (Efron & Roberts, 1989) provides excellent descriptions of the problems facing immigrants. Missing, however, in these journal articles is any reference to the ways immigration differs for men and women, or to the hardships specific to immigrant women as a consequence of intertwined racist and sexist policies and practices. Therefore, the comprehensive assessment includes the impact of gender on women's life experiences, power imbalances in relationships, and possible violence within the family.

When marriage and family therapists speak of power in couple relationships and "women holding all the power," generally they are referring to women's capacity to support their partners emotionally and the enormous pain their partners experience when that support is withheld. Children too are described as having great power because of their ability to drain parents and "triangulate," or come between parents. However, in terms of "absolute power"—that is, the capacity to effect or influence change, the ability to generate income comparable to a man's, decision-making power regarding finances, ability to control violence by partners or parents, and choices over their own lives—women and children are anything but powerful.

Appreciating Crisis Potential When Counseling Victims of Violence

Working with abuse involves addressing ongoing or intermittent crises: in which there is the ongoing potential for physical injury or even death. During a crisis, immediate danger must be assessed. The counselor needs to determine the nature of a woman's injuries, past and current; the most serious injury; whether or not medical care has been required; whether or not there have been threats to kill; whether or not the husband has threatened to use or has ever used a weapon; and whether or not substance abuse, particularly alcohol, has been involved. Use of alcohol or another disinhibiting substance, severity of injury, increasing violence over time, and threats to kill are predictors of the potential for killing. The woman will need information regarding the laying of charges and the possible outcomes of such charges: imprisonment, fines, probation, mandated counseling, or some combination of these. Physical injuries will need to be treated and documented. Information regarding involvement of police and the medical community needs to be obtained. It is also important to determine whether or not the wife has informed anyone else of the abuse and what the response has been to this information. Frequently, women experience extremely inappropriate responses, which the counselor will need to counteract. For example, "Leave the animal" fails to appreciate the ambivalence women feel for their partners. These men are not monsters, although they sometimes behave monstrously. Typically, abused women value the beautiful elements in their partners and wish to end the violence, not their relationships. In contrast, "You must return or you'll shame the community" fails to appreciate the magnitude of the suffering experienced by battered women and child witnesses. It must be kept in mind that *any* directive to battered women further disempowers them and denies them choices over their own lives, just as their husbands have denied them such choice.

Another element of crisis work is normalizing the woman's responses. Denial, depression, fear, withdrawal, disorientation, and numbing are all natural coping strategies in dealing with trauma and ongoing abuse of all forms. Above all, an abused woman needs to know that she is not to blame, that she has not failed as a wife, and that she has not provoked her husband's behavior. Battered women believe that they are to blame for a number of reasons. They have been socialized to believe that they are responsible for the well-being of family members, and that if anything goes wrong, they are to blame. Abusers externalize responsibility for their actions and continually attribute them to their wives' inadequacies. A frequent response to women's disclosure is a question to them about what they did that brought on such behavior by their husbands. Finally, valuing their partners, and men in general, battered women readily believe the statements of their husbands (Pressman, 1984).

Because of battered women's low self-esteem, erroneous self-blame, fear, and lack of supports, ongoing counseling involving group support has been found to be most helpful for these women. Until women feel safe enough or comfortable enough to join such programs, individual work before (and possibly concurrently with) group work will be required. The group work involves restoration of personhood; information regarding the impact of abuse on women and child witnesses; understanding of the dynamics of abuse, which reflect men's need to maintain control over partners; and empowerment of women through self-help and mutual support, rather than a focus on information and support derived from the therapist/expert.

Immigrant women, ethnic women, women of color, and aboriginal women may be reluctant to seek group support from mainstream agencies staffed primarily by white therapists. As well, they may be financially unable to travel to organizations beyond the confines of their immediate neighborhoods. Therefore, outreach is critical to provide services to women from different cultural and ethnic groups. Ethnic churches, multicultural centers, Native centers, and Native women's shelters are places where outreach can begin. Professionals and shelter workers experienced in the treatment of victimized women can provide training to grassroots workers and can promote involvement of paraprofessionals from the same backgrounds of the respective women discussed. Women who are abused are already isolated and feel different from others; for an abused ethnic woman to enter a group where she is the only ethnic member can compound this sense of differentness and isolation. Paraprofessionals facilitating groups for women of the same background as the facilitators can provide models of women in positions of leadership, promote self-help, and validate that each woman is not alone or crazy or different.

Fitting Therapeutic Interventions to Clients' Needs

Therapeutic interventions must be consistent with clients' needs and experiences, rather than reflecting strict adherence to theoretical models that may ignore critical issues or may even be harmful. Although I was trained in a traditional psychodynamic model and in the systems theory of marriage and family therapy, none of my training prepared me to treat violence against women. Nor did these theoretical orientations adequately explain such violence. In fact, many tacitly blamed women by viewing relationship problems as stemming from intrapsychic phenomena or as a function of joint responsibility. Missing was an analysis of problems that incorporated the socioeconomic and political context of women's lives. The inattention to gender inequality has been addressed by many writers (Bograd, 1984; James & McIntyre, 1983; Miller, 1986; Taggart, 1985).

Therapeutic models to explain and treat violence against women need to include recognition of and explanation for the pervasive and extensive nature of such violence. They must also address the myriad treatment issues that exist for abused women and for perpetrators as well. When the many related issues are ignored (e.g., stereotyped views of male–female relationships; embracing the societal value that power means control over others, rather than control of the self and inner power; low self-esteem; an unaddressed childhood history of trauma), especially for perpetrators, there is the danger that women will not receive needed validation of their experiences, and that abusing (controlling) men and sexual perpetrators will not receive the most effective therapy. Consequently, these men will continue to be a threat to women and children (Pressman, 1992).

Recognizing Political Implications of Various Clinical Responses

The models and respective interventions a therapist chooses are highly political in nature (Pressman, 1989). Emphasizing intrapsychic phenomena or interactional patterns in treating wife abuse renders therapy a political act. Not only is the sociopolitical context of people's lives ignored, but mammoth social issues are reduced to individual problems, to identification with abusing fathers, or to couple issues and communication patterns. Thereby, individual and conjoint therapy may depoliticize the act of violence in the home by focusing on the immediate situation, rather than exploring the ways in which wife abuse reflects the societal values and inequities that endorse, legitimize, and foster violence against women and children. Although a conjoint approach may end violence in certain situations (Goldner, 1992), I have deep concerns about couple therapy. Even couple therapy that connects a man's history to his present abusing behavior and addresses the impact of violence on his partner may fail to focus sufficiently on male privilege, on the societal endorsement of controlling behavior toward women, on the values instilled in men that promote violence against and control of women, on the many forms that abuse takes, and on the need to end all forms of abuse.

Even when couple or individual therapy involves challenging a man's sexist thinking and behavior and involves consciousness raising, neither of these approaches can afford the potential for the emergence of sexist thinking that group therapy can. In a group composed minimally of eight men, it is almost impossible for a session to transpire without some member exposing sexist attitudes or acts through his words or experiences. Expressions such as, "She's on the rag," or objectifying and dehumanizing a partner by referring to her as "the wife," are likely when a number of men are together. Some men also disclose a belief in their entitlement to sexual gratification by partners, and feel deeply aggrieved when wives do not wish to fulfill this want. Although many would not express such thinking openly, invariably at least one man will talk in these terms. When he does, it becomes an important opportunity for other men to explore such attitudes in themselves. There is an increased willingness for such disclosure in the presence of other men who have risked this honesty. People are largely socialized in groups—family, peers, and organizations (such as places of worship and schools). Since much of the work with abusing men involves resocialization to new values of maleness, I believe that group therapy is the optimal form of therapy.

In addition to challenging legitimized sexism, male privilege, and gender inequality, therapy needs to appreciate the trauma to the individual who has been abused, the consequent damage to self-esteem, and the coping behaviors employed (which may interfere with daily functioning). Finally, therapy needs to respect the fact that women in abusing relationships frequently wish to end the abuse, not the relationships. However, couple counseling is not the only way to respect this wish. Recommending separate counseling does not equate with recommending marital separation, and counselors can explain that ending violence is a dramatic way to improve relationships.

Even when it is requested specifically by a couple, I believe that couple work is inappropriate until a number of conditions have been met. Namely, the woman must feel safe; she must be able to assert her needs and concerns; her partner must have learned to hear her words without interpreting them as disrespect, castigation, or rejection; and the man must end all forms of abusing behavior. Some therapists subscribe to couple work sought by both partners when the man acknowledges the inappropriateness of his behavior (Lipchik, 1991) and when "the violence is not so pervasive or severe; the woman still has some agency and power within the relationship and outside of it; and the man shows some readiness and capacity to take genuine responsibility" (Goldner, 1992, p. 58). Even under these conditions, however, there is the danger of inadequate attention to a woman's eroded self-worth; the danger of missing her reluctance to express rage in a couple session about former behaviors that still trouble her (Pressman, 1984); and the danger of obscuring the ways in which wife abuse is destructive to child witnesses (Jaffe, Wolfe, Wilson, & Zak, 1986; Rosenbaum & O'Leary, 1981).

Furthermore, most abusing men place enormous expectations on their partners to fulfill their need for nurturance and emotional support, while isolating their partners from others. This expectation becomes an enormous burden for women, who frequently complain that men do not correspondingly attend to their emotional needs. Helping men become nonviolent involves helping them develop nurturing behavior, openness with their feelings, and openness with their need for others. Expressing the need for others is expanded to include not exclusively relying on their partners, but also turning to other men. This necessitates challenging the beliefs that expressions of affect (other than anger) and the need for others are indications of weakness and unmanliness. A group is a most effective forum for practicing new beliefs and behaviors. Most critical in establishing these new behaviors are the endorsement, encouragement, and support men receive from one another.

Shin (1991) raises yet another political concern related to "mainstream" approaches to violence against women. For women from cultural communities different from white North America, "mainstream" approaches generally fail to conceptualize intrafamilial violence against women in the context of racism, economic poverty, and social and political violence toward women. Consequently, a number of immigrant women, ethnic women, and women of color have organized at the grassroots level to correct the shortcomings of traditional approaches to treatment of abused women. Illustrative of a group that incorporates the expanded analysis of violence against women is a Latin American women's project in Edmonton, Alberta, called "Proyecto Soledad." This group begins its discussions on wife assault by presenting an analysis of all forms of violence, including economic, military, political, and social oppression (Shin, 1991). The term "wife assault" itself is redefined to reflect the realities of immigrant and ethnic women, some of whom experience abuse by in-laws, fathers or brothers, adult children, or others. Women who work as domestic workers may be victims of abuse by their employers. Some women have been brought to North America as "mail-order brides" by white men, and face both racism and abuse from their partners.

Appreciating How Poverty Limits Choices

Poverty limits choices and results in the involvement of many social services in families' lives. One of the most pernicious consequences of racism is poverty. Black males experience the highest job loss rates in the labor force; even among those who are employed, the number engaged in managerial and professional jobs is relatively small. However, they are subject to the same societal expectations of all other men: that they be successful earners in order to be successful men. In fact, black males may have to expend great time and energy trying to provide minimal survival necessities for their families (McGoldrick et al., 1989). However, it is critical to emphasize that the sociopolitical context offers only an explanation—never an excuse or justification—for violence against women.

For many black, ethnic, immigrant, and Native women, the shortage of money makes even public transportation difficult and sometimes impossible, limits mobility, and renders child care inaccessible. Because of the costs of public transportation, the time involved in going to a variety of services in different parts of a community, and consequent difficulties when needing to bring along small children, women are then denied access to numerous, spread-out services. Therefore, a therapist wishing to make services accessible can do so by bringing the various services to one location. Many shelters, for example, have been successful at bringing representatives from welfare agencies and low-cost housing into the shelters on a regular basis.

It is also common for ethnic women to experience patronizing demeanor and hostility from social service providers (A. Martel, personal communication, May 11, 1992). Consequently, therapy may involve advocacy work. Advocating a woman's needs when she is not heard by other professionals is not a usurping of her voice but an augmentation of it. In situations where racism prevails, advocacy confirms that a client's needs count and that the therapist is willing to employ every means available to increase the likelihood that the client will have a hearing in forums where the client's voice is being dismissed or ignored.

Empowering Women

Because disempowerment is endemic to women's life experiences, therapy must routinely empower women. To ensure that therapy does not further disempower women, especially women who do not speak English, it is critical that their invisibility and silenced voices not be reinforced. Careful attention must be paid to elements estranging them from their children and disempowering them *vis-à-vis* partners. Consequently, women may need to be linked with affordable educational facilities or volunteers who will tutor them in English. These may be available in multicultural centers, which would also provide them social supports. Moreover, they may wish for training opportunities that will allow them to develop their economic potential.

Because of language limitations, the use of interpreters may be required; however, judicious use of interpreters is advised. Engaging a male interpreter for women who wish to discuss very personal issues, possibly regarding their bodies, can be deeply embarrassing and intimidating. Also many nuances and biases may be introduced in the interpretation. Therefore, whenever possible, female interpreters should be engaged for immigrant women.

Another highly affirming experience for women is group therapy. In a group, women can learn that they are not alone, not bizarre for remaining with abusing men, not deserving of abuse, and not to blame for abuse. They can also become very much an important resource and source of information, comfort, and knowledge to one another.

Validating Women's Experiences

Therapists should validate women's experiences rather than pathologize them or blame them for their own difficulties and family problems. Commonly, women present in therapy with visible symptoms of depression, concerns regarding their marriages, or concerns regarding their children. It has been the norm to blame women for the problems in these relationships, instead of viewing women in the context of possible controlling relationships and a sexist society (Avis, 1988; Caplan & Hall-McCorquodale,

1985; Dye Holten,1990). Women's presenting concerns about depression frequently reflect erosion of personhood, resulting from repeated whittling down of their self-esteem by words denigrating their mothering, their appearance, their housekeeping, and their fidelity—the very elements by which many women gauge their worth as women. Routinely, women seek counseling to become "better wives," with the mistaken belief that if they were acting differently, their abusing, controlling partners would become caring, supportive people.

It is the norm as well that women do not even recognize that they have been abused until questions such as those suggested in Appendix A reveal the abuse and until therapists *name* the experience. Although this process is extremely painful, it is also validating and allows women to make sense of their feelings of distress, depression, and dissatisfaction. They begin to question long-held beliefs that economic provision by husbands, absence of alcoholism, freedom from physical abuse, and partner fidelity should be sufficient to create a satisfactory relationship. They are not "crazy" for feeling sadness and discontent when these conditions prove limited. Abuse, they also learn, takes many forms, all of which are devastating.

Highlighting Women's Strengths

Therapists should recognize women's personal strengths and assets, and those derived from their respective cultures and ethnic backgrounds, by promoting and advocating coordinated services and holistic approaches to therapy. Aliseo Martel, a doctor from Central America who counsels immigrants in an immigrant support program sponsored by a Kitchener, Ontario, church, observes:

> We have coped with experiences far more severe than most North Americans will ever experience. We have all the coping skills we need. We've coped with the worst horrors. Even with these skills, we still will have transition difficulties when adapting to a totally new environment and culture. What we need is not coping strategies but support and recognition of the enormous upheaval in coming to a foreign land where we must learn a new language and new customs. (personal communication, May 11, 1992)

Native people, many immigrant groups, and black people value the involvement of and support derived from extended families and kinship bonds. For blacks, reliance on kinship networks—which are not necessarily drawn along bloodlines—remains a major way for coping with the pressures of an oppressive society. These networks afford black families life-long support, cooperative domestic exchange, coresidence arrangements of multiple families, and bonds to three-generational households (McGoldrick et al., 1989). Consequently, therapists need to expand their definition of "family" to include such kinship networks. McGoldrick et al. (1989) point out as well the valued involvement of a child's aunts, grandmothers, and other relatives in shared child care. To assume that this is dysfunctional or indicates a breached boundary ignores the positive features of a family style that mitigates the problems and difficulties emerging from very limited economic resources. Therefore, when a therapist is helping a woman who needs to establish her executive role in the family, it is important to do so without demeaning or dismissing essential external supports. A very useful technique in establishing the significant people in women's lives is the genogram; however, as noted above, black families' genograms seldom conform completely to bloodlines (McGoldrick et al., 1989).

To foster self-healing and acknowledge the strength of Native peoples and their traditions, white therapists can to turn to healers, elders, and Native healing ceremonies. These are the essential resources for Native clients in reclaiming their roots, pride in their heritage, and ultimately pride in themselves. In Toronto, the Native Community Crisis Team is an innovative mental health service through which Native counselors, with the clinical backup of an on-site psychologist and the Toronto East General Hospital Crisis Intervention Unit, provide counseling within the community as an alternative to service within a traditional hospital setting. The outreach approach increases accessibility to counseling for a population that is underserved by existing programs. The growing need of Native people to share "collective pasts" renders Native counselors a valuable but rare resource, for they are critical in guiding Native people returning to their cultural traditions (Koptie, 1991).

Shin (1991) points out that services for battered women and sexually abused women are frequently provided by separate agencies whose services are neither near to each other nor coordinated. Although battered women were not necessarily victims of abuse in childhood, those who were abused physically or sexually are at increased risk of marrying abusing men (Pressman, 1989). Moreover, as pointed out earlier, refugee women are often victims of rape as well as wife assault. These women require comprehensive services by one organization that is responsive to their multiple needs, rather than disjointed services by several different organizations.

Understanding Unresponsive Behavior in Therapy

Seeming unwillingness to cooperate in therapy, disclose information, or conform to a therapist's interventions does not reflect "resistance" so much as fear, distrust, and the need of oppressed people to protect themselves from further contempt and abuse. Every fearful person with whom I have worked has invariably suffered abuse, and has realistically recognized that people are not always well-meaning and the world in general is not a safe place. A key element in therapy, therefore, is painstaking and possibly lengthy trust building, to enable a healing experience with another human being and to foster trust in others.

Overcoming Isolation

Overcoming isolation is a key to ending violence. Isolation is an ally of abuse in the home. Since the extended family and the community may have been critical parts of the life experience of the ethnic family culturally, historically, and in the country of origin, an important element of therapy is creating bridges between women and community supports. It is important to recognize that it may be especially difficult for women to make new connections and friendships when they are accustomed to ready-made extended family supports. Consequently, they may lack knowledge of the ways to make friends—ways that may seem quite natural to North Americans, who traditionally have learned how to connect with and establish ties with those outside of extended family.

Piazza and delValle (1992) point out that community may be a supportive context for the family, just as the family is a supportive context for the individual. They urge that administrators and educators introduce the context of community into clinical work by recruiting staff members with a knowledge of the community in which clients live; by developing relationships with a wide range of community leaders; and finally by involving these staff members and leaders in program planning and staff training. They further stress that community is not to be confused with class, race, and ethnicity. Recruitment of staff should be based not exclusively on these variables, but also on potential staff members' knowledge of community support structures and knowledge of ways to enlist the help of these systems.

Addressing Trauma

Violence engenders trauma and loss (Herman, 1992). A glaring shortcoming of classic systemic thinking is failure to acknowledge trauma and its destructive impact on the individual's self-esteem and sense of well-being (Pressman, 1989). Therefore, respectful therapy will incorporate knowledge of post-traumatic behavior; coping strategies, such as numbing, minimizing, and repression; damaged self-esteem; and lack of trust. Abused wives who were abused in childhood or traumatized through torture will require much longer therapy than abused women without such histories.

Understanding Minority Women's Political Loyalties

Women from minority groups within the majority culture identify with the struggles of their people against oppression, not exclusively or primarily with the struggles of women. Unlike white middle-class women, who experience no racial, ethnic, or class discrimination, women of color, ethnic women, aboriginal women, and immigrant women feel very identified with the persecution and prejudice experiences of their male counterparts. The consequence is very close identification with the men in their common suffering and in their struggles to end inequality within the societies that encompass them. Unfortunately, this identification is sometimes misunderstood, and some white "mainstream" feminists view minority women as male-oriented when in fact they are oriented toward the oppression of all their people, male and female. Until this oppression has been addressed, they are unwilling to focus on discrimination against them as women and on "private" violence, such as wife abuse, that will potentially generate further contempt toward their people (Bannerji et al., 1989; hooks, 1989).

Addressing Cultural and Ethnic Differences between Therapist and Client

As therapists, we must engage in dialogue with clients regarding cultural, ethnic, race, and class differences between ourselves and our clients' and the clients' concerns about seeking therapy. We cannot heal the wounded psyches of ethnic people without healing the racist community that is the source of much of that wounding. It is analogous to treating a child incest victim's symptoms of trauma and maintaining the child in the home with the perpetrator without first ensuring that the perpetrator has ended the abusing behavior. Just as perpetrators tend to deny and invalidate their victims out of shame and a wish to distance themselves from their heinous acts, so many of us white therapists unwittingly deny and wish to avoid those realities that are painful to us. The dilemma for us as white therapists becomes our duplicitous role of oppressors/wounders. However, we must validate oppressed persons' experience and our part in that experience if we are to be honest and real with ethnic people who seek our help. Moreover, since the very act of seeking help may encompass fear of persons in authority, any such concern about therapy needs attention.

CONCLUSION

This chapter has attempted to describe how immediate violence in the lives of immigrant women, ethnic women, aboriginal women, and women of color is an extension of the violence against them in North American society and their countries of origin. How we think about, understand, and define violence against women ultimately determines how we counsel. Whether or not we incorporate the ethnic, cultural, racial, and societal context of women's lives into our analysis will determine whether or not these problems are reduced in scope and whether or not women's experiences are validated.

The material presented and the suffering of clients described here may seem overwhelming. They are so only if a therapist believes that therapy is the means to transforming societal values and ending institutionalized racism and sexism. Therapy is not the solution to massive societal problems. Therapists striving to change the world outside of their offices will need to leave their offices and become activists there.

Despite the limitations of therapy in "curing" social problems, there is enormous pressure on therapists treating perpetrators to be the means for ending male violence. There is corresponding pressure on those attending to victims of violence to ensure women's and children's safety. Therapy alone cannot ensure the end of male violence or guarantee women's safety. However, it is a significant way of responding to the suffering generated by destructive social structures and values. It is a means of providing validation, comfort, support, information, tools for healing, and tools for unlearning violence. It is also a means of challenging those societal structures and values that support and promote violence against women and children. Although these therapeutic offerings in and of themselves will not change society, they are responses to violence that can contribute to far-reaching social change.

APPENDIX A
Assessment Questions to Expose Violence and Controlling Behavior

Questions Regarding the Relationship

- *Companionship:* Do the husband and wife have time together as a couple? How often? What sorts of things do they do together?
- *Affection:* How is this expressed? By whom? Has it been satisfactory for each?
- *Sex:* Has this been satisfactory? If not, what would make it so? Does the husband read pornography?
- *Support networks:* Does each partner have separate friends? Is each comfortable when the other goes out separately? Is jealousy frequently expressed? By whom?
- *Sharing:* Is each partner able to talk openly about hopes, fears, worries, upsets outside of the relationship, and concerns regarding the other? Is the response to such sharing satisfactory?

Questions Regarding Decision Making, Family Roles, and Power Imbalances

- Do both partners work outside of the home?
- Are chores within the home shared?

- If a wife does all the inside work *and* works outside, how was this arrangement decided?
- Who nurtures whom in the family? To whom does each person turn for support?
- What emotions are expressed in the family? How are they expressed and by whom?
- What is the husband's involvement with the children?
- How was that decided?
- How are decisions in general made?
- How are decisions regarding money made?
- Does one partner have a greater say than the other?
- If there is a family car, does each partner have access to the family car and a separate set of keys?
- When differences arise, how are conflicts resolved?
- When there is a difference and someone gets angry or upset, how is anger expressed? Does anyone get hit or pushed or grabbed, or have hair pulled? Does anyone yell? Are any objects thrown, walls kicked or punched, doors slammed, fists slammed on a table, fists raised?
- What is the impact of that behavior on the partner toward whom it is directed and on children?
- Does a woman have a history of abuse in the past? What are her current experiences of abuse both in the community and in the home?
- What positive qualities does a woman value in her partner?
- What are her primary concerns or criticisms of her partner?
- If the partner were present, what would he say he values in her?
- What would he criticize about her?
- Does he have difficulty accepting ideas or opinions of hers that differ from his, or criticism from her or other people? (Abusing men very often interpret differences as put-downs, indicating lack of respect or disregard for their position as head of the household.)
- When she differs, or he perceives a difference, what is his response?
- Is the extended family a part of the household or decision making?
- Do extended family members have a voice that transcends that of the woman being interviewed? Who is most influential in the family?
- What is the impact of the arrangement described above on the woman? On her relationships with her husband? On her relationships with her children?
- What attitudes toward authority are instilled in children in the woman's country of origin? (These may make submission especially natural and defying an abusing man particularly difficult.)
- Are there cultural values that expect couples to remain married, regardless of circumstances?
- What is the nature of the woman's relationship with her in-laws? What is their decision-making role within the family, if any? What is the impact of this role on the woman?
- What is the nature of the woman's relationship with her children? What impact has acculturation had on the woman's executive role in the family? Are there any controlling behaviors by children?

- What is the woman's sense of herself before her marriage? How has she changed since marrying?

APPENDIX B
Assessment Questions for Abused Immigrant and Ethnic Women

- How long has the client lived in Canada?
- How was life in the country of origin different from life here?
- What has been the most difficult part of the move?
- What has been most missed since the move?
- What has changed for each family member since moving?
- What specific experiences have been related to refugee status?
- Were there supports here to help in the adjustment to a new country?
- What or who were those supports?
- Was more support needed than provided?
- What type was needed, and would this kind of support be useful now?
- What aids would have been helpful, or could be helpful but are not yet in place?
- What are the cultural strengths and assets present for the client: cultural values and practices; involvement with social networks, support systems, and extended family; and effective coping strategies in difficult times or situations in the past?
- Is the violence at home in some way connected with the move, the transition due to migration, or immigration itself?
- To what extent is the client's understanding of the violence based on a cultural explanation?
- Is the abuse considered normal within the culture, or is it considered inappropriate?
- How are marital problems or family problems usually addressed in the woman's tradition or culture?
- What are the client's financial and educational resources?
- To what extent is the violence reflective of environmental shortcomings or lack of access to resources and supports?
- Have there been specific experiences in the new country of racism and discrimination?
- What specific effects has acculturation had on family development? Have there been relationship problems as a consequence of differential acculturation?
- What is the nature of the client's relationship to her partner? To her children?
- Have these changed since the move?

REFERENCES

Allport, G. W. (1958). *The nature of prejudice.* Garden City, NY: Doubleday/Anchor.

Anderson, D. (1991). *The unfinished revolution.* Toronto: Doubleday Canada.

Avis, J. M. (1988). Deepening awareness: A private study guide to feminism and family therapy. In L. Braverman (Ed.), *A guide to feminist family therapy* (pp. 15–46). New York: Harrington Park Press.

Bannerji, H., Brand, D., Gupta, N., Khosla, P., & Silvera, M. (1989). We appear silent to people who are deaf to what we say. In N. Gupta & M. Silvera (Eds.), *The issue is 'ism: Women of colour speak out* (pp. 9–29). Toronto: Sister Vision.

Bograd, M. (1984). Family systems approaches to wife battering: A feminist critique. *American Journal of Orthopsychiatry, 54,* 558–568.

Brownmiller, S. (1976). *Against our will: Men, women and rape.* New York: Bantam Books.

Caplan, P. J., & Hall-McCorquodale, I. (1985). Mother-blaming in major clinical journals. *American Journal of Orthopsychiatry, 55,* 345–353.

Chambon, A. (1989). Refugee families' experiences: Three family themes: Family disruption, violent trauma and acculturation. *Journal of Strategic and Systemic Therapies, 8*(2), 3–13.

Chapman, C., & Nadeau, D. (1987–1990). *Family violence training kit.* Vancouver: Native Education Centre.

Davis, A. (1983). *Women, race and class.* New York: Vintage Books.

Davis, M., & Krauter, J. F. (1971). *The other Canadians: Profiles of six minorities.* Toronto: Methuen.

Davidson, T. (1980). *Conjugal crime: Understanding and changing the wifebeating pattern.* New York: Ballantine Books.

Dobash, R., & Dobash, R. P. (1979). *Violence against wives.* New York: Free Press.

Dufresne, M. (1992). Choosing accountability to battered women. *Vis-à-Vis,10,* 5–6.

Dye Holten, J. (1990). When do we stop mother-blaming? *Journal of Feminist Family Therapy, 2,* 53–60.

Efron, D., & Roberts, J. (Eds.). (1989, Summer). *Journal of Strategic and Systemic Therapies,* Special Bonus Issue (8).

Fornazzari, X., & Freire, M. (1990). Women as victims of torture. *Acta Psychiatrica Scandinavica. 82,* 257–260.

Freire, M. (1989). Latin American refugees: Adjustment and adaptation. *Canadian Woman Studies, 10*(1), 55–57.

Freire, M. (1991, June). *Violence in the lives of refugee women.* Paper presented at Violence in the Lives of Immigrant and Refugee Women: Cross-Cultural Views Conference, Hispanic Council of Metropolitan Toronto.

Goldner, V. (1992, March–April). Making room for both/and. *The Family Therapy Networker,* pp. 55–61.

Hare, S. (1991). Breaking free: A proposal for change to aboriginal family violence. *Canadian Woman Studies, 11*(4), 79–80.

Herizons. (1992, Summer). Native women's association demands equality. p. 13.

Herman, J. L. (1992). *Trauma and recovery.* New York: Basic Books.

Hines, P. M., & Boyd-Franklin, N. (1982). Black families. In M. McGoldrick, J. K. Pearce, & J. Giordano (Eds.), *Ethnicity and family therapy* (pp. 84–108). New York: Guilford Press.

hooks, b. (1981). *Ain't I a woman.* Boston: South End Press.

hooks, b. (1989). *Talking back: Thinking feminist, thinking black.* Boston: South End Press.

Jaffe, P., Wolfe, D. A., Wilson, S. K., & Zak, L. (1986). Similarities in behavioral and social maladjustment among child victims and witnesses to family violence. *American Journal of Orthopsychiatry, 56*, 142–146.

James, K., & McIntyre, D. (1983). The reproduction of families: The social role of family therapy? *Journal of Marital and Family Therapy, 9*, 119–129.

Koptie, S. (1991). The Native community crisis team. *Canadian Woman Studies, 12*(3), Spring, 44–45.

Lipchik, E. (1991, May–June). Spouse abuse: Challenging the party line. *The Family Therapy Networker*, pp. 59–63.

Mann, S. A. (1988). Slavery, sharecropping, and sexual inequality. In M. R. Malson, E. Mudimbe-Boyi, J. F. O'Barr, & M. Wyer (Eds.), *Black women in America* (pp. 133–157). Chicago: University of Chicago Press.

Martin, D. (1983). *Battered wives*. New York: Pocket Books.

McDougald, E. J. (1973). In defense of black women. In G. Lerner (Ed.), *Black women in white America: A documentary history* (pp. 169–171). New York: Vintage Books.

McGoldrick, M., Garcia-Preto, N., Moore Hines, P., & Lee, E. (1989). Ethnicity and women. In M. McGoldrick, C. M. Anderson, & F. Walsh (Eds.), *Women in families* (pp. 169–199). New York: Norton.

McIntosh, P. (1988). *White privilege and male privilege: A personal account of coming to see correspondences through work in women's studies* (Work in progress, No. 189). Wellesley, MA: Stone Center, Wellesley College.

Miller, J. B. (1986). *Toward a new psychology of women* (2nd ed). Boston: Beacon Press.

Ministry of Indian Affairs and Northern Development (1980). *Indian Conditions: A survey*. Ottawa: Author.

Narayan, J. (1991, March 13). *Immigrant women from a feminist perspective*. Talk given at the Faculty of Social Work, Wilfrid Laurier University, Waterloo, Ontario.

Ng, R. (1988). Immigrant women and institutionalized racism. In S. Burt, L. Codie, & L. Dorney (Eds.), *Changing patterns: Women in Canada* (pp. 184–203). Toronto: McLelland & Stewart.

Piazza, J., & delValle, C.M. (1992). Community-based family therapy training: An example of work with poor and minority families. *Journal of Strategic and Systemic Therapies, 11*, 53–69.

Pinderhughes, E. (1989). *Understanding race, ethnicity, and power: The key to efficacy in clinical practice*. New York: Free Press.

Pressman, B. (1984). *Family violence: Origins and treatment*. Guelph, Ontario: University of Guelph Press.

Pressman, B. (1989). Power and ideological issues in intervening with assaulted women. In B. Pressman, G. Cameron, & M. Rothery (Eds.), *Intervening with assaulted women: Current theory, reserach, and practice* (pp. 9–45). Hillsdale, NJ: Erlbaum.

Pressman, B. (1992). [Review of C. Madanes (1990), *Sex, love, and violence*]. *Journal of Feminist Family Therapy, 4*, 99–103.

Rosenbaum, A., & O'Leary, K. D. (1981). Children: The unintended victims of marital violence. *American Journal of Orthopsychiatry, 51*, 692–699.

Riutort, M., & Endicott Small, S. (1985). *Working with assaulted immigrant women: A handbook for lay counsellors*. Toronto: Education Wife Assault.

Schecter, S. (1982). *Women and male violence.* Boston: South End Press.

Shin, M. Y. (1991). Immigrant and racial minority women organize. *Canadian Woman Studies, 12,*(1), 55–57.

Silvera, M. (1989). Silenced. In N. Gupta & M. Silvera (Eds.), *The issue is 'ism: Women of colour speak out* (pp. 70–82). Toronto: Sister Vision.

Subcommittee on the Status of Women (Standing Committee on Health and Welfare, Social Affairs, Seniors and the Status of Women). (1991). *The war against women* (First Report of the Subcommittee). Ottawa: House of Commons Canada.

Taggart, M. (1985). The feminist critique in epistemological perspective: Questions of context in family therapy. *Journal of Marital and Family Therapy, 11,* 113–126.

Walker, L. E. (1979). *The battered woman.* New York: Harper & Row.

York, G. (1990). *The dispossessed: Life and death in Native Canada.* London: Vintage U.K.

17

Poor Women: Making a Difference

MYRTLE PARNELL
JO VANDERKLOOT

. . . women are a Third World wherever we are: low on capital, low on technology, labor intensive, . . . a source of raw materials, maintenance . . . underpaid or unpaid production for the more powerful.

—GLORIA STEINEM (1988, p. 19)

We have spent the majority of our professional lives treating the poor. Over the years we have asked ourselves, "What makes the issues of race, ethnicity, and poverty so difficult to talk about and to resolve? Are the problems we encounter among a very poor and diverse population purely of these persons' own making? Or is there a message for the rest of society in the nature of these problems?"

POVERTY IN CONTEXT

According to Senge (1990), we all have mental models with deeply ingrained assumptions, generalizations, or images that influence how we see the world and how we take action. These models determine our perception of how things can and cannot be done. Mental models are particularly important in a multicultural society, because when we define difference as defective, we miss many important messages about what is happening in society at large. We then find ourselves seriously off the mark, focusing on intrafamilial dysfunction and missing the cues about the meanings of particular problems in the larger social context. For instance, as poor black families became increasingly headed by single female parents, they were defined as "deviant," and psychotherapy was frequently prescribed to deal with this "problem." In the last 20 years, however, white families have followed in the footsteps of black families, becoming increasingly poor, single-parent, and female-headed. Black families were the harbinger of the unraveling of the social fabric. We missed 30 or 40 years of cues about family disintegration because we could not conceive of how poor black women could possibly have anything to do with white families.

The perception of the poor woman is that there is a deficit in her psyche that has caused a predicament, which requires outside intervention. Whether her children are in foster care, she is an abused woman, or she needs medication for anxiety, depression, or psychosis, there is something within her that needs to be fixed in order for her to function independently. This perception is maintained, despite massive evidence that the social fabric itself is giving way—institutional failures, breakdown of family and community. We still continue with the same treatment models, insisting that the problem is inside the woman, and then we define her as resistant when she drops out of treatment. We must ask, "Who is the crazy one in this process?" Little children receive the same treatment. Although they frequently live in families, communities, and states that are dysfunctional, the children are singled out—most often in school, for play therapy. For what purpose? What message does this give to such a child about where the problem lies?

What is clear to those of us working with poor women and their children is that they believe that in the larger society they are viewed as burdens who are resented for taking up time, space, and resources. The larger society persists in its judgments against the poor, with the belief that there is "equal opportunity" for all, and therefore that the problems of poor people are of their own making. We clinicians have peddled this idea so long that most people have come to believe it, and policy makers develop initiatives and programs based on this assumption. The two of us have become convinced that the approach to treatment with the poor must be redesigned and expanded, in order to be at least appropriate and at best effective. The existing body of knowledge for working with the poor is a caricature when compared to the realities of poor women and their families. Moreover, poor women do not believe that the therapeutic models typically provided to them are helpful:

That powerful global and unitary body of knowledge, the *Diagnostic and Statistical Manual of Mental Disorders,* Third Edition (American Psychiatric Association, 1980), which is centrally established and encoded in economic, medical, and educational systems, is practiced at the most local level—in the relationship between [a] social worker and a client. When the social worker is required by an agency's funding needs or by by the rules of third-party payers to attach a diagnostic label to a client, a powerful and privileged classification system has entered this relationship and has in all likelihood affected the worker's professional objectivity, the relationship, and the client's self-definition. (Hartman, 1992, p. 483)

What often follows is a negative experience for both client and clinician, which leads to a distorted clinical picture, suggesting a lack of motivation and resistance on the part of the client.

The current medical paradigm in which the helping professions operate suggests a belief that all knowledge is objective and comes from science alone. This medical model is no longer adequate to solve the myriad of psychosocial problems in the postmodern world. It overlooks the environment in which poor women struggle to survive. It ignores the collapse of our institutions and the impact this has on people who depend daily on those very institutions for their survival needs. It ignores the fact that most jobs programs are not real jobs, but employment programs for the middle class; that the medical needs of the poor are high and cannot be covered by the salary of a menial job; that there is anarchy in poor neighborhoods, leaving people too fearful to leave their homes unattended; and that there is inadequate or no child care available—a not insignificant issue when there is no safe place for children. These times call for innovative approaches to the human services. We call this a need for a paradigm shift—a transformation in our way of thinking. Capra (1982) has described it as a "profound change in the thoughts, perceptions and values that form a particular vision of reality" (p. 30).

The poor do not have the kind of control over their lives that has, until recently, been enjoyed by the middle class. Because of this, it behooves us as clinicians to know about the constraints that militate against the upward mobility of poor women, so that we can validate their perceptions when this is warranted and educate them when this is needed. Knowledge and validation are empowering to middle-class women, but they are essential for poor women who are struggling to improve living conditions for themselves and their children. Society itself in many ways maintains poverty through its false myths, which cruelly deny that poverty is more than an individual problem, and then unmercifully blame a poor woman for her situation. How do we label as pathological people who are very different from ourselves, and who live and survive in a world about which we know little or nothing? How can we really distinguish pathology from adaptation? What is pathological in response to living in a domestic war zone? If we are looking for pathology in the individual, we will find it, but what then? Can this be an adequate basis for a treatment plan when it fails to account for the overwhelming social realities that must be dealt with? Instead, our treatment must validate poor clients' reality by addressing their situation of collapsing institutions and disintegrating communities. Viable families cannot exist without viable communities to support them. Homelessness is an indication of the disintegration of formerly viable communities. Housing the homeless in shelters outside of their own communities further adds to the breakdown.

Because it is most likely that middle-class clinicians lack a common ground on which to communicate with people whose life conditions and frames of reference are so very different from their own, it is essential that such clinicians be very careful about making assumptions about poor clients' pathology. There are very different ways of surviving in different segments of society. Initially, a middle-class clinician might best look upon a poor client as a person from a foreign country who speaks a different language, especially in respect to the social realities the client experiences. The treatment process, then, of necessity, must be a collaborative one in which the clinician and client interact and learn from each other.

GENERAL TREATMENT CONSIDERATIONS

Our treatment of poor families illustrates a mix of many techniques we have evolved over a period of time working in very poor communities. Our approach has been strongly influenced by the family systems concepts of Hartman and Laird (1983); by Milton Erickson's concept of the unconscious as the reservoir of all life's experience and creativity (see Carter, 1982); and by Albert Scheflin's (1981) levels of organization.

Erickson's unconditional positive regard for the client, and his belief that all people are okay just as they are, constitute the cornerstone of our work with the poor. This means starting with the assumption that people have integrity and generally do the best they can with the options they perceive as available to them. For example, we have yet to meet two people who come together, have a family, and intentionally try to make their lives and those of their children worse than it was for them when they were growing up. Yet this happens all the time. Sometimes the harder such people try, using the only skills they know, the poorer the results, and the more likely the escalation of the very behavior they are trying to prevent. They get stuck in patterns that have negative consequences, and need help in creating positive ways of interacting. When people are behaving in a way that is counterproductive, our approach identifies the behavior pattern and the function it serves, and helps the clients shift the pattern so that the outcome is positive.

Next, we pay close attention to the context in which the symptoms occur. This means taking into consideration everything that may have an impact on the system. The social environment of the neighborhood, community, state, and even perhaps the nation may be part of the context that maintains the symptom. Only after the context is examined and understood can a client's behavior be fully understood.

Learning to sidestep resistance is essential in working with the poor. Resistance is often a client's first way of communicating that a clinician's hypothesis is not complete or that an intervention is not helpful (Anderson & Stewart, 1983). It is important to look behind clients' resistance in order to find a way for them to cooperate in their own treatment. The more difficult the presenting problems, the more likely clinicians are to push in a particular direction to assuage their own overwhelming feelings of frustration. It is precisely at these times that it is necessary to rethink the hypothesis and intervention to find what has been left out in the initial assessment and treatment plan. When people have requested help and feel understood, resistance is usually not a major problem.

An important issue regarding resistance and working with the poor is that those who are dependent on social services for survival are intruded upon in ways never imagined by the clinician who is not familiar with the lives of the poor. Poor people make it their business to know which programs work and which do not. Resistance, then, may be a client's way of letting a clinician know that there is something wrong with the program. A social work student of ours once said that when she worked in a foundling hospital, she was feeling hopeless when dealing with the children because their backgrounds were so bleak. She said that she held out the hope of survival for these children in the school system. After reading Kozol's (1991) *Savage Inequalities,* which talks of the terrible state of schools in poor communities, she realized how foolish that was. Yet many clinicians and policy makers continue to blame the children for not doing well.

The family we use for the case example that constitutes the bulk of this chapter lives in one of New York City's more violent communities—one that is losing the battle for order and civility. The drug dealers have moved in and taken over. They hang out on street corners, outside the schools, and in the parks, so that children rarely go anywhere unescorted. Even 12-year-olds continue to be escorted to school by adults, and the adults' presence severely limits the children's already limited world. The children mostly play indoors year round, no matter how beautiful the weather. Drive-by shootings have terrorized the population, and children are used to the sound of gunshots during the night. They are taught to stay away from windows and to "hit the floor" at the sound of shots.

THE CASE OF RICARDO AND HIS FAMILY

Ricardo, an adorable 6-year-old first-grader, was referred to us by his teacher because of recent highly disruptive behavior and increasing inattentiveness in class. She believed that his mother, who is Latina, was in a lesbian relationship with a black woman, and that the relationship was not going well. Ricardo's mother and her partner took turns picking him up after school, and each had seemed very stressed lately. Ricardo was and is a beautiful child, with large brown eyes, dimples, and an impish smile. He is open and outgoing and seems very comfortable with adults, always ready for and expecting hugs.

Ricardo's mother, Yolanda, agreed to our request that she bring everyone in her household to the first meeting. She came with Ricardo and
Evelyn, her live-in lover. Yolanda, an attractive, articulate 25-year-old
woman, had moved about 6 months before from her mother's home (where
she had lived since Ricardo's birth) to an apartment with Evelyn. Yolanda
and Evelyn had met in a Narcotics Anonymous (NA) meeting. Evelyn,
aged 30, is a slender, athletic black woman; like Yolanda, she is very bright
and articulate. She had completed a long-term rehabilitation program, had
been drug-free for 2 years, and attended NA meetings five to seven times
weekly. Yolanda had been drug-free for 1 year, but was less regular in her
attendance at NA meetings. This was one of the ongoing issues between
them.

Evelyn, the spokesperson for the family, presented their major concern
that Ricardo was not concentrating in school and sometimes disrupted the
class. Although both women were obviously concerned about this behavior, there was a sense that the focus on Ricardo was a distraction from
important issues between them. This sense came in part from the way in
which their presentation skirted their present relationship, although they
talked very freely about their lives as drug addicts, their efforts to abstain
from drug use, and their goals for themselves in terms of education and
employment.

Exploring the Genogram

Although some clinicians do not believe that one should use genograms
when first meeting with a black family because of issues of trust, we find
that working with chaotic families in chaotic communities requires all the
leverage we can get. The clients' context and patterns of function are
essential to this process, and time is of the essence. If we are unable to hook
the family members in the first session in a meaningful way, they rarely
return. Their environment is so compelling that they need to believe that
we have something meaningful to offer immediately. Information gathering is an engagement tool, because we not only are requesting information,
but are providing information about a new understanding (context) in
which to view the problems and potential solutions. It is useful not only for
our own understanding; it is equally important in educating the clients
about family systems, our hypotheses, and the patterns within their families
that have coalesced over generations and led to a coping style that will be
the focus of our work together.

Another reason why genograms have proved useful in engaging the
clients is this: They are relieved to learn that some personal, innate deficit is
not what has caused the misery that brings them to treatment. Sharing our
knowledge and hypotheses about their family systems is respectful, and
invites them to continue to have input into their treatment. Clients general-

ly experience this process as validating and empowering. Family-of-origin work broadens the frame and focuses on processes of interaction, rather than on who is to blame. What processes and patterns get in the way of the family members' having a positive interaction with one another and with service providers? We then identify a pattern of functioning and coach the family to do more of what works.

In constructing the genogram in this case (see Figure 17.1), we discovered that Yolanda is the youngest of three children. Yolanda's mother, Helena, was the oldest girl in her family, and had been raised with all the responsibilities traditionally prescribed for the Latina female. Yolanda described her maternal grandmother as a very hard worker who neglected and physically abused the children, especially Helena. She described her grandfather as a man who had a rosary in one hand and a whip in the other.

Yolanda's grandmother had had 14 children. Helena herself told us in her first session (to be described later) that her family consisted of 95% chemical abusers, with the remaining 5% extremely obese. Abuse in this family was rampant in all forms throughout these three generations. There were murders, incest, betrayal, and verbal as well as physical abuse. Helena's younger sister had announced her intention to take Yolanda's grandmother in when she was old and had Alzheimer's disease. Instead, she took the grandmother's disability checks and deposited the grandmother at the entrance to Bellevue Hospital, where she died a short time later.

Helena's personal history turned out to be essential to understanding and working on her daughter's problems. Because Helena's mother worked long hours, Helena was confined to the home immediately after school, did not have friends, and very rarely was able to play. So confined was she that when she was in her early 20s, she met someone her age who had lived two doors away from her while she was growing up and had never seen or heard of her. Also in keeping with traditional Latino culture, the males in the family had the prerogative of demanding caretaking from the sisters, and could reprimand and inflict corporal punishment at will. Helena was frequently beaten by her older brother, and only very recently had had a confrontation with him in which she informed him that she would no longer take his abuse and that he was no longer welcome in her home unless he learned to respect her and her children.

Helena became pregnant at 19 by her first cousin, whom she then married. He was described as a nice person who loved his children, but also as a multiple-drug user who worked only sporadically, leaving the burden of family care and support to Helena. She worked when and where she could. She was and continues to be very overweight. In order to cope with many life stresses, she sought medication and was prescribed combinations of amphetamines and tranquilizers, which she took as needed. This led to frequent blackouts of varying durations.

While growing up, Yolanda developed a style of "coping" in which

Lesbian Couple – Abusive Background

African-American   Loss / Abuse / Boundaries   Puerto Rican

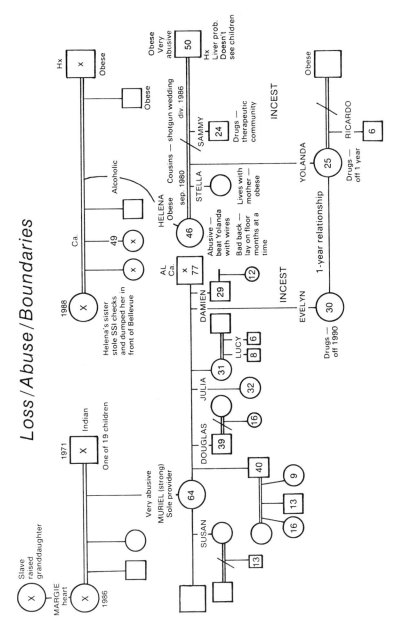

FIGURE 17.1. Genogram for Evelyn, Yolanda, and Ricardo.

she too would fade out—not from medication, but rather in reaction to very high levels of stress within the family. She described herself as having a poor memory; it became clear that Yolanda responded to tension by fading out, and therefore experienced herself as very forgetful. During those growing-up years, she "faded out" so frequently that there were (and still are) large gaps in her knowledge of what happened. Evidently the pain of living in her family was often unbearable, if we are to judge by the style of both mother and daughter. Yolanda did remember in great detail the physical and verbal abuse she received from her mother, which was frequent and extremely harsh (Helena sometimes beat her with wires). However, she had almost no recall of the the difficulties her mother was having or of the ongoing conflict between her parents. There was never a problem of sexual abuse, according to mother and daughter. Yolanda's blanking out seemed to occur when her parents were fighting. She did not recall, for instance, that her father once attempted to strangle her mother and another time tried to stab her, and was only prevented from doing so by her older sister. The parents separated when Yolanda was 14 and divorced when she was 20.

Yolanda's first sexual relationship with a girl began at age 10, when she and her sister, Stella, shared a bed. She started abusing drugs at age 13, and soon after began engaging in prostitution to support her habit. She became bulimic and anorexic during adolesence. She was slightly overweight at intake, but said that she managed her weight with normal dieting.

Evelyn's portion of the genogram shows similar issues of abuse. She is the youngest girl of nine children, born to two fathers. The children feel that the family is split along paternal lines. Neither of the fathers ever lived with them, but did visit from time to time; though they did not offer consistent financial support, they did help out in times of special need or crisis. The mother worked long hours as a domestic to support the family. Her own family had been extremely poor, and had had to take her out of school in third grade so that she could pick cotton.

Evelyn's mother was excessively neat and clean, as Evelyn continues to be. Her mother was further described as having been physically abusive to all the children, beating them with switches, inner tubes from bicycle tires, and electric cords. Physical punishment was not frequent, but was very severe when it occurred. Evelyn recalled that she was once beaten for hours for some minor infraction. Criticism and verbal abuse were daily occurrences. In addition, Evelyn said she felt that she was neglected by her mother in a way that the others were not. She did not understand why she was singled out for this "special" treatment. When Evelyn was 5 years old, she slipped and fell on some glass, sustaining many deep cuts in her left arm and severing a nerve. She was taken to a hospital emergency room by a relative, who reported the physician's recommendation was that Evelyn have an operation in order to achieve full use of her left hand. The mother, it seemed, was phobic about hospitals and refused to permit the operation. From that time on, Evelyn hid her left hand because it was smaller than the right one, and she was very self-conscious about it. In treatment, we suggested that she was reacting to the stigma she felt as her mother's least favorite child. Evelyn then stopped hiding her hand and was surprised that others did not notice the difference. It was the way in which she favored the arm that had called attention to it.

At age 17, Evelyn had a lengthy operation during which two large cysts were removed from her uterus, and she was treated for "blood in her urine." The mother did not visit her in the hospital. The mother's phobias also extended to attending funerals: She did not attend the funerals of any of her close relatives, even her parents. Evelyn reportedly was sick at the time of each funeral, and therefore did not attend either. We speculate that Evelyn stayed home to comfort her mother and later suffered from not having a full experience of grieving.

In addition to the physical abuse by her mother, Evelyn was sexually abused by an older brother and his friends, beginning when she was 6. She was raped by someone in the neighborhood at age 15 and again at age 18. By this time she decided that she had "had enough" and took up body building. By the age of 19, when the next attempt occurred, she was more than able to defend herself. At age 10 she had had a sexual encounter with a 13-year-old girl. She liked it and decided then that she would continue having sexual relationships with females.

Evelyn's use of drugs had begun very early in adolesence and continued until 3 years earlier, when she entered a long-term rehabilitation program, as noted above. She remains committed to recovery, and wants to go for training as a drug and alcoholism counselor. Virtually all of her new friends are in recovery. She attends meetings all over the city of New York.

Relationships in Evelyn's family of origin remain quite strained. The sisters and mother all live within walking distance of one another and have frequent contact, but are very critical of one another. They can rarely cooperate in anything, and the negotiation on any subject is verbally abusive in the extreme. The men are all doing better financially than the women are: They all have jobs that enable them to support their families, and they own their own homes.

The Situation at Intake

Evelyn was the primary homemaker and disciplinarian of the household and the couple's interactions concerning housework and discipline constituted excellent examples of how abusive systems work. Evelyn, like her mother, demanded very high standards of cleanliness, releasing a lot of her own pent-up anger through scrubbing and polishing. She demanded the same commitment to housekeeping chores from Yolanda, who spent most of her day in computer school, had homework to complete, and needed to spend some time every day with her son and attend NA meetings several times a week. Yolanda also worked 12 hours every weekend in a laundromat. The issues of cleanliness and house cleaning were at the center of an ongoing battle.

The following was a typical example of this interaction: Yolanda finally decided to spend one day out of the weekend cleaning. She did a thorough job and was tired, but pleased with herself. Evelyn, upon returning home, immediately noticed that one of the window sills was dusty. She began a tirade, completely ignoring the shine and polish in the rest of the apartment. The attack on Yolanda was not limited to the cleaning incident, but escalated into a torrent of criticism: Yolanda did not attend NA meetings as often as she should; she had a poor memory; she did not try hard enough at anything she did. Evelyn continued yelling: She, Evelyn, was left with the burden of child care; Yolanda did not spend enough time with Evelyn; and Yolanda did not speak up for herself among friends. As she typically did, Yolanda withdrew and sat in the corner on the floor rocking and crying. Evelyn also was hurt and angry, and repeatedly declared that she was tired of this relationship because she did not get anything from it. The denial of anything positive in the relationship is very characteristic of abusive relationships. Evelyn only focused on what Yolanda did not do.

Interventions with Evelyn and Yolanda

In treatment, we asked each woman to study what her part was in getting her partner to do what she said she did not want her to do; each was asked to track only her own behavior. This proved initially to be an almost impossible task. What eventually became clear in the sessions in which tracking was the focus was that neither of them could permit closeness and intimacy in their lives, and thus each had a repertoire of abusive behaviors to push the other away. This pattern had to change if they were to have a better life, together or apart. Tracking was also a homework assignment, given when the partners were stuck in blaming each other. After many attempts, they finally "got it," and this signaled the beginning of real change. What is typical in these kinds of abusive cases is that one party focuses only on what is wrong, while the other feels so needy that she focuses on her desperate need and what is good about the relationship. This is the process by which abused women remain with spouses who beat them. When an abusive incident is over, they block out all the times they were beaten, and remember the times the spouses were kind.

What was evident about each of these women was that they cared about each other and about Ricardo, and very much wanted their lives to be different. In situations such as these, we need to remind ourselves constantly that if people are not behaving in ways that are constructive, it is not because they do not want to or do not care, but because they have learned an interpretation of reality and a pattern of behavior that precludes their achieving what they say they want.

The discipline of Ricardo was the focus of much of the couple's abusiveness. Yolanda, in keeping with Latino culture, was a devoted and indulgent mother, who saw her 6-year-old as a baby and felt both pleasure and sadness with each growth step. The initial child care arrangement required Evelyn to be responsible for Ricardo (except during school hours) from early morning to late afternoon, when Yolanda returned from computer school. Evelyn was very strict with Ricardo, in what we originally thought was simply in keeping with lower socioeconomic black culture. Only later did we learn of the extremes to which Evelyn would go to "spy" on him with reprimands and punishments. Each misbehavior, no matter how minor, was reported to Yolanda with the demand that she punish him. After being away from her son all day, however, Yolanda was more inclined to talk and play with Ricardo than to punish him. This scenario was repeated several evenings a week, leading to Yolanda's withdrawing in tears, and feeling like a failure as both mother and lover. Evelyn herself felt left out and unappreciated once again. At first she never connected her lonely feelings to her own behavior and how it pushed everyone so far away. Later, she was astounded to discover the role she played in her own misery.

Woven into our foci on the abusive pattern, discipline, and parenting were the generational issues of unresolved mourning, which further impaired the development of healthy, trusting, intimate relationships. Parents who have not adequately mourned their losses are wary of close personal relationships, out of fear of suffering another loss. Unbeknownst to them, they transmit a distant style of relating and communicating to their children, who learn it and pass it on to the next generation. This generational pattern is easily illustrated through their genograms.

Enter the Larger System

Six weeks into treatment, a major crisis erupted. Ricardo went to his maternal grandmother, Helena, for a weekend visit and was not returned. Yolanda's efforts to contact him were thwarted by whoever answered the phone. It took 48 hours to confirm that the Child Welfare Administration (CWA) had given Helena temporary custody of Ricardo, because bruises had been found on his buttocks. Apparently he had been taken to the doctor for another reason, which remained unclear. Yolanda had not been told that he was ill. The doctor noticed the bruises and filed a report with the child abuse hotline. An investigation and hearing were pending.

Yolanda was devastated to realize that her own mother would actually take her child from her. She was so hurt by this that we were concerned that there would be irreparable estrangement. In poor communities in particular, contact with the extended family is very important for help with child care. With all the pressures and stresses in this family, the loss of regular contact with his grandmother would have been devastating for Ricardo. We contacted the CWA; in a subsequent letter, we gave our assessment of the couple and Ricardo, outlined our treatment plan, and described the couple as very cooperative clients who seemed committed to forming better family relationships. The CWA responded with mixed messages to us and to our clients about their procedures, their findings, and their investigations. A court hearing was scheduled.

One of the most frustrating aspects of involvement with public social service agencies is that it is rare to have contact with the same worker twice. Like most bureaucracies, the system is set up in such a way that no one is clearly accountable for anything. For example, one worker told us that Ricardo stated that he had been beaten, did not want to see his mother or Evelyn, and had specifically requested to live with his grandmother. A court hearing was scheduled to determine whether continued custody should be granted. On the same day Yolanda was told that she could see her son, but then no such arrangements were made. The following day, a third worker informed us that Helena would not gain custody, because the bruises were not recent and Ricardo confirmed that he had not been spanked in a long time. However, a court hearing was still scheduled, and visitation by Yolanda was still not arranged. As this confusion continued, it became clear how the system, in trying to carry out its responsibilities, was inadvertently abusing all concerned. It certainly did not help Ricardo to be caught in the mire of confusing messages to his family, to have no way to sort out what was happening to him, and to have no one to help him with his feelings.

Evelyn was not allowed to attend the hearing because she was not legally related to Yolanda and Ricardo. She assumed that she was not included because she was black and a lesbian, and thus not worthy of respect. (To be a lesbian and a poor woman of color is for an individual to have three strikes against her in terms of mainstream white culture. However, in terms of family and community relationships, these three strikes are usually not an issue, as survival needs occupy center stage; all else has little importance for people who daily negotiate a minefield.) As for Yolanda, she felt intimidated by the judge and humiliated by her mother's "performance" in court. Helena described Yolanda as an incompetent mother and a former drug addict, and as incapable of caring for Ricardo. A legal aid lawyer was assigned to Yolanda for the next hearing.

Yolanda and Evelyn were certain that the lawyer was Jewish and made some very derogatory comments about this. Since there is such antagonism in New York City between the Jewish and African-American communities, we were concerned that this might become an unspoken issue that could jeopardize the outcome of the hearing, with devastating long-term effects on this family. We were specifically concerned because Evelyn is a very bright, articulate, and angry black woman who already felt invalidated by being left out of the first hearing. It was possible that she might be contentious in a way that would be detrimental. We suggested that we accompany them to the first meeting with their attorney; they readily agreed to this. The meeting turned out to be quite positive. We modeled a way of handling the issues, and Evelyn felt protected by our presence. She was able to present her viewpoint confidently and calmly, and was only mildly challenging. Members of minority groups are generally intimidated by the legal system, as there are few people of their own race in authority; moreover, the system itself is confusing, intimidating, and often disrespectful.

The attorney was open to our participation in the meeting and responded positively to our goals and suggestions. We felt confident that we could help this family resolve the custody issues, if Helena would join the sessions. The attorney agreed to take this suggestion to the judge at the next hearing. The judge agreed, and required 6 months of family therapy for Yolanda and her mother as a step toward deciding custody. These sessions were in addition to the weekly sessions between Yolanda and Evelyn.

Therapy with Yolanda and Helena

The first two sessions with Yolanda and her mother, Helena, were very tense. Yolanda turned away from her mother, and spoke disparagingly about her mother's lack of love and availability and her physical abuse of the children. Our focus was on the abusive patterns, getting additional information from Helena about her life (see "Exploring the Genogram," above) and again educating the pair about family systems. They were stunned to see the recurring pattern. As with all the clients we see, we first establish from their own history that they have tried mightily to do a good job with their children and other family members, but have not been successful. The genogram spells out the transmission process in a way that enables clients to understand the process and how to change it.

Helena and Yolanda learned that together they had the ability to short-circuit the abusive pattern and to write a different script for Ricardo, in which he would have the opportunity to form more loving and satisfying relationships. We constantly emphasized that unless they changed their abusive behavior toward each other, Ricardo would experience the same pain as they had felt and were still feeling. Caring about him as much as they did gave them the strength and motivation to look at their own process.

There were continuing problems with Ricardo's visits to Helena and with harsh accusations from Yolanda about Helena. Ricardo was caught in the middle. The loyalty issues were too stressful for him, and he began having difficulty in school again. Evelyn and Yolanda became harsh and demanding with him, doling out daily punishments and deprivations. Our goal was to extricate Ricardo from this difficult position. Part of Yolanda's style of coping with abuse was to find someone to blame for it and then do battle with that person. She carried this out against her mother by keeping Ricardo informed of all slights and injuries, making certain that he understood that the offending person was *intentionally* causing hurt or harm. Yolanda saw this as an essential part of her mothering role and did not hesitate to tell Ricardo that his grandmother was "lying" to him. As Yolanda saw it, a major responsibility of a parent is to prepare her child for the harshness of the world, so that the child can develop the necessary protective skills and defenses.

In abusive systems, the smallest error is magnified into a major event. There is no such thing as an innocent mistake. If someone is hurt, it is perceived as intentional, and there must be retribution. Every slight is responded to as though it were life-threatening. It took a while for Yolanda to grasp that although her intentions were positive, she was teaching Ricardo the abusive patterns that she and her mother wanted to break between themselves. We helped Yolanda and Helena to understand that if they persisted in transmitting their current world view and behavior pattern, Ricardo would be as unhappy as they, and most likely would become an abusive husband and father someday. We repeatedly emphasized that they had the power to change the script by shifting their pattern of interaction. This was a powerful intervention, one that re-established their focus and commitment. The pattern between mother and daughter began to shift following several crises like the one described above. Much of the early work focused on arrangements for visits to Helena, which started with 6 hours on alternating weekends and progressed to full weekends every other week.

Another major crisis ensued over a weekend in which Yolanda sent Ricardo to Helena with 3 hours of homework, without first getting her mother's agreement to supervise this. Helena did not see this as a grandmother's responsibility; she had had her fill of it with her own three children. She was, moreover, not familiar with the kind of work Ricardo was doing, and was not certain whether what they had done together was acceptable. After phone calls in which messages were transmitted through other people, Helena said to Ricardo that the homework might have to be done over when he got home. Needless to say, this 6-year-old boy was more than a little unhappy about this prospect; when he arrived home, he was angry and unresponsive to Yolanda and Evelyn, which made them feel incompetent and enraged. This started a new round of accusations that Helena had "lied," and was presented as more evidence that she was trying to hurt Ricardo.

The session in which this material emerged revealed the pattern of abuse to its extreme. Yolanda screamed at her mother for most of the session, completely tuning us out. Helena sat quietly crying as Yolanda got even by threatening to deny her mother access to Ricardo—no more weekend visits; only 6-hour visits from now on; and then only when she, Yolanda, felt disposed to grant them. Again, we pointed out that Yolanda was teaching Ricardo how to be abusive to a parent. No parent is perfect, and if mistakes are not allowed, would she, Yolanda, be surprised if one day Ricardo did a similar thing to her? There was a pause. The session quieted and ended without resolution.

Actually, this was the beginning of a major shift. In the next session, we were able to discuss what went wrong with the last visit. Both women were able to listen as we talked about the necessity for clear communication. They each readily agreed to talk directly to each other by phone, rather than allowing messages to be transmitted by other people. They also agreed to write down any requirements regarding the visits, such as what Ricardo should eat, and how many and what kind of snacks he should have. Finally, it was agreed that Helena had to be contacted in advance if Ricardo had homework, regardless of her willingness to help with the homework. Both mother and daughter were pleased with this plan. It has since worked well and has resulted in a significant improvement in the mother–daughter relationship. On meeting Helena at the office the following week, Yolanda spontaneously gave her mother a hug, and this has continued in each successive meeting.

An important fact to remember in dealing with abusive systems is that at some point in the treatment, the client will attempt to abuse the clinician. In a later session, the abuse again took the form of completely screening us, the clinicians, out; Yolanda and Helena screamed at each other throughout one session, despite our strong efforts to intervene. After about 40 minutes of this, we made it clear that this was a form of abuse and that we would not allow anyone to abuse us. We ended the session and gave them another appointment. Yolanda and Helena appeared very relieved and were very apologetic the next week. They learned that the pattern could be disrupted; it did not have to be a duel to the death. We reminded them that abusive behavior is a pattern that takes more than one party to sustain, and that we refused to participate.

So far, Yolanda and her mother have not repeated the abusive behavior toward us. The sessions continue at this writing, and we expect more crises before a new pattern takes hold. We are optimistic that the members of this family will give themselves a new beginning—one in which the future generations will have greater possibilities for intimacy, flexibility, and supportive relationships. The family members have worked very hard in treatment, never missing a session, despite the fact that they travel a great distance to see us.

Summary

In summary, our first concern was Ricardo's school problems. This was the point of entry and the easiest part to resolve. Yolanda and Evelyn quickly came to realize that in order to be most helpful to him, we would have to focus on their relationship. Although they came from different cultures with different child-rearing practices, they shared not only problems regarding drugs, but also a similar history of abuse in their own families. Their extremely abusive style and pattern of behavior was having a negative impact on Ricardo's emotional well-being and his ability to concentrate in school. While recognizing the abuse, we also acknowledged Evelyn and Yolanda's love and caring for each other and their desire for a better relationship.

In response to the custody conflict, we intervened in the courts and child welfare system, avoiding potentially destructive interactions and a possibly permanent estrangement between Yolanda and her mother. As Yolanda's relationship with her mother has improved, the interaction between Yolanda and Evelyn has also changed. Yolanda is less needy and less accepting of the one-down position *vis-à-vis* Evelyn, who in turn initially became more abusive. This is a common pattern: As one person in a relationship changes, the other does more of what she usually does to prevent the change. Yolanda will not back off from the changes, because she feels that too much is at stake. There is talk of a possible separation. Ricardo is staying with Helena until the living arrangements are worked out between Yolanda and Evelyn. Helena is able to provide a more supportive and nurturing environment for Ricardo at the moment, because she is on temporary disability following hand surgery and is at home with him.

CONCLUSION

In conclusion, we accepted the members of this family as they were—acknowledging their love and caring for one another, while noticing the generational patterns of severe abuse, which hindered their ability to have a loving and supportive relationship. We also recognized the role that chaotic external systems in general play in the maintenance of the abusive cycle, and coached the family in how to deal with these external systems (courts, school, welfare, etc.) in ways that would maximize their effectiveness and minimize the abuse. When clinicians pay attention to all areas of abuse in a family's life, the family members are more likely to change in ways that are permanent.

Working with poor women, even in a safe community, is very difficult; it becomes even more so when the treatment takes place in an anarchic community, where the stress level of clients, therapists, agencies, and the community is unbearably intense. Working with chaotic systems requires that each intervention be specifically tailored to fit the unit in question, harnessing a skill that is already available. People living in chaos do not readily learn new behaviors, but are capable of doing more of what works. Those of us working in chaotic communities not only have an obligation to bring all of our creative energy to bear for our clients, but also have an obligation to the community—to the common good—to help poor women and their children function in the most optimal way, despite the chaos. When we fail these clients, we fail the larger community and thus further jeopardize our society, which now hangs by a very slender thread. There is no "they"; there is only "we" now.

REFERENCES

American Psychiatric Association. (1980). *Diagnostic and statistical manual of mental disorders* (3rd ed.). Washington, DC: Author.

Anderson, C., & Stewart, S. (1983). *Mastering resistance: A practical guide to family therapy.* New York: Guilford Press.

Capra, F. (1982). *The turning point.* New York: Bantam Books.

Carter, P. (1982). Rapport and integrity for Ericksonian practitioners. In J. Zeig (Ed.), *Ericksonian approaches to hypnosis and psychotherapy.* New York: Brunner/ Mazel.

Hartman, A. (1992). In search of subjugated knowledge. *Social Work, 37*(6), 483–484.

Hartman, A., & Laird, J. (1983). *Family centered social work practice.* New York: Free Press.

Kozol, J. (1991). *Savage inequalities: Children in America's schools.* New York: Crown.

Senge, P. (1990). *The fifth discipline.* Garden City, NY: Doubleday.

Scheflin, A. (1981). *Levels of schizophrenia.* New York: Brunner/Mazel.

Steinem, G. (1988). Introduction. In M. Waring (Ed.), *If women counted* (p. 19). New York: Harper & Row.

18

Empowerment Work
with Homeless Women

ALICE K. JOHNSON
JUDITH A. B. LEE

Toward the end of a group meeting in a New York City shelter for homeless women, the group members—six young women of color—spontaneously sang the rap song "The Message" by Grandmaster Flash and the Furious Five (Fletcher, Glover, Robinson, & Chad, 1982). The song describes living in poverty with "no choice" and growing up "in the ghetto living second-rate," witnessing hopelessness, squalor, and the ravages and temptations of drug addiction and violence: ". . . it's all about money, ain't a damn thing funny. . . ." The refrain echoes, "Don't push me 'cause I'm close to the edge. I'm trying not to lose my head," accompanied by hollow, eerie laughter. The social worker recognized the song and repeated the refrain with them. She added, affirming their reality, "The song tells it like it is." Carla, an insightful and articulate member, said softly, "It's the fruits of oppression." The worker said that it was, and added that she understood that the group members were feeling "on the edge." They spoke of feelings of desperation and anger at their plight. The worker empathized and asked them to "hold on" as they developed a group that could address these fruits of oppression (Lee, 1986, 1987).

Homelessness is the fruit of oppression. It cannot be said better than Carla said it. Her story speaks to understanding the complex interplay of socio-economic, interpersonal, and personal resources in the context of oppression. Homeless women are among those most oppressed at the bottom of society who continue to experience socioeconomic disaster and its toll on human growth and development (Anderson, 1990; Wilson, 1987). This challenges those who would help homeless women to develop both clinical and political knowledge and skill, in order to facilitate the women's personal and political empowerment.

In the first part of this chapter, the socioeconomic and political context of homelessness for women is discussed. The second section identifies racism, sexism, ageism, domestic abuse, substance abuse, mental illness, and the lack of dependability of support networks as conditions resulting in homelessness for diverse groups of women. Third, the chapter discusses the current shelter-based treatment environment for homeless women. Next, a feminist empowerment approach for working with homeless women—one that is both clinical and political—is proposed. The chapter ends with some illustrations of differential intervention in an agency that uses this empowerment approach in working with homeless women.

AFFORDABLE HOUSING AND POOR WOMEN

The affordable-housing crisis and the feminization of poverty are two common problems uniting all types of homeless women (Sullivan & Damrosch, 1987). The low-income housing crisis started when the Reagan administration made policy decisions designed to get the federal government out of the housing business. Adjusted for inflation, the federal low-income housing budget has been cut more than 80% between 1978 and 1988, and available low-income rental units have declined by 19% since 1970 (Leonard, Dolbeare, & Lazare, 1989). This loss can be traced to several causes, including urban renewal (Johnson, 1992b); the demolition of single-room occupancy hotels (Kasinitz, 1984); gentrification processes in old city neighborhoods (Adams, 1986); condominium conversion and displacement (Wright & Lam, 1987); arson and abandonment (Brady, 1983); and inadequate new construction levels (Hartman, 1986). As the supply of housing has diminished, housing costs have soared. By 1983, half of all low-income renters were paying more than half of their incomes for rent. In 1987, the rent burden for single-parent renter families had reached 58% of their income. One million families are currently on waiting lists for public housing, and in many major cities waiting lists for subsidized housing are closed (National Housing Task Force, 1988).

The 41% growth in the number of single parents, especially women and children, between 1980 and 1990 (U.S. Bureau of the Census, 1990) has resulted in an increased demand for affordable housing. At the same time, state and federal aid cutbacks, combined with quickly rising rates of inflation from 1974 through the mid-1980s (Apgar, 1989), have placed housing out of the financial reach of many women. The purchasing power of income from Aid to Families with Dependent Children (AFDC), for example, has decreased by more than 30% over the past 18 years, and AFDC benefits are not sufficient in any state to bring the income of recipients above the federally established poverty level (Wolf, 1989). For women with disabilities, cutbacks in Supplemental Security Income (SSI) and food stamps add to their level of poverty. For example, approximately 160,000 of chronically mentally ill former SSI recipients (12%) were dropped from the rolls during the Reagan administration, and tighter eligibility requirements hinder new applicants from obtaining benefits (Burt & Pittman, 1985). More recently, states such as Ohio and Wisconsin have discontinued general assistance programs for poor single persons.

Housing assistance, unlike welfare benefits, is not available for all who need it; only one-third of eligible households currently receive federal housing assistance. At the same time, gender interacts negatively with a woman's need for affordable housing:

> As a group, female householders constitute more than 40 percent of the nation's housing problem. Being a female householder means that a woman has a one in three chance of being cost burdened and a one in eight chance of living in an inadequate dwelling. . . . If she is a single parent, she has more than a 50 percent chance of having a housing problem. (Birch, 1985, p. 44)

In addition to the negative effects of changes in public policies for dependent women, changes in the labor market also affect homeless women. Some may be disheartened workers still unemployed after the twin recessions of 1979 and 1982. According to McChesney (1991), other macroeconomic issues having a disproportionate impact on poor women are the inadequate coverage of unemployment and disability insurance, secondary labor market employment in uncertain jobs with no benefits, plant closings due to deindustrialization, and racial and gender discrimination in employment. Single mothers are especially affected economically by working in occupations where women are paid less than men, as well as by the failure of fathers to pay child support. In short, women who are without labor market skills, or who are underpaid and without male support, are forced to turn to welfare for economic support and medical care. This income is so small that the recipients live below the poverty line. In summary, homelessness results when there are too many poor female-headed households and not enough affordable housing:

> . . . they are too poor . . . to be able to pay the market rate for housing—in the context of a shortage of affordable housing . . . because they are unable to work (sick, disabled, or without child care), because they are unable to find work (involuntarily unemployed, discouraged workers), or because they are unable to find work that pays more than a poverty wage (working poor). (McChesney, 1991, p. 164)

A GENDER PERSPECTIVE ON HOMELESSNESS

Although women are recognized as a sizeable and underserved portion of the heterogeneous homeless population (Stoner, 1983), they are underrepresented in the literature—so much so that "gender status is sometimes subsumed under the nongender specific, depersonalized status of the homeless" (Milburn & D'Ercole, 1991, p. 1161). Lee's (1986, 1987) work identifies racism, classism, sexism, ageism, and the lack of dependability of support networks as conditions resulting in homelessness for women. For conceptual purposes, it is useful to think of three different types of homeless women, although these are not mutually exclusive groups: single women, young minority mothers, and battered women.

Single Women

The very few homeless women during the 1970s were alcoholics noticeable in the skid row areas of cities (Garrett & Bahr, 1973). By the early 1980s, middle-aged and elderly mentally ill women were also homeless (Baxter & Hopper, 1984). Their presence on the street was encouraged by de-institutionalization policies that closed mental hospitals and that failed to provide adequate funding for community residences as a backup. Since "shopping bag women" rarely use social services, their preference for social isolation adds to the difficulty of providing shelter and services for them (Schein, 1979), and the funding cuts for community mental health centers have left them even more isolated. The inflexibility of most shelters regarding "rules of the house" is also prohibitive. For example, one homeless woman lived on the street for years with her dog, as no shelter would accommodate both of them. She would also not abandon the shopping cart containing all of her possessions at the front door.

Although alcoholic skid row women and mentally ill bag ladies are two distinct types of older women, Johnson and Kreuger (1989) have used the presence or absence of children to differentiate women who are homeless alone (unaccompanied women) from women who are homeless with dependent children (accompanied women). Research in St. Louis shows that unaccompanied women are generally older white women with higher levels of individual dysfunction, whereas accompanied women are typically younger women of color. Unaccompanied women, compared to mothers with dependent children, have been homeless longer, are more likely to have received outpatient mental health services or inpatient psychiatric services, and are more likely to have a drinking problem. Robertson (1991) found that unaccompanied women are also more likely to admit to a substance abuse problem.

Many unaccompanied women grew up in foster care, and most have previously been married (Crystal, 1984). Some unaccompanied women are mothers whose children are in foster care, and some accompanied women have just gotten their children back from child protective services. Unaccompanied women do tend, however, to keep contact with their children and with a small number of women friends and female relatives— "affiliation and concern for their children was their principal interest" (Russell, 1991, p. 106). With the exception of bag ladies, women express a greater need for social support and utilize a wider support network than homeless men (Calsyn & Morse, 1990).

There is tentative support for the hypotheses that single women, like single men, drift downward toward literal homelessness. This slow deterioration at the margin of society stems from personal backgrounds that include some types of mental illness, attempted suicide, substance abuse (including prescription drugs), and/or a history of victimization in abusive relationships (Benda, 1990; Brown & Ziefert, 1990). Because many shelters have specialized in serving women with children, unaccompanied women have had to seek shelter in programs that are not sensitive to their needs (U.S. Department of Housing and Urban Development [HUD], 1989b), and these single women have been increasingly shut out of family-oriented shelters because of violation of shelter rules, sexual acting out, mental illness, and violence (Johnson & Kreuger, 1989). Shelters have also specialized in serving only women—for example, in New York City and Hartford, Connecticut. Some shelters in Hartford serve unaccompanied women alongside homeless mothers, as long as neither type is actively abusing substances.

Young Minority Mothers

Although women who are homeless are a heterogeneous aggregate, young poor women of color, often with children, make up the largest category of homeless women. The typical homeless mother is a young woman of color with a high school education or less and a poor job history; she is the single parent of at least two children, one of whom is a preschooler. Since the birth of her first child, the mother has supported her children through AFDC (Burt & Cohen, 1989). Minority mothers, especially African-Americans, are disproportionately represented among homeless women (Bassuk & Rosenberg, 1988).

Compared to housed poor families in New York, homeless families recount a greater incidence of spouse abuse, higher rates of child abuse, greater use of illegal drugs, more mental health problems, higher rates of physical abuse as children, and weaker social support networks. There is evidence that some homeless mothers exhaust their social support networks prior to turning to public shelters (Shinn, Knickman, & Weitzman, 1991). In other cases, mothers turn to shelters in an attempt to leave unsafe neighborhoods, where gang violence, crime, and drug dealing threaten the welfare of their children. Drug-addicted mothers can become homeless when their children are removed from their care by child protective services and the income support of AFDC is interrupted. Others enter shelters with their children (as a ticket to admission?), leave them there to get high, and then lose their children (Johnson, 1992a). The substance abuse problems of unemployed male companions may also be superimposed on these women's situation of homelessness (McChesney, 1992).

Interpersonal conflict in living quarters, combined with the shortage of affordable housing, also leads to family homelessness. When difficult housing problems such as substandard housing and eviction disrupt their previously stable tenancy, some families double up with other families in order to maintain their housing. However, interpersonal conflict ultimately leads to the dissolution of doubling up and thus to homelessness (Johnson, 1989). The growing number of female-headed homeless families is illustrated by the fact that the number of sheltered families more than quadrupled between 1984 and 1988, to over 60,000 (HUD, 1989b). These women with children need extensive socioeconomic and psychosocial supports, including low-income housing, public entitlements, parenting skills, day care, and job training. Intimidated by the fear of having their children taken away by protective services, and aware that the presence of dependent children gives them access to financial assistance, health care, and counseling, homeless mothers make every effort to keep their children with them (Anderson, Boe, & Smith, 1988).

Battered Women

The literature on homeless women rarely mentions woman battering as a major cause of homelessness, yet battered women and their children are well represented in homeless shelters (Zorza, 1991). A 1988 national survey (HUD, 1989b) estimates that on an average night one-fifth of sheltered single adults are homeless because of domestic violence, and that among sheltered families with children, about one-half of the adult heads of households are victims of domestic violence. In fact, "no other problem was as prevalent" (HUD, 1989b, p. 14). A sample of 80 homeless families in Los Angeles (McChesney, 1992) identifies abuse as a key factor leading to mother–child homelessness. Mothers, living previously in stable housing arrangements with men who supported the families, often leave these relationships because of abuse. Mothers who were homeless as teenagers often experienced severe abuse in their families of origin, followed by multiple and abusive foster care placements, which were terminated by running away. Many survived on subsistence prostitution until the birth of their first child, which made them eligible for AFDC.

The lack of attention to the problem of abuse among homeless women is the result of several factors. First, the social problem of battered women, though existing for centuries, was only recognized in the 1970s (Davis, 1987). Nonetheless, by 1984 the Family Violence Prevention and Services Act (P.L. 98-457) provided federal funds for temporary shelter and such emergency services as counseling, food, clothing, child care, and transportation (Davis & Hagen, 1988), and shelters and services for battered women were already operating at a time when recognition of the contemporary problem of homelessness was just gaining public attention (Stern, 1984). In this early period, it was assumed that women fleeing abuse were a distinct population appropriately served by the existing service network; in reality, however, battered women often seek refuge in emergency shelters designed for the more general homeless population. In some instances, shelter directors refer these women to a "safe house," because the addresses of shelters are well known in the community and safety cannot be assured. Second, researchers have often categorically exempted battered women's shelters from cross-sectional studies on the assumption that abused women have homes to return to, and are therefore technically not "homeless." Finally, family researchers have not been able to gain access to battered women's shelters because the shelter operators themselves do not consider "safe" houses homeless shelters, or because they wish to keep these locations secret in order to protect the women and children sheltered there (see Stanford Center for the Study of Families, Children and Youth, 1991).

Despite these service delivery issues, long histories of abusive victimization among single women and homeless mothers are now well documented (see D'Ercole & Struening, 1990; Goodman, 1991). The presence of domestic abuse inserts a legal issue into the situation of homelessness for women; that is, an abused homeless woman must choose whether or not to file charges against her batterer. Those who do not pursue legal charges often go back to abusive relationships because they are frightened, have not learned to manage alone, or are economically unable to find a permanent alternative to this dangerous situation (Zorza, 1991).

THE TREATMENT ENVIRONMENT

Shelters and Services

Emergency shelters, originally conceived as a crisis response to the problem of homelessness, have become institutionalized as the entry-level treatment environment for homeless persons. These short-term shelters, often located in armories or church basements, usually provide food, shelter, showers, clothing, and supervision. Midlevel shelters, with a length of stay of 1 to 3 months, provide case management services, training classes, referrals to community-based services, and some on-site counseling. Transitional shelters, identified by a longer length of stay of 6 to 24 months, provide individual and group counseling in addition to case management and a host of other on-site services designed to help clients obtain housing and acquire the socioeconomic supports necessary to maintain it (Johnson, 1990). The types of shelter services offered are usually associated with the types of persons served and the implied reasons for their homeless situation. Specialized shelters and services for single women are less common than shelters for single men (HUD, 1989b). Some comprehensive outreach and treatment programs for dually diagnosed homeless women have been developed as demonstration projects by the National Institute on Alcoholism and Alcohol Abuse (see Blankertz, Cnaan, White, Fox, & Messinger, 1990).

In most cities, shelters can be described, at best, as a loosely organized network. Usually there is no central point of authority or accountability, except in cities where coordinating mechanisms for inclement weather have been established (Institute of Medicine, 1988) or where lawsuits have forced city governments to respond to the problem (see Johnson, Kreuger, & Stretch, 1989). Nationwide, the number of homeless shelters has increased 190%, from 1,900 in 1984 to 5,400 in 1988; total capacity has been expanded by 180%, from 100,000 to 275,000 shelter beds; and private agencies provide an unwavering 90% of these beds (HUD, 1984, 1989b). The private sector has also initiated sophisticated services such as health care for the homeless (Stoner, 1988), but funding comes from a mix of private and public sources, including purchase-of-service contracts from local governments (Johnson & Banerjee, 1992).

Generally, services for homeless mothers focus on obtaining housing and the resources needed to maintain it. Case management is used to help these women obtain welfare entitlements and low-cost housing. Although this approach is effective in dealing with the socioeconomic causes of homelessness, case management tends to leave the personal causes of homelessness untouched. Johnson and Castengera (in press) argue that work with homeless families should include group work to deal with psychosocial issues, and that both types of social work interventions should be integrated at the programmatic level. Homeless women receive such services in several places, but such programs are not yet the norm.

Although shelters for battered women did not exist in most communities until late in the 1970s, the emergence of these new organizations, spurred largely by the advocacy of feminist groups, was quite rapid (McShane, 1979). Feminist shelters are organized around egalitarian norms and informal relationships as a means of empowering staff and residents alike (Srinivasan & Davis, 1991). Other types of battered women's shelters grew out of the voluntary work of individuals or were created by redesigning institutions or existing programs for an alternate use. These shelters tend to lack the group support and advocacy focus provided in shelters operated by feminist groups (Higgins, 1978). There are over 700 government-funded shelters for battered women, but the demand for shelter consistently exceeds the supply (Gross & Rosenberg, 1987). The primary goal of battered women's shelters is to provide emergency care, consisting of crisis phone lines, information and referral centers, and work with hospital emergency rooms and police departments. Case management, a process by which each woman's situation is assessed and her specific needs are identified, is critical in linking her to the numerous service delivery systems. For example, a battered woman may need police protection and legal assistance simultaneously, or medical care, emergency shelter, and temporary financial assistance, in that order (McShane, 1979). In contrast to marital counseling or psychodynamic work, counseling is based on a feminist, empowerment-oriented model that focuses on the psychological needs of women. According to Davis and Hagen (1988), battered women are adequately helped to face their psychological dependency, but little is done to stop economic dependency. What is lacking is "a framework that psychologically empowers women while simultaneously assuring them the resources, such as jobs, housing, and child care, necessary to become economically independent" (p. 615). Although federal legislation has ignored the battered woman's need for transitional or long-term services, battered women's shelters are better funded than other types of women's shelters because state programs underwrite the cost of shelter (HUD, 1989a). In summary, case management services for homeless families tend to deal with the practical needs of income and low-cost housing, but do not deal adequately with homeless women's psychological needs. In contrast, feminist-led battered women's shelters address these psychological dependency needs, but fall short in addressing housing and economic needs. Both may fall short of raising political consciousness.

A FEMINIST CLINICAL APPROACH

Empowerment Work

It is no accident that homeless women with children often have not completed high school, have weak job histories, and have their first or second child during their teen years. Their life chances and options have been severely limited, and the lack of adequate low-cost housing is one further insult in a chain of events related to poverty, racism, sexism, and classism in this society. Benda and Dattalo (1990) point out that women are victimized by patriarchal society and obstructed by its unequal opportunity structures. A feminist perspective that seeks to empower, therefore, is appropriate for understanding and helping these victimized and oppressed women, no matter what the particular reasons for their situation. The feminist skills of reconstructing, renaming, and recreating reality to redefine the self as strong, capable, and powerful are particularly pertinent for homeless women (Johnson & Richards, in press). Empowerment is attained through individual and group actions that help women attain their fair share of the resources needed to live, including the establishment of a home (Lee, in press). Feminist practice follows feminist values: such as viewing the personal as political; renaming; valuing process as equal to outcomes; and reconceptualizing power (Bricker-Hooyman & Jenkins, 1986; Van Den Bergh & Cooper, 1986).

As noted above, an empowerment approach to clinical and political practice with women who are homeless utilizes individual, group, and community approaches. It begins with the clinician's raised consciousness of oppression (Lee, in press). In the case of homeless women, the clinician must understand the oppression of women and minorities of color in this country, as well as the stigma that accompanies mental and physical illness and female substance abuse. A homeless woman's consciousness may or may not be raised in these areas, but she is the expert by virtue of lived experience. Together, the worker and the woman engage in dialogue, take action, reflect on that action, and take action again—a process known as "praxis" that frees and liberates those who engage in it. The worker takes an ego-supportive approach to utilizing and developing strengths in coping with the burdens of oppression and the situation of homelessness. She uses cognitive-behavioral strategies, such as problem-solving skills and the cognitive restructuring of false beliefs caused by internalizing oppressive valuations, so that potentialities may be actualized as the environment is changed. Finally, she promotes collective/political action.

Homeless women's experiences of direct and indirect power blocks, which render them powerless to direct their own destinies, must not be minimized. Direct power blocks are inherent inequities and discrimination in systems needed to sustain life: the provision of basic financial resources, health care, day care, education, employment, housing, and so on. Indirect power blocks are the result of internalizing the negative valuations of the oppressor, of experiencing a lifetime of unequal opportunity structures, and of unique personality characteristics (Solomon, 1976; Lee, in press). Moreover, responses to homeless women need to go beyond the provision of housing, necessary as this is. Professional expertise is needed to assist women who are without homes in empowering themselves, both personally and politically. The feminist principle that "the personal is political" can be operationalized in programs and in practice, so that professionals can use both clinical and political knowledge to help women empower themselves.

Empowerment strategies are aimed at releasing and developing the potentialities of the person and family *and* at changing oppressive societal structures, such as discrimination in the provision of basic survival resources (e.g., housing). The empowerment approach recognizes that people must empower themselves. In helping a homeless woman with children, the whole family unit must be envisioned; in cases where a male partner is not present, help should be offered to him as well, for he will rejoin the family once it is housed. Differential assessment ability is also needed to recognize diagnosed and undiagnosed mental illness, including patterns of migrating from state to state and shelter to shelter (trying to "outdistance" illness) and substance abuse (even when it is denied). Workers must also be able to appreciate genuine crisis situations and the exceptional coping skills needed to deal with the precipitants; to understand the stark realities of living in shelters or on the streets; and to respond accordingly. Moreover, empowerment work with homeless women must include an understanding of the woman's cultural and "ethclass" heritage (the latter term was coined by Gordon, 1978, to refer to the social connection and identity of persons segregated within their own social class and ethnic group), and of the wealth of resources this provides. Knowledge of family systems, particularly the extended and augmented systems of minority cultures, is also necessary.

The ability to see and build on strengths, and to provide incentives for motivation and the expansion of life chances and options, is critical in working with homeless women of color and their families. The application of feminist principles to the helping process differentiates the empowerment process from other types of helping, where the "helped" is in a "one-down" position. As parity in communication is observed, personal stories are shared as they may apply, and a sister-like relationship is offered as evidence of the fact that women struggle over issues common to all in varying degrees.

This use of the one-to-one relationship and the provision of supportive group experiences offer homeless women who lack dependable support networks a new chance at attachment and connection, as well as at collective action (Lee, 1986, 1991, in press). A detailed family history and the use of a genogram (Hartman & Laird, 1983) are important and often revealing regarding attachment and perceptions of attachment to significant others. For homeless women, dealing with these issues comprises the "treatment" part of personal empowerment. For example, in the transitional living facility for women and children in Hartford, Connecticut, 50% (11 out of 22) of the women accepted into the 2-year program in 1991 and 1992 had experienced the loss and absence of a mother during childhood as a result of death, divorce, or placement (in the foster care system or with extended family, kin or nonkin). These women shared profound feelings of loss and abandonment, as well as ongoing issues of anger and disappointment with their mothers if they were reunited at a later point. Although some of these alternative family situations provided both stability and love, and others did not, the subjective perception of each woman included feeling unwanted and unloved. Only 5 of the 22 women (these 5 were Hispanic) described warm, nurturing mothers who continued to provide support for them. Most (19) of the women had their children in the residence with them, and several expressed concern about their own parenting. Most (10 out of 22) expressed anger at estranged, physically and emotionally abusive, or long-gone male partners as well. Yet these 22 women had the desire and ability to get on with their lives, plan for the future, and enter into dialogue with other women about common issues.

Dealing with Substance Abuse

Promoting empowerment, however, does not mean being blind to "pathology." In contrast, it must be identified in its myriad forms—not as internal baggage to be shed while the oppressive forces remain untouched, but as a transactional problem between women and their oppressive environments. The ecological perspective, advanced in social work by Carel Germain (Germain, 1979, 1991; Germain & Gitterman, 1980), sees social problems as interactive between persons and their environments. Psychologists Toro, Trickett, Wall, and Salem (1991), among others, define the transactional nature of homelessness and suggest that multiple interventions in the person–environment configuration are necessary to solve the problem of homelessness. The stance of the feminist clinician is to stand side by side with women who are homeless, poor, and usually of color, in order to challenge oppression as coequal investigators of reality and actors in the situation (Friere, 1973; Pence, 1987; Lee, in press).

For example, a significant number of women who are homeless suffer from substance abuse problems. Many shelter providers estimate that 90–100% of homeless men and 50–70% of homeless women with and without children are substance abusers. The higher estimates include those dually diagnosed with both mental illness and substance abuse problems. Many also suffer from the effects of substance abuse on their male partners or in their families of origin. Sometimes the family structure weakens until it can no longer maintain housing for its members. In other cases, strong, viable families expel substance abusers because the families have reached their tolerance level for drug- and alcohol-related behaviors. Domestic violence precipitating homelessness is often related to substance abuse. Every shelter provider is aware of the importance of substance abuse as a factor in homelessness, yet it is underreported in the literature for many reasons. Such data are difficult to collect, since the self-reported rates of substance abuse are much lower than those observed by shelter providers; this discrepancy is a result of abusers' denial or minimization of their illness (which comes with the territory), as well as their fear of stigma and denial of shelter. Furthermore, until recently it has been "politically incorrect" for workers to name the reality, out of fear of the public's tendency to blame the victims and to withhold resources and services.

Professionals in the field, and sufferers themselves, know that addictions are biochemically based diseases with multiple causation on many levels, including a response to the no-win situation of oppression and discrimination (Wright, Kail, & Creecy, 1990; Hanson, 1991); they are not matters of "willpower" and morality. Blau (1992), an advocate for the homeless, affirms the high prevalence of substance abuse among the homeless, but sees it as an effect rather than a cause of homelessness. Whether or not one can establish chicken-and-egg relationships and multiple causality, the fact remains that any political–clinical response to homelessness must provide for treatment of addiction. One woman in a Hartford shelter put it succinctly after a difficult and lengthy wait for subsidized housing: "It's easy to get the housing; it's harder to keep it." She was making a second attempt at recovery from alcoholism and cocaine addiction. Some providers have begun to gather accurate statistics of substance abuse based on observation as well as self-reporting, and have concluded, as the title of Hanrahan's (1991) master's thesis puts it, that "homeless families need more than a home."

Differential assessment must be utilized so that adequate treatment is provided. Empowerment approaches to addicted women must motivate and assist them to enter drug and alcohol treatment and recovery, and must advocate with them for residential and outpatient treatment facilities and follow-up services that serve women with their children. The mind *is* a terrible thing to waste, and it must be drug-free to grapple with issues of political and personal change.

Empowerment-Oriented Practice: My Sisters' Place

My Sisters' Place in Hartford, Connecticut, is a three-tier agency serving diverse groups of homeless and formerly homeless women with and without children. It utilizes an empowerment approach with individuals and groups of women, which addresses the transactional nature of the problem of homelessness and personal–political change issues (Lee, in press).

As is typical of agencies serving homeless people, this agency was not started by professional clinicians, nor did it employ any in its beginning years. It was started in 1983 by a group of feminist-oriented women interested in helping other women. The core of this group consisted of Sisters from different religious communities who worked and lived in the north end of Hartford, a working-class, poor, predominantly African-American community. They were known for their compassion as well as their political activism in areas of peace and justice. In concert with community leaders, they obtained a lease on church-owned property and opened a home-like shelter that accommodated 15 homeless women and their children (if children accompanied them) in private and shared rooms. Initially, the length of stay was limited to 1 week, but is now based on an individual assessment; some women stay only briefly, while others stay for several months. The shelter was initially operated entirely by volunteers, and an atmosphere of equality among women, compassion, and political activism to address the housing crisis prevailed. Homeless women were treated as sisters and guests instead of "clients." Staff members easily "went the extra mile" to help women. They also elicited clients' participation in political activities, such as protesting, lobbying, and testifying at the legislature. One of the early volunteers (who later became the shelter director, and then the executive director of this triprogram agency) also engaged in civil disobedience with other housing activists to bring attention to the plight of homeless persons in the richest state in the Union. Without conceptualizing it as such, the agency enacted feminist and empowerment-oriented practice.

Eventually, faced with baffling and complex behaviors among the guests—who ranged from profoundly mentally ill single and accompanied women, to families and unaccompanied women in crisis, to substance abusers with or without families in tow—the shelter hired a professionally trained social worker. The agency moved toward differential assessment and programming, and in 1988 it was funded to open a scattered-site residential support program for homeless and formerly homeless chronically mentally ill women. In this program, women hold their own leases and receive intensive support services, both individually and in a group. A clinical social work consultant was engaged, and thus began the mutual development of an empowerment approach to working with homeless women (Lee, in press). By 1991, the agency renovated a devastated factory building not far from the shelter and opened a 20-unit apartment complex. At this transitional living facility, women with children and unaccompanied women can reside for up to 2 years as they complete their education and job training and receive supportive services; these services include day care and empowerment counseling, both individually and in groups called "empowerment groups." Intense clinical counseling is provided in-house as well as by referral.

Although the agency now employs six professionally trained social workers, a day care director, a housing coordinator who obtains housing for and with the women and other homeless people, and several other persons (some with expertise in drug and alcohol counseling), it retains the empowerment perspective with which it began. Others who work with the various program shifts, including graduate social work students, a variety of other students, and a host of volunteers, are trained in empowerment work. Homeless and formerly homeless women are viewed as residents and guests; they participate in hiring practices, and also sit on the board of directors. Their opinions are sought as the need for new policies or policy change develops. "Alumnae groups" of shelter "graduates" meet to continue their empowerment work and stay in contact with the agency. Residents of the transitional living facility have published their own newspaper, *New Voices*.

The empowerment groups offer opportunities for staff and residents to struggle with issues of oppression, raise consciousness, and take actions together. They have taken part in national and local demonstrations, spoken at the legislature, and lobbied at the state capitol. State representatives such as Marie Kirkley-Bey, as well as U.S. Senator Christopher Dodd, have come to My Sisters' Place and entered into dialogue with the women. Women in each program are challenged to enter a process of personal and political action and change. Entering as homeless women, they leave in the process of becoming empowered women. Empowerment work is done on a one-to-one basis and in the group. The following examples illustrate empowerment-oriented practice at work.

EXAMPLES OF DIFFERENTIAL INTERVENTION

The Shelter Empowerment Group

The first example shows a shelter empowerment group at work. Since the membership is open-ended, the workers need to explain the empowerment purpose of the group in each meeting. The aims are to make clear the personal and political levels of the work the group members can do together and to begin a consciousness-raising process. Often five to eight women remain over a lengthy period of time, so that the issues raised can be considered in some depth. This group meets weekly, and the members also attend a weekly housing group where the focus is specific to obtaining housing. There is weekly individual work with each resident. This group usually has a single leader, which enhances member-to-member participation and worker-to-member relationships. Present at the meeting described here were two coleaders for the group, both professional social workers: an African-American woman who was learning to work with groups, and a white (Franco-American) woman who was experienced in this approach and who summarized this meeting (she is the "I" in the summary below). Both workers were in their mid-30s. They played complementary roles, with the African-American worker attending to the content of oppression while the white woman attended to the group processes. (Identifying oppression as external helps to reduce self-blame and stimulate action while encouraging responsibility for personal change.) Eight women were present: five African-Americans, two Puerto Ricans, and one white woman (Italian-American), aged 19–36. All had their children with them except Maria, the white woman. The children were in the next room with a volunteer. The workers' primary statements are given below in italics, and the skills these statements illustrate are in parentheses.

After a welcome and introductions, *I said, "Everyone here has had a difficult time before coming here"* (empathizing). I described the group as an opportunity to talk about the things they have experienced and the problems they face that make or may make them feel powerless. I said that this is an empowerment group, which means that work can help them develop the power they need to make it and to change things for themselves and others. *"Some of the problems are personal, like the ones with relationships you have already described, or trouble with drug and alcohol abuse for yourself or someone close to you"* (pointing out the common ground, offering handles to get the work started, developing the contract).

Daria said sadly, "That's me!" She elaborated on her drug and alcohol problems, and added that she was glad the shelter was drug-free and had a policy of residents' attending Twelve-Step programs. Maria said, "Me too—I just got out of a drug program and I had nowhere to go. This is what I need now." *I said, "It was courageous to share that; it is a very hard struggle, and one we will work on together here"* (contracting and offering encouragement on sharing personal struggles). *My coworker said, "Drugs are oppressive. They keep our people down"* (making a political statement). Daria said, "They made me a slave." She said she raised her children with her mother's help, but now her mother had given up on her and she needed help. Maria said, "Drugs made me a fool too." She shared her story. She told Daria she needed a residential drug program. *My coworker said she would help Daria look for a program* (providing information and access to help).

Janine said, "My mother married a guy who drinks. He gets nasty and makes a play for me." She elaborated as the others sympathized. "That's why I left. But what I'm upset about is that they lost my application for a Section Eight certificate and I have to start all over again." Mary said, "No, you don't. You should contact the supervisor. I bet they'll find it." Others echoed this advice. *I said, "The systems you have to deal with are often inadequate or inefficient and cause frustration"* (empathizing regarding the system's abuse). "Helping each other to deal with these systems is an important part of our work too. *But sometimes this kind of treatment represents bigger things that go on in our society, like racism and sexism, or prejudiced feelings against people who are poor. These create barriers to getting what you need, and can also influence how you feel about yourselves and actions you may need to take"* (developing the wider political level of the work). They were nodding, and Matilda said, "You feel like you're no good." *I said, "This is the time to talk about and question such things and get an understanding of what's going on. You're up against big barriers to your success"* (suggesting a critical approach, defining part of the struggle). Janine said, " 'barrier' is a good word for it. I think the secretary I spoke to is prejudiced against blacks." She elaborated. "I think I'll go in person so she can at least see me. Maybe I'll offer to help her look for it." After the laughter, my coworker said, "Going in person is a good idea—to make yourself known as a person." She shared an experience from her own life in which a personal appearance made a difference. *She then told a story of a storekeeper's rudeness to all of his black customers. She stood her ground, and this stopped his behavior* (disclosing her own experiences with oppression and how she handled it). Mary said, "It's hard to stand your ground. That was brave." *I said that it was and that these are good examples of handling oppression* (clarifying, naming).

Mary asked, "What does 'oppression' mean? Is it like depression?" *I said that oppression, or discrimination or disadvantage because of race or sex or being poor, can certainly cause depression or deep sadness. I then asked what oppression was to them* (defining and asking them to define). Matilda said, "Oppression is living in one room with four kids, and no heat or hot water. That happened to me, and I got so depressed someone had to rescue me and pull me out of that building. I thank God for that person and for this shelter." Janine said, "It is oppression to be disregarded." *I asked, "Lost in the shuffle?"* (clarifying, reaching for feeling). Janine said, "Exactly. Like a piece of useless paper." Daria then began to cry and say, "That's how I feel, and all I can find to rent are ratholes!" Everyone drew close to her. *My coworker said that substandard living conditions are oppressive* (defining). Mary said, "I get so mad I want to hit the landlord with my fist and make him do right by us." Janine said, "Or slap him with a big fine, take him to court! We pay the rent, we should get the services!" Everyone agreed. *I said, "Now you're talking"* (validating the feelings and beginning to define and encourage action). I went on to explain how we could take action together on the housing issues they raised. Three of the members agreed to testify at a legislative hearing on the state's Rental Assistance Program.

A Middle-Phase Empowerment Group Meeting in Transitional Living

In the group meeting described below, the social worker was an African-American woman in her mid-30s who was also the director of the transitional living program. The group consisted of eight women: four African-American women in their 20; three Puerto Rican women ranging in age from 23 to 43; and Pat, a white woman of Irish-American background in her mid-40s, who had been in the program 2 months. In this model, a worker asks critical or consciousness-raising questions, along with using a range of helping skills. The critical question posed at this particular meeting was this: "What power blocks contributed to your homelessness?" Pat's openness brought the group into a taboo area that the members had previously avoided. Again, the worker's primary statements are given in italics, and the skills these statements illustrate are in parentheses.

Pat said, "My husband had all the power. Do you know this is the first time in my life I've ever been free and on my own? I got married when

I was 20 years old. . . . This is the first time that I've ever had to do anything for myself. I didn't have to pay for the car [she began to sob] or the rent. He hasn't given me any money since we broke up and it's been so hard." Nilsa gave her some tissues and was crying with her. *I said, "It's okay to cry. It's hard to be on your own when you're used to someone doing everything for you"* (empathizing and generalizing the theme). Pat then said, "How could I have been so stupid to fall for this guy? You know my worker gave me an article about recognizing the signs of a batterer. He lost his mind and practically killed me. The signs were all there."

I asked, "Would you like to tell us what some of those signs were, Pat?" (creating an opportunity for work, asking her to share information). She replied, "Well, he began to not want me around my family, and I used to just think that it was because he loved me so much that he wanted to spend time with me. When I met him he seemed to be the nicest guy because he always bought things for me. Now I see it was all about control. I used to have to have sex with him every damn day and every damn night. It wasn't love, it was control, just like the article said. If I resisted he would threaten me. That's when I knew he was sick. Just the thought of it, I hated it." She began to sob again. *I was watching the expressions on Marta's face. Her eyes lit up and widened when Pat described being made to perform sexually. Our eyes met* (scanning the group).

Marta began nodding her head in agreement. "I know what you mean. My husband, he started trying to control me. He became very jealous. He made me quit my job, and he tried to keep me to himself all the time. When he started hitting me, that's when I said that I wasn't going to continue to let it happen. He'd always say, 'I'm sorry,' and he would do better for a little while but then in about a week he would start up again." Debby said, "That's how men are. They can look at any women they want to, but they don't want you to look at anyone. My kids' father know that I don't like a man who drink and do drugs. He used to do that and want to fight me. He hit me too. But he doesn't do that any more because I won't take it." Sandy said, "I don't take anything from a man because they try to own you and control you. I work and can get anything I want for me and my kids." Pat said, "I sometimes say to God, 'Why did you let this happen to me?' but I believe that everything happens for a reason. If I hadn't had this experience, I wouldn't have ever felt good about myself again. . . . Now I know he was the sick one." The women reflected on how they were made to feel crazy when they tried to leave their abusive partners. Marta said, "I know leaving him was the smartest thing I ever did!"

At the end of the meeting I said, "I would like to thank all of you for sharing your hurts and some healing with each other, and Pat for shar-ing the information about battering with us. Several of you began to recognize the signs and grow in awareness." They nodded. Then I said, "You did

some good work here tonight" (encouragement and crediting the
work).

Brenda Gary, Activist: A New Home and a New Identity

Brenda Gary is a 39-year-old African-American woman who has chronic
paranoid schizophrenia and multiple disfiguring physical problems. She
experienced periods of acute psychosis and intermittent homelessness for 5
years. Leaving her children with relatives, she travelled cyclically from
psychiatric hospitals to the streets to shelters, including My Sisters' Place. In
1988, Brenda became the first resident of My Sisters' Place scattered-site
residential program for chronically mentally ill homeless women. With the
program's daily visits, assistance in activities of daily living, case management, and individual and group support, Brenda's life stabilized. She was
soon able to have her children visit regularly on weekends, her most
important goal. On occasion she becomes mildly delusional, despite her
medication, but she has not needed hospitalization since she entered the
program. Moreover, she has gained the friendship and respect of her peers
for her abilities to write and speak about issues relevant to homeless and
mentally ill women. She is experiencing a new sense of self-respect, dignity,
and identity.

Recently Brenda volunteered to testify at public hearings on proposed
state cutbacks of mental health programs. She had gone to the legislature
with her empowerment group on other occasions, but never felt able to
speak. She surveyed group members and composed a statement, which she
read at the hearing after patiently waiting 2½ hours to be called upon. This
is an excerpt:

> "We need our programs to keep us aware of life's possibilities. No
> matter what you want to be, it's possible. I used to live on the streets.
> . . . These programs kept me on track and looking forward to life. If
> the state cuts these programs, the state also cuts the good that they do.
> . . . We have a women's group every week. We talk about what goes
> on in our lives—the problems we experience and solutions to them by
> getting feedback from other group members. . . . These programs are
> essential. . . . Please maintain these programs for the many people that
> need them."

Brenda's legislative testimony was powerful and moving. The press sought
her out for further interviews.

In the next empowerment group meeting, the worker had group
members reflect on Brenda's action and their support in accompanying
her. They read the entire article in the newspaper to one another with

her. They read the entire article in the newspaper to one another with pride, applauding at quotes from Brenda. Vickey said, "Oh, it was wonderful. . . . Brenda represented all of us. She was a leader." Brenda beamed and reminded the group that she used their comments as well as her own. Ida said that because they all went, they had a presence as well as a voice. Brenda added, "It's good to know that I can accomplish things even with a mental illness. I live with the illness, but this does not mean I am not able to take care of business!"

Brenda Gary is an empowered woman. She has a home, friends who care about and respect her, a good relationship with her children, and a sophisticated level of political understanding and activity. She manages her illness, and still she gives back to her community. Not all women who participate in one or more of My Sisters' Place's three programs obtain empowerment, but all have the opportunity.

CONCLUSION

Programs and helping professionals that serve homeless women need to look beyond meeting housing needs to providing opportunities for empowerment. Empowerment is not only psychobiosocial, but socioeconomic and political. Empowerment includes developing a raised consciousness and taking action to change the multiple internal and external oppressive forces that create and permit poverty and discrimination against women, people of color, and people who are different. Helping professionals must support and challenge personal growth and change, even as they support and take part in collective/political actions that stop oppression. Differential assessment, intervention, and program development that acknowledge the transactional nature of "homelessness" is essential. Together, empowered women called clients and those called professionals can eradicate homelessness.

In conclusion, the goals of intervention are to help the woman who is homeless to obtain and develop the external and internal resources to find and maintain housing; to complete her education; to obtain job training and employment; to parent her children; to deal with her specific mental health and health problems, including substance abuse; to manage on her own; to identify how she may have internalized the views of her oppressors; to raise her consciousness regarding the manifestations of oppression in her life, including situations of domestic violence; and to join with other women in refusing to accept oppression and in taking action against it. As feminist clinicians, we must go beyond providing "therapy" to individuals, families, and groups, to promoting the empowerment and liberation of each woman we work with. Only then can we all hope to be free.

ACKNOWLEDGMENTS

We wish to acknowledge Judy Beaumont; the entire staff of My Sisters' Place, Hartford, Connecticut; and especially Gail Bourdon, Jean Konan, and Robin Taylor for sharing their practice with us.

REFERENCES

Adams, C. T. (1986). Homelessness in the postindustrial city: Views from London and Philadelphia. *Urban Affairs Quarterly, 21,* 527–549.

Anderson, E. (1990). *Streetwise: Race, class and change in an urban community.* Chicago: University of Chicago Press.

Anderson, S. C., Boe, T., & Smith, S. (1988). Homeless women. *AFFILIA: Journal of Women and Social Work, 3,* 62–70.

Apgar, W. C. Jr. (1989). Recent trends in housing quality and affordability: A reassessment. In S. Rosenberry & C. Hartman (Eds.), *Housing issues of the 1990s* (pp. 37–62). New York: Praeger.

Bassuk, E. L., & Rosenberg, L. (1988). Why does family homelessness occur? A case-control study. *American Journal of Public Health, 78*(7), 783–788.

Baxter, E., & Hopper, K. (1984). *Private lives/public spaces: Homeless adults on the streets of New York City.* New York: Community Service Society.

Benda, B. B. (1990). Crime, drug abuse and mental illness: A comparison of homeless men and women. *Journal of Social Service Research, 13*(3), 39–60.

Benda, B. B., & Dattalo, P. (1990). Homeless women and men: Their problems and use of services. *AFFILIA: Journal of Women and Social Work, 5*(3), 50–82.

Birch, E. L. (Ed.). (1985). *The unsheltered woman: Women and housing in the 1980s.* New Brunswick, NJ: Rutgers University, Center for Urban Policy Research.

Blankertz, L. E., Cnaan, R. A., White, K., Fox, J., & Messinger, K. (1990). Outreach efforts with dually diagnosed homeless persons. *Families in Society: The Journal of Contemporary Human Services, 71*(7), 387–397.

Blau, J. (1992). *The visible poor: Homelessness in the United States.* New York: Oxford University Press.

Brady, J. (1983). Arson, urban economy, and organized crime. *Social Problems, 31*(1), 1–27.

Bricker-Jenkins, M., & Hooyman, N. (Eds.). (1986). *Not for women only: Social work practice for a feminist future.* Silver Spring, MD: National Association of Social Workers.

Brown, K. S., & Ziefert, M. (1990). A feminist approach to working with homeless women. *AFFILIA: Journal of Women and Social Work, 5*(1), 6–20.

Burt, M. R., & Cohen, B. E. (1989). Differences among homeless single women, women with children, and single men. *Social Problems, 36*(5), 508–524.

Burt, M., & Pittman, K. J. (1985). *Testing the social safety net.* Washington, DC: Urban Institute.

Calsyn, R. J., & Morse, G. (1990). Homeless men and women: Commonalities and service gender gap. *American Journal of Community Psychology, 18*(4), 597–608.

Crystal, S. (1984). Homeless men and homeless women: The gender gap. *Urban and Social Change Review, 17*(2), 2–6.

Davis, L. V. (1987). Battered women: The transformation of a social problem. *Social Work, 32,* 306–311.

Davis, L. V., & Hagen, J. L. (1988). Services for battered women: The public policy response. *Social Service Review, 62,* 649–667.

D'Ercole, A., & Struening, E. (1990). Victimization among homeless women: Implications for service delivery. *Journal of Community Psychology, 18,* 141–152.

Family Violence Prevention and Services Act. (1984). P. L. 98-457.

Fletcher, E., Glover, M., Robinson, S., & Chad, J. (1982). *The message* (sung by Grandmaster Flash and the Furious Five). New York: Sugar Hills Music.

Friere, P. (1973). *Pedagogy of the oppressed.* New York: Seabury Press.

Garrett, G. R., & Bahr, H. M. (1973). Women on skid row. *Quarterly Journal of Studies on Alcohol, 34,* 1228–1243.

Germain, C. B. (Ed.). (1979). *Social work practice: People and environments.* New York: Columbia University Press.

Germain, C. B. (1991). *Human behavior in the social environment: An ecological view.* New York: Columbia University Press.

Germain, C. B., & Gitterman, A. (1980). *The life model of social work practice.* New York: Columbia University Press.

Goodman, L. (1991). The prevalence of abuse in the lives of homeless and housed poor mothers: A comparison study. *American Journal of Orthopsychiatry, 61,* 489–500.

Gordon, M. (1978). *Human nature, class, and ethnicity.* New York: Oxford University Press.

Gross, T. P., & Rosenberg, M. L. (1987). Shelters for battered women and their children: An under-recognized source of communicable disease transmission. *American Journal of Public Health, 77,* 1198–1201.

Hanrahan, V. D. (1991). *Two paradigms of housing: Homeless families need more than a home.* Unpublished master's thesis, Yale University.

Hanson, M. (1991). Alcoholism and other drug addictions. In A. Gitterman (Ed.), *Handbook of social work practice with vulnerable populations* (pp. 65–100). New York: Columbia University Press.

Hartman, A., & Laird, J. (1983). *Family centered social work practice.* New York: Free Press.

Hartman, C. (1986). The housing part of the homelessness problem. In E. L. Bassuk (Ed.), *New directions for mental health services: No. 30. The mental health needs of homeless persons* (pp. 71–85). San Francisco: Jossey-Bass.

Higgins, J. G. (1978). Social services for abused wives. *Social Casework, 59,* 266–271.

Institute of Medicine. (1988). *Homelessness, health and human needs.* Washington, DC: National Academy Press.

Johnson, A. K. (1989). Female-headed homeless families: A comparative profile. *AFFILIA: Journal of Women and Social Work, 4*(4), 23–39.

Johnson, A. K. (1990). *Homeless shelter services in St. Louis.* Unpublished doctoral dissertation, Washington University, St. Louis, MO.

Johnson, A. K. (1992a). *Interviews with formerly homeless families.* Unpublished manuscript, New Haven Home Recovery, New Haven, CT.

Johnson, A. K. (1992b). Urban redevelopment law and the loss of affordable housing: A reassessment. *Journal of Law and Social Work, 3*(1), 29–43.

Johnson, A. K., & Banerjee, M. (1992). Purchase of service contracts for the homeless: The development of a city-wide network. *Journal of Applied Social Sciences, 16*(2), 129–141.

Johnson, A. K., & Castengera, A. R. (in press). Integrated program development: A model for meeting the complex needs of homeless persons. *Journal of Community Practice: Organizing, Planning, Development and Change.*

Johnson, A. K., & Kreuger, L. W. (1989). Toward a better understanding of homeless women. *Social Work, 34*(6), 537–540.

Johnson, A. K., Kreuger, L. W., & Stretch, J. J. (1989). A court-ordered consent decree for the homeless: Process, conflicts, and control. *Journal of Sociology and Social Welfare, 16*(3), 29–42.

Johnson, A. K., & Richards, R. N. (in press). Feminist practice with homeless women. In N. Van Den Bergh (Ed.), *Feminist practice in the 21st century.* Washington, DC: National Association of Social Workers Press.

Kasinitz, P. (1984). Gentrification and homelessness: The single room occupant and the inner city revival. *Urban and Social Change Review, 17*(1), 9–14.

Lee, J. A. B. (1986). No place to go: Homeless women. In A. Gitterman & L. Shulman (Eds.), *Mutual aid groups and the life cycle* (pp. 245–259). Itasca, IL: F. E. Peacock.

Lee, J. A. B. (1987). Social work with oppressed populations: Jane Addams won't you please come home? In J. Lassner, K. Powell, & E. Finnegan (Eds.), *Social group work: Competence and values in practice* (pp. 1–16). New York: The Haworth Press.

Lee, J. A. B. (1991). Empowerment through mutual aid groups: A practice grounded conceptual framework. *Groupwork, 4*(1), 5–21.

Lee, J. A. B. (in press). *The empowerment approach to social work practice.* New York: Columbia University Press.

Leonard, P. A., Dolbeare, C. N., & Lazare, E. B. (1989). *A place to call home: The crisis in housing for the poor.* Washington, DC: Center for Budget and Policy Priorities and Low Income Housing Information Service.

McChesney, K. Y. (1991). Macroeconomic issues in poverty: Implications for child and youth homelessness. In J. J. Kryder, L. M. Salamon, & J. M. Molnar (Eds.), *Homeless children and youth: A new American dilemma* (pp. 143–173). New Brunswick, NJ: Transaction.

McChesney, K. Y. (1992). Homeless families: Four patterns of poverty. In M. J. Robertson & M. Greenblatt (Eds.), *Homelessness: A national perspective* (pp. 245–256). New York: Plenum.

McShane, C. (1979). Community services for battered women. *Social Work, 24,* 37–41.

Milburn, N., & D'Ercole, A. (1991). Homeless women: Moving toward a comprehensive model. *American Psychologist, 46*(11), 1159–1169.

National Housing Task Force. (1988). *A decent place to live.* Washington, DC: Author.

Pence, E. (1987). *In our best interests: A process for personal and social change.* Duluth: Minnesota Program Development.

Robertson, M. J. (1991). Homeless women with children: The role of alcohol and other drug abuse. *American Psychologist, 46*(11), 1198–1204.

Russell, B. G. (1991). *Silent sisters: A study of homeless women.* New York: Hemisphere.

Schein, L. (1979). A hard-to-reach population: Shopping bag women. *Journal of Gerontological Social Work, 2*(1), 29–41.

Shinn, M., Knickman, J., & Weitzman, B. C. (1991). Social relationships and vulnerability to becoming homeless among poor families. *American Psychologist, 46*(11), 1180–1187.

Solomon, B. B. (1976). *Black empowerment: Social work in oppressed communities.* New York: Columbia University Press.

Srinivasan, M., & Davis, L. V. (1991). A shelter: An organization like any other? *AFFILIA: Journal of Woman and Social Work, 6*(1), 38–57.

Stanford Center for the Study of Families, Children and Youth. (1991). *The Stanford studies of homeless families, children and youth.* Stanford, CA: Stanford University.

Stern, M. J. (1984). The emergence of homelessness as a public problem. *Social Service Review, 58,* 291–301.

Stoner, M. R. (1983). The plight of homeless women. *Social Service Review, 57,* 565–581.

Stoner, M. R. (1988). The voluntary sector leads the way in delivering health care to the homeless ill. *Journal of Voluntary Action Research, 17*(1), 24–35.

Sullivan, P. A., & Damrosch, S. P. (1987). Homeless women and children. In R. D. Bingham, R. E. Green, & S. B. White (Eds.), *The homeless in contemporary society* (pp. 82–98). Newbury Park, CA: Sage.

Toro, P.A., Trickett, E.J., Wall, D.D., & Salem, D.A. (1991). Homelessness in the United States: An ecological perspective. *American Psychologist, 46*(11), 1208–1218.

U.S. Bureau of the Census. (1990). *Statistical abstract of the United States* (110th ed.). Washington, DC: U.S. Government Printing Office.

U.S. Department of Housing and Urban Development (HUD). (1984). *A report to the Secretary on the homeless and emergency shelters.* Washington, DC: HUD, Office of Policy Development and Research.

U.S. Department of Housing and Urban Development (HUD). (1989a). *A report on homeless assistance policy and practice in the nation's five largest cities.* Washington, DC: HUD, Office of Policy Development and Research, Division of Policy Studies.

U.S. Department of Housing and Urban Development (HUD). (1989b). *A report on the 1988 national survey of shelters for the homeless.* Washington, DC: HUD, Office of Policy Development and Research, Division of Policy Studies.

Van Den Bergh, N., & Cooper, L. (Eds.). (1986). *Feminist visions for social work.* Silver Spring, MD: National Association of Social Workers.

Wolf, L. A. (1991). The welfare system's response to homelessness. In J. J. Kryder, L. M. Salamon, & J. M. Molnar (Eds.), *Homeless children and youth: A new American dilemma* (pp. 271–283). New Brunswick, NJ: Transaction.

Wilson, W. J. (1987). *The truly disadvantaged: The inner city, the underclass and public policy.* Chicago: University of Chicago Press.

Wright, J. D., & Lam, J. (1987). Homelessness and the low income housing supply. *Social Policy, 17*(4), 48–53.

Wright, R., Kail, B. L., & Creecy, R. F. (1990). Culturally sensitive social work practice with black alcoholics and their families. In S. Logan, E. Freeman, & R. McRoy (Eds.), *Social work practice with black families* (pp. 102–222). New York: Longman.

Zorza, J. (1991). Women battering: A major cause of homelessness. *Clearinghouse Review, 25*(4), 421–429.

19

Women's Struggles in the Workplace: A Relational Model

IRENE PIERCE STIVER

When 50 female psychoanalysts were asked the simple question "Would you refuse an invitation to speak publicly?", 50% said that they would refuse to speak (Moulton, 1977); this stood in stark contrast to 20% of male psychoanalysts polled who would refuse to speak. In an early study (Crandall, Katkovsky, & Preston, 1962) with latency-aged boys and girls, it was found that the brighter a boy was, the better he expected to do in the future, and the more he thought his good scores were a result of his ability. In contrast, the brighter a girl was, the less she was apt to think that her good performance was a reflection of her competence, and she did not expect to do better in the future. These studies began to scratch the surface of women's struggles at work.

Despite such observations, women rarely come to therapy with a presenting problem related to work. Men who have difficulties at work seem to see them as a legitimate reason for entering therapy. Women more typically come into therapy because of a concern about a personal relationship, and it is only as the therapy progresses that work issues come into focus.

Women have entered the paid work force in unprecedented numbers in the past 35 years. In 1985 they accounted for 44% of the work force (Bureau of National Affairs, 1986). Yet they continue to experience conflict and varying degrees of distress in their jobs. In the literature on women and work, there is a propensity to focus on women's deficiencies in adapting to the workplace, and consequently women are often blamed for their struggles at work. The major effect has been to make women feel worse. In this chapter, I address several facets of women's work experience. I hope we can consider more complex and appropriate explorations of women's struggles with work, without reducing them to additions to the list of "problems women have."

WOMEN AT WORK: A RELATIONAL MODEL

To understand women's work completely, we would have to understand the structure and forces of our economic, cultural, and occupational institutions. I do not review that large body of material here, but limit this discussion to some of the problems women tend to bring to us as therapists in our clinical practices.

Are women's problems about work different from men's, and if so, how? What is immediately apparent is that for men, work has been a means of enhancing their experience of themselves as men and supporting their identities as men; work has always been an important source of their self-esteem. The successful man is perceived as more masculine than the man who is less successful. Many women, on the other hand, experience considerable conflict between their sense of self at work and their sense of self in their personal lives. Until recently, middle-class white women have not typically experienced their achievements at work as the major source of their self-esteem; even with the changes that have more and more legitimized women's presence in the work place, white women still see their relational capacities and fostering the growth of others as their major sources of self-esteem. African-American women have been able to integrate work more positively into their sense of self and self-esteem, in a different way from both white middle-class women and African-American men (Turner, 1984).

The Male Yardstick

In the current literature about women and work, the suggested resolution of women's problems usually involves helping women learn more about how to be more competitive, to take more power, to be more assertive, to become more task-oriented, to act more impersonally, to develop more invulnerability to feedback, and to think more analytically. I question this strategy, because I believe it contains the source of the problems rather than the means of resolving them. That is, it says both explicitly and implicitly that women's style, which is often less openly competitive, more person-directed, and more emotionally expressive than men's, is a sign of a defect or deficiency that must be overcome. This perspective sets the stage for women to feel inadequate in adapting to standards that are less congenial to their personhood and are not always exemplary in themselves. In our search to understand more fully women's experience and behavior at work, I would like to offer another perspective from which to look at women's style, to explore its foundation and dynamics.

The Relational Model of Female Development

In recent years, the writings of Jean Baker Miller and her colleagues at the Stone Center (e.g., Miller, 1976; Jordan, Kaplan, Miller, Stiver, & Surrey, 1991), and of Carol Gilligan and her colleagues (e.g., Gilligan, 1982; Brown & Gilligan, 1992), have brought to our attention the fact that much of our understanding of female experience and development has been based on a masculine model; data for this model were typically gathered from samples in which women were greatly outnumbered or were not included at all. Drawing from research with women subjects and clinical experience with women seen in psychotherapy, these authors have highlighted how the inequities between women and men in a patriarchal society are reflected in significant differences in how women and men are socialized. The very qualities encouraged in women in our culture, such as their relational, empathic skills, are at the same time demeaned and devalued by a male-oriented society.

Current developmental theory has stressed the importance of separation, individuation, and achievement of independence as the hallmarks of maturity (Mahler, Pine, & Bergman, 1975). Yet this model seems more applicable to male than to female development, and overlooks the significance of human relationships as a propelling force in women's psychological growth. Miller (1976) has emphasized the significance of personal relationships to women and has stressed that "women's sense of self becomes very much organized around being able to make and maintain affiliation in relationships" (p. 83). Such conceptualization of the female experience has led to the development of a relational model that provides a new theoretical understanding of female development. In this model, the "relational self" is seen as the core self-structure in women. Rather than becoming more "separate" or "individuated," the developmental process proceeds through an increasing self-differentiation in women, *within a context in which the maintenance of relational ties remains central.*

Since for women the need to feel emotionally connected to others—to be caring, empathic, and attentive to the needs of others—is central to their sense of self, their developmental goals are different from those of men. For men the goal of development is the assertion of differences and separateness, autonomy and independence; for women, it is rather to achieve "increasing levels of complexity, structure and . . . articulation within the context of human bonds and attachment" (Surrey, 1991, p. 36). Self-esteem in women is more a function of their effectiveness in establishing and maintaining relatively mutual and emotionally gratifying relationships than of their achievement and mastery *in relative isolation.* Women's search, then, is for relationships both at home and at work that are characterized by mutual empathy and mutual empowerment, rather than by independence and increasing separation from others.

ISSUES AND CONFLICTS IN THE WORKPLACE

I would like now to identify what I believe are some of the central issues and conflicts that women face in the workplace, and to explore them within the context of this relational model.

Self-Doubts

One of the most pervasive indications of women's struggles at work is the extent of their self-doubts. It is striking how often women express enormous doubts about their abilities and their competence. Women still repeatedly minimize and negate signs of their effectiveness—what they know and what they can do. Occasionally their intelligence and conviction overcome their discretion and they speak up, but then they begin to ruminate about whether they have made fools of themselves. They worry about whether they were too aggressive; whether they should have said this or that; whether they should have spoken so long or so little or so much. If anyone recognizes them for saying something worthwhile, they are gratified at first but then begin to worry that they are phonies and frauds, and that someday people will find them out. Women typically also attribute their successes to chance events and say that they happened to be at the right place at the right time, or they were just lucky.

Betty Rollins (1986), television writer and producer, expresses the feelings of many working women when she reports that she has always had a

> fear, that is, of screwing up. Of not coming through. After all these years fear—and sometimes terror—continues to rise like steam with the onset of each new assignment, whether it's on camera or on paper. Not until a task is done do I ever believe it *can* be done and, past experience not withstanding, I usually believe it can't. Which is to say, I usually believe I can't. (pp. 233–234)

What is particularly interesting is how much women resist changing such attitudes about themselves in the face of contrasting information. Why do women hold on to the sense of themselves as inadequate and helpless? Dowling (1981) angrily accuses women of overstating their helplessness and dependency, since they believe that a strong man will respond to this show of helplessness and rescue them. She also says that such a man will never come, and that women must become "independent" and strong. Certainly there is some truth to the idea that our culture supports a woman's assuming a dependent role and presenting herself as helpless. She is seduced by the promise that she will be rescued and taken care of, but she ends up deeply disappointed. This seductive fantasy may indeed be so gratifying that women hold onto a helpless position. I believe, however, that this formulation is deceptive and reflects a misunderstanding of the meanings of women's "dependency."

In our culture, we too readily equate the need to be related to other people with dependency. From the perspective of the relational model, we understand that a woman's need to feel related to others is a crucial aspect of her identity; however, her attempts to form relationships are often mislabeled as expressions of dependency. It is also true that assuming a dependent position has been the only mode available (i.e., acceptable) to many women, particularly in establishing relationships with men.

The term "dependent" is used pejoratively in our culture, because dependency is seen as more of a female than a male characteristic. When women have a quality that is not seen as frequently in men, it is named as a "deficiency" and devalued. Yet both men and women are vulnerable to regressive pulls and seductive promises of being "taken care of." Women acknowledge it more because it is more permissible for them to do so. But, paradoxically, men live it out more. In marriage, emotional dependency needs are more often gratified by wives than by husbands. Women are better trained to be nurturant caretakers. At work, too, men are surrounded by secretaries and assistants, primarily women, who also "take care of" them. Thus the successful man gets taken care of, and the successful woman is considered to be someone who can take care of herself.

Disavowals of Women's Skills

There are also powerful forces in the workplace that, in a variety of ways, profoundly puncture women's self-esteem and exacerbate their self-doubt. Despite apparent progress in the opening up of wider work arenas for women, women's competencies and contributions are often not seen, not acknowledged, and not recognized (in terms of promotions, equitable salaries, and other external signs of success). Furthermore, women's "relational" talents—their interpersonal skills, their attunement to those factors that contribute to good morale and greater creativity at work—are typically not appreciated, if noted at all.

Faludi (1991), in exploring the prevalence of "backlash" in the work arena, demonstrates the extent to which men are significantly threatened by women's effectiveness at work. As a consequence, men's devaluation of women's performance has intensified in recent years as more women move into traditionally male arenas. Women then internalize these attitudes, since it confirms what they have heard all their lives—that they do not measure up.

Women from a less advantaged social class, and women of color, are even more vulnerable to not being seen or heard and to being devalued in the workplace. Women from working-class families, African-American women, and women from other minority groups may in some instances feel less conflicted about work, since from an early age they saw their mothers' work as a sign of strength and competence. These women do often feel supported in their own communities. Yet in the more typical white-male-dominated workplace, racism interacts with sexism in powerful ways. Women of color are thus confronted with even greater instances of devaluation, which intensify their self-doubt and lower their self-esteem.

Assigning Priorities

Work versus Family Tasks

Although women seek opportunities for advancement, they also often experience such opportunities as burdensome obligations, and feel both gratified and resentful when they arise. The underlying reasons for this perspective is often misunderstood, and women are criticized for having difficulties in assigning priorities to tasks. Again, the literature tells us that women have all sorts of "blind spots" about recognizing opportunities and challenges (e.g., Hennig & Jardim, 1977). Are women more naive in the working world? Have they not been trained sufficiently as competitors? And do they have blind spots about recognizing new possibilities? I think the answer lies elsewhere. Women continue to carry significant household responsibilities even when they are working, despite the changes in some households, where men have assumed more domestic tasks. Also, women's involvement in these family tasks is often not understood sufficiently.

Family tasks represent more than the sum of hours required to execute the tasks. In addition to carrying out the tasks themselves, women typically take on the chore of thinking about and planning what needs to be done, when, where, and by whom; they also feel the need to monitor whether these tasks get done. All of this involves considerable preoccupation and emotional energy. When we also take into account the importance of relationships to women, we see how much the intensity of the emotional bonding with those at home consumes women's involvement with family tasks. Thus the "wrenching away" from home to work and from work to home takes more of a toll on women than men. Because of this struggle, women often develop a precarious balance between what they do at home and what they do at work. If anything occurs to threaten this balance—for example, one more demand at work—many women experience enormous anxiety and begin to feel that they do not have things sufficiently under control. Every new obligation and every new task carry the potential of creating a disequilibrium in that balance.

Since the workplace is typically not very supportive of the struggles women face in juggling motherhood and their other relationships with the responsibilities of their jobs, women may appear not to value their work responsibilities sufficiently. This struggle begins when a woman becomes pregnant and continues to work. At work she often experiences a double bind. On the one hand, there is a climate of criticism suggesting that she is not attentive enough to her unborn child and may be "overdoing" it; perhaps she is seen as too ambitious to be sufficiently motherly. On the other hand, if the woman shows any indication that she is getting tired or is not as fully available as she may have been before, she may be perceived as someone who cannot truly take her work seriously. After the child is born, this theme continues. Of course, the general negative and unsupportive attitudes in the workplace and the culture at large about paternity leave underscore this message.

We are all familiar with very competent, responsible women who simply cannot work after the hour at which they have to pick up their children from day care. When children are ill, or when important events occur in the family, women are terribly torn, especially if there are no other adults who share in the family responsibilities. Women are typically criticized and devalued for their "poor planning" or whatever terms are used to explain away these powerful struggles. Women, in turn, see their difficulties in finding easy solutions as indications of their inadequacy as both mothers and workers.

A woman I see in therapy told me that she had to miss attending an important evening meeting when her daughter came home from her first day at school; she was very upset and needed to tell her mother all that had happened. This woman felt she could not leave her daughter that evening. The next morning she met her daily walking companion, an accomplished scientist. The companion's daughter had been ill the day before, but the companion decided to go to work anyway, since she felt her babysitter was competent. My patient immediately began to compare herself unfavorably to her companion, saying that if she were really dedicated enough to her work and gave it the high priority it deserved, she would have been able to get to the meeting and talk to her daughter another time. She was not able to see on her own how much her empathic responsiveness to her daughter was a powerful strength—a strength she also brought in a variety of ways to her work performance.

Such dilemmas are further exacerbated for those women who are more isolated and disadvantaged economically. Single mothers, women in marriages that are not supportive and mutual, women who cannot afford the kinds of day care and home care necessary for their children—all these will suffer even more powerfully as they attempt to pursue their interests and ambitions at work and at home.

Putting Others First

Another factor that affects how women set priorities, both at work *and* at home, is that they are taught that they should be attentive to the needs of others before themselves. Consequently, if they do something for their own advancement ahead of something for other people, they feel selfish and opportunistic. A brief vignette illustrates this dilemma.

> Susan is a 35-year-old divorced woman with two young children. After the divorce she decided to apply to graduate school, but did this with some trepidation, feeling unsure of her ability to juggle the responsibility of running a one-parent home and becoming part of a very competitive program. During this time she became involved with a man who was already an established professional in the field. He, too, was divorced with two children. Since his wife had custody of the children, he lived a bachelor-type existence; he was hard-working and ambitious.
>
> In one session, Susan reported that over the past weekend her ex-husband had taken the children, and that for the first time in a long time she would be able to catch up on her work. However, she and the man with whom she was involved typically spent weekends together, since the weekdays were so busy for each of them. She knew he expected them to spend a relaxing weekend. He had had an unencumbered week devoted entirely to work, but she had gone to class, run errands, visited her daughter's school, called on her mother (who was ill), helped out a friend in distress, and so on. She wanted to tell him that she could not spend the whole weekend with him, but felt this would seem selfish and overly ambitious.
>
> Still, she mustered her courage and did tell him. "Of course," he said; "work would always come first with me." His reaction was very surprising to her, since it was so foreign to her perspective. Although she was grateful that she could do her work without "guilt," she felt he could not understand her dilemma. She could not imagine taking that position herself (work was *not* always most important to her), but she also felt that perhaps her inability to do that was a sign of her failure in her work. Susan wanted to be responsive to her partner's needs, and at the same time to be able to take her work seriously without feeling she was hurting him. To act for herself, however, made her feel she was being selfish and destructive to the other person. She could not value her capacity to be caring and attentive to her relationships, even when

they were not always consonant with her intellectual interests and ambitions. She continued to feel torn between her strong investment in her career and her wish to be responsive to all the important people in her life.

"Professional" Behavior

Another type of conflict centers around what I call "professionalism." Unlike men who are successful at work, competent women worry excessively about whether or not they have behaved "unprofessionally." In attempting to adapt to the work setting, many women internalize a set of values about acceptable behavior at work that is often polarized, with stereotyped masculine characteristics at one end of the continuum and feminine characteristics at the other. Masculine characteristics are considered "good" at work; feminine ones are "bad" and must be kept separate. For women, to show too many "feminine" characteristics at work feels dangerous.

In most work settings, men are more numerous and more often in power positions, and thus set the climate for acceptable behavior. Women have difficulty adapting to what they believe are the expectations for "professional" behavior, which often conflict with their own experience, inclinations, and talents. For example, a woman often believes that it is not appropriate to include personal feelings about colleagues when making work decisions. This reflects the woman's conviction that in order to be effective at her job and in dealing with her male colleagues, she must adapt to the masculine model and separate her personal feelings from her professional responsibilities.

Yet men do act on their "personal opinions" in work situations. But men and women differ in the types of personal concerns they allow to influence their decisions. Women feel they are behaving in a professional, male-sanctioned manner if personal considerations do not influence their job decisions. Yet men do allow their personal considerations to influence their decision making. Personal considerations for men often center around issues of power and competitiveness. For example, a male colleague pounded his fist on a table, angrily and forcefully explaining his decision to fire someone because "he does not accept my authority." This was clearly a decision based on "personal" and emotional considerations, since the employee's competence was not at all in question; yet the employer felt perfectly comfortable in his justification for firing him.

One of the greatest fears a woman has—the worst example of "unprofessionalism"—is of crying on the job. A friend told me of a situation where she was one of the few women at a meeting. She was feeling scapegoated; tears welled in her eyes (which made everybody nervous); and the man who was running the meeting ended it prematurely. As the participants were leaving, one man turned to her in a patronizing way and asked, "Are you all right?" "I would have been a lot worse if I hadn't cried," she said. He was a little startled at that! Thus women's perception that emotional expressiveness in the workplace is dangerous is validated often enough to reinforce their reluctance to put themselves forward on emotionally charged issues.

Women can become so constrained in attempting to measure up to some fictional, exemplary masculine role model of objectivity and unemotionality that they lose touch with their relational strengths.

About 1 year after Joanne had terminated therapy, she returned to see me about a crisis at work that had caused her considerable anxiety. She had an executive position at a company she had been with for 12 years, and she supervised a large staff. I knew she had given birth to a baby 6 months earlier, because she had sent me an announcement, but she spoke only of the issues at work. She was troubled by the hostility she felt from the junior staff, and she thought it could be attributed to her having recently been given more responsibility in the company. She expressed considerable anger at members of her staff, who she felt had always been her friends, and she was quite upset at the thought that they disliked her now.

After two sessions of talking about this, I noted that Joanne had hardly said anything about her new son. Even she was startled by how little she had mentioned him, since she had intense feelings about him and about dividing her time between home and work. What soon emerged was that the complaints from her staff were that she had become aloof and uncaring, in sharp contrast to her style before her son's birth. She became aware that she had considerable difficulty in leaving her baby to come to work, as well as in proving she could combine motherhood and a career. At home, she had turned over the care of her son to her husband and housekeeper when she was working. At work, she had curtailed her nurturing, sensitive feelings toward her staff, in order to prove her ability to continue her career and "be professional" after having her son. Joanne felt that she had to suppress her concerns for others to prove that she was effective; however, she became less sensitive to her staff and less effective as a consequence.

How to communicate in the work arena is also troublesome for many women. When women communicate with a strong emotional tone, they are often called "hysterical," and the message is quickly discarded. For women, the expression of feeling is as central to their communications to others as the content of what they say (e.g., intensity of affect may express how important the topic is to the woman, and/or how energized and even frustrated she feels about the task at hand). Emotional communication is generally hard for men to hear, however.

The ultimate result of this climate in the workplace is that it silences women who do not feel free to use their authentic voice—the voice of reason *and* passion. Since emotional expression is an integral ingredient of gratifying relational interactions, women feel distanced from others when they deliberately curtail it. Yet when they do communicate with feeling, they end up disempowered, not heard, and humiliated. We know, however, that one can both be cognitively effective and express strong affect (Jordan et al., 1991). It is most important that women learn how to carry this message to the workplace, despite men's clear difficulty in listening, tolerating, and responding to women's communication of ideas with emotional expression.

Competition

Still another troublesome area for women is competition. Compared to men, women are more likely to avoid competitive situations, less likely to acknowledge their ambitions and competitive wishes, and less likely to do well in competition. Since the assumption is that male competitiveness is a positive work characteristic, women are told that they should learn to be more competitive and become more skilled at it. Rarely do "experts" address the value of women's relational skills, which help them work collaboratively and empower others to be more effective.

For several reasons, it is difficult for women to be competitive. First, when a woman is openly competitive, she frequently experiences herself as aggressive and destructive. Fearful that others will perceive her that way, she believes that the worst thing she can be called is "a castrating woman." But it goes deeper than the labels other people give. Women are trained to be concerned about other people and to be empathic, so that it is very hard for them to enjoy vanquishing rivals if they are at the same time empathic with those rivals. Furthermore, women who move ahead in the workplace often feel very isolated, in sharp contrast to their desire to feel connected in collaborative endeavors. Finally, because some women need to idealize men and see them as stronger and more powerful for the sake of the "rescue fantasy," it is too threatening to outdo the men they want to idealize.

Interestingly, although women are not given the permission to compete the way men are, women are allowed—and even encouraged and groomed—to compete with other women for men. Yet when women compete with women, they are also competing with the very people they want for support. Also, they are competing symbolically with their mothers, and (as I discuss more fully below) women may experience their successes as threatening their connection with their mothers.

Sexual Harassment

Although the term "sexual harassment" was not coined until the mid-1970s, the phenomenon has characterized the workplace for as long as women have been in it. Yet it is primarily since Anita Hill's allegations against Clarence Thomas during Thomas's U.S. Supreme Court confirmation hearings in 1991 that sexual harassment became legitimized as a very serious concern of women. Statistics indicate that anywhere from 40% to 90% of women will experience some form of harassment during their employed lives (Hamilton, Alagna, King, & Lloyd, 1987).

> The day after Hill made her statement, a woman opened our therapy session by telling me that she had endured a year-long affair with her boss in her first job after graduating from high school. She felt then that she could not refuse him and keep her job, which was vital to her, since she was contributing significantly to the family finances. Although I had been seeing her in therapy for 6 months, she had never told me this story before; she said she had felt too ashamed. Listening to the hearings confirmed her belief that she would only have been blamed had she told her family or anyone else about that harassment at that time. As we explored this further, it was clear that she blamed herself for what happened. Since she was sure she was the only one who had had such a thing happen to her, she concluded that it was because she must have appeared "too sexy."
>
> Listening to Anita Hill began the process of freeing this woman from her own self-condemnation. Once she found her voice in speaking to me about it, she began to talk with other women who had had similar experiences. She was then able to move out of her long history of isolation and shame.

Harassment is now beginning to be understood as an expression more of power and aggression than of sex per se. In work settings defined by the masculine model, the exercise of "power over" and competitive struggles are encouraged and valued far above sensitivity to others and collaborative efforts. Power is maintained through holding on to old stereotypes and prejudices toward those who have less power—namely, women and minorities. As Hill (1992) has herself noted, "harassment crosses lines of race and class. In some ways, it is a creature that practices 'equal opportunity' where women are concerned" (p. 32). The continued perceptions of women as "sex objects," and the belief that they must welcome sexual advances, create the settings that foster harassment and support the needs of those in power to devalue women and keep them in powerless positions. As women move ahead in work settings, the need to "keep them in their place" may intensify these expressions of sexual harassment. It is of interest that women with graduate education experience more harassment than do less educated women (Hill, 1992).

The reasons why women so readily become victims of such harass-ment, keep silent, and are resistant to take action and "go public" can be understood more fully if we look at women in terms of the relational model as well as the power dynamics in our society. When a woman experiences sexual harassment within a significant relationship, such as that with her boss or mentor, she is faced with the danger of a rupture in this relationship if she rejects his advances and indicates any displeasure. This rupture in an important relationship has major consequences for the woman. Not only does she fear being left alone and unprotected, but she also blames herself for somehow leading the man on, or for hurting him when she resists his overtures. To speak up threatens the woman's relatedness and makes others both uncomfortable and critical (Hamilton et al., 1987). Finally, the woman believes (often correctly) that she will be blamed and shamed if others know about the harassment.

Women, we know, have been socialized to be accommodating and responsive to the needs of others. Such behavior both helps them feel better about themselves (i.e., as caring and not "selfish" people) and offers them the opportunity to have some kind of relationships and sense of intimacy with other persons. However, such compliance and accommodation, when not acknowledged or especially when exploited, leave women feeling powerless and resentful; nonetheless, they fear the relational consequences of disclosure. This dilemma has silenced women for years, and they have avoided conflict at all cost. In work situations in particular, almost any expression of difference or airing of conflict by a woman is viewed as her "making a fuss." This has often been men's justification for dismissing the content of women's objections and expressions of difference. Given this dynamic, it becomes easier to understand why so many women have tried for so long to put up with the various manifestations of sexual harassment—without feeling the freedom to say "no," without feeling entitled to tell anyone, without the right to "make a fuss" and file charges.

Women feel very exposed when sexual advances are made, especially out of the context of a mutually caring relationship. To talk about the harassment to others feels very shaming to many women, since it is ex-perienced as an exposure of their sexuality. Yet women often believe the male view of their sexuality—that is, that women should want and enjoy all sexual advances. As a result, when women feel resistant and unresponsive, they fear being identified as frigid and unwomanly. At the same time, we know that women are often seen as seductive and responsible for the harassment. Thus women feel both blamed and inadequate, and believe that there must be something wrong with them for appearing either too "seduc-tive" or too "frigid."

Women are also threatened both economically and professionally if they "make a fuss" about the sexual harassment. Clearly, sexual advances are used by those in power to threaten women's job security and advancement in their organizations. If their jobs and economic viability are at stake, it is easier for others to "excuse" women for not leaving their jobs, or for "putting up with" the sexual demands of those men who have power over them. What are much harder for both men and women to understand and respect are the instances when women put up with sexual harassment in order not to risk undermining their career goals. Such a stance exposes them as ambitious persons—a characteristic not respected and valued in women. A man who is openly ambitious is seen positively as a "go-getter," a self-initiator. An ambitious woman, however, is readily labeled as too pushy and aggressive. I believe that the initial lack of understanding of and empathy with Anita Hill was in part attributable to a reluctance to recognize the enormous importance of her career to her, and her commitment to making a difference in equal rights for all people. Her career goals would have been seriously jeopardized if she had reported sexual harassment at the time it allegedly occurred.

At every turn, it is dangerous for women to function effectively in a system that typically discredits, blames, and humiliates them. Thus, if a woman does report instances of sexual harassment, she realistically does not expect to be believed; worse, she fears being accused of seductiveness or of making things "difficult." Yet if it is learned that the harassment occurred and she did not report it, she is criticized for staying in the situation.

These issues of excessive self-doubts, apparent difficulty in setting priorities, overconcern and self-consciousness about behaving "professionally" (i.e., objectively and unemotionally), and conflicts centering around competition have been typically misunderstood and have occasioned critical and demeaning evaluations of women's style in the workplace. Finally, the more recent focus on sexual harassment has highlighted very poignantly the ways in which women feel misunderstood, exploited, and disempowered in most work environments. Together with my colleagues at the Stone Center (Jordan et al., 1991), I have offered the perspective of a relational model to understand women's struggles at work. This model reframes the meanings and the potential value and strength of those characteristics that seem so troubling to women, as well as to the men who form the attitudinal climate in most work settings. I would like now to address another dynamic that can help us understand further the conflicts and struggles women face at work.

The Role of the Mother–Daughter Dynamic

In order to explore the role that identification with and differentiation from their mothers play in women's struggles with work and the pursuit of a career, it is necessary to elaborate further on the relational understanding of female development. Chodorow (1978) has noted that little girls are encouraged neither toward independence, nor toward achieving a separate identity from their mothers, in the same way as little boys. Since mothers tend to experience their daughters as more like and continuous with themselves, there often develops a particular bonding of mothers with daughters, with expectations of mutual caretaking and mutual empathic interactions and interdependency. Surrey (1991) discusses how mothers teach their daughters mothering behaviors. Both mothers and daughters learn early in the socialization process that they are expected to accommodate and "take care of" others. It is not surprising, then, that girls continue to experience strong attachments to their mothers.

The other side of this strong connection is that women also struggle against identification with their mothers, who are seen as devalued; as a consequence, however, women often feel alone and lost. Two examples from my practice are illustrative.

One woman, a physician, told me that as a resident during rounds, she made a rather dramatic correct diagnosis. People were surprised and impressed by her ability to do this. Clearly, she had made quite a coup. She was exhilarated—and yet she suddenly experienced enormous anxiety, had to retreat to her office, and felt acutely alone and isolated. Another woman had recently returned to her career in her 40s and was timid in work situations, but she began to speak up more and more. At one conference where she expressed her thoughts more fully, her contributions were appreciated, and she felt encouraged and pleased. But that night she had a nightmare in which she was lying in bed, helpless and immobilized, calling out desperately for her mother. Her mother had died about 2 years earlier.

I believe that both of these women came in touch with their strong yearnings for connection with their mothers at the moment that they felt more empowered, more competent, and more valued; it was as if they saw these signs of competence as a threat to their strong connection to their mothers, who seemed less competent.

The dynamic of the mother–son relationship follows another developmental path. Since a mother often experiences her son as different from her, and she is under both inner and outer pressures to affirm this difference, she feels that she must help her son achieve a strong masculine identification and independence through pushing him away from her. This role often conflicts with her natural inclination to maintain her connection with him while affirming the differences between them. Because mothers feel they need to help their sons move away from them and go into the world, they try to fulfill their needs for more direct interpersonal connectedness through their attachments with their daughters.

The more positive aspects of the mother–daughter bond, however, are countered by the mother's tendency to project her feelings of inadequacy onto her daughter. Although this may give the mother more license to hold on to the daughter and to "mother" her, it contributes to the highly ambivalent aspects of mother–daughter interrelations. Thus, mothers may express their ambivalence by holding on to their daughters to "take care of them," and at the same time they are quite critical of them. Such criticism often reflects both a mother's own negative self-image projected on her daughter and her need to keep her daughter "like her" and "with her." Also, mothers can become competitive and fearful, *as well as gratified,* as they see their daughters move forward in a positive and competent fashion. And daughters, as one often hears in psychotherapy with women, often struggle to defend themselves against their identification with their mothers, whom they see as critical, devalued, and unhappy. Yet these same women fear betraying their mothers, and experience considerable guilt if they move ahead and demonstrate "differences" from their mothers.

In attempting to break this highly ambivalent bond with their mothers, some women may feel that the only alternative is complete independence and an identification with the more valued masculine model. Those women appear very counterdependent and play out rather stereotyped masculine roles in the workplace. But they are left feeling absolutely alone in the world, without any support and with a significant sense of loss in disconnecting from their mothers. A woman may also try to deal with this ambivalent bond by looking for a strong man who will take care of her, which often results in considerable disappointment. Efforts to gain vicarious gratification through identification with the powerful man only leave the woman with long-standing resentments centering around giving up her own intellectual interests and pursuits; her self-esteem is diminished, and again she experiences a deep sense of disconnection from other women.

Fear of the Consequences of Success

The influence of the notion that success jeopardizes women's femininity and attractiveness to men cannot be overestimated, but it also merits re-examination (Horner, 1972). Again and again, women report the feeling that a successful woman alienates herself from both women and men. Single heterosexual women often feel that the more successful they get, the narrower their choice of acceptable men becomes.

The literature suggests that women who have very supportive fathers are typically more likely to become successful (e.g., Hennig & Jardim, 1977). However, in my clinical experience, when there is a struggle between their daughters' personal and professional lives, these fathers suddenly stop being very supportive.

This theme emerged with a woman I was seeing in therapy who was very successful in her work. Her father had always encouraged her to pursue her career, and he took pride in her success. She had earned an important promotion in her job, and she felt that she had to bring work home on evenings and weekends to get the job done. She was also having trouble with her marriage—the original reason for her coming into therapy. After the promotion, tension between her and her husband seemed to increase, and she finally talked to her parents about this. Her father was furious. He told her that the recent promotion had been too much, that she was putting work ahead of her family, and that her husband should come first. Furthermore, if she stopped all this nonsense and put her energies into her marriage and not into her work, things would be different. She was devastated. Her father's reaction was unexpected, but it confirmed her belief that her personal life was compromised by getting ahead in her career.

In attempting to help women challenge this fear of consequences of success, various writers have again exhorted women to become more like men in their strivings. A paper by Hoffman (1972) says, "Driving a point home, winning an argument, beating others in competition, and attending to the task at hand, without being sidetracked by concern with rapport are all hurdles women have difficulty jumping, no matter how innately intelligent they may be" (p. 140). The clear implication is that women have to change their attitude in order to get ahead; however, this perspective does not recognize the importance or value of relationships to women's growth and development.

Success, as defined by our culture, threatens the relational self in women by engendering fears of feeling disconnected from others ("It's lonely at the top"). In an effort to be more consonant with the needs and values of women, we can consider other models of success. For example, women can learn to value their relational and empathic skills and their emotional expressiveness, and to use these adaptively at work. Rather than offering "assertiveness training workshops" for women, we might develop instead more advanced "relational training workshops," emphasizing the utilization of collaborative processes in work settings for both men and women (Godfrey, 1992; Helgesen, 1990).

In doing psychotherapy with women and work issues, it is important that we as therapists validate the intrinsic conflict between success as defined in our culture, and the qualities that women value for themselves. It is crucial to help women see how deeply they have internalized assumptions, attitudes, and stereotypes of what is valued and not valued, based on a masculine model of success, which may be sometimes destructive and often inhumane. At the same time, we must recognize that most work settings present women with a masculine model that emphasizes independence and autonomy, and that places high value on impersonal, unemotional, objective, and competitive attitudes.

EMPOWERING WOMEN IN THE WORK SETTING

How can women find the strength of their authentic voices at work, given the powerful attitudes that inform male-oriented work settings? How can women be effective if they feel isolated and see no way to get support or to check out inaccurate perceptions? I believe that women need to look to other women, through networking groups of one sort or another, for mutual support and the opportunity to counter the status quo. Even if that is not possible, a woman's finding just one other woman to talk to, to check out perceptions, and to validate her experience can offset those profound feelings of isolation and inauthenticity. This connection with other women is the first step in empowerment at work.

Women who feel devalued and isolated from supportive relationships may submit too readily to the prevailing atmosphere, with resignation and depression. In such a context, it is unlikely that they will be able to demonstrate the full extent of their talents. However, through a relational process with other women, they can begin to believe that what they are doing and how they are doing it is worthwhile; they then *can* take action, feeling empowered and courageous even in alien territory.

This perspective is powerfully illustrated in Nan Robertson's (1992) book about the class action sex discrimination suit brought against *The New York Times* by a dozen women in the newspaper's unofficial Women's Caucus. Ten years after the suit was settled, in 1988, this group of women—who had maintained connections through the years—had a reunion to assess the agonizing experience of going through this suit, and its impact on the subsequent policies of *The New York Times*. The strength of the voices of those women who spoke at this reunion is inspiring. They tell the tale of the importance of relational connections for women, as well as of the enormously empowering effect of women joining together.

Anna Quindlen, the first woman op-ed columnist at *The New York Times,* said:

> The fact is that in some ways . . . we are all different and in some ways, which we all know and understand, we are better. We ought to use those ways in which we are better to help make [the] newsroom a better place. There are plenty of boys there to do the things that boys do, but in those rare cases when there are women in positions of power, they have a moral obligation to not only help other women, but to foster some of the special qualities which make us do an exemplary job as executives. (quoted in Robertson, 1992, p. 218)

Another woman, Sharon Yakata, asked, "Why do we [still] need a women's group? [Women] need a support group such as the Women's Caucus to define and push for their goals: promotions, equal salaries, child care, flextime, elderly parent care" (quoted in Robertson, 1992, p. 222). But she also stressed that a women's group could serve "as a teaching arm of the company, an army of employees to retrain colleagues and managers with more traditional, archaic attitudes about the role for women in the company" (quoted in Robertson, 1992, p. 222).

What these and other women said was that the group and its accomplishments helped them recognize the importance of the gains they made for themselves, as well as for other women who joined the *Times* after the suit. I believe that the group efforts, the feelings of connection with others, resulted in a growing sense of empowerment—action in the service of innovative change. Finally, these women's recognition of what they contributed to the women who came after them added immeasurably to their self-esteem and effectiveness in the world, both at work and at home.

Let us continue to explore the struggles women face at work and search for new forms of support and change, rather than put pressure on women to adapt to a model that is uncongenial with their relational selves and that leaves them feeling stressed, inauthentic, devalued, and alone.

ACKNOWLEDGMENT

This chapter is a revision of *Work Inhibitions in Women,* which was originally published in 1984 as Work in Progress, No. 3, by the Stone Center of Wellesley College, Wellesley, MA, and later appeared in Jordan et al. (1991).

REFERENCES

Bureau of National Affairs. (1986). *Work and family: A changing dynamic.* Washington, DC: Books Demand, Universal Microfilm International.

Brown, L. M., & Gilligan, G. (1992). *Meeting at the crossroads: Women's psychology and girls' development.* Cambridge, MA: Harvard University Press.

Chodorow, N. (1978). *The reproduction of mothering: Psychoanalysis and the sociology of gender.* Berkeley: University of California Press.

Crandall, V. J., Katkovsky, W., & Preston, S. (1962). Motivational and ability determinants of young children's intellectual achievement behaviors. *Child Development, 33*(3), 643–661.

Dowling, C. (1981). *The Cinderella complex.* New York: Summit Books.

Faludi, S. (1991). *Backlash: The undeclared war against American women.* New York: Crown.

Gilligan, C. (1982). *In a different voice: Psychological theory and women's development.* Cambridge, MA: Harvard University Press.

Godfrey, J. (1992). *In our wildest dreams.* New York: HarperCollins.

Hamilton, J., Alagna, S., King, L., & Lloyd, C. (1987). The emotional consequences of gender-based abuse in the workplace: New counseling programs for sex discrimination. *Women and Therapy, 6*(12), 155–182.

Helgesen, S. (1990). *The female advantage: Women's way of leadership.* Garden City, NY: Doubleday.

Hennig, M., & Jardim, A. (1977). *The managerial woman.* Garden City, NY: Doubleday.

Hill, A. (1992, April). The nature of the beast. *Ms.,* pp. 32–33.

Hoffman, L. W. (1972). Early childhood experiences and women's achievement motives. *Journal of Social Issues, 28*(2), 129–155.

Horner, M. S. (1972). The motive to avoid success and changing aspirations of college women. In J. Bardwick (Ed.), *Readings in the psychology of women* (pp. 62–67). New York: Harper & Row.

Jordan, J. V. (1991). Empathy and self boundaries. In J. V. Jordan, A. G. Kaplan, J. B. Miller, I. P. Stiver, & J. L. Surrey, *Women's growth in connection: Writings from the Stone Center* (pp. 67–80). New York: Guilford Press.

Jordan, J. V., Kaplan, A. G., Miller, J. B., Stiver, I. P., & Surrey, J. L. (1991). *Women's growth in connection: Writings from the Stone Center.* New York: Guilford Press.

Mahler, M., Pine, F., & Bergman, A. (1975). *The psychological birth of the human infant: Symbiosis and individuation.* New York: Basic Books.

Miller, J. B. (1976). *Toward a new psychology of women.* Boston: Beacon Press.

Moulton, R. (1977). Some effects of the new feminism. *American Journal of Psychiatry, 134*(1), 1–6.

Robertson, N. (1992). *The girls in the balcony: Women, men, and The New York Times.* New York: Random House.

Rollins, B. (1986). Women at work. In N. R. Newhouse (Ed.), *Hers: Through women's eyes* (pp. 233–236). New York: Harper & Row.

Surrey, J. L. (1991). The relational self in women: Clinical implications. In J. V. Jordan, A. G. Kaplan, J. B. Miller, I. P. Stiver, & J. L. Surrey, *Women's growth in connection: Writings from the Stone Center* (pp. 35–43). New York: Guilford Press.

Turner, C. (1984). *Psychosocial barriers to black women's career development* (Work in progress, No. 4). Wellesley, MA: Stone Center, Wellesley College.

20

It's a Question of Dollars and Cents: Prioritizing Economic Issues in Women's Treatment

ELANA KATZ

We lived in this 23-room house with 10 bathrooms, but my dad would count out the money so close . . . that she kept this jar in the closet and that's where the change from the grocery store would go . . . so the only way she had her own savings account was that she used to roll nickels and take them to the bank.
—FROM A THERAPY SESSION WITH A 24-YEAR-OLD WOMAN
SPEAKING ABOUT HER MOTHER

We resonate with the contradictions of both exciting and frightening feed-back about the current economics of women's lives. Over 4.1 million businesses in the United States are now female-owned (Berger, 1990), and businesses owned by women are increasing at a rate that is 1.5 times that of businesses owned by men (Michals, 1989). A prominently featured *New York Times* article (Apple, 1992) noted that more women—with more money—were running for political office, and that their chances of victory were substantially improved because tens of thousands of other women were giving them money and working in their campaigns. Although a recent survey (Rubenstein, 1989) of women's attitudes toward money noted that many women had grown up with an expectation that someone else (usually a man, and probably a husband) would take charge of the finances in their lives, many more women were embracing the control and subse-quent security inherent in managing their own finances.

WOMEN'S ACCESS TO MONEY

However, that same survey also brought with it more worrisome informa-tion. Although Rubenstein (1989) strongly suggested that the sample group was more knowledgeable and better established economically than the average woman, a third of the respondents believed that they would not have enough money to live comfortably for most of their lives, and the fear that they might be homeless someday was acknowledged by 28%. In a similar vein, *60 Minutes* (DeBoismilon, 1992) recently aired a riches-to-rags story about homeless widowed and divorced women between the ages of 55 and 65 who were living out of cars they now parked in some of the exclusive Los Angeles suburbs where they once lived. Unprepared for the job market and too young for Social Security, these women told some harrowing stories about their financial ruin in the absence of the men in their lives.

As the recent recession has affected nearly every family in the United States, and spending power has been cut in half during the span of many people's careers (Lee & Siegel, 1986), many women and men live with the worry that they will never feel financially "safe." However, since the national median income for women is $10,618 compared to $19,878 for men (Rubenstein, 1989), the opportunity to protect oneself against these uncertainties is different for a woman than it is for a man. Indeed, U.S. women represent two-thirds of all poor adults (Faludi, 1991). Women are far more likely than men to live in poor housing and to receive no health insurance, and they are twice as likely to draw no pension. Black women earn an average of 76% of what black men earn, and a 1987 survey (Otten, 1989) reported that pay for all white working women was just 52% of that of white working men. Even though a very recent *New York Times* article (Nasar, 1992) claims that women's income rose to 72% of men's by 1990, and suggests that it will continue to grow, the picture is more promising for younger than for older women.

Bringing the issue (uncomfortably) closer to home, the 1991 results of a fee and practice survey (Landers, 1992) revealed a wide gap between the income of male and female therapists in full-time practice:

Social workers: men, $57,273; women, $47,000
Psychologists: men, $81,818; women, $62,500
Marriage and family therapists: men, $61,538; women, $47,419

Michele Bograd (1991) has suggested that when female therapists do not charge full fees to clients who can afford them, they are respecting societal mandates to be self-sacrificing, "good" women, and honoring the premise that women should care "naturally." She notes that women as a group are not yet fully accustomed to having power and to being direct about the economic needs and motivations that are part of work life.

The degree to which women and men have different access to money is indeed one measure of the discrepant access to power they have in their lives. Money shapes where we live and how we live, as well as our hopes and fears for the future. Since it is the basic commodity we exchange to meet many of our needs, our access to it has profound implications. It seems incumbent upon us as therapists to listen to, and more carefully elicit, this dimension of our clients' lives.

DIFFERENT WOMEN, DIFFERENT STORIES

I recently worked with a black woman who described her approach to finding a man as "Romance without finance is a nuisance," thereby reflecting her desire for a mate with a good job. However, she also made it very clear that she and her sisters had *all* been raised with the expectation that they would learn to take care of themselves and be able to provide for their children. This premise—that one must be prepared to earn and manage one's own money—was echoed by other black women as well. Black women are very aware of the fact that black men have experienced greater discrimination and therefore have had a harder time integrating into the workplace. Black men are more threatening to white society than black women; as a result, black women report tremendous pressure to secure employment and support their children.

Even when a black family begins to achieve more economic success, there is rarely enough money to share with one's network or kinfolk, or to put aside to provide some assurances for one's future or one's children (Boyd-Franklin, 1989). In addition, the prejudices that continue to limit resources and opportunity mean that job security and advancement are precarious. One client was most distressed about her difficulty in establishing credit; not having ready access to credit meant that buying a house (often the cornerstone of "moving up" in U.S. society) was out of the question. These kinds of experiences leave many black people with the disturbing conclusion that money is inevitably transient. No one really expects it to last; at best, one may have stories to tell and embellish about the "good old days," when one did have money to spend (B. Dorsey, personal communication, April 4, 1992).

There are unique constraints that inform financial realities for lesbian women as well. Because lesbian couples are left out of the mainstream institution of marriage, they cannot share tax returns or health insurance plans, and one partner cannot automatically assume rights of survivorship if the other dies. In fact, there is currently a legal case pending against a major corporation in which the surviving mate is being denied life insurance benefits, even though she was the named beneficiary and the couple had raised two children together (Patten, Rothberg, & Williams, 1992). Lesbian women face special hurdles because any financial arrangements they create can be challenged or denied in court. Markowitz (1992) has described the way in which this lack of external validation partly shapes a gay couple's own expectations and concerns about having an enduring relationship: "This [financial] separateness makes . . . a relationship feel more temporary, as if there is less glue holding [a couple] together" (p. 53). Interestingly enough, one of the recommendations of the Gay and Lesbian Study Group at the Ackerman Institute is to use money to demonstrate and document family ties (Patten et al., 1992). In our consumer-oriented society, if both women in a lesbian couple have a track record of buying clothes, paying medical bills, and making other routine expenditures for a child, this financial record may offer some protection in the event that parenthood is ever challenged. However, the societal impediments sometimes make it too difficult for some women to realize their personal and familial desires.

> In one case seen by a supervisee of mine, a lesbian couple planning to have a child faced a combination of pressures. Clearly there was a risk for the woman who hoped to take time off from building a career to bear the child and assume the primary caretaking. For the other woman, the risk was emotional—she could not legally adopt the child or otherwise ensure her parental rights. Each woman was concerned that, should anything happen to her mate or the relationship, she would be left too vulnerable and unprotected. These problems proved too daunting for them to proceed, and they decided not to have a child.

At times, the norms of different cultures severely constrain the therapeutic conversation about money.

> I recently treated a Puerto Rican husband and wife who were experiencing a lot of distress in their first year of marriage. One of the areas of disagreement focused on the financial support the husband provided to his first wife for herself and their children. I felt that I had been responsive to the monetary issue, and I had developed a line of inquiry that, in addition to more familiar questions, included information about their careers and their finances. However, in a subsequent session alone with the wife, I learned that part of her despair about money was that during the course of the couple's marriage, her business had prospered while his had suffered. The net result was that she was the one who had been providing the support for her husband's ex-wife. When asked why she chose to share this material in an individual session, she responded, "I could no sooner have said this to you in a session with my husband, than . . . well, I might as well have made a billboard for him to wear up and down the street saying 'I have no [genitals].' " Breaking her silence in an individual session was a first step toward the wife's seeking a new balance between the cultural mandate to respect the traditional role of the Puerto Rican male (Garcia-Preto, 1982) and her own need to validate and respond to her tangible contribution to the financial well-being of her family.

Rita, another Hispanic woman, described to me the different messages she had received about money. Although Rita's mother had been abandoned by her husband when she arrived in this country, and she had had to raise her children on welfare, she was against a woman's working or going to school; according to her, a "good" mother stays home and protects her kids. When Rita, as an adult, went back to college while her children were young, her mother was too upset to attend the graduation. Rita's boyfriend's mother, Carmela, had a seemingly different perspective, as she had always worked outside the home. Nonetheless, Rita recalled that when Carmela took her family out to eat, she gave the check, and *her* money, to one of her sons: "It would have been shameful for her to be the one paying."

However, in her own life, Rita wanted to take financial autonomy a step further: "Surviving in a poor culture, you don't grow up planning for the future . . . just for the moment. My mother had the [welfare] system, and I won't have that." She noted that "some people grow up learning about insurance and investing," and now, in her early 40s, Rita was beginning to embrace that idea too. And what was she teaching her daughter? She was advising her to learn to support herself: "There's no guarantees in life about anyone taking care of you, and that's the bottom line."

CLINICAL IMPLICATIONS

Although the barriers for some women are unquestionably more daunting than for others, and the messages about women's autonomy are cautionary in some cultures while insistent in others, there are those who feel strongly that women are more similar than different in the premises that restrict their financial thinking and actions (R. Hayden, personal communication, July 7, 1992). Clearly there is an enormous gap between what many women have been taught to believe will keep them financially safe, such as being "good enough" or "loving enough," and the lack of financial safety many women actually experience. Yet many of us continue to see women in our practices who are still proceeding as if one day a man will arrive on the scene who will take care of money matters. This is often equally true for women who earn good salaries and yet have not devoted a fraction of the time to financial planning that they spend thinking about their relational hopes and goals. As one of my clients phrased it, "We're there for them, we bear their children . . . can't they just help us on with our coats and pay for our dinners?"

I believe that we have an obligation to ask questions in therapy that will help women afford their own dinners. As Ruth Hayden, a financial consultant, notes in a 1992 book, economic viability and the resulting power women experience to make choices in their lives are what actually keep them safe. Faludi (1991) also speaks of the significant impact of economics on women's lives. For example, she cites a study of 3,000 singles that found women earning high incomes almost twice as likely to *want* to remain unwed as women earning low incomes. She also reports that when the National Center for Health Statistics examined three factors—employment, marriage, and children—employment had by far the strongest and most consistent tie to women's good health.

I have often heard it said that if you want to see an unhappy man, find a man who is unhappy with his work; if you want to see an unhappy woman, talk with a woman whose relationships are not working. I believe that the data Faludi cites, as well as the demographic realities noted earlier, challenge our basic assumptions and invite us to be more inclusive in our thinking as we consider what needs to be addressed clinically. If finances and employment are part of women's health and well-being, then they also have an important place in therapy.

The importance of attending to economic viability in marital treatment has been well discussed. Betty Carter (1992) has clearly stated that an awareness of gender inequality means that a discussion of money is always clinically relevant. In working with couples in traditional roles, Carter has suggested an actual transfer of assets between a husband and wife until the wife is financially secure enough to negotiate emotional issues *as an equal*. Monica McGoldrick (1991) also takes a clear position that therapists cannot understand marital problems unless they know the economic viability of each partner. Clearly, a therapist challenging a relationship that a woman client cannot afford to lose risks creating an inauthentic therapeutic exchange.

I believe that discussions about money are also important in our work with individuals and families, as in this example:

One young woman I treated came to me with a variety of concerns. She aspired to a career in the arts, and at the same time was having difficulty at the office job she held to support herself as she pursued her goal. In the face of these obstacles, she had returned home and was living with her parents. They had serious concerns about her career choice, and they worried about the lack of a man in her life—as did she. She reported a great deal of friction in her family relationships. I imagine that if I had seen her several years ago, it would have been easy for me to focus my therapeutic efforts more narrowly on the relationships involved, and I might have looked for some connections between her relationships with her family members and her concerns about her personal life. Instead, early in the course of therapy, I included a conversation about the results of the above-mentioned study from the National Center for Health Statistics (cited in Faludi, 1991), and together we discussed just how shaky she felt—to herself, and to her concerned family—in the absence of secure employment. Four weeks later, she reported the exciting news that she had found a wonderful day job, one that afforded her ample time and money to pursue her career; 2 months after that, she moved out. To her surprise, her parents were "okay." "They're basically supportive," she reported. "I think that down deep, they just want me to be happy." Although there were issues that we subsequently worked on to strengthen the family ties at this time of transition, my client now saw herself in a far more successful light, and her parents were responding to her with significantly less anxiety as they witnessed the steps she had taken to secure her own future.

Hare-Mustin (1987) has noted that the way the therapist thinks about the world is the most powerful factor in family therapy. As we focus on the pragmatics of women taking charge of their lives, issues that we might have left in the background for our women clients suddenly seem perfectly in place in the foreground. One of the most useful approaches we can offer is to help our clients access and examine the premises that—knowingly or unknowingly—shape their most personal thinking and decision making about money. What do our clients believe about their abilities to earn and manage money, and what do they see as the consequences of avoiding the subject or becoming more knowledgeable? When given the opportunity to examine their internal financial road maps, many women echo the premise that if they become too successful, their success will hamper the possibilities of future relationships (Stern-Peck, 1992). It is as if being financially successful seems incompatible with being with a man. Other women worry that if they find a man who is comfortable with a woman who is economically successful, he will be looking for a free ride. Still others identify a range of messages in their family, their culture, or the culture at large (Berger, 1990) that say that, in one form or another: Money is part of a male fraternity, and that talking about it (never mind working at it) is something that "nice" people (i.e., women) just do not do (Lee & Siegel, 1986).

The broader cultural issues include the low expectations that our educational system sets for the performance of females in science and math. Biases in the educational experience are detected as early as age 9 and are reported throughout academic training, as women studying science and math at coeducational colleges report being ignored by faculty members and not being taken seriously (Tilghman, 1993). In 1992, Mattel marketed a Barbie doll that said "Math is tough" when poked in the stomach; this doll has since been taken off the shelves (D. Wild, personal communication, January 31, 1994). Cues like these convey to many girls and women that familiarity with and understanding of numbers, inherent to managing money, are beyond their reach.

If a woman has an opportunity in therapy to discover and consider her unique premises about money, and she concludes that these premises are not working, a therapist can help her deconstruct the problematic attitudes and beliefs she has held about what she as a woman can or cannot do. Hayden (1992), in her book, also invites women to challenge their learned beliefs rather than criticize themselves. This enables women to reassess their potential and develop plans to become economically viable.

A client of mine decided that she had "listened to fairy tales long enough," and she no longer wanted to rely on a man for support. However, she could not afford the training she needed to advance. We brainstormed together about different options, and she arrived at a plan that enabled her to barter several hours of her computer skills for the classes she needed. It was also helpful to ask her whether she knew other women who had become skillful at developing their careers and managing their economic lives. This normalized the steps she was taking (Tomm, 1987), and it also opened the door for some of the pragmatic coaching to continue outside of treatment.

Through this type of willingness to help clients anchor themselves in work and money, we can help them become mistresses of their own lives.

What will happen in a society where women really have economic viability? As the young woman whose quote I shared at the beginning of this chapter later noted, "In almost every relationship, the money and the power seem to go together." Perhaps as we begin to ask the questions, and help the subject of money come alive in our work, we can do something more about the power that shapes and is shaped by women's lives.

ACKNOWLEDGMENTS

I would like to thank Nancy Boyd-Franklin, Barbara A. Dorsey, Carmen Goraz, and Vicki Brower for their assistance with background information and research on this topic, and Peggy Papp and Marcia Sheinberg for their suggestions on earlier drafts of this chapter.

REFERENCES

Apple, R.W. (1992, May 24). Sisterhood is political. *The New York Times,* Section 4, pp. 1, 5.
Berger, E. (1990, March 12). Why women fear money. *Newsweek,* p. 10.
Bograd, M. (1991). The color of money: Pink or blue? In T. J. Goodrich (Ed.), *Women and power* (pp. 203–209). New York: Norton.
Boyd-Franklin, N. (1989). *Black families in therapy.* New York: Guilford Press.
Carter, B. (1992). Stonewalling feminism. *Family Therapy Networker, 16*(1), 64–69.

DeBoismilon, A. (Producer). (1992, April 5). Lost in Bel Air [Transcript of *60 Minutes* segment]. New York: CBS Television.

Faludi, S. (1991). *Backlash: The undeclared war against American women.* New York: Crown.

Garcia-Preto, N. (1982). Puerto Rican families. In M. McGoldrick, J. K. Pearce, & J. Giordano (Eds.), *Ethnicity and family therapy* (pp. 164–186). New York: Guilford Press.

Hare-Mustin, R. (1987). The problem of gender in family therapy theory. *Family Process, 26*(1), 15–27.

Hayden, R. (1992). *How to turn your money life around.* Deerfield Beach, FL: Health Communications.

Landers, S. (1992, April). Survey eyes therapy fees. *National Association of Social Workers News,* pp. 1, 8.

Lee, B., & Siegel, P. (1986). *Take control of your money.* New York: Villard Books.

Markowitz, L. (1992, September–October). Money, honey: Lesbian and gay couples face special economic challenges. *The Utne Reader,* pp. 53, 62.

McGoldrick, M. (1991). For love or money. In T. J. Goodrich (Ed.), *Women and power* (pp. 239–244). New York: Norton.

Michals, D. (1989, May). She's the boss. *Ms.,* pp. 58–61.

Nasar, S. (1992, October 18). Women's progress stalled? Just not so. *The New York Times,* Section 3, pp. 1, 10.

Otten, A. (1989, April 17). Black women narrow the earnings gap. *The Wall Street Journal,* p. B1.

Patten, J., Rothberg, B., & Williams, D. (1992, May). [Presentation by the Gay and Lesbian Studies Group]. New York: Ackerman Institute for Family Therapy.

Rubenstein, C. (1989, May). Smart money. *Ms.,* pp. 51–57.

Stern-Peck, J. (1992). A room of one's own . . . and 500 pounds. *Journal of Feminist Family Therapy, 4*(1), 79–93.

Tilghman, S. (1993, January 25). Science vs. the female scientist. *The New York Times,* Section A, p. 17.

Tomm, K. (1987). Interventive interviewing: Part II. Reflexive questioning as a means to enable self-healing. *Family Process, 26*(2), 167–183.

21

Female Adolescents and Sexuality: A Look at Teen Sexual Behavior, Its Consequences, and Pregnancy Prevention Programs

JOYCE R. LAPPIN

You are 14 years old. You are an African-American or Hispanic teen. You are packed into the auditorium of an inner-city school with 300 other kids. You want out. But the lights are low and two of your classmates—a boy and a girl—are on stage. They are talking about having sex. So you decide to stay.

"C'mon, baby," he pleads, looking deep into her eyes, "you know I love you."

The audience hoots; chaos reigns. "Go for it." "Do her." "No, no, don't listen to him." "Ask him where—where you're gonna do it!"

This is a play, but in real life our children write the next lines of this familiar story. Their coauthors may be friends, television, movies, lyrics from a hit song or music video, or behavior that they have observed among the adults in their lives—all of whom or which may promote an unsafe view of sexual behavior. But in this urban production of an everyday American scene, the drama is not taking place in a car or at a party, or on a beach after prom night, but on a stage in the heart of Camden, New Jersey. The concept is an innovative one: The teenage audience views a vignette and then explores the consequences of having sex.

This chapter looks at two innovative prevention programs, which attempt to challenge the problems of teen pregnancy and to foster hope amidst the overwhelming odds of poverty, racism, misogyny, and culture-bound mythologies. The chapter starts with a consideration of teen pregnancy and its consequences.

TEENAGE PREGNANCY: AN OVERVIEW

The causes of, and issues surrounding, the problem of teenage pregnancy are complex and serious. The facts are alarming. Each year over 1 million teens—one out of every 10 female adolescents—get pregnant in the United States. In 1988 it was estimated that each day 3,000 teen girls got pregnant, 1,300 gave birth, 1,100 had abortions, 26 girls aged 13–14 had their first child, and 13 girls aged 16 had their second child, with low-income, minority teens being at highest risk (Edelman, 1986; Forrest & Singh, 1990). In 1971, 28% of girls aged 15–19 were sexually active, as compared to 42% in 1982 (Dryfoos, 1990; Hayes, 1987; Forrest & Singh, 1990). These statistics become even more startling when we realize that other developed nations' teen pregnancy rates are a fraction of those in the United States (as discussed in a later section).

The introduction of effective, reversible methods of birth control, and the legalization of abortion with the 1973 *Roe v. Wade* decision, afforded women the ability to control their fertility and take advantage of the expanding economy that offered more jobs. Many women expected equality of sexual expression and fulfillment. Cohabitation and premarital intercourse became more prevalent. Separation and divorce increased as the rate of first marriages decreased (Dryfoos, 1990; Hayes, 1987). For some, shame no longer dictated that a young woman faced with an unplanned pregnancy had to give her child up for adoption in secrecy, or jump hastily into a marriage that was likely to fail.

Sadly, however, societal priorities, resources, and government policies lag behind changing needs. Many states have eliminated Medicaid funding for abortions. Few schools have school-based health clinics, and still fewer provide contraceptive services and/or prenatal care. Good day care is difficult to find and often unaffordable. Health care is not always accessible or available. Family planning and prenatal clinics are underfunded, which then makes them understaffed and overcrowded. Sex education is lacking or nonexistent in schools. The mass media do little to balance this grim picture. Sex is portrayed as desirable, romantic, and carefree, and responsibility is rarely a theme. Ads for contraception are practically nonexistent.

Although the problem of adolescent pregnancy and childbearing affects all economic and social groups, it is especially difficult for those living in poverty. Teens in poor urban areas are more likely to experience earlier onset of sexual activity and intergenerational patterns of early childbearing and parenting; they are also more likely to encounter public resources and services that are unavailable, inaccessible, or inadequate. Teen parents face interrupted education as well as this lack of services, which then means that their children are more likely to experience health and development problems, along with an increased chance of living in poverty.

Adolescent childbearing affects us all through higher public costs and complex social problems. More than 50% of the families that receive Aid to Families with Dependent Children (AFDC) began with the birth of a child to a teen mother (Burt, 1986). It is estimated that the public cost of early childbearing in 1988 was more than $20 billion (Center for Population Options, 1989). Though huge, this figure only includes AFDC, Medicaid, and food stamps, not the support costs involved with foster care, social and protective services, housing, special education, and so on (Hardy & Zabin, 1991).

Aside from the personal tragedies, the physical and emotional complications, and the scholastic and economic setbacks, the real injustice is that much of the heartache and most of the cost could be prevented. For every year adolescent childbearing is delayed, these expenses can be reduced. For example, every federal dollar invested in family planning services and pregnancy prevention programs can save an average of $4.40 over the next 2 years in social welfare costs, such as medical services, welfare subsidies, foster care, and nutritional services (Family Planning Association of New Jersey, personal communication, April 1991).

Adolescent childbearing is rarely viewed as desirable, but in a situation where the family rallies around the teen and provides support for her to finish school, work, learn parenting skills, and complete her development as an adolescent, the outcome is far more favorable.

OPTIONS FOR THE PREGNANT TEEN

When a teenager becomes pregnant, she is faced with difficult and complex decisions. Whatever her choice, early intervention is crucial to the health and safety of the adolescent.

Continuing the Pregnancy

A teen may continue her pregnancy, either by deliberate choice or by default (i.e., by denying the pregnancy). She is then faced with a host of possible problems, at least some of which can be eliminated by early intervention.

Health Complications

Within the medical community, a teen pregnancy is generally considered a potentially high risk, because many adolescents have unhealthy lifestyles and exhibit typical teen behaviors that can complicate a pregnancy. These high-risk behaviors include poor eating and sleep habits; experimentation with drugs, alcohol, and cigarettes; and lack of access to regular medical care. In addition, a teenage girl is still growing, which puts her in competition for nutrition with the developing fetus.

Once an adolescent acknowledges her pregnancy, adequate prenatal care frequently does not occur early enough to eliminate many of the complications. Typically, half of pregnant teens receive late or no prenatal care (March of Dimes, South Jersey Chapter, personal communication, April 1991). As a result, many teen mothers experience health problems such as anemia, underdeveloped cervix, prolonged labor, and toxemia (pregnancy-induced high blood pressure) (Hardy & Zabin, 1991). The death rate from complications of pregnancy is 2.5 times higher for girls under 15 than for older women (Dryfoos, 1990; Hayes, 1987).

For the babies born to teen mothers, the picture is equally grim. They are twice as likely to be premature and of low birth weight as children born to women in their 20s. Low birth weight is associated with early death, underdeveloped organs, birth defects, and learning disabilities (Dryfoos, 1990; Hayes, 1987; March of Dimes, South Jersey Chapter, personal communication, April 1991). Timely and comprehensive prenatal care can reduce the risks of pregnancy for the adolescent, as well as the risks to her child.

Economic and Other Complications

Usually, teen parents do not fare as well economically as mothers who wait until their 20s to have children. They are more likely to drop out of school; to have more births closer together; and to have lower job status, fewer marketable skills, and a greater chance of dependency on AFDC (Hardy & Zabin, 1991; Dryfoos, 1990; Hayes, 1987).

Children born to adolescent mothers also face more economics-related and other problems than children born to women in their 20s. They tend to have lower achievement in school, more emotional problems, and greater poverty (McCormick, 1992; Stone, 1990). Studies indicate that there is also a trend for these children to become teen parents themselves (Dryfoos, 1990; Horwitz, Klerman, Kuo, & Jekel, 1991).

Teen Fathers

Even though the teenage girl is the one who gets pregnant, it is important to acknowledge that there is a male involved. Few data exist on adolescent fathers, since they are harder to reach and less reliable about reporting pregnancy history than adolescent mothers are. Many times a teen father is a school dropout and/or is unemployed, though not necessarily because he is a father (Hardy & Zabin, 1991).

Adoption

Today, fewer than 4% of pregnant teens choose to place their children for adoption. Typically, the teen mother who opts for adoption is white, comes from an advantaged or working-class background, and views educational and occupational success as important (Kalmuss, 1991). Such teens have more traditional attitudes about adoption, which are usually shared with their parents and boyfriends (Hardy & Zabin, 1991). The birth mothers are mainly concerned that their children live in a two-parent home with mature parents who are not struggling financially. In many cases, birth parents can select adoptive families from pictures and written profiles compiled by the adoption agencies.

Most agencies require in-depth counseling for birth parents considering adoption; this is especially important for adolescents. Counseling ensures some safeguards for all parties involved: the birth parents, the adoptive parents, and the child (S. Loumeau, Catholic Social Services, Diocese of Camden, personal communication, April 1991).

Abortion

Of the 1.5 million legal, induced abortions performed in the United States annually, women 20 years old and younger account for 28.5% (Hardy & Zabin, 1991; Stone, 1990). Forty-two percent of pregnant teens choose legal abortion. Over 90% of all abortions are performed in the first trimester, but teens tend to have a higher proportion of later, more risky procedures. Abortion at any stage is safer for a teen then childbearing is (Stone, 1990). Of course, any medical procedure carries the risk of some complications, and those for first-trimester abortions occur about 1% of the time. Possible complications include infection, retained tissue, perforation of the uterus, hemorrhage, cervical laceration, missed abortion, and postabortal syndrome (Boston Women's Health Book Collective, 1984).

A review of the literature (Hardy & Zabin, 1991) concluded that adolescents rarely experienced a negative psychological outcome as a result of abortion. When problems did ensue, they appeared to be related to pre-existing emotional characteristics and not necessarily to abortion per se. In one controlled study (Hardy & Zabin, 1991), teens who chose abortion after unwanted pregnancies did better economically, educationally, and psychologically than peers who chose to continue their pregnancies. The teens who chose abortion also became better users of contraceptives than those who continued their pregnancies.

In some states, teenagers now have to deal not only with the difficult decisions related to unplanned pregnancies, but also with laws requiring parental notification and permission for minors to have abortions. Evidence is growing that parental consent laws cause teens to delay abortions, sometimes to the second trimester, which may result in increased health risks

(Donovan, 1992). Some states also have a 24-hour waiting period, which is a major problem for teens in rural areas, or areas that have no clinics or doctors.

Although teens need some kind of adult assistance in making these decisions (55% of teens having an abortion have informed at least one parent), mandating parental involvement will not guarantee the right help (Stone, 1990). Some laws go as far as to require consent from a noncustodial parent. In the tradition of "blaming the victim," the youngest women with the fewest resources are consigned to the human services' equivalent of the "scarlet letter."

FACTORS ACCOUNTING FOR TEEN PREGNANCY IN THE UNITED STATES

For all of us, adolescence is like a high-wire balancing act. Some seem to glide effortlessly across the wire; others remain frozen to the platform. With a little coaching, most achieve a sense of balance and arrive on the other side, a little out of breath, but intact and optimistic. When it comes to traversing the sexual arena, however, teenagers find little coaching and fewer supports—an act without a net. Parents and other family members who were once supportive can suddenly become mute or angry when faced with their adolescents' sexuality. Schools, where teens spend most of their time, are either unprepared or unwilling to provide the help the teens need. Friends usually have only stories and inaccurate information to offer.

Among various industrialized nations, the United States has the worst overall track record on teenage pregnancies, births, and abortions. This was demonstrated by a major study (Jones et al., 1985) by the Alan Guttmacher Institute, a corporation for research, policy analysis, and public education. The United States was compared with five Western countries (Canada, England/Wales, France, Sweden, and the Netherlands) that are similar to the U.S. dominant culture and stage of economic development. The United States led all the other 5 countries in the rates of teen pregnancies, teen abortions, and teen births. The rates for white teens alone are significantly higher than the overall rates of the other five countries. Finally, Jones et al. showed that the biggest difference in birth rate occurred among the youngest and most vulnerable group, those under 15 years of age. What factors might account for these differences?

The Guttmacher study (Jones et al., 1985) revealed that government policies and regulations in the other countries in the study reflected an attitude that teen childbearing and abortions are undesirable. In this respect, they were consistent with the U.S. position. What was different (and what thus begins to account for the tremendous disparity in statistics) was how the other countries attacked the problem societally as well as individually.

At the societal level, these countries created a context of openness by providing contraceptive information and services to all teens, complete and comprehensive sexuality education, and a balanced view of sexuality in the mass media. On the individual level, when a girl did get pregnant, her choices were more easily implemented. If she opted for an abortion, the services were free or subsidized. If she chose to continue the pregnancy, prenatal care and medical services were readily available and also usually free. If needed, welfare benefits were far more generous than in the United States. All of this contrasts sharply with U.S. policies.

In the United States, the goals and policies of the government have traditionally been directed at preventing teenage sexual activity. In the 1980s, U.S. policies seemed to reinforce the view that providing contraceptive services encourages sexual activity. Therefore, forcing a girl to continue an unwanted pregnancy was seen as appropriate punishment for her crime of sexual activity. The efforts made in this country to legislate chastity, in effect, during the Reagan and Bush administrations failed miserably.

Mixed Messages

American society consistently conveys mixed messages about sexual intercourse (Harris & Associates, 1987). On one hand, the mass media suggest that sex is exciting, desirable, and appealing through shows that present an illusion of a beautiful life involving spontaneous and spur-of-the-moment sex, with no consequences. Advertisements and commercials imply that buying the right product will make one sexually desirable, and that sexual activity is the ticket to a happy life. On the other hand, the message from some adults is that sex is something to be hidden and not discussed. It is loud and clear that sex is okay for boys but that "good girls don't."

These media effects are compounded, since teens spend more hours in front of the television than they do in the classroom, viewing sexual innuendos, seductive behavior, and suggested acts of sexual intercourse—approximately 20,000 in one year (Center for Population Options, 1984). There are few or no references to or information about how to prevent pregnancy, sexually transmitted diseases (STDs), or HIV/AIDS, or even indications that one should be worried about such things (Harris & Associates, 1987). Ironically, television executives have no problem allowing ads for vaginal infection and feminine hygiene products, hemorrhoidal preparations, and jock itch, but refuse to run commercials for methods of contraception. Even public service announcements directed at pregnancy prevention are rare, because these topics are deemed too controversial and offensive to their audiences (Brown, 1986; Cone, 1986).

Parents often fear that talking about sex encourages teens to become sexually active, and that discussing birth control is like giving permission to have intercourse. In an effort to try to delay premature sexual intercourse, parents and other adults present only the negative consequences, in hopes that guilt will control sexual behavior. Studies show the opposite to be true, however (Howard & McCabe, 1990; Jones et al., 1985; Newcomer & Udry, 1985). Although guilt does not prevent sexual activity, it does prevent the use of reliable contraception. For adolescents, planning intercourse in advance, and getting and using a method of birth control, are seen in a negative light; if they are "swept away," then sex is not premeditated and is thus perceived to be more acceptable.

Poverty

Poverty itself is the cause of many problems and can make teenage pregnancy even more difficult. Girls growing up in poverty tend to be ambivalent about getting pregnant and being pregnant. Regularly heard in family planning clinics is "I didn't really plan to get pregnant, but if it happened it would be okay." Girls are pressured by their partners to have babies, because for many poor, disenfranchised young men, the only path to manhood is to father children. For the young women themselves, motherhood is often used as a way to get their own psychological needs met ("I want something to love, something that is just mine"). They may also see no way out of poverty, or no good reason *not* to have babies. Others have babies because their friends are doing so, and because motherhood can bring status in some groups.

Sexuality Education

Sexuality education has been shown to be an important component in the prevention of "too soon" adolescent sexual activity and unplanned pregnancies (Howard & McCabe, 1990; Jones et al., 1985; Steinberg, 1989). Education is the balancing pole for teens who must traverse the adolescent tightrope. They must learn to balance their own physical sexual feelings; the voices of their parents and clergy, who tell them to wait; and the media and their friends, who tell them to go ahead.

The number of states that mandate sexuality education in public schools increased from 3 in 1985 to 23 in 1989 (deMauro, 1990). Unfortunately, even in these states, many school systems fail to provide adequate, comprehensive, developmentally appropriate curricula that meet the needs of the students. A good sex education program is positive; accepts diversity; provides thorough, relevant, up-to-date information; and conveys sexual development as a dynamic, lifelong process that is part of healthy human development. It must include cognitive, affective, and behavioral components, and must be written with input from the students.

Contraceptive Neglect

Even though there was an increase in sexual activity among U.S. teens during the 1980s, the teen pregnancy rate remained stable, indicating an increased use of contraception (Forrest & Singh, 1990). However, a 1988 Children's Defense Fund special report (Pittman & Adams, 1988) estimated that at any time only 50% of sexually active teens will use some form of birth control.

Teens are resistant to the use of effective contraception for many reasons, as suggested above and as described further below. Access to contraceptives and to health services is hampered by lack of and cost of transportation, location of services (if they exist at all), and expected cost of the services and/or supplies. Adolescents also fear judgmental reactions from clerks in stores and staff members of clinics, and fear as well that their confidentiality will be breached. Some teens are embarrassed about and afraid of the medical procedures associated with the physical exam, or have unrealistic fears of the side effects of hormonal contraceptives. All of these factors demonstrate that in order for teens who are sexually active to avoid unplanned pregnancy, birth control must be affordable and accessible, and incorporated into the context of the adolescents' daily life (Zabin & Clark, 1981).

TWO TEEN PREGNANCY PREVENTION PROGRAMS

The Planned Parenthood Federation of America and its 164 affiliates have always had a profound concern with the problems associated with unplanned teenage pregnancy. They have worked on a national level to establish federal guidelines that would make prevention the primary focus; to improve contraceptive services to all sexually active adolescents; to encourage comprehensive sex education in schools; and to urge television networks and the other media to present a more balanced view of sexuality, including contraceptive advertisements. Two teen pregnancy prevention programs implemented by a Planned Parenthood affiliate at the local level are described in this section.

The Peer Teen Center

Planned Parenthood, Greater Camden Area (PPGCA), in 1978, developed a unique project—the Peer Teen Center (PTC)—to address two issues that have long contributed to unplanned teen pregnancy: (1) lack of information and education about sexuality, reproduction, and contraception; and (2) lack of access to confidential and affordable contraceptive services.[1] The

PTC is an educational/counseling program whose mission is to delay premature sexual behavior and to encourage safer sex among those teens who are sexually active. It works toward achieving these goals by training and hiring teenagers to counsel and educate other teens. At present, as the teen coordinator for PPGCA, I supervise the PTC.

It was obvious that we could not change the poverty level in the city of Camden, improve the quality of the schools, or change the mass media. It even eventually became clear that such a small program probably could not have an effect on large numbers of teens in the city. So the PTC focused on helping the teens who became peer counselors to delay early sexual intercourse, prevent unplanned pregnancy, and develop a healthy adult sexuality. We hoped that what they learned would be spread to their peers, their families, and eventually their children, so high-quality sexuality education was the key to the program.

One useful strategy of the sexuality education program is to "level" the educational context. Even though the adult educators have more knowledge of sexuality, they acknowledge that the teens know more about the dilemmas of being teens. This shapes a teaching context that is codeveloped and equal. Increasing opportunities for dialogue is a critical component of good sex education and good relationships. Typically, the discussions teens have with adults and/or teachers focus on factual information, whereas their discussions with peers deal with sexual behavior. At the PTC, a topic is introduced by presenting factual information in a variety of ways (e.g., movies, group activity, or a game). This then opens the door for the peer counselors to engage in open discussion about feelings and behavior. This combining of facts and feelings is then reflected in the operation and services of the center.

Operations and Services

The PTC operates a drop-in center at the PPGCA facility in Camden, New Jersey. It is staffed by male and female teens who are hired and trained to work as peer counselors/educators. At any given time, the peer counselors are 85% African-American, 10% Hispanic, and 5% white—a division that closely parallels the proportions of these groups in the urban population. Recognizing that peer pressure has a great deal to do with adolescent behavior, the PTC provides a comfortable place where teens can talk with other teens their own age or a little older—ones who have accurate information, the skills needed to negotiate interpersonal relationships, and a desire to help their peers.

Available to teens at the site are information and programs dealing with human sexuality, birth control, pregnancy and prenatal care, STDs, AIDS/HIV, abortion, puberty, peer pressure, decision making, assertiveness, communication skills, and many other related topics. They may choose to watch a video, which is then processed by a peer counselor; to get brochures or literature; to participate in group rap sessions; to use the resource library to write school reports; or to talk on a one-to-one basis with a peer counselor. All the services and programs at the PTC are free and confidential.

Nonprescriptive methods of birth control—condoms, foam, and sponges—are available at no cost. No examination is needed with nonprescriptive methods; they have no serious side effects; and they provide some protection against STDs and HIV/AIDS. The peer counselors give both oral and written instructions to those teens receiving over-the-counter birth control methods at the center.

Again, teens do not use birth control for many reasons. Many simply believe that they will not get pregnant, because a common developmental feature of adolescence is belief in one's own invincibility. Others have false information about pregnancy prevention and believe myths such as these: It cannot happen the first time; simultaneous orgasms are required to become pregnant; withdrawal is a reliable method of birth control; standing up after intercourse will cause the semen to drain out; and urinating after intercourse will wash out the sperm. Others rationalize that there is no need to bother with birth control because it is not totally effective (Zabin & Clark, 1981).

The reasons teens themselves give for not using contraception, even when they have an accurate understanding of pregnancy, include the following: fear of the physical exam or of their parents' finding out; cost; lack of a clinic near the community or school; embarrassment in purchasing contraceptives; and inability to talk with their partners or belief that it is the partners' responsibility. Some teens have an unrealistic fear of the side effects of oral contraceptives, which they then generalize to every method; however, all forms of birth control are safer for a teenager than pregnancy, labor, and delivery (Mason, 1992).

By giving presentations and doing demonstrations on the different contraceptive methods, the teen counselors dispel the myths and help to make contraception a more acceptable part of everyday life. This is especially true of condoms. One technique the teens use is to answer questions in an advice column style. Together, the peer counselors collaborate on writing letters that reflect real-life situations in which a person has to deal with a resistant partner, either male or female. Here is an example:

Dear Peer Teen,
    My boyfriend and I have just had sex for the first time, and I am really worried. We did not use a condom or any kind of birth control. He said not to worry, but in school we learned about AIDS and other diseases, and how anyone can get them. For me it was the first time, but I know he has had other girlfriends. Should I be worried? What should I do?

Worried

As part of a program, a peer counselor gives this letter to a visitor to read. With the peer counselors or individually, a letter is written to "Worried" giving her some suggestions on what to do. For example, it might be suggested that she and her partner use condoms the next time they have intercourse. The peer counselors then conduct a short demonstration on condom use (including how it prevents pregnancy and reduces the risk of STDs), and discuss its advantages and disadvantages. The next action is to role-play how to respond to a partner who is resistant to the use of condoms.

Many different scenarios have been played out in this activity, especially since the boyfriend's views are not known. He has been played as accepting and caring, as uninformed but open to the idea, and as belligerent and despicable. Each situation opens the way to talking about even more topics, such as positive communication, assertiveness, male and female sex roles, disease prevention, and goal setting. The role play also provides an opportunity to practice the communication skills needed to negotiate a sexual relationship in a safe environment. After hearing possible responses from a partner, the participants practice ways of dealing with those responses. This again illustrates how both factual and affective learning take place.

Some wonderful discussions between the male and female participants have come from this activity. They have honestly shared each other's concerns, fears, and problems, and have sometimes expressed surprising feelings. It is difficult to convey in writing the energy of these discussions when the two sexes argue over who is right, or the frustrations of not being heard; the joy when someone truly experiences another's perspective; and the overwhelming satisfaction of giving young people a new skill or new tool that will be used throughout their lives. And how can I describe the pride we adults feel when the peer counselors conduct a group so well that no one wants the session to end?

Training Peer Counselors

The core of the PTC is the peer counselor training, which is conducted for 30 hours over a 6- to 8-week period. The training has two objectives. One is to prepare the teens for their role as peer counselors/educators who help normal teens deal with the normal problems of growing up. We do this by providing them with accurate, relevant information about human sexuality and by training them in nonjudgmental, active listening skills. The second objective is to help them learn attitudes and values that are crucial to making responsible decisions about their own sexual behavior, and, more broadly, to help them incorporate a sense of responsibility and concern for others into their lives.

The training is activity-based and not dependent upon lectures, so the trainees learn by doing. These activities can take the form of debates, role play, oral reports, homework with family members, brainstorming, demonstrations, small-group activities, and projects. A few examples follow.[2]

Activities for Exploring Sex-Role Stereotypes. As the teens enter the room, an adult leader is casually reading the newspaper. Once they are settled, the leader says,

"Hey, guys, this is the strangest thing. There was a bad car wreck on the turnpike last night, and a woman and her son were seriously injured. They took the mother to one hospital and the son to another. But when the son was wheeled into the emergency room, the nurse started to cry and said, 'Oh, my God, I can't help with this patient. It's my son.' How could that be?"

It usually takes a few minutes of sometimes creative solutions before the trainees "get" that the nurse was the boy's father. This challenging of stereotypes opens the way for further discussions of how we make assumptions and how important those assumptions can be.

Peer pressure to conform to rigid stereotypes can lead to conflicts for teens who are exploring their adult roles, and whose true feelings are not reflected in the stereotypes. Pressure on males to perform and keep feelings inside, and pressure on females to be sexy but nonsexual, play their part in the high rates of unplanned pregnancy and abortion. Adherence to these sex-role stereotypes does not provide an opportunity for planning a sexual encounter that involves the use of effective contraception.

Next, the trainees are divided into groups of males and females. Each group is assigned to make lists of "things I do not like about boys/girls" and "things I do like about boys/girls," with each group writing about the opposite sex. After 10 minutes, the groups are brought together and the lists are compared. The ensuing discussion is usually lively, full of emotion, and often revealing, as each group shares insights into understanding the opposite sex.

The session concludes with a "fishbowl" activity, in which the females form an inner circle and the males form an outer circle. The girls are instructed to go around the circle and say one thing they do not like and one thing they do like about being female. The outer circle is instructed to observe and listen carefully, as the males will be allowed to comment after the females have finished. The boys are then allowed to make one comment about what was said. The two groups then switch places, and the process is repeated with the boys in the center.

As a homework assignment, each teen is asked to interview an adult in his or her family concerning three situations that challenge sex-role stereotypes. The teen is to ask the adult how the adult feels about the situation and how the adult might have responded during his or her teen years. Examples of such situations include the following: a girl asking a boy out on a date, a boy asking his date to go "dutch," and a boy playing with dolls.

Slang Activity. At the beginning, many trainees are uncomfortable discussing anything dealing with sexuality. Like most teens (and many adults), they giggle and become embarrassed at the mention of genitalia. This discomfort is compounded by the facts that they are in a mixed group of males and females, and that few of them are used to adults who are open in discussion about sexuality.

The "slang activity" is used early in the training to increase comfort with terminology and to build group cohesiveness. Correct terminology for some female and male genitalia, the words "sexual intercourse," and the word "elbow" are written on separate pieces of paper that are posted around the room. Each person writes all the slang words he or she knows for each of those terms on each sheet of paper. The slang and correct words are then read aloud.

To process the activity, the group is asked how the terms are the same and/or different for the two genders; why there are no slang terms for "elbow"; why people laugh at sex jokes; what it is like to have permission to write those words; what is it like to say them out loud; whether the words tend to be positive or negative; whether any of the words are abusive; and what it means when people use these words.

When discussing how it feels for them to do this activity, the teens are most uncomfortable saying the words in front of the adult leaders, since this is not usually an acceptable practice. But the leaders' comfort and acceptance allow the teens to get beyond their discomfort, and also model the behavior the teens will need when working with their peers.

This comfort is important when using "swing language." When in conversation with teens who are not familiar with correct terminology, the counselors use a slang term, then immediately follow it with the correct terminology. This lets the teens being counseled know that they are understood, and it helps them begin to learn and become comfortable using correct terms.

Communication. Later in the training, the many skills the counselors will need to help their peers are introduced: active listening, positive communication skills, decision making, and assertiveness training. Using the factual information they have already learned, they practice these skills with each other in role play. During this phase, it is emphasized that they are not "urban Freuds" and that their job is not to cure or to provide therapy; rather, it is to help their peers look at options and the consequences of each choice, and to encourage further discussion with an adult in the peers' lives. Each peer counselor has information about local resources and services. An adult supervisor is always available on site.

It is impossible to cover every topic during the training, so during regular in-service presentations (which continue after training), a more in-depth look is taken at rape and sexual abuse, dating violence, human sexual behavior and sexual functioning, the media's impact on sexuality, and critical television viewing.

Teaching through Games

The most innovative project of the PTC has been the development of games used to teach sexuality. They are interactive, provide factual information, and make learning fun.

These games use the basic structure of popular television and board games. "Password" and "Body Bingo" require an understanding of human sexuality terminology. "Body Building" is a card game in which each player collects parts of the male or female reproductive system, names the parts, and explains the physiology in order to win.

In the "Family Life Feud Game," two groups, teams, or even health classes compete against each other to answer complex, multipart questions. First, one member from each team competes to answer a simple question to gain control of the play—for example, "Who tends to start puberty first, boys or girls?" The first team with the correct answer decides whether to play or pass. That team must then answer a more complex question, such as "Name five physical changes girls experience during puberty." Many times, the teams are given books and printed material in order to find the answers. If they do not give the correct answer, the other team has the chance to answer and to receive the points.

Teen Information Life Theatre

In another effort to reach even more teens with accurate information about sexuality, PPGCA has developed a teen improvisational theater group called Teen Information Life Theatre (TILT). By dramatizing, in a safe setting, life situations that teens may encounter, and using suggestions from the audience to solve those problems, TILT can help its audiences to experience and gain knowledge about difficult situations. Here is an example.

> On the stage are seven actors, three male, four female. They are arranged over the stage, frozen in a variety of poses. A female actor, playing a character named Cate, comes to center stage and talks to the audience.

"I have a boyfriend. He is *sooo* cute and wonderful. Even my parents think he is great. He is a smooth dancer, with all the right moves. And what a bod. He just makes me *hot*. Which is great. Except he doesn't want to just kiss any more. I think he wants more, but I am so confused, I don't know what to do. I don't want to lose him, but I don't know if I'm ready for sex."

One by one, each actor unfreezes, calls Cate over to him or her, and offers an opinion:

"Go ahead, girl, everyone else is doing it."

"What if he breaks up with you and tells everyone about your sex life?"

"It will make your relationship stronger."

"What if you get pregnant or get a disease?"

"He turns you on, doesn't he? Well, then it will feel real good."

"What if your parents found out? They would be so disappointed."

"You must only have intimate sexual relationships within the sanctity of marriage."

"What's wrong with you? Do you want to be a virgin forever?"

"Go ahead, it will make you a woman."

"Don't do it! It's not worth the risk."

"Do it!"

"Don't do it!"

As Cate again approaches center stage, the other actors slowly come closer, saying "Do it!" or "Don't do it!" louder and louder, until they surround Cate and she yells, *"Stop!"* Cate then goes to the audience to ask for help in trying to figure out what she should do.

Each suggestion the audience gives on how to handle the situation is explored. If it is suggested that Cate should delay sexual intercourse, then the actors who have lines to support that decision engage in dialogue with the audience and Cate, to try to get her to see their side. Sometimes the suggestions from the audience are incorporated into the skit. For example, someone may suggest that Cate talk with her mother. Once the audience defines the role of Cate's mother, she is played by one of the actors or by a member of the audience.

During each performance and the discussion that follows, the players remain in character. For instance, in the example given above, the girl who plays Cate must continue in the role of the confused teenager during the discussion. When portraying a negative or unpopular character, some players are concerned that members of the audience will assume that they are playing themselves. For that reason, a very important part of the presentation is the introduction of the actors' "real" selves to the audience at the closing of the program. This highlights that although the content is important, the characters are fictional and do not necessarily represent the actors.

Under the direction of the PPGCA teen coordinator (myself), the

TILT players write the skits and develop the story lines and characters. In order for them to write and process each skit, they must have factual knowledge about the content of the problem depicted in the skit. They gain this knowledge during the PTC training, which is required of TILT players. They also learn how to evaluate a situation from multiple perspectives by looking at the people involved and what effects they have on each other. During skit development, many different views of what is right or wrong, good or bad, moral or immoral are discussed. This discussion helps the players clarify their own values.

For example, the skit introduced at the beginning of this chapter was written to illustrate the importance of assertive, honest communication in a sexual relationship. The full skit is as follows:

> The scene opens with a boy and girl on the stage, wrapped in an embrace, kissing. He starts to pull her shirt out of her jeans. She pulls back.
> "C'mon, baby," he pleads, looking deep into her eyes, "you know I love you."
> She hesitates, then says, "I love you too." The hugging resumes, but then she says in a soft voice, looking at the floor, "James, I don't know."
> "It's okay. I'll take care of you. It will be all right."
> Again they embrace; again he pulls at her shirt. The two actors freeze. Then the girl stands up and talks with the audience. "I do really love him, but I'm not ready to have sex. I know he had sex with his last girlfriend, so he probably expects it from me. He *is* 16, you know. But I have rights, too. How can I tell him and not make him mad?"
> She then asks members of the audience for suggestions on how she can tell him she is not ready for sex without losing him, and the actor playing the boyfriend asks the audience how he should respond. The scene is played over and over again, using as many of the audience's suggestions as possible. Not all of the possible scenes end positively: In one important scenario, the boyfriend dumps her. The two then talk with the audience about how they felt in each situation, about other possible options, and about the audience's reactions.

CONCLUSION

There are few other topics that will get the national blood boiling faster than how to prevent teenage pregnancy. And there are even fewer topics that are both so personal and have such far-reaching public consequences. It is not surprising, then, that given this complex context—this cauldron of emotions, politics, and lives—it is difficult to see the picture clearly.

Some adults still advocate a campaign of "Just Say No" and a government policy that focuses only on the prevention of adolescent sexual activity. Such a plan, however, has no provision to change the mass media's image of sexuality; to change adult behavior, which is emulated by teens and incorporated into their lives; or to empower young people to take control of their sexual lives.

Contrary to assertions from the conservative factions in this country, it has been demonstrated that sexuality education and the availability of birth control are not the causes of teen pregnancy. Countries that have the most liberal attitudes toward sex, the most readily available contraceptive services for teens, and the most comprehensive sexuality education have the lowest rates of teen pregnancies, abortions, and births (Jones et al., 1985). It has also been proven that scare tactics do not prevent adolescent sexual activity, but that they do prevent responsible use of contraception (Newcomer & Udry, 1985).

Some teens plan for and are prepared for pregnancy. For others, unplanned pregnancy can result in economic setbacks, interrupted education, medical complications, dependency on welfare, more births, and less space between births. With strong supports, good prenatal care, and continued education, many teen mothers can overcome the odds and lead happy, successful lives.

Some pregnant teens choose to terminate their pregnancies, most with few or no physical or emotional complications. But for the 25% of adolescents who say they cannot talk with their parents about abortion, this choice is becoming less available as states pass parental notification acts that restrict teen access.

In her latest book, *Adolescents at Risk: Prevalence and Prevention*, Joy Dryfoos (1990) argues that teens must have knowledge, access, and motivation in order to prevent unplanned pregnancy. The PPGCA teen programs provide these elements for the teens who participate. These programs cannot improve the quality of public education, provide health services for everyone, guarantee employment, or decrease the poverty level of the community they serve, but they do provide opportunities for area teens. Through open and honest educational programs such as the PTC and TILT, many youth are learning to negotiate the sexual arena. They are acquiring skills that will help them to delay first sexual intercourse, and information on how to use effective methods of contraception when they do decide to be sexually active. All this will help prepare them for the adult decisions they are confronted with as teens.

ACKNOWLEDGMENTS

I would like to thank Marsha Pravder Mirkin for her editorial wisdom, clarity, and patience; G. Lynn Brown, Betty Lou Hanna, and Deena Kutcher for their assistance on countless "reads"; my sons, Jeffrey and Timothy, for pitching in at home;

my husband, Jay, for his support, encouragement, and ideas; and all the peer counselors who shared a bit of their lives with me and taught me how to dance.

NOTES

1. In 1990, PPGCA established Teens on Track (TNT) to educate, motivate, and change the behavior of adolescent males in the area of sexual responsibility, through educational programs, recreation and athletic activities, and medical services.
2. Many of these activities have been around for such a long time that I do not know their original source.

REFERENCES

Boston Women's Health Book Collective. (1984). *The new our bodies, ourselves*. New York: Simon & Schuster.
Brown, J. D. (1986, Winter). Sex in the media. *Planned Parenthood Review*, pp. 5–8.
Burt, M. R. (1986). *Estimates of public costs for teenage childbearing*. Washington, DC: Center for Population Options.
Center for Population Options. (1984). *The facts: Broadcast media, teenage awareness and sexuality*. Washington, DC: Author.
Center for Population Options. (1989). *Teenage pregnancy and too-early childbearing: Public costs, personal consequences*. Washington, DC: Author.
Cone, S. E. (1986, Winter). TV decision makers ambivalent about sex. *Planned Parenthood Review*, pp. 14–15.
deMauro, D. (1990). Sexuality education 1990: A review of state sexuality and AIDS education curricula. *SIECUS Report, 18*(2).
Donovan, P. (1992). *Our daughters' decisions: The conflict in state law on abortion and other issues*. New York: Alan Guttmacher Institute.
Dryfoos, J. G. (1990). *Adolescents at risk: Prevalence and prevention*. New York: Oxford University Press.
Edelman, M. W. (1986). *Families in peril*. Cambridge, MA: Harvard University Press.
Forrest, J. D., & Singh, S. (1990). The sexual and reproductive behavior of American women, 1982–1988. *Family Planning Perspectives, 22*(5), 206–214.
Hardy, J. B., & Zabin, L. S. (1991). *Adolescent pregnancy in an urban environment: Issues, programs, and evaluation*. Washington, DC: Urban Institute Press.
Harris, L., & Associates. (1987). *Sexual material on American television 1986–1987* (Study No. 864021). New York: Author.
Hayes, C. D. (Ed.). (1987). *Risking the future: Adolescent sexuality, pregnancy, and childbearing* (Vol. 1). Washington, DC: National Academy of Sciences.
Horwitz, S. Mc., Klerman, L. V., Kuo, H. S., & Jekel, J. F. (1991). Intergenerational transmission of school-age parenthood. *Family Planning Perspectives, 23*(4), 168–172.

Howard, M., & McCabe, J. B. (1990). Helping teenagers postpone sexual involvement. *Family Planning Perspectives, 22*(1), 21–26.

Jones, E. F., Forrest, J. D., Goldman, N., Henshaw, S. K., Lincoln, R., Rosoff, J. I., Westoff, C. F., & Wulf, D. (1985). Teen pregnancy in developed countries: Determinants and policy implications. *Family Planning Perspectives, 17*(2), 53–61.

Kalmuss, D. (1991). Adoption versus parenting among young pregnant women. *Family Planning Perspectives, 23*(1), 17–23.

Mason, V. (1992). Battling teenage pregnancy, STDs requires special skills. *Contraceptive Technology Update, 13*(9), 133–148.

McCormick, M. C. (1992). The health and development status of very-low-birthweight children at school age. *Journal of the American Medical Association, 267*(16), 2204–2208.

Newcomer, S. F., & Udry, J. R. (1985). Parent–child communication and adolescent sexual behavior. *Family Planning Perspectives, 17*(4), 169–174.

Pittman, K., & Adams, G. (1988). *Teenage pregnancy: An advocates guide to the numbers* (Special Report, p. 27). Washington, DC: The Children's Defense Fund.

Steinberg, A. (Ed.). (1989). Teaching children about sex. *Harvard Education Letter, 5*(5).

Stone, R. (1990). *Adolescents and abortion: Choice in crisis.* Washington, DC: Center for Population Options.

Zabin, L., & Clark, S. (1981). Why teens delay getting birth control help. *Family Planning Perspectives, 13*(1), 205–217.

22

Epilogue:
The Maternal Presence
in Therapy

MOLLY LAYTON

*Family therapy is, among other things, a moral endeavor. That is,
family therapy is based on a vision of human life and of the environment best suited to produce and nourish human life. Women have had
little part in creating that vision and scant opportunity to develop one
they could recognize as their own. Feminists work for that opportunity, and for the next step: a way for that vision to have its day.*
—GOODRICH, RAMPAGE, ELLMAN,
AND HALSTEAD (1988, p. 33)

THE CASE OF LILY

Several years ago, a woman I will call Lily asked to come into treatment
with me. She struck me then as a very talented woman—vibrant, almost
incandescent—but she was breaking up with a man who was emotionally
abusive. Then, too, she was living from hand to mouth; she did this partly
as a kind of ethical statement, but also because even though she was 38 years
old, she did not know how to use her considerable talents to make a more
reliable living.

After Lily and I had met for a month or so, she confessed that she had
been thinking about treatment with me for some time, and what had finally
convinced her was reading about my relationship with my adolescent
daughter. I had written an account of my experiences as a mother, trying to
explain what it felt like, at least for myself, to develop as a mother. Here's
the passage that led Lily to my particular door:

My transformation into the mother of adolescents was far more dramatic
and demanding than I had anticipated: it seemed one day Rebecca was

sunny and open and the next day she was dashing through the living room with a face preternaturally bright from rouge and slamming the door on her way out. The tiresome question was whether to let it go, confront her later, or get up to follow her out the door. On these dreary occasions, I hated many of the feelings I had: I hated it when someone was not home when they agreed to be home, I hated worrying about accidents and city psychopaths, I hated seeing college applications languishing under piles of phonograph records, I hated the worry about drugs and alcohol. So I learned to follow Rebecca out the door. . . .

[Then I describe how intense it is to be around adolescents, how I could not merely be a nice mom:] I had always admired Rebecca with a mother's ready admiration for sweet youth itself: her clear peachy skin, her demure smile, her tender sympathies. But when Rebecca became convinced that her body was ugly, I found that it did no good to reassure her sweetly that she was attractive. Instead, I learned to fight with her, sometimes on the soapbox, ranting about Twiggy and Jane Fonda and Kim Chernin, sometimes yelling at her when she complained that a perfectly molded thigh was somehow "too big." Finally, whenever she had doubts, she would come to me, serious and trusting:

"How do I look? Truthfully!"

"You look wonderful. The truth."

She took me in by fighting. (Layton, 1989, pp. 31–32)

So Lily told me that reading about my fights with Rebecca convinced her that I was the right therapist for her. Inwardly, I groaned; I do not willingly sign on for trouble. But in beginning to know Lily I was beginning to understand what she was asking for. Sometimes she struggled with bulimia. Starting in early adolescence, after her brother had sexually abused her, she became heartbreakingly vulnerable, with no notion of boundaries or protection. She became sexual prey—for example, to the next-door neighbor, presumably a responsible family man. Her parents were pediatricians; their marriage was miserable; and during this period Lily's mother was involved in open trysts with visiting medical students. By Lily's account, her parents were absorbed in their own adventures. It was the 1960s.

So it seemed to me that Lily was asking whether I would notice. Would I get up and follow *her* out the door? Would I challenge her about what she was doing? Would I fight with her? And, indeed, does one fight with an abused woman?

It seemed to me that Lily was asking me to fill in a missing piece of experience for her. And it seemed to me that the questions for Lily and any therapist were these: How much of Lily's grief was just tough luck, something to name and then to miss and mourn? And how much was a matter of filling in the missing piece, gratifying the need? And where did Lily need to go for such caretaking? Back to herself? To her mother? To her father? To her friends? To a new lover? And to me—should she turn to me?

I came to feel that Lily wanted a particular fighting experience with me. She felt that she was mostly a good, caring, earnest person, optimistic and energetic, and her friends loved her. But she also felt that if she got any more complicated than that—if she became darkly pessimistic, if she were tough and angry about something, or if people started to look weak and disgusting to her—then she imagined that she was becoming too much trouble. And it was this troublesome person that she was holding in check, often taking to her bed depressed and crying.

There had been, in another round of therapy years ago, a series of confrontations with her powerful and angry father, and consequently her father had written her off completely. The parents had divorced by then, and several years later her mother died. She made a few attempts to imagine confronting her brother, but had always gotten bogged down: How could it have been abuse, how could she accuse him, when she had so willingly gone along? The sexual abuse had in fact been the "best" period between the two of them, because during the time when her brother was sexually interested in her, he was also not hitting her and not throwing tantrums.

It took a long time for Lily to start fighting; surprisingly, the fights themselves were short and swift, like summer storms with a fine clearing afterward. The fights were mostly about how she spent her money and how she could not work too hard. For example, here's a fight I did not win. Lily was coming in, week after week, crazy with anxiety about how little money she was making, and then she announced that she was buying a $500 sewing machine to make her own clothes. "It'll be great," she said, with characteristic optimism; "I love to sew." I said, "Look at how you're setting yourself up." She replied, arms folded, "So what?" Now I felt like the mother of an adolescent all right: She was saying, in effect, "Make me care!" I knew this landscape dishearteningly well. She egged me on; we went round and round; I could not make any headway with her about her judgment; she left, she bought the sewing machine; she made two dresses; she got depressed about money. I was gracious enough not to say, "I told you so." I figured that we were learning how to go at it.

The ability to fight is at its best the contestants' ability and willingness to engage each other over matters of importance. Some observers, including mothers and daughters themselves, see the infamous fighting of a mother and daughter as a kind of battle over turf—the turf in this case being the daughter's soul. These observers often note the strong pull of *identity* between the two participants, and so judge the fighting as the daughter's push toward separation. Terri Apter (1990) has written about these fights, seeing in them not merely the daughter's effort to define herself as *separate,* but more as the mother and daughter's struggle for a kind of mutual recognition—a fighting that struggles to define each other's strength. In this characterization, the story is more mutual; potentially, each is an admirer of the other. And in truth, daughters surely have no real stake in their mothers' weakness. It is that pesky issue of identity again, seen now in its pro-grammatic sense: "As it goes for her, so it goes for me." It is the mother's *strength* that interests the daughter. The lives of girls and women are indeed hopelessly intertwined: the daughter's source flowing out of her mother, the mother's hope for a bright future played out in the daughter, neither to be easily denied.

The real foundations for a good fight lie in a robust history of attach-ment between two people, where the fact of caring has already been established. At her best, a mother argues with the part of the daughter that would sabotage herself; a mother has credibility, she has money in the bank, to the extent that the daughter knows that the mother is not *merely* critical. And sometimes such a mother's strength lies in her capacity to hang in there, like a dog hanging onto a bone.

With Lily, the fight I wanted to win—the fight that both of us wanted me to win—was the fight about work. If Lily worked too hard, then she felt robbed of her freedom and creativity; she felt depleted and hopeless; she felt her spirit taken away from her. At the same time, she could not help noticing that as a hard-working therapist, I apparently had different stan-dards about work from hers. So she defensively bridled as she described turning down work. She said, as if I had challenged her, "You don't understand. It robs me of something." And I said, "But what if I were here for you? What if we both watch to make sure that you don't disappear forever?"

THERAPIST AND MOTHERS

If I brought you, the reader, in on my own internal processes while I was going through all these hours with Lily, we would find strands of this teaching and that supervisor, certain theoretical beliefs, and a goodly chunk of my own personal experience of therapy as well. But there would also be contained, in my feelings and relationship with Lily, my real experience of myself as a mother—an experience that I often find very orienting in therapy sessions. Now I am supported in this illusion, if you will, by some theory: specifically, Winnicott's (1965) ideas, which unabashedly describe how a therapist can be a good mother. It is this theory (namely, object relations) that allows me to explore what the therapist means to her clients.

But there is a broader issue beyond the curve of any theoretical bent. If therapy is about growth and change and even healing, then it should not be surprising that at least some of our assumptions about the duties and skills of a change agent, a growth agent, should come from the day-to-day experiences in our culture with changing and growing. If we can think of therapists as coaches and car salesmen, which some family therapists have done, then why not also explore the experiences and metaphors of mothering? Despite all the differences in theory, is there not necessarily a maternal presence in therapy? And furthermore, in our fear of the "D word," dependency, and in our cultural ignorance of mothers and their thinking, is not this maternal presence often denigrated or hidden in our own thinking as therapists?

Rereading Lois Braverman's (1989) article on mothering, I was caught this time around by her description of the early advice given to mothers by John B. Watson in 1928. He wrote a widely accepted book on child care, laying out the kinds of inflexible demands and pompous prescriptions we now find so irritating: Infants should be fed only at certain times; infants should sleep only at certain times; in order to develop character, infants and children should not be indulged with too much gratification and touch. In particular, Watson advised mothers to give their children only one kiss a day, at bedtime, and to shake their children's hands upon arising in the morning. (Or vice versa?)

And in sizing up all these demands—about time and touch and gratification and boundaries—it struck me for the first time that these strictures seemed remarkably similar to the kinds of rules laid on me when I was a beginning therapist. Early on I had trained with a series of male therapists who saw therapy as a kind of battle of boundaries. Thus it occurred to me that at least some kinds of therapy (and certainly our culture's mainstream idea of therapy) are constructed on a model of the Victorian parent—in particular, I suspect, on the model of the Victorian papa. And so I have wondered, and still do, about which models from family and social life construct the positions of therapists in the various modes of family and individual therapy. Surely the therapist is not constructed *ex nihilo,* out of nothing, the way God made the world.

So I think it behooves us to question and compare what we know about caretaking: caretaking as a skill, as a philosophy, as a kind of thinking and behavior shaped by the demands of caring for growing people. As a good example of such exploration, the work of the women at the Stone Center—conversations, dialogues, "works in progress" that by their very definition resist our primitive longings for a papa who knows best—has enriched our vision of the intricacies of connection in our lives (Jordan, Kaplan, Miller, Stiver, & Surrey, 1991).

Sara Ruddick (1983), too, has written from this perspective, describing the ways that people who are mothers *think,* describing not the heart but "the head of the mother" (p. 76):

> I speak about a mother's *thought*—the intellectual capacities she develops, the judgments she makes, the metaphysical attitudes she assumes, the values she affirms. A mother engages in a discipline. That is, she asks certain questions rather than others; she establishes criteria for the truth, adequacy, and relevance of proposed answers; and she cares about the

findings she makes and can act on. Like any discipline, hers has *characteristic* errors, temptations and goals. (p. 77)

Indeed, if we understand that all thought arises out of social practice, out of a given context such as the task of mothering children, then we can see how the general interests of "preserving, reproducing, directing, and understanding individual and group life" (p. 77) constitute a particular reality, a particular set of values, to which the caretaker must respond.

Let us imagine, then, that we read certain passages about mother and child in Ruddick's article, but instead substitute "therapist" and "client." For example, we could then read *à la* Ruddick that "[therapists] develop an attitude of 'holding,'

> an attitude governed by the priority of keeping over acquiring, of conserving the fragile, of maintaining whatever is at hand and necessary to the [client's] life. It is an attitude elicited by the work of [and here Ruddick quotes Adrienne Rich] "world protection, world preservation, world repair . . . the invisible weaving of a frayed and threadbare family life." (p. 80)

Is this not at least some of what we do as therapists—holding, conserving, weaving?

In our rereading, Ruddick might also write: "A [therapist], in order to understand her [client], must assume the existence of a conscious continuing person whose acts make sense in terms of perceptions and responses to a meaning-filled world" (p. 82). And as therapists, like mothers, do we not indeed search for continuity and meaning? Is therapy not becoming more and more a kind of conversation in which lives are not so much "worked through," as if to drain them of emotional intensity, but rather explained and narrated and reconstructed in healing ways? Are we not remaking the scrapbook?

In looking at the role of mothering in therapy, I am not suggesting that a therapist becomes first and foremost a mother to her clients. The process of therapy is structured by many other, broader considerations, including the therapist's long education in the many eccentricities of human development, the sweeping shape of culture and class, and the history of psychotherapy itself. But if the role of mother does not structure therapy, it can certainly *inform* it, illuminate its way, like a light on a path.

But there is for me an existential piece as well, something having to do with being a real person in a real place. I am in fact a mother. It is a description that fits me comfortably now, so comfortably that it has become one of the strongest ways in which I know the world. However, in the beginning, the kind of knowing and strength that can be in mothering was strangely inaccessible to me—centrally important, but still maddeningly inaccessible. I grew slowly into mothering.

When I was first a therapist, I was also very insecure. I was 33 years old when I saw my first client, and the beginning years were so scary that I made a rule, which I actually announced to my fellow trainees: I would hang on as a therapist, I would assume that I was not doing irreparable harm, unless somebody jumped up and ran out of the room screaming. One day in a nerve-wracking family session, the adolescent in the family jumped up, arrogantly yelled something at his hard-bitten grandmother, and ran out of the room. And instinctively I ran after him, yelling at the guard in the waiting room of the clinic to stop him. And I continued to see the family. Somehow I evidently was not ready yet to give up trying as a therapist.

For me, my development as a mother and my development as a therapist have been close enough in time and similar enough that slowly, over the years, each experience has begun to flow into and illuminate the other. In both areas, I have had to struggle with much confusion, a pervasive sense of inadequacy, many doubts, and much questioning of myself, held together sometimes merely with the bald curiosity of wanting to experience and understand everything. All these doubts dogged me so that the agonizingly slow shift into the powerful self of the caretaker came finally, thankfully, not so much a relief as a kind of *realization,* a coming into real and honest form.

But even given my personal history, I do not believe that the problem is just mine. I think that in the field of psychotherapy we have generally more to understand about the shift, the growth, of the human self into the powerful, caring self, including the healthy maternalized self. Certainly the epidemic proportions of eating disorders, alcoholism, and other self-destructive behaviors suggest that something has gone awry in our culture's capacity to preserve life, to foster growth. Nowadays, the treatment of people who have been victims of incest and abuse has developed a new generation of therapists who are willing to bring a more active, committed presence into the therapy relationship. I hope that in our move toward managed health care, we leave room for the kind of soulful therapists who work with victims of early trauma. So I am suggesting that we keep a clear head not only about the people who come for help, but also about the people who are charged with both comforting and challenging them.

So I want to continue to sketch out a particular instance of the use of this hard-won maternal self in therapy—the case of Lily.

THE CASE OF LILY, CONTINUED

So Lily's idea was that she would take me in by fighting. And this sort of "taking in" is what she started to do. For example, I often found myself astounded at what little vision Lily had about her considerable talents, and I found myself encouraging her in a motherly way: "You could do that." She would always say, "That's amazing. I never think that I could do that sort of thing." So I knew she was open to this kind of input.

Finally one day Lily came in to report that she had met up with some old friends now living and working in Costa Rica, and as they were renewing old times, the talk led somehow to the need for some specialized teaching down in their school in Costa Rica. Lily was astounded to report that she heard my voice, clear as a bell (she said that to me over and over, "It was clear as a bell!"), saying to her, "Lily, you could do that." So she found herself collaborating with her friends to be hired for some week-long workshops in Costa Rica, a place she would love to visit. She said, "I never would have imagined doing that by myself."

What I have learned to appreciate, both as a mother and as a therapist, is a kind of patience for this taking-in process—introjection. Ideally, we take in supportive and challenging pieces of people in our lives all along: our mothers, our fathers, our lovers, our friends, maybe a therapist or two—the bad as well as the good. And so Lily was taking me along in her heart. It was a good version of me, to be sure-my best supportive stuff. I think Lily came to me because she needed something better inside her heart, and because she wanted the kind of emotional stimulation (in this case, it was fighting) that would allow the heart to open up and take something in: "Make me care."

But that's not the whole story on introjection. Here is the whole story: Several weeks after Lily heard my voice in her, she had another experience of drawing on something strong within herself. She was applying for a training grant (she was on a roll by now), and, surprisingly, she found herself remembering how clever and efficient her mother had been in convincing people to bankroll her special projects. Lily found herself using some of her mother's techniques in her grant. This part was what I really appreciated: It was the first time in over a year of therapy that I could see Lily identifying in a good way with her mother. Up to this point, her mother had been dismissed as weak, immoral, indifferent.

I have seen this development over and over again—often enough to know that the two events are connected. A client has a good experience with being cared for, and then finds herself able to reconstruct an old important relationship in a healing way. What I think was going on was that Lily had been carrying around with her the piece of her mother that she had taken in, but it did not feel good to her. There were too many unresolved issues, too many traumas left uncomforted; there was also Lily's despair over some of her mother's choices and behaviors.

As Lily's therapist, as her new "mother," I learned how to engage her, and I learned how to be the right mother for her. So Lily finally had an experience of taking something into her heart and using it to be strong. But in feeling that internal strength now located in herself, Lily also began to have access to other aspects of her mother that carried important meaning for her—for example, her mother's cleverness and energy. It seems to me that our relationship helped Lily to use the mother that was there all along. Her experience with me was added on to her experience with her mother, and there was no longer a split between the "good" therapist and the "bad" mother. Rather, there was a continuity in her experience, a range of good and bad, shades of gray, dots finally connected. I think, too, that in her experience with me, she came to know a bit more about how it felt to be a good daughter. At least at this point, for this moment, her grief ("Why couldn't you come out the door after me?") was comforted. And it was all going on in her heart. Lily's mother had died several years ago.

And here too, at this point, as the therapist I felt as if I were participating in a community of mothers, a community of people—all imperfect people, all of us—who loved and cared for Lily. We did not exhaust the people who might someday be involved, including Lily's father and perhaps a lover. Maybe, too, Lily would eventually adopt a daughter, and then she would find herself on the other side of the mirror.

Mixed into the progress of Lily was my own progress as well. I participated as a caretaker, and found echoes of my relationship to my own son and daughter in my relationship with Lily. And I especially felt the poignancy of Lily's lament: She had said about work, "You don't understand. It robs me of something. It takes away my spirit." In my own struggle to grow up, that was not exactly how I felt, but as I recall my own insecurities, it is breathlessly close enough. So I remembered how other people have supported me—my husband's care, for example, and the generous kindness of good friends, and the excitement of good teachers. These experiences eventually guided me back to connect with my own mother in a fresh way. And, miraculously, all these experiences of caring for and being cared for have spiraled around and, augmenting one another, echo back and forth.

There is, I think, an intriguing issue about point of view here, the shift into and out of the persona of a mother. It seems that the same old stories get repeated over and over, in my life, in my clients' lives: stories of loss and ordeal, stories of celebration and hope. Only we change our places in the drama: Sometimes I am the comforting mother; sometimes I am the tearful child; sometimes I am the villain, or the friendly sidekick, or the wise old woman, or the beginner, or the fool. Every shift in perspective adds another layer of meaning, a community of meaning. Lily was starting to build this community of meaning for herself.

CONCLUSION

As therapists, we undoubtedly have a lot to learn from all of us, and from all the many roles, big and little, that come to us in life: daughters, fathers, grandmothers, lovers, husbands, sisters, friends, teachers, neighbors, classmates. But in this space I have tried to show some ways in which therapists and mothers share some particular interests: in preserving and holding, in fostering growth. And I have tried to think about those questions, as I did with Lily: How much of our grief is just tough luck, something to name and then to miss and mourn? And how much is a matter of filling in the missing pieces, gratifying the need? And where do we go—where do we all go—for such caretaking?

REFERENCES

Apter, T. (1990). *Altered loves: Mothers and daughters during adolescence*. New York: St. Martin's Press.

Braverman, L. (1989). Beyond the myth of motherhood. In M. McGoldrick, C. Anderson, & F. Walsh (Eds.), *Women in families: A framework for family therapy* (pp. 227–243). New York: Norton.

Goodrich, T. J., Rampage, C., Ellman, B., & Halstead, K. (1988). *Feminist family therapy: A casebook*. New York: Norton.

Jordan, J. V., Kaplan, A. G., Miller, J. B., Stiver, I. P., & Surrey, J. L. (1991). *Women's growth in connection: Writings from the Stone Center*. New York: Guilford Press.

Layton, M. (1989, September–October). The mother journey. *The Family Therapy Networker*, pp. 22–35.

Ruddick, S. (1983). Maternal thinking. In H. Trebilcot (Ed.), *Mothering: Essays in feminist theory* (pp. 76–94). Totowa, NJ: Rowman & Littlefield.

Winnicott, D. (1965). *The maturational processes and the facilitating environment*. London: Hogarth Press.

Index

Aboriginal people, violence against, 362–366
Abortion, 256–281
  in adolescent pregnancies, 466–467
    psychological effects of, 270–271, 275
  ambivalence about, 268, 272
  and analysis of fetal protection laws, 259
  and biases of therapists, 279–280
  counseling on, 271–275
    for adolescents, 275
    postabortion, 275–279
  decisions by battered women, 265
  economic reasons for, 263–264
  in failure of birth control, 266
  heterosexual relationships affecting, 264–265
  incidence of, 256–257
  judicial decisions on, 84
  and power issues in reproductive freedom, 257–262
  psychological effects of, 266–271
    in adolescents, 270–271, 275
  racial and class factors in, 259–261
  in rape victims, 265–266
  roadblocks to, 260
  and traditions concerning individual rights, 298
Abuse
  against children
    damaging effects of, 68–69
    in unwanted children, 262
  sexual. See Sexual abuse
  violence in. See Violence
Adolescent females
  abortions in, 466–467
    counseling on, 275
    psychological effects of, 270–271, 275
  anorexia in, and goals of therapy, 79
  attitudes toward mothers, 87–88
  body image in, 83–87
  conflict avoided in, 79

connection needs in, 78–83
  identity development in, 87–93
  in immigrant families, 89–90, 356
  lesbian, 85
  peer group affecting socialization of, 247, 249
  pregnancy in, 463–470
    and decision to place children for adoption, 466
    economic problems in, 465
    health problems in, 464–465
    incidence of, 463, 467
    prevention programs, 470–479
  rape attempts on, 84
  and role of mother–daughter dynamic, 446–448
  self-denial in, 80–81
  separation and individuation of, 78–83
  sexuality of, 83–87
    mixed messages on, 468–469
    and resistance to contraceptives, 469, 470, 471
  views on womanhood, 87–88
    and story construction for new image, 91–93
Adoption of children from adolescent mothers, 466
Ageism
  manifestations of, 96, 106
  and negative views of older women, 96, 322
  and youth equated with beauty, 323
Aging. See Older women
AIDS, 237–253
  community interventions in, 249–253
  in disintegrating communities, 241–246
  drug abuse as factor in, 240–241, 246
  and factors affecting social behavior, 240
  parental deaths from, 249
Anger toward men, as legacy of misogyny, 66–68